THE
WRESTLING
OBSERVER
YEARBOOK
1993

Online: F4Wonline.com

Twitter: @davemeltzerWON

Twitter: @WONF4W

Email: dave@wrestlingobserver.com

THE WRESTLING OBSERVER YEARBOOK 1993

THE YEAR OF MAJOR BEGINNINGS AND MAJOR ENDINGS

Dave Meltzer

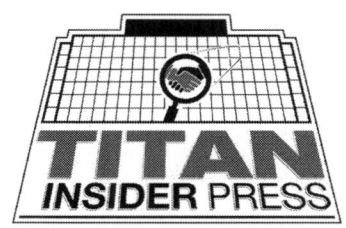

TITAN INSIDER PRESS

CONTENTS

	Preface	9
1	Legal Wranglings	11
2	WWE Revamps Cable Lineup	29
3	Ric Flair Leaves WWF for WCW	31
4	Behind the Scenes Turmoil in WCW	35
5	The Steroid Scandal	51
6	Pancrase Forms	81
7	Hulk Hogan Saga	83
8	Lex Luger Debuts in WWF	95
9	The Tragedy of Kerry Von Erich	99
10	SMW Working With WWF	119
11	The Death of Andre the Giant	123
12	Yokozuna Controversy	135
13	WWF Invades USWA	137
14	Vader Legal Issues in Japan	143
15	Jumbo Tsuruta's Health Declines	147
16	Dino Bravo Murdered	149
17	Antonio Inoki Comeback	153
18	Jim Ross Signs for the WWF	157
19	Business Down Across the Board	161
20	The Fading Influence of the NWA	171
21	Wrestling in Oregon	177
22	Wally Karbo Passes Away	181
23	SMW Thriving	183
24	AJW on Fire	187
25	Violence Levels in Wrestling Increase	193
26	The Early Days of ECW	201
27	AAA Surpasses All Expectations	207
28	Vince McMahon Resigns as Head of WWF	215
29	Issues with WCW Taping in Advance	219
30	The Destroyer Retires	225
31	New Japan Doing Big Business at the Box Office	227
32	Mean Gene Okerlund Leaves WWF for WCW	233
33	Shawn Michaels Quits WWF	235

34	Launch of the UWFI	239
35	Randy Savage Blasts Hulk Hogan	243
36	EMLL 60th Anniversary	249
37	900 Numbers and Consumer Fraud	251
38	Sid Stabs Arn Anderson	255
39	Oro Dies in the Ring	263
40	Texas Wrestling Turns Back the Clock	267
41	Jerry Lawler Indicted	269
42	Bobby Heenan Leaves the WWF	275
43	British Bulldog Fired by WCW	277
44	Bits and Pieces	279
45	Ins and Outs	305
46	1993 Year in Review	317
47	Supercard Summary	329
48	The Big Shows Directory	355
49	Wrestling Observer Newsletter Awards	365

10 YEARS OF THE WRESTLING OBSERVER

Dear Readers,

A few weeks ago, we celebrated the 10th anniversary of this newsletter. I don't want to make a big deal about it, but do want to take this time to thank everyone involved especially in putting this together or in just being interested enough to spend time every week reading. Whatever impact or accomplishments, breakthroughs, or whatever else anyone wants to credit or not credit to the idea and existence of this publication is up to others to decide. All I want to say is to thank all of you for your interest in wrestling and this publication for the past ten years, particularly those of you who have been here from the start. I started publishing a wrestling newsletter when I was 12-years-old. I started this specific newsletter while in college, because it was an idea I felt whose time had come. The past ten years have more than proven that hunch to be correct. For those who still don't believe that's the case, then welcome to the 20th century. But you'd better hurry up, because it's almost over. This isn't the oldest newsletter in existence, but it was the first to cover wrestling in the manner it did. There are so many people who have been such a major part of this over the years that I don't want to mention any names, because I'd forget someone important, because the most important ones still wouldn't want to be mentioned, but I want to thank you for teaching me, for helping me, for being friends and for offering encouragement.

The Wrestling Observer is a lot more than just a newsletter to me. It's the single most rewarding thing I've been involved in my entire life. Looking back, whatever sacrifices I've had to make for it have all been worth it. The experiences and pleasure I've derived from it weigh a lot heavier on the scale than any sacrifices. There are many other people in this business who have sacrificed major portions of their lives for the betterment of the profession, and you all deserve a lot more credit than you have received. For those who have taken selfishly, and there are many, whatever may be able to be derived from it on one end is balanced out by the lack of respect on the other end. In 1985 I received a job offer, which, combined with a mistaken view of where the business was headed, caused me to not have enough time, and interest, I thought, to devote to this newsletter. I learned a valuable lesson from that. It was a mistake, and one which, in the succeeding years, I haven't repeated nor have considered at any time repeating. This newsletter is not a stepping stone, or a means to an end. It is the end. All the fun, all the experiences, things I've been fortunate enough to see and place I've been fortunate enough to travel to and all the friendships which can be credited to this publication are things I feel lucky to have been a part of. I've never regretted this path, not even for a moment. There are times I have to stop and think about how fortunate I've been, and after ten years, this is one of them. Even the bad times and stress involved with dealing with unscrupulous people over the years have in the long run, always turned out to have been a positive. They've all turned into learning experiences that both myself, and hopefully others in the same field, have been able to benefit from. And for those who in the field who haven't, I'm really sorry they haven't paid closer attention, because aside from being fun, these past ten years have been a wonderful education.

There really is a lot to learn from this business that relates to far more than just pro wrestling. The most important thing about wrestling, entertainment in general, and really life, that I've learned, is that the minute you think you understand it completely, it means that time has already passed you by. You're done. It's always changing. It has to always change, because the world always changes and time doesn't stand still. If you want to stop paying attention to the present and don't care to open yourself up to accept new concepts relating to both the present and the future, the door is there on the left. This business has changed completely over the past ten years. The next ten will bring changes probably just as significant. Don't decry these changes because you long for the way things were in the past. Not only does time, particularly in the entertainment world, not stand still, but it definitely doesn't go backwards. Decry the changes when you believe they aren't for the better, and many of them won't be. But don't close your mind to them simply because they are new.

We're going to be here for another ten years, and hope as many of you as possible will stay along for the ride.

Your Friend (in most cases),
Dave Meltzer

PS: For the few of you who have come to the conclusion at this point that "Dave's sure trying to get himself over," I feel sorry for you. I think you should consider taking a week off and heading to the beach. It's not very healthy going through life and not being able to differentiate between a shoot and a work, especially when it should be obvious. That is meant very seriously, not sarcastically. Being unable to differentiate here means you are probably seriously misjudging many things far more important. Maybe I'll see you there, if you can wait until March or April.

CHAPTER ONE

LEGAL WRANGLINGS

JANUARY 4

On 12/5, Jesse Ventura, the former wrestler and current mayor, actor and wrestling announcer was interviewed by Mike Tenay on the Wrestling Insiders radio show, mainly regarding his lawsuit against Titan Sports. The following is a transcription of the interview.

MT: Jesse, we want to get your thoughts on many subjects this evening. First, let's concentrate on your upcoming lawsuit against your former employers, Titan Sports and the WWF. Tell us what's behind your claim that you feel you're entitled to receive residuals on your announcing work from the WWF?

JV: What it is, it's simple. Vince McMahon wants to be in the normal entertainment world. He talks like he is and like he's a big operator within it. But he wants to play by his own set of rules. He doesn't want to play by the normal rules of the entertainment industry. If I do a film and that film goes to videotape, I get royalties from that. If I do a TV show, if that show is shown in reruns, I get royalties from that. Vince McMahon has put out over 150 wrestling videotapes. I would venture to guess I'm on at least 135 to 140 of them and I haven't received one penny. It's my voice from beginning to end on many of them. When I signed to do things for Vince McMahon, I was paid to do the live events, the individual shows. Not to have him tape these shows or pay-per-views where he makes money. Two years ago I think it was, he was bragging in Sports Illustrated how he's made $100 million in the videotape industry. Yet he's paying no one any royalties.

MT: Speaking of royalties. It seems many of the WWF's merchandising deals always come under question from many of the wrestlers. In your opinion, did you get your fair share of the money that was received from dolls, t-shirts, calendars and the like?

JV: Not at all. That's also part of my lawsuit. I was put on two calendars and never received any royalties for my picture being in a calendar. The original wrestling dolls, the thing I'm going to court about on that is that we were never given the opportunity to negotiate. If you were to do some merchandising like that out in Los Angeles, chances are the talent would get anywhere from 25 to 33 percent of what the parent company would get, which in this case is Titan Sports. On the original dolls that the WWF put out in 1985-86-87, we weren't even getting I believe one percent. It was never negotiated. That's the point I'm going to make in the trial. Vince McMahon has done a lot for wrestling and he's also changed wrestling a tremendous amount. Nobody was marketed prior to Vince McMahon. Us as wrestlers had no idea what marketing was worth. We had no idea what a percentage was and we had no idea what contracts were. Vince McMahon would market something and he never gave anyone the opportunity to negotiate that marketing. There may be certain people who were allowed to negotiate, but on general principle, nobody was allowed to negotiate anything. It was whatever Vince deemed he felt like giving you. I don't think that's right. The other thing Vince changed in wrestling is signing guys to exclusive contracts. I think this is going to come out in the trial, too. How can he call wrestlers independent contracts when they're signed to exclusive contracts? If you were truthfully an independent contractor you could wrestle for the WWF one week and for WCW the other week.

MT: I guess that's probably the main reason why you think pro wrestlers should be considered employees of the WWF or WCW instead of as independent contractors.

JV: Absolutely. That's my opinion. An independent contractor is like being a plumber. You would go out, get your own work, negotiate your own price and everything like that and you wouldn't be held binding that you could only work in a particular neighborhood. If you're truthfully an independent contractor you can contract to work for anyone. How can you be signed to an exclusive contract and then for tax purposes be called an independent contractor. What it does is it saves Titan Sports seven percent on paying taxes.

MT: Let's discuss contracts. Explain your contractual status with the WWF.

JV: Really, I have no contracts with them other than the one in 1984 that I was forced to sign with them as a wrestler. When Vince went across the country and plucked the talent from the AWA and the different portions of the old NWA, he never told us out front when he brought us in that at some point he would want to sign us to exclusive contracts. Up until that time there had been no contracts in wrestling. If there had been, I had never been involved in any. All of a sudden, as Titan and the WWF started to grow, Vince all of a sudden came out with these bogus one-sided contracts that give the wrestler nothing and give Titan Sports everything. They had given me three or four of them and I had refused to sign them. I kept putting it off and putting it off until one night at the Mecca Arena in Milwaukee, Gorilla Monsoon comes up to me two minutes before I'm due to go into the ring and puts it in front of me, and says "This is straight from the old man," meaning Vince, "If you don't sign this, you don't wrestle." I looked at Monsoon and said, "You mean to tell me if I don't sign that I don't go to the ring right now?" He said, "Nope, you're done." I looked at Gorilla and said, "Okay Gorilla, I'm signing this under duress and I'm signing out of my free will." I scribbled my name on it. It isn't my normal signature but I did sign it because I was forced to sign it essentially. At that point in my career I couldn't say no. I'd already burned my bridge with the AWA with the help of Vince McMahon. So there was no real places for we as talent in the WWF would have been accepted because that was at the height of the war. That contract expired after two years. After that point I was never signed to anything ever again. That doesn't cover my broadcasting which I fell into a little later. It's a whole different deal. It's not wrestling.

MT: When and where is the case scheduled to be heard?

JV: It's scheduled to be heard in February at Fourth District Court in St. Paul in front of judge Paul Magnuson. I'm not sure if that's the right district but it's in St. Paul under judge Magnuson.

MT: Who can we expect to see deposed coming up?

JV: I've already been deposed and me and my attorneys have already deposed Vince McMahon and other personnel at Titan Sports. I think the final depositions will be this coming Friday (Dec. 11)

MT: This is going to be a precedent setting case. It could be a landmark decision with everyone else getting a fair piece of the pie also.

JV: That's all any of us wanted from day one is a fair slice of the pie to whatever to help Titan Sports achieve the success it did. All we ever asked for was a fair cut of the pie in return but Vince doesn't like to do that. He enjoys making all the money. But wrestlers or announcers, If I whip him in court in February, feel free to come back because it'll be easy to get money then.

JANUARY 4

Phil Mushnick of the New York Post had a column mention on 12/28 about the Nailz incident: "Here's some pro wrestling news you won't read the "The Slammer's column: The wrestling headliner known as Nailz (real name Kevin Wacholz) was fired by the WWF on Dec. 14--about the same time he filed a report with the Green

Pay police stating that he pushed WWF president Vince McMahon to the ground after McMahon tried to sexually assault him. The incident is alleged to have taken place in a locker room at Green Bay's Brown County Expo Center prior to a WWF show. The latest in a string of drug, sex and child abuse charges against WWF executives and/or employees has been dismissed by a WWF spokesman as a case of Wacholz attempting to extort money from McMahon. Green Bay police are investigating. Wacholz, according to the police report, claims McMahon sexually assaulted him on another occasion--last month at MSG." . . Wacholz, under advice from his lawyer, has yet to make any public comments. The $150,000 Wacholz was allegedly trying to extort from McMahon at the time of the incident that was talked about by a Titan p.r. firm was, according to one WWF source, money he wanted paid in advance for putting Undertaker over every night at the house shows. The Summer Slam pay-off Wacholz was unhappy about was reportedly $8,000. Another major star the Titan office put in contact with us but asked anonymity because he was afraid of possible reprisals from other wrestlers stated that just recently, during a drug test, Wacholz was complaining about the drug test being unconstitutional and allegedly made the statement that the only way to make money in this company was to claim that somebody grabbed your you know what.

FEBRUARY 15

Phil Mushnick in his New York Post column on 2/8, had another item regarding Titan Sports which read as follows: "Jim Hellwig, recent-day WWF superstars who performed as the 6-3, 300-pound Ultimate Warrior, is about to file a multi-million-dollar lawsuit vs. Vince McMahon and the scandal-soaked WWF, according to sources of the up-close and personal kind. Hellwig, we're told, will claim breach of contract and other, nastier things, with the help of Manhattan lawyer Michael Kennedy. Kennedy's client list includes Ivana Trump and Jean Harris. Both Hellwig,who lives in Arizona, and Kennedy declined comment. The suit is expected to be filed before the end of the month.

FEBRUARY 22

Based on newspaper stories over the past week, it seems as though this past week and this coming week are going to be filled with major lawsuits regarding pro wrestling. Based on an item in the New York Daily News, it appears that Titan Sports is going to sue Kevin Wacholz (Nailz) for slander and while Titan wouldn't confirm this, others have reported to me that a suit has been filed, and the story indicated it wouldn't be the only one. The lawsuit involves the incidents on 12/14 in Green Bay, WI which resulted in Wacholz' firing. Wacholz was reportedly involved in a heated discussion about money and grabbed McMahon and threw him down physically when it was broken up. Wacholz then called the police and reported McMahon attempted a sexual assault on him. The Green Bay District Attorneys office refused to prosecute the claim due to a lack of evidence. Wacholz' claim was generally not believed within wrestling and Titan provided an eye-witness, referee Earl Hebner, who claimed to have seen the entire incident and said that Wacholz claim was false.

FEBRUARY 22

Vince & Linda McMahon filed a major publicized lawsuit against Geraldo Rivera, David Shults and several others regarding the "Now It Can Be Told" segment on pro wrestling that aired April 3, 1992; Jim Hellwig, formerly known as Ultimate Warrior, is expected to file a lawsuit against McMahon and Titan Sports imminently according to an item in a Phil Mushnick column reprinted here last week; and the New York Daily News reported on Friday that Paul Heyman (formerly and currently known in many circles as Paul E. Dangerously) would be serving WCW with papers of an intention to sue early this week.

The suit that has generated the most publicity due to the names involved is the McMahons suit against Rivera and several others, which was the subject of a front page story in the Entertainment section in Friday's USA Today. The suit, filed 2/9 in Superior Court in Stamford, CT (where the WWF's home offices are located), claims Rivera and those working for him, along with Shults, were involved in a scheme to extort $5 million from McMahon in order to keep the charges made by former referee Rita Chatterton, which the suit claimed were fraudulent and is also named in the suit, from going public.

Rivera was quoted in many places as saying, "It's a mark of honor to be sued by the WWF. I will body slam them in court."

"We stand by the story," said Jeff Erdel, a publicist for Rivera. "We repeatedly asked Mr. McMahon to appear on the program to counter the allegations. He repeatedly refused."

In a story in Friday's Hartford, CT Courant by Jack Ewing, Eileen McGann, the attorney for Shults, said: "David looks forward to finally forcing McMahon to testify under oath about these absurd claims as well as other serious outrageous acts which will be the subject of counterclaims." McGann also said Shults called McMahon "a well-known bully" and said the charges in the suit are "bizarre" and "hysterical" and claims he'll counter-sue.

McMahon's attorney, Jerry McDevitt, in the same article, said the significance of the lawsuit goes beyond issues of extortion and sexual assault. "The larger issue is the use of tabloid television programs to make stories where none exist. They have nothing to do with journalism."

The 13-page complaint names as defendants, Rivera, Brooke Skulski (the producer of the piece "Wrestling's Ring of Vice" that aired on "Now It Can Be Told" in early April), Tribune Entertainment Company (which distributed and syndicated the now-defunct "Now It Can Be Told" program and the "Geraldo" show, and also was part-owner of the two shows, which saw Chatterton appear as a guest), Investigative News Group, Inc. (a company owned by Rivera which also was part-owner of the shows), Chatterton and Shults.

The main claims in the suit are as follows:

- Chatterton was dismissed as a referee in or around 1986 because she wasn't a competent referee and posed a danger to herself in the ring
- Shults' contractual relationship with Titan was terminated in 1985 because of his erratic and violent behavior which included but wasn't limited to the incident with John Stossel
- In or around 1988, Shults hired Anthony Toce (the former deputy chief of police in Bloomfield, CT) as a private investigator for the purpose of attempting to obtain negative information about McMahon and Titan Sports. Toce conducted a tape recorded interview with Chatterton in or around 1988 in which Chatterton made no allegation of sexual misconduct against McMahon
- In early 1992, Shults granted interviews where he promised to expose alleged sexual preferences and sexual improprieties of Titan employees. In these various appearances, he never named names
- Shults also entered into an agreement with agents of Rivera to provide the show with disparaging information about McMahon and Titan Sports.
- Shults contacted Chatterton to "induce her to make a false claim that McMahon had raped her while she was still affiliated with the WWF"
- Chatterton agreed to make the accusation for the first time on the "Now It Can Be Told" show
- Chatterton was promised legal counsel to represent her in an attempt to secure money from McMahon not to air her story
- Shults arranged in March of 1992 for Chatterton to make a tape recording purportedly to have been the one done in 1988 in which Chatterton would claim she had been raped
- Shults directed Toce to go to a hotel in Connecticut on or around March 19, 1992 to interview Chatterton. Shults instructed Toce to hide two tape recorders in the room and keep both recorders on at all times. The third tape recorder was to be the only one seen by Chatterton. The concealed tape recorders were designed to pick up everything said in the room, even when Chatterton believed she wasn't being recorded
- On or about March 19, 1992, Chatterton, Shults and Toce conducted the interview and manufactured an audio tape to make it sound as if it had been done in 1988. During the interview, Skulski called the hotel room to make arrangements with Shults to have Chatterton brought to New York City to meet with agents of Rivera
- On the same day that the interview took place, a caller who identified himself as being affiliated with a TV

show contacted Titan and informed a Titan employee that he possessed three tapes of former referee Rita Marie in which she said some pretty nasty things about McMahon that were to be broadcasted on national TV pretty soon. The caller asked if Titan would like to buy the tapes. Titan refused

- After the interview, Shults arranged for Chatterton to travel to New York to meet with agents of Rivera. Rivera's people offered to pay and provide other considerations to Shults and/or Chatterton for her story
- On March 20, 1992, agents of Rivera saw to it that Chatterton spoke to a lawyer selected and controlled by Rivera
- On March 23, 1992, Lisa Pelosi, a lawyer controlled by Rivera, contacted Titan to discuss Chatterton's claim. This March 23, 1992 call was the first time Chatterton had made a claim against McMahon. This call was made despite Pelosi's knowledge that the statute of limitations on a rape case (since the incident Chatterton described allegedly took place in July 1986) had expired and as such the claim had no legal value
- Chatterton's counsel (Robert Wolf, an Albany-based attorney) demanded $5 million to settle Chatterton's claim and that Chatterton wouldn't appear on the "Now It Can Be Told" show if the claim was settled. McMahon refused to settle
- Titan learned about the attempt to fabricate a 1988 tape being done on March 25, 1992
- Titan contacted Charles Sennet, the General Counsel of Tribune Broadcasting and specifically told him of all these matters. Sennet contacted Skulski and informed her Titan was aware Shults and Chatterton had attempted to fabricate evidence to support her claim
- Skulski contacted Shults and told him Titan's story. Skulski asked Shults to secure a sworn affidavit from Chatterton that the tapes were made in 1988
- At various times between March 25 and April 3 (air date of the show), Titan repeatedly provided Sennet with "truthful information regarding Chatterton's allegations." Sennet refused to disavow an intent to broadcast Chatterton's accusation
- "Now It Can Be Told" aired on April 3 with Chatterton's allegations and Chatterton appeared on an April 10 taping of "Geraldo."
- The suit claims all the defendants acted with malice in that they knew Chatterton's accusations were false and/or reckless disregard as to whether or not they were true
- Vince McMahon has suffered severe emotional distress and/or other injuries including but not limited to mental anguish, anger, embarrassment, shame, humiliation, depression and loss of sleep. The same basic complaints were made regarding Linda McMahon.

Sennet, who had not seen the suit at the time he was contacted by the Hartford paper, said the show was "carefully researched and carefully done."

Dangerously's suit that, according to a column in Friday's New York Daily News by Bob Raissman, would serve WCW with papers sometime this week claiming wrongful termination, professional disparagement and ethnic discrimination. In the article, Dangerously claimed, "I was shafted for the simple fact Bill Watts wanted to cut costs. Watts' message was clear. Conform to his ways or he'll break you. He broke me." Watts couldn't be reached for comment by the paper.

MARCH 1

Lawsuits galore to report on next week. Ultimate Warrior filed his $5 million plus suit against Vince McMahon and Titan Sports with many interesting claims and pieces of evidence such as a letter from McMahon to Jim Hellwig saying that Hellwig would always be the highest paid athlete in the WWF (this letter was written when Hogan was still around).

McMahon has also sued Kevin Wacholz over the incident in Green Bay and Phil Mushnick and the New York Post over the many articles Mushnick has written in the last 19 months. The latter suit garnered a lot of publicity in the New York area.

Entertainment Tonight led its Tuesday night show off with the story on McMahon's lawsuit against Geraldo, Shults and Chatterton. It was a dumb move for McMahon to go for the publicity on this one unless or until

Chatterton changes her story, because the largest audience ever saw Chatterton claim to have been raped and it only brought the story back.

MARCH 8

There were two major suits, both of which will likely garner significant publicity, filed the previous week, both involving Vince McMahon, and another suit filed earlier which we didn't get details on until last week.

In the latter, which is the simplest and most straight-forward of the three, McMahon is suing Kevin Wacholz (Nailz). According to the complaint filed in Brown County Circuit Court in Wisconsin, McMahon claimed Wacholz perpetrated a violent attack and assault upon him with great force and violence. As a consequence of the attack, the suit claims, McMahon suffered pain and bodily injury as well as embarrassment and humiliation. McMahon also claimed the defendant filed a false police report claiming he had been sexually assaulted and the police report compounded the anguish and humiliation because the police reported was published in various media outlets.

Lawsuit No. 2: James Hellwig (Ultimate Warrior) filed a $5,819,500 lawsuit against Titan Sports Inc., World Wrestling Federation and Vince and Linda McMahon. The 19-page suit was filed about two weeks ago in U.S. District Court for the Eastern District of New York.

The main claims and allegations involved in the suit are:

- Hellwig claims to have created the name and image of Dingo Warrior while in Texas, which included the unique pattern of face-paint and brightly colored strings wrapped around his biceps
- Hellwig signed a two-year contract with Titan on September 23, 1987, which provided for automatic one-year renewal upon conclusion
- Hellwig was re-named Ultimate Warrior, but the paint pattern on his face and bicep strings were remained and were largely unchanged from his pre-WWF sting as Dingo Warrior
- The original contract was automatically renewed on September 23, 1989 and September 23, 1990
- Hellwig claimed he began to experience illegal and unfair treatment by the defendants, claiming he was overworked and underpaid in comparison with other wrestlers of his acclaim, skill (I don't know why I found that word in this context so humorous) and status
- On July 13, 1991, Vince McMahon agreed to increase Hellwig's compensation and lessen his workload in a novation. The novation, written by McMahon, which was introduced as part of the suit, had 1) McMahon agreeing to pay Hellwig $550,000 for his participation in Wrestlemania VII (The semi-main event on the card against Randy Savage at the Los Angeles Sports Arena); 2) Agreeing that with the exception of special events, Hellwig would receive four days off every other time off period; 3) His pay on house shows would increase to four to five percent of net, effective immediately, with the understanding that no other WWF athlete would be paid at a higher rate and that no other WWF athlete would be paid at a higher rate than him on pay-per-view events (keep in mind this includes Hogan); 4) His royalty rate on merchandise would be increased; 5) His compensation from the Warrior 900 line would be identical to Hogan's from his 900 line.
- On August 26, 1991, the defendants refused to honor the terms of the written novation
- Hellwig was then suspended without cause by the defendants for 90 days. Although the parties later renewed their professional relationship, defendants illegal and unfair treatment of plaintiff continued
- On or about March 31, 1992, Hellwig and Titan entered into a second booking contract, a two-year deal to last until March 31, 1994
- On October 28, 1992 and October 30, 1992, Hellwig and McMahon had discussions regarding Hellwig's desire to pursue commercial activity in which the promoter is not otherwise engaged. Those included opening a gym, making a workout video, and releasing a poster. Verbal agreement to be able to use the name Ultimate Warrior on these projects was obtained by McMahon
- On November 6, 1992, Hellwig's attorney, John Goodson of Phoenix, sent a letter to McMahon memorializing these conversations. McMahon never signed the letter
- On November 9, 1992, McMahon terminated Hellwig's contract immediately. The basis of the termination,

according to McMahon, was Hellwig's alleged involvement in a scheme to import Human Growth Hormones. Hellwig claims McMahon knew these allegations were false

- Hellwig said he began using anabolic steroids in 1982 as a bodybuilder and continued to use them as a wrestler. The use of steroids was commonplace among the other wrestlers and employees of the defendants including Vince McMahon
- The defendants acquiesced and encouraged the wrestlers to use anabolic steroids in order to improve their appearances. Often McMahon discussed his own use of steroids with Hellwig and with other wrestlers
- After the Zahorian trial, Titan instituted an anti-steroid policy and drug testing for both steroids and other illicit drugs. However, after this policy was instituted, steroid use continued with both the knowledge and acquiescence of the defendants
- McMahon continued to use anabolic steroids and other controlled substances in violation of his own drug policy
- Titan discriminately imposed the so-called drug policy by punishing certain wrestlers for testing positive for the use of anabolic steroids while allowing others to go unpunished
- At the time the defendants anti-steroid policy went into effect, Hellwig ceased the use of anabolic steroids
- Certain wrestlers and other Titan employees then began using Human Growth Hormone (HGH) to circumvent the drug policy without detection
- At certain times during Hellwig's employment, McMahon asked him if he knew of any source to obtain HGH. Hellwig replied that he didn't
- In May 1992, Hellwig inquired into securing HGH for his own personal use. He was not successful and never attempted to obtain HGH again. At no time did Hellwig ever use HGH
- On or about October 10, 1992, Hellwig told McMahon of his unsuccessful attempt to obtain HGH
- In Hellwig's contract, the only guidance to how much he was to be paid was a phrase stating "An amount equal to such percentage of the gate receipts for such event as is consistent with the nature of the match in which wrestler appears ie. preliminary bout, main event, etc.; the prevailing practice of the United States professional wrestling community; and any standards promoter or others establish specifically for such event."
- Wrestlers under contract to Titan were never told by the company and/or its agents of the amount of compensation or the percentage of the gate they were to receive for participation in exhibitions. The wrestlers learned of the amount of their payment on receipt of the checks
- On August 29, 1992, Hellwig was booked by Titan as a headline attraction in the Summer Slam PPV show. Despite Hellwig appearing (and in the main event against Savage), Titan never paid Hellwig his percentage of the total receipts for this event. Hellwig claims he is entitled to $1 million for this event
- Hellwig is also asking for the following amount for matches he has yet to be paid for: October 16 Nassau Coliseum ($2,000); October 23 Denver ($1,200); October 25 Peoria ($850); October 26 Springfield, IL ($1,200); October 27 Terre Haute, IN ($1,200); October 28 Louisville ($1,500); November 5 San Antonio ($1,250); November 6 Minneapolis ($1,200); November 7 Cincinnati ($800); November 8 West Palm Beach ($850); November 8 Orlando ($850)
- Hellwig's booking contract states that he "shall receive 25 percent of licensed products net receipts
- Hellwig received in royalties, about $150,000 for the last quarter of 1991, $99,392.99 for the first quarter of 1992 (at which time he wasn't even an active wrestler), $50,113.66 for the second quarter of 1992 (at which time he was working). The lawsuit contends the defendants purposely withheld monies owed to Hellwig according to the contract under the section regarding merchandise royalties
- Hellwig asks that an accounting be ordered by the court from Titan Sports in the areas of domestic concession sales, mail order sales, licensees, toys, domestic Coliseum and Canadian Coliseum for the period starting with the third quarter of 1991 through the second quarter of 1992
- During a phone conversation between McMahon and Hellwig, McMahon stated his reason for termination was that his attorneys had advised him to terminate the contract because of some alleged intent on behalf

of Hellwig to distribute anabolic agents. Defendants knew this allegation was false
- At no time has McMahon provided any reason in writing as to why Hellwig's contract was terminated
- With no cause for termination, Hellwig is claiming wrongful breaching of contract
- For the terms of the contract, Hellwig would have been a headline attraction in one more PPV show in 1992, four in 1993 and two in 1994
- Plaintiff is asking for $1 million for his participation in each Survivor Series 1992 and 1993, $400,000 for each Royal Rumble 1993 and $1 million each for the 1993 Wrestlemania and Summer Slam
- The contract also stipulates an obligation to book at least ten bookings per year, so based on the full year of 1993 and the first quarter of 1994 that is 13 bookings and they are asking $1,500 per booking
- Hellwig claims he began his pro wrestling career in Texas in 1984 as Dingo Warrior. Dingo Warrior garnered some national recognition and eventually became noticed by Titan Sports
- Hellwig's initial booking contract along with his second contract contain a section regarding trademarks. This section attempts to differentiate between pre-developed intellectual property of Hellwig and of intellectual property developed during the course of being under contract to Titan Sports
- Section 3.1 of Hellwig's second contract states that "intellectual property" belongs exclusively to Titan Sports for the term of the contract. This includes all names, trademarks and identifying indicia
- Section 3.2 of Hellwig's second contract lists items that make up name and likeness and provides these items belong to Titan Sports forever. The contract states "If promoter develops such service marks...and distinctive and identifying indicia for wrestler, they shall belong to promoter in perpetuity
- Therefore, Hellwig contends, since Dingo Warrior, the pattern of the face paint and strings around the biceps were not developed by Titan Sports and the contract has now been breached by Titan Sports, Hellwig owns and is entitled to use, for purposes of commercial exploitation, the name Dingo Warrior, the face-paint pattern and the strings
- Titan Sports promoted Summer Slam '92 on November 25, 1992. Hellwig was to be a headline attraction in most of the promotion for this event. Employees of Titan Sports indicated on WWF television shows that Ultimate Warrior "quit the Survivor Series."
- Hellwig contends he didn't choose to quit the Survivor Series. Hellwig contends he has been, and will continue to be irreparably harmed if Titan or Titan employees continue to state Ultimate Warrior dropped out of his own accord from Survivor Series
- Hellwig is asking that Titan Sports be permanently enjoined from using or exploiting the name Dingo Warrior and/or its likeness for any purpose and that Titan Sports be permanently enjoined from making any public statements that either imply or directly state that Ultimate Warrior left Titan Sports either on his own volition or due to an act of cowardice

Basically how I read this is that at some point there will most likely be some form of settlement at least when it comes to Hellwig getting paid for the last PPV and last run of house shows that he already worked. Aside from that, he is obviously seeking not so much to use the Dingo Warrior name, but perhaps the Warrior part of the name, but to continue to use the Dingo Warrior costuming if he chooses to wrestle in the future. As far as damages and the rest, that's another story. The amount he's asking for the PPV events sounds to me to be a lot higher than what one would think he would have earned, but at the same time, knowing the grosses from the cities on his last run, the amount he's asking for is well under the four to five percent as stipulated in McMahon's written novation. For example, the gross in Nassau was about $160,000 and he was asking for $2,000, which comes out to 1.25 percent rather than 4-5 percent, although the novation does stipulate net rather than gross, but it's hard to believe Titan's net on a $160,000 house comes out to $40-50,000. The fact that his gimmick check was almost double during the quarter that he wasn't even working than during the period after he returned is unusual. But it may be able to be at least partially explained in that Warrior's popularity wasn't the same after he returned as it was before he left, and the business itself was in the midst of a tailspin, but that he earned twice as much when he wasn't even appearing on television then he did when he was on television and involved in the biggest pushed angle in the company at the time is still curious. Another interesting statement was in going over his history, Hellwig's suit listed him as beginning his wrestling career in 1984 in Texas as a member of a tag team called The Blade Runners. That technically is incorrect, as Hellwig's career began in November 1985 in Tennessee as a member of a tag team called Power Team USA, The Freedom Fighters. In January 1986, the team was re-named The Blade Runners. He went to Mid South in March 1986, which did promote in Texas, but it wasn't until a few months later that he went to Texas where he was re-named Dingo Warrior.

From reading the suit and accompanying evidence and what little knowledge of the situation as it existed that has gone public, it appears that in July of 1991, Hellwig held up McMahon for a huge payoff from the Wrestlemania of a few months earlier (where the $550,000 figure comes in) and a guarantee he'd basically be the highest paid guy in the company on all PPV shows and get the highest percentage of anyone on house shows (remember Hogan was still around at this time), McMahon agreed to it in writing (the written novation), but then got rid of him immediately after the Summer Slam PPV show for what was reported as unprofessional conduct. He was brought back at Wrestlemania in 1992. On October 28, 1992, in Louisville, he allegedly had a meeting with McMahon where a letter from his lawyer indicates McMahon gave him verbal approval to use the name Warrior Gym in an upcoming business venture, and wanted to put out a workout video and release a poster. From what I gathered, he would not use the Warrior name or gimmick in the latter two endeavors. Titan's plan at that time was to turn Warrior heel and have him wrestle Hulk Hogan at this year's Wrestlemania. Hellwig wasn't in agreement with the change and his contract stated that "Promoter shall (develop and enhance)..the value of wrestler's performance as professional wrestler and his/her standing in the professional wrestling community, all of which shall inure to the benefit of wrestler." Hellwig's belief was the future objective to turn Warrior heel would hurt the image of the character, not enhance it. However, in return for Hellwig agreeing to let Warrior turn heel, he was asking Titan to cut down his house show schedule to a bare minimum which would allow him to pursue an acting career unrelated to the Warrior character and the WWF.

Hellwig wanted all rights to the characters and likenesses that he portrays in any acting endeavors and for Titan to have no claim to any of them. Hellwig in return agreed that he would not do any projects in which he plays a character with a likeness to The Ultimate Warrior. Hellwig only wanted to be booked on PPV events and would devote a reasonable amount of time before the shows to promote them. Hellwig agreed to make himself available to work house shows only in emergency situations and provided these house shows didn't interfere with his outside commitments. So anyway, based on the wording of the letter, we are led to believe McMahon agreed to these terms verbally in Louisville, was sent a letter by Hellwig's attorney to get it in writing, then four days after receiving the letter, terminated Hellwig allegedly on the HGH distribution charge. Actually, one can understand McMahon's side to all this if his slant was that Warrior only agreed to turn heel if McMahon wouldn't book him on all but emergency duty house shows, because there is no point in keeping someone around to work on top at PPV's when they won't work on the road because it just takes up a slot for someone who will work full-time to get their character over. Still, I can't imagine Hellwig not at least receiving a settlement based on the shows he's already worked and not been paid for although the $1 million asked for the Summer Slam PPV sounds awfully high on the surface.

Hellwig was interviewed on 2/27 on John Arezzi's Pro Wrestling Spotlight radio show in New York. A caller brought up the subject of anabolic steroids and Hellwig claimed the last time he used steroids was August 26, 1991. He said he considered them like vitamins, that he was aware of the dangers but felt it was a sacrifice he was willing to make to be successful. He said that at times he had thoughts that he was using too great a quantity of steroids at one time but when he talked with other steroid users, he believed he was using less than many others were. It should be noted that August 26, 1991 date was just a few days after McMahon told myself and a few other journalists (and a few others masquerading as such) that there was no possible way that any of his wrestlers were still using steroids (and three months before half the wrestlers failed the first steroid test, and you still wonder why McMahon's credibility is where it is) although it was about six weeks after Titan's first public announcement regarding steroids. So this does slightly contradict what is in the suit about Hellwig ceasing use when Titan announced its policy, if you take his claim at face value. Hellwig also said that he won't be wrestling in the United States at anytime in the near future, but did talk of possibly wrestling overseas. He said WCW had contacted him but indicated there had been no real discussions. Hellwig started Monday filming a martial arts movie in Southern California called "Firepower." In regard to his career, Hellwig made an attempt to separate himself from The Ultimate Warrior the wrestling character and also when talking about his Wrestlemania match with Hogan in 1990, first said the Warrior beat Hogan, then thinking, immediately corrected his wording to that The Ultimate Warrior was the only man chosen to beat Hogan.

Lawsuit No. 3: Vincent K. McMahon and Titan Sports vs. The New York Post and Phil Mushnick, a 13-page document filed February 17, 1993 in U.S. District Court for the state of Connecticut although as of the weekend, I believe neither Mushnick nor the Post had actually been served papers.

The suit claims:

- The defendants had a tortious, systematic and ongoing campaign to maliciously destroy the business of Titan Sports, Inc. and the life of its owner
- Beginning in or around July 1991, Mushnick and the Post targeted plaintiffs to be victims of a character assassination of the type practiced by the Post
- With respect to the attacks made on McMahon and Titan, Mushnick never asked for comment from either Titan or McMahon. Mushnick and The Post also refused to print retractions when provided with specific evidence that factual statements they had published about McMahon and Titan were false and erroneous
- Defendants have falsely portrayed Titan, its executives, its employees and its talent as an evil empire involved with organized crime and operated and staffed by sexual criminals, homosexual predators and child molesters
- Defendants have smeared WWF fans by publishing false and malicious statement about WWF fans implying that no right-headed person would attend or purchase WWF products
- Defendants have also made and published false and malicious statements about wrestlers affiliated with the WWF and the process by which they are selected by implying by innuendo that wrestlers must submit to a homosexual casting couch sponsored by corporate management of Titan in order to become affiliated with the WWF or succeed in it.
- Defendants have repeatedly and viciously defamed McMahon by direct statement or provable innuendo, Mushnick has written or orally stated McMahon was a child abuser, a child molester, homosexual criminal sexual offender, a liar in general, a man practiced in the art of deception, cold-blooded, devoid of honor and propriety, a member of organized crime and worse than the fictional character Hannibal Lecter
- Mushnick made all these statements although he doesn't know McMahon, refused McMahon's request to meet and talk, and has never spoken to him in person
- Mushnick claimed part of the business of Titan was to transport minors across state lines for sexual purposes and that such a claim has legal legitimacy as evidenced by a claimed impending lawsuit. No such lawsuit was ever filed or served on Titan or on any person affiliated with Titan
- Mushnick falsely implied McMahon had been charged with rape and that charges had been made against another person involving the sodomy of a minor. No lawsuit has ever been filed by or on behalf of any minor claiming to have been sodomized by a person affiliated with the WWF
- Mushnick and the Post implied or stated in stories with bold headlines "Wrestling Hit by Gay Sex Scandal" and "Boy-Sex Scandal Rocks Wrestling" that high-ranking officials of the WWF have sexually abused teenage employees
- After publishing these articles, Mushnick and Post falsely reported McMahon would make a full admission that certain sexual misconduct charges made in these articles were true, thereby giving false credence to the charges
- Mushnick and/or persons acting at his request or direction or on his behalf offered financial inducements, job promises and the allure of money to be obtained by lawsuits in induce third parties to fabricate accusations of sexual misconduct by WWF personnel
- Mushnick and Post consistently failed to identify their sources for attribution so as to preclude specific rebuttal and prevent any question about the motives and veracity of their sources

- Upon information and belief, Mushnick's sources included convicted felons, a fugitive from justice with a history of crimes against trust, a confidence man of considerable achievement with an easily ascertainable past which includes judicially noted perjurious tendencies, former disgruntled employees or third parties with known desires to retaliate against plaintiffs and a variety of other persons who shared improper and malicious financial motives for their actions and statements
- Mushnick attempted to persuade government agents to take adverse action against Titan and has promised favorable articles to such agents
- When Titan learned of Mushnick's tactics, Mushnick responded by calling for a federal investigation into Titan and McMahon
- Mushnick took steps to fabricate evidence to support his statements and to enhance and influence the likelihood of success for his demand of an investigation and indictment of Titan Sports and McMahon. To do so, Mushnick affiliated himself with Lee Cole, a convicted felon who had been a fugitive from justice during his early dealings with Mushnick
- Mushnick and Cole devised and implemented a calculated plan to induce an individual to stretch the truth and claim he had been sexually abused while a minor by a person formerly affiliated with the WWF. As part of this plan, the person was offered a job and other consideration
- As a result, McMahon has suffered severe emotional distress, severe mental anguish, anger, embarrassment, shame, humiliation, depression and loss of sleep
- During the course of his campaign, Mushnick has been provided with specific evidence in the form of a letter from the Department of Justice proving the falsity of certain statements he has made in his column. Despite such proof, Mushnick refused to retract those statements or inform his readership of the letter
- Mushnick printed an accusation of criminal homosexual conduct by McMahon despite the fact other writers from the Post refused to publish the charges after being provided with specific information that the charge was false and fabricated. Mushnick also made no mention of the information provided the paper indicating the accusation was false and fabricated
- Mushnick knew he was publishing false statements with actual malice and/or reckless disregard for truth

Many of the points in this suit are frivolous in that a columnist is not only allowed, but encouraged to print his opinions. Others lack the very same specifics the suit charges Mushnick with. Others we can at least try and comment on with whatever knowledge we have of the proceedings as they took place during the time period they took place.

Since I haven't seen what is referred to as specific evidence that factual statements they have published were false and erroneous, I can't comment on it. If they were statements made that were provably false, and no retraction was printed, then there is certainly a case. Since no specifics were noted or evidence offered, I don't know of any evidence such is or isn't the case. It's no secret to anyone who knows something about this story that the main witness for both Titan Sports and for Phil Mushnick is the same person, which makes it very difficult for either side to say the main witness that Mushnick used was a bad source since Titan's key source against Mushnick is the same person.

Mushnick has the right to state Titan is an evil empire if that is his opinion (and it is his opinion, and he has the right even if it isn't his opinion, although that would be a poor example of being a columnist) and the charge he smeared Titan's fans is equally ludicrous. I may have missed it, but I believe I've seen just about every column Mushnick wrote regarding this subject, but I can't recall any column stating or insinuating McMahon himself was a child abuser or child molester or a member of organized crime (there was one mention where Billy Graham talked about the investigation and said they were asking him questions along those lines but it was never stated as far as I know point blank or insinuated that was true, just that at one point the idea of it was, according to Graham, being investigated, a huge distinction). He did state there was a police report filed by a wrestler (Kevin Wacholz) and the contents of that report certainly would give one that impression. But the existence of such a report was fact, even though I know of few people who believe the act described actually took place. As far as being a liar in general, I'd think any person who sees a tape of the Larry King show today knowing the facts in hindsight could reasonably reach that conclusion let alone the contradictions between that show and the different Vince McMahon on Donahue. If I recall correctly, the article in which that was stated had specifics to back up that claim.

A man practiced in the art of deception? How can that even be argued? Pro wrestling is the art of deception and there's nobody better than Vince in that art. Quite frankly, that should be a compliment, even though it certainly wasn't meant as such. Devoid of honor and propriety? If I recall, the article written in which that line was stated backed up that statement. Worse than Hannibal Lecter? Hopefully by now we should have all realized that reality is reality and fiction is fiction and any comparison between the two is ridiculous. Mushnick did refuse McMahon's request to meet and talk. How that is applicable to this I'm not entirely sure, but it is a fact. It is untrue, however, that Mushnick never called Titan. The claimed impending lawsuit about transporting minors across state lines for reasons of moral corruption that the suit stated was never filed was at least believed to be part of Tom Cole's claim against Titan that was settled out of court. Saying no lawsuit was filed is pretty flimsy for something that at least based on information I've received was a verified complaint that resulted in a settlement, or some legal agreement that constituted something similar to that in that Cole agreed to drop his claim. Mushnick implied McMahon had been charged with rape? Rita Chatterton had already made her charge on television. Mushnick never stated, as far as I know, that a legal charge of rape was made. I don't even recall him using the word. But what would you describe what Chatterton said in interviews on several television shows and in at least two magazine interviews? To the best of my knowledge, to this point Chatterton has not recanted her story. Whether the story is true, false, or there is a shade of gray to it, we may or may not at some point find out but Chatterton certainly said what she said. Mushnick implied charges had been made against another person involving the sodomy of a minor? Yes, no lawsuit was ever filed. Yes also, that person did go on at least two radio shows with the specific claim.

Muchnick and Post implied that high-ranking officials of the WWF have sexually abused teenage boys? If I recall from the "Now It Can Be Told" show, that it was Tom Cole's lawyer, after the settlement or whatever the correct legal term was for the agreement that had been reached with Titan, in asking that Cole's tape not be played as part of the show, who implied this from the wording in his letter read on the air stronger than anyone. Mushnick and Post falsely reported McMahon would make a full admission that the charges were true? McMahon never made a full admission, so the report that he would certainly turned out to be false. Mushnick and Post failed to identify the sources? I'd need specifics to comment on this although as a general rule, this is pro wrestling, and if all stories were done with identified sources, the vast majority of what you would read would approximate the near-fiction published elsewhere on wrestling, and incidentally, in McMahon's own wrestling and defunct bodybuilding magazines, which means his claiming publishing false information would be like the pot calling the kettle black to begin with, although the fiction in those magazines is not defamatory per se. Mushnick and/or persons acting at his request or direction offered financial inducements, etc. to fabricate accusations? This was the first I've heard of this so can't comment on it. Mushnick's sources? Convicted felons, a fugitive from justice, a con man whose past includes perjurious tendencies, former disgruntled employees, etc. I think I know which pegs fit into which holes here, and it should be noted in almost every case (the fugitive from justice being the exception), these so-called non-reputable people with horrible pasts were hired by Titan Sports after their convictions and con man pasts. As far as the others, at least a few are pretty credible individuals. As far as the rest of the charges, they are things I'm not aware of so can't comment on.

"I stand by what I've written," said Mushnick. "Vince McMahon is a well-known liar. I am not."

Attempts to reach Titan lawyer Jerry McDevitt regarding both aforementioned suits went unanswered.

To win the case, Titan has to be able to prove four things: A) Falsity; B) Reckless disregard for the truth in that the reporter knew what he was printing was false and printed it anyway; C) Malicious intent; and D) Results of this were injurious to the plaintiff. All four must be proven for libel to exist. D is a given, but if this was based on actual truth or what the reporter honestly perceived as truth (absence of malice), it is not libel. My own belief, based on dealings with most all of the above-mentioned people is that B is absolutely not the case and the charges of his attempting to fabricate evidence as being even more ludicrous. As for A, while in hindsight there are some sources whose credibility one has to question and thus some stories emanating from them where the credibility of such is questionable, there are many others that, in hindsight, were credible. The plethora of people who came out indicate either a pattern of something, which, unless every charge were untrue, would at the very least show dishonesty emanating from those formerly affiliated with Titan Sports which at the least gives some credence to Mushnick's conclusions.

My belief is that some of what has come out was exaggerated and probably there is at least one or two cases of outright lying. Much of Mushnick's work during this period was reporting and commenting about steroid use and abuse within the WWF. That not only has been confirmed by numerous sources, but it is a given that the basis for these stories is factual from numerous published interviews, not to mention the Zahorian trial or just from observing the obvious. A major crux of Mushnick's reporting during the period in question, in regard to steroid use in the WWF, was not even mentioned in the suit. It is also worth noting that this same job of reporting was the first item mentioned in the Village Voice story just a few weeks back on Muchnick naming him New York's sports columnist of the year. But, as stated before, the main source of information based on the lawsuit appears to be the same source of a major portion of information on the other side, which makes this a very ugly situation.

MARCH 15

Expect considerably more mainstream media coverage of the lawsuits, particularly the ones involving Geraldo, Mushnick and Hellwig, in the upcoming weeks. The 3/1 Media Week did an article saying that the scandals and lawsuits haven't diminished advertiser interest in the WWF but the falling ratings may. The article stated the WWF as attributing part of the recent increase in ratings to the lawsuits against Rivera and Mushnick. They had quotes from two major ad reps, one of whom said the 1992 scandals weren't an issue when it came to buying time on WWF telecasts and that he hasn't heard any ad reps talking about it. The other said exactly the opposite, that everyone is talking about it and eventually all the bad publicity has to affect sponsor buys. The article noted the WWF syndicated package dropped 26 percent in viewership in 1992. Kids 6-11 held up best, dropping only seven percent, so the loss of Hulk Hogan had very little affect on kids viewing. However, teenagers and males 18-34 showed devastating viewer drops. I've got to presume those are the audiences that the muscles were a larger lure while young kids are more into the exaggerated characters so the elimination of the steroid boys and shrinkage of those still around was a key reason, if not the key reason. Interesting also to note that during 1992, WCW also had its ratings drop only slightly less by percentage, but their major losses were Kids 6-11 and WCW's ratings held up in both the teenagers and males 18-34 category.

MARCH 22

More news was made in the bevy of lawsuits that have been filed around the wrestling world. Jim Hellwig's lawsuit which was the subject of significant space in the 3/8 issue, was dropped just hours before Titan Sports was going to give a written response to it. We have no other details on that (and not for a lack of trying) other than Hellwig has told people the suit was dropped because he's changing lawyers. The timing of the suit being dropped makes that curious. Hellwig's former attorney who filed the suit, Michael Kennedy, was in court until the middle of this week and has yet to return any media calls as of press time, and Steve Planamenta of Titan Sports said he had no additional details on the case.

MARCH 22

Both the Hartford Courant and Fairfield County Advocate, both located near Titan headquarters in Stamford, CT, had lengthy stories regarding the different legal action taken both by Vince McMahon and against McMahon. Both stories were non-committal in editorial slant. The Hartford story was the lead story on page one of the newspaper on 3/8, which had the tongue-in-cheek beginning and ending that many wrestling stories have, but was serious the rest of the way. Rita Chatterton told both reporters that she would like to talk but was advised against it by her attorney, Robert Wolf, who didn't return a phone calls from either newspaper.

Wolf's legal assistant, Roberto Cardenas, was quoted in the Fairfield County piece as saying McMahon's charges about Chatterton fabricating her story were "completely wrong" and also denied the charge in the lawsuit that Wolf works for or has ever worked for Geraldo Rivera. McMahon's claim on Entertainment Tonight that Rivera allegedly gave him two choices, come up with $5 million (the amount Wolf requested from Titan as a "settlement" prior to the story running) or they would air Chatterton's story, had to have been based on the premise that Rivera and Wolf were working together and the lawsuit said Wolf was "within the network of attorneys controlled by (Rivera)." Rivera's spokesman, Jeff Erdel said in the Fairfield County story in regards to the suit, that "If I filed a suit against you claiming you were an alien from the Planet Venus with three heads, it would have as much truth as this legal action. Our attorneys feel it doesn't have any merit. There's no truth to the charges. Erdel repeated earlier statements that he believed the Now It Can Be Told piece was fair and accurate and that McMahon had been given repeated opportunities to appear, claimed Chatterton was credible and said they stand behind the story.

Jerry McDevitt, the attorney for McMahon, said the company is still calculating the damage they believe was caused by the Rivera story and the stories by Mushnick but predicts the figure will be in the millions. One interesting thing to note about assessing the Mushnick damage is that throughout the time period when Mushnick was writing the articles, the WWF attendance in New York's three metro arenas were the only major arenas in which the gates didn't plummet in 1992. "In plain English, we were sick of it," he said to the Fairfield paper. "Bashing Vince McMahon has become a cottage industry. Geraldo said to Vince, `We've got a women here who claims you raped her. Do you want to come on and deny that?' What kind of choice is that? It gives it dignity if he appears. And it's bullshit."

The Fairfield newspaper also talked about the August, 1991 suit filed by Jim Stuart, McMahon's long-time limo driver, who had been fired by McMahon the previous year. Stuart wouldn't say anything on the record other than he wouldn't retract anything he's said previously (in the Penthouse story). In a deposition in March 1992 with Titan's lawyers, Stuart charged WWF officials with extensive use of "illegal substances," although the only name he said specifically was McMahon's. He claimed he was fired because he knew of a move to dump someone who was his friend. Stuart was vague in his deposition on almost everything, saying he was worried about retaliation. McDevitt responded saying Stuart "couldn't get over the fact he was just a driver."

Both stories also covered the much-publicized Murray Hodgson lawsuit, which apparently still exists. Hodgson didn't return calls from either publication, although both pointed out the charge he repeated on several television shows about being fired for rejecting a homosexual advance was dropped from the suit, although neither publication were aware that the charge was dropped due to a legal technicality well before Hodgson had ever talked to anyone publicly. This isn't to give credence to his story, just that he didn't drop the claim, the claim was stricken from the suit on a legal technicality by the Titan lawyers because of certain legal procedures regarding sexual harassment cases in Connecticut.

Both stories also printed McDevitt's most colorful paragraph in his lawsuit against Mushnick and the New York Post. In it, the suit claims Mushnick has "written or orally stated that Mr. McMahon is a child abuser, a child molester, homosexual, a charged heterosexual rapist, a miscreant, a homosexual criminal sexual offender, a liar in general and in specific respects, a man practiced in the art of deception, devoid of honor and proprietary (sic), a member of organized crime, and worse than the fictional character Hannibal Lecter, who killed and ate his victims." As mentioned in the 3/8 issue, I'm not aware of Mushnick ever stating or writing some of those statements, only made a comparison between the two. The strongest words he did write were these, from his March 16, 1992 column: "The WWF is so powerdrunk in the knowledge that its autonomy fully enables it to violate every standard of human decency because right-headed humans possess neither the time nor the inclination to do anything about an industry they've always viewed with bemused disregard. Never will you encounter a human more cold-blooded, more devoid of honor and propriety than Vince McMahon, America's foremost babysitter. In your wildest, most twisted dreams, you won't meet up with the likes of McMahon, a miscreant so practiced in the art of deception, the half-truth, and the bald-faced lie as to make the Artful Dodger appear clumsy. A George Steinbrenner or a Don King pale by comparison. So help us. Indeed, Hannibal

Lecter is the only fictional character who comes close." In the Fairfield story, Mushnick said, "the suit is full of shit and I'm waiting for my chance to prove it in court." Mushnick claimed to have talked to McMahon for hours in the story, McMahon said it was more like minutes and that Mushnick refused a face-to-face interview. I can recall, from talking to both shortly after their lone conversation, that both described it at the time as lengthy, although from what I recall, neither gave the impression it lasted more than two hours.

The Hartford paper also talked of a suit by Bill Eadie and Randy Colley in New Haven, who claimed McMahon never paid them what he promised for the ring characters they claimed to have created (Demolition).

David Shults interviewed with the Hartford newspaper and said he never even received a copy of the tape of Chatterton (in the lawsuit it claims Shults wanted to tape a Chatterton conversation in 1992 and claim it was taped in 1988 to lend credence to her rape story; Chatterton did a 1988 tape for Shults that was said to have been "very colorful" whatever that means, but she never claimed to have been raped) from Anthony Toce, the former deputy police chief of Bloomfield, CT who was hired by Shults as a private eye to investigate McMahon. Toce hasn't commented on the charges.

The Hartford story mentioned the federal investigation when Shults' attorney, Eileen McGann said she was contacted by an assistant U.S. attorney who told her he is looking into allegations of illegal drug use, sexual harassment and sexual abuse in the WWF and that a prosecutor wanted to talk with Shults. When McDevitt was asked if he knew about a federal investigation, he said he couldn't comment.

McMahon, who is doing heavy publicity on his and his company's charity work in order to upgrade both his and the company image, refused a request for an interview for the Hartford story. He did, however give a lengthy diatribe for the Fairfield reporter, which stated: "I just think it's extremely unfortunate (what the Post and Geraldo did). To coin a phrase, it's tabloid terrorism, the worst aspect of media these days. To see your name written in such a light as `worse than the fictional flesh-eating character Hannibal Lecter' is demeaning to say the least. And it makes you feel very bad that someone who doesn't know you, and hasn't made an effort to know you, would write these dastardly things that are totally untrue. It hurts big time. It hurts me, every member of my organization, and it hurts my family. You say to yourself, for whatever reason, maybe that's it, maybe this will be the last one, the last outlandish thing (Mushnick's) going to say. You try and make dialogue, try to make contact, but that doesn't go anywhere. And it just keeps going on and on. Finally you say you have to do something about it because it's so unfair. You seek whatever redress you have, and, unfortunately, in this case it's the courts...People keep asking me, `Vince, what did you do to this guy (Mushnick) to make him the way he is? I have no idea. I've never met him, although I've tried. When does it end?"

McMahon claimed in the story that the WWF started drug testing in 1986 (actually it was 1987) and when steroids became illegal, he put them on the banned list (steroids were actually illegal in many states dating to the mid-80s, black market distribution has always been illegal and distribution for muscle-building purposes was made illegal nationwide in 1988 although many states had prior laws existing on that as well, personal use was illegal nationwide by early 1990; the first test wasn't until November of 1991, at which time use was somewhere between substantial and epidemic). When it comes to steroid use in the WWF, McMahon said, "We have had the finger unjustly pointed at us. Not to say that at one time, when steroids were legal, there wasn't use in the WWF, and perhaps even something of prolific use. But when it became illegal, we addressed it very strongly. There's nothing that's even close to what we do." McMahon also maintained his previous stance when it comes to his own use of anabolic steroids that "I experimented with them when they were legal. They're not legal now. I don't take them and haven't. And that goes with any other kind of a drug."

MAY 31

Latest on the legal front. New York magazine ran a short blurb headlined "WWF has Mushnick on the ropes" with Titan lawyers saying Phil Mushnick had failed to show up for a deposition. Titan attempted to get default judgements in both its case against Mushnick and also its case against Kevin "Nailz" Wacholz, in both cases claiming the defendants failed to respond to the suit within the prescribed period of time. In both cases Titan's request was turned down. In the case of Wacholz, the judge ruled that the process server didn't take adequate measures to reach Wacholz. The summons for the lawsuit was served to Wacholz' sister rather than Kevin himself. According to the newspaper article than ran about the court hearing, Wacholz has filed a countersuit against McMahon and Titan Sports based on his claims made regarding the incident in Green Bay last December.

JUNE 7

Tom Cole, the WWF ringboy who was largely responsible for much of the negative publicity that surrounded the WWF last year, filed a $1.6 million suit against Titan Sports, Pat Patterson, Mel Phillips and Terry Garvin this past Tuesday. This is a long, involved story with many twists and turns. The lawsuit is a three-parter. Part one re-opens the claims of sexual harassment of a homosexual nature by top WWF officials. Cole first brought forth these claims last year in a front page article in the San Diego Union. The story didn't name any names, but did detail certain situations and had other ringboys claim sexual abuse was prevalent. Almost immediately, Patterson, Phillips and Garvin, who were the three men Cole's initial claims were about but whose names had yet to be brought out in the public, resigned their positions. Patterson was brought back several months later but Phillips and Garvin never returned. Cole's attorneys brought forth a complaint that was settled before a lawsuit was ever filed. The settlement was an agreement between Cole and Titan Sports last year in which Cole received $55,000 and was rehired as a ringboy and offered a try-out as a ring announcer.

As part of the settlement, according to the complaint, Cole agreed to never bring up his charges again and Titan agreed never to ask him to retract his initial charges. The lawsuit claims Titan breached that settlement agreement by failing to give Cole a try-out as a ring announcer which is largely the crux of the new lawsuit, a breach of contract, and also said Titan continually attempted to get Cole to go public and retract his sexual abuse and harassment charges. The third part of the suit claims that Titan officials attempted to get Cole to sign an affidavit stating things that weren't true about his brother, Lee Cole, who at the time was going on several radio stations making claims. Tom Cole in the suit claims he didn't want to sign it but finally did because Titan wouldn't allow him to leave a room until he signed it and the suit claims he was falsely imprisoned.

While this isn't certain, given the wording of the Titan lawsuit against Phil Mushnick, it can be ascertained that the statements Cole signed claimed Mushnick and Lee Cole had conspired against Titan and induced Tom to create an untrue story, which may have been a key point in the lawsuit against Mushnick. Given the circumstances of what came out publicly during that time, that specific charge of imprisonment sounds curious on the surface since it was well-known publicly at the time of the split between Tom Cole and Lee Cole. This new suit also does not name names when it comes to specific harassment charges by specific individuals as the previous complaint did, and also doesn't detail incidents of sexual abuse as the initial complaint did which is also curious.

JUNE 14

Tom Cole, who filed the lawsuit two weeks back against Titan, is apparently still on the company payroll.

JULY 12

In an item in the August WWF Magazine that was released this past week as well as sent to various employees of the company in a separate letter, a statement read: "The World Wrestling Federation Magazine has always been published with entertaining and informative articles for you, our fans. However, in the upcoming issues, TitanSports Inc., and the World Wrestling Federation will address some malicious issues that have confronted and unjustly challenged our company over the past two years. There have been libelous remarks and vicious newspaper and magazine articles written. The tabloid media has had a field day with us, and we have been subjected to tactics bordering on McCarthyism. We have spent a great deal of time, effort, energy and money combating the lies and innuendo, countering with our own lawsuits, and we are continuing to investigate the reasons for this witch hunt. Now it's time for us to tell our story about Tom Cole, Rita Chatterton, Murray Hodgson, Superstar Billy Graham, Dave Schultz (sic) and others who have aided and abetted in spreading gossip and lies. Starting next month, we will do just that."

The first article in what appears to be a series will be released the first week of August. While I've got little doubt that some of the stories that came out lacked credibility, others, in particular those talking about widespread steroid use within the company both before and after the federal law changed (and after many states had ruled use of the drugs and dispensation for non-therapeutic reasons as illegal) were quite credible. What will be most interesting is to see if these stories attempt to be written with credibility in being balanced as to weeding out the credible for the stories lacking credibility, or if they'll be written in a manner as to try and portray every issue and every story as one in which the company was unjustly portrayed.

JULY 26

Titan's legal department has picked on some strange targets this past week. Jason Shepard, 16, who ran fan clubs for Mr. Perfect and Shawn Michaels received a threatening legal letter regarding such and asking him to turn over all monies received from those endeavors since the WWF holds trademarks to both names. While this is in their legal rights since they own the trademarks, it probably could have been handled in a less-threatening manner. Wade Keller of the Pro Wrestling Torch also received a threatening letter. Two months back Keller, in an ad in his newsletter for Torch t-shirts, made a joke that if you wear a t-shirt and sit in the first rows at a WWF taping, you may get a free WWF t-shirt. This was a comment based on existing and longstanding WWF policy when it comes to those wearing t-shirts of rival company wrestlers at tapings. Titan's lawyers tried to imply that Keller was saying the WWF endorsed and/or sponsored his t-shirt sale, a conclusion that nobody with half a brain could have come to and demanded he state that Titan Sports neither endorses nor sponsors either his t-shirts or his newsletter. I think that statement is more of a recommendation for a newsletter than a retraction.

AUGUST 2

Sometime this past week there was a demonstration with picket signs in front of Titan's office building in Stamford, CT done by the family of Tom Cole. From the sounds of things, it apparently turned into a circus.

AUGUST 16

Billy Graham had some comments to make about the WWF Magazine article on his life story that is in the current issue. "I could nitpick and pull things apart but I think you (Wrestling Observer) did a good job (in last week's issue) on the major issues." Graham was most upset about the line about him never holding a regular job in his life, saying it speaks volumes for how Titan and other promoters feel about their wrestlers. "They don't consider being a wrestler a legitimate job, but that is the history of the relationship between promoters and the wrestlers. They showed total disregard for my career, never mentioning sellout after sellout or when Bruno and I set the (attendance) record at the Spectrum for the cage match. It's true that I wasn't the best worker. I never claimed to be a good worker. My appeal was as a speaker, my charismatic appeal, the clothes, the interviews.

I can't think of any other business with as much distrust between the employers and the employees. They didn't bring up the issues that created this in the first place. If one of their fans read the article, I don't think they could even figure out what it is all about." The story did make valid points as far as Graham's legal action against both Titan and George Zahorian in that he used steroids for many years before he was in the WWWF or had met Zahorian, but never addressed any of the issues that were publicized regarding Graham in the media.

SEPTEMBER 13

Mike Quinn, the WBF bodybuilder who finished in unofficial last place at the second contest, is suing Vince McMahon and Titan Sports for $750,000. Many of the ex-WBFers have been critical in recent muscle mag interviews of how the WBF was run. In his interviews, Quinn claimed he was fired after the second contest (and the WBF subsequently went out of business) for failing a cocaine test administered the day of the show and because Titan claimed a hotel employee had found syringes and Growth Hormone in his hotel room. Quinn is claiming innocence on both accounts.

DECEMBER 6

Former wrestling legend Edouardo Carpentier filed a $127,000 lawsuit against Titan Sports in Quebec Superior Court on 11/26. Carpentier, whose real name is Edward Wieczorkiewicz (which I guess tells why he didn't use his real name although his original wrestling name was shortened to Eddie Wiecz), 66, is claiming wrongful termination. He handled the French commentary on the WWF's syndie shows from December 7, 1984 through October 27, 1992. Titan, in the letter firing him, claimed he was negligent, incompetent and disinterested in the product and claimed he was offered $1,669.20 in severance pay but then never received it. Carpentier is asking for $52,868.70 as his salary for the 14 months remaining on his contract when he was fired, $25,000 for defamation, $25,000 for age discrimination and $25,000 in punitive damages. Raymond Rougeau has handled the French announcing since Carpentier was dropped.

CHAPTER TWO

WWF REVAMPS CABLE LINEUP

JANUARY 4

The new Saturday morning television show on USA Network, which originally was going to be called Slam & Jam, will instead be named "WWF Mania" because WCW beat them to the punch calling their record album Slam & Jam.

JANUARY 20

After a fourth quarter in which its television ratings failed to show the expected seasonal increase, and coming off before that the lowest ratings in its history, the WWF decided to revamp its cable line-up starting the weekend of 1/9. The new Saturday Morning show called WWF Mania debuted in the 10 a.m. time slot on that day. The show is similar to All-American Wrestling in that it is simply taped matches and interviews, most of which had already aired previously in syndication, hosted by Todd Pettingill (not sure of spelling). Pettingill's segments are decided aimed toward young kids, which considering the time slot, is probably a good idea. But I was disappointed in the show because it's simply more of the same, rather than any kind of a change. With the state of the industry in 1993, more of the same on television is definitely not better. The show opened with a poor 0.8 rating and a two share, barely better than WBF Body Stars did in the same time slot during its abortive run. First week ratings aren't indicative of anything, but I didn't see anything on the show to indicate people should go out of their way to see it.

On 1/11, they debuted the new Monday Night Raw, a one hour show which replaces Prime Time Wrestling. As a concept, the live show idea is good. The first show wasn't. The main problem was Rob Bartlett, a New York disc jockey comedian who is part of the Don Iamus morning show on WFAN. Bartlett's comedy isn't funny, but that wasn't the problem. The problem is he was totally unprepared. Not only that, but Vince McMahon seemed off, such as when Bartlett asked if Shawn Michaels would be in the Royal Rumble and McMahon didn't even know, when Michaels had been announced to wrestle Marty Janetty weeks ago. When an announcer doesn't know Rick Steiner from Scott Steiner, he really shouldn't be put out there live. Maybe he'll catch on, but he definitely came across as someone far more interested in getting himself over and with nothing but disdain for the vehicle (in this case the WWF) that was giving him the time to get over. I'm not sure making jokes about the promotion's killer heel needing a bra and having a wedgie is going to help get him over as an awesome monster. It's also questionable if in 1993, when one of the major problems is the lack of believability causing a lack of heat and interest and a collapse of the business (and 30 to 50 percent decline in attendance does qualify as a collapse), that making an obvious joke out of the profession is the answer to regaining heat and interest. Even under good business conditions, if it was a Buddy Rose-like comedy figure, that would be one thing, but not Yokozuna, when he's figured in as a main event heel for the next year or so.

The real problem isn't Bartlett, because it's obvious from the concept of the show that the idea of the major selling point will be the toilet humor. There's a place in this world for it and an audience, and the wrestling audience probably isn't the worst audience to aim it toward. I'm just suspect of the timing. They tried the same thing a few years back with the Bobby Heenan show and it flopped royally, and Heenan was a whole lot funnier than Bartlett, because Heenan had the ability to make himself the butt of the jokes while Bartlett is being put in the position that he makes the jokes and that his jokes are more important than anything else on the show. The ratings for the first show were pretty good (2.5) based on curiosity and I suspect for the first four to six weeks they'll stay that way. But unless the shows improve during that period, the curiosity will end and they'll be back to the hardcores, and hardcore WWF numbers are no longer impressive.

CHAPTER THREE

RIC FLAIR LEAVES WWF FOR WCW

JANUARY 4

The status of Ric Flair in the WWF has been the subject of a lot of speculation over the past week including one semi-erroneous report that he has already jumped from the WWF to WCW. Flair's WWF contract doesn't expire until September. There have apparently been discussions between Flair and Vince McMahon about getting a release before that time. To the best of my knowledge as of press time, Flair has not received a release and Flair is booked on WWF shows as far out as the bookings have been completed (through early March) in a top spot. He will be moved down from headline status probably by the end of January or mid-February to second from the top status on the tour either in singles against Mr. Perfect or in tags with Razor Ramon against Perfect & Tatanka, which may mean a serious pay cut and likely means him doing frequent jobs since Tatanka and Doink are going to get the mega-pushes these next few months. Presumably, and this all depends on many factors like size of gates or emergency situations which happen every day in wrestling and might force him back on top, one would think the odds are he would be able to earn more money in WCW by the nature of the contract they would no doubt offer him and almost surely would be able to earn more over the long run with a WCW contract. To say there has been contact with WCW would be to indicate WCW has tampered with a wrestler under contract to WWF, which is illegal. I think we all realize illegal acts like that are commonplace in the wrestling business under the guise of social conversations. As of press time, there is smoke, but no fire, to the story.

JANUARY 15

Several major news items since our last issue. Although two world titles changed hands, no doubt the biggest news is that Ric Flair will most likely be returning to World Championship Wrestling in mid-February. While no contract has been signed, Flair has received a release from his World Wrestling Federation contract that expires in September which would allow him to join WCW after 2/15, which means his most likely debut date will be the SuperBrawl PPV show in Asheville, NC. Flair will be finishing up all scheduled matches against Bret Hart and Mr. Perfect with his last date expected to be around 2/8 after completion of the WWF's European tour. His final WWF appearances in the United States will be on the final weekend of January, including the 1/29 Somalia benefit at Madison Square Garden against Mr. Perfect. Flair is expected to sign a multi-year contract with WCW which includes an undisclosed guaranteed annual salary said to be well above the $1,000 per night maximum Bill Watts had originally stated would be the most he would pay any wrestler, and also minus the four month contract review period intervals which Watts talked about as guidelines for all wrestlers on new contracts. Flair is expected to be put into a babyface role upon his arrival in WCW and feud with Barry Windham and Big Van Vader.

Flair left the WWF on amicable business terms with Vince McMahon according to several sources on both sides. The WWF party line story is that McMahon a few weeks back asked Flair, who turns 44 on 2/25, to retire to a front office position because he respected Flair's talents and his position as one of the sports legends so much that he didn't want to see him become a preliminary wrestler, but that he could no longer use him on top. That story is hard to fathom. It is well known behind the scenes that WCW has made several major plays in recent months to try and bring Flair back, with the major hold-up being his Titan contract although Flair had been having thoughts of returning to WCW since Bill Watts returned and had felt all along he could get out of his Titan contract at any time if he needed to which makes the Titan party line seem like a way of saving face although, as mentioned, sources on both sides confirm the personal parting of the ways between McMahon and Flair was amicable.

Losing Flair has become a very divisive issue within Titan, however, since the company's stated goal was to improve the wrestling quality and Flair was still one of the two or three best workers in the promotion, which has little depth when it comes to quality workers who can headline. Sportscaster Harold Johnson of WSOC-TV in Charlotte, who is known to be a friend of Flair's and was the sportscaster who talked of wrestling fans boycotting WCW events in Charlotte in 1991 because of the treatment Flair received when he was fired, reported on 1/6 that Flair agreed to a multi-year deal (believed to be either two or three years) "that will pay him considerably more than he was making when he left" WCW. That would be hard to believe, since Flair's old contract was in the $750,000 per year range, although figures of $375,000 to $400,000 have been bandied about, which would be considerably more than he could have earned in the WWF.

JANUARY 20

Although no contract has been signed at press time, it now appears to be close to a sure thing that Ric Flair will start with WCW, most likely at the SuperBrawl III PPV show on 2/21 in Asheville, NC. I don't believe Flair has received his written release from Titan Sports, however, as reported last week, it appears he and Vince McMahon have split on amicable terms. Apparently the meeting between the two several weeks back wasn't so much McMahon wanting Flair to retire, but explaining how he'd be used, which appears to be mainly to work semifinals and third from the top and generally putting younger talent over, and when the time is right, and unlike what was reported here last week, that time wasn't now, he'd be given a front office position. Flair cut a deal with Bill Shaw of TBS to return as a featured performer, and it does appear to be in a babyface role with a natural feud with Barry Windham and eventually Big Van Vader.

JANUARY 25

The latest on Ric Flair is that he still hasn't signed a contract with World Championship Wrestling. Flair was on the road this weekend finishing up his commitments with the WWF and a new contract was supposed to be waiting for him when he returned home. While it is expected the deal to be consummated and Flair to start on the 2/21 PPV show from Asheville, NC, it is not a done deal at least as of press time. Even Jim Ross of WCW, when commenting about the reports of the deal on the 900 number said deals have been known to fall apart at the last minute. Flair's WWF departure was explained within the storyline when on 1/18, he lost a loser leaves town match with Mr. Perfect at the Manhattan Center for the 1/25 airing of Monday Night Raw (which can't air live because the WWF will be taping television in San Jose, CA that night). The match was said to have been excellent, lasting about 20:00 and Perfect juiced (the blade seems to be back in use minimally in both WCW & WWF), with Perfect winning with the Perfect plex.

Titan pulled a coup out with the way they handled this. First off, they established Monday Night Raw as a television show with the angle on 1/18 and the blow-off of a major feud on television the next week. Theoretically, the 1/25 show should draw a big Clash-like rating, probably in excess of a 3.0. Some of the momentum from that rating and the interest garnered in the show itself should carry over for several weeks. In addition, it won't look as though Flair jumped from WWF to WCW to the casual fan. It will look as though Flair lost his job with WWF and had no choice but to return to WCW, which is established again as the second-rate circuit. I don't know whether or not Flair had the choice in whether to handle his departure like this or his release was based on him doing this on the way out, but this particular clean job in a match that will be viewed by millions, rather than by just a few thousand hardcores in a few cities, many of whom don't take wins and losses seriously, will have an effect on Flair's image upon his return. While Flair's first interview in WCW (and this is dependent upon him going there) may erase much of the stigma of the loss to a degree, the clean loss to Perfect in a match that "forced him to leave" rather than him deciding to seek more lucrative pastures in the fans eyes will establish him in some eyes as damaged goods for his return. Give Flair credit because in a scenario that wasn't designed to get him over, he put on his typical performance.

FEBRUARY 1

This week's Ric Flair update is that as of press time, Flair has not signed with WCW. I expect it to still happen and the timing of everything to be basically what has been listed here previously, although it doesn't appear that the signing is just a simple formality at this point, either. The plan on both sides is still for Flair to debut on 2/21, probably just doing an interview which may turn into an angle. WCW did officially sign Davey Boy Smith on 1/19 and garnered a lot of mainstream publicity in the United Kingdom for signing the country's most popular wrestler. I haven't seen the stories, but apparently they were along with lines that Smith wanted serious wrestling competition and insinuating that the WWF was a circus. Hey, just because a guy dressed up in a clown suit is being pushed as a main eventer doesn't mean it's a circus. You want proof positive it isn't a circus? Okay, how many circuses have you been to during your life in which you get to listen to a preacher give a sermon? They have a policeman, but that doesn't make them a precinct. They have a dressed up Indian, but that doesn't make them a Western movie. They have Bret Hart and Shawn Michaels as singles champions, but that doesn't make them a wrestling promotion.

FEBRUARY 8

Ric Flair signed his contract with WCW this past week and is expected to debut at the PPV show. I believe they'll make the announcement on the 2/13 TBS show that Flair will be back on the PPV and will announce Davey Boy Smith appearing at the PPV this coming weekend. He still hasn't signed his WWF release papers for whatever that is worth.

FEBRUARY 15

What may have been a hang-up involving Ric Flair coming to WCW surfaced this past week. According to several WCW officials and confirmed on the Jim Ross 900 line on Saturday, Flair has yet to receive an official written contract release from Vince McMahon, even though reportedly McMahon gave him a verbal okay months back. WCW received a release from Titan, however the release wasn't signed. Going under the assumption that it was an honest error, it was sent back but this time the release that came back wasn't notarized. Apparently this second miscue happened early this past week and caused several WCW officials to re-evaluate the situation and wonder if someone wasn't dealing in good faith. Word was given to the PR department to eliminate all references to Flair, all advertising of Flair or talk of Flair beginning at SuperBrawl until the situation was settled. While this was going on, Flair was in Europe finishing up his WWF commitments with his final date being 2/10. Originally the announcement of Flair's return at SuperBrawl was scheduled for the 2/13 TBS show, but everything is now on hold until a legal release from Titan is received. Since the final two Saturday TBS shows before SuperBrawl were taped on 2/8, it would require late additions if Flair could appear at SuperBrawl (which would be in a non-wrestling role) that wouldn't air until the day before the show. If things aren't straightened out this week, that appearance would be in serious doubt. The reason Lex Luger, whose contract with WCW didn't expire until March 1, 1993, was able to start with Titan on January 24, was because Watts released him from the last five weeks of his contract period. Luger had appeared on a few WWF telecasts as part of the WBF immediately after jumping from WCW, however then-WCW VP Kip Frey filed suit against Luger which prevented him from appearing on any wrestling telecasts until March 1 due to the release Frey had signed with Luger allowing him to leave WCW one year early.

FEBRUARY 22

Everything has been finalized as far as contracts and releases regarding Ric Flair's return to WCW. Flair's officially becomes part of the WCW payroll on 2/16 and debuts Sunday at the PPV. Flair apparently obtained his official release from Titan Sports upon finishing his European tour on 2/10. Since the final television taping for airing before SuperBrawl was done two days earlier, there will be no televised announcement of Flair appearing at SuperBrawl, something the company was hoping to be able to put in at the last minute to increase late buys. No word on what Flair's role will be on the PPV but he won't be wrestling. For whatever this is worth, the rumor among the wrestlers is that Flair signed a three-year deal at $425,000 per. Davey Boy Smith's opponent for the show has been finalized as Bill Irwin. In another possible change, the arthroscopic surgery to Ron Simmons' rotator cuff (shoulder) showed more damage than originally thought and while it's not 100 percent certain, it is expected he won't be able to wrestle Dustin Rhodes at the PPV as advertised. WCW actually got this word after the final taping as well so it may not be able to make this correction before the show if such a correction is needed. Actually, they can always insert promos and it would be good-will to the fans if somehow an insert is put in the show Saturday during the Control Center to at least, if Simmons won't be there, indicate what his injury is and that his appearance is questionable. No word on a possible replacement.

MARCH 8

Flair returned to WCW on 2/21 in Asheville and made his first television appearance on the show taped 2/23 that aired this past Saturday. Flair just said that he was back, and only hinted of his initial role which will be to do an interview segment called "A Flair for the Gold," which not-so-coincidentally was the subtitle for Starrcade '83 (and should be for Starrcade '93 if they play their cards correctly). Obviously something at some point will happen that will lead to him getting back into the ring, with general speculation being his first match taking place on the 6/15 Clash of Champions from Norfolk.

CHAPTER FOUR

BEHIND THE SCENES
TURMOIL IN WCW

MARCH 24

Three were a lot of fireworks this past week on the 900 line. Bill Watts and Steve Beverly ripped into Mark Madden, who wrote a parody that appeared in Pro Wrestling Torch. It has become commonplace for Watts to rip into newsletters, because he apparently never learned how to take criticism, only to dish it out, but never mentions them by name, although he broke that rule in this instance. I found Madden's piece one of the funniest things in a newsletter in a while. Bill and Erik Watts along with Dusty and Dustin Rhodes were the subject of the parody which was built around a fictitious last TBS broadcast where each had one last chance to push their son. I realize some found one specific paragraph in bad taste where Erik was in a video and was crucified but made a comeback with the crawler on the screen "Erik Watts, arising on the third day at an arena near you" as a satire on one of the Watts videos that aired a few weeks back on television. There is a difference between satire and seriousness, even when the satire is delivering a serious message. Having been through all this before many times, trying to obfuscate legitimate criticism of someone's decisions or performance by attempting to create the idea that the criticism is based on personal dislike (and sometimes it can be, other times it's a total con job to hide the real issue) can be an effective defense if you change the real issue, of which there is no legitimate defense for, to the fake personal issue so the real issue is forgotten.

In this case with Bill Watts, thus far his record is there in dollars, sense, ratings and attendance. In seven months at the helm, he's had some successes and more failures. Overall, the quality of the house shows have gone down. The Saturday Night TBS show has improved but Main Event has been inconsistent. Based on the syndication I've seen, it has gotten worse. Attendance has gone down. Gates are down even more. Ratings hit all-time lows but have increased since but that can largely be explained by seasonal variation since they are still way down from last year. The quality of the talent is down. The buy rate for the October PPV was encouraging. Overall interest in the product has decreased, and that is what should be judged. This lashing out at those who report these numbers to create a "war with the media" is just a way to camouflage what the real facts state about his job performance.

As far as Erik Watts goes, Bill Watts isn't the first promoter to overpush his son. He won't be the last.

Promoters have gone out of business because they couldn't see past their own blinders in pushing their son. Erik Watts may become a good wrestler some day. He may not. The fact that Dustin Rhodes was overpushed early in his career because of who his father was and is now a good wrestler, or even that the same happened with Dory and Terry Funk, who became all-time legends, is not a defense. The fact that there have been wrestlers with even less potential or less ability pushed harder in the past is also not a defense. Erik Watts is taking a lot of personal heat that he doesn't deserve for anything he's done. But it is a natural reaction based on the position he's been put in--a position he also doesn't deserve at this point.

JANUARY 25

Paul E. Dangerously (Paul Heyman) was officially fired 1/15 by WCW by a letter faxed to him from Bill Watts. Watts, in the letter, claimed that WCW's investigation of Dangerously's expense reports turned up falsified reports at the Ramada Hotel Atlanta Airport South for dates in April, May, June and July of this past year. Watts' letter also claimed that the Ramada Hotel confirmed Dangerously wasn't registered as a guest on the dates claimed in his expense reports and "it appears that you induced Ramada Hotel to provide false information that you did stay at the Hotel to support fraudulent expense reports and attempt to obtain improper payments of approximately $1,200." Watts also claimed that it appears Dangerously may have falsified other expense reports as well.

Reportedly, during that four-month period, Dangerously turned in receipts from the hotel totalling $1,162.50 for 39 dates. According to a hotel official we contacted, there is no question Dangerously stayed at the hotel during that time period, although the official claimed they would be unable to prove how many dates.

Dangerously signed a two-year contract with WCW and Kip Frey on April 1, 1992 worth, between base salary, performance incentives and expenses, well in excess of $200,000 per year. The contract also listed him as a TBS employee, rather than an independent contractor. This would have made him the only performer in the company designated as such so the contract was somewhat precedent setting for a pro wrestling performer. The employee's contract provided that work-related expenses, such as medical expenses, road expenses and promotional expenses be paid for by the company. Shortly after Watts took over the reigns of the company, Dangerously found himself phased out of the spotlight. It has been heavily speculated that the size and terms of the contract, which no doubt Watts never would have given to any manager, spelled his downfall, similar to Jim Cornette's $225,000 per year contract with WCW being a large part of his initial downfall under Jim Herd, who felt no manager was worth that kind of money and Cornette was phased down which made Herd's feelings into a self-fulfilling prophesy. Nevertheless, the investigation of Dangerously was known about by some within the industry for several months. It wasn't a quickie deal by any means.

In an interview on Friday in the Charleston Post-Courier, Dangerously claimed that Watts attempted to bury his career in an attempt to make him settle on a contract buyout.

"They made that allegation (of falsified expense reports). It is 100 percent untrue. It is false, and it is a lie. The only discrepancy at all on my expense reports is the fact that for several years, several members of the organization have stayed at a particular motel in Atlanta, never got receipts, and that was the maximum amount the company would pay us to stay at the motel anyway. They asked for further documentation, and I got from the hotel itself a letter acknowledging I had been there on the dates in question, and all of a sudden even that is not good enough for WCW. This has been a witch hunt for five months because I refused to renegotiate a contract I signed with that company because I refused to take less pay when I had already committed myself for two years under an agreement. I had no problem renegotiating this deal on April 1, 1994, when this contract expires. It would have been stupid to renegotiate a contract that had already been signed by both parties in good faith.

"In my contract, there is a buyout clause in which they have to buy me out at a certain price even if there is just cause, which there isn't. They have to pay me six months severance (in excess of $100,000) up front. In an attempt to get me to lie down like a dog so that I don't chase after even that, this company is holding the treat of criminal prosecution to make me go away. I am going to seek all legal recourse, not only to enforce the stipulations and provisions of my contract, but for damages to my professional standing and reputation for this blatant attempt to blackmail me and ruin my career because I wouldn't buckle under Bill Watts' pressure. We're going to litigate."

The last statement concerns two items. First, Dangerously claims his contract calls for him to be given 30 days notice in the event of termination and severance pay equal to slightly more than six months salary, a combined figure in the $120,000 range. Secondly, in Watts' termination letter, Watts said that WCW is not waiving its right to process criminal action in regard to the case.

Delaine Dunovan, the General Manager of the Ramada Hotel Atlanta Airport South, was worried that the entire situation may have been a misunderstanding because wrestling personalities often check in under pseudonyms so they can avoid being bothered by fans.

Dunovan, who, when contacted Monday, wasn't aware Dangerously had been fired over the incident, but knew of the WCW investigation, said the problem may have been that the office computer would have no records of any cash purchases if made under pseudonyms unless they were asked to pull out the records knowing the pseudonym used on the specific night. She recalled that Dangerously was a regular customer at the hotel, saying she even recalls personally checking him in on several occasions.

"I don't know too much other than they were investigating his records," she said. "They (Turner investigations) talked with our comptrollers office to pull the records. They took it back to the office. I haven't heard anything since that time. He (Dangerously) didn't have the receipts. He had a letter (from hotel management) saying he stayed here. They (Turner investigations) were looking for back-up copies of the receipts.

"All the guys stay here under different names. They don't want the fans to find them. Sometimes they don't want their families to find them. He definitely stayed here. The problem is some of the dates don't coincide with the dates he turned in. Sometimes guys rent rooms late at night and pay cash. It's hard to pinpoint unless you know the name they used and look for it on the specific date. If he signed in as Joe Blow, for example (it should be noted Joe Blow was a well-known sign-in name of a specific wrestler at the hotel), we would have no way of pulling those records up. He could have been his own worst enemy. It was really kind of a screwy deal on both parts (sides).

"He had stayed here. We never had any problems with him when he was here. I know he stayed here because I've personally checked him in. Without knowing the dates and the name he used, we can't go back and look. But the guy stayed here for a long time. It (the investigation) got out of my hands and into the owners' hands. I had no control over it. Without paying by credit card or knowing what name he used on specific dates, there's no way to prove he stayed here."

JANUARY 25

Bill Watts sent out a five-page letter to all talent two weeks back. He made some good points, such as "I didn't get my wake up call from the front desk at the hotel" as not being a valid excuse for missing flight connections and thus missing bookings and talked about heavily fining the wrestlers who used that excuse and missed the Charlotte card on 12/27. On the other hand, Watts' continued his harangue blaming guaranteed contracts for all the problems in the business which don't hold water based on applied practices within the industry both currently and over the past few years. In addition, he quoted NFL parallels once again, which held no water because his statements about NFL contracts once again were factually incorrect and even if they were correct, the NFL and pro wrestling aren't the same thing. The most blatant statement that he's repeated often and continues to hold no water is that the NFL "attempted guaranteed contracts to high draft choices way back in the 60s and found them to be an expensive failure. A lot of teams ended up with No. 1 picks that rode the bench and collected big bucks. They do not do that anymore."

In reality, it's now the 90s and No. 1 picks in the NFL draft still get huge signing contracts, many times larger, even adjusting for inflation, to the contracts from the 60s. He also said that football, baseball and basketball are all entering a crisis situation--declining attendance, declining TV ratings, declining revenue, apathetic self-serving athletes and free agency and predicted the current situation to self destruct the system in those sports.

That's what we were all told in the 60s and 70s if free agency were to exist and players would have freedom of movement, yet in both baseball and basketball, the period following free agency turned into the period of the greatest revenue and popularity increases in the history of both sports. Basketball is flourishing more now than ever. Baseball and football attendance is basically the same as in previous years, although television oversaturation has hurt ratings and killed the golden goose of those big money network contracts. Things are going to have to change in those industries because they're starting to face a day of reckoning because of getting used to television income that will be dropping over the next few years.

FEBRUARY 8

Bob Dhue and Bill Shaw are taking a more hands-on approach at WCW and expect some noticeable changes over the next few weeks. A lot of them may be big changes.

FEBRUARY 15

The expected major bloodletting at World Championship Wrestling took place in a meeting on 2/2, resulting in a significant changing in the corporate hierarchy including loss of power for both Bill Watts, and more particularly, Jim Ross.

Bill Shaw and Bob Dhue, who were put in charge of the company nearly one year ago from the now-retired Jack Petrik, have taken more of a hands-on approach in recent weeks rather than leaving much of the decision-making to Watts. They've divided the company into three categories, a pay-per-view division headed by Sharon Sidello, a television division headed by an as yet unnamed individual who is expected to be named this week, and a wrestling product division headed by Watts. Sidello and the television division head, whose title will be Executive Producer of WCW, will have the final say-so on all matters relating to their divisions including the matches that air on television and on PPV shows. Since, in reality, television is the most important facet of a wrestling company, the new Executive Producer may wind up as the most powerful front office employee. The Executive Producer apparently will either be Keith Mitchell, David Crockett, Tony Schiavone, Eric Bischoff or someone not currently working in the company at present. Speculation within the company over the weekend is that Mitchell or Bischoff had the best shot at the position. In addition, the largest booking committee in recorded history was put together to put together storylines and decide on who gets pushed.

The official corporate ladder shows Shaw on top as WCW President. Underneath him and answering to him are Dhue, Sidello, the new Executive Producer and Rob Garner (who will head the syndication division). Answering to Dhue will be Watts, Bryan Mitchels (the comptroller) and Dusty Rhodes (head booker). Jim Barnett, Ross and Tim Willet (recently hired from Titan) will work underneath Garner, while the announcers and television show producers (Schiavone, Bischoff, Keith Mitchell and Greg Gagne) will answer to the new Executive Producer. The Event Coordinators (local promoters) will report to Sidello.

Jim Ross, whose official title had been Vice President in charge of television, took the biggest fall of anyone. Ross will be removed as a personality from all TBS shows effective March 1, and will no longer be part of the announcing team on Clashes and pay-per-views with his final major assignments being the 2/21 SuperBrawl III show from Asheville and the 3/7 PPV air date of the January 4 Tokyo Dome card. Ross had been the lead announcer on every Clash since the series began in 1988, and had been part of the announcing team for every pay-per-view event in company history in addition to being voted Announcer of the Year in the Wrestling Observer Newsletter poll by a wide margin the past five years. Most sources seem to believe that Watts and Ross took tremendous heat from management because of criticism that all the television shows continue to have a similar look. The decision to replaced Ross as lead announcer, and in fact eliminate him from all TBS broadcasts appears to be related to his falling star in the front office, when the two different demotions should have probably been judged on each's individual merit rather than collectively. I suppose those who look at a wrestling show like the 6 p.m. news may knock Ross because of his accent or because he doesn't look like Bischoff, but that would be missing the point that the stars of a wrestling show are supposed to be the performers. The announcer is not akin to a news anchorman and unless Schiavone and in particular, Bischoff, are as adept at announcing wrestling matches and getting the points that need to be gotten across to the audience better, this decision makes little sense. Schiavone does come across as less offensive than Ross to those who don't like Ross and there is an argument can be made that he would fit in better in the No. 1 slot (which he occupied on TBS from 1985 to 1989). Ross rubbed some people the wrong way with what many felt was excessive self-promotion on television, but it appears his being replaced may have had more to do with upper management unhappiness regarding the similar looks to all the shows.

Few would argue that when it comes down to announcing a key match, Ross may be the best in the business (the only possible exception being Vince McMahon of those who speak this language, and McMahon comes across on television as more abrasive than Ross) and is definitely the best in the company. Ross being taken off completely and Bischoff's role being expanded is a little harder to justify. In addition, Ross' decision-making position was eliminated and he was re-assigned into becoming a syndicated television salesman, a position which will entail spending most of his time going around the country making sales calls to local stations to pitch the two syndicated shows. WCW released a revised partial list of announcing assignments starting in March, and Ross' name was listed with Jesse Ventura as hosts of World Wide Wrestling, but I'm told this is far from a definite and if it does materialize, will initially only be a trial run. Tony Schiavone and Larry Zbyszko will become hosts of WCW Saturday Night. Schiavone and Ventura will become the lead announcers on the Clashes and PPV shows. Eric Bischoff and Michael Hayes will take over the Sunday Main Event show. Announcing assignments for WCW Pro Wrestling and Power Hour have yet to be officially announced.

In addition, a huge booking committee was put together. Officially on the committee are Watts, Dusty Rhodes, Greg Gagne, Bill dundee, Jim Barnett, Keith Mitchell, Ole Anderson, Ross, Zbyszko, Sidello, Mike Graham, Bischoff and Hayes. In addition, it is expected that if the Ric Flair deal doesn't fall through, that Flair will be added to the committee. Sid Vicious was also promised a spot on the committee should he sign with the company. Vicious and WCW officials have spoken numerous times although no official deal has been reached as far as we know. No word as of yet if Lord Littlebrook, Eddie Gilbert, Cowboy Bradley, Happy, Grumpy, Dopey (well, I guess he's already in there somewhere), Sleepy, Sneezy, Dancer, Prancer or anyone else was promised a spot if they were to come in as well.

On the surface, this all seems like a recipe for total chaos in a company in which Chaos, and not Championship, has been the real "C" in the WCW name almost since the inception of the company. Based on conversations with many wrestlers and officials, by and large the moves were popular because both Watts and Ross were extremely unpopular personally by many within the organization. Actually, in the case of Watts, by most everyone. However, whatever glee there is in seeing Watts and Ross taken down a peg by these changes needs to be thought about more carefully because the current structure with nobody in charge and everyone in charge at the same time may result in a more disorganized company. In addition, management laid down a new doctrine, aimed at mainly Watts but also Rhodes. There can be no yelling or swearing at employees or overall bombastic behavior within the office, and that executives (ie Watts and Rhodes) can no longer wear jeans, Zubaz pants, sweat pants or t-shirts to work and must wear suits and ties. Watts is still technically in charge of contract negotiations, at least in theory, although going over his head and having him overruled doesn't seem to be unusual. For instance, Watts and Dhue's apparent decision regarding wanting Rick Rude to apply for workmen's comp while injured rather than receive his wrestling salary while injured seemingly was overruled by Shaw, since Rude received a check for all the money he would have earned the past month while he was mending his neck injury. So all negatives regarding Rude's return have been settled and Rude returned the U.S. title belt, which Dustin Rhodes is now wearing, and will be back in action when the injury heels in the next few weeks. In addition, Shaw was involved in the negotiations in some fashion with Johnny B. Badd, who it now appears likely to be staying when one week ago it seemed better than 50/50 that he'd be going to the WWF when his contract expired in a few weeks.

In my opinion, for a wrestling company to have a true sense of direction, it needs one person who knows exactly where he's taking the product long-term and has a focused idea of how to get there. While the Saturday television show has been very good for the past five or six weeks and there have been some solid talent acquisitions (none of which have been put over in a manner that could create them as new faces on top), overall, based on the eight month period Watts has been in charge of the company, the results, when it comes to television ratings, house shows and PPV buy rates, have not been there. Recognizing the positives of Watts, it was painfully obvious almost from the start that his motivational methods, dealing with personnel both in the office and talent and overall old-time wrestling double-talk, carny strategy came off as behind the times and he seemingly had no inclination to adapt, rather wanted the both the company's employees and the world to adapt to him.

Nevertheless, if Watts isn't the person, and one way or another things not related to the wrestling product decisions themselves were going to fell him most likely anyway, my own opinion is that they needed to bring in another person, not put several different people, all of whom are going to have their own specific ideas, agendas and friends and relatives to push and own perception of what pro wrestling should be in 1993 and how to get to that point, in charge. In this case, too many decisions will be those of political compromise, there will be far too much second-guessing too early in the game, and it will be next to impossible to establish a long-term direction. The vast booking committee only makes the unwieldy decision-making process that much worse. Maybe that won't be the case, but after speaking with many who have been involved in the hierarchy of successful organizations in the past, none believe this is a viable solution.

FEBRUARY 22

Bill Watts resigned as Vice President of Wrestling Operations for World Championship Wrestling on the morning of 2/10 and in a meeting of WCW department heads on 2/12 it was announced that Ole Anderson (Alan Rogowski) would take Watts' position and Eric Bischoff was named as Executive Producer of all WCW television.

The aftermath of the announcement of company restructuring on 2/2 and the resignation of Watts leaves the WCW company headed by Bill Shaw (President), Bob Dhue (Executive Vice President) and the four department heads, Sharon Sidello (pay-per-view), Bischoff (television), Anderson (house shows and wrestling personnel) and Rob Garner (syndication).

Watts' resignation was largely expected by most in the company to be imminent after the restructuring was announced and his power diluted. The official company statement was: "Turner Broadcasting does not, by policy, comment on personnel matters." The resignation came just as at least four different media sources were working on a story based on statements made by Watts more than 18 months ago that were along with lines of statements made by Marge Schott, the Cincinnati Reds baseball owner, which had become front page news in recent weeks and resulted in her one year suspension from baseball, comments about her statements and that her suspension was just a slap on the wrist from Henry Aaron, the all-time home run record holder, and the coincidence of Aaron (who at the time had no idea about the statements Watts had made) being involved with the WCW Starrcade PPV on 12/28 at the Omni while the Schott controversy was going on.

The interview in question was by Watts in the Pro Wrestling Torch Summer 1991 annual. In addition, an interview published in the past few months by Watts in the Wrestling World Examiner newsletter contained comments by Watts regarding Adolf Hitler and Nazi Germany that were eerily similar to remarks Schott made and was heavily criticized for just one day after Watts' resignation on Prime Time Live. The interview was faxed to Aaron on 2/9 by Torch columnist and Pittsburgh Post-Gazette sportswriter Mark Madden, who asked Aaron for his comments on the interview. Aaron took the interview to TBS President Terry McGuirk and the announcement was made of Watts' resignation early the next morning. Those close to Watts say the decision to leave was his. The stories, which would have broken most likely toward the latter stages of this week had Watts not resigned, would have proven to be a major embarrassment for Turner Broadcasting. It would have shown that Turner, who was one of the owners sitting on the board to decide Schott's fate, had hired someone to run one of his companies after someone had made published statements that could be classified as even more offensive.

Watts, in the Torch interview, stated: "If you own a business and you put the money in, why shouldn't you be able to discriminate? It's your business. If free enterprise is going to make or break it, you should be able to discriminate. It's your business. It should be that, by God, if you're going to open your doors in America, you can discriminate. Why the f--- not? That's why I went into business, so that I could discriminate. I mean, really. I mean I want to be able to serve who I want to. It's my business. It's my investment. So they come in and say no. I can't tell a fag to get the f--- out. I should have the right to not associate with a fag if I don't want to. I should have the right to not fire a fag if I don't want to. I mean, why should I have to hire a f---in fag if I don't like fags? Fags discriminate against us, don't they? .

"Sure they do. Do Blacks discriminate against Whites? Whose killed more Blacks than anyone? The f---in Blacks. But they want to blame that bull---- "Roots" that came on the air. That "Roots" was so bull----. All you have to do if you want slaves is hand beads to the chiefs and they gave you the slaves. What is the best thing that has ever, ever happened to the Black race? That they were brought to this country. No matter how they got here, they were brought here. You know why? Because they intermarried and got educated. They're the ones running the Black race. You go down to the Black countries and they're all broke. Idi Amin killed more Blacks than we ever killed. You see what I mean. That's how stupid we are. But we get all caught up in all this bull---- rhetoric. And so, it's ridiculous what's happening to our country. Lester Maddox (former Alabama Governor who was most famous in the 60s for blocking a school door and not allowing Black children into a formerly all-white school) was right. If I don't want to sell fried chicken to Blacks, I shouldn't have to. It's my restaurant. Hell, at least I respect him for his stand."

Aaron, in an interview Wednesday with Madden, said about Watts' resignation: "I think there was a little pressure put on him. Not by me. What I did yesterday after you and I talked and I got the thing and took it down to Terry McGuirk, to the proper people. I guess they were very disturbed by the language that was being used. This is too big a company and it stands for too much to have something like this stand in the way."

In regard to the statements by Watts in the Torch interview, Aaron said: "It was horrible. They were horrible statements. In this day and age, for anybody, regardless of whether he made them or anyone else, it is just despicable, really. Regardless of whether you work for a company or work for yourself or whether you're independent." Aaron compared what Watts said with the statements Schott made that got her banned from baseball and said, "It's the same thing. It's one and the same. I can't say Marge was worse."

Aaron believed had those doing the hiring known Watts had made those statements, that he never would have been hired in the first place. Aaron said that Shaw had talked to some people about the interview, that he had gotten wind of it, but didn't know what to think of it because he never saw it. "I'm sure if he had known about it, no way he would have hired him."

Ironically these statements and Watts' subsequent departure from the company bring up another point that has been made frequently over the past few years. On numerous occasions over the years WCW has used race-baiting angles to sell wrestling tickets. In the overall scheme of things, which is really more damaging and offensive, portraying this behavior in a quasi-realistic setting in front of millions on television in order to attempt to inflame race relations or making some ill-advised statements in the Torch? In addition, those statements were talked about by a lot of people both inside and outside of the WCW organization upon Watts' hiring. While Shaw and Dhue being ignorant of the statements may well be true, it's a sad commentary about the organization that it took what could have been some highly embarrassing publicity to get the heads of the department to be aware of an interview that had been most controversial and talked about extensively within the industry regarding their department head. Perhaps it was only the strange coincidence of Aaron's involvement in Starrcade during the timing when he was so outspoken regarding Schott that even brought these comments once again to people's attention.

Perhaps in response to this, Shaw issued a directive that only himself and Mike Weber (head of publicity) are allowed to speak to the media on any matters relating to company policy.

The news of Watts resigning for the most part set off celebrations among both the wrestlers and many of the front office employees since Watts was almost universally disliked, particularly among the wrestlers for his my-way-or-the-highway attitude. Even though Anderson was definitely not popular, or particularly successful, in most circles during his reign as booker (May through December 1990), the dislike of Watts was such that morale in most cases underwent a major upswing Wednesday that continued unabated by the announcement of Anderson and Bischoff in the key decision-making positions. Ironically, one of Anderson's first moves when he was booker in 1990 was to create a wrestling angle built around inflaming racial tension. There is definitely a lot of skepticism toward the new moves, since Bischoff is largely unproven in a decision-making position and there are questions about his knowledge and background in regard to this business. Anderson, one of the all-time great heels in the Southeast, while admittedly an intelligent person, hasn't achieved any success in behind in a key decision making position in a wrestling company since the early 80s and his last reign was heavily criticized for implementing more behind the times ideas and angles and bringing in wrestlers who were well past their prime than Watts' most recent reign.

The resignation of Watts seemingly ends the talent trading cooperation with Smoky Mountain Wrestling. Watts had attempted to book a limited amount of house show dates in the SMW territory and there were plans for a limited amount of talent trading between the two groups. From almost all accounts, the Rock & Roll Express vs. Heavenly Bodies match on the 2/21 PPV will spell the end of any trading of talent between the two offices because SMW head Jim Cornette did all his dealings with Watts and has been very much outspoken about the rest of the WCW organization. There is no way of knowing what the change in leadership will mean with the WCW/New Japan alliance.

FEBRUARY 22

Watts' former protege, Jim Ross, saw his position fall even farther this past week as the decision was made to remove him from all television effective immediately. Ross' last television broadcast will be the Saturday Night show that airs this coming weekend. Ross was pulled from the announcing line-up for the 2/21 Asheville, NC SuperBrawl PPV and was also removed from consideration for hosting World Wide Wrestling and would be off television in all forms completely. One week earlier WCW had released to the press new announcing line-ups listing Ross and Jesse Ventura as hosts of World Wide. As of press time, the only announcing line-ups that seem to be official are that the TBS Saturday show will be hosted by Tony Schiavone and Larry Zbyszko and the Sunday show by Bischoff and Michael Hayes. Schiavone and Ventura will become the lead announcers for all Clashes and PPV shows starting with Sunday's card. No official announcement has been made regarding the future of Ross' 900 line, which has been for years the most called item on the Hotline, although most expected it would be gone within a month or two. Ross' Sunday evening wrestling radio show on WSB in Atlanta and his football announcing are his own personal deal independent from WCW, so those positions will be unaffected by recent developments.

WCW BUSINESS UNDER BILL WATTS
WATTS' RECORD VS. PREDECESSORS (JIM HERD & KIP FREY)

(A comparison of the Bill Watts era (June 1992 through February 1993 compared with the same months the previous year ie June 1991 through February 1992, mainly the Jim Herd era and the first two months of the Kip Frey era)

AVERAGE ATTENDANCE
Watts 1,594 (-2.7%)
Predecessors 1,638

AVERAGE HOUSE
Watts $14,158 (-27.2%)
Predecessors $19,444

SELLOUT PERCENTAGE
Watts 2.4
Predecessors 4.5

AVERAGE CABLE TELEVISION RATING
Watts 2.04 (-19.4%)
Predecessors 2.53

AVERAGE CLASH RATING
Watts 3.15 (-19.2%)
Predecessors 3.90

AVERAGE PPV BUY RATE
Watts 0.55 (-40.9%)
Predecessors 0.93

Overall measurable interest level decline during Watts era: 21.9%

Editors note: There is no truth to the rumor that Gary Rossington and Johnny Van Zant of the legendary rock group Lynrd Skynrd have been added to the WCW booking committee in exchange for shilling for the musical quality of the Slam Jam record album.

MARCH 8

Jim Ross, who has been the face of World Championship Wrestling for the past five years, officially resigned from the company on 2/25. The resignation wasn't unexpected since the new regime in charge made it abundantly clear they had no plans to use Ross on the air, and instead re-assigned him to a role as a salesman for the syndicated television division. Ross, who signed a three-year contract with the company at a price rumored to be between $150,000 and $200,000 per year shortly after Bill Watts was brought aboard as Vice President of Wrestling Operations, reportedly asked Bill Shaw and Bob Dhue if he could get out of the contract because he didn't want to give up broadcasting, something his new job would make it very difficult for him to continue. I'm not sure if the details of the release have been completely worked out, but part of the deal may include a no-compete clause, which would make it impossible, at least for a time period that would probably be in the six month range, for Ross to join Titan Sports, which would be the obvious place he'd look for employment. Ross told friends during the week that he had no definite future plans but apparently was talking about moving back to the Tulsa area within a matter of a few months and trying to pursue radio work in the area.

From WCW sources, Ross left the company on amicable terms in particular with Shaw and Dhue. If Ross' contract also included the same 90 day review period that Watts' wrestlers contract had in them, which meant Ross and his big salary could have been dumped for poor job performance as a salesman in syndication, and selling syndicated wrestling shows these days with the current television attitude toward the product could have made being a success fairly difficult. For the time being, Ross will continue his weekly wrestling radio show in Atlanta. He'll also continue on the WCW 900 line for a short period of time, probably just a few weeks, until WCW had find a replacement on Saturdays. This was probably close to a mutual disillusionment since both Ross and Dennis Brent (WCW Magazine and head of hotline) were moved out of their offices in the WCW wing of CNN Center over the past two weeks, prior to each leaving the company. Brent resigned Tuesday, shortly after that decision was made, although he apparently felt much pressure from external forces to lead to that decision. Friends of his say he felt the new regime wanted those closely aligned with Bill Watts and those aligned with Jim Herd out of the company, and Brent fit both bills to an extent.

The booking committee has been pared way down. The only names on the initial list that I know are no longer involved are Ross and Larry Zbyszko (who quit because apparently he had philosophical problems with the direction certain things were headed) but there are others as well. Zbyszko was also replaced by Jesse Ventura on the Saturday Night show, although Z will continue on WCW Pro and Power Hour and he and Schiavone will do the match announcing on Main Event although Michael Hayes will host the show doing an on-location type deal similar to Gene Okerlund and Bobby Heenan on All-American wrestling.

Eric Bischoff is either going to take himself off television completely, or severely limit his on-air role with his new job as producer. Several people have been interviewed for being new play-by-play announcers since if Bischoff removes himself completely, Schiavone is the only one left in the company. Ring announcer Tony Gilliam is taking over Bischoff's role doing the WCW magazine segments.

APRIL 19

The most talked about non-wrestling item revolves around a front page story this past week in the Atlanta Journal talking about the potential sale of the Turner Empire to Time-Warner and TCI. How this may or may not affect the wrestling operation at this point is only speculative but people are talking.

MAY 3

Scriptwriters started writing some of the interviews the guys have to do this past week. Expect more cute puns and less "I hate your guts and here's why" interviews. Just a hunch, but that would seem to me to be a sign of Eric Bischoff's power as opposed to Dusty Rhodes and Ole Anderson.

MAY 31

While nothing has been confirmed, expect major changes within the structure of WCW to be announced imminently. It appears that from 7/5 to 7/16, WCW will be taping 48 hours of television in Orlando at Disney Studios. If that is for syndication, WCW Main Event and Power Hour, it means that they'll be taping shows more than three months in advance. If it's just for World Wide and WCW Pro, then we are talking about taping some shows six months in advance. This lends itself to an entirely new structuring of the wrestling business. If an angle doesn't work, it can't be refined. No turns, angles or title changes can happen at house shows unless they are well planned out ahead of time. Injuries or people leaving the company or people holding out, quitting, simply not renewing their contacts or whatever, which happens with frequency in this business, can't be accounted for if television is taped so far in advance.

In addition, expect changes in the way house shows are done, but what they will be is uncertain at press time. Those within the company have been talking of severe cutbacks in number of house show dates and even a possible complete elimination by the fall. It's another example of the heavy duty losses the company has suffered for so many years causing major internal changes that are going to change wrestling as we know it. May has been probably the worst month ever when it comes to arena business in WCW history, and that's saying a mouthful. A recent show in New Brockton, AL drew fewer than 100 paying fans, and this past Thursday and Friday night in Baltimore (going head-to-head with "Cheers" finale) and Philadelphia drew each city's lowest crowd in history, of roughly 1,000 and 600 respectively. A company simply can't go along piling up such heavy financial losses and a day of reckoning was going to happen.

JUNE 28

After its television show reached a new low in retarded wrestling angles on Saturday, the hierarchy of World Championship Wrestling needs a thorough housecleaning.

The problem isn't trying to identify who wrote and came up with the scenario in which Sting, Davey Boy Smith, Sid Vicious, Big Van Vader, Harley Race and Col. Rob Parker were involved in a reported $80,000 mini-movie production to build up the 7/18 Beach Blast PPV main event. The problem wasn't even in the decision to go with the same idea (a mini-movie) to build up the PPV for the third time in nine months, after the second such expensive attempt failed miserably. The problem is with an organization which has so many supposed checks and balances in its hierarchy yet absolutely no understanding of what its product is, what its audience is, and that none of those checks and balances stopped the mini-movie that everyone I've spoken with both in and out of the organization admits was a total embarrassment, from airing.

For those of you lucky enough to not see the most flawed PPV angle in history, it went something like this. The heels, mad because Sting & Smith didn't show up for a pep rally, went to a mysterious island where Sting & Smith were doing charity work. It's bad enough when wrestling people and other celebrities use charities simply to promote themselves in a positive light as a reaction to negative publicity, but at least in those cases they do donate time and/or effort to charity. In this case, the "charity work" consisted of playing volleyball with some child actors. Parker assured the rest of the heels that he had a plan that would keep Sting & Smith from appearing at Beach Blast. Little did he know that plan would only keep viewers from buying the show. It wound up with a dwarf wearing an eye patch swimming with a shark fin putting a bomb on a boat that Sting & Smith used to get to Gilligan's Island. Two very young girls saw the dwarf. The heels then took a boat ride to Gilligan's Island, and the only thing positive about that is that they didn't let Harley drive the boat. After a confrontation where the heels demanded the faces retire and the kids acted like they were going to cry if the faces would retire, one of the little kids told Sting about the funny man who was hanging around the boat. As Sting went to check, somehow one of the little girls told Smith about a ticking noise, and Einstein himself started sprinting down the beach, which was a sight in itself, and knocked Sting out of harms way just seconds before the bomb exploded and the boat blew up.

One would think when looking at any business venture, one would look at how the same business, especially a world wide one such as pro wrestling, is run both successfully and unsuccessfully in different places. Instead, the company is being run by people who haven't a clue about 1993 wrestling. It's run by some who are very knowledgeable about 1985 pro wrestling in the Southeast, and some who aren't knowledgeable about any aspect of pro wrestling whatsoever. There are plenty of companies still very successful in this industry, although none in this country right now. None are taking this path. That isn't necessarily bad, because a company has to forge its own way. However, this isn't forging its own way. We already have a role model to examine when it comes to putting endless stupid skits on television what the end result is. The Global Wrestling Federation. A group that, despite having a national television outlet, had no interest in its product whatsoever, and has to give away 30,000 tickets every week just to get 2,000 people to show up on Friday nights. The saddest part of all this isn't that WCW is copying Global. The saddest part is the people running the company are so ill-informed of the goings on in their own industry that they most likely don't even know what they are doing has already been tried and was and is a miserable failure. I'm convinced in those skits where they go to skid row, they aren't really searching for Cactus Jack. Knowing the TBS track record in picking people to run WCW, they're actually searching for replacements for the current company hierarchy when this group gets run out in the wake of what are sure to be disastrous ratings over the next few months.

Amidst the phone messages from some long-time fans who vowed this show marked the end of their interest in wrestling, and/or WCW, the calls to wrestling radio shows over the weekend, and messages from those in the business who couldn't believe how unwatchable the entire Saturday night television show had become, was one by Jim Cornette who begged to be quoted regarding said skit.

"Three of the wrestlers who comprise the wrestling talent in that thing I have the highest respect for their work and think they're fantastic, but anybody that would take part in this thing for any price or for any contract is crazy. Anybody responsible for that f---ing abomination should not only be shot but be forced to watch that abomination over and over again until they puke up their toenails before being shot. And they wonder why they can't do any business? I think everyone involved should suffer the most horrible painful death possible because of the money they're taking out of all our pockets who are trying to preserve this business that is rapidly going down the tubes."

No one skit is going to, in and of itself, destroy pro wrestling or even damage it noticeably. And in reality, the wrestlers themselves had little input or option in this or similar scenarios like the one with Cactus Jack. However, this direction is going to be one of many things that will take the company down to yet even greater depths.

WCW needs somebody who has an open mind, knows the year on the current calendar, understands what the word continuity means and understands why wrestling fans watch television and go to arenas in control. They also need to keep those who have no idea why pro wrestling is successful in places and times when it has been successful, why wrestling fans even attend and what they're looking for in a television and live product from giving their expert decisions to muddle up all the work needed to save a business that could be just months away from truly critical condition.

If not, I've got three words to say about WCW. Better off dead. Those words are being written taking into account just how terrible it would be for the wrestlers and their families, and the industry as a whole to have another company bite the dust with such few job openings left in this industry. They take into account that WCW still has the ability to put on entertaining events such as the recent Clash. They take into account that the current time period is one where the future of the WWF, WCW's main alternative, is itself in its most cloudy state in history. But an abrupt death, allowing others to start up, hopefully learn from the mistakes, and get rolling as quick as possible is better for the industry than a slow, painful damaging death that slows the process or prevents these things from happening by turning more people off to the product producing silly skits like we've been seeing. But the real and best possible solution is for the company to higher people in a decision making position that have at least a semblance of both respect and understanding for and toward its consumers.

JULY 5

The continuing soap opera that is World Championship Wrestling took several more turns this past week. Rumors abound about the future of nearly everyone in a key decision-making position after a week which saw:

- An almost but-not-quite debut of a new tag team called The Possee (formerly the Ebony Experience in GWF) managed by Col. Rob Parker. The original idea was for The Possee to be brought out in chains and shackles, to give the visual impression of a white southerner leading two black men in chains and shackles. The idea, which was the brainchild of one Sid Vicious who was so impressed when working with the duo in a tag team match at the Adkisson Memorial show in Dallas on 4/2, had wanted to bring the duo in with the gimmick of them being escaped murderers managed by Parker (Robert Fuller). The idea was all dressed up and ready to go on television when Eric Bischoff, who apparently didn't know the extent of the angle, nixed it just as it was about to be taped. When WCW President Bill Shaw found out about the idea which almost ran, which no doubt would have caused even more negative phone calls, he found a finger-pointing upper brass all trying to blame others for giving the approval of the idea. While Booker T and Stevie Ray are going to keep their jobs with WCW, when they appeared at the television tapings Monday night, they were instead called Chitown Heat (yeah, I know the punch line, they're bringing in the Power Twins as Music City Showdown and renaming The Black Hearts "Halloween Havoc") and had masking tape over their prisoner uniform numbers and they will no longer be pushed as former prisoners.

- Higher-ups in the company caused cancellation of any repeating of the Beach Blast mini-movie on TBS, and also on Thursday canceled all future "Search for Cactus Jack" features, although it was too late to eliminate the most recent one from the Saturday television show and I've heard talk that this coming weekend's segment may still air since the show may have already been produced.

- In television shows already taped to air through late July, there is a considerable increase in emphasis on retired wrestlers Dusty Rhodes, The Assassin and Thunderbolt Patterson. Based on what has already appeared on television and using logical thought, it appears the company is already primed for a major run using Dusty Rhodes in the ring as a lead face. However, all sources within the company insist that such a scenario won't be taking place because TBS won't allow its booker to be an active wrestler. They have already let him get himself over in a manner to set the stage which only makes things appear even more ridiculous if Rhodes isn't allowed to come back. My own opinion when it comes to Rhodes in the ring is that for mid-card 5:00 matches, he's been gone long enough and was a big enough star that his return may pique some interest. However, if his return is in a serious capacity as one of the top faces, based on how he looked when he finally was put out of the ring years ago and how he performed, whatever short-term benefit will be gained by his coming back will work to the company's detriment after the first time around the horn. In addition, at this point in time, no wrestler's name is strong enough to make a significant impact either at the gate or in television viewing patterns. The idea of a retired superstar making a comeback in a major grudge ala Bill Watts in 1984 or Crusher many times over in the Midwest and countless others that has been traditionally a successful promotion, will have only a minimal effect if any nowadays as witnessed by the return of both Ric Flair to WCW and Hulk Hogan to WWF, each of whom drew an initial big television rating and largely disappointing gates at the arenas.

- WCW champion Big Van Vader, NWA champion Barry Windham and TV champion Paul Orndorff all missed the week's house shows due to injuries. Vader is still recovering from what has now been diagnosed as a herniated disc in his back. Vader will work the Beach Blast PPV show but won't be working any house shows until then, and word is he'll be out of action for a significant length of time after Beach Blast as well. We've heard word Vader may work the Orlando television tapings for World Wide next week, but nothing definite on his recovery. Windham blew out his knee on either 6/20 or 6/21 (contradictory stories) and may face major surgery, in which case he'd be out of action for six months similar to the major knee injuries suffered in recent years by Sting and Robert Gibson. Windham is also going to be off until Beach Blast, and even though injured, is reportedly going to go through with his match with Ric Flair working on one leg, then have the surgery which, depending on the severity, could keep him out of action for six months or more. Orndorff is still suffering from re-aggravation of the torn groin muscle that has been bothering him for more than one month. At the weekend house shows, since Sid Vicious wasn't originally booked, Vader's place was taken for scheduled title matches with Davey Boy Smith by Big Sky (Darryl Karolet), who was flown in from Canada. Orndorff's place in TV title matches was taken by Dick Slater. Windham's place in NWA title matches was taken by Lord Steven Regal. To make matters even worse, at the beginning of all the house shows this week, an announcement was made in each city that the three would not be appearing due to contractual problems, instead of telling the truth about all being injured. While certainly not the stupidest decision of recent months, it was yet another act of stupidity. Fans who paid up to $15 for ringside tickets in all the towns obviously don't like paying for advertised talent that doesn't appear. However, even though they will be unhappy, if they are told someone is injured and believe it, they can accept it. They may not believe it because when one lies too often, even when they tell the truth people take it as a lie. But the one thing they don't want to hear is that someone advertised won't appear because of a contractual dispute because it makes them believe they have paid to see a what may be a Mickey Mouse unstable operation. When three wrestlers don't appear for that reason, it removes all doubt. WCW has done many things over the past five years to drive away what was a very loyal hardcore audience base, and the sad part is that after five years, they are continuing to make all the same mistakes, only now at a much more rapid pace.

- Everyone in the creative capacity looked exhausted at the 6/28 tapings, since apparently the previous night they were meeting until 5 a.m. because they had to re-book all the line-ups for the arenas because of the injuries, redo all the television shows since the bookings had changed and several video segments had to be eliminated by orders of the higher-ups, and had to re-program the entire Beach Blast show because several things on paper that would lead to other things can't take place for the previously mentioned reasons.

JULY 26

The major talk of the past week has been regarding the booking at both World Championship Wrestling and the World Wrestling Federation. WCW interviewed Terry Funk on Friday about what is believed to be the position of booker, although at press time it appeared the chances of Funk getting hired for the slot were less than 50 percent. It is believed Jerry Jarrett is also under consideration for that slot and that either way, the remaining two creative heads of WCW, Ole Anderson and Eric Bischoff, were going to maintain their positions and the overall hierarchy would stay status quo with the possible exception of a new booker. WCW is akin to a bicycle with two flat tires and stripped gears. Changing one spoke in one tire, no matter who is brought in, isn't going to make the bicycle ride.

JULY 26

Sharon Sedello was replaced as head of merchandising and arena booking although she's still in the power position in marketing. The arena bookings will be handled by Don Sandifer, who formerly did bookings for the PGA tour, with help from Gary Juster and Georgia Davidson.

AUGUST 2

While no decision has been made at press time, it is believed WCW will be making a major announcement within the next week concerning a new booker. Both Terry Funk and Jerry Jarrett were interviewed of late for Dusty Rhodes' booking job. Funk pretty well has publicly stated he believed himself to be out of the running which led to speculation regarding Jarrett getting the position to run rampant throughout wrestling. Most believe Funk isn't being considered because he made it clear in a meeting with Bill Shaw that he didn't like having to clear all his booking ideas through Eric Bischoff before they could be implemented. If Jarrett were to get the position, what that would mean as far as the USWA, which Jarrett owns a majority interest in, and his owm business relationship with Titan Sports, is unknown. If Jarrett is hired, besides likely WCW turning into a more Memphis-oriented promotion, which means heavier on the gimmick matches and run-in finishes, but faster moving angles and talent being brought in and out at a more rapid rate, is that it means one more son will be getting pushed as a top babyface. At press time, it was believed that Jarrett, who reportedly was in Atlanta during the early part of the week in meetings with WCW brass, was far from a sure bet to take the position.

AUGUST 9

After much discussion and speculation over the past week, World Championship Wrestling has reverted back to a booking committee composed of those already involved on the previous booking team (Dusty Rhodes, Ole Anderson, Eric Bischoff, Greg Gagne, Mike Graham, etc.). It appears the final decision-making power rests with Bischoff, who seems to be the most influential individual in the WCW organization since Bill Shaw is crediting the Disney tapings as a major success and Bischoff is getting the lion's share of credit for the shows. Both Terry Funk and Jerry Jarrett were spoken with by Shaw and/or Bob Dhue over the past few weeks about a spot in the organization, but to the best of my knowledge, neither were actually given a firm offer of a specific spot. Among many things, Funk felt coming in with Bischoff having the final decision-making power wasn't an environment he wanted to be part of.

AUGUST 9

Jim Barnett is negotiating with Prime Network which could be a huge international deal. Prime has the leading satellite sports network in Asia and the deal would put WCW on television throughout the world. Prime claims WCW would be on television throughout the world in three years. In return, they want a long-term deal of all promotional rights to all live events outside of North America and England, all licensing and merchandising rights outside of North America and England.

SEPTEMBER 6

Eric Bischoff received a promotion based on the Clash rating to Senior Vice President. David Crockett was also promoted to Executive in charge of all television production.

SEPTEMBER 27

Ole Anderson really isn't much a part of the key decision-making process. Eric Bischoff has the ultimate power although Dusty Rhodes is thought by the wrestlers as still being the most influential since most believe Dustin is still going to wind up as the person unifying both world titles.

SEPTEMBER 29

Much discussion within the company about the "plan" to make Dustin Rhodes world champion. Nobody has anything bad to say about Rhodes as a person and most everyone compliments him as being a good worker, but you'd be hard pressed to find many who see him as someone to be put in the position as world champion, particularly when his match was the focal match when the TBS ratings dropped back down. The rating for this past Saturday may be looked at as if it isn't good, that'll make two of three weeks with TV being built around him that didn't draw and this is a company where Saturday TV ratings are looked at ahead of and almost to the exclusion of every other business criterion.

NOVEMBER 8

Eric Bischoff sent Antonio Pena a three-page fax wanting to put together a deal with AAA where Bischoff said they'd get Pena a weekly cable television show in the United States and put his wrestlers on their PPV shows. Pena wanted no part of it because he felt the company had no direction with its own product, so how could it be of a benefit to a product it had no understanding of. In reality, WCW had a deal with New Japan, which worked a style and had talent that would translate much better into an American-style show and screwed it up, so one wonders how it could have made an alliance with AAA work to anyone's benefit. One of Pena's assistants and Ron Skoler, who heads the organization that promotes AAA in the United States, were vehement about both Bischoff and Terry Funk (who it is believed went to Bischoff with the idea) for going behind their backs in trying to put together a deal. Skoler said that one of his business partners, who is long-time friends with Bob Dhue of WCW, called Dhue and told him AAA would never have any dealings with WCW as long as Bischoff is in the company.

NOVEMBER 29

Some changes in WCW hierarchy. Sharon Sidello will work most of the year out of Europe selling syndication. Mike Weber will take her duties in marketing and PPV, and Chris Potenza takes Weber's p.r. duties. Feel sorry for him.

DECEMBER 27

Ted Turner addressed the wrestling company, both wrestlers and front office, for the first time ever in a meeting held on 12/16. There was nothing of major importance discussed other than it being a pep rally with Turner vowing that the entire Turner Home Entertainment empire would be backing WCW and that with the exception of CNN, every aspect of the empire would be involved in cross-promotion. He vowed that as long as he was around, the company would never go out of business, which uplifted everyone's spirits. There was talk about doing a special card for TNT and a lot of talk about this being the year that WCW overtakes the WWF. Basically Turner execs and WCW heads have made similar pronouncements throughout the five-years Turner has owned the company, but this was only the third time Turner has ever made an appearance having to do with wrestling and the first time he's ever addressed the company. In 1989, Turner posed for several publicity shots with Ric Flair, and later Turner was on hand for a press conference for publicity shots where WCW announced the signing of El Gigante. Vince McMahon did a similar pep rally for WWF office employees on 12/17.

CHAPTER FIVE

THE STEROID SCANDAL

JANUARY 15

The Justice Department has been calling in more and more personnel for its probe into the WWF. It also hired an ex-police officer and ex-wrestling promoter named Thomas Parker specifically to investigate the WWF.

JANUARY 15

Hulk Hogan, ended his long silence with a one hour interview on 1/4 on the Miller and Company talk show on the Nashville Network. In a very controversial interview, Hogan blamed the Arsenio Hall show's time constraints for all the controversy over his statements in July of 1991 regarding his use of anabolic steroids that led to the controversy which saw him take an extended hiatus from the business and which led to aftershocks that were partly responsible for the collapse of Titan Sports' business nearly one year later. Hogan claimed he was going to talk about more use of steroids than he did, but he simply ran out of time. Anyone who remembers the Arsenio Hall interview can readily see that this wasn't the case, however, since Hogan denied any use of steroids aside from three times in 1983 while recovering from a bicep tear. Hogan stated to host Dan Miller, who had no clue as to what was going on, that on the Hall show, "I said yes, I did use steroids." Hogan claimed he experimented with steroids and blamed the medical profession for saying it was okay and that he stopped when the profession found out steroids were dangerous, basically using the same line of defense Arnold Schwarzeneggar did a few months back in a Newsweek cover story, which was heavily criticized as being dishonest within the bodybuilding community.

Hogan also said that if he was going to return to active wrestling, it would be in Japan. Although he took credit for the Rock & Wrestling Connection, saying it was his idea and not Vince McMahon's when the host credited McMahon with it, and said he had to convince McMahon to play the Rocky music as his original entrance music in 1984, he was still defensive of Titan Sports. He was critical of the People Magazine article by Irv Muchnick although never mentioned any specifics as to why. He claimed he was responsible for preventing people from using steroids (there have been articles claiming that besides Schwarzeneggar and Ben Johnson, that Hogan was the most influential as a celebrity hero among teenagers who were using steroids). He said that McMahon had been drug testing since 1987 (which is the case, although steroids weren't included in those tests until November, 1991 and it was the only policy in sports that I know of which only took punitive action against those whose levels of steroids increased in tests rather than simply judged positives based on simply the existence of steroids in the urine). Hogan also claimed the WWF grossed $1.7 million last year in merchandise (the WWF itself, which is known to heavily exaggerate revenue figures, lists the figure at $200 million and the real number probably is nowhere close to that).

Perhaps the most questionable statement he made during the show was when the subject of drug testing was brought up. Hogan said that the Olympic testing was getting better but basically called the NFL's drug testing a joke. "The guys in the NFL," he said, "if they were under Vince's test, there wouldn't be anybody left on the field." From my own standpoint, that latter statement got me extremely hot because grouping 1,600 NFL players together with a statement like that is stupid to begin with but also because it hits home with me personally. Because of Hogan's status of being the biggest drawing card of our era and because at least to a lot of the wrestlers he's never acted stuck up to them in spite of all of his financial success, there are many who will defend him no matter what he says. There are also many who won't. Ironically, the statement within the profession that will cause the most controversy was also probably the most honest thing out of the entire interview. When the subject of real vs. fake came up, Hogan said, "I'm not going to insult anyone's intelligence. It's a controlled situation. It's an exhibition. It's acting, charisma and good athletes. It's a show. A lot of the wrestlers are friends. If you want to call it (what he just said) exposing the business, call it whatever you want. I call it good business."

JANUARY 20

Hulk Hogan presented yet another story in regard to his use of steroids in an article in the 1/7 Buffalo News. The article, which was mainly publicity for the movie Mr. Nanny, which opens this week, had Hogan quoted as saying: "You go on a show like `Arsenio' and you only have a couple of minutes to talk about something like steroids, and it's not enough time..."If Arsenio Hall would have given me the whole hour I would have told him: `Yes, I used steroids throughout the 80s. And many of the athletes that I know used steroids, because they were legal. They used them sometimes for injuries, sometimes just to keep yourself going. Doctors prescribed it for bodybuilding. Just because the government and the medical profession smarten up and say, `OK, you can take steroids today, but tomorrow if you have this foreign subject in your body, you're a criminal,' well, I think it's hypocritical."

If Hogan would have said this 18 months ago, the entire wrestling world would be a different place today. It's a major cop out to blame the Arsenio Hall people, since Hogan time-after-time in promoting Suburban Commando echoed the same statement when reporters surely weren't stopping him from talking due to time constraints. The Hall show gave him 14 minute on very short notice and a producer who was caught up in the controversy after the show told us that what he said he was going to say before the show started and what he said on the air were two different stories. It's even more a cop out to blame the medical profession. However, after 18 months, Hogan seems to be telling the truth when it comes to personal use, although it isn't like that truth hadn't already come out from many sources in 1992. Honest, but seemingly unwilling to accept responsibility for his earlier dishonesty.

As far as the medical profession goes, the medical profession has been decidedly negative about using steroids for bodybuilding purposes dating back to the early 60s, although celebrities and bodybuilders were always able to find doctors who wanted to be hangers-on (and in some cases with bodybuilders and other athletes, a whole lot worse) to prescribe it to them and it was legal, but considered in many cases and by most doctors to be unethical, to do so until the federal law changed in 1988. It should also be pointed out that in Florida, where Hogan has lived most of his life, and in many other states, the state law regarding steroid prescribing and usage had changed several years before that, so what everyone is saying was legal during a time period, with legal being the defense, was not legal in many cases.

Use with a prescription was legal until that point (actually use was legal until 1991), however much of the use pre-1988 and all post-1988 use was through dealing in black market distribution, which has always been highly illegal, so a lot of claims about using them when they were legal in many cases is a very hazy area, because what was being done in many cases wasn't legal. Besides, the issue all along has never been legal vs. illegal or even steroids themselves per se, but honesty vs. misleading statements and outright deception. However, this week's statements should pretty much close the book on that subject as it relates to Hulk Hogan.

FEBRUARY 8

WCW will have its first steroid test on 2/15. Hopefully everything will be handled fairly in that the guys weren't told about any testing and there are many drugs that stay in the system longer than two weeks. Hopefully positives, if there are any, won't be penalized until they've been given a chance to get the stuff out of their system. This isn't the WWF which told everyone to get off in July and told tests would be forthcoming and then they didn't have a test until November and even then the positives were overlooked. This came from corporate higher-ups who have seen the problems this caused and is currently causing Titan Sports and realize there are a few neon signs on television every week that say "we're asking for legal problems for the company."

FEBRUARY 15

A federal probe into the WWF apparently has intensified. At least one New York-based investigator was in the deep South last week to interview ex-WWF headliners. Feds don't spend air fare on witch hunts. Word is that the initial focus of the probe--the WWF's systematic involvement with steroids--has grown to include tax evasion, violation of child labor laws, pedophilia, the exchange of sex for employment and the illegal drug and use distribution beyond steroids." In his 2/5 column, Mushnick had a short regarding New York State Athletic Commissioner Randy Gordon which read: "To listen to New York State Athletic Commissioner (and inveterate braggart) Randy Gordon crow to WABC-Radio's Mike Kay about his stringent drug tests for boxers in his jurisdiction, you'd think Gordon was McGruff, the Crime Dog. But if Gordon's such a force in the war on drugs, how is it that the World Wrestling Federation's performers, pumped up on steroids to outrageous proportions, wrestled with impunity in New York, not only under Gordon's jurisdiction, but under Gordon's very own eyes?"

MARCH 15

The U.S. Justice Department is continuing its investigation. Honkytonk Man called up John Arezzi's radio show on Saturday about this subject unbeknownst to Arezzi, who tried to get him off the subject immediately. Actually this, while being potentially the biggest story in the business of the decade (or it could be not a story at all), is one nobody wants to talk about because nobody except those involved really know what's going on, where it's headed and what the intended end result will be. All their info is supposed to be confidential. We just know interviews are continuing. Honky talked about him being flown into New York two weeks ago and being subpoenaed (which shows things are getting more serious) by the government and said he was interrogated by two FBI agents and answered every question with as much truthfulness as possible and "gave them the answers they needed." . .

MARCH 22

Muscle Mag International in its gossip column (5/93) talked about the departure of several suspected steroid boys from the WWF and the drop in gates (attributed to this newsletter's stats) and came to the conclusion: "The two things that are clear from this is that roid-enhanced physiques were the bottom line in the WWF's climb to the top and that there are many users that will go where they make less money in order to stay on the juice." It also stated that supplement Met-Rx (a legal food supplement that is being advertised as the latest magic food in bodybuilding pubs) was over big with WCW wrestlers. Actually I know of two WCW wrestlers who were using the stuff and one told me it was totally worthless and said he gave most of his away after trying it.

APRIL 5

The major topic of conversation in wrestling dressing rooms these days, now more than ever, is in regard to the U.S. Justice Department investigation of Titan Sports. Everybody has their read on the situation, but all of these "conclusions" based on a lack of information, and should all be dismissed as groundless at this point, unless they have come from someone who has extensively testified and knows where the questions are going and what the answers that have been testified to are and has been told in specific anything regarding that. I believe that to be nobody aside from those working on the case, since everything has been tight-lipped and nothing more than hints have been dropped.

Whether or not devoting the first 12 minutes of Monday Night Raw on 3/22 to Vince McMahon producing a piece on himself regarding the Michael Landon Awards and his company's so-called charity work (some of which was charity work, other of which, like Headlock for Hunger, would be more accurately described as a very expensive Public Relations and Image Repair bill which happened to also do a lot of good for some people) was coincidental to the apparent heating up of the investigation or not, most everyone in wrestling that I've spoken with during the week and the talk in the dressing rooms was that it was just that. The Raw piece resulted in multiplying the dressing room gossip regarding the investigation five-fold over the past week. As written here earlier, this could be the biggest wrestling story of the decade or it could wind up not even being much of a story. But one way or another, there is still only a little that can be said or written about it today of any real substance.

Several more ex-WWF wrestlers were subpoenaed over the weekend by the Justice Department at an independent show in the New York area. Several dozen interviews have already taken place. Honky Tonk Man (Wayne Ferris) went public that he, along with another ex-WWF wrestler, were subpoenaed and granted immunity from prosecution in exchange for their testimony, and flown into New York about a month ago for several hours of questioning. The subject matter of that questioning hasn't been made clear. About the only information at this point that I'd feel confident in reporting is that much of the investigation has to do with drugs, not just limited to anabolic steroids but much of it steroids, but it goes much deeper than just drugs and into all of the allegations that went public about one year ago.

My impression is that Vince McMahon has made many public comments in the media that were not in his best interest, some of them recently, particularly in the Fairfield County Advocate, both in his erroneous statements about legality but also in his statements regarding his own company's drug testing program. The key individual involved in the investigation, Tony Valenti of the Brooklyn office of the Justice Department, called this past week and said that the Observer has been the only media source covering this story that has been accurately reporting the legalities, or lack thereof, in regard to anabolic steroid use. More specifically, the defense that anabolic steroids were used in the WWF (or WCW, or bodybuilding or football for that matter) at a time they were legal is in many cases, not only false because use continued well after the federal laws changed, but the statement that they were legal before those specific laws changed is in many, probably most cases untrue.

While the federal law re-classifying steroids as a Code Three controlled substance went into effect in early 1991, personal use of anabolic steroids for non-therapeutic purposes was illegal in many states dating back years earlier, including some of the states that Dr. George Zahorian sent packages to the biggest names of the business into. Obtaining steroids without a prescription was illegal dating back before that. Information gathered in the prosecution of Zahorian showed that 96 percent of the steroids and barbiturates he distributed had no accompanying prescription. In addition, possession of drug paraphernalia (syringes for injections in specific) has also been illegal dating back many years. Being involved with black market dealers has always been illegal. It has been a felony since 1991 for management or coaches in sports to encourage use of steroids.

There can be a strong argument made that based on who was getting the biggest pushes and making the most money and who was getting hired at that time that steroids were still being encouraged well after 1991 by some wrestling offices, and not just in the WWF but surely more in the WWF than anywhere else. Let's not try and pussy-foot around the issue, everyone reading this knows what type of bodies were being pushed from 1984 on in the WWF, why they were being pushed, and the means the wrestlers went through to achieve them, and knows when the changes came in the selection of who was being put over. This was around the summer/fall of 1992 when all the obvious suspects started dropping off into independent never-never land, or more than one year after the law went into effect. This law has never been tested as far as I know and the WWF would hardly be the most guilty athletically oriented organization in this regard, but it would be in the upper echelon. That doesn't make the organization not guilty of encouraging steroid use based on who was being pushed in the top money positions simply because they aren't the most guilty.

APRIL 5

Our beloved head of the President's Council on Physical Fitness and Sports just three weeks ago promoted a bodybuilding contest called the Arnold Classic with huge prize money going to the top place-winners. Not only were none of the male contestants drug tested, but it is well-known that one couldn't even be competitive at that level without not only steroids, but other drugs that are a lot more dangerous. One of the contestants in that show, Mike Mattarazzo, was so water depleted from dehydrating drugs that in his own words one week later he stated that if it weren't for the medical crew in attendance, he would have died that night. It wasn't too many months earlier in a similar situation that the winner of a pro contest in Europe died within hours after winning from dehydration. The fact that similar arguments can be made about bodybuilding, American Gladiators, the 100-meters or the shot put as can be made about some wrestling promotions, and today's WCW is surely included in that statement, is not a valid defense if one is prosecuted under the terms of that law and the letter of the law is strictly interpreted. The fact that others may be just as guilty and even more guilty doesn't make someone else who violated the same law innocent.

APRIL 26

A few clarifications need to be made regarding the laws involving anabolic steroid use as it relates to what was reported here in the 4/5 issue. First off, the 1990 Anabolic Steroid Act originally contained a provision which specifically stated that a physical trainer, adviser, manager, coach, etc. who encourages, persuades or induces an individual to possess or use anabolic steroids would be in violation of the law with a maximum term of two years in prison. However, that specific part of the act wasn't voted into law. It was reported in many bodybuilding magazines and here on two occasions, including 4/5 that it was the law. However, according to DEA agent Paul Sehafer, there are already laws on the books that cover encouraging, persuading or inducing use of controlled substances (a category anabolic steroids now fall into) and he said that, for example, if a coach tells a player to use steroids or provides a connection, whether it be a doctor or other source where a player can get steroids, than he can be prosecuted as a felony for conspiracy and aiding and abetting use of a controlled substance so a similar law was largely already on the books covering it.

As far as rewarding use through financial incentives based on who has what spot as would be the case in some sports and at certain points several pro wrestling organizations have to fit into this category, that can't be prosecuted under that law unless the encouragement was done specifically telling the person to use steroids and not simply telling someone they need to gain weight to get a job or the implication based on who is making the most money that using steroids would be a good thing for someone on a professional basis. As far as how this law applies to the current U.S. Justice Department investigation of whatever it is involving Titan Sports in some fashion that is being investigated, simply the rewarding of top spots in a manner that encouraged steroid use, even after the 1991 law, wouldn't fit into the category of what could be prosecuted under federal law unless there was specific aiding and abetting that use, which is a correction from the 4/5 issue.

By the way, in regard to that investigation, anything you may hear as far as gossip or whatever in regard to what the end result will be is uneducated speculation, as outside of government officials, I don't really believe anyone else has a clue. As far as the question as to whether steroids were a legal drug as has been used many times by various people as an excuse to justify prior usage ("I used them, but they were legal then"), in many cases, that was incorrect. Steroids themselves have never been a legal drug without a prescription, although the federal law regarding possession being a felony didn't go into effect until 1991. Before that law was enacted, most states had individual laws regarding use and what was categorized as proper dispensation (in many states that had those laws, using them for muscle building purposes didn't qualify as proper dispensation) and possession and it varied by the state. Possession for non therapeutic reasons was specifically illegal in many states dating back several years. As far as the use of syringes and the legality of such, which was brought into question since the 4/5 issue, according to Sehafer, they fall into the category of possession of drug paraphernalia, thus possession would be illegal, unless there is a proper medical reason such as a diabetic needing insulin and that law also goes back prior to the federal anabolic steroid laws.

MAY 3

The Wyandotte (MI) News-Herald did a story on Vinnie Vegas, who is from nearly Trenton, MI and was called Kevin Nash in the story. The subject of steroids came up and Nash said in the story that WCW began testing for them last year, which would be news to everyone else in the company.

MAY 24

The Warlord (Terry Szopinski) appeared in court on 5/10 on a possession of steroids charge stemming from a November arrest that went unreported. At that time, postal agents in Chicago intercepted a package containing steroids mailed from England to Szopinski's house in Eagen, MN. The police then arranged for the package to be delivered to its destination, and shortly after, went to Szopinski's home for a search and found 11 different varieties of steroids. The 31-year-old Szopinski was charged with a felony for drug possession and released without bail at Dakota Country District Court in Hastings, MN. Szopinski has a second court date set for 6/7 at which time he'll have to enter a plea. Under sentencing guidelines, he faces a maximum one year in prison. Since the arrest made the wire services during the week, Szopinski went on John Arezzi's Pro Wrestling Spotlight radio show on 5/15 and claimed that he hadn't used steroids since the arrest seven months ago and claimed he needed them to maintain his physique while being on the road 300 days per year. Warlord wrestled for the WWF for nearly five years until the relationship dissolved one year ago, which is believed to have been in some way related to steroids. At 320 pounds and with a near 600 pound bench press to his credit, Warlord may have been the largest muscular specimen in the history of wrestling and certainly would have been among the first names speculated on by anyone when it came to steroid use in pro wrestling.

JUNE 14

It has been about the worst kept secret in wrestling that the NBC news division began working on a story should the current investigation lead to charges being filed. NBC has tried to contact several former WWF wrestlers now working for WCW, and also those who have already testified before the Grand Jury. For the most part, the wrestlers contacted have largely avoided cooperating with the story. The thinking among the wrestlers behind the scenes right now is that with the precarious state the wrestling business is already in, anymore negative publicity would be devastating. WCW seems on a train headed nowhere and there is considerable talk about how long things can go on in that company without an upturn in interest, and nobody has any confidence that the people running the company are capable of that. Certainly everyone involved is worried about considerable cutbacks when it comes to talent and future contracts, which may leave WWF as the only place, save for a chosen few on top at WCW with existing contracts, to make money in this business. The fear of something happening in regard to that option, ie, WWF taking another hit which would result in business collapsing to new depths, ie potential payoffs collapsing, has been considerable. There are some who feel that in the long run for the overall health of the wrestling industry, that this scenario could be beneficial long-term, although few in wrestling think long-term. The theory is that if WWF were to have to retrench to being a Northeastern regional office (and for the month of July, based on the touring schedule, it largely will be), it would theoretically open up the rest of the country for new offices to open, which would mean more jobs for new and old wrestlers and more fresh talent constantly being developed which years down the road would alleviate the staleness that has been a factor in a declining business. But that scenario of a WWF downfall being good for the wrestling business is theoretical at best and may be more wishful thinking than anything else. Until the smaller offices that already exist can show signs of being consistently profitable, there is no indication there are more than a few people out there who can operate a wrestling promotion in the 1990s on a regional basis and maintain it at a healthy financial level, or that such a market even exists for small-time wrestling territories to the level it can be profitable enough to be a full-time occupation for the dozen or so workers needed.

All that aside, discussing of what would be good for the pro wrestling business has nothing to do with this story other than speculation on possible effects of this story. The real story is this. If illegal activities were taking place, whatever they may be, the effect it may have on this industry's future should not be considered as a justification for covering it up or ignoring it. Whatever entertainment value a promoter or company has is not justification for ignoring criminal activity. And if there wasn't any wrongdoing, it is the best thing for it to all come out in the open so the cloud of suspicion is removed. Speculation has it will be in the fall if anything does occur, and we can put a close to this bizarre chapter of wrestling history, or open a new chapter of the biggest wrestling story of the era.

Steroid use in pro wrestling, encouragement of which and ignorance of which was in many ways the catalyst of all these problems, had been largely ignored by WCW, despite all the negative publicity Titan suffered regarding the same subject. WCW instituted a written anti-steroid policy in early 1992 under then Executive Vice President Kip Frey. When Bill Watts took over in June, his initial move was to scrap the policy, which he based on Frey's awarding bonuses to wrestlers to stay off steroids. Watts, when he first came in at the helm, largely ignorant of all goings-on in the business of the previous five years, chose the route of ignoring the apparent (and in some cases apparently rampant) use, which had been the position all wrestling organizations had taken when Watts left the business. Watts' initial statements in regard to steroids were of the lip service variety but he largely ignored it as an issue and in many cases pushed the biggest guys, even when in some cases they lacked talent and/or charisma, which tacitly encourages the medium-sized and smaller guys to try and become big guys in order to improve their financial lot. A drug test which specified all illegal drugs (steroids being among many) was held in November of 1992, in the wake of the problems with Jake Roberts. According to an interview with Watts and also several other WCW sources, several wrestlers in key positions on the Starrcade card failed the test showing a positive for steroids. The reason none were suspended according to Watts' interview after being removed from office in Wrestling Flyer, aside from the fact it would have crippled the planned line-up, was that with Frey's policy out the window, WCW had no policy in regard to steroids. That statement may not hold water since the company almost surely had a policy in regard to illegal drug use and steroids fall under that umbrella even without a specific policy regarding steroids. Watts had planned a second test, but it was canceled as his resignation took place a week before the test and the new regime chose to ignore the situation and even hire a few walking neon signs for apparent steroid abuse.

Last week Bill Shaw wrote a memo to all WCW employees regarding a new drug policy, which was passed out to all the wrestlers at the Center Stage television taping on 6/7. The policy prohibits employees from using steroids and other illegal drugs specifically mentioning Human Growth Hormone (which is virtually impossible to detect in urine drug tests) and food supplements containing illegal substances. Also mentioned in the policy were abuse of prescription and over-the-counter medications and possession of any illegal drugs. It also prohibits use of diuretics and any other "masking" drugs known to hide the presence of steroids in the urine. Whether this is a serious policy, or another example of lip service to try and simply protect the company against the negative publicity that is surely on its way, will become obvious shortly if the physiques of the most muscular wrestlers start changing as they did in Titan when the wrestlers started getting off, or if they don't change but the obvious neon signs start getting suspended.

The penalties according to the policy for a positive drug test of any kind are rehabilitation and counseling for a first offense, suspension without pay until completion of rehabilitation for second offense and termination for a third offense. In addition, all new WCW contracts as a prerequisite to WCW signing wrestlers will be based on the wrestler passing a drug test. Testing will be random, according to the policy, based on reasonable suspicion, with the wording being those who either look like or act like there is reason to believe they may be on steroids or other illegal drugs. There will be monitors watching the drug testing urination, which a lot of people believe to be demeaning, but is necessary because without it, it is far too easy to bring someone else's urine in and pull a switch, as has happened in other sports and allegedly in the WWF in the past.

If the obvious physiques don't change, having a policy that isn't enforced will do nothing to circumvent prospective negative publicity, as we have already seen with Titan Sports. Marijuana, which is an illegal drug and is not at all foreign to pro wrestlers because of the widespread belief that it helps then relax and sleep while on the strange schedule that wrestlers live on in which they are often all amped up at night because they perform at night, yet have to sleep because they have to wake early often for travel to the next city, was not specifically mentioned in the policy to the best of my knowledge. Titan Sports fines wrestlers for marijuana, which has a longer half-life in the system than cocaine, thus is easier to detect in tests, but doesn't suspend them. If traces of any illegal drug in the system constitutes a positive, then by definition, marijuana would be subject to the same penalties as the other drugs. This is going to cause a change in people's lifestyle if this policy is legitimately enforced.

One WCW wrestler in discussing the policy said most wrestlers won't take the policy seriously (in regard to steroids) until they see a name suspended, and many of the names one would suspect are figured into key roles in major shows months in advance so suspending them would throw major plans asunder. From several accounts, Titan ignored its own drug policy on at least one occasion just prior to the 1992 Wrestlemania in regard to Sid Justice aka Vicious. Justice was allegedly caught cheating on the drug test using someone else's urine, which by drug policy definition, would have meant a six week suspension for first offense, but still worked the main event at Wrestlemania, the subsequent European tour, and continued to work house show bookings until he himself walked out on the promotion. In other cases, Titan has suspended headline wrestlers for similar drug policy violations such as Hawk and Davey Boy Smith.

JUNE 21

We've received a complete copy of the WCW Substance Abuse policy. The policy lists anabolic steroids and related substances, Growth Hormones, Clenbuterol, Diuretics (water weight loss pills), masking agents, food supplements containing banned substances, illegal drugs as being banned substances. It also lists misuse or abuse of prescription and over-the-counter medications, alcohol or any other drug, as being on the banned list. Individuals will be tested upon entering WCW, at random during their tenure and at anytime when they show signs that would make them reasonably suspicious candidates for using banned substances. While policy states that a first positive will be punished by a reprimand and by the wrestler being required to attend rehab and counseling at his own expense, a second positive brings both rehab and counseling and suspension without pay until rehab is completed and he can't return until he tests negative. A third positive results in a termination. The policy gives the office the option to terminate on a first offense if the office deems it appropriate. Failure to take a scheduled test or efforts to evade or distort the results will be penalized more heavily than a positive test result. WCW management is prohibited for condoning, encouraging, supplying or otherwise facilitating the use of any substances prohibited by the policy. I wonder if whomever wrote the policy when writing that last sentence looks at the main event of the next PPV show. Hopefully management can look at that main event and figures out a way to fool themselves into believing that main event doesn't constitute both condoning use of steroids and encouraging those underneath what a quick way to get ahead is. All wrestlers will be tested prior to being offered a contract or starting date. There is also reasonable suspicion testing and random testing, which, by the wording of the policy, seems that two wrestlers every month will be tested at random.

From speaking to several doctors and policy administrators in other athletic organizations, the consensus is a policy is as strong as the frequency of tests, although nothing if foolproof. WWF policy is mandatory tests roughly every four to six weeks for everyone. This policy is testing two at random every month. Results of positive tests are to be kept confidential to the office, although the policy recognizes that individuals who are disciplined may gain media attention. Nobody involved with the program (doctors involved and those in charge of reading test results) is allowed to publicly disclose or allude to any information gathered in testing or to comment publicly to the news media on this subject. Anyone violating this policy, or any WCW employees who divulge either directly or indirectly information gathered as a result of test results are subject to fines up to and including firing. In other words, the policy, by its own wording doesn't allow for any media scrutiny. Given the credibility of how testing has been handled in the past, both from this organization and Titan Sports makes the credibility of the policy itself somewhat suspicious from the start. At the very least, if there are no changes in the physiques on top, a change in who is pushed on top, or disappearance of several similar to the mass disappearances of the most muscular wrestlers in the WWF during 1992, then this policy should, and will, be viewed with heavy suspicion.

JUNE 21

Shane Douglas did an interview for Wrestling Flyer newsletter that also appeared on the Real Wrestling Hotline where he said pro wrestling still has a steroid problem and that WCW management has only paid lip service to it. He also said that right now he had no desire to get back in the ring and that even though he's been a life-long fan. Douglas was married a few weeks back and apparently is going to settle on a more normal life as a school teacher. Douglas said this last experience with WCW left a bad taste in his mouth, that WCW will lose more top talent in upcoming months to WWF and replace it with non-talent. He was also critical of Hulk Hogan's behavior during the steroid controversy saying that since he's going back to being a school teacher and he can see the impression star athletes and other role models have on kids and that they owe them the truth about these types of subjects. Douglas said the entire time he was in WCW that there was only one drug test (the November test) and that he knew of many wrestlers that were on steroids at the time and nothing happened. In a previous interview, Bill Watts talked of several wrestlers testing positive for steroids in November but claiming there was no discipline handed out because WCW didn't have a steroid policy in effect

JULY 26

As one can tell by the physiques on the PPV, most wrestlers consider the new steroid policy as the latest policy not worth the paper it's printed on put out by WCW. Guess where they killed the policy was bringing in the new wrestlers and from what we speculated last week and were later told this week, didn't test them despite the policy specifically stating all new wrestlers are to be tested and have to pass the test before they can be offered a final deal.

AUGUST 9

It's ironic that just days before the test, Titan Sports in its WWF Magazine that hits the newsstands this week (that subscribers have already received at press time), published the first in its series of articles purporting to tell "the true set of facts" regarding the attacks on the WWF since the summer of 1991. The story in this issue was largely a very negative two-page profile of Superstar Billy Graham.

As far as facts are concerned, the story is largely accurate, with most of the information on Graham's past coming from his own mouth in his recent depositions for his lawsuit, or from his own mouth in the lengthy interview in this publication in January 1992. However, the facts are items simply on Graham's background and don't even discuss any of the issues or allegations Graham went public with in 1992. The story never addresses any of the statements made by Graham that garnered so much publicity, ie the rampant use of steroids within the WWF and Hulk Hogan's denying steroid use on the Arsenio Hall show, both of which were confirmed by many on-the-record sources in many different publications during that time period. The veracity of his statements on those subjects are known at this point to be true. In fact, the rampant steroid use was later admitted to on the record by Vince McMahon when he admitted half the wrestlers in the WWF failed the first steroid test to the Los Angeles Times and other media sources and by Hogan himself earlier this year in the Buffalo News, when he admitted he used steroids for virtually the entire decade of the 80s.

The story is a defense, and a strong defense at that, of Titan's position and also the position of Zahorian, who the story was surprisingly defensive of, in regard to the lawsuit Graham has outstanding against both. Titan claims, which is true, that Graham only spent a little more than one year as a wrestler for Titan Sports since his 1970s WWWF stint was for Vince's father's company, Capitol Wrestling Corporation, out of the 23 years he used steroids, although realistically he spent about four years, three months of his career largely as a headliner for the WWF, and that he had used steroids for more than a decade before he ever met Zahorian.

The story misrepresented Graham's connection with the Zahorian trial claiming "pretrial publicity heightened when Eldridge Coleman, a/k/a Superstar Billy Graham, arrived on the scene and indicated that he would testify as a rebuttal witness on behalf of the government at the trial." The fact is, pretrial publicity heightened when it was revealed Hulk Hogan and Roddy Piper, two of the biggest names in pro wrestling in that time period, were subpoenaed by the government in regard to their connection with Zahorian and possible steroid use (Hogan's subpoena was then quashed days before the trial, which caused the trial to receive far less mainstream media publicity than it would have). The name Billy Graham, which was only identified as a witness beforehand in one mainstream media publication (the wrestling column I wrote in the now-defunct National Sports Daily), had nothing to do with any garnering any significant pretrial publicity. Not only that, but Graham didn't even arrive on the scene of the trial in Harrisburg, PA until several days into the trial, nor was it publicly revealed he would testify until the day before he did.

The story then talked of Graham's lawyers demanding a $1.25 million settlement, which Titan refused, to avoid the filing of a lawsuit, which is true. A deadline date was given and the deadline past, and it was several months before a lawsuit was filed. The story revealed Graham, from Graham's own depositions with Jerry McDevitt, that he had multiple suppliers of steroids while in Phoenix in his pre-wrestling days. Graham had already gone public years ago admitting 20 years or so of heavy steroid use. The story claimed "Graham presents himself as if he were a professional wrestler associated with the World Wrestling Federation throughout that 23-year-period (where he used steroids)," when in fact, Graham never did anything of the sort. The story said, "Our investigation has revealed that he (Graham) is a high school dropout and has never held a regular job. He has a well-documented past of tax liens as well as non-support orders for the two children he left behind when he married for the fifth time."

If we are to assume that is true, the statement in the WWF Magazine about Graham never holding a regular job after a career as a wrestler that spanned 20 years as largely a main eventer throughout North America and Japan speaks volumes about the regard the WWF holds professional wrestlers in. Graham was called "...one of the few wrestlers of that era (1970) to use steroids and, ironically, is substantially responsible for the subsequent spread of steroids to other wrestlers." The fact is that steroid use in wrestling dated back to the early 60s and many major names and minor names of that era had experimented with them although when Graham broke into the business in Calgary in 1969, use was minuscule in comparison to 15 years later. Certainly Graham's use in the 70s was more regular and more prolific than most in the profession at the time. His look with the massive muscularity which was unique during its time frame and the fact that he was one of the biggest box office draws of the 70s and perhaps the most charismatic wrestler of his era no doubt did encourage others to copy his act, which included using steroids to copy the physique, as both Hulk Hogan and Jesse Ventura could attest to.

No doubt Graham's popularity during his heyday, and the fact the wrestlers of his era knew him as a major steroid user, did encourage others to use. But the explosion of steroid use in wrestling came around 1984, at which point Graham was no longer one of the most charismatic and influential wrestlers around. If wrestlers are to be blamed, and that in itself is unfair since it was the promoters who decided who to push to the top of the cards, who to hire and what look is in vogue, the most influential in this explosion were Hogan and the Road Warriors, who were massively muscular and pushed to the top, in the case of the Road Warriors, with virtually no experience. Graham's influence in the steroid problem in pro wrestling pales in comparison with the influence of McMahon's, and for the WWF Magazine to blame Graham for much of wrestling's steroid problem is a case of unmitigated gall.

The story said Graham "was pretty much washed up as a wrestler (during his October 1982 to April 1983 stint)" with Titan, and was a drug addict and unreliable and let go. Graham was never anything special as a worker during the 70s, and his work had deteriorated and he physically looked to be in poor health, apparently because of his drug addictions, which he fully admitted to, during that stint. But it should be noted that in spite of all that, he was pushed by McMahon as a headliner and top title contender much of that run and drew many sellout crowds against Bob Backlund. The story went on to say that Graham defrauded McMahon in 1984 when he came back for his final run saying he was fit and able when he needed a hip replacement. The fact that Graham wasn't physically in good shape and was barely mobile in the ring was well-known throughout the industry. Between his WWF stints, Graham worked as largely a headline performer for NWA territories in both the Carolinas and Florida, and got by largely on his interview ability and name value. As the story stated, Titan did pay approximately $30,000 for Graham to get his hip operation and paid Graham $1,000 per week during his convalescence. It didn't state that the hip operation itself was used by Titan as a promotional angle and that when Graham returned, that money was taken out of his wrestling paychecks until he had paid all the money back to McMahon. "When Graham improved, he tried to wrestle for about six months and was not very good at it." Certainly true again, but if he wasn't good, and as a worker during that time period he surely wasn't, that doesn't explain why he was pushed as a headliner during most of that run as well.

If Titan felt that Graham had damaged the company last year, and he did somewhat, although it's hard to pinpoint to what degree, the company certainly has the right to defend themselves against his charges. But by ignoring most of Graham's claims rather than addressing them, the most important of which have been substantiated, this article, entitled, "Now It's Our Turn..." comes across more as personal revenge and trying to cloud up issues rather than trying to clear anything up. For that reason, with the exception of stating Titan's position regarding Graham's lawsuit against the company, a lawsuit which has received virtually no publicity at all, it's hard to figure out what the purpose even was for it.

AUGUST 9

In response to much heated criticism in recent months, WCW held a comprehensive drug test for both steroids and street drugs on 8/2 in Atlanta for all wrestlers. The wrestlers knew about the test several days in advance, which, because of well-known written ways to beat steroid tests, makes the results less foolproof than doing an unannounced test. Earlier this year, Shaw outlined a new drug program, with specific guidelines requiring all new wrestlers to pass a steroid test before they could be offered a position with the company. Many new wrestlers had debuted since the policy was issued, and it is believed none were steroid tested first. It seemed that "look" one gets when on steroids was a major factor in many of them being hired in the first place, which made the written policy appear to be just another in a long series of "works" and misleading statements by the two major promotions when it came to the steroid issue since the trial of Dr. George Zahorian in 1991.

With some high-level media publicity in the works once again regarding the subject of steroids and pro wrestling, WCW was under the gone to act on its policy as a defense against what could have been and still may be negative major publicity. Although the results of this testing will be kept confidential, it puts WCW in a bad position credibility-wise. With tapings already completed through November, suspending any key wrestlers will be just one of what will be many problems with tapings being outdated by the time they hit the air since it is entirely conceivable that wrestlers involved in headline spots on PPV shows that angles and interviews and publicity have already been done for are on steroids, and that is putting things mildly. If nobody is suspended, everyone will believe the policy to be a fraud because it's virtually impossible to comprehend that there is no use at present of these drugs in WCW. Nevertheless, with the advance warning, it is possible the tests can be beaten by those currently using. The NFL, which has about 1,400 players, tests regularly for steroids and maybe two or three per year fail a test, yet nobody believes the steroid use in the NFL is at as low a figure as would be indicated by positive test results.

It has already been reported here and elsewhere, and confirmed in an interview by Bill Watts, that when he was running WCW, the most recent drug test (held in November 1992), that several wrestlers tested positive for steroids but no disciplinary action was taken because WCW had no written steroid policy in place. In early 1992, Kip Frey had implemented a steroid policy, but Watts dropped the policy upon taking command because of his initial belief, which he apparently later changed, that the company needn't worry about whether its wrestlers were using felonious drugs in order to gain competitive advantages. Indeed, judging by who is pushed on top, the "steroid look" (unnatural muscle size combined with extreme definition and body hardness that can't be achieved through weight training and diet even when not when constantly on the road), has become as much a competitive advantage in today's WCW as it ever was in the past with this company, although probably not to extreme the look was in the heyday of the WWF.

AUGUST 30

Former WCW Executive Vice President Jim Herd was brought in by the Justice Department to appear before the Grand Jury in the investigation of Vince McMahon on 8/19. According to Herd, who is currently part-owner of "The Real Wrestling Hotline" (of which I'm involved with as well) , he was questioned largely about Tully Blanchard's departure from the WWF in 1989 and Herd subsequently pulling the previously-offered $250,000 per year contract from Blanchard. If you recall, during the summer of 1989, Blanchard & Arn Anderson held the WWF tag title as The BrainBusters (or known in Japan as the Vertical Suplexes). Both gave notice because they received big money offers from WCW through Herd and booker Ric Flair. Blanchard, in fact, was actively recruiting and believed he had commitments from nearly a dozen WWF wrestlers to jump with him. At that point Blanchard, after immediately dropping the tag title back to Demolition was suspended for the duration of his notice for failing a cocaine test. At that point Herd pulled the contract offer from him feeling it wouldn't have been good p.r. to hire someone the WWF got rid of for cocaine, or at least I believe that is the gist of what he told the Grand Jury. Herd told the Grand Jury that neither McMahon nor Pat Patterson had ever spoken to him about this situation, which may have been what they were trying to get at. This investigation is now about 17 months old, and whatever is going to happen is thought to be going to happen around October.

SEPTEMBER 27

Apparently the WCW steroid test is being judged on the "lowering levels" standard. In other words, a positive on the recent first test isn't cause for disciplinary action (which, if tests were really foolproof which they aren't, would have meant several suspensions high on the cards) as long as the next test shows a lower level of steroids in the system. Several doctors involved with drug testing told me when WWF used those standards that judging on those parameters is largely a fraud because the testing procedure isn't sophisticated enough to accurately detect levels dropping.

SEPTEMBER 29

An article in the New York Observer, a small New York City weekly publication, that came out on 9/8, spawned short items in USA Today and the New York Daily News the next day and provided some insight into potentially the biggest news story to hit the pro wrestling business in the United States in many years.

The article, believed to have been the product of a public relations agency working for Titan Sports, alleged that the U.S. Justice Department and NBC News are facing allegations that a Justice Department investigator and a NBC news producer "may have jointly committed legal or ethical violations while trying to substantiate charges of misconduct in the World Wrestling Federation." The story tried to compare an upcoming NBC news magazine piece investigating Titan Sports with the NBC "Dateline" story on the exploding G.M. trucks which was later revealed to be in some ways fraudulent and caused the network to publicly apologize. The story named the investigator as Anthony Valenti of the U.S. Attorney's Office of the Eastern District of New York, who has been heading the grand jury inquiry into Titan Sports, Vince McMahon and the World Wrestling Federation, and the producer as Len Tepper of the new NBC magazine show called "Now," hosted by Tom Brokaw and Katie Couric. According to the story, Titan and McMahon have accused Tepper and Valenti of sharing information protected by grand jury secrecy to advance their independent investigations, and of improperly wielding the power of the Government to coerce witnesses into giving them information about the company.

The story, in the same basic form, was a short picked up the next day in USA Today, a newspaper that for years has come under heavy criticism for its seemingly biased coverage whenever issues involving Titan Sports have come to light, ie. lack of coverage of all negative stories, yet strong coverage of all Titan responses to negative stories reported elsewhere, almost, as in the case of the steroid issue, in one case of a story defending Titan completely contradicting a key item in another story (in regard to the ability to test for Human Growth

Hormone) in the same sports section printed on the same day. The New York Daily News also ran a short item the next day, talking about the New York Observer story with a response by NBC spokesperson Beth Comstock saying the story was "silly," and basically saying it wasn't unusual for companies being investigating by a news show to respond in this manner.

The story noted WWF attorney Jerry McDevitt has written letters to both NBC News President Andrew Lack and network President Robert Wright complaining about Tepper. In an 8/11 letter to Lack, McDevitt wrote: "We have reason to believe that confidential and secret information before the Federal grand jury has been revealed to Mr. Tepper.

It is also our conclusion that Mr. Tepper has reached an accommodation with the Government agents whereby he receives confidential information which could feud the Government's investigation and, in turn, fuel his news story." McDevitt also claimed in the letter that if the investigation would result in legal charges, he would call Tepper to testify based on "direct evidence that he has acted as a government agent." In an 8/24 letter to Wright, McDevitt wrote, "The activities of Mr. Tepper which have come to light indicate some rather unusual improprieties in connection with what appears to be a joint venture between Mr. Tepper and a friend of his who is a Federal agent on the case.

Pursuant to that friendship, Mr. Tepper apparently feels comfortable calling in the power of the grand jury to obtain evidence that witnesses are unwilling to give him for the show."

The key item the story revealed was an apparent videotape involving Mel Phillips, the former ring announcer who resigned along with booking assistant Terry Garvin (Terry Joyal) and Vice President of talent Pat Patterson (Pierre Clermont) when the scandal first broke in the San Diego Union-Tribune in March, 1992. Patterson later rejoined the company in his former position in August. The tape, in the possession of a former WWF employee, was apparently told by the employee to an NBC employee that it contained footage of Phillips caveating with some ring boys. The employee agreed to send the tape to NBC via federal express, but changed his mind and stopped the delivery. Tepper went to the fed-ex office to try and claim the tape, but was unsuccessful. Later that day, Valenti appeared at the fed-ex office and took custody of the videotape.

The story noted the WWF has long been the center of controversy regarding steroid use and sexual assault by its executives. Source/s identified in the story only as "WWF's defenders" claimed the charges of sexual abuse were resolved in the March, 1992 settlement out-of-court with Tom Cole and that "the company acknowledged its use of steroids three years ago--before the muscle-building pills were made illegal because of their dangerous side effects--and has since instituted a policy banning such drugs from its organization." In reality, the Cole case is the subject of a pending lawsuit, and the WWF's first acknowledgement of any steroid use within the federation came at a press conference in July, 1991, months after federal law has made steroids illegal throughout the United States and years after possession and use for non-medical purposes had been banned in many states. Even to this day, in several interviews, WWF spokespeople and top wrestlers have consistently tried to use the misleading defense that the prior use was during the period steroids were legal, when half the wrestlers in the company failed a steroid test long after the federal law had gone into effect, and it well-known that the type of steroid test being used at the time was hardly infallible when it comes to being beaten.

The attempt by Titan apparently to stop proceedings by both NBC and the Justice Department seems to have failed. NBC has indicated it has no plans to cancel the segment and the Justice Department investigation is continuing with more witnesses scheduled to be brought before the Grand Jury this week. The NOW segment as yet doesn't have a scheduled air date, nor is their any indication how much longer the government investigation will continue before it is either dropped or charges will come out. Titan's reaction is just the latest in a string of attempts by the company to try and obfuscate and confuse the real issues involved in a legitimate investigative news story concerning allegations of sexual harassment and/or sexual abuse of minors and almost institutionalized steroid use in the past within the company and a government investigation that is in its 18th month by attempting to point an accusing finger at those doing the investigations. The attempt to bring this story public before the Grand Jury questioning of witnesses has even been completed, let alone many weeks before any potential indictments or conclusions could possibly be reached seems to indicate major concern over what the results of the investigation and the contents of the news story will contain.

OCTOBER 5

Another steroid story, of which some allegations have been thrown around as to include unnamed pro wrestlers, has surfaced over the past ten days in the Atlanta area. It actually stems from a murder case of Simon Ijiwoye this past May. As part of an investigation of Ijiwoye's death, defendant Tony Langston's attorney, John Matteson, has filed a motion requesting the state turn over information relating to Ijiwoye's alleged steroid and drug trafficking. Matteson claimed Ijiwoye was a well-known steroid dealer for area pro wrestlers and Atlanta Falcons football players. The only name which has gone public in the investigation, injured Falcons quarterback Chris Miller, denied knowing Ijiwoye, any use of steroids or even the ability to recognize steroids if he were to see them and the Falcons released a statement during the week saying that none of the players knew of Ijiwoye or a "Dr. Simon." As the week went on, one local television station also added unnamed area high school football coaches to the list of those obtaining steroids. There have been allegations from the defendant's side regarding some major wrestling personalities that go much deeper than simply personal use of steroids in connection with Ijiwoye, who it is claimed would purchase the drugs in Cancun, Mexico, smuggle them into the country and sell them in the Atlanta area. Weekend television news reports didn't identify any wrestling names other than linking "some people connected with pro wrestling" to the list of possible steroid recipients.

OCTOBER 11

Bret Hart was on "The FAN" radio, an all-sports station in Toronto this past week and made some comments that are bound to cause more than a little controversy in many quarters. When the host asked "What about the other federations, are they the minor leagues?," Hart replied: "I would say so. I don't mean that in a nasty way. There's the WCW, which is probably the only other form of wrestling next to the World Wrestling Federation, but I couldn't hold them close to the World Wrestling Federation when it comes to actual production and wrestling. They have some good wrestlers. A lot of times the wrestlers are interchangeable, but I don't think they have as good a product. I hate to bring it up, as far as even the drug testing, for example, the WCW, their drug testing must be pretty shoddy because you can tell by looking at the guys in the WCW that they're all obviously drug abusers. There's no hiding that.

In the World Wrestling Federation, every single wrestler is drug tested just like Olympic athletes, every seven or eight days, and there's absolutely not one single wrestler taking any kind of drugs. That's any kind of drugs, period, from amphetamines, you can barely get away with caffeine, I think." The host then brought up the subject of steroids and all the steroid talk in the WWF in the past, and Hart replied, "And all that steroid talk was pretty much true. I think it worked in my favor. For example, a few years ago, there were all these huge guys that were on steroids. Hulk Hogan is an example. These guys were huge, maxed out on steroids, which wasn't right. It wasn't fair to guys like myself. I was strictly known for my wrestling ability, not a muscle-body, a physique, which is what it had become. It worked in my favor that they cleaned that end of it up. I think it worked in everybody's favor, even the wrestlers. You'll see now there's a lot of these big muscle guys who have since departed the World Wrestling Federation and they're in the WCW and that's because they couldn't pass the drug testing."

At this point they went to a caller who disputed Hart's claim of being the best there is, was, etc. and said that Ric Flair was the greatest wrestler of all-time. Hart replied, "What could you possibly see in Ric Flair? I mean this. This is the truth. Ric Flair was the most overrated wrestler there ever was. If you've seen Ric flair wrestle one time, you've seen him wrestle a million times. He's the most uncreative, unimaginative wrestler there ever was. He was the pits. You are wrong. You don't know anything about wrestling if you think Ric Flair is a great wrestler. (Wrestling) Ric Flair was the biggest letdown of my entire career. I've wrestled all kinds of wrestlers everywhere and I thought when I stepped in the ring to wrestle Ric Flair that I was going to be wrestling a legend, like one of the greatest of all-time. On a scale of one-to-ten, I'd rate Ric Flair as about a three. He sucks. I'd even say Jerry Lawler quite conceivably has at least a little more imagination than Ric Flair. Ric Flair, I don't hate him or anything, I hear that all the time that Ric Flair is the greatest, Ric Flair is the greatest. I don't know how anyone could even begin to think he was good. If you've seen Ric Flair wrestle one time, you've seen Ric Flair's whole show."

Arguing about WWF vs. WCW when it comes to product mix is largely a matter of taste. There's little argument WWF is world's more effective when it comes to production, promotion, booking, overall interest, etc. As far as the wrestling itself, while the WCW product quality has dropped a lot of late, for pure wrestling, the WCW Wrestle War PPV show was better from top-to-bottom than any WWF PPV show this year. As far as the drug situation, when it comes to steroids, no doubt the WWF has done a much better job of cleaning up its problem than WCW. The reasons for this are obvious. The WWF has been under a lot more pressure and scrutiny regarding the subject, which admittedly is unfair on one hand. However, WCW officials and dozens of wrestlers weren't involved in a major steroid dealer bust, and then caught making ridiculous statements, attempts at major deception and outright lies left and right on the subject which came back to haunt them. In regard to that subject, WCW's announced policy, first implemented in January, 1992, has turned into a complete joke.

However, making a statement that not one single wrestler is taking any kind of drug in the WWF is something that is ridiculous, although it may also be a response along the "company line" because of all the negative publicity of the past. The very nature of wrestling (physical punishment, heavy travel) makes Percoset, Percodan, Halcion and other downers almost second nature, not to mention that alcohol is a drug. This is not meant as pointing fingers at anyone in a derogatory fashion about usage of these drugs because it's the nature of the beast, some of the drugs are legal with prescription and alcohol and some over-the-counter sleep-aids are legal without, and many drugs have positive qualities to athletes if use is kept under control. But saying any group of 50 or so adults, often very wild human beings in their 20s, 30s and early 40s, many of whom had more then a little familiarity with drugs in their past, and making a blanket statement that not one of them is on any kind of drug is a pretty strong statement no matter what the results of any drug tests are. There are many drugs which can't be tested for and aren't tested for, so saying they all have to pass tests is no evidence of non-use. Hart's statement about all these big muscle-guys who left the WWF for WCW because they couldn't pass their drug test, while in theory that would be the case with WCW's obvious preferential hiring of late of muscleheads which encourages steroid use, there are really only two wrestlers who fit that bill. The blanket statement that they're all obviously drug abusers is really unfair to many WCW wrestlers, because I'm sure some aren't, although his criticism of the WCW drug testing policy and the results seems valid.

As far as the comments on Flair go, that isn't the first time Hart has made comments like that regarding Flair and it's doubtful it'll be the last time. He's got the right to his opinion, although my experience is that if you'd ask every active pro wrestler today who the greatest all-around worker of all-time was, Flair's name would be mentioned far more often than anyone else's. This may be part of the root of the problem. Hart is unquestionably an excellent performer and would probably be considered by most as one of the two or three best active performers in the country today, and as the best by many. To reach that level in a profession such as this requires a lot of ego and sacrifice, and having a lot of one and doing a lot of the latter could easily make one tired or frustrated with the constant comparisons, often unfavorable, of his own ability to work a match as compared to Flair.

OCTOBER 18

Bret Hart was on Jim Ross' radio show 10/9 reiterating his remarks regarding drug use in WCW and Ric Flair. It turned into a cheap shot since they kept phoning the Jacksonville Coliseum (where WCW was that night) to get a hold of Flair to give the impression that Flair wouldn't defend himself against the remarks knowing full well WCW wouldn't allow of one of its wrestlers to appear on the rival promotions' broadcast. Hart's remarks did cause a lot of heat in the WCW dressing room, although comments I heard were people laughing off the remarks about Flair. The comments that got people hot were the ones about the company's wrestlers being all drug abusers.

NOVEMBER 8

On the WWF Radio show, a caller asked about the policy regarding suspended wrestlers still wrestling at television tapings and Ross said that he didn't know for sure but he believed they could wrestle on television and not get paid, so that seems to confirm what we all strongly suspected the new drug suspension policy is only for house shows and doesn't include being suspended from television tapings.

NOVEMBER 8

Newsday, a Long Island-based daily newspaper, ran a page three story with a page one photo on the investigation of the WWF, centering the story around steroids. Actually the biggest surprise is that the story, which was released nationally on the wire services the next day and was the subject of an unfunny Saturday Night Live spoof that evening, was even prominently featured. First, Newsday never ran any stories on previous WWF scandals. Second, they didn't have a story and instead mostly recycled testimony and evidence from the Zahorian trial (nearly two-and-a-half years old). The stories' lead, which was the one of only two paragraphs of substance, said that federal authorities are investigating allegations that the WWF and its owner, Vince McMahon, illegally dispensed steroids to wrestlers. The only other paragraph of substance stated that in an attempt to discredit the investigation, McMahon's attorney, Jerry McDevitt, complained that an unnamed criminal investigator has misused his position by leaking information to an NBC news producer, which is the same charge reported on elsewhere weeks ago in another New York newspaper. Nevertheless, the publicity from the prominence of the story garnered a strong reaction by the WWF on its radio show that night, loaded with the "we test" more aggressively than anyone defense from one of its doctors, David Lee Black of Nashville, and from Lex Luger. Host Jim Ross at least gave the impression he was attempting to be as fair as his position would allow him in some aspects, acknowledging the reported allegation of McMahon dispensing the drugs and saying that he knew they hadn't heard the last of this subject.

Of course his position prohibited him from bringing up obvious points, especially when Luger, who gave the same misleading use when legal quotes he gave all summer, is being used as a spokesperson for the company in its anti-physique enhancing drugs stance. Luger claimed he'd be willing to take a test for anyone at anytime. Black talked about the WWF's drug testing as being the most stringent in any sport, which may very well be true today, but is no defense at all when the allegations brought up in the story were during a time period when this wasn't the case. Black, who was never asked about potential policy loopholes such as undetectable drugs, compared the current policy favorably compared with the NFL and IOC policy because of more frequent testing which seems to be a valid point when it comes to being a deterrent against steroids if the policy is enforced uniformly. While both the NFL and IOC's tests have come under serious scrutiny numerous times, at least NFL and IOC officials will admit what McMahon has denied on numerous occasions, and that is that no testing policy is foolproof. When the current drug stack of choice for professional bodybuilders growth/ muscularity purposes (and allegedly some pro wrestlers) has moved away from the category of anabolic steroids to a combination of Growth Hormone and Insulin, using steroid tests as a defense to the claim that nobody is using illegal drugs without qualification is even more suspect than ever.

NOVEMBER 29

THE CHARGES AGAINST VINCE MCMAHON
- Conspiracy to distribute anabolic steroids and to defraud the United States Food and Drug Administration (during the period from 1985 to February, 1991). Maximum penalty: Five years in prison
- Illegal possession of anabolic steroids with intent to distribute (October 24, 1989). Maximum penalty: Three years in prison. Maximum personal fines against Vince McMahon for both charges: $500,000

AGAINST TITAN SPORTS
- Conspiracy to distribute anabolic steroids and to defraud the United States Food and Drug Administration

(during the period from 1985 to February, 1991. Maximum fine: $500,000
- Illegal possession of anabolic steroids with intent to distribute (October 24, 1989). Maximum fine: $500,000.
- Additional maximum penalty against Titan Sports for one or both counts: Forfeiture of the land, office building, and everything in it located at 1241 East Main Street in Stamford, CT (aka Titan Towers). Estimated value of office building: $9.5 million

In what could be prove to be a landmark steroid case, both Titan Sports owner Vince McMahon and his company were indicted on two counts apiece of steroid law violations.

The case is believed to mark the first attempt by the U.S. government in enforcing its steroid laws to charge the owner or a key management figure of a sports organization, and the organization itself, which allegedly benefitted financially from its athletes usage of steroids as conspirators for that use.

McMahon, in denying the conspiracy charges, claimed the charge was an attempt to make him responsible for the actions of Dr. George Zahorian III, the Harrisburg, PA osteopath who was convicted of 12 counts of illegally dispensing steroids and other controlled substances in a well-publicized 1991 trial. Zahorian, who is currently serving a three-year sentence, was believed to have been the main and most well-known supplier of steroids, but was not the only supplier, to WWF wrestlers from the early 1980s through his 1991 arrest. The indictment named Zahorian, as well as others who weren't named, as unindicted co-conspirators.

McMahon and Titan Sports were arraigned Tuesday morning, 11/23 in Brooklyn. McMahon plead "not guilty" on all charges and was released on $250,000 bond before U.S. District Court Judge Jacob Mishler. A May 2, 1994 trial date was set. At the arraignment McMahon refused to answer any media questions on the advice of his attorney but called the entire proceedings "unfair."

In a statement issued through his lawyers, McMahon claimed the government's prosecutors "are now trying to make me responsible for what the doctor (Zahorian) did. I did no such thing."

In a statement released to the press, McMahon said, "To turn my personal use into a crime, they claim I shared some of those steroids with a friend and that somehow made me a dealer."

The indictments, which resulted from an at least 20-month long Justice Department investigation of McMahon and his company, never alleged McMahon sold steroids, but that on several occasions around or between March 1988 and October 1989, McMahon and Titan Sports distributed and caused to be distributed the steroid Nandrolone Decanoate (better known as Decadurabolin or "Deca" for short) to a WWF performer known to the Grand Jury whose name wasn't listed in the indictment. There is widespread belief within the wrestling industry of who the performer is, and his name was in at least one major media report originally before lawyers for that media service took the name out. If the performer in question is one believed to be within the industry, it would contradict many public statements that performer has made in the past in regard to his involvement with the drugs.

McMahon, who after the indictment acknowledged sharing steroids with a friend, but admitted to committing no crimes, contradicted an interview in the Boston Herald a few days before the indictment, when he addressed the potential of a charge for dispensing steroids.

"Of all the things that have been rumored, the vicious rumors and the lies that have been said about me and this company, no one's ever said that before. Not one wrestler or anyone. So if I had ever given anyone steroids, distributed steroids or anything along those lines, that would have been one of the very first things that someone could have said, `Yes, he did it to me.'"

McMahon, whose age was listed in all published reports as 47, but is believed to really have turned 48 in August, had, in a July 1991 press conference in the wake of the Zahorian trial where the first announcement was made that Titan would steroid test its wrestlers, and in more than one statement to the this publication in 1991 and early 1992 admitted personal use of Decadurabolin acquired from Dr. Zahorian but categorized the extent of his use as briefly experimenting in 1987.

On the WWF's Saturday night radio show, Jim Ross early in the show listed the charges against McMahon, read the company's prepared statement and then largely dropped the subject for the remainder of the first hour.

During the opening of the second hour, Ross complained that the government should have had better things to do and that both McMahon and the WWF claim the allegations are groundless and plan to contest these allegations.

However, the pleas hardly make a May trial date a certainty. At this point business negotiations will take place (ie plea bargaining). There are many who believe a trial, win or lose, would prove devastating for the McMahon Empire because it would require numerous wrestlers to testify to their own use of steroids including the possibility or most of the company's top drawing cards from its heyday. The name Hulk Hogan becomes a key factor. The Zahorian trial suddenly became front page news in USA Today and was scheduled to be covered as significant news in many mainstream media outlets when it was believed Hogan would be testifying. When Hogan's subpoena was quashed, the story took on far less significance initially, although not in the long-run. If Hogan were to be called on to testify in a trial with McMahon on the subject of steroids, it would become a huge media event.

McMahon is going to continue as lead television announcer and in his CEO capacity with Titan Sports in the wake of the indictments.

"The government does not allege that I or my company have done anything wrong since the use of steroids became illegal nearly three years ago," McMahon said in a story that ran Thursday night on the AP wire. "The World Wrestling Federation does not condone or tolerate the use of steroids."

The question of legality of steroids has been misinterpreted by media and misrepresented in statements by many leading wrestling personalities since media scrutiny and controversy regarding the drug being abused by wrestlers started in the wake of the Zahorian trial.

Since this is a federal case, various state laws regarding use or distribution of the drug aren't applicable to these indictments. Statements made by many wrestling personalities regarding steroids themselves being legal during certain periods was often not the case even before changes in federal law because of state laws in many instances.

Simply put, steroids in an of themselves have never been a "legal drug" during any of this period except for specifically specified instances. Prior to 1988, dispensing steroids was under the jurisdiction of the FDA (Food and Drug Administration). Dispensing steroids was only legal before 1988 under one condition, when use was supervised by a licensed medical practitioner acting within a legitimate doctor-patient relationship. During the Zahorian trail, one of the government's key points against Zahorian was that his manner of dispensing steroids did not fall within that framework.

In November, 1988, after a congressional hearing, because it was felt doctors were abusing that specific instance and acting unethically in writing prescriptions and dispensing steroids to healthy athletes, the drugs were placed under the jurisdiction of the DEA (Drug Enforcement Administration). The law was tightened up at this point to only allow steroids to be dispensed or to be possessed with intent to distribute for the specific purpose of treatment of disease in human beings. Any other type of dispensing or distribution was considered a felony.

In early 1991, another law was enacted making it a felony for any kind of possession of steroids or use of steroids by individuals for anything other than the treatment of disease. There are no charges in these indictments relating to this final law change.

McMahon's statement that the government doesn't allege any wrongdoing by him or his company since use (the key word is "use," making his statement true) of steroids became illegal is apparently trying to confuse the press and public and in some cases may have succeeded in regard to the final law change of 1991, which isn't applicable to this indictment, with the fact that other laws pertaining to the legality of the drug had been in effect since the 70s.

The press release sent out by the U.S. Justice Department's Eastern District on 11/18 announcing the indictment specifically stated, "at all relevant times anabolic steroids have been classified as prescription drugs under federal law and could not be dispensed without a valid medical prescription." It later went on to state, "The indictment announced today charges McMahon and Titan with violations of federal law both before and after the enactment of the 1988 statute."

McMahon's attorney, Jerry McDevitt, who was the attorney for Hulk Hogan and responsible for getting him out of testifying at the Zahorian trial, in a New York Daily News article called the indictments, "Cockamamie," and claimed, "We're going back into ancient and revisionist history to fashion an indictment against Vincent McMahon."

The charges against McMahon and the company are significant in the sports and quasi-sports world. If McMahon were to be convicted as being part of a conspiratorial role during the years stated, it would not seem to be a stretch to argue that during the same time frame, college football coaches, bodybuilding promoters and others in ownership or personnel-decision making capacities in sports where steroids offer a competitive advantage or the steroid look increases box office marketability, along with the institution, particularly if somehow a strength coach or administrator provided funds for their purchase, of which they represent could conceivably be guilty of the same offenses. Previous steroid indictments have largely been made against the pawns of a system that creates steroid use from those who strive to reach the top of their profession--doctors supplying them in order to be friends and get favors from celebrities and athletes--and athletes--rather than those who control the field of play and the criteria of how to get ahead. McMahon can be more closely tied to Zahorian because he himself purchased steroids from the doctor and was clearly knowledgeable of the situation that Zahorian was dispensing steroids to his wrestlers and seemingly took no actions to discourage use in his company until after Zahorian was convicted and media pressure followed.

Perhaps even more potentially devastating from an industry-wide standpoint then the charges against McMahon personally, who is largely seen as the most powerful and influential individual worldwide in the industry for most of the past ten years and arguably in its history, are the charges against the company itself.

Besides a maximum of $1 million in fines, Titan Sports is facing a possible forfeiture of its $9.5 million office complex known as "Titan Towers." The latter, because of the costs of replacing the office and everything in it, would most likely leave the company in a severely financially weakened position and almost force the company into downsizing and rebuilding from a much lower level.

A recent conviction of a Puerto Rican baseball team owner for selling cocaine, with the claim he used the team's offices to do so, resulted in the government seizing the entire team from the owner and putting it up for auction.

The indictment claimed the object of the conspiracy was "unlawfully to provide WWF wrestling performers with steroids to enhance their size and musculature, and thereby to increase the ticket sales for WWF exhibition and the profits to Titan and McMahon."

Titan Sports' involvement in the distribution indictment was caused by the allegation within the indictment that on several occasions between March of 1988 and October of 1989, McMahon ordered and caused to be ordered Nandrolone Decanoate from Zahorian, and the indictment claims, in order to evade the detection of these transactions, McMahon utilized Titan funds or resources to cause the purchase of bank checks used to pay Zahorian for the shipments, which were then distributed to both McMahon and the unnamed WWF performer.

By virtue of the Drug Forfeiture Act, the government, upon a conviction of Titan Sports on either of the counts, is attempting to seize Titan Towers, because it is alleged that office property was used or intended to have been used to commit or facilitate the violations.

The indictment also noted that in December 1989, Titan officials and McMahon learned of the federal investigation into Zahorian's activities and warned him of the investigation, and at that point prevented him from appearing at future WWF shows. A Titan executive known to the Grand Jury, with knowledge of the investigation, instructed another executive to ensure that Zahorian didn't attend a show in Hershey, PA that he was scheduled to be the attending physician at, and to consider warning Zahorian of the existence of the investigation. McMahon also discussed this situation with the Titan executive, and the Titan executive phoned Zahorian and told him to destroy any records of Zahorian's contact with the WWF and with WWF wrestling personnel.

In the Zahorian trial, Zahorian's attorney, Bill Costopoulus claimed that Pat Patterson called Zahorian to tell them that wrestlers were being investigated and at that point Zahorian turned over all his files on wrestlers to a lawyer. When the FBI raided Zahorian's office the following March, there were no files or records relating to medical treatment or contact with WWF wrestlers that Zahorian was dispensing steroids to. It was the acquisition of Zahorian's Fed-Ex receipts which was loaded with names of pro wrestlers, including major names like Hulk Hogan, Randy Savage, Roddy Piper, Ultimate Warrior and Curt Hennig, and most prominently 36 pounds worth of shipments to McMahon and others at the Titan offices which led to pro wrestling being tied into the trial and ultimately led to these indictments.

In the Boston story days before the indictment, McMahon said, "This oppressive investigation for over 19 months has cost us millions and millions of dollars. I would not want to wish what we have endured already on my worst enemy. Ever. Because it's been unfair, unjust and as far as I'm concerned, un-American."

NOVEMBER 29

There was considerable mainstream media coverage of the McMahon/Titan indictments on Thursday night, with coverage on both the NBC and ABC national newscasts, a brief mention on "Prime Time Live" that evening by Sam Donaldson after a piece of steroid use among high schoolers, and coverage nationally on both CNN and ESPN nightly sports reports. The NBC coverage, ironically from the network that carried WWF specials for years, was the strongest. CBS was planning on a more in-depth feature for its Friday night newscast but it was pulled ten minutes before air-time because of a Bill Clinton press conference and may be run sometime in the next week. Coverage was strongest on a local basis in the New York market where all the leading stations carried the story and at least two stations opened the newscast with the indictments as the leading story. Local television and radio carried the story in many markets, although none to anywhere near the same level as New York. On the tabloid scene, "Inside Edition" ran a five-minute feature the next day, using tape of a previous piece done in 1991 on the Zahorian trial and updating it only with the announcement of the indictments of McMahon.

Newspaper coverage was less significant. The AP ran at least two different five-paragraph brief stories on the indictment and another 11-paragraph story on the arraignment which were covered throughout the country, but usually just one or two sentences in the local paper. In the New York media on Friday, the New York Post, which covered this story from the beginning and eventually was sued by McMahon, had a banner cover headline "Muscle Bind--Feds indict wrestle king in steroid pump-up scam" with McMahon's photo, and ran two stories on page five. It followed up by another story on Monday, which had a quote from Ken Patera saying, "Everybody used steroids. If you didn't use them, you couldn't work for McMahon. He wanted everyone to look like a cartoon character."

The most amazing quote in the story came from Craig Peters of PWI, not that it would surprise me he believed it, but that he'd say it for attribution in a newspaper, was, "I don't know if McMahon gave wrestlers steroids, but there was an implicit message that the bigger the bodies, the more impressive the physique, the better chance you have for getting a job with the WWF." Ultimate Warrior was quoted as saying McMahon never told him to use steroids, but that the road schedule and pressure to maintain the Ultimate Warrior character encouraged him to take advantage of every edge, including steroids. The New York Daily News also ran a page five story, while the New York Times limited its coverage to four paragraphs. USA Today, which has been long known for its decided pro-WWF coverage sometimes to the point of being beyond fiction, and complete lack of negative coverage, ran a one-paragraph item in the Entertainment pages in its early editions, but had pulled the item by the time it ran its West Coast edition. The Boston Herald ran a lengthy interview with Vince McMahon on Sunday, an interview done days before the indictments, where McMahon called the investigation a witch hunt. Forbes Magazine is scheduled to do a piece this week. The Miami Herald pulled its weekly wrestling column on Sunday, deeming the subject matter "too controversial."

The story also received and will receive a surprising amount of coverage in the Japanese press, which largely buried the Zahorian trial story and subsequent follow-ups that were major news in the U.S. Ellis Henican of Newsday ran easily the best written piece I've seen, a Sunday feature on Billy Graham, which was the only newspaper story that really captured the essence of the real story. The plight of Graham, as a 50-year-old ex-steroid user for two decades, has to be noted as at least to this point, to be the unfortunate exception, rather than the rule of thumb long-term result. Up to this point, Henican's article had also proven to be the unfortunate exception.

The arraignment on Tuesday was being covered heavily on local New York television and news radio segments, and is expected to lead to further stories this week.

The most ironic thing about the media coverage is this. If a media source never covers pro wrestling to begin with for whatever reason, beneath its dignity, sports editor doesn't think it's sport and entertainment editor doesn't think it's entertainment, etc., it is hard to fault that source for not covering this story, because no mainstream source at press time has understood tying in the conspiracy indictment against McMahon and the company with ramification to many mainstream and cult sports organizations. At some point, those ramifications make this potentially a major sports story, particularly if there turns out to be a conviction on the conspiracy charge. However, any source that has given significant coverage to the industry, particularly during its heyday that these indictments coincide with, has no argument toward not giving the indictment of the company itself and of the most powerful man in the business at least that same amount of coverage. It does point to the sad state of journalism itself in too many cases when the same reporters covering the fantasy aspect run like hell from examining the reality.

Many others seem to have confused the issue stemming from the indictments, thinking the ramifications of this story and long-term effects are based on the amount of coverage it received. Media coverage of certain aspects was the significant determining factor in 1992 when allegations were going public. It is almost completely insignificant when it comes to indictments. The only significance when it comes to indictments are the end results of the indictments.

As with many drugs, steroids are largely misunderstood by the public and media. Because of their ability to enhance performance in numerous sports where speed and or power are prime elements, their use recreationally and athletically is fundamentally different from other drugs. Attempts to legislate them may be in a vain attempt to keep the proverbial playing field level than to protect society from devastating side effects.

While taken for long periods of time in high dosages is presumed to be quite unhealthy, very little in the way of medical research is out there that conclusively proves anything one way or another in regard to either long-term or short-term effects. This allows those who want to justify personal use as claiming there is no proof of what the warning labels claim, and allows those on the other side to exaggerate toxic effects because there is no proof to contradict them, either. Those who use the drugs have quickly learned to shun medical research, which for years claimed no performance enhancing capabilities to the drugs while athletes were blowing out previous bests in their speed and strength sports while on them. The results of the early research was the first of many lies to be told, as some of the earliest researchers have since gone forward saying the original claims of no bulk or strength increases were actually falsified by those in the medical profession for fear it would create an epidemic among athletes if the truth were to come out. When the epidemic took place anyway some years later, attempts were made to exaggerate side effects, but in many cases that had little effect as a deterrent, and now many athletes don't listen to anything the medical profession says on the subject because of lost credibility.

In May of last year, I attended the wedding of a childhood friend in Southern California, a former competitive bodybuilder who once placed in the Collegiate Mr. America bodybuilding championship and was a strength coach at a major steroid-laden college sports program. Both himself and his older brother, who I also grew up with, had used steroids for competition purposes. His brother also used steroids and was still using steroids having nothing to do with competition due to the fact he had the type of personality that would cause somebody to use steroids and brag they enabled him to get it on 32 times in an eight day period. In the wedding party were several other competitive and former competitive bodybuilders, and in that company steroids is usually the prime subject of conversation anyway, but made more cognizant because it was just a few weeks before what was being heavily publicized locally as a drug-free bodybuilding contest being put on by Vince McMahon (more on that later) the very idea of which was laughable to all. They were joking, knowing without having any tangible proof of what later came out in the bodybuilding mags, but truly knowing from experience if you get my drift, the misleading nature of that advertising. I made a comment that wasn't meant at all as funny, and that is that the most prevalent side effect of not only using steroids, but just being involved with those who use is not hair loss, acne increase or increased aggression, but a huge increase in lying, particularly when the subject comes up.

As every new report comes in and every new statement is made, whether it be by Vince McMahon, or Hulk Hogan, or some members of the medical profession, or athletes in other sports, or many, but certainly not all, wrestlers who have spoken publicly on this subject, it always seems to be suspicious. It often is even a direct contradiction with the same people's previous statement. Charting the history of Titan's statements, both in regard to the WWF and WBF, and attempts at misrepresentation and outright fantasy in them has been done numerous times in these pages. Rather than repeating the obvious, the key points are:

- Titan Sports' popularity was built on the back of anabolic steroids. There would be no Hulk Hogan if Terry Bollea had not used anabolic steroids. Take Hulk Hogan and everyone else whose character was pushed due to their physique during that time period out of the equation and Titan Sports would have never achieved anything close to the level of popularity and mainstream appeal it had before the walls of mainstream interest came tumbling down in 1992. Take Terry Bollea out of the equation as the leading star of the company probably would have been another exceptionally big man with a steroided-up physique, as every attempt but one as an heir apparent to Hogan has been. Popularity of most, but not all, of the key draws during that time period was based on physiques that could not have achieved or maintained on the arduous schedule without steroids.

- Vince McMahon was fully aware of all these factors as both a bodybuilder, bodybuilding fan and steroid user himself. His decisions on whom to market and ability to market more than any other promoter during that time period were based largely on physique which led to what virtually all sources in that time period will concede was far more use within the WWF than any other wrestling company. However, steroids were used regularly in all promotions during that time period and were a competitive advantage across the board and in numerous other sports. To say the WWF when it comes to steroid use is guilty of something other sports organizations aren't would be unfair, although it was more of a prerequisite to get in and get to the top than in most. The only difference is, its pusher got caught, its media and a few members of the mainstream media weren't as apt to let its lies go unchallenged, its owner was a user and its owner got to choose who won and lost and how and thus was in complete control over who was and wasn't a star. In a few sports, like bodybuilding, use was probably more rampant then the WWF.

- Use of steroids today in the WWF is minimal, if at all. Steroid tests aren't foolproof. There have been numerous public statements made to the media on this subject that have turned out to be totally untrue, and not just misleading. There have been questions raised about their accuracy and if enforcement of failures is uniform. If there is truth to those questions, and it has already gone public in a few cases that there has, that would not be unique to the WWF either. Questions have been raised by officials and participants in track, football, and all sports with testing policies and everyone knows about the dragging its feet WCW has done the past two years. Just this past week the NFL was sued by former player Terry Long, who is one of only a handful of players who has been suspended in the past few years for failing a test, back in the pre-season of 1991. Long claimed steroid use is encouraged on certain teams, rampant among players, and tests are arbitrarily enforced by the league. His suit claims to have examples of players who failed tests but were never suspended, because they legally challenged the tests and the league ruled the positive results as inconclusive. He even claimed his first test failure (for a higher testosterone level than testing regulations allow) didn't result in a suspension but his second test, which had a more normal level, did, because then the doctors re-evaluated the results first test. But the policy as is administered in the WWF today is a strong deterrent and certainly current use among existing employees is strongly discouraged. The recent attempt to build the promotion around Lex Luger does present a strong case that it is still to a young wrestlers' advantage if they want a job to use the stuff, pump the weights, and hope the genetics are there to get ones' foot in the door. Once they get in they are most likely not going to get away with use for any length of time.

- Nothing have to do with this story and these charges have anything to do with what is going on in the WWF today, but laws that are alleged to have been broken years ago. The current drug testing procedures are not relevant to the time period noted in the indictments.

There are so many stories, some of which were frustrating to cover at the time because the subject leads to one work (read that lie) after another and this is hardly limited to wrestling but all aspects of the issue of performance enhancing drugs in sports, that in looking back, become really humorous, regarding statements made not only by Vince McMahon and wrestlers, but by other major celebrities.

One of the funniest stories involving McMahon has to do with the World Bodybuilding Federation. The WBF announced its formation in January, 1991. At its inaugural press conference, Tom Platz (whose position with Titan would have been equivalent to Pat Patterson's in the wrestling end), said the WBF would regularly steroid test the bodybuilders. This was nearly six months before the Zahorian trial, and there was little mainstream publicity on the subject applied toward either wrestling or bodybuilders and steroids. This statement was made even though there were no plans at all to steroid test, that the word within the industry was "Bodybuilding the way it's supposed to be," (the WBF's original theme) was a way of saying bodybuilding without steroid testing. At the time, the rival Weider group had just had its first (and as it turned out last) Mr. Olympia, the 1990 version, with the guys drug tested. Even though virtually everyone used the juice to prepare and some were said to be on as late as days before the show, the flaws of testing are such that only four of 21 failed and had to forfeit their spot. When the competitors came out, the truth didn't stop the p.a. announcer from saying how all these physiques were drug-tested and steroid free, which brought out the biggest howl of laughter the entire night. It appeared all the guys had to limit their intake in order to beat the test instead of the traditional "going-for-broke."

The fans of the drug-gorged sport were disappointed because the quality of the physiques was the lowest in recent memory. Without ever making an announcement, the Weider organization dropped drug testing from the Olympia, claiming it was cost prohibitive but largely because of fear attendance the next year would drop. However, nobody knew Weider would drop drug testing when the WBF was formed. In the first few months of the WBF, there were no steroid tests. A few months later, in a USA Today article before the first WBF show, Titan again said that all competitors would be tested for steroids before the show. Once again, no tests. It was the WBF lies that made those who followed Titan closely wary when the wrestling tests were announced later that year.

A few months after this, after much media pressure on the wrestling company in the wake of the Zahorian trial, the WWF held its first drug test. During that same period, I had a lengthy discussion with McMahon and the subject of bodybuilding came up and McMahon told me the bodybuilders would be drug tested just like the wrestlers, and in fact, because they were smarter in techniques of beating the test, even more stringent than the wrestlers. He talked about a meeting he had just had with all the bodybuilders a few days earlier where he told them that they'd be subject to the most stringent drug testing in the history of professional sports, about things that had happened at the meeting, etc, and that all the bodybuilders grudgingly accepted they were being pushed as ambassadors of health, thus it would be hypocritical to be on the juice. He said it might take him one or two years, but his goal was to present the first professional steroid-free bodybuilding show.

During the same conversation, he mentioned that he had just signed Lou Ferrigno of TV's "Incredible Hulk" fame to the WBF, what a great guy he was, invited me to a press conference in a few days in Los Angeles when the announcement would go public, and mentioned that Ferrigno would be appearing a few days after that on Johnny Carson. Ferrigno went on with Carson and brought up drug testing in bodybuilding, saying that's why he decided to come back to competition after a 17-year absence, and chose the WBF, because it would have "the strictest drug testing in all of professional sports." The funny part of all this is that, as time will show, in Ferrigno's mind, and in the mind of the WBF bodybuilders at the time, "the strictest drug testing in all of professional sports" line that so many were seemingly willing to say actually in the minds of many meant no drug testing at all. I can't even speculate what was in Vince McMahon's mind at this point in time.

You see, the meeting with the bodybuilders he was giving me details on never happened. Well, actually, that isn't true either. McMahon may have met with the bodybuilders around the time Ferrigno signed. I don't know if he spoke about steroids or not but it couldn't have been a major factor because none of the bodybuilders believed they were ever going to be drug tested until a months later. But McMahon did have that meeting he was telling me about. Several months later, when the entire situation regarding Titan Sports and steroids had changed again due to even more adverse media publicity. According to descriptions of the meeting months later in the bodybuilding mags, the most amazing thing is that some of what McMahon told me "happened" in the meeting "a few days earlier," really did "happen" when the meeting took place months later, almost as if in his mind he was preparing to choreograph reality and as he often has done, to an extent, succeeded. This was in the spring of 1992, when the media publicity regarding steroids in the WWF, Hogan being less than truthful exploded with stories in the San Diego Union-Tribune, New York Post, Los Angeles Times, People Magazine, Miami Herald and syndicated in numerous other papers around the world.

While this was going on, McMahon had his meeting with the bodybuilders and told them he'd have to start testing. It isn't clear what he said but it was reported everywhere that the bodybuilders were told it was because he was getting negative press and mainly for fear of what would air on the company in an upcoming 20/20 special if they pushed the bodybuilders without testing them, which wound up being far more influential because of reactions for fear or what would appear than for what actually appeared. Some of the bodybuilders claimed later they thought he had told one of them what to say beforehand and he directed the meeting, a work unknown to all but the orchestrator. A funny thing happened at the meeting. Most of the guys freaked out about being told to give up all their drugs just three months before a contest, despite many willingly spouting the drug-free company line. Preparing for a contest without drugs simply didn't exist in their world. Most knew they'd look, well comparatively, like crap on stage (which by the standards of the industry, most of them did, and the few that didn't were largely accused by the others of figuring out a way to beat the testing) and it would hurt their reputations. One guy more then freaked out. He walked out. Lou "I came back because they were doing the strictest drug testing in pro sports" Ferrigno was about 320 pounds at that meeting, just a few months away from being the biggest man ever to get in contest shape. Ferrigno challenged Gary Strydom to take off his shirt and posedown right there because nobody would look good in the real contest, and reportedly telling people that if any of them get caught failing a drug test, it means nothing, but The Incredible Hulk got caught and it went public, as a kids hero, he'd be ruined. The idea of competing without drugs, as he was so proudly talking of on Carson months earlier, apparently wasn't even considered as an option. Ferrigno quit the WBF after the meeting. Something about him suffering from carpal tunnel's syndrome and needing an operation (which, in fact, he was suffering from and was operated on, but had nothing to do with his leaving the WBF), and shortly thereafter joined the Weider organization.

McMahon was able to achieve his goal of promoting the first "drug-free" bodybuilding contest in history a year quicker than he told me he thought he'd be able to. Unfortunately, not all the participants were cooperative but that didn't change the way McMahon marketed the show. The "drug free" was screamed as if it were the words "Wrestlemania" in hyping the ill-fated first and last WBF PPV show. The fact that eight or ten weeks before the show, either nine or ten of the guys who were in the contest failed the steroid test, didn't even have an affect on hyping the show as "drug free" both beforehand, and constantly during the show. The guys who failed were suspended for six weeks, which meant nothing to the show with the contest eight or ten weeks away, and all but one scheduled participated and it wasn't for failing a drug test but because he was hospitalized. The guys were also suspended from their paycheck, which was serious punishment to the guys, but the company continued to mislead the fans that the contest and all the guys were drug-free. They continued to appear on the WBF television show hyping the PPV, doing exercise routines and talking about being steroid tested and drug free. While the idea of promoting a show where the majority of participants had recently failed a steroid test as drug-free on the surface was both ludicrous and fraudulent, the funny thing is, when show time came, it appeared that in the preparatory period for the show among the crew, there was less steroid use than at any contest of that level in recent years.

The two questions I've been asked the most in the past few days are:
- How is this going to affect the wrestling industry?

- What's going to be the end result from these charges?

The answer to both is the same. It's premature to speculate. But given a few possible case scenarios, here's at least an attempt to answer those questions.

Assuming no plea bargaining, which is by no means a safe assumption, the end result of this will be the trial. Until that point, don't expect much of an effect on this business. This is not a case where media coverage, whether it be strong, weak, informed or uninformed, is relevant. The decision of the jury, if it goes that far, supersedes everything said or written beforehand. If it goes to trial, everything hinges on what happens during the trial, the verdict and eventual punishment if there are guilty verdicts.

That directly leads to question No. 2. Vince McMahon and Titan Sports had knowledge of Zahorian dispensing drugs. By pushing Hulk Hogan and others with steroid physiques, the decisions encouraged use by most wrestlers hungry for the big money. Whatever dangers steroids have over the short and long-term, they are hardly the most unhealthy things wrestlers will do in order to get a push. But can a case go to a jury with no knowledge of the subject and be proven beyond a reasonable doubt that this was a conspiracy between McMahon, the company, the doctor and others to get most of the wrestlers on steroids? There were most likely wrestlers during that time period that didn't use steroids and were pushed, although they were probably a distinct minority, but it did exist. A Grand Jury, to get an indictment only needs a majority vote, or 12 of 23 members. A conviction needs a lot more agreement. On this case, I can't even begin to speculate other than it is going to be extremely difficult for the prosecution without being able to supply strong background of the organization and strong witnesses.

As far as dispensing, there are no allegations that Vince McMahon sold steroids to wrestlers, or even widespread gave steroids to wrestlers, although there is an allegations that during a time frame he on several occasions gave steroids to a specific wrestler. If this allegation is true, if McMahon and his attorneys are able to convince the jury that all it was, was sharing with a friend, they may be able to get a sympathetic reaction and minimal if any real problems resulting from it even though it would be technically a felony. The jury may react as if it isn't like he was randomly selling cocaine to anyone on the street or anything. If the prosecution is able to convince that this was a promoter giving one of his employees and leading draws (provided this wrestler was one of his leading draws during the time period) steroids in order that he'd be more over and people would buy more tickets to see him perform, thus earning the promoter more money, it could be viewed in a very negative manner, particularly if the company purchases, as the allegations charge with McMahon, could have also been a way to eliminate all paper trails tracing the drugs back to that performer and even make it so that even Dr. Zahorian didn't know who his steroids were going to.

Either way, it's really the same thing and it all comes down to how the jury interprets it. If the jury believes the charge to be true, it may still come down to who gets the jury's sympathy at the end. Vince McMahon is a master at controlling people's emotions, yet he has a track record of past statements on this subject that could come back to haunt him. Enough evidence could go public than even a not-guilty verdict wouldn't be enough to not damage the company. A guilty verdict has the potential, if McMahon is eliminated from the business and the office is seized, to entirely reshape the wrestling world. But if there is a guilty verdict, will the fact McMahon has spent so much money to alleviate the problem currently be applicable when punishment is meted out, or will the belief be the current philosophy of serious testing was largely a reaction to media publicity and getting truly serious on the subject to the point the habitual users either had to get off or leave was concurrent with the Justice Department investigation of the owner and the company on the very subject?

McMahon in some circles has a reputation as something of a "teflon don" with some who don't understand what has happened to the business of Titan Sports the past few years. Some see him as having been invulnerable to all the negative publicity that has come his way in the past two-and-a-half years. The reality is the company has already lost millions of dollars in revenue and been financially knocked down several pegs in the wake of the negative media publicity of the past two years. According to McMahon, he's already spent millions of dollars more attempting to defend himself in regard to legal fees because of the Justice Department investigation. He's taken a terrible hit the past 20 months already and it may have been more because he's played his cards wrong more often than not when it comes to the steroid story almost every step of the way. That track record shouldn't lead to overconfidence in these proceedings, yet the public "we aren't going to sell this indictment" attitude of many in the company comes across as just that. Judging from the past two years, that public posturing may have already wound up creating the biggest problem of all. The inability to learn from one's mistakes has taken much larger companies than Titan Sports and much bigger fish than Vince McMahon down the tubes.

DECEMBER 6

The New York Daily News on Wednesday named Hulk Hogan as the unidentified WWF performer known to the grand jury who allegedly was supplied anabolic steroids from Titan Sports and Vince McMahon between on or around March 1988 and October 1989.

It was believed by most wrestling insiders Hogan was the recipient and that Hogan would become a government witness in the case against the promoter and company that marketed him to millions worldwide. Hogan's name was given to the News by McMahon's former limo driver, James Stuart, through his attorney, Frank Riccio. Riccio noted that Stuart said McMahon once ordered him to deliver a shipment of steroids to Hogan.

According to the newspaper, "(Stuart) was told by McMahon to pick up some prescriptions, he might have gone to the doctor first, and then he...took the prescriptions to Hulk Hogan," Riccio said. They believed the incident took place in 1988, and that he understood Hogan cooperated with the Justice Department's investigation that indicted McMahon.

Attorneys for both Hogan and McMahon declined to comment on whether or not Hogan was the WWF performer allegedly supplied steroids and that he had cooperated with the government in the case. McMahon, after his indictment, admitted "sharing" steroids with an unidentified friend who was a wrestler but denied doing anything illegal. There were laws prohibiting distribution of steroids except in specific circumstances--by a doctor with a prescription before 1988, and after 1988 by a doctor with a prescription only for the treatment of disease. It is not expected that either Hogan, who most believe will be a reluctant witness, nor McMahon will say anything publicly about each other before the trial provided Hogan is the wrestler in question. My own opinion is it would be in Hogan's best interest to call a press conference and tell the complete truth before the trial, at least if it becomes apparent there really will be no plea bargaining and the trial will go forward, rather than put himself in the position of his credibility being destroyed on the stand because of previous statements.

However, if it comes to trial and the Daily News story is accurate and Hogan is a government witness, Hogan's own previous statements regarding personal use and the dichotomy of being a pitchman for children's vitamins using a physique developed through more than a decade of steroids could be used against him. The ultimate of all ironies is the possibility of the two men who seemingly profited the most from the method of marketing Hogan on opposite sides in a trial that threatens to at the very least cripple aspects of the company that made both men famous. There will be numerous other ironies if that comes to pass, not the least of which is attorney Jerry McDevitt, who represents McMahon, is the same attorney who represented Hogan before the Zahorian trial and got Hogan out of testifying at the trial.

This also seems to at least be a plausible explanation for the Randy Savage interview on Radio WWF and later on Monday Night Raw where he was critical of Hogan as being only out for himself, calling him a liar, and claiming Hogan was in some way responsible for Savage's divorce, although that hasn't even been hinted at by anyone, but has become the subject of much speculation since the Daily News story. Hogan has also been removed from the opening of WWF Superstars although he still has a merchandising deal with Titan.

If Hogan is the wrestler in question, as mentioned in last week's Observer, it once again contradicts numerous statements he's made regarding his personal use of steroids. As is well known, on a July 16, 1991 appearance on the Arsenio Hall show, Hogan said, in a response to the media questions when he was named as a steroid recipient in the Zahorian trial after the judge excused him from the trial, that the extent of his steroid use was a few times in 1983 to rehabilitate a torn bicep and refused to comment on whether he had received the drugs from Zahorian, instead blaming his being mentioned as a possible steroid user from the trial saying that the doctor and others had lied in the trial and that the media had lied and that his connection with Zahorian was simply posing for a photo with the doctor that was in the doctor's office and when the FBI raided the office, they saw the photo, and that's how Hogan's name was dragged into the trial. In numerous interviews with various media outlets for the remainder of that summer, both Hogan and WWF spokesman Steve Planamenta repeated that Hogan's use was limited to that specific rehabilitation incident even though it was expected that Graham would come forward in September to contradict Hogan's story. In late August, Planamenta, when it was suggested it would be in Hogan's best interest to tell the truth before Graham would come forward with the truth, told the Observer, "Who do you think the public is going to believe, Hulk Hogan or Billy Graham?"

It wasn't until January of 1992 when Graham and David Shults were the first to say publicly (although hardly the first to say privately) that Hogan's comments were a sham, with Shults claiming that in the early 80s when the two were friends in the AWA that he had shot Hogan with steroids more than 100 times. Hogan refused to comment in the wake of a tremendous media barrage which included front page stories in the Los Angeles Times and San Diego Union-Tribune, the former of which was syndicated in newspapers around the world, and a lengthy article in People Magazine. During that same period, McMahon blamed Hogan for the comments on Arsenio, saying "I think he told the truth, but maybe there's a question from the media if it was the complete truth," on the Phil Donahue show, but had earlier stated to the Observer that he didn't want to call "Terry" a liar because he considered him a friend but that he was devastated watching the interview on Arsenio, comments he then later denied making. McMahon also claimed to have wanted Hogan to clear the air in the Los Angeles Times story, but that Hogan refused to talk to anyone in the media during that time period.

Before Hogan made his aborted wrestling comeback in February, 1992, he quietly rescinded his earlier remarks blaming the producers of Arsenio Hall for not giving him enough time and admitting to using steroids virtually the entire decade of the 80s in a newspaper interview in Buffalo, NY and on a Nashville Network television show. It was done so quietly that virtually the entire media when reporting on Hogan's name in regard to the recent McMahon indictment reported that Hogan had denied using steroids when in fact he had admitted lengthy use numerous times over the previous year. However, in his first interview on television after returning, he once again refused to accept any blame for his situation, placing the blame on "tabloid terrorists," ironic since the article on him that was carried the most widely was the Los Angeles Times story. After leaving WWF for what may be the last time in August, in promotional work for the movie "Mr. Nanny," Hogan claimed to have ceased using in 1988 when he claimed doctors found out the side effects from steroids and the drugs ceased to be legal. He claimed to have always used his steroids under a doctor's care and monitoring. The statement about the side effects holds no water since the vast majority of steroid's supposed side effects were known in the late 60s and early 70s to virtually all users but ignored, but it has become a convenient alibi athletes who have been caught or have supposedly turned over a new leaf ala Arnold Schwarzeneggar have used so often that many in the media accept it to be a valid point.

If the allegations in the indictment are true, Hogan's claim to have ceased using steroids in 1988 appears to be dubious since the indictment talks about steroids being distributed to the wrestler known to the Grand Jury as late as October, 1989. Studying changes in physique, which isn't anywhere near 100 percent accurate, but is probably far more accurate than statements by users with this kind of a track record, it appears Hogan's physique changed significantly between January 1992 and late February of the same year. There are other periods before that time where he also appeared to be off steroids, such as the summer after the Zahorian trial, but by the fall had suddenly gained lost size and muscularity back. That could be healing of a neck/shoulder injury which he was suffering from during the summer, which would make heavier training possible and thus an ability to regain lost size, although because Hogan himself has apparently been less than forthright on the subject, it leads to speculation based on how he looks. It also may validate the statement that seemed ridiculous on the surface made by Zahorian in his 1991 trial and after the trial that he believed he had weaned Hogan off steroids in 1988, that Hogan had a serious steroid abuse problem before that time, and that he believed Hogan had been steroid free since that time. If the statements in these indictments are accurate, it very well could mean that Zahorian himself didn't even know the ultimate recipient of the steroids he was allegedly sending to the

WWF office and believed since he his last fed-ex package to Hogan was in November, 1988, that Hogan had given up steroids at that point.

History may view McMahon's "coming clean" in a July 16, 1991 press conference as being much different than Hogan's interview on Arsenio, but there is reason to believe maybe it shouldn't. In that press conference, McMahon claimed his personal steroid use was limited to briefly experimenting in 1987 with the steroid Decadurabolin that he received from Zahorian, but quickly gave it up because he didn't feel "natural." The indictment indicates McMahon allegedly received the drugs during a lot longer period than he indicated when he supposedly came clean at his own press conference. In an interview with Ken Patera published in last week's Pro Wrestling Torch, Patera claimed having conversations with McMahon where McMahon acknowledged personal use as far back as 1976. After the indictment, all McMahon said about his personal use was that it ceased before 1991, when the federal law making use for non-therapeutic purposes a felony went into effect, which, if nothing else, the Justice Department hasn't been able to get any evidence to contradict because if they had some, you know they would use it. Even though it is McMahon and not Hogan who is under indictment, McMahon's personal use is not a subject that is germane in the big marketing picture of Titan Sports. McMahon never spent ten years marketing his own physique, if steroids had a hand in building it, to an audience of largely young children. He was strictly a television announcer, a fully-clothed one at that. Steroids played no part in how the public reacted to his announcing. McMahon never used his own physique to sell marketing gimmick after marketing gimmick. He used the physiques of others and it's the steroid use of others, not McMahon, that is relevant to the building and marketing of Titan Sports.

DECEMBER 6

There was a lot of television publicity in the wake of McMahon's arraignment, particularly on numerous local NBC newscasts which featured an interview with Tully Blanchard where he stated that the look Vince wanted of his wrestlers, which is skin stretched over cinder blocks is a look you can only get from steroids. He said when he was there the company tested for cocaine but anything else went. He said that was a problem for him because he enjoyed cocaine. Blanchard said that because they brainwashed a generation of kids, he prays to God every night that someone takes the business down, which came off as a very strong statement.

Forbes Magazine will have a piece in this week's issue and The Oregonian and New York Daily News will have feature pieces in upcoming days. Sports Illustrated was planning on a Scorecard feature for this week but my gut feeling is it won't be happening. The NBC NOW piece won't air because most of the key footage was already released to NBC news stations around the country for local and national newscasts. It is said that a few tabloid TV shows are working on pieces as well. The London Daily Mirror tabloid ran a feature filled with errors such as a photo of Bret Hart labeled "Macho Man Randy Savage" and listing Andre the Giant and Sgt. Slaughter as among current stars of the WWF.

The entire Hart Family was on with Regis & Kathy Lee and Regis avoided the subject like the plague.

Bob Mathews, a Rochester, NY newspaper sports columnist/radio talk show host announced who has given weekly wrestling news updates going back eight or nine years announced this past weak that due to the sleazy nature of the business and the things that had happened in recent weeks that he would no longer have anything to do with it.

USA Today did its obligatory two sentences on the arraignment.

Entertainment Weekly listed the story as the seventh most talked about news story of the past week, but then dismissed addressing is seriously by saying, "why give real hormones to fake athletes?" There was also a literal ton of publicity in Montreal, although virtually no mention of any indictments, because Jacques Rougeau had gone crazy having promised the Quebecers first match in town with the belts would draw a big house and he came through with 13,800 fans paying $114,000. Quebecers got cheers the nearly blew the roof off the building when they came out, and Steiners were 100 percent booed, which surprised everyone who expected a mixed reaction to both since the Rougeau wrestling family are legendary faces in Montreal, but the kids see what's on television today. The Quebecers worked the match as complete heels and managed to turn the crowd as the match went along, with them doing the Dusty finish at the end where it appeared Steiners had won the belts but instead it was a DQ.

DECEMBER 20

The United States Supreme Court ruled Monday morning in a case totally unrelated to the U.S. Government vs. Vince McMahon and Titan Sports as to the constitutionality of drug property seizures. In a 5-4 ruling which was the lead story on many national newscasts that day and reported as being a major blow to the government's so-called war against drugs, the court ruled that the government couldn't confiscate property used in drug dealings without the convicted party getting a hearing.

In the case of Titan, this relates to the most severe possible penalty in the case, the government's attempt upon a conviction of either of the two charges against the company, to seize Titan's $9.5 million office complex because of belief it was used to facilitate illegal drug dealings. In the case of a conviction on either of the two charges against the company (conspiracy to distribute steroids and purchasing with intent to distribute), the government can still attempt to seize the building, although it's power to do so was taken down a peg and a hearing would have to take place before the government would have a right to seize the building.

Not much else of substance has taken place in the past two weeks, although rumors are swirling out of control. Several newspapers have written columns regarding the story that have painted Titan in a negative light and both Forbes Magazine, ESPN and Sports Illustrated came out with pieces in the past week. Since Forbes is a movers-and-shakers trade journal, the short article, which largely talked more about the decline of Titan Sports business then the indictments, is the kind of thing that may make advertisers squeamish, although the indictments will be more powerful in that regard than a magazine short. The SI piece was actually weak considering the potential ground-breaking nature of the case as a steroid story, since it just mentioned the indictments and instead used its short Scorecard item to pretty much say the popularity of wrestling is over and acted embarrassed that at one point wrestling had any popularity in the first place, and even brought up names like Murray Hodgson and Rita Chatterton, who have nothing to do with what's going on today. The New York Daily News ran a gossip item about Hulk Hogan as it relates to his potential testimony affecting his current acting career.

As a clarification, Vince McMahon did not acknowledge "sharing steroids with a friend" after the indictment as was stated here three weeks back which therefore means he didn't contradict his denial of any type of distribution of steroids that he made in the days before the indictment in the Boston Herald. McMahon simply stated that the government alleged he had shared steroids with a friend, which isn't what the government indictment or anyone in the government to this point has alleged in the first place. If an awful lot of people had spent more time telling the truth in the beginning instead of trying to make misleading statements, do you think pro wrestling would be in this position right now? I can tell you one thing with almost certainty. As things get hotter, people will revert more and more to their roots (which, in most cases in this business is still the con man mentality) and there will be less and less learned from what should be obvious lessons that lying only leads to further problems, and more and more damaging mistakes made from all sides

CHAPTER SIX

PANCRASE FORMS

JANAURY 15

Shinji Jin, who was the front office leader responsible for the break-up of the second UWF (1988-90 version) because of his dispute with Akira Maeda, is the money man behind the new group that Masakatsu Funaki and Minoru Suzuki are forming in Japan. All the PWFG wrestlers with the exception of Yoshiaki Fujiwara and one prelim wrestler jumped, however Fujiwara is still planning a 1/16 Korakuen Hall show plus big shows over the next two months although I don't know how he can pull off big shows with no native wrestlers. The foreign wrestlers, mainly Florida wrestlers and Wayne Shamrock, will stay with PWFG. While no deal has been made, don't be surprised to see Fujiwara work a program on some New Japan shows in exchange for talent help similar to WAR.

MARCH 8

It appears the backing for Minoru Suzuki and Masakatsu Funaki to start their new group has fallen through, so right now they are in limbo. Funaki is so talented and charismatic and has superstar potential so he won't be left out in the cold for long most likely.

Word has it that the wrestlers from PWFG will join with Rings, including Bart Vail, Wayne Shamrock and the other Americans. Yoshiaki Fujiwara may not work in Rings, but wants to send his prelim Japanese wrestlers to work underneath and he'll work in their corner on Rings shows, but he doesn't want to commit himself in the ring because he still may wind up with New Japan to work with Tenryu, Fujinami and Choshu as potential feuds.

MAY 24

Masakatsu Funaki officially announced the formation of his own new promotion sometime in the fall called World Pan Class Creation (WPCC). The word Pan in the title is short for Pantheon, which was an event in the ancient Olympics which was pretty much free fighting with wrestling, kicking and boxing included. Funaki said that Karl Gotch came up with the name which I guess shows they are going to try and use Gotch's name and reputation to bolster the group much as UWFI uses Lou Thesz. He also announced that Wayne Shamrock would be with the group when it starts up and in newspaper interviews said it would be a harder style of fighting than either RINGS or UWFI.

OCTOBER 4

Pancrase wrestling debuted on 9/21 before a sellout 7,000 at Tokyo Bay NK Hall with a very unique show. It sounds very markish to say Pancrase wrestling is real shooting, because groups that claim to be that all seem to be something less. But the reason Minoru Suzuki and Masakatsu Funaki formed the new group and quit Pro Wrestling Fujiwara-Gumi at least publicly was because they didn't want to have pre-planned winners. Anyway, the card itself was described to be as an amazing show, even though the five matches only lasted a total of 13 minutes of wrestling time which made it surprising and different from any other style in Japan. I'm not sure what else they did and some fans couldn't have been happy paying $135 ringside for 13 minutes of wrestling. Main event saw Wayne Shamrock beat Masakatsu Funaki with a sleeper in 6:15.

OCTOBER 25

Pancrase Wrestling, which is at least believed to be by those who tell me the only "pro wrestling" promotion where the winners and losers aren't predetermined, had its second show on 10/14 in Nagoya. I'm told they go until either a knockout or they lock on a submission, similar to UWFI and Rings rules, although it's obvious by how the matches go that this is a different breed because nobody "sells" and attempts are made to always defend, move like a boxing match, and to block moves, which you don't see on UWFI and Rings shows in the marquee matches. All the wrestlers have dropped a lot of weight and look more like light heavyweight boxers because all the training is done for conditioning rather than muscle bulk which would be the case if one was training for a legitimate combat sport. The entire five-match card had only 23 minutes of wrestling, most of which were in the main event (Wayne Shamrock vs. Yoshiki Takahashi going 12:23). Because of the belief that it is real, the 11/8 match in Kobe with Suzuki (who was a champion amateur wrestler before going pro) vs. World Karate Association world heavyweight champion Maurice Smith (yes, another kick boxing world champion) is getting a lot of publicity with the magazines pushing it strongly as being a legitimate contest. They don't call any other groups illegitimate, but by emphasizing this match as being a shoot, doesn't it pretty much say that all others must not be? At the November 29, 1989 UWF card at the Tokyo Dome, Suzuki was knocked out by Smith in a mixed match which was a shoot

DECEMBER 6

Masakatsu Funaki of Pancrase Wrestling in what everyone is reporting as a legitimate shooting match, made World heavyweight Kick Boxing champ Maurice Smith of the United States submit with a sleeper/body scissors combination in 1:50 of the first round after taking him off his feet in a mixed match held at an All Japan Kick Boxing Association show which drew an overflow crowd of 7,450 fans to Tokyo Bay NK Hall. Several years ago the two had fought to a six round draw in a mixed match at the Tokyo Dome which probably had a worked finish before 25,000 fans. On 11/8, Smith had destroyed Pancrase wrestler Minoru Suzuki with a third round knockout in what was said to have been a shoot kick boxing match, a match where Suzuki clearly had no chance in. There are rumors going around already of a possible combined promotion of Pancrase and the Gracie Family (Royce Gracie, who won the Ultimate Fight held in Denver and on PPV on 11/12, and his brother, who promoted the PPV) for next October at the Tokyo Dome where Gracie would face Funaki on top. Both Akira Maeda and Masaake Satake (Japan's No. 1 martial arts hero and holder of another version of the World heavyweight karate championship) were at the show. Satake formerly worked for RINGS. Maeda said watching Funaki beat Smith made him for the first time regret that the UWF folded. In previous magazine interviews, Maeda had always tried to put UWF in his past and talked of RINGS as the present, but talked of how proud he was to see Funaki, who was a mid-card wrestler with the old UWF, come so far.

CHAPTER SEVEN

HULK HOGAN SAGA

JANUARY 25

Latest on the Hulk Hogan speaking tour. A few weeks back, Hogan was interviewed by the George Michael Sports Machine television show (will air in February) and said he wanted to come back to wrestling and get the world title back. When asked if he could do it all over again, would he have handled the steroid controversy the same way, Hogan said he'd do the same thing all over again and blamed all the problems on the media. The Rockford Register-Star quoted Hogan as saying, when asked if he'd return to wrestling, "I just don't want to go wrestle. I want to win the belt back. I want to be the champion. They've got a guy named Bret "The Hit Man" Hart who's champion now. I could beat him with my eyes closed. He couldn't even lace my boots up." In the photo that accompanied the article, Hogan looked much smaller than in his wrestling days, although he says he's around 270, which he may be since he's 6-6 and still a huge guy. He was about 250 in the movie, which will be out shortly. Most believe that if Hogan comes back, it would only be for a few major shows per year at a huge price tag (well into six figures) per appearance. Even with only a few appearances per year, the part about him wanting to be champion again appears to be something of a shoot.

FEBRUARY 1

Speaking of The Hulk, most of the rumor mill is that he's negotiating with WCW (I've heard that rumor from many sources in the past two weeks, and Ted Turner even told Jim Herd that specific thing last week) or planning on getting involved with Angelo Poffo's promotion based in Florida that is looking at running shows in Europe. Some think Hulk himself wants those stories out, like the negotiations with Japan that seemingly fell through, because it'll up the ante for a return to wherever he decides to return. The only advantage WCW can offer is if the Turner organization promises him movie work as part of the deal to wrestle a few major shows, because long-range, acting, not wrestling, seems to be his primary goal. Those who are friends of his say he does want to come back, but only to work five to ten dates per year. Titan hasn't wanted him back under those circumstances because Hulk would overshadow what they are trying to build for the future and bring to the house shows.

FEBRUARY 8

Hulk Hogan was reported in the Atlanta Journal-Constitution to have been in a restaurant last week that happened to be on the bottom floor of CNN Center, although word we get is he was in CNN Center to negotiate a movie deal rather than a wrestling deal, although there has been at least preliminary discussion involving Hogan and WCW over the recent weeks.

Hogan's long-time friend, Brutus Beefcake, returned to the WWF on Monday Night Raw on 2/1 doing an interview that sure made you think Hogan was on the way back to the WWF. Beefcake said he was going to return to the ring and talked about his parents dying, his accident, and his wife leaving him and taking all his money. This didn't come across that well alive as the crowd was really sarcastic in its response to him and the reaction when he brought up Hogan's name was 50 percent boos. Beefcake's face was destroyed in a July 4, 1991 para-sailing accident. He attempted a comeback a year later but a decision was reached at the time that it wasn't a good idea. Hogan's nephew, Mike Bollea is on the road full-time as a prelim wrestler. Hogan was supposedly in the Titan offices on Thursday with Beefcake although we have been unable to confirm any agreement was reached, but WWF policy of not talking about anyone unless they are on the way in makes one think an agreement was reached.

The interview seems to be a sign that the buy rate of the last PPV show opened the doors regarding Hogan's return wider. Beefcake vs. Ted DiBiase will be the headline match on the 2/15 show, but it was actually taped on 2/1 (because WWF will be doing a regular television taping in Southern California on 2/15 and because the 2/8 Raw will be pre-empted by a dog show). Beefcake had the advantage the entire way when IRS interfered using his briefcase for the DQ. The two double-teamed Beefcake until Jimmy Hart came in and ordered them to stop (they teased the Hart babyface turn on 2/1 TV) that they've done enough damage. IRS threw Hart to the floor. DiBiase then held Beefcake while IRS ran toward him with the briefcase and nailed him right in the face. Beefcake went down, bladed (this is becoming a more frequent occurrence on television these days), and eventually did a stretcher job with Hart (now a babyface) consoling him. Also on next week's show is a Battle Royal. It came down to Ramon, Santana and Tatanka when Giant Gonzales showed up and threw the two faces out of the ring while Ramon ran and hid. After Gonzales left, Ramon came back into the ring to be declared the winner. There were loud chants at four different times during the two hour taping of "We Want Flair." . . It was reported in the 1/29 New York Daily News Slammer column that Hogan would be returning at Wrestlemania which is certainly what I'd expect given how the TV was handled.

FEBRUARY 15

From almost all accounts, Hulk Hogan will be returning to the ring after a one year absence at Wrestlemania, teaming with Brutus Beefcake against Ted DiBiase & IRS. Jimmy Hart, whose babyface turn will air on 2/15, will manage Hogan and Beefcake. Word we get is that Hart, who specializes in p.r. work well beyond the call of duty, has been wanting to switch face so he can fit into the p.r. end of things better. Traditionally, the role of babyface manager has been the kiss of death long-term. Since Hogan & Beefcake are obviously going over, since Hogan isn't coming back to lose, then this match will either be non-title or DiBiase & IRS will lose the titles before WM. Hogan is expected to make a few television appearances before the show, starting perhaps as early as the 2/22 Monday Night Raw show or the television tapings the previous week in California. Most believe now that whatever negotiations Hogan was doing with Turner Broadcasting was just leverage to strike a better deal with Titan. Part of the reason for Hogan's return could be to re-solidify his wrestling following before the release of the movie Mr. Nanny in June, because if that movie doesn't do business, and its release being held off six months wasn't a good sign of the studio's confidence in it, it will dim whatever star Hogan may have in Hollywood.

New Japan Pro Wrestling is also expressing interest in Hogan once again. There has been talk in Japan of trying to get Hogan for the 5/3 Fukuoka Dome card. Unlike the Tokyo Dome, which sold out well ahead of time without Hogan, the Fukuoka show can use Hogan box office power because they have 68,000 seats and are in a mid-sized city nine hours from Tokyo rather than in one of the largest and most wrestling-mad cities in the world. Even more interesting is the talk of a double main (which has yet to be announced, nor is anything even close to the point where it would be announced) is Antonio Inoki vs. Genichiro Tenryu along with Hogan vs. Big Van Vader. The latter match is incredibly politically sensitive because it would result in the name most associated with the WWF facing the WCW champion. One would suspect Hogan would have to go over, which, if Vader is still WCW champ at that point, would cause a lot of political problems to the point I can't envision it happening. Another political headache is the deal McMahon and Tenryu reached for WWF talent to work only for WAR, although since WAR and New Japan are working closely together, maybe that's a minor hurdle. Yet another hurdle in putting together the match is that Vader reportedly has received a huge money offer from UWFI in Japan to work just eight dates. If he takes that deal, then any work for New Japan is out of the question. However, New Japan has the talent trade agreement with WCW. With Vader being under contract to WCW (if he indeed renews his current deal that expires in just a few weeks, and considering how much WCW has built around him, one would think they are going to everything they can to insure that happens), how will that effect trying to sign a limited date independent contract?

In what apparently is a related deal, New Japan signed Horace Boulder (Hulk's nephew Mike, who is also working regularly with WWF under a hood as The Predator) to debut on the March tour. Boulder had been a regular for FMW. Both All Japan and New Japan had shied away from using FMW regulars, in particular Big Titan and The Gladiator (Mike Alfonso) who have a lot of potential to be superstars in either group because they were with the "lower-rated" FMW group. Hogan had turned down a reported $250,000 offer to work three dates for New Japan in 1993, the 1/4 Tokyo Dome, the 5/3 Fukuoka Dome and a September indoor show in Yokohama. At that point it appeared New Japan had lost interest in booking Hogan, but coming into the Fukuoka show with all those tickets to sell, interest seems to have picked up.

FEBRUARY 22

Hogan is set to debut on 2/22 at the Monday Night Raw show at the Manhattan Center. Hogan's deal is apparently to work all PPV shows and a few major shows as well which I will assume includes the 3/7 Fox Network live special from Fayetteville, NC (I'm not sure that is a certainty or not, have heard it isn't confirmed and that it is). Hogan's presence probably helped in getting a special since the last Fox special, before the Survivor Series, bombed in the ratings. In addition, talk is that there will be at least one PPV show added this year since Hogan is back in the fold.

MARCH 1

Hogan returned at Monday Night Raw doing both a live interview and a taped interview where he basically blamed the tabloid media, alluding to but not specifically mentioning Phil Mushnick, for digging into his past, but admitted he made a lot of mistakes both in his professional and personal life.

MARCH 8

Lots of news regarding some of the biggest names in both today's wrestling business, and of the modern era. Both Hulk Hogan and Ric Flair have returned to the WWF and WCW within the past weeks. Hogan returned on Monday Night Raw on 2/22, doing two interviews, the latter of which was replayed throughout syndication over the weekend. Hogan & Brutus Beefcake will face Ted DiBiase & IRS (who almost surely won't have the tag team titles by that time) at WrestleMania, which will be Hogan's first match back, although he'll appear live at two or three more television tapings before that show. The current plan, and I'm not sure how much of this is finalized, is that Hogan's next match after Mania will be the 5/3 Fukuoka Dome show in Japan, probably as a tag team with Antonio Inoki, and that he'll start working weekend house shows for the WWF, likely against Yokozuna although I'm not sure anything is close to finalized about that, from June through August.

Hogan's return will pop big houses, something that has been almost non-existent in this country of late, and should significantly help the Mania orders. How long he's willing to stay this time is unclear, but it is expected he'll appear on all PPV shows from this point forward and the WWF is adding the June PPV show from Dayton to the regular four. After Mania, Hogan will be filming a television pilot called "Thunder in Paradise," by the producers of Baywatch. If that series is picked up, it would surely necessitate another leave from wrestling. Besides doing his regular shtick interview on the Raw show, he also did a fake-shoot studio interview. I'm torn between admiration for just how good Hogan delivered the interview (if you're a fan of this business and you accept it for what it is, you have to give credit to the best workers both in the ring and on the mic and Hogan's sincere interview delivery is the best in the business) and disdain for the public message he was trying to deliver. I still see this as someone who is blaming the messengers for the fact he was caught with his hand in the cookie jar. Then he put himself in a very public position and tried a work and got caught. Then he quietly, nearly two years later, in recanting his original story, never admitted any personal blame for trying the work but instead tried to blame it on the producers of the show and the reporters who wouldn't accept the lie at face value, while at the same time praising all those who did.

MARCH 29

Hulk Hogan was on the cover of this week's Gong Magazine which pretty well stated he was going to work the 5/3 Fukuoka Dome show. The rumors of Hogan headed to New Japan go back well over a year and have been the subject of a decent amount of negotiation during that time. To the best of my knowledge, no contract has been signed although Masa Saito will be going to Florida at the end of the month with contract in hand to officially finalize the deal. Talk is of Hogan either working a tag team match teaming with Antonio Inoki, or a singles match against Great Muta. Nothing conclusive as to what their opponents would be in a tag match, however word we're getting is that Genichiro Tenryu will probably not be involved and instead work a singles match as a semi-main event. All the major angles will be finished probably with the 4/6 Sumo Hall show and the line-up will probably be announced at that point.

APRIL 12

The magazine advertisements for the 5/3 Fukuoka Dome list Hulk Hogan as appearing, plus it has already been reported that Brutus Beefcake and Jimmy Hart would be there as well. However, in a post-WrestleMania press conference, when Hogan was asked about it, he said he'd love to go but said that he hadn't signed a contract yet. New Japan was looking for Hogan to sign a deal before Mania for Fukuoka Dome plus two more shows in 1993, most likely one of the seven nights at Sumo Hall in August and the 9/23 show at the Yokohama Arena.

APRIL 19

The announcement was made over the weekend on WWF syndicated television that Hulk Hogan would be keeping the title. Hogan will work a few house shows in May (Philadelphia and Pittsburgh that I know of) which I believe will be tag team matches against Money Inc., and I believe his first title defense will be at the June "King of the Ring" PPV show against Yokozuna. Hogan has recently been filming a two-hour CBS television pilot called "Thunder in Paradise." If CBS picks up the series, Hogan would leave wrestling in October for about 13 weeks of production. Hogan also signed this past week for the 5/3 show at the Fukuoka Dome where he'll face IWGP champ Great Muta in what I would guess to be a non-title match. Most reports are that Hogan, starting sometime in June, will go back on the road working with Yokozuna on a fairly regular schedule (three days per week) with Jim Duggan filling in the program when Hogan isn't booked.

It appears that WrestleMania did about a 2.1 percent buy rate, which would be about 430,000 buys or roughly a $5.8 million gross for Titan. The buy rate would be the lowest of any previous WM, as was expected but the amount of the drop between this year and the previous year would be less than has been the case for the past several years. In comparison with dropping buy rates across-the-board on WWF PPV events, this small drop should be considered a success and again show that when it comes to PPV, because of his mainstream name appeal which others' lack, Hogan makes a huge difference. One could estimate that Hogan's appearance at this show was worth somewhere in the neighborhood of $1.2 million to Titan based on PPV and a hard to determine additional amount when it comes to live gate.

While Caesar's Palace appeared both live and on television to be packed, our reports from the past week indicate more freebies in the crowd than initially thought. While on a Las Vegas radio show this past weekend, a caller/subscriber called to claim that just hours before the show that he was part of a group that received 400 $150 tickets in the first few rows as comps because it was so close to show time and they knew it was too late to sell them. In addition, the host claimed he called the box office 30 minutes into the show asking if tickets were available and they said they were. I believe Caesar's received a lot of tickets to give to their high-rollers as well, although they paid Titan a substantial rights fee (well over the cost of what the tickets would have brought if Titan had sold them) for holding the event. Between the rights fee and the live gate, Titan probably made out a lot better financially from the live house, whether sold out or not, this year than last year in the Hoosier Dome which had 62,000 in the building.

As for the aftermath, as judging from the poll's results and responses to just about everyplace else, it didn't seem as if too many people were happy with the show and quite a few were furious. Still, you've got to figure that the $1.2 million worth of business that Hogan brought to the table with him, that a good percentage of those folks are going to be happy since the person they paid to see came out on top at the end.

APRIL 26

Hulk Hogan is working just three WWF dates in May. He's teaming with Brutus Beefcake vs. Money Inc. in Pittsburgh on 5/21, Philadelphia on 5/22 and at the Meadowlands on 5/22 which is sort of strange for the WWF champion to be challenging for the tag team title. I don't know of any singles matches until the 6/13 PPV show but Hogan will be working something of a regular schedule (3-4 times per week) starting in June.

MAY 10

The other big show in the past few days, "Wrestling Dontaku," took place 5/3 at the Fukuoka Dome before 55,000 fans, so they failed to break the Japanese all-time attendance mark by booking a building larger than the Tokyo Dome. The building, which could hold at least 68,000 for wrestling, was legitimately full everywhere that was opened up, however the outfield bleachers section wasn't opened. The card name comes from the "Hakata Dontaku" festival which is held in early May every year in Fukuoka which attracts tourists from around Japan. The most intriguing thing when it comes to U.S. fans was it was the first time ever for Hulk Hogan and Sting to work on the same show.

In a non-title match featuring the two world champions of the two biggest money wrestling promotions in the world against each other, Great Muta pinned Hulk Hogan. You didn't really believe that, did you? If you did, you haven't been paying attention. Of course Hogan won with the axe bomber (lariat), which has always been his finishing move in Japan, in 15:55 after a legdrop and a foot to the face. Muta got the best reaction of anyone on the card. Told the match was super when judged against Hogan's typical U.S. match, and was even one of the better matches on the show. Hogan did a lot of wrestling and seemed like he felt he had something to prove as a wrestler and was using this match and his post-match interview trying to make drive home a point that he was a good worker. Muta did all his signature moves plus a tope and the 40-yard sprint on the ramp into a clothesline. It was one of Muta's "on" matches since Muta is a lot like Randy Savage in his prime when it comes to on and off matches. Hogan kicked out of Muta's moonsault before going to the finish. Hogan got a decent reaction, but everyone was surprised that is nowhere near the level of Muta, who got the biggest pop on the entire show. It was also clear that the fans "wanted" Muta to win and reacted to him like he was the superstar in the ring. It should be noted that at the post-match party for the VIP's (sponsors and their families, etc.) that Hogan was mobbed for photos and autographs far more than anyone else. I'm told that from listening to the crowd before, during and after the show, that it was this match more than the tag team main event that people were talking about the most. It took a long time in his post-match posing routine before the crowd even started to react and it was never more than a polite response.

The biggest news after the show was the interview Hogan did with the press after the show, in which, well, you be the judge. These are not direct quotes because what he said was translated into Japanese, then translated back, which means a lot can be lost in double translation. The gist of his interview was he was very happy to be back with New Japan. He said he started wrestling in the United States when he was trained by Hiro Matsuda, but he considers his wrestling home to be New Japan. Now he's back after eight years of being a big success in the U.S. as a wrestling star, movie star and television star. Everyone has something in the back of their mind that they always want to do. For me it was to come back to New Japan (the six-figures per match deal had nothing to do with it, it was just something he had in his heart). The Japanese have always accepted me so well and I felt I needed to return. I'm still the best wrestler and best showman. While I was gone for eight years (forgetting he's worked several shows in Japan since 1990, including three Tokyo Domes against Tenryu, Hansen and the Road Warriors), a whole new generation of wrestling fans has grown up in this country. I want every one of them to think of Hulk Hogan when they go to bed thinking about who the best wrestler is. I'm a five-time WWF champ (shows the belt). To me, this (WWF belt) is a toy, like a Christmas tree ornament. The WWF belt is like a Honda. The IWGP belt is like a Rolls Royce. It's the real world championship belt. Winning this (WWF belt) was very easy. The IWGP belt is very hard to win (Hogan was the first IWGP champ winning the initial tournament in 1983 before losing it in 1984 to Inoki). No bullshit. I can wrestle. They say you can't teach an old dog new tricks. I'm the old dog, but I know all the tricks. I never quit wrestling. I'm not one of those guys coming back disgracing my former reputation. I'm still the best wrestler. The match (with Muta) today was fun, but it was easy. He is a star, but I beat him 1-2-3 in the middle. I should be wearing the IWGP belt. I want to wrestle every top name in Japan and hopefully wrestle Mr. Inoki again.

At that point Hogan went on and on about Inoki. However, when Inoki did his post-match interview, he only talked about wanting singles matches against Tenryu and Fujinami and never mentioned Hogan's name. While Hogan vs. Inoki would certainly be a big draw at next year's Tokyo Dome, how can you put together the finish? Which of the two will be willing to sacrifice himself?

MAY 17

The New Japan television show this past Saturday which aired both Hulk Hogan vs. Great Muta and Yoshiaki Fujiwara vs. Hiroshi Hase from the 5/3 Fukuoka Dome show, also featured an interview with Hogan, speaking English. Hogan, while not as direct as in the press conference after the match which was written about last week, did call the WWF title a stepping stone to the real world title, the IWGP title. In several media interviews, Hogan continually put forth the story that his wrestling career had begun with New Japan and that he hadn't wrestled in Japan in eight years, and that now he's going to finish up his career with New Japan. It was really confusing since many of his matches in the past eight years were considerably well publicized, particularly the match with Stan Hansen at the Tokyo Dome in 1990. This caused wrestling fans, and others who aren't even fans, who saw those interviews to be really perplexed on why Hogan would say things on television about something that everyone knew to be false. It's really hard to figure out what's going on here other than something is going on.

MAY 24

For those who think Hogan can't draw at the houses, you'll be proven wrong most likely this coming weekend. The show at the Meadowlands is expected to draw the biggest regular house show crowd for any U.S. show in months, although nowhere near capacity, but those days of drawing 21,000 for a regular house show are over. Hogan will be working four house shows during June besides the PPV and one set of tapings--Minneapolis, Winnipeg, Chicago and Boston.

MAY 31

This was the weekend of Hulk Hogan's return to house shows and the results have to be classified as slightly disappointing. Hogan worked on Friday night in Pittsburgh and did a double shot of Philadelphia and the Meadowlands on Saturday, all in tag team title matches with Brutus Beefcake against Money Inc. Reports we received were that the matches were terrible, with the obvious heel DQ ending. In Pittsburgh, a crowd of about 6,600 paid, or about 2,000 less than the March house show in the same building. In Philadelphia, Hogan's return drew 8,415, which was about 300 fewer fans than the March house show at the Spectrum, although the gate was significantly down because this card had the kids $3 off all tickets pricing gimmick. The Meadowlands show was the lone success, drawing about 11,000 people and $180,000, or roughly the same as the much more heavily publicized "Headlock on Hunger" card drew in Madison Square Garden in late January. Although they did no live angles to promote it, it was announced in the arena that at the next Philly show in July, that Hogan vs. Yokozuna would headline. In reality, Beefcake, DiBiase and IRS were an anchor tied to Hogan's drawing power although most nostalgia acts that have drawing power usually can't sustain it in a market after the first show, so Hogan's "easiest" houses should have been these. A singles match with Yokozuna won't be that anchor. Still, when Hogan's first match back in the company's best-drawing markets draws these numbers, it does lend credence to the argument that him getting the belt wasn't the best idea after all.

MAY 31

5/8 television show which included the Hogan vs. Muta match from Fukuoka Dome drew an 8.4 rating. Saw three of the Fukuoka Dome matches and nothing was that impressive. Fujiwara vs. Hase was *1/2. Fujiwara has the unique charisma because people believe he's so dangerous but he really didn't do much. Hogan vs. Muta was interesting because Hogan did some wrestling, was tons smaller than ever before (estimated around 255 with thin by comparison arms). I'd only give it **3/4 because it wasn't really that good, although Muta's sprint along with ramp into a clothesline was even better than the match with Chono. The reaction to Hogan was nothing compared with Inoki, Choshu and Muta. Inoki & Fujinami vs. Choshu & Tenryu was worth about ***1/4 because Choshu & Tenryu were really intense in the ring. They sold big for Inoki, who physically looked younger than Hogan even though he's really more than 10 years older. They made Inoki look great, which was their role.

JUNE 14

Hulk Hogan's second weekend of house shows has to be labeled as a major disappointment. Hulk worked 6/4 in Winnipeg, drawing about 6,500 paid; 6/5 in Minneapolis, drawing about 3,300 paid; and 6/6 in Albany, NY (as the main event on the show where Shawn Michaels regained the IC title) drawing about 3,000 paid. Only the Winnipeg gate can be labeled a success. Hogan still had the anchor of being in a main event with Brutus Beefcake and Money Inc., who simply aren't capable of working on top and selling tickets at this point, so we'll have to see what happens next month when he has the singles matches with Yokozuna. Same finish with Money Inc. getting DQ'd. But just putting the name Hogan on the marquee without a match people want to see isn't going to bring in casual fans anymore. Hogan made the gossip column of the Winnipeg Sun on 6/7, as after his Friday night match, he attended a strip club with Jimmy Hart, Beefcake, Papa Shango, Virgil and Ted DiBiase. Speaking of Hogan, Mr. Nanny opens nationally on 6/30.

JUNE 14

King of the Ring, which takes place 6/13 in Dayton, is largely a two-event show. The King of the Ring finals and the Hulk Hogan vs. Yokozuna WWF title match main event. One week out, these scenarios appear to be the most likely for the summer plans leading to Summer Slam: 1) The heel Japanese referee Masao Hattori causes Hogan to lose the title to Yokozuna, setting the two up for a third meeting at Summer Slam. At this point, depending upon Hogan's outside commitments, a decision can be made to either screw-job the finish of that match, and feed Yokozuna to another babyface (likely being Bret Hart) to lose the title, or have Hogan regain the title once again, and make occasional house shots in between his acting commitments; 2) Despite the Japanese heel referee, Hogan retains his title, setting up the Hogan-Bret Hart match at Summer Slam. This is the most likely scenario. Despite the apparent legitimate professional differences the two had and may still have, any speculation that this would lead to "shooting" is ludicrous. It won't happen. Both are too professional. As far as talk that one wouldn't do the job for the other, while it may very well be that neither would be thrilled about it, whatever direction the company is wanting to go will determine the outcome. If they want the belt from Hogan, I don't see him not giving it back. Likewise, if they want Hart to do the favor, he's professional enough that I can't see him refusing.

JUNE 21

Hulk Hogan worked three shows this past weekend besides the PPV show, all with the tag team match teaming with Brutus Beefcake vs. Money Inc. and doing the DQ finish. In Richmond on 6/11, the pairing only drew

1,850, the next night in Indianapolis drew about 2,500 and at the television tapings in Columbus, OH on 6/14 they drew about 3,700. The singles rematches with Yokozuna, which start this coming weekend, are going to be the acid test on whether Hogan can still draw the masses, as there is a strong argument that Beefcake and Money Inc. being in the main event match with him was keeping fans home. Either way, with the exception of Winnipeg and the Meadowlands, Hogan's return to house shows has thus far been a box office flop

JUNE 28

In the wake of the King of the Ring tournament, Hulk Hogan's future with the WWF is up in the air. Early last week Hogan, along with his associates Brutus Beefcake and Jimmy Hart, pulled themselves from all his previously committed dates with the exception of shows this coming weekend in Chicago and Boston and a European tour that starts in five weeks. In addition, another man working in the same Wrestlemania and house show scenario, Ted DiBiase, officially gave notice that he'll be leaving after the Summer Slam PPV event to work as a regular for All Japan Pro Wrestling. Since it was too late to adequately get the word out in those markets that Hogan, who faces Yokozuna in both cities and is the main ticket seller on both shows, wouldn't appear and tickets, the trio will fulfill those commitments. Since the European tour, with Hogan's name advertised, had such huge advances based largely on Hogan's name (including more than 20,000 advance tickets sold for an outdoor soccer stadium show in Germany), those commitments as well will be fulfilled. However, Hogan, Beefcake and Jimmy Hart pulled themselves from all previously advertised July house shows in which he was scheduled to face Yokozuna. In those markets Hogan will be replaced by Bret Hart.

Hogan also pulled himself and company off the SummerSlam PPV show. Hogan was scheduled in the main event against Yokozuna on the card which takes place 8/30 in Auburn Hills, MI, although no advertising had gone out for that specific match. Hart will not be moved to the main event at Summer Slam, but instead will work the semifinal against Jerry Lawler and it appears the two matches underneath that will be Shawn Michaels vs. Mr. Perfect for the IC title and Steiners vs. Head Shrinkers for the tag team titles (which changed hands twice more this past week with Money Inc. beating Steiners on 6/16 in Rockford, IL and Steiners regaining the belts on 6/19 in St. Louis, making three tag title switches in five days and six title changes in all in one month). Most likely Yokozuna's opponent will be made public after an angle is shot on 7/4. Best guess is that one of the bigger heels will turn and represent the USA and slam Yokozuna ala the Mr. Perfect turn when the company was in desperate shape before the Survivor Series when Ultimate Warrior and Davey Boy Smith left the company. However in any case the opponent is supposed to be a major surprise.

Hogan and his associates were known to be unhappy with the direction the company was going and because of the differences with Vince McMahon in regard to direction, decided it was time for them to pull out while leaving the door open for future business. In reality, Hogan had to be tremendously disappointed in how the business in general was doing the past few weeks, and in specific on the shows he headlined. From an entertainment career standpoint, it may be the best move possible for Hogan to not be associated with the current wrestling business. If movie producers or television producers come to realize that Hogan isn't even drawing wrestling fans anymore, then his perceived value in drawing people to other entertainment ventures would greatly decrease. It's better from a Hogan perspective to give the illusion that the WWF was a booming business that collapsed when he left it and that he simply went to New Japan, where business is still booming and he can take credit for still being associated with a thriving wrestling enterprise, rather than be associated with a business on a downward slide, let alone whatever bad publicity may be forthcoming in the fall. A reconciliation could happen at any time provided those differences can be worked out and Hogan won't be quitting, at least at this point, because it will allow both sides to benefit from each other as far as merchandising and licensing the Hogan name in conjunction with WWF. The end result for that to happen would be a major increase in Hogan's power on the wrestling end of the company including a possible role as booker.

There will be no official announcement apparently, at least at this point, from either side as to Hogan taking another hiatus because word of Hogan being gone could seriously adversely affect merchandising and licensing, of which his name is by far the hottest property the WWF has. Even if and when Hogan's proposed television vehicle, "Thunder in Paradise" starts filming, the scheduled would be filming four days per week in the Tampa area so he would still be available to work weekend wrestling dates or if he chose to.

JULY 5

Hulk Hogan's WWF wrestling career came in like a lion. After just a few television taping appearances, in his first house show match in 1984 in Madison Square Garden, he won the WWF title from the Iron Sheik in about 4:00. Nine-and-a-half years later, in what was his final weekend appearing for the WWF on U.S. soil for the present, and in what probably only he knew for sure whether or not it was his final U.S. appearances as an active wrestler, Hogan's WWF career went out like a lamb. Hogan worked before crowds of 3,800 and 3,500 in Chicago and Boston respectively. In both cases, Hogan didn't seem to be taking matters seriously. In Chicago, Hogan brought Horace Grant of the Chicago Bulls into the ring from the crowd and let him pin Ted DiBiase to signal the end of his tag team match. The next night in Boston during a tag match, while Brutus Beefcake was in the ring battling Money Inc., Hogan jumped off the apron and began a conversation with some ringside fans instead of acting like he was heavily involved in what was an advertised main event match. Hogan still has a series of European matches against Yokozuna starting in about four weeks before what at least at this point appears to be the end of his WWF tenure for the foreseeable future.

Hogan's departure came in the midst of a week where much discussion has been made about the future of the WWF. For reasons that have been gone into in past issues, the complaints among the top wrestlers because of the time demands of doing the localized face-to-face segments combined with smaller pay due to the declining houses have continued and even escalated.

In addition, several changes in house show scheduling as soon as August are already in the cards. How widespread these changes are isn't clear at press time, although several major market shows during August and September were canceled. While this is not a hard rule of thumb, we've been told the idea is to cut each market back to three house shows per year. Obviously the major markets like New York, Philadelphia, Los Angeles, Chicago and SF Bay Area will get more than three shows and other markets that don't draw will get less than three shows, but three is said to be the target rule for an average market. Judging from announced future line-ups of August house shows that they seem to be changing the philosophy of putting two "equal" touring troupes to one "strong" troupe in big markets and a secondary smaller troupe with fewer major names in medium and smaller-sized markets, but this is just something ascertained from the few line-ups for late August that have been made public rather than anything told to me as officially a new policy. There has been a lot of talk about cutting back to one show per night, but thus far the schedules still have two shows. Several Sundays in August are off, however, so there are fewer shows being run. Perhaps they will use Sundays to tape the face-to-face interviews, thereby giving the wrestlers the extra day off in mid-week (Tuesdays of non-TV weeks) that was taken away when the segments started, although it will be offset by losing one payoff per week by working the one less show. Obviously there is no perfect formula here.

Reportedly an even stronger emphasis is being placed on garnering television ratings. Logic tells you that you have to rebuild your television numbers as a precursor to getting fans back into the building. If they aren't watching the syndicated shows (where the local cards are promoted as opposed to the cable shows which can't promote shows in individual markets), by and large they won't be attending the house shows. Syndicated numbers are weak in many markets. So, being that television is the key to this business, there will be upgrades made in the shows and major emphasis placed on angles solely derived to increase a particular show's one-night rating ala The 1-2-3 Kid vs. Razor Ramon angle which drew an excellent 3.1 rating on 6/21's Monday Night Raw and the 7/4 Stars-and-stripes bodyslam challenge to air the next evening on Raw. Obviously things of this ilk will also have to happen on syndication. Also a greater emphasis is supposed to be placed on garnering mainstream media attention to boost interest in the product in specific markets since the local promoters' television and radio advertising budgets were cut back, which some have blamed as at least partially for the latest drop in arena attendance that took place concurrently with the house show advertising cutbacks.

JULY 12

The reason they brought up Hulk Hogan's name on the list of contenders for Yokozuna is because Raw also goes to England where Hogan vs. Yokozuna is the headline match in early August.

JULY 19

This week's Hulk Hogan stories. Besides going to New Japan, Tokyo Sports this past week ran a story saying that Hogan, Jimmy Hart and Hiro Matsuda would be starting up their own wrestling promotion in Tampa. There certainly would be no shortage of veteran talent from both major groups ready to make a move just about now. Also, this week "Hulk Hogan's Wrestling Boot Trash Can Band" will be recording with Brutus Beefcake, Jimmy Hart, Typhoon and Hillbilly Jim. The pilot for the show "Thunder in Paradise" will be released as a 104 minute video on 9/22 with a $2 million national advertising campaign behind it according to an ad in a video trade journal.

AUGUST 16

The European tour that ended 8/6 in Sheffield, England spelled the end of at least this WWF stint of Hulk Hogan, who beat Yokozuna via DQ in the title matches at every spot on the tour. Hogan's (and WWF) merchandise sold like crazy during the tour, as has been the case for the previous European tours. Next tour will be in October. The Hogan-Yokozuna matches were in the DUD to * range most nights I was told. The cards themselves weren't said to be any good with the Bam Bam Bigelow vs. Tatanka matches saving the show on most nights. Bigelow pulled out a lot of Japanese moves and was over pretty much as a babyface in several of the cities. Although Jim Duggan vs. Bastion Booger was the worst match most nights, Duggan was second only to Hogan in popularity.

SEPTEMBER 6

Hulk Hogan & Jimmy Hart have signed a deal with Arista records. Hogan made a personal appearance at Brian Blair's Gold's Gym in Tampa recently that drew about 5,000 to 8,000 people. No word on his next move in wrestling, but if it was WWF, then Luger would have definitely won the title at Summer Slam. AAA sources claim Hogan contacted that promotion about work, but they weren't interested because the price was too high, plus it would have meant they'd have to use Brutus Beefcake and Jimmy Hart.

OCTOBER 11

Hulk Hogan made the media rounds this week to promote his movie. In Montreal last Thursday, Hogan dropped a hint that he'd be bringing New Japan Pro Wrestling to the United States, but by Monday on Regis, Hogan talked about returning to the WWF to challenge Yokozuna for the title. Hogan had a lengthy meeting with Antonio Inoki and TV-Asahi about promoting internationally during the Japan tour. Hogan did acknowledge his matches in Japan on Regis saying he's been wrestling there and that the Japanese take their wrestling a lot more seriously than the Americans, but that he still won all his matches because he's in better shape than the Japanese. That's not entirely untrue. He keeps winning because he's in better financial shape and can afford to balk at doing jobs (as if anyone would even dare suggest it to him), rather than better physical shape.

OCTOBER 18

This was the week that Hulk Hogan made his media blitz for the movie "Mr. Nanny," which opened nationwide on 10/8. The movie, which didn't even crack the top ten in its opening weekend (finishing in 12th place grossing $1.9 million in 1,293 locations, which the AP weekly box office rundown described as an "anemic" showing), may not have been a box office or artistic success, but Hogan was all over the country including Regis & Kathy Lee, Jay Leno and Joan Rivers television, Larry King on radio, and countless local shows and newspaper interviews this pats week. On the subject of wrestling, he wouldn't commit himself to anything and said the only thing he's agreed to do was the January Tokyo Dome. He tried to talk about New Japan on Leno, but Leno first made cracks about them all being 5-6 or 5-7, and then tried to make like Hogan was fighting sumo wrestlers so he gave up realizing it was a futile attempt to discuss that subject and did almost a pro wrestler interview plugging opening night. He admitted in a newspaper interview in Montreal that New Japan had discussed with him the idea of being part-owner of an American company that would promote New Japan live shows in the United States but he acted as if he didn't have time for it right now, and also mentioned WCW and independents along with WWF as being interested and he could pick and choose what he wanted to do. Many thought Hogan was going to appear the Saturday prior to the event on WCW to promote the movie, but he decided against it, apparently not wanting to rub anyone at WWF the wrong way since WWF heavily pushed the movie on television and surprised both Hogan and Jimmy Hart with a two-page spread on them in a recent magazine even though they weren't working for the company. Hogan's schedule is tied up with the television series, but he gave the impression he's up for an occasional big show like a Wrestlemania and said he and Vince McMahon have an understanding that he can come back whenever he has the time but that McMahon can't build the company around him anymore because he won't work enough dates.

The subject of steroids came up in almost every interview which shows that the public still associates Hogan largely with that subject. On CBC radio in Canada Hogan made the same speech he's done in the past comparing WWF testing with the NFL saying WWF tests every week and NFL tells you six months in advance they'll be testing in June and said in the WWF if you do any drugs you're out. That's not accurate at all on many levels. The NFL during the season random tests every week and does off-season testing as well and hasn't done testing the way Hogan keeps describing it in four or five years, when in fact, the NFL did have a steroid system that was largely a joke. But he also said that the WWF grosses more money then the NFL, which speaks for itself when it comes to accuracy. In the Los Angeles Times, when responding to the steroid question, Hogan said, "That was a tremendous hit my career took. You have to understand the situation. Prior to 1966 (I believe that date is a misprint because in other interviews, the year he continually used was 1988), steroids were legal (which isn't entirely true, but isn't entirely false either as it varied by state and different aspects of use and distribution were both legal and illegal dating back to the early 80s depending on the location). Growing up in the 60s, 70s and 80s there was a lot of peer pressure. Everybody was doing it. Me, being at the top of my profession, they picked Hulk out and said, you represent the whole world. You're a role model. But I got through it. A lot of people thought it was just Hulk doing it. Now they realize the whole sports world in the 80s was doing it. I survived it and I'm going to be around for a while." Hogan also had a wax statue of himself put into the Movieland Hall of Fame this past week.

NOVEMBER 8

The WWF was advertising Hulk Hogan for a February, 1994 tour of Israel, but has now stopped the advertising since it appears relations with Hogan and WWF have ended.

NOVEMBER 22

Hulk Hogan has signed a deal with Disney to film "Thunder in Paradise" in Orlando. The show's first 20 episodes will be taped from January 10 to June 6 and will debut on television worldwide in March. With that kind of a schedule, don't expect Hogan to do much wrestling during that time frame. In addition, when it comes to all the rumors of Hogan starting a new wrestling company, while it's a possibility at some point, the time constraints are such that there is no way it's going to happen anytime soon.

CHAPTER EIGHT

LEX LUGER
DEBUTS IN WWF

FEBRUARY 1

Lex Luger debuted on Superstars. They bring in a 7-foot mirror before he comes out and he enters to music similar to Rick Martel. Really, this character is just too similar to Michaels and Martel. Anyway, he looks at himself in the mirror and poses. He beat Mark Ming with a forearm smash and the gimmick is the agents have to give the jobber smelling salts to awaken him from the knockout blow. Luger got no reaction at all. Everyone knew who he was, but nobody seemed to care.

MAY 3

On television they showed the X-rays of Lex Luger's forearm but announced they were powerless to do anything about it. I believe in late summer Luger is having the plate removed, so you've got to figure they'll be working an angle around that.

JUNE 28

They are really hyping the Stars and Stripes Challenge where they are trying to bring in several athletes from other sports to try and slam Yokozuna on 7/4. McMahon already announced Bill Fralic of the Detroit Lions, who is good friends with Jim Ross, along with one other football player and a hockey player as going to try. I believe they've got a few retired Jets and Giants agreeing to do it as well, as well as, for comedy purposes, they are trying line up some jockeys and for pubilcity purposes, trying to get Nadia Comaneci. They are trying to get other athletes as well asking practically everyone in the organization who may have connections with pro athletes for help. Apparently they are only offering trans + accomodations, so in most (probably not all) cases, this isn't a case of big money being thrown around to get the people to participate. I guess the idea is to associate Yokozuna not being able to be slammed by "real athletes" is a way to give him and wrestling sports credibility and get mainstream press. The association with celebs in 1984 is one of the things the company was originally built on, and they need the mainstream attention to turn fortunes around.

JULY 5

Most of the hype this week was built around the Stars-and-Stripes challenge, a heavy xenophobic angle where Yokozuna challenges any American athlete to slam him. Besides the wrestlers, they've got about 15 others, both active and retired football players and a hockey player and jockey thrown in, although the only athletes of any name value on the list are Bill Fralic of the Detroit Lions and Reggie Roby, a punter with the Miami Dolphins. For those who don't understand the concept of doing a bodyslam, it's pretty much impossible to slam anyone of that size unless they go up for it. In other words, nobody can slam the guy unless he lets them, but if he lets them, almost anyone could. It's kind of funny when people are impressed with bodyslamming a big guy like Andre in the wrestling ring because a strong 200 pounder could have slammed Andre if he had gone up for them. How else did Greg Gagne at 190 slam Jerry Blackwell at 420? They really buried Hogan in the video clips over the weekend concerning the slam challenge which was interesting.

JULY 7

As started on 7/4 and as will be made obvious over the next several weeks, the World Wrestling Federation has decided to go all the way with Lex Luger.

The 7/4 "Stars and Stripes Challenge" gimmick, an idea originally to set up Yokozuna's opponent for the Summer Slam PPV show, changed in nature when Hulk Hogan decided to pull out of the WWF. The decision was made to take Luger, who some wrestling experts had been tabbing as the next Hulk Hogan almost from the day he debuted in late 1985, and give him the biggest push the promotion has given any wrestler since Hogan's initial return in late 1983. Many feel that Hogan's lack of drawing power upon his return this year signalled the end for pushing him as the promotion's major star and there is considerable question as to if he'll even ever return to the WWF. While details are sketchy at press time, apparently Luger will be pulled off the road shows until Summer Slam on 8/30 in Auburn Hills, MI when he faces Yokozuna for the title and gets to begin his reign as the focal point and top babyface of the promotion. Luger and Yokozuna will also be the feature match coming off Summer Slam for the fall and early winter at all the house shows.

In the interim, Luger will be sent on a tour bus and go from major city to major city doing a local media tour which will be put together by a former Rock & Roll promoter with extensive experience in this genre. This will be an expensive, and some say desperate attempt to turn him into a mainstream celebrity in two months, because it's questionable if using tradition wrestling promotion methods that he'll be able to become a celebrity, although turning him into a heavily cheered babyface is a piece of cake. But the mainstream appeal is needed because right now a double main event of Luger vs. Yokozuna and Hart vs. Lawler won't be able to do much of a buy rate, nor right now does Luger have the kind of appeal needed to carry the company on his back. The tour starts 7/15 in Stamford, CT and goes to Philadelphia, Washington D.C., New York, New Haven, Boston, Syracuse, Utica, Buffalo, Erie, Cleveland, Youngstown, Pittsburgh, Detroit, Flint, Grand Rapids, Chicago, Milwaukee, Madison, Minneapolis, Sioux Falls, Rapid City, Denver, Sacramento, San Francisco, Anaheim, Los Angeles, Albuquerque, St. Louis, Springfield IL and finishes up on 8/30 for Summer Slam in Auburn Hills. Whether the choice of Luger for this role was the right choice can be debated, but to the WWF's credit, they are sparing no expense and came up with a creative angle, although heavily xenophobic in nature, with the 7/4 bodyslam challenge and the tour in order to make the choice a home run.

After several athletes, both pro wrestlers along with several current and former NFL football players, a jockey, a basketball player and two Ice Hockey players were involved in a heavy anti-Japanese angle that obliterated the line of bad taste on Independence Day attempting to slam the 500+ pound Yokozuna, it appeared the show onboard the U.S.S. Entrepid would end without the bodyslam. Just at that moment, a helicopter flew onto the boat with a stars and stripes decked out Luger, who gave an interview turning himself babyface, and then getting into a melee with Yokozuna, ending by hitting him with the forearm and slamming him.

Naturally this decision is going to be heavily second-guessed over the next two months, and moreso if it doesn't pan out. As one person close to the scene surmised, this is either going to be a major success or a total failure, but no in between. Luger has been pushed, both as a rookie in Florida and later on-and-off with WCW, as the focal point of the promotion before, with a noticeable lack of success in both cases, unlike Hogan, who had already proven to be a huge drawing card in Japan and the AWA before getting his chance. However, unlike The Ultimate Warrior and Sid Vicious, who in one case was given the chance to replace Hogan as the top star and in the other originally would have been given the chance, Luger seems a lot more mature and stable so the chance of him walking out in the middle of this opportunity appears minimal if at all. There is certainly the questioning of replacing Hulk Hogan with another blond-haired muscle man, as opposed to trying to go with something completely different to avoid the obvious comparisons (Bret Hart being the obvious choice here). However, as history has shown, the WWF was built on muscles, the public has been brainwashed to believe the physique equals ring ability and attempts to push actual ring ability last fall met with the worst run of business in company history. Luger's incredible genetics are such that he looks as physically impressive off steroids as all but a few wrestlers do on them, and is really the only wrestler left in the company who can be pushed, sans steroids, on his physique alone.

This brings up the obvious comparison with Bret Hart, who would have been the "other" possible choice for the role, and will be moved down a peg on the pecking order. In nearly every category one would want to make a comparison in, whether it be work rate, charisma, psychology, interviews and overall crowd appeal, Hart has a sizeable advantage over Luger. In addition, while his run on top didn't prove to be a success at the gate, Hart's popularity and respect did appear to grow from the point of time last October when Ultimate Warrior and Davey Boy Smith left and he was thrust into the top spot. But the key point is that Hart already had the opportunity and from a financial standpoint, it didn't work. Luger, on the other hand, was pretty much a flop as far as getting the crowd to care about him one way or the other in his heavily-pushed role as "The Narcissist." One of wrestling's traditional sayings is that if someone isn't over as a heel, they aren't going to get over when they're turned. While sayings such as these aren't always correct, this specific one is correct more often than not. But building around Luger is "something new" to the WWF audience, although Luger actually has been a major spotlight performer on a national basis longer than Hart. Luger just turned 35, while Hart just turned 36. But more than anything else, the difference is the admission that the physical difference between the two, both in size (about three-and-a-half inches and probably 30 pounds) and muscularity overrode all the advantages Hart possessed.

It also appears the WWF has a secondary goal for the month of August besides trying to turn Luger into a drawing card capable of carrying the company. Striking back at those who came forward or were involved in the various scandal-related activity which precluded the company's drop in popularity during the summer of 1992.

JULY 26

Lex Luger is getting some media attention for his tour, which in many cities coincides with an existing WWF house show. On those nights, he's been saving Bret Hart after Yokozuna and Mr. Fuji are double-teaming Hart. The whole scenario of Luger at children's hospitals and kissing babies and being friendly to wrestling fans is hilarious to everyone who has formerly worked with him. It's probably going to be more effective than a traditional wrestling push, although a report from the Saturday night show in Philadelphia when they brought up the Lex Express said it got no reaction other than fans thinking they were shoving him down their throats. However, when he made the save later in the card, they popped big for him.

AUGUST 2

Supposedly interviews have already been taped with Lex Luger regarding the subject of steroids, so he doesn't repeat the mistake that felled Hulk Hogan. Luger was also on "Live with Regis and Kathy Lee" on 7/20, although the appearance was uneventful. Largely his media tour has been met with little response as far as mainstream stories, but it's made for some effective television footage as far as getting him over to wrestling fans.

AUGUST 9

If the Lex Luger thing doesn't get over huge, it isn't because it hasn't been done to perfection. It's also interesting to note that unlike Hulk Hogan, they are through interviews trying to portray him as a multi-dimensional human being rather than a one-dimensional cartoon hero.

AUGUST 16

Luger has been drawing good crowds to his public appearances, which he has largely been arriving 30 to 45 minutes late to (blamed on the schedule makers not allotting him enough time to train and tan before his start time). Reports from readers we've received are mixed, although WWF officials say they're very pleased with Luger's performance. Luger did an interview with the Fairfield County (CT) Advocate by the same reporter (Jim Motavalli) who did a WWF scandal story a few months back, where Luger claimed to be a proponent of steroid testing: "We get fully tested every 10 days. Steroid use was a problem at the WWF; Vince admits it was a problem, but it's fully cleaned up now. We have real pants-to-the-ankles testing for marijuana, coke and steroids by men in white coats--there's no faking the urine samples. It seems demeaning at first, but you eventually realize it's a good thing. Whether you like it or not, you're a role model, and it's great to be able to say for the record that you're not on drugs and the physique you have is one you built yourself." In an interview with Mark Madden in the Pittsburgh Post-Gazette, Luger once again focused on steroids, saying, "When (steroids) were legal, in the quest to be big and strong, yes, I used them, but now that I'm not using them and I can see the results of what I can do without them, I realize you don't need shortcuts. That's what I tell kids now. Using steroids was a mistake. I wasn't an abuser. I wasn't a heavy user year-round, but there's no safe way to take steroids. They're illegal.

That's (drug testing) my vindication. I'm always lumped in with a lot of guys, guys who look a lot different than before drug testing, but I basically look the same." Talk about making statements that are "politically correct." He can't deny use because everyone saw what happened when Hulk Hogan did that, but most wrestlers (not all) who try to clarify it as "use when legal" are being either misleading or outright deceptive when it comes to actual legality of such use. The reality is that Luger may never have even gotten in the wrestling business in the first place if he had never used steroids, and almost certainly wouldn't have been pushed as hard from the start and given the immediate publicity which led to being put on top in a national promotion before he knew how to work. Even with his superior genetics and consistent training and disciplined diet, he was recruited in and has consistently received a huge push because he had a freaky physique, which steroids were responsible for a percentage of. This is not meant as a criticism of him for using steroids, because that was the system in those days and in many ways still is the system. Luger was just a byproduct of that system, and not the cause. But just once I'd like to see a big star be completely honest and up-front on this issue. For quoting in a newspaper for someone in his position, you can't say that steroids have enabled you to get a job making $300,000 to $500,000 per year at something you've never proven to be that good at, but I wonder if in reality, if Lex could turn back time, if he would have never used steroids given the financial rewards they've enabled him to achieve.

CHAPTER NINE

THE TRAGEDY OF KERRY VON ERICH

FEBRUARY 1

Kerry Von Erich was apprehended on 1/13 on a Heath & Safety Code violation, which, according to the Dallas County District Attorney's office, is a drug charge. No specific details as to the drug are available until the substance has been laboratory tested. Von Erich was released after posting a $5,000 felony bond. If the tests show the drug to be an illegal substance, Von Erich will appear before Judge Larry Baraka, who has a reputation for being one of the toughest judges in the area in drug cases. Von Erich is currently serving ten years probation for a conviction on forging drug prescriptions, so a conviction in this case would revoke his probation and could be his final strike. Von Erich is making all his scheduled bookings.

FEBRUARY 1

There was a wrestling convention held over the weekend in Philadelphia with Formerly known as the Ultimate Warrior, Formerly known as the British Bulldog, Currently known as Road Warrior Animal, Would be Currently known as Kerry Von Erich if he could remember his name and what city he's in, Sid Vicious, Terry Funk, Woman and others. Kevin Sullivan no-showed for reasons not having to do with the promoters or Sullivan and Road Warrior Hawk no-showed as well. Funniest story from the card was they asked Von Erich to fill in for Sullivan against Sal Bellomo. Von Erich was supposed to wear a mask as Woman's secret weapon. Von Erich went to the ring wearing the mask, but had a ring jacket with "Kerry" on the back. As silly as that sounds, he was stopped backstage before he got out and someone told him that his name was on the ring jacket and he's supposed to be a masked guy so take the jacket off. Von Erich took the jacket off, walked about ten yards, seemingly forgot, put the jacket back on, and then went through the entrance way to the crowd and worked about a 1:00 match.

FEBRUARY 8

The substance Kerry Von Erich was caught with on 1/13 was analyzed and found to be a controlled substance (cocaine). He had a court date set for 2/1 on possession charges.

FEBRUARY 15

Kerry Von Erich's charge of possession of a controlled substance from 1/13 will be sent to the Grand Jury on 2/15 to decide on whether or not to have an indictment. If he's indicted, a trial date will then be set.

MARCH 1

"Somewhere along the way, a cute marketing concept decayed into a macabre body count." -- Irvin Muchnick, Penthouse Magazine, in a 1988 article "Born Again Bashing" about the Von Erich family

"I was shocked that Kerry killed himself. But I wasn't shocked at all that he died." -- Terry Simms, pro wrestler and one of Kerry's closest friends

Fantasy vs. reality. For most people in the real world, for the most part, they know the difference. In pro wrestling, among both its performers and its fans, sometimes the line gets a little blurred. Often that's dismissed as simply harmless. But sometimes when the line is blurred for long enough, or the difference is no longer perceptible, or even worse, when the fantasy becomes the reality, it creates a situation of potential danger. The danger is that the day may come when the bubble is burst and the fantasy is over and one isn't equipped to deal with the reality.

The bubble must have come close to bursting several times over the past decade for Kerry Gene Adkisson, who had lived in many ways the ultimate fantasy life up until he was in his mid-20s. The reality after that period was the harshest imaginable. Three brothers died. His other brother suffered a near death experience. One of his brothers' children died at birth. He was involved in a motorcycle accident that left him crippled. The company that was his by birthright went out of business, ending with him having little money left to his name. The superstardom that was seemingly his not only by birthright but through ability and charisma as well, slowly slipped away. Because he was broke, he hooked up with the biggest wrestling company in the world, and for a time, he was getting to relive his past fame. But in doing so, they originally planned to take away his beloved family name. While he kept his name, the legendary status of it and favored treatment the name Von Erich meant were no longer the case. Slowly the reality that he wasn't what he once was moved him from superstar to preliminary status. The recreational drug problems continued. Soon, the drugs that created his beloved physique were banned as well, causing his beloved muscles to shrink to ungodlike normality. Eventually, he lost that job as well, and the money that went with it, and was only working once or twice a week, earning the kind of money that he often blew nightly during his years of living the ultimate fantasy, on good times. He was broke, and was in trouble with the IRS to the point that he was auctioning off his wrestling memorabilia from his famous title win over Ric Flair at wrestling conventions. His parents, the cornerstone behind the so-called perfect family unit, split up. His own marriage had its ups and downs. Yet in his own way, he was able to somehow shield himself, at least to a point, from reality by drawing upon the fantasy.

The fantasy was that he was Kerry Von Erich, the Modern Day Warrior. He was one of the great athletes in the world. He had the perfect physique. He was nearly unbeatable at wrestling, and in fact, was the uncrowned World champion. He was the second-youngest man ever to hold the most famous and prestigious wrestling belt in the world and he won it from the greatest wrestler of our time in the most emotional setting and in front of one of the biggest crowds and in one of the most famous matches the wrestling world had ever seen. He was loaded with charisma. He'd have gone to the Olympics in the discus if Carter hadn't called for the boycott or if some heel wouldn't have stomped on his shoulder just before the try-outs that in reality he was never going to attend in the first place. He was rich. He had the hottest car. He could literally do no wrong, because even if he did, since he was a Von Erich, it would always be taken care of. Whatever he wanted, someone would take care of for him because he was Kerry Von Erich, son of the greatest wrestler the world had ever seen and son of one of the wealthiest and most influential men in the community. He was the object of desire for every female in the state of Texas, and plenty in other states as well. Everyone else wanted to be his friend. Anywhere he went he was mobbed by autograph seekers. Every night he stepped into the ring, the cheers were as loud for him as nearly anyone in the history of a business that was his. He was born to be a demigod. Hell, he was a demigod, at least he was every night when he stepped into the ring in the minds of most of the people in the building and to enough hangers-on out of the ring that he was able to never have to leave the fantasy. He was born into the perfect Christian family, inherited the greatest athletic genes, and through his never-ending search for athletic perfection, achieved dizzying heights of fame. He and his brothers were going to rule the wrestling world.

On Wednesday, February 17, the fantasy world of Kerry Von Erich was about to end. He was indicted that morning on cocaine possession charges stemming from a January 13 arrest. He was already serving ten years probation for forging drug prescriptions during a time about one year earlier when he was supposed to be attending rehab. While it was not a guarantee, the odds were very good that his probation would be revoked and he would be sent to prison. It appears Kerry at least believed that was going to be his future. In prison, there would be no evenings where hundreds of women would screech every time he took off his ring jacket. No women would send him roses and fantasize or realize time with him. There were no world title matches to be won. No ugly heels were going to sell big when he said "discus." There was almost no family left. The drugs that made him a modern-day Warrior, the steroids, weren't going to be available. The drugs he took, just because they were available and plentiful, and the ones he took to numb both the physical and mental pain, were going to be gone. The drugs he took to escape from the reality were also going to be history. He could no longer lie and con, traits that had been instilled in him at a young age because the marks would always believe a Von Erich because they fought the fans' fantasy enemies, nor have everyone that surrounded him believe he was something that he wasn't. Perhaps the worst thing of all was he'd have to come to grips with the fact that the fantasy that was his professional life and became much of his personal life wasn't reality. He'd have to face what the reality really was. The night of his death, a long-time family friend theorized that if Kerry hadn't have taken his life that afternoon, he would have almost certainly done so in his first week in prison.

When he learned Thursday morning of his indictment, he apparently set out to kill himself. But those who knew him well, or even casually, seem to believe this wasn't a spontaneous decision.

Many of his friends recalled in the past few days Kerry would come over, for seemingly no reason, hug them, say "I love you," and then leave. Some were confused by his actions initially. In hindsight, they realized he had been saying his good-byes. It may have seemed unusual, but unusual in Kerry's case wasn't unusual. Terry Funk, who saw Von Erich a few weeks earlier in Philadelphia, remembered him coming up to him and reminiscing about when he and his brothers feuded with Terry and his brother in Amarillo during the early days of his career, talking about it being some of the happiest moments of his life. On January 27, one week before is 33rd birthday, he and his probation office, Gary Hunter, had their routine meeting and he talked of suicide.

"He talked about it then," Hunter said in an article in the Dallas Morning-News. "He said he missed his brothers and said he just didn't feel like going on." Hunter said Kerry rejected his advice to seek counseling for his suicidal feelings and his continuing drug addictions.

"In his own way, he came to say good-bye to me on Monday," remembered Terry Simms, a Dallas wrestler who was one of his best friends. "He came into the (health) club, hugged me and said, 'I miss you when you're not around.' It bothered me for a couple of days because it was really strange. His hair wasn't combed. He hadn't shaved. He looked terrible. I'm sure that everyone he came in contact with the last two weeks thought the same thing.

"He didn't want to go to prison. He had told people that if he got indicted, he'd kill himself.

"Is prison really that bad? So he may have had to spend a year in prison. It may have been the best thing that ever happened to him. He had two daughters that he loved deeply. Anyone who was ever around him could tell that in a second."

His father said Kerry had frequently mentioned taking his own life. His wife Cathy, whom he had an on-again, off-again relationship with over the years, hid all the guns from the house. He said the same strange goodbyes to the woman and her mother whom he had been living with the past few weeks, and headed to his father's ranch.

As he had done with everyone else he felt close to, when he arrived at 1:30 p.m., he hugged his dad and told him he loved him, borrowed the .44-calibre Magnum handgun he had given his father for Christmas in 1991 and borrowed his father's jeep telling him that he needed to find a quiet spot to do some thinking.

About 45 minutes later, his father, who in his own fantasy life was the legendary Fritz Von Erich, got worried. Jack Adkisson had built a company largely to package and hype his alter ego as the greatest wrestler of all-time and his children as the prodigal sons. He was the father of the ultimate fantasy family of athletes, but in reality he had already lost four of his six sons, none of whom saw their 26th birthday. He knew Kerry had to pick up his two daughters, nine-year-old Holly and six-year-old Lacy, from school. He searched on his ranch and found that the jeep was empty. Then found the body partially hidden from the thicket. Apparently Kerry had shot himself in the heart.

The death marks the end of one of the most bizarre family stories any of us will ever know. The story is far beyond the significance of simply the pro wrestling world that the family was once among the most powerful and recognizable members of. The Von Erich dynasty, what at one time seemed to have been a brilliant marketing plan by Jack Adkisson dating back to the late 60s, saw the seeds bloom on Christmas night of 1982, and for the next 16 months he owned the hottest and most innovative wrestling company in the world. The cornerstones were his three young, athletic and at the time almost interchangeable sons. The youngest of the three, Kerry, was rivalled by only Hulk Hogan in Minneapolis and Jimmy Snuka in New York as the most popular wrestler in the country. Certainly, in terms of attracting new fans and a young audience, "The Modern Day Warrior" stood as almost a sure-bet to become the biggest wrestling star in the world before too many more years were finished. While other promotions quickly caught up and surpassed Jack Adkisson's company, the marketing plan was still in tact for a successful regional business. The Von Erichs were still the kings of North Texas. The first Wrestlemania, which rocked the nation, died in Dallas. The Saturday Night Main Events of the WWF, at the time a ratings success story around the country, was destroyed head-to-head by Adkisson's local television show on KTVT. The life didn't immediately get squeezed away from the territory, but instead lives themselves started ending, one after another, a body count that engulfed the wrestling world with morbid fascination. The dynasty pretty well ended in April of 1987, with the death of Jack's fifth son, Michael, and third to die, at the age of 23, a suicide caused by overdosing on Placidyl. Michael had been involved with frequent scrapes with the law during the last year of his life, and his death had been eerily predicted just two weeks before it happened by Jack's booker, Frank "Bruiser Brody" Goodish. Goodish was the only wrestler in the glory era who rivalled the sons' popularity in Texas and in a bizarre turn of fate, he would be murdered just over one year later in a Puerto Rican dressing room.

Less than one month after Mike's death, the fourth annual David Von Erich Memorial Parade of Champions took place at Texas Stadium. Only it was changed to the David and Mike Von Erich Memorial show. Even the Dallas fans, who had a national reputation for being the most blindly loyal fans to the family of any fans in the world, suddenly woke up. Three years earlier, when David's death was memorialized at Texas Stadium and drew what was at the time the second-largest gate in pro wrestling history (32,123 fans live paying $402,000 trailing only the Bruno Sammartino vs. Larry Zbyszko 1980 match at Shea Stadium), many of Jack's former closest friends and fellow compadres in the admittedly seedy business, were repulsed at the attempt to make money capitalizing on his sons' death.

"When I was down there (late 70s), I thought Jack was as great a man as I'd ever known," said Denver sportscaster Steve Harmes, who worked for a Dallas television station at the time and eventually became a referee, play-by-play announcer and close personal friend of Jack Adkisson while his sons were first breaking in. "I was really disillusioned when they had the Memorial after David died. After that I mainly followed them in the Observer. They lost touch with reality. The marks who would go to the shows twice a week got fed up when he faked the heart attack and with all the Memorial shows. When I'd go down there on vacation and talk to the fans, that's what I kept hearing."

But the Dallas area fans themselves largely didn't notice the exploitation at the first David Von Erich Memorial Bash on May 6, 1984. Even with the family photos and David memorabilia being sold at inflated prices, including a rushed out 45 record called "Heaven Needed a Champion" being sung at the show and sold at the dozens of merchandise tables, a record cut by one of Jack's gospel singing friends and released literally days after David's death, exploitation was not on most wrestling fans' mind. After all, in their own world of fantasy, their long-awaited dream that had been teased for about two years for most, and for nearly two decades for the older fans that followed Fritz' career, a Von Erich finally winning the NWA world heavyweight title, was about to take place. Just a few miles down the road, the NBA Mavericks were in a do-or-die playoff game with the legendary Lakers of Kareem and Magic fame in a game that shocked the local sports community because it didn't sellout. Even during its heyday, the local community didn't understand the emotion and impact to so many that the world title and the Von Erichs meant, as more than twice as many fans attended the wrestling show.

Kerry, who had teased fans for more than four years with his incredible near-misses in world title matches against both Harley Race and Ric Flair, had promised his fans he'd win the title in memory of his recently deceased brother. While Flair and Kerry rushed through a 13:00 match which was nowhere near the level the two usually had, it ended up as probably the most famous match either would ever be involved in. Kerry won the belt and was mobbed by the Texas babyface wrestlers and received one of the most emotional pops in history. At the age of 24, he was the second youngest man ever to hold the world heavyweight wrestling title (Lou Thesz in 1937, at the age of 21, being the youngest). As tears filled the eyes of the fans while Kerry walked down the aisle, Jack (who wrestled his final match ever that afternoon as the legendary Fritz Von Erich) and Doris met him halfway. Wrestling has never duplicated a scene like that, and may never again. For that one moment, Jack's fantasy world had taken such a hold that it actually became not only his family's and his loyal audience's reality, but reality for much of North Texas. Little did any of the 32,123 fans, wrestlers, Kerry or Jack himself realize that single moment, at which point they were on top of the world and their future under the 100 degree Texas sun seemingly would burn bright forever as the premiere family and promotion in the world, that this was actually the beginning of the end.

As the other end of the business deal that resulted in that crowning moment of his wrestling career, Kerry dropped the title back to Flair on May 24 in Yokosuka, Japan.

Facing the reality that the moment when Kerry, Jack and Doris embraced before 32,123 cheering and teary-eyed fans was their apex came in the same spot, some three years later. Jack's World Class Championship Wrestling was overtaken by the Titan Sports and Jim Crockett Promotions. The compassion from the community at large when Mike nearly died from Toxic Shock syndrome over Labor Day weekend of 1985 turned into the general public's realization that something very serious was wrong when he was rushed into a heavily hyped public appearance several weeks later at the Cotton Bowl to wave and thank the fans during a major outdoor spectacular that drew 25,000 fans. The main event was a double hair vs. hair match in which Kevin & Kerry beat Gino Hernandez & Chris Adams. As Gino tried to escape from his haircut, the youngest brother, Chris, then 15, but only about 5-foot-3, participated in his first major angle to set the stage for his future stardom by tackling Gino at ringside. Gino was dragged back into the ring and shaved bald. Barely three months later Gino Hernandez, 28, the company's top heel, was dead of a cocaine overdose.

Kerry's crippling injuries in the motorcycle accident preceded Mike's suicide, which made the tragedies into something only the densest marks couldn't see had turned into a pattern. While the loyal live-and-die with the Von Erichs fans remained, their numbers dwindled. The thousands of Texas teenagers who flocked to Reunion Arena for the first time in 1982 and nearly rioted when Kerry was screwed out of the title, then cried their eyes out when the newspapers, unaware of the phenomenon, devoted just a few short paragraphs buried in the back of the sports section to the death of David (which only became a front-page story in the local media on the second day after his death, after the local media realized just how much of an affect a Von Erich death had on the community), largely gave up in the wake of the death of Mike. Only 5,900 fans came to Texas Stadium on May 3, 1987 to see the David and Mike Von Erich Memorial Parade of Champions. Eight days later, Kevin passed out and nearly died in a Fort Worth ring, only to be saved by CPR from wrestler Tommy Rogers. Another angle was created. His opponent when he collapsed, Brian Adias, who ironically was Kerry's real best friend from childhood but had recently turned heel, had developed a deadly Oriental tool punch that nearly killed his former best friend's older brother.

About the time Mike first took ill, and with Kevin floating in-and-out of the business due to injuries and lack of interest, a phony Von Erich was created, the model-like Lance Von Erich, real name Kevin William Vaughn. Lance was said to have been the cousin of the boys and the son of Waldo Von Erich, a one-time big-name wrestler himself who was the fictitious brother of Fritz Von Erich. Lance ironically suffered from the Von Erich curse as soon as he adopted the name, with a series of strange illnesses, traced largely to his heavy use of steroids, interfering with his own wrestling career. After a dispute with his "uncle," Lance quit to work for an opposition group in Dallas, at which time a bitter and bombastic Fritz Von Erich, against all good judgement, went on the television show and said that Lance wasn't related to the family, that his real name was William Vaughn, and that he used the family in order to get a break in wrestling. Unbeknownst to Fritz, that outburst ended the family's credibility even more except to the dwindling never-say-die fans, some of whom still remained as late as this past week. Kevin Vaughn then fell in love while on a wrestling tour of South Africa, and has lived there ever since.

On Christmas night of that year, with the territory in shambles, the booker during the company's glory days, Ken Lusk (known in wrestling as Ken Mantell), bought into the territory. The idea to turn things around was on Christmas night, several heels would attack Fritz Von Erich and beat him nearly to death. Fritz faked that he had suffered a heart attack and was rushed off to emergency. While Dallas fans celebrated their holiday season, on the wrestling broadcast they were told of yet another impending Von Erich tragedy, only in this case, not only were the causes lied about, but the entire story was a work. On television the next few days, the announcers told how Fritz is touch-and-go and may not make it through the night. Even local television stations and newspapers fell for the act at the beginning, but Jack's magic with the local media was such that the truth never came out publicly, just like the truth about David's death was still the worked version in all media reports this past week. Outside of wrestling, he was never criticized for the stunt. Later the media and the promotion amended the story to have been a blow from a cane caused temporary paralysis which was originally thought to have been a heart attack. Even Jack's closest friends in the wrestling business, none of whom were saints and all of whom specialized in stretching the truth and creating their own fantasy worlds for a buck, had long turned against this level of exploitation. It was too much to use the family's many tragedies that had moved the fans and attempting to create another near-death, as a means to get the territory off its back. Crowds did pick up as Kevin and Kerry sought to gain revenge on the perpetrators. That was the last time Fritz Von Erich set foot in World Class Wrestling rings (he worked in Kerry's corner once in 1991 on a WWF show, but that was long after the family's magical image was gone). The death of the Von Erich legacy, which occurred more than five years before its brightest star took his own life, was also the death of North Texas wrestling.

"I don't think there will ever be anything big here as far as the wrestling business is concerned," said Simms. "WWF and WCW can draw elsewhere but when they come here, they can't draw. The people here are saying `It's a screwed up world you're in and we know about it.'"

The story of the Von Erichs really started in 1949. Jack Adkisson was a back-up offensive guard at Southern Methodist University and set a school record in the discus. But he lost his scholarship by violating team rules and getting married to the future Doris Adkisson. The two took off for Canada, where he played Canadian football with several future wrestling superstars including Gene Kiniski and Wilbur Snyder. In 1954, he learned wrestling from Stu Hart in Calgary, and he, Doris and son Jackie Jr., lived in a trailer park on the Hart property. A few years later, he created the persona of Nazi heel Fritz Von Erich, and with his large hands, he became the master of the deadly "Iron Claw," when post-World War II Nazi and Japanese heels were the rage. While Nazi heels came and went, the 6-3, 275 pound powerhouse with agility, charisma and a certain demonic sneer that exuded toughness and danger, became one of the country's biggest drawing cards. While working out of Buffalo in 1959, son Jackie, then six, touched a live wire while he was outside during a storm, was given a major jolt and was knocked unconscious. He fell into a puddle and drowned to death.

Personal tragedies aside, Fritz Von Erich became a worldwide superstar in the 1960s. He held the AWA world title for a short period of time (he and Kerry remain to this day the only father-son combination to each have held a major world heavyweight title although in the NWA's lighter weight divisions the Guerrero and Dantes family also accomplished the same thing). One of the most famous faux paus ever in Japan was during a brutal main event match where Fritz was wrestling Giant Baba for the International title (which Fritz is one of the few men in history to hold), Baba went to blade himself to sell the Iron Claw, but instead of getting his forehead, he cut up Fritz' finger. Fritz' finger bled like crazy and the Japanese press created what is now a famous story of Fritz suffering from a hangnail during this now-legendary match. Due to real estate investments during a few Dallas-Fort Worth area building booms, he also became a millionaire. In the 1960s, he became a phenomenal drawing card in Texas for promoters Ed McLemore and Morris Siegel. In 1967, he pulled his big power play. Adkisson rallied all the North Texas wrestlers and pulled out the rug from under McLemore to start his own company. After winning a bitter promotional war, largely through the help of NWA President Sam Muchnick who sided with his good friend and top draw, Adkisson hired McLemore and, learning from Muchnick that it's best to make peace with your former enemies, kept McLemore's name out front as the supposed promoter. Siegel, who sided with McLemore, passed away of a heart attack shortly thereafter.

Fritz Von Erich largely stopped touring at that point, mainly confining his ring activities to his own company, in which he quickly became (surprise, surprise) the top babyface. His promotion did consistently strong business by the early 70s matching Fritz against whatever heel he could make money with, from a Johnny Valentine to a Mongolian Stomper to a Professor Boris Malenko, and eventually running them out of town. The annual climactic world title matches against Kiniski and later Dory Funk Jr., which he'd come within a hair of winning, before either being screwed or going to the time limit, were moved outdoors to Texas Stadium because no indoor arena in the market could hold the crowd. A 1973 match with Funk, a 60 minute draw in 100 degree heat, set the state attendance and gate record with 26,339 fans paying $96,000. The attendance record stood until Kerry won the title in honor of brother David 11 years later. The gate record was first broken in Flair and Kerry's famous Christmas 1982 match. A rematch one year later drew 23,000 fans. At the same time, he was channeling his sons into sports and himself and his family into religion.

Official Von Erich mythology has it that Jack was deeply moved by a sermon in 1974, and shortly thereafter a divine voice guided him to open his Bible to Psalms 23. Not long after that, the same powerful force somehow made him pull his car over to the shoulder of a highway one day and ponder his sin, beginning the Von Erichs famous link with religion. A former friend of Jack's, and his many detractors who believed him to be less than sincere in his constant religious talk, will tell the story somewhat differently. Doris, who was deeply religious, had or was about to throw Jack out. Jack, who by this time had already began to conceptualize the company being built around his All-American family image, to save his family and his dream, became born-again.

Just as the first media story, in Penthouse Magazine, which looked underneath the largely worked mythology that the local media had never examined, was about to be released, Ken Lusk, Jack's then-partner in the office, said to the Dallas Times-Herald that "anyone who says the Von Erichs aren't a Christian family, well, that's a crock. An outright lie.

Being a Christian doesn't mean you are perfect, doesn't mean you haven't made mistakes in your life. There's another book that says, 'Let he who is without sin cast the first stone.'"

Perhaps since many influential in Texas traditionally protect their own, and nobody was more Texan than the Von Erichs, the sons of the ex-Nazi heel, even with five sons now dead, the local media has never examined this strange phenonemon as anything more than a series of tragic random coincidences to a family that somehow was jinxed. The truth is that these tragedies were patterned, frequent and predictable with some obvious and other not so obvious root causes. Ironically, when the kids one-time running mate in drugs and wrestling main events, Hernandez, passed away, his life story of drugs, drugs and more drugs, was an open book in the local media worthy of an award winning newspaper story. When it came to the sons of Jack Adkisson, different rules seemed to prevail.

At about the same time his kids were the high school studs at small Lake Dallas High, Jack Adkisson was named the new NWA President, replacing Muchnick who decided to step down from power since he was in his late 60s. People remember Jack bringing Kevin, David and Kerry, whose ages ranged from 18 to 15 at the time, to the NWA conventions in Las Vegas, in which the various NWA promoters would alternately kiss-ass and back-stab their compadres, and telling the other NWA promoters, almost arrogantly, how his kids would all be future NWA world champions. At the time Kerry, then in 10th grade, was rumored to already be heavily into steroids. Whether it was simply parental obsession to create a string of super athletes, or he (and perhaps his brothers as well) fell into the steroids on their own, the three oldest were bonafide high school sports stars, facts that Jack made sure were constantly mentioned on his television shows, in his programs, in programs of other influential NWA promoters, and in wrestling magazines.

David, named for Doris Adkisson's brother that passed away as a teenager from brain cancer, was 6-6, but thin as a rail when he entered the ring first, in the summer of 1977. He had received a basketball scholarship to North Texas State University in nearby Denton, but red-shirted as a freshman and quit school after one year to work for his father. Kevin, 6-2 with a somewhat slight build, but with tremendous muscularity, followed a few months later. He was the starting fullback at North Texas State as a freshman and had legitimate potential, but a series of concussions and knee injuries caused him to quit school and join brother David in the ring. Kerry, who was already taking on the dimensions of a bodybuilder in 10th grade, was a high school football star and, like his father, threw the discus. Kerry was both state and junior national champion as a senior in high school, setting a small high school state record that stood for more than a decade. He received a football and track scholarship to the University of Houston. But, like his brothers, he only lasted one year in college before pro wrestling came calling. He red-shirted in football, but starred in track, including winning at the discus in the Texas Relays.

All three brothers had become national superstars through Adkisson's company, re-named World Class Championship Wrestling, getting national syndication in 1981 and 1982 through a state-of-the-art television production from the Dallas Sportatorium. The first slick wrestling program preceded TBS and WWF in fast-paced slickly-edited productions complete with hard rock entrance music which attracted a largely teenage audience, with a heavy percentage of girls, to see Jack's three heartthrob sons. By the time Michael made his pro debut on November 18, 1983, the promotion was the hottest in the land and his brothers were all local mega-celebrities and national wrestling superstars. The Von Erichs, along with Hogan, Flair and the Road Warriors, dominated the covers and the coverage in all the national wrestling magazines during that time period. Behind the scenes, within wrestling, the outside the ring bizarre stories of the Von Erichs, largely based around drug problems, were legion.

"I remember going with Gary Hart, Kerry, Kevin, Gino and David on road trips," recalled Harmes. "We'd go to the hotel. David, Kerry and Gino would load up on quaaludes and placidyls. They had a doctor who provided them with anything they wanted and as much as they wanted. I remember once being in Fritz' office when Gino called and needed 400 quaaludes and he got them that afternoon."

Within wrestling, it was generally believed the father was in denial about his son's drug problems. Stories are legion that his lieutenants in the company would beg the father to open his eyes but he would never believe his sons would do such things. Even during the glory years of 1983 and 1984, Kevin, David and Kerry, who were in huge demand as local celebrities for public appearances, developed bad reputations among local merchants for either showing up incoherent, or not showing up at all. The company was making big money running two spot shows per night in area high schools, usually using local non-profit organizations as sponsors, which at one point consistently drew consistently large and phenomenally enthusiastic crowds to see the Von Erichs in the flesh. The idolatry was so out of control that banners like, "On the eighth day,

God created the Von Erichs," at matches, were not the exception. Unfortunately that business started falling off as the sons frequently no-showed the cards and the sponsors, feeling burned, lost interest in World Class wrestling.

"Whenever anything came up about Kevin and Kerry from the Lake Dallas Police Department, Fritz always said it was the police's fault," Harmes recalled. "Once Kevin drove his car into a lake. The next day, he had a new car and it was like nothing had happened. But they were the model children around their dad's friends. They were the most polite and friendly kids you can imagine."

In June of 1983, Kerry was arrested at DFW Airport coming back from his honeymoon with Cathy in Puerto Vallarta, Mexico. Customs agents found him with 18 unmarked tablets in his right front packet. He was hiding nearly 300 assorted downers like Percodan and Codeine pills in a plastic bag in the crotch of his pants, had ten grams of Marijuana and 6.5 grams of an undetermined blue and white powder. The incident made the newspapers, with Kerry going on television begging fans not to believe what you read in the newspapers. The most hardcore Von Erich marks dismissed the story, believing Kerry's insidious enemy, Freebird Michael Hayes, must have planted the drugs on him. Not so surprisingly, the evidence somehow disappeared from the police station and all charges were dropped.

Adkisson's territory was only a moderate small-time promotion in the North Texas area, built around himself and his three soon-to-be famous sons in the early 80s. When, at age 53, he decided to hold his big retirement show at Texas Stadium in the spring of 1982, just 6,000 fans attended. Four months later at Reunion Arena came the first major sign that the seeds of his family marketing concept were going to pay big dividends when more than 10,000 fans came to see Kerry's two out of three fall double disqualification with Flair, after which Fritz labeled Kerry as the uncrowned world champion. Unlike at Texas Stadium a few months earlier, which drew a traditional wrestling crowd, this crowd was filled with high schoolers and younger. The younger kids, most of whom had never attended a live wrestling show before, clicked in by relating to Kerry, at the time just 22, in his chance to win the world heavyweight title for Texas. A rematch was scheduled for a few months later, but Kerry's knee went out and he needed minor surgery at the time Flair was booked into Fort Worth. Older brother David took his place and vowed to win the title for Texas. When Flair attacked the still on-crutches Kerry and began stomping on his recently operated knee, causing a near riot among the new fans who discovered this pseudo-sport, David lost his cool and got disqualified. On Christmas night, Jack Adkisson's slot machine came up cherries to the tune of state record gross of $105,000 for the Flair vs. Kerry cage match for the NWA title.

The legendary match ended when Terry Gordy slammed the cage door on Kerry's head, a finish imitated many times over the next decade but never with the same results. The resulting Freebirds vs. Von Erichs marraige became one of the hottest feuds in pro wrestling history. It also made World Class the first American promotion that captured the quality and set the standard for the wrestling of the future.

From that point forward, the Friday night cards at the Sportatorium became weekly sellouts. Spot show business picked up even more with the young roguish Freebirds as the natural foes. The three shows at Reunion Arena the next year all sold out at near $200,000, setting a state gate record each time out of the box, with several thousands turned away at each show. On Thanksgiving night, the loser leave town match with Kerry vs. Hayes not only sold out a few days in advance despite, but thousands of those turned away stayed out in the zero degree weather outside the arena watching through the glass to watch the television monitors to see what was going on inside.

Because of the success, Adkisson's power increased within the alliance and his dream of having a son as world champion started being closer to reality. Of course, Adkisson wasn't going to be satisfied with that, as he wanted, at one point, everyone of his sons to get the belt. It appeared David, who wasn't as good an all-around athlete as Kevin or Kerry, but was the smartest, the most reliable, and the best worker, would be the first to get the chance. Apparently David, the one pushed as "being the most like Fritz," was promised the title in 1983 from Harley Race, but through maneuverings of Jim Crockett, Flair got the title for a second time that Thanksgiving night at the first Starrcade. The Flair-David match on Christmas night of 1983 was again sold out well in advance, despite a week-long ice storm. The predictable over-the-top-rope DQ save-the-title finish climaxed the company's most profitable year ever.

The same week Flair got the title back that David was destined for, Michael made his pro debut. Immediately, a match was set up between Flair and Michael for Fort Worth in January, 1984. It was a 10 minute match, and if Flair won, David would never get a return match. If Mike won, or lasted 10:00, David would get a title match and he could pick the time, place and all stipulations. David went one step farther, saying if he couldn't beat Flair this time, he'd retire from wrestling. Mike, at 19 years old and all of 180 pounds, not only lasted the 10:00, but had Flair out with a sleeper when the bell expired in what had to be one of the most forgettable and regrettable matches of the latters' career. One week later David, who had won the United National title (one of three All Japan singles belts later unified into the current Triple Crown title) and was apparently set to dump the belt to Genichiro Tenryu, thereby setting Tenryu up as a No. 1 contender when David eventually returned as world champion, left for All Japan Pro Wrestling.

David went to Ribera Steak House in Tokyo, a hangout for wrestlers, on his first night in Japan with Bill and the late Scott Irwin (who were working as The Super Destroyers at the time). He was drinking heavily. On February 10, he wasn't in the lobby for the bus taking them to the arena on the opening night of the tour. Ref Joe Higuchi along with Bruiser Brody and Jerry Morrow broke into his hotel room and found him dead on the floor. He was 25. Brody immediately flushed the drugs down the toilet. It was reported in Penthouse, that the drugs were Placidyls, the same drug his brother Michael would eventually overdose on as well.

The mythology machine went to work immediately. To this day, the official press reports, that were still used in all newspaper stories about Kerry's death, reported the death from an inflamed intestine, technically known as enteritis. The enteritis story originally was released as occurring from a hard kick in a match in Japan, which was definitely a lie since David died the night before his first match of the tour. Over the ensuing years, the Von Erichs in different press interviews have changed the story many times about David's death, including calling it a stroke, a heart attack after a strenuous match in Japan, food poisoning from sushi and an injury suffered and ignored by David just before leaving for Japan in a match he and Kevin had against the Road Warriors in San Antonio. There was nothing even close to true about any of the above stories, since he of course hadn't had his first match on the tour, Ribera's doesn't serve sushi, and he and Kevin had never wrestled the Road Warriors. David's funeral, open to the public, drew 3,500 wrestling fans, the largest funeral procession in North Texas in many years. Within days, "Heaven Needed a champion" was released and Texas Stadium was booked for one of the biggest wrestling spectaculars ever.

"David was the one he (Jack) saw as taking over the business," Harmes remembered. "He wanted David to become the NWA champion so he could have some time making big money. David wasn't in love with being in the ring. His love was horses. He saw wrestling as a way to set himself up for a great life. Kevin and Kerry were always their own biggest marks. David was a more stable guy."

At about this time, Kevin started becoming a different wrestler. The most gifted athletically of the entire family, the bare-footed Kevin specialized in flying moves which would be considered normal fare by the top wrestlers today, but by the standards of the time were spectacular. His dropkicks rivalled Jim Brunzell's as the best in the business. Most wrestlers, however, didn't like working with him because he worked stiff, didn't like to sell much despite being around 225 pounds, and injured people. Many observers from that time believe that when Kerry was given the title shot at Texas Stadium that was originally scheduled for David, it was the first sign that the three-way parity that the brothers were always pushed as having was out the window and a public sign from either the promotion or the Alliance itself that Kerry was a bigger star than Kevin. Kevin at least appeared genuinely despondent that he wasn't the one who was going to get to win the title in his brother's name since he was the older brother. Even if it was all simply a work, he was never the same wrestler after that point. Kerry became the superstar of the family and Kevin slowly faded in-and-out of wrestling over the next few years with less and less notice each time. The tragedies, and the public nature of them seemingly got to him more and more as the years went by. He used to tell people that when you're a regular person, you have skeletons in your closet. When you're a Von Erich, you have them dangling in your front yard.

While Jack may have deluded himself that his sons could do no wrong, apparently the sons in many cases believed they couldn't do enough right. Growing up and having to then live with the Von Erich name, they apparently believed they had to live up to a standard of athletic and moral perfection that few could attain. Those within the Texas wrestling scene have always pointed at Fritz as the villain in the family story. The usually jovial Boyd Pierce, who worked for years in Dallas as a television and ring announcer and is well-known in wrestling for not having anything bad to say about almost anyone, used to joke that Will Rogers never met Fritz Von Erich (in reference to Will Rogers' saying that he never met a man he didn't like). Certainly the combination of the permissiveness in the upbringing, protection from having to deal with their mistakes, combined with the destiny of their future drummed into them from childhood that they couldn't live up to made them ill equipped for coping with the real world. They were taught that David and Jackie were in a better place, and it was no work that the brothers were all close with one another and, one by one, maybe it became time to join them. No matter what the real background reasons were, this was one screwed up family. Even before the deaths, that was the general consensus within wrestling. But even his fiercest critics and enemies have to admit that for whatever deceptions and abuses he propagated throughout the years, and there were many, that he has paid for them in personal grief many times over.

Still, the talk of Fritz Von Erich, the villain of the Von Erich story, largely came after the death of Michael. Unlike his brothers, Mike was not a good athlete. That only meant the Von Erich mythology would have to be more creative. Mike was billed as having been the best amateur wrestler and best all-around athlete of the brothers. He was said to have broken Kevin's record for the most points in the high school district track meet, which Kevin probably didn't set in the first place. None of this was true, as Mike never competed in track beyond the junior varsity level and played special teams on his small high school football team. He was said to have the potential to surpass all the others. Mike, who was 6-1, but resembled David greatly, was thrust into the spotlight faster than ever because there needed to be three Von Erichs on top, and David was gone. When the announcers would fawn all the praise on Mike about being a better athlete than his brothers, he would stand there embarrassed about the praise and nervous on his interviews. From all accounts, Mike never wanted to be a wrestler. Soon he was pushed as a main eventer, a world title contender, held the group's American title, beat all the top heels and virtually never did any jobs, all at around 190 pounds and as one of the poorest main event performers of the era. Even at that, on July 4, 1984 in Fort Worth, Mike participated in the match of the year, a six-man tag, against The Freebirds.

The Penthouse article stated the pressure led Mike not only to dangerous doses of steroids to increase his size, but to uppers and downers as well. He was forever separating a chronic bad shoulder, suffered in a high school sports injury when he tumbled over hurdles. The trouble started piling up. In May 1985, he was charged with two counts of misdemeanor assault against an emergency room physician. A Denton County jury acquitted him. In September he contracted the toxic shock syndrome that nearly killed him. The greatest crime came in July, when he was, amidst incredible hype, put back into the ring. The return of Mike to Reunion Arena drew 10,000 fans. In November, he totalled his Lincoln Continental when he ran off an embankment but escaped with only a minor head injury. Kevin went on television the next week discussing the incident and blamed himself, saying he kept Mike up too late that night studying wrestling videotapes. He was later arrested and spent five hours in jail on drunk and disorderly charges. A few months later, criminal mischief charges were dismissed against him when he agreed to pay a Fort Worth man $900 for kicking in the door of his car. On April 11, 1987, Mike left a bar in Denton and was swerving severely while driving home. An officer pulled him over and found a small bottle of marijuana, two bottles incorrectly labeled that actually contained 78 pills of five varieties, mainly painkillers. Mike tried to bribe the cop, but when that failed agreed to a blood test. While it showed his alcohol level at a legal .05, it also showed several drugs, presumably placidyls, barbiturates and Valium or its equivalents in his system. He was arrested for drunk driving and controlled substance charges. When he was released, it was the last time he was seen alive. While a suicide note was found before his body, the promotion announced at a spot show in Lubbock after Mike had disappeared but before his body was found, that he was missing and foul play was suspected. The attempt, which didn't succeed this time, was to work the story once again. The cause of death was an overdose of Placidyl, self administered.

Chris Adkisson had been around wrestling dressing rooms for as long as anyone could remember. While growing up, it was considered a given that one day he'd be a superstar wrestler. But unlike even Mike, who at least played some sports in high school, Chris' asthma kept him away from athletics. He always palled around with older brother Mike and wore his hair and dressed like Kerry. Chris was even smaller than Mike, at about 5-5, 165. On a religious television show about the Von Erichs in early 1986, Fritz was on bragging about Chris was the best amateur wrestler of the group and had only lost once as an amateur, to a boy seven years older than him. The host, who had heard Fritz going on and on about the sports accomplishments of Kevin, Kerry and Mike, by this time was even incredulous and when Fritz started his spiel about little Chris, sarcastically said, "and he never lost an amateur wrestling match." By the time Chris got out of high school, Kevin and Kerry had nearly put the company out of business and Jerry Jarrett took over as a partner and was in control of the office and didn't want to use Chris, who had done some independent work. It ended in a messy split when Jarrett tried to push his son Jeff and phase down Kevin and Kerry, and eventually both the Von Erichs and Jarrett wound up out of the market with Global in control. Just before the Von Erich/Jarrett split up, Jarrett finally relented and booked Chris in a few gimmick matches, mainly against Percy Pringle.

Simms trained Chris, who, surprisingly, had virtually never been in the ring until a few weeks before his debut and his matches with Pringle (now the WWF's Paul Bearer).

"He had a suicidal mind," Simms remembered about Chris. Chris was hampered by his asthma, and his medication caused him to lose muscle tone. The police believed the combination of an arm injury suffered a few weeks before his death and the medication caused him to become despondent of him losing his physique, and he was having a difficult time coming to grips with the fact he wasn't going to be able to make it as a wrestler.

On September 12, 1991, Chris called up Kevin and was very despondent. At 9 p.m., Kevin and Doris found Chris about 150 yards from the family ranch. He had shot himself in the head with a 9 mm pistol. He was rushed to East Texas Medical Center in Tyler, where he passed away at 10:27 p.m. Investigators found a one-page hand-written suicide note, where Chris wrote that his family was not to blame for his suicide and that he was sorry. In the note, he wrote about his three older brothers who had died, but there was no indication that played a part in his decision to take his own life. He was 21.

"I remember right after Chris shot himself that Kerry and I went to eat with his two daughters," recalled Simms. "We started talking about Chris and he said Chris had a lot of balls. I asked, `Why do you say that?' He said, `It took a lot of balls to put a gun to your head.'"

Bruce Hart, at least in some ways, grew up in a similar environment as the Von Erichs. His father was a legendary wrestler and became a promoter. His brothers all wrestled at one time or another. Like Kerry, one of his brothers eventually became world champion. He even had a tragic death, brother Dean at age 36, although it was not drug related or self-inflicted, and some other brothers who had their own problems, some of which went public.

"I can relate to the pressure," said Hart. "Maybe the difference is we were able to see it was a work. I remember talking with Kevin and Kerry and we talked about our similarities and it's pretty weird. My biggest perception of the difference was the drugs, but it's a cause and effect thing. Most of us were pretty clean which enabled us to deal with our problems less traumatically. Our father also never allowed us to deify ourselves. Fritz was relentless in pushing them. They weren't bad kids. I saw them as being pretty sensitive. Kerry always seemed to be reaching out for a life line."

As a performer, Kerry was somewhat green, but carryable, but loaded with a certain dumb-jock charisma that appealed to teenage girls that no promotion has been able to duplicate since. At the same time, he wasn't pretty enough to alienate the guys when he started clicking as a draw in 1982. He worked with the best and learned from the best over the next two years until the time that he became one of the best himself. By early 1985, he and Ric Flair toured several territories--Hawaii, Missouri, Mid South and of course his home

World Class area and put on the state-of-the-art matches for that time period. The World Class television and the Von Erich name was so strong that Flair and Kerry were able to sell out Honolulu for their 60:00 draw, sell out St. Louis for a 65:00 draw, and draw a $175,000 house at the Superdome in New Orleans, all out of Kerry's home territory, in the first few months of 1985. Most were classics, but not all. One night Flair and Kerry had to work a 60:00 draw in Fort Worth and nobody could find Kerry. Eventually they found him passed out in his car. They managed to revive him and get him into the ring, but he was zombie-like and Flair had to carry him through perhaps the worst 60:00 draw of his career. Kerry was brought into Chicago for an AWA card at Comiskey Park that drew more than 20,000, and got a bigger pop than any of the regulars. Every promoter in wrestling wanted to be a part of the Kerry Von Erich gravy train. Still, in early 1986, unexplainably, his performance started wavering.

In June 1986, Kerry was involved in a serious motorcycle accident. He was traveling at an unsafe speed riding his bike wearing nothing but gym shorts and no shoes. He made an ill-advised pass and crashed into the back of a patrol car. After 13 hours of a new process called microsurgery, they transplanted muscle and skin tissue from Kerry's back to restore circulation and try to save his foot. He also suffered a dislocated hip, a crushed right ankle and many internal injuries. Nearly every specialist put to rest any hopes of him ever coming back to the ring.

The promotion, at this time on a noticeable downslide and feeling the pressure from the expansion of the WWF, Mid South and Crockett all coming into North Texas, put the big lie back into effect. The Von Erich mythology, as given by Kevin on television, was that Kerry was in a motorcycle accident as everyone had already heard, but it wasn't serious and he'd be back in the ring in about a month. When that month was up, Kevin would say Kerry would be back in about another month or two. The fear was that if fans were told it would be a year, or maybe never, before Kerry could return, they'd tune out of World Class and either forget wrestling, or turn to the opposition groups which had their own stable of superstars. By Thanksgiving, Kerry showed up on television on crutches and took about two baby steps on his own. It seemed well past insanity one month later when it was announced Kerry would return to the ring on a major show in Fort Worth against his former best friend Brian Adias. On crutches, Kerry came into the building, then, according to Penthouse, a doctor filled a syringe with enough novocaine to numb Secretariat, and Kerry walked to the ring, and basically immobile, worked a 5:00 match, winning of course. But the news was mainly bad. The Von Erich magic was gone to the masses in Dallas. Kerry's return drew only 2,326 fans. And in the process, his ankle was rebroken. Four months later, his foot was supposedly permanently fused into a walking position. Miraculously enough, Kerry returned to action on Thanksgiving of 1987 and toured Japan with Kevin a few weeks later. All things considered, the very fact he could still work, let alone work at an acceptable level, although he was never able to come anywhere close to his 1985 peak, may have been, in reality as opposed to fantasy, the thing he should be most admired for. In the fantasy world of his own promotion, Kerry became a world champion once again. Kerry had beaten Al Perez on March 6, 1988 in Dallas to win the World Class title, since the promotion by this time had split with Crockett, who controlled the NWA title. Kerry traded it once with Jerry Lawler and Tatsumi Fujinami during the year, before the title was done away with after Lawler won a PPV unification match in Chicago.

Somewhere along with way, Kerry's bad foot was amputated. It's not clear whether the microsurgery, which was at best a 50/50 proposition in those days, failed to be successful, or if he did so much damage making his ill-advised comeback match with Adias and the operation that it was released as having to fuse to foot was actually the amputation. Most likely it was the latter, since many in wrestling have said that Kerry being put into the ring with Adias well before he was ready played a part in his losing his foot. It was largely unknown in wrestling circles, although a few people working for the Dallas office had suspicions since Kerry never removed his boot, even while showering. One time some of the wrestlers told the story of going into a pool with Kerry, who went in with his boot on, and when he got out of the water, there was an incredible amount of water coming out of his boot. The world, or at least the inside wrestling world, first heard the story in the summer of 1988 when he was on an AWA show in Las Vegas against Col. DeBeers. DeBeers grabbed Von Erich by the boot of his right foot, and suddenly, the boot came off, revealing a sock without a foot in it. DeBeers, and the fans at ringside who saw this, were taken aback, a hush drew over the stunned crowd. Von Erich grabbed his boot, put his leg under the ring to hide it, and put the boot back on. When the word leaked about the incident, which initially was only reported in this and one other publication, denials came everywhere. Rob Russen, who was doing publicity for the AWA denied the story, despite the fact he was sitting right in front when it happened. Jerry Lawler, who was feuding with Von Erich at the time, claimed he had seen the foot, that it was all scarred up and that's why Von Erich never took the boot off. Because of the denials, this turned into one of the most controversial issues of late 1988. The WWF even got involved, as before the Lawler-Von Erich PPV match, they went to the Illinois commission and tried to get Von Erich banned from wrestling because of an ancient statute in the books about boxers and wrestlers with amputated limbs being unable to perform. The commission avoided the issue by scheduling a hearing for Von Erich after the match date, by which time everything was forgotten since there was no political advantage in blocking Von Erich from wrestling other than screwing with the show. The two had an excellent match, with Von Erich losing when the ref stopped the match because he was bleeding. Before the match even started, Kerry was fooling around with the blade backstage and somehow sliced up his arm, which was bleeding as he came to the ring forthe match. A few weeks before the match, Von Erich told Bill Apter that he could photograph him with his boot off after the match to end the controversy. All night Von Erich continued to stall until finally he told Apter just to tell everyone that he saw him with his boot off and to tell people he had seen his right foot.

In early 1990, WCW called up Kerry to bring him in, thinking they could bring back the Flair-Kerry feud and hope that it still had its box office magic. However, Kerry no-showed his first scheduled TV appearance and WCW chalked him up as a lost cause. A few months later, WWF came calling and Kerry grabbed the chance to resurrect himself as a national star. Vince McMahon, who no doubt wanted Kerry as much as almost anyone when he started his national expansion in 1984 (McMahon's own magazine occasionally reported on the Von Erichs while ignoring the existence of every other promotion) talked Kerry into leaving Texas. As irony would have it, at almost the same time, Brutus Beefcake suffered a para-sailing accident and Kerry, now renamed The Texas Tornado, took his place against Mr. Perfect to capture the Intercontinental title at Summer Slam of 1990. The reign was short-lived, and Kerry slowly moved his way down the cards. In February of 1992, his father called the WWF and said his son was having drug problems and needed rehab. At the same time, Kerry was arrested for forging prescriptions. The much-publicized drug raid of the WWF dressing room in St. Louis was largely caused on a tip that was believed to have been related to Kerry, who no-showed the card since it was during the period Titan had given him off for rehab. Kerry finally went through the rehab, and apparently it made a difference over the short run. But by the summer, WWF let Kerry go. Kerry was a time bomb ready to explode and the WWF was in no position to be able to not be seriously damaged by the explosion.

"We did everything we could for him," said WWF spokesperson Steve Planamenta in August when the company released him.

Four hours after Kerry's death, Jack Adkisson had to come up with the final chapter of the Von Erich mythology. Jack admitted that his son had his right foot amputated, who said everyone at the hospital and the physical therapists had all been sworn to secrecy about.

"No one knew. It was extremely painful at first," he said in the Fort Worth Star-Telegram. "Kerry's had a drug problem since that accident, and no one was ever about to tell why." He said Kerry didn't want anyone to tell because "Fellas might think he was weaker." The story that nobody knew was another example of not accepting what was going on in the real world and accepting only self-created fantasy. Kerry's predicament was a major story in late 1988, and was even reported in one Dallas newspapers shortly after the incident with DeBeers in Las Vegas. Still, the Dallas television media acted stunned at the revelation. The story of his drug problem beginning with the accident is also not accurate.

Grey Pierson, promoter of the Friday night shows at the Sportatorium, immediately went public hyping a Kerry Von Erich Memorial show for the next evening. Kerry had been scheduled in the main event on the card against Dave Sheldon, who ironically uses the ring name Angel of Death. That afternoon, Kevin Adkisson, 35, the lone living son of Jack, who flew home the day before from a wrestling tour of the Virgin Islands, went to the Dallas media and decried the event. Kevin said that he, his father and his mother disapproved of the event, wouldn't be at the event, and accused Pierson of trying to capitalize on his brother's death. "I want the people to know that the Von Erichs don't have anything to do with that at all. In fact, I think it's terrible to try and exploit something like that." The irony of that statement was lost on very few. Many of the 3,038 fans, still heavily papered but it is expected it was the most paid at a Sportatorium wrestling event in a long time, particularly women, sobbed at ringside during the 45 minute ceremony. Simms, Sheldon, Jack's long-time lieutenant in the glory days, David Manning, Chris Adams, Japanese photographer Jimmy Suzuki and Dallas City Councilman Al Lipscomb all delivered eulogies in a ring decorated with flowers and plants with a huge photo of Kerry, with one of his wrestling robes and a pair of his boots on display. A shocking number of fans, the ones who, like Kerry, were unable to let go of the fantasy despite one news story after another over the past decade, still wouldn't allow themselves to face the truth. Many believed somebody shot him, and that the drug stories involving him were all concocted.

The reality was that Kerry Adkisson was a likeable guy according to those who knew him best, if you could get past the fact he was sheltered in almost a Peter Pan like existence where he didn't have to grow up. But you had to accept that about him. He wasn't particularly intelligent, but that was part of his charm to the fans and his friends, and he had a lot of both, and part of the funny stories that he'll leave behind. He was hardly a saint. Certainly he wasn't particularly honest, but some of that can be traced to his upbringing where he was taught to con the marks at all times and yet con himself into clinging to the fantasy. Not clinging to the fantasy of wrestling, but to the fantasy of the Von Erichs, to the same bitter end that, sad to say, was his destiny, almost no different than Andre the Giant. He was a great athlete, and maybe under different circumstances would have been the biggest stars in this profession, a spot he was seemingly destined for a decade ago. But if he ever had reached that spot, the travel and the pressures of the spotlight probably would have self-destructed him in one form or another. The one thing, ironically, that as an athlete and as a competitor he deserves the most credit for, being able to come back to the ring with one foot and still perform better than many, no matter how ill-advised it probably was, had to be hidden because it, too, would have meant facing reality. Some of the bizarre things, like the night after his wife served him with divorce papers when he grabbed the house mic at the Sportatorium and told the fans that his wife was divorcing him so he'd be collecting phone numbers in the back, were probably less based on ego and arrogance as much as naivete and stupidity. Others, like when he would go to a spot show and say he would let fans take Polaroids with him for $5 and that all the money would go to charity, but somehow the money never went to charity, may have been as much based on his upbringing in regard to fans simply being marks to be conned. But it was those same fans that gave him his world. It was the only real world he knew. It was the world where he was Kerry Von Erich, the Modern Day Warrior. It was the only world he could survive in. And that world was coming to an end.

Kerry Adkisson was buried alongside his brothers on February 22 at Grove Hill Memorial Park in East Dallas. Of the many major deaths in wrestling in recent years, none received the amount of media coverage as this one. Ironically, neither World Championship Wrestling, which ran a pay-per-view event on Sunday, nor the World Wrestling Federation, which ran its live Monday Night Raw show the following evening, acknowledged the death of the man who not all that many years ago was one of the three or four biggest stars in its world. Even under the most real of circumstances, they still had to ignore it on the grounds it might interfere with their fantasy. Maybe in that way, Kerry Von Erich did the only thing he had learned, protecting his fantasy world to the bitter end.

FEBRUARY 8

The funeral for Adkisson, who committed suicide four days earlier, was held on 2/22 at the First Baptist Church in Dallas before about 500 onlookers in a ceremony open to the public. Many Dallas area wrestlers attended, although the only out-of-towners that were there were Jim Hellwig (Ultimate Warrior) and Bret and Owen Hart. Other wrestling personalities in attendance included Scott Putski, Terry Simms, Steven Dane, Calvin Knapp, retired wrestler/referee Bronko Lubich, former referee/booker David Manning, Bob Beddow (promoter in Southeastern Texas), Toni Adams and Jimmy Papa (musician behind the WCW Slam Jam album). Pall bearers included Hellwig, Bill Collville (long-time family bodyguard) and Kerry's ex-father-in-law. There were no speakers at the service.

Hellwig, who became friends with Kerry in 1986 when he wrestled for his father in the World Class promotion as Dingo Warrior, has talked about starting a trust fund for Kerry's two daughters, since Kerry left the family with no money.

In addition, The Global Wrestling Federation will be presenting a benefit show on 4/2 at the Dallas Sportatorium with all proceeds going into a trust fund for Kerry's two daughters. Promoter Grey Pierson started the trust with a $1,000 donation and Max Andrews, the former television syndicator for the Von Erichs' defunct World Class Championship Wrestling promotion, added a $500 donation. Peace was made with Kerry's family as brother Kevin will work the main event and father Fritz will make his first appearance at a pro wrestling show in more than two years and his first at the Sportatorium since he gave us his company four years ago to appear in Kevin's corner. The promotion (Grey Pierson, 817-265-7771) is looking for any independent name wrestlers who would like to appear at the benefit and will help provide transportation to the event for out-of-towners. They are also going to try and get cooperation from both WWF and WCW and hopefully both groups will supply talent for this benefit show. The normal free passes which make up the large bulk of the Friday night Sportatorium audience each week will be eliminated on this show and ticket prices will be increased. On the tasteless end of all this, at this past Friday's show at the Sportatorium, Scandor Akbar, who no doubt will wind up managing Kerry's opponent and be in the opposite corner from Fritz on the 4/2 card, did a live interview saying that he had no sympathy for Kerry Von Erich and he agreed with Judge Larry Baraka's statement about Kerry taking the coward's way out. Baraka, who was the judge scheduled to hear Kerry's case, was quoted in the Dallas Morning News the morning after the death as saying that Kerry took the coward's way out, which infuriated the hardcore wrestling marks in the area. Akbar then proclaimed himself the real king of Dallas wrestling (as opposed to Fritz). They can't let it go, can they? I guess it can be rationalized by saying Kerry would have wanted it that way, which is probably true.

APRIL 5

The GWF also announced its complete line-up for the 4/2 Hollie and Lacy Adkisson Benefit show at the Dallas Sportatorium as Kevin Von Erich & Chris Adams managed by Fritz Von Erich vs. Michael Hayes & Buddy Roberts managed by Scandor Akbar, Sid Vicious & Motor City Mad Man vs. Ebony Experience, Dingo Warrior (Ultimate Warrior Jim Hellwig) vs. Black Bart, Awesome Kong & King Kong vs. Steve & Schaun Simpson, Iceman King Parsons & Action Jackson vs. Bobby Duncum Jr. & John Hawk, Rod Price vs. Scott Putski, Tim Brooks vs. Terry Simms, John Tatum vs. Chaz Taylor, Calvin Knapp vs. Alex Porteau, Johnny Mantell vs. Francis Buxton and Bubba Fangman vs. Ed Robinson. According to someone who spoke with Hellwig on Monday, he was saying that he wasn't going to be wrestling on the card, saying that he would have worked the show but that nobody from GWF had ever contacted him. So as it turns out, from the names previously billed, Jake Roberts and The Fantastics won't be appearing and Hellwig may not be either so the only major names working the card out of the ordinary are The Freebirds and Vicious. We were originally told Warrior vs. Vicious as the semi-final match, but the line-up was changed. The card will be taped for home video with the proceeds also going to benefit the children of Kerry Adkisson. Fritz Von Erich was scheduled to appear Saturday night on the Wrestling Insiders radio show, then at the last minute, pulled out and had Kevin do the show in his place. The only thing of note was when the subject of religion was broached, Kevin almost matter-of-factly said that he and his father weren't religious.

APRIL 12

The other major show of the weekend was the Hollie and Lacey Adkisson benefit card on 4/2 at the Dallas Sportatorium. The show drew 1,720 (1,570 paid) and raised approximately $15-16,000 for the children of Kerry Adkisson. Although the GWF has often drawn larger crowds in the Sportatorium, most of the tickets are giveaways and it'll certainly be the largest paid crowd in the building in a few years. There were a lot of problems with the card, which was highlighted by the return of Michael Hayes & Buddy Roberts to Dallas as The Freebirds. First, the Jim Hellwig (Ultimate Warrior) situation. Hellwig was well-known as being one of Kerry's best friends both in Dallas when he achieved some fame as Dingo Warrior and in the WWF. Hellwig was advertised for the show even though the promotion actually had never contacted him. The promotion claimed they called him several times and he never called back, which may very well have been true, except that they didn't even get his phone number until a week or so before the card, and they had been advertising him as appearing for several weeks before even making the call. Hellwig was out of town (he lives in Arizona) in New York this past week, which was reported on the Pro Wrestling Spotlight radio show over the weekend as several days worth of meetings with the Justice Department, so if he was called, he wasn't there to receive them. It was estimated that one-third of the crowd came specifically to see him, and no announcement was even made at any point about his not being there.

I don't know that the situation was with Jake Roberts and The Fantastics, whose names were mentioned on TV promos, although neither were being advertised by the promotion in the final week. Sid Vicious had his first match in almost one year on the card, teaming with guy billed as Johnny Rotten, who I believe was an old friend who taught him how to wrestle (insert your own punch line here). The two ended up losing to the Ebony Experience, with Rotten naturally doing the favor.

The main event was Kevin Von Erich & Chris Adams against Hayes & Roberts, managed by Scandor Akbar. Hayes & Roberts got a huge face reaction coming down, actually much larger than Kevin, Adams & Fritz got, although once the match began they turned the crowd as heels. Finish saw Kevin put the claw on Roberts while Hayes was beating up Adams in the corner and Fritz had the claw on Akbar. Kevin pinned Roberts (who I'm told looked really good in the ring, which is saying something since it's been years since he's wrestled regularly), at which point Angel of Death did a run-in to save Adams from Hayes. The idea was to use the match to shoot the top angle for this group's future, with Akbar having a reason to place a bounty on Angel. There was at least some consternation in that all the wrestlers were working the show gratis as a benefit for Kerry's daughters, and while Kevin did thank the wrestlers, Fritz never did, and neither ever said anything on the house mic to the fans. This show was also taped for home video.

APRIL 19

The saga of the Von Erich wrestling family was covered in depth on 4/11 and 4/12 in a five-page two-part series entitled "The Von Erichs: An American Tragedy" in the sports section of the New York Daily News. The story, by hockey writer Barry Meisel, included numerous quotes from Jack (Fritz), his former wife Doris, Kevin and Kerry's ex-wife Cathy. The story did give what appeared to be some new insight into one of the most tragic and bizarre stories in the history of the wrestling profession, particularly in certain attitudes in the aftermath of the death of David in 1984. However, all quotes from Jack and Kevin, given the track record, have to be taken with more than the standard grain of salt. In other areas, the story was lacking, particularly in factual research regarding certain well-chronicled occurrences in the family's history. Perhaps the biggest negative to the story was all of the neon-sign obvious messages that can be learned about confusing reality with fantasy and the problems of achieving too much fame, particularly fame stemming from such heavy manipulation too fast and the aftermath of when its gone, were nowhere to be found. At times the story read like just the latest media chapter in the Von Erich mythology. Overall the reporter did a good job of writing an interesting story while having little background on it going in, but there was so much missing that shouldn't have been hard to find.

The Daily News story stated that Kerry had said over and over again that he would kill himself before he'd ever spend a day in jail. It also said that he had lunch just hours before committing suicide with his ex-wife that day and told her that he'd kill himself she wouldn't agree to get back together with him, although he had said that to her on numerous occasions previously in an effort to get her to take him back.

"I think people are getting awfully simplistic when they start looking for a reason," said Doris Adkisson, Kerry's mother, in what was probably her first newspaper interview since the death. "You're talking about a lifetime of all current emotions. To say it's all so-and-so's fault is awfully simplistic. It's like saying it's all my fault because I married him. It's all my fault because I married him at 17 instead of waiting until he was 30. And maybe then it means it's all Fritz's mom's fault for having him. Or all my mother's fault for having me in the first place. There are no real answers."

However, the Von Erich mythology was still evident, particularly in the thumbnail sketches of the five sons. It listed Kevin's 1987 concussion in the ring in Fort Worth as attributed to having his head run into the ring post, which, while more believable then being hit with a dreaded Oriental tool punch, is no more accurate. It listed David's death as being from acute gastroenteritis and claimed he was the most popular wrestler in the family (Kerry was the most popular although David was the most popular among promoters because he was the most reliable and considered the best worker). It also listed David as playing football and basketball at North Texas State University, which isn't technically true. He went to the school on a football/basketball scholarship, but didn't play football as a freshman and was redshirted in basketball his freshman year, then quit college and started pro wrestling at the age of 19. It listed Kevin as the first brother to turn pro (actually David was, Kevin joined him a few months later, both in 1977 although the article listed Kevin as 1978 and David as 1979, admittedly minor errors).

It listed Kerry as turning pro in 1980 (actually it was Thanksgiving of 1978 when he started during college break but was full-time by the summer of 1979) claiming he dropped out of college when President Carter ordered the boycott of the Moscow Olympics since the article claimed he was an Olympic discus prospect. He could have been a possibility, although the odds against it would have been strong, given continued improvement over the years, but not until the 1984 or 1988 Olympics. There are plenty of state high school champions and even state record holders, and very few spots on the Olympic team. Kerry would have been only 20 at the time of the 1980 games and his best collegiate throw of 178 feet was nowhere close to what would have been needed to have made the U.S. team. His coaches thought he did have the athletic potential, but for every top athlete, there are often dozens with equal or more potential that don't go as far. His discus prowess and the subsequent boycott were put together as part of the family mythology used for wrestling angles. He was talked about as a medal favorite on the wrestling shows in early 1980 before the Olympic trials when heels "injured" his shoulder just prior, keeping him from attending the tryouts he was never going to in the first place. Kerry had been wrestling full-time and had given up serious discus training long before the boycott was called, although his former college track coach confirmed that his father wanted him to stay in college. It listed the crowd at Texas Stadium for the famous Flair-Kerry match in 1984 as 43,013 when it was actually 32,123. That 43,000 figure has been used so many times over the years that like many exaggerations in every form of media, when repeated often enough, it "becomes" the truth. Admittedly it's hardly the first exaggerated crowd figure used in the entertainment world but the real number isn't much of a secret either.

In the story, Jack swore that he never wanted his sons to follow him in the ring. This contradicts the fact he seemingly had planted the seeds for it when they were teenagers by talking about them and featuring them on television before they even started wrestling and even as much as got other NWA promoters who were his friends like Sam Muchnick to begin talking about his sons when they were still in high school or the ridiculous push all received long before they were ready. When Kevin, David and Kerry were 18, 17 and 15 respectively, Jack introduced them at the NWA annual convention telling the other promoters that his three boys would all be future NWA champions. After Jack's retirement match in 1982, all five sons were brought together in an interview and Fritz saying how all five would someday be NWA champion.

"Man, I did everything in the world to keep my kids out of this damn business," he said. "But it was all they knew. A lot of boys don't want to follow in their father's footsteps. But there are those who do.

Everybody likes recognition. They saw me getting a lot of it. They idolized me. I trained, was on television, a big name, why wouldn't they want the same thing? It was as natural as anything in the world.

If somebody has the gall to say that I forced my kids and I'm responsible for their deaths in any way, shape or form, it makes me want to get a .45 and shoot somebody right in the ass. It burns me up."

The story quoted Kevin as saying David's death was the beginning of the end. Kevin claimed David's death burned out his heart while Jack, who ran the promotion, said that he lost his initiative and desire. For all real purposes, Jack got out of the wrestling business after the death of Mike although still had a major financial interest in the company and did the infamous heart-attack angle after Mike's death. Jack also talked of a fight the two had just before Mike's suicide. Jack claimed Mike was drunk when he sternly scolded him for his series of legal transgressions which went public after his near-fatal bout with toxic shock syndrome. Mike responded by kicking his father in the groin and Jack knocked him down. It also noted that Jack was the only member of the family not mentioned in Mike's suicide note. It did note that Mike wasn't particularly athletic. The story of how heavily hyped his return to the ring after suffering brain damage and a loss of equilibrium from the toxic shock with Jack pushing him as "The Living Miracle" and promising he'd return to win championships, which some would say was the most telling sign of all about things being out of control, wasn't brought up. It talked of Chris' suicide as despondency after being told by doctors that he couldn't wrestle again. The sidebar story also talked of benevolent endeavors that had become the family's trademark.

APRIL 26

From several reports, Kevin Adkisson (Kevin Von Erich) held up GWF promoter Grey Pierson for $1,000 cash before the show on the 4/2 benefit show at the Sportatorium for his nieces. All the wrestlers had agreed to work the card with no payment since it was advertised that all the proceeds would go into a trust fund for the two young daughters of his late brother Kerry. Pierson had agreed to reimburse wrestlers for transportation costs and had told wrestlers that if they had to cancel a prior booking in order to appear on the show, that he would reimburse them for missing the booking. None of the wrestlers on the show asked for any money for either transportation or reimbursement for canceling a prior engagement besides Kevin. Kevin claimed he had a prior booking that night in Birmingham, AL which brought with it a $1,000 payoff. We have no record of any such a show in Birmingham on that evening that Kevin would have been booked on, let alone had been promised that kind of a payoff, which would be labeled as very unusual in the independent market for a wrestler of Kevin's calibre, but not necessarily impossible. Kevin is believed to be on a tour of Nigeria so nobody has heard his side of the story. According to other reports, there was no show in Birmingham and the promotion paid him the money before the show figuring his no-showing that particular event would cause numerous problems, especially with the potential fear that should he not appear that his father might choose to leave with him.

Wrestlers holding up promoters at the last minute and promoters underpaying wrestlers what they promised ahead of time is as old as the wrestling business itself, which doesn't make it correct, but in many ways this is almost inherently in many cases an unscrupulous business. However, this particular incident of doing so on a benefit show where everyone else on the card gave up their Friday night and worked for free on a benefit show for ones own nieces does seem to set new record in that regard. Speaking of the Von Erichs, Texas Magazine, a Sunday newspaper supplement similar to Parade, will be doing another major feature on the family. Based on what I'm told, Jack Adkisson is a lot more open about certain things in this article as compared with previous ones.

MAY 17

The television show "A Current Affair" will be doing a segment on the Von Erichs tentatively either on Monday, 5/17 or Thursday, 5/20 according to the latest reports from those with the show. The piece will definitely run during May because the show feels the story is prime sweeps material.

MAY 24

"A Current Affair" ran its entire 5/17 show on the Adkisson/Von Erichs, which revolved around interviews with on 5/17, which revolved with Jack and Kevin. The piece has already come under heavy criticism because of what was left out, but in defense of the piece, and only a little defense is deserved, there was only so much you can air and say in 30 minutes on a story that would need to be a four-part mini-series to do justice to. The interview of Jack was really telling and deserving of the time allotted. They spent too much time interviewing Kevin and left unanswered all the questions that a viewer would be interested in after seeing the piece, many of which have answers. Overall I'm not as negative on it as most, although there was a lot left out that the producers knew about that probably needed to somehow be included. The story couldn't be done without making clear that Jack owned the wrestling company his sons worked for and controlled the fact that his sons were always on top and won almost all of their matches. Their superstardom was not a result of their athletic ability (although some were good athletes) but of Jack's marketing the family name and his obsession with making his sons the superstars that they weren't equipped to be. How that key point could be left out no matter how tight things were hurt the story.

While a minor point, reporting that the Kerry Von Erich-Ric Flair match drew 43,000 people, no matter how many times it is reported, is not true, and by virtue of the fact that producers had the issue of the Observer in their hands putting together that piece, there is no excuse for that error, no matter how minor. It also had Jack talk about how nobody knew about Kerry wrestling with a prosthetic leg. This was reported in a Dallas newspaper in 1988 and was the subject of major controversy within the industry that year, which also was mentioned in that same Observer. But the capper, which would have ruined the piece no matter what, was Maureen O'Boyle's closing line about Kevin still being an international superstar who only works in this country on charity shows. Yes, the producers of the piece were aware of what happened at the Sportatorium when Kevin held up promoter Grey Pierson at his own niece's benefit show for a $1,000 payoff claiming a canceled booking that there is no evidence existed. And to classify Kevin Von Erich today as anything but a superstar of a decade ago who has fallen to the ranks of being a non-entity in the wrestling business would be inaccurate. For whatever positive and negative one can say about the piece, the final line sealed it as overall negative.

MAY 31

Another correction or retraction. After viewing the "A Current Affair" piece twice more this week, last week's comments on the piece were far too favorable. While the piece was well produced visually and interesting to watch, the overall impression it gave is misleading and it seemed they ignored any evidence that would answer the questions the viewers wanted most. Watching the piece left me with the impression that the deal that was made to get all the classic home footage and wrestling footage included going along with Von Erich mythology in most cases without question, and in some cases with just perfunctory questioning.

CHAPTER TEN

SMW WORKING WITH WWF

FEBRUARY 1

The long-awaited return of Jim Cornette to TBS will air on the Saturday Night show on 2/5. The return was taped on 1/25 at Center Stage. Cornette, Stan Lane, Tom Prichard and Bobby Eaton came in unannounced through the crowd, knocking down a security railing and Cornette went into a tirade about how the Rock & Roll Express stole the Smoky Mountain tag team titles and he wanted to wrestle them right now. Bill Watts came out (to a chorus of boos) and Cornette went into a 5:00 WCW Bill Watts tirade. Apparently the highlight was when Cornette said that Watts wasn't fit to run the company and should be cleaning the toilets out at CNN, only because of the big crowd pop for the line on the look on Watts' face. Although Watts was booed like crazy coming out, the boos turned to cheers when Cornette was poking Watts in the chest and Watts grabbed his hand and gave a line about how he didn't know where that finger had been. This is similar to the 1984 Cornette-Watts feud which drew more money than any feud ever in the old Mid South promotion. It wound up with Rock & Roll wrestling Lane & Prichard, with Eaton interfering for the DQ and Cornette knocking out both Morton & Gibson with the tennis racquet. Quality wise I'm told this wasn't one of their better matches, but the heat was the best in the building in a long time.

FEBRUARY 15

Although it was one of the hottest television angles in a long time and the match was great, the Rock & Roll vs. Heavenly Bodies deal on television was somewhat marred because the people who edited the show cut out four sentences by Cornette (which is why when watching the show it appeared the mic kept going out, what they did was muted the Cornette lines because certain people felt they didn't want someone who doesn't work for the company going on television and knocking the company, not understanding that was part of the reason why the angle was so good). What was cut out was Cornette saying he hated Jim Herd, he broke up the Midnight Express because the company was trying to turn them into something they weren't, threatening to sue Watts, TBS and everyone else (that suing is something everyone is a bit touchy about nowadays) and they also cut out the line when Cornette was yelling at Morton & Gibson and said that they'll settle it 2/19 in Knoxville (which was an SMW card) although it made no sense when Watts came back and told him not to be talking about something "our fans" don't know or care anything about. Watts had OK'd all those lines beforehand. Cornette ended up going on Jim Ross' radio show Sunday night and got his digs in on Herd and got to plug all his SMW dates for February.

AUGUST 2

Hell froze over for the second time in less than one year as Jim Cornette and the Heavenly Bodies debuted for the World Wrestling Federation at the Monday Night Raw tapings on 7/25 in Alexandria Bay, NY. The Bodies (Tom Prichard & Jimmy Del Rey) will be announced in upcoming weeks as the opponents for Rick & Scott Steiner in a WWF tag team title match at Summer Slam which will be pushed for the first time in WWF recent history as an interfederation match-up. Originally the Steiners were to face The Head Shrinkers, however that match had to be canceled due to a serious leg infection suffered by Fatu out of the ring that will keep him out of action indefinitely.

In addition, Cornette was also announced as the new "spokesperson" (read that manager) for WWF champ Yokozuna. This took place during a "contract signing" for the Lex Luger vs. Yokozuna WWF title match at Summer Slam, where Mr. Fuji brought in Cornette as a surprise and the storyline was that Cornette worked the contract with a clause that this would be Luger's only chance at the title, which pretty well guarantees the finish. Since the WWF is pretty much rolling the dice and putting everything down on Luger's back, it's important for this title win to garner as much interest as possible to start things off on the right foot and it is no secret that Mr. Fuji's promos aren't strong enough to carry such an important angle. In addition, Luger vs. Yokozuna will probably be the headline match all fall at the house shows after Summer Slam and somebody needs to be able to do strong interviews to get it over and Fuji wasn't going to be that someone. There had been rumors throughout wrestling dating back for months that the WWF was looking for a new manager to work with Yokozuna, realizing Fuji wasn't nearly at the level needed for the heel the promotion was focusing so much on. Cornette will be doing all the promo work for Yokozuna starling on the television that airs either 8/2 or 8/9. On the 7/26 tapings in Utica, Cornette did an interview for Yokozuna which saw several babyface wrestlers come out (Luger not being one of them) waving the small flags (they again passed out flags before the show to the fans as well) while the sound system played "Stars and Stripes forever."

Cornette and the Bodies were acknowledged by the WWF announcers as being from Smoky Mountain Wrestling, called "the hottest wrestling promotion in the South," on their first two nights in. Bobby Heenan, who did the interview with Cornette on the program that will air on Raw on 8/2, acknowledged his SMW feuds with the Armstrongs and the Rock & Roll Express. This marks the first time in modern history that the WWF has on television acknowledged by name another wrestling organization. It is believed that acknowledging his own promotion and talking of it on television in a positive light was the key to getting Cornette to agree to come in. In addition, the WWF is going to plug the SMW house shows in Knoxville on its local TV show in that market. In addition, some WWF talent will be made available to work SMW major shows ala the WWF relationship with USWA. Supposedly the only deal made was that Cornette and the Bodies were to work four dates as independents for the WWF, the three television taping dates, the Raw taping on 7/25, the Superstars taping on 7/26 in Utica, NY and the Challenge taping on 7/29 in Plattsburgh, NY and Summer Slam. On 7/26, they held a dry run match with the Steiners vs. Bodies for the tag team title, ending with Cornette interfering for the DQ in a match that was said to be only okay. The deal, which was kept a secret from all other SMW employees, was put together between Cornette and Bruce Prichard (Tom's younger brother), and originally simply consisted of the Bodies and Cornette being brought is as a team from another federation challenging a WWF babyface tag team (likely being the Smoking Gunns). With the injury to Fatu combined with Fuji's incompetence as a manager in such an important scenario, the original plans changed drastically. The deal probably stemmed originally from Cornette's attempts to use Big Bossman on a few SMW house shows in August. Supposedly Cornette will be taping some of the Events Center promos for Yokozuna's matches while at the three days of taping, with any additional interviews being taped from home rather than being brought into Connecticut. Cornette on at least two prior occasions had turned down WWF offers, the most recent coming in late 1991 when he was offered the spot to manage Ric Flair in his series against Hulk Hogan when Bobby Heenan pulled himself from the road, in the spot that eventually went to Mr. Perfect.

On the surface, this looks like a deal that helps both promotions. SMW, which is struggling at the gate, gains whatever credibility, whether it be positive or negative and that can be argued, of having three of its headliners appear on the most widely viewed wrestling show in the country and on a major PPV event. A similar circumstance took place earlier this year when Cornette and the old Heavenly Bodies along with the Rock & Roll Express did two WCW television tapings and the Slamboree PPV show and its really hard to see if that turned out to be a boost or not for SMW, although a lot of the higher-ups in WCW didn't like the idea of using non-WCW talent in a key position on a PPV show. It's ironic only because Cornette, since the inception of SMW has claimed numerous times in interviews to be wanting to avoid anything that make it seem SMW is associated with either WWF or WCW, feeling that people have associated those two organizations with cartoon wrestling, bad shows, and an overall negative stigma and that to be successful his company has to give the impression it has nothing to do with them. To protect that belief, in both the WCW appearance and in this one, it will be emphasized that Cornette and company are outsiders and not involved with the Fed. This working agreement will probably result in SMW using WWF talent to augment its big shows. With Titan cutting back to one show per night on 8/15 and adding so much new talent at the same time, there will be a tremendous number of wrestlers who will receive infrequent bookings, or in many cases, no bookings at all, and that translates into little or no money. Titan, in order to keep a contractual hold on that talent can and will be looking to book the talent out to independents like SMW and can even work out a deal where some may even appear regularly in the SMW territory. The WWF will get to finally test the waters of working what can be promoted as an interfederational feud, the kind which has proven to be immensely successful financially in recent years in Japan. Many, including myself, felt this should have been the hook used in the 1991 Flair-Hogan series, but instead it wasn't, which seemingly detracted from the luster of that "dream" match-up after just a few weeks. In addition, Titan has someone who presumably can garner additional heat and interest in its most important match-up of the year. However, it is hard to believe that the WWF would give so much television air time to Cornette, let alone violate its most basic long-lasting rule in regard to acknowledging by name another wrestling group, for only a one-shot deal, no matter how important Summer Slam may be. Cornette's role behind-the-scenes at SMW requires so much time that he simply couldn't work any kind of a regular schedule with Titan and still have enough time left to do justice to SMW.

AUGUST 9

The biggest question of the past week is how does the appearance of Jim Cornette and the Heavenly Bodies in WWF affect this group. There was a lot of talk, some of it not positive, among some in the group about the "surprise" during the past week. None of the wrestlers were informed about it beforehand, which probably should have been handled better because it created a week's worth of what may have been unnecessary worrying and speculation that got out of hand and guys had to fend off rumors that went way past ridiculous. The first time Cornette saw most of the guys since it happened would have been Friday night's house show and whatever comments were made to him personally were of a positive vein. But this is the wrestling business so that doesn't mean there are no negative feelings about it, since Cornette had been adamant in the past about his views on the WWF. Any relationship does increase the chances of SMW wrestlers getting a shot with WWF, as the USWA relationship has resulted in people like Well Done and Men on a Mission getting gigs. One thing people have to realize is that between running the business, booking the television and house shows, and honing his own stuff, Cornette eats, sleeps and breaths SMW 24 hours per day. Anytime spent on outside activities is going to cut what is already a tight schedule. In August, Cornette only has three WWF dates, a television taping on 8/18, one trip to Connecticut to cut face-to-face promos, and Summer Slam on 8/30. Theoretically that is a light enough schedule that it should be manageable. However, if that schedule gets much heavier, or starts including weekend road trips, there simply isn't enough hours in the day where it won't cut into his necessary time spent running SMW.

After watching the angle on Monday Night Raw, which was good (and Bobby Heenan was fabulous tripping over his chair), although not nearly as good as the unedited (or even the edited) initial angle he did in WCW with Bill Watts, this is a good opportunity for himself. The timing couldn't be better since there are no top-flight managers working the national scene so Cornette will stand out now more than ever before, when people like Heenan, Hart, Dillon and Dangerously were around. It's a nice ego boost that he got Vince McMahon to plug his product on WWF telecasts, but that alone doesn't mean a hill of beans when it comes to improving SMW's business. Bringing in WWF talent to SMW under the right circumstances can help business. But it has to be done carefully and in a manner where the WWF talent isn't portrayed as being superior major league talent, because that will then make the SMW wrestlers minor league in their own territory which will kill them, but certainly Cornette is smart enough to avoid that obvious pitfall.

In addition, if the WWF talent coming in when it's in the SMW territory isn't willing to put over the local boys (which doesn't necessarily mean doing jobs, although on occasion they would need to), it'll be detrimental if the relationship lasts a long time. Another pitfall is the danger of Cornette himself getting overexposed in his own territory. Cornette has been all over every SMW television show and involved in all the strongest angles since the company's inception. When watching the tapes, even though he is the best piece of talent in the company when it comes to getting angles over, he's many times been right on the border of overexposing himself at times just on his own television. Throw in being all over WWF television that runs in many of his key cities, and as talented as he is, if this is a long run, he'll run the risk of being overexposed in his own territory. At that point, whatever he says and does will start yielding less and less when it comes to results. His initial appearances on WWF should be of slight benefit to the territory, particularly if things that happen in the WWF are worked into the SMW storylines. Regular appearances all over both group's television over a long period of time isn't to his benefit in his own neck of the woods.

CHAPTER ELEVEN

THE DEATH OF ANDRE THE GIANT

FEBRUARY 8

One of the largest men and biggest gate attractions in the history of pro wrestling, Andre the Giant, passed away on January 27 in his sleep of an apparent heart attack. Andre, who was 46 at the time of his death, was probably the second most famous pro wrestler on a world wide basis, and correspondingly, probably the second biggest drawing card internationally, in the history of the business.

Known in the business simply as "The Giant," Andre wrestled professionally for 28 years, and was an international superstar attraction for most of that period. During the 1970s, Andre was undeniably the most famous wrestler in the world, the biggest international box office attraction and the highest paid performer. He was also one of the most recognizable athletes on the planet. Andre headlined before the largest recorded paid wrestling crowd in history, the 90,817 paid fans who sold out the Pontiac Silverdome on March 29, 1987 for his Wrestlemania III main event match against Hulk Hogan. The bout was the first million dollar live gate in history ($1,599,000), was the largest closed circuit gate in history ($5,200,000) and set a pay-per-view buy rate record (reported at 10.2 percent, but probably closer to eight percent legitimately, which has since been broken by boxing, but the figure hasn't been even approached again in wrestling). The closed-circuit and buy rate figures appear to be safe bets to remain on the books for many years. On February 5, 1988, Andre's rematch with Hulk Hogan from Indianapolis aired on the first live prime-time network special in the United States in more than 30 years, and the viewing audience, 33 million, made it by far the most viewed pro wrestling match in U.S. history. That record also appears safe for many years to come.

The story of Andre the Giant's life was the ultimate Faustian bargain. Only, his destiny was determined, almost at birth. Born Andre Rene Rousimoff on May 19, 1946 in Grenoble, France, Andre was born with a rare glandular disease known as acromegaly. The disease comes from the body's continual oversecretion of Growth Hormone. It caused him to grow and grow and be one of the largest and most powerful men around. He became what doctors would say would be the ultimate result of too many megadoses of Human Growth Hormone, both in positives and in side effects. But once he could no longer grow in height, his body would turn against him. The continual growth would go to his head, his hands and his feet, causing them to continually thicken and somewhat distort his already unique oversized proportions, known as some circles as "giantism." He would start aging extremely fast at this point. And it was doubtful he'd ever see his 50th birthday. Although the most famous, Andre was not the first wrestling attraction to suffer this fate. The famed French Angel (Maurice Tillet), who was much shorter, had the big hands and huge, misproportioned face perhaps even more than Andre. Although he was never any kind of a worker, Angel was a major box office attraction, and also died at a relatively young age.

In his youth, the size and power from the acromegaly made Andre one of the biggest and, in some ways, one of most powerful men in the world. The upside was that wherever he went, he was always the center of attention and loaded with friends and hangers-on. The downside was that this would all be short-lived and the long-term results would be as the years go by, almost grotesque physical features, tremendous physical pain from joints having to carry around so much weight, a depressing rapidity in the aging process and ultimately a shortened life span. When he was in pain, the same public was still mesmerized by his transforming look. In many ways, Andre was luckier than most with the same disease because he was able to live life to its fullest during his short period as a veritable superman among men. He saw the world, earned tons of money, was recognized everywhere, loved and admired by millions, and in his passions, eating and drinking, he was able to consume more than just about anyone he came in contact with. In the world he lived, pro wrestling, a world filled with tough guys, the youthful Andre the Giant was respected not only because he was an amazing athlete for his size, and also because it was well-known in the business that "you don't f--- with The Giant." It's really hard to say just how strong he was or just how tough he was. He was almost never really challenged. But certainly when he first hit his stride in North America around 1973, just from the looks of things, he may very well have been the most physically intimidating man around. Almost from the start in the United States, he became the most famous figure, the most popular figure and biggest drawing card in the game, going from territory-to-territory around the world.

Andre left Europe in late 1970 to live in Montreal. Later he moved to a 200-acre estate in Ellerbe, N.C. where he raised longhorn sheep and quarterhorses. He lived on his farm for the remainder of his life. He received word on January 9 that his father, Boris Rousimoff, who was in his early 80s., was on his deathbed. Andre flew home to France two days later, and on January 15, his father passed away. Andre had decided to remain with his family for two more weeks, before he was scheduled to return home. He went to sleep on Wednesday night and when his chauffeur showed up Thursday morning, Andre never answered the phone in his hotel room. Finally the staff broke down the door and found him dead. No autopsy was performed so there is no official cause of death, but it is believed he went to sleep and never woke up, dying of heart failure. Andre had requested being cremated 48 hours after his death, but as of Tuesday, this hadn't occurred because they couldn't find a place in France that could accommodate someone of such size. Lawyers are currently working on getting that taken care of. His ashes, by his request, are to be scattered on his farm, where a memorial service will be held. The service has not been confirmed, but they are looking at around Feb. 16.

Andre was from a family of five, two brothers and two sisters. His father was 6-foot-2, his mother 5-2. The remaining siblings were all normal size. Legend has it that Andre inherited his size from his grandfather, who died before Andre was born, but reputedly was 7-foot-8 and more than 500 pounds. Of course, like many of the tall stories surrounding the most physically imposing man on the planet who was prime subject material for a world of tall-story tellers, it's hard to know where truth ends and fiction begins.

Many men claim to have started Andre in wrestling, to have first discovered him in France, to have talked him into entering pro wrestling, to have brought him to the United States, etc. His beginnings are somewhat mired in mystery. Already 6-foot-3, Andre left home at the age of 12. Because of his size, he tried rugby, soccer and even a little boxing, before falling in with a crowd of wrestlers. His first pro match was in France in late 1964, at the age of 18. At the time, he was about 6-foot-7 and 245 pounds, certainly a huge man for his age, but nothing out of the ordinary. How big he wound up itself will forever be part of the legend of Andre the Giant.

Andre will forever be known as being 7-foot-4 and 520 pounds. His size and his legend may even grow bigger as the years go on. At times, particularly in his later years, that weight figure was probably accurate. Some say his weight was in excess of 550 pounds at the time of his death. He was not 7-foot-4, or even close to that height. The 7-4 figure, created when he first came to Montreal in late 1970, was probably because the most famous tall athlete in the world at the time, basketball superstar Lew Alcindor (who became more famous as Kareem Abdul-Jabbar), was 7-2 and promoters wanted to bill him as the tallest and largest athlete in the world. At his tallest, he was probably around 6-10, maybe he could have been 6-11 before he ever made his mark in North America. Basketball players who met him generally estimated his height at around 6-9, although he was proportioned completely different than any 6-9 man around with relatively short legs, a long torso and huge head, their estimates could have been deceptive. In a photo with 7-2 Wilt Chamberlain and Arnold Schwarzeneggar taken when both were in Mexico City around 1984, Wilt appeared to have Andre by about three inches, although Wilt was bare-footed in the photo while Andre was wearing thick heels. Arnold looked like a small midget in between them, although Andre appeared to have basketball's goliath by about 150 pounds. In the mid-70s, Andre appeared in a TV series called "The Six Million Dollar Man," playing the character "Bigfoot." Later that season, "Bigfoot" was brought back for a return bout with Steve Austin, the hero character played by Lee Majors in what was at the time one of the most popular shows on television. The second "Bigfoot" was the late actor Ted Cassidy, who was always billed at being 6-9. Cassidy was most well-known for his role as Lurch on the Adams Family television show in the 60s. Comparing the two episodes it was obvious Lurch was taller than Andre. In 1976, when Andre had his famous boxer vs. wrestler match at Shea Stadium against Chuck Wepner on the undercard of the Muhammad Ali vs. Antonio Inoki fiasco, legitimate sportswriters who took notice of Andre for the first time estimated him at 6-9, 370. However, later in his career, Andre posed in numerous photographs with Shohei "Giant" Baba, and he appeared to be around an inch or two taller than the 6-foot-8 Japanese giant. Those photos were taken in his later years, after gravity had taken its toll on his aching spine and lower back. It would probably be fair to say his size was his gimmick, the reason for his popularity and his drawing power. Yet, there have been a few wrestlers who were legitimately taller, yet to this point, none ever even made a mark in the business. There were a few who were heavier, some of whom, the original Haystacks Calhoun comes to mind, turned out to be genuine attractions, but certainly nothing comparable to Andre.

In the mid-60s, when Andre "The Butcher" Rousimoff started wrestling in France, there was no such thing as international news or communication. He actually wrestled for about six years before all but the most ardent wrestling fans and promoters in North America were even aware he existed. Although legend may have that differently as well. Frank Valois, who was Andre's best friend and business manager during his wrestling barnstorming heyday, said that he first met Andre in 1966 while he was wrestling as a headliner in France and brought him to England and Germany with him the next year before bringing him to Montreal in 1971. Edouardo Carpentier was always given credit for discovering Andre as part of the first legendary "worked" story introducing him to fans in Montreal. Carpentier claimed Andre approached him in France in 1964 and Carpentier saw to it that he got started in the business. Carpentier claimed that he went back to France in 1969 and set up bringing Andre to North America. Carpentier claimed he told Valois about Andre after the 1969 meeting, at a time when Andre was already a well-known name in Europe and put the two of them together.

In Japan, the story was always that Isao Yoshihara, the president of the International Wrestling Enterprises, at the time the distant No. 2 promotion in a two-party Japanese wrestling world, was in Europe scouting talent for his annual Grand Prix tournament. Yoshihara had "discovered" other European attractions and gotten them their first notice in the Western World, most notable of which was Billy Robinson a few years earlier. Billed as the 7-foot-tall Monster Rousimoff, Andre debuted in Japan for the IWE on January 3, 1970 as part of a six-week tour which included Michael Nador, a European star, and Jim Shields, an AWA wrestler known in the U.S. as Bull Bullinski. In early February, during the final week of the tour, Verne Gagne, who supplied the IWE with talent, arrived in Japan to defend his AWA title against the IWE's top star, Shozo Kobayashi. Gagne got his first glimpse of Monster Rousimoff, and immediately saw the dollar signs, but not where you'd think. Verne talked with young Andre, who was at the time a physical specimen at 335 pounds, and wanted to turn him into a boxer, figuring the boxing world was at the time desperately in search of a white heavyweight title contender, and a white giant would be that much the better at the box office. Boxing fans could be just as much marks for size as wrestling fans, witness Primo Carnera. Andre didn't take Verne's advice, but in Japan the story was Verne was the first American promoter to find out about Andre, and then sent him to Montreal to live, since at the time he only spoke French, and brought him in a few times as an undercard attraction for major shows.

But that story may not have been true either. Andre, as Monster Eiffel Tower, had already appeared in New Zealand and did great guns as an attraction there in 1969. By early 1971, American wrestling magazines started showing pictures of this "7-foot-4, 385 pound" superman, who in Montreal was given the ring name Jean Ferre, the always-smiling giant, with little bodyfat, who could do dropkicks. He went back to the IWE in Japan from March to May of 1971 for the annual Grand Prix tournament which included such luminaries as Billy Robinson, Karl Gotch and Don Leo Jonathan. Rousimoff had a draw with Robinson and wins over Gotch and Jonathan to send him into the finals against Kobayashi. The Gotch match is remembered to this day in Japan, because there was a ref bump, and Gotch picked Rousimoff up in a perfect german suplex but there was no ref to count the fall. Andre came back to attack Gotch from behind and score the pin to get him into the championship match. Kobayashi won the two out of three fall match, via count out in the third fall.

Jean Ferre, who was billed upon arrival as "The Eighth Wonder of the World," was an immediate sensation in Montreal. He arrived with the famous Paul Bunyan-like storyline. Carpentier, whose real name was Ed Wiecz but took the name Carpentier after a famous French boxing contender and became in the 50s the biggest draw in wrestling-mad Montreal, introduced him to the new world. Carpentier said he was driving around in the French Alps when a huge redwood tree had fallen in the road. Carpentier, who although only 5-7, was one of the most muscular men of his era, said he tried in vain, but couldn't even budge the tree. Suddenly out of the woods came the biggest man he had ever seen, who lifted up the redwood tree as if it were a twig and Carpentier befriended him and brought him to Montreal to become a wrestler. The young Giant got over fast as Carpentier's big buddy, and started making big money and living life like there was no tomorrow. Carpentier, now 67 and still living in Montreal, remembered when he first made it big.

"Andre was really living fast," Carpentier said in an interview with the Montreal Gazette. "As soon as he started making money, he bought a big white cadillac and drove it all over town. He'd have a stogie (cigar) in his mouth and had women draped all over him. I used to worry about him living so fast but I guess he felt he didn't have a long time to live so he had to make the most of it."

Jean Ferre was usually booked in handicap matches against two men, or in 3-on-2 matches teaming up with Carpentier, who was the most popular wrestler in Montreal. He occasional singles matches were limited to the huge heels of the time, which in the Montreal territory were either Killer Kowalski or Don Leo Jonathan. Photos of this huge newcomer who made the giant Kowalski look like a skinny midget hit all the wrestling magazines. News of his box office potential started leaking to the United States promoters when Ferre was booked in his first main event, billed as "The Match of the Century" in the Montreal Forum against Jonathan. The Battle of the Giants with Andre (billed as 7-4, 385) against Jonathan (billed as 6-9, 320, although he was legitimately closer to 6-5 and 285 at the time) set Canada's indoor wrestling attendance and gate mark with more than 20,000 fans selling out the Forum. Officially, the always-smiling Ferre "lost his temper" for the first time in that match, and was disqualified with every wrestler on the undercard trying in vain for moments to pull his huge hands off Ferre's throat, with one swat of the huge paw sending one big wrestler after another flying. The idea was set in stone. He's the nicest guy in the world, but if you get him mad, there is nobody or nothing that can physically stop him. During that time period Ferre worked some big-card matches as a special attraction on major AWA spectaculars, which was actually his first foray into the United States.

Jonathan, real name Don Heaton, now 61 and living in Delta, British Columbia, was known at the time as the most agile big man in the game. "What I remember most about wrestling Jean (Andre) was how far it was to the canvas when I was over his head. He was so big and so tall, it was nearly impossible to get the leverage you needed to get him off the ground. We met maybe 20 times during our career. We had some awfully hard matches over the years, but I never lost respect for him. I remember Jean with much fondness. I knew him fairly well in the early years, and we came to travel together in Montreal, Texas, Europe and Japan. I'm really, deeply sorry that I haven't had the time in recent years to speak with him. I always wanted to tell him that I considered him a friend, but you know, you're always a day late."

Just before his first meeting with Vince McMahon Sr. and being christened Andre the Giant, Jean Ferre was given a shot at headlining a few AWA towns in singles matches against that territory's top heel, the ever colorful and controversial Superstar Billy Graham.

"I was probably the first person he ever let take him off his feet," remembered Graham about their early meetings. "At the time, nobody ever took him off his feet. It wasn't a planned spot, either. I was holding him in a bearhug and he said, `lift me up and take me over to the ropes.' I told him, `I can't do that.' He just told me to do it. I was amazed at the time he let me do it. He was a real nice person in that if he liked you, he'd let you do things with him in the ring. I don't believe there was ever anyone in wrestling who could impress you as much by looking at him like Andre the Giant in his prime. He was a super athlete, for his size, when he was still able to move. For a man that huge, he was a little clumsy, but he was light on his feet. And he was a great worker in that he never hurt anyone. You'd never hear of anyone getting an injury against Andre. He'd throw that big punch with that big paw and never threw a potato. His hand was so big but you'd never feel it."

The name Andre the Giant was born in 1973. The Montreal territory, which had been going great guns behind Ferre, had started to falter because fans didn't believe there was anyone who stood a chance against him. The promoters knew they had to get him out of the territory because no heel could get any serious heat, because he was so physically impressive nobody was even perceived as a threat to him. But his gimmick drawing power was gone because everyone had seen him for a few years week-after-week. Frank Valois, a wrestler who had been a major star in France during the 60s, became Andre's caretaker, taking care of everything for him. Valois represented Andre and set up a meeting with Vince McMahon Sr. McMahon Sr. changed his name from Jean Ferre to Andre the Giant, debuted him in Madison Square Garden where he became an immediate sensation, and realizing the mistakes that had been made in booking him in Montreal because of overexposure, sent him on the road around the world doing one-night stands working every territory that was affiliated with the NWA, WWWF and AWA, which in those days meant just about everywhere, and not only in North America. McMahon Sr. booked The Giant during the days when all the major promoters cooperated with one another, and Andre toured the world, staying a week or two in each territory until the wrestling war broke out in 1984 and Vince McMahon Jr. no longer allowed Andre to work for any other promotion aside from his New Japan tours. Andre, on his first go around, was billed as 7-4, 424 pounds of solid muscle and before he'd hit a territory, the promoters would air a photo of him with his long arms outstretched with two women wrestlers apparently sitting down in each arm, to give the illusion that with his arms outstretched he was easily holding up about 300 pounds of weight in each arm. Of course the photo was gimmicked in that the weight of the four wrestlers wasn't really totally supported by Andre's two arms. As if his size needed any illusion added to it, often the announcers would sit down while interviewing him with only a shot from the chest up which made him appear to be eight-feet-tall. All this illusion would have worked once in every territory, if there was nothing to the live package.

"People went to see him originally as a novelty," said Valois, now 71 and living in St. Marguerite, Quebec. "But after seeing him, they recognized he wasn't a one-night stand."

But by the time he hit New York, and then the rest of the United States, the dropkicks and the like went out the window. "I remember being amazed at seeing a man that big do a dropkick," noted Wladek (Walter) "Killer" Kowalski, one of Andre's first major opponents in Quebec. "But when he moved to the WWWF they told him, `We only want you to be a big hulking monster who goes into the ring and destroys people.'"

Actually, Andre's life was a series of one-night stands as promoters couldn't get enough of him. His first go-around the territories in 1973-74 as the ever-smiling Giant saw him break attendance records throughout the country. He was generally booked in handicap matches and Battle Royals and kept away from the top heels so as not to damage the territory for the long-term. In most cases, his opponent in the handicap matches would be Valois, his manager, who would call the match, and a local small preliminary wrestler who would take all the bumps. In the Battle Royals, which at the time were the biggest drawing gimmick match, he more often than not was put over. When Eddie Einhorn in the mid-70s challenged the entire wrestling establishment with his ill-fated IWA, Andre was booked in whatever town the IWA would run so the established NWA or WWWF promotion could run head-to-head and keep the IWA from getting a foothold. He was the most in-demand wrestler in the world. Every promoter booking a major event wanted Andre in as the so-called French dressing. The Guiness Book of World's Records used to list Andre as the highest paid wrestler ever with documented earnings of $400,000 in 1974. In later years, when Andre spent more time working the major Northeastern arenas, his income probably topped the $500,000 mark and he certainly earned more than that during the mid-80s when Titan Sports went national. Sam Muchnick, then president of the NWA said that Andre, Buddy Rogers and Jim Londos were the three biggest drawing cards in wrestling history.

"He was like a big, loveable baby," Valois recalls of his days barnstorming with The Giant. "I used to treat him as a son and he used to treat me as his father." Barnstorming wasn't even the word, as Valois recalls days where he had to get The Giant to a Saturday afternoon booking in Sydney, Australia and then to a Sunday, afternoon booking in Toronto. While it wasn't always like that, life was hectic and Valois' main job was to make sure Andre made the arenas, even when it took chartering flights to get there.

Somewhere along the line, the ever-smiling giant also became the undefeated giant. Wrestling legend has it that he was never pinned until that fateful Pontiac Silverdome match with Hulk Hogan. While not entirely accurate, Andre did exceedingly few jobs during his career. He certainly lost a few during his early years in Europe, since in the early days he was a big, but not monstrous, young, green guy. Kowalski and Jonathan scored gimmicked wins in backwater Quebec towns as part of programs to build up returns. Kobayashi and Jerry Lawler scored count out wins during the 70s. Antonio Inoki and Seiji Sakaguchi pinned Andre in Japan in 1974 during his first tenure as a monster heel for New Japan, a totally different role than in the U.S. but one where he was every bit as much of a sensation in. Inoki probably pinned him on at least a second occasion as well. Valois and later Arnold Skoaland, who became Andre's caretaker and business manager after Valois left the road, took care of Andre in Japan and worked at ringside as heel managers for his matches against Inoki and company. The Sheik, when he never lost in Detroit and Toronto, beat Andre in blow-off matches in feuds during his early touring days, although obviously the finishes were heavily gimmicked. Harley Race may have pinned him for single falls in best-of-three fall matches when Race was NWA champion. I believe it happened once in Houston, if not again. Stan Hansen beat him via count out in a New Japan tournament in the late 1970s. Canek pinned Andre after a bodyslam in a famous match at El Toreo bullring for the UWA title match somewhere between 1982 and 1984. Inoki had a famous submission victory over Andre in June of 1986 with an armlock during Andre's final tour with New Japan. There was the famous Hogan match at the Silverdome. He also put over Otto Wanz in Graz, Austria, although that may have been via count out. The only other jobs Andre did were probably a few dozen less than one minute jobs to the Ultimate Warrior in late 1989, during Andre's final go-around as a main eventer for the WWF.

As the years went by, people no longer wanted to see Andre laugh through comedy matches with undercard wrestlers and he'd start going into territories and face the top heels. His best drawing matches would be against men who were at least close to his size, with famous feuds with the likes of Big John Studd, Hulk Hogan (when Hogan was a heel not only in his first WWF tour but even earlier in Alabama and Georgia as Terry Boulder and Sterling Golden), Blackjack Mulligan, Killer Khan, Bruiser Brody, Superstar Billy Graham and perhaps his biggest opponent during the 1970s, Ernie Ladd, a 6-9, 320 pound former all-pro football lineman whom he drew many big gates against in Battles of the Giants. Ironically, because Ladd had achieved so much fame in football before wrestling as his real height of 6-9 was known, promoters never tried to exaggerate his height as would have normally been the case in those days. It was funny, because Andre at the time was billed as 7-5, yet the two were roughly the same height. Some wrestlers have said Ladd was actually a shade taller.

In the late 1970s, Valois went back home and Frenchy Bernard, a former referee out of Florida, became Andre's road mate and lived with him until the time of his death. Valois still received a check from the New York office until Sr. passed the torch to Jr. in 1984, at which point he was cut off and lost touch with Andre.

"I never took it personally," Valois said. "He was such a huge attraction at the time. He was a great friend. I lost touch with him in 1985 or 1986. We never had a falling out. Life just took us in different directions."

Within wrestling, stories of Andre are legion. While there are stories of his awesome presence and strength when he was still in his 20s, before the disease that made him famous turned on him, the most famous stories are eating and drinking stories. There would be fighting stories as well, but Andre got into such few fights that the stories were more like a fight about to break out, Andre showed up, and the fight ended before the first punch was thrown, so Andre stories mainly revolved around drinking. A rare fighting story came out of South Africa, where the country's most popular wrestler, Jan Wilkens (who naturally doubled as the promoter), who held that country's version of the world title for most of the 70s, apparently wanted to embarrass Andre to build his own reputation, or perhaps believed in his own self-created hype. The story has it that Andre threw once punch, and Wilkens woke up three days later. Another story was out of Los Angeles, when Andre had a match against "The Monster," a guy named Tony Hernandez who dressed up in a Frankenstein outfit with huge boots to make him look about 6-7 and doing an indestructible gimmick. Apparently Andre wanted to unmask him, not realizing the promotion had billed the man as a Frankenstein built in a laboratory rather than as a masked man, and the guy fought for all he was worth to avoid it because it would kill the gimmick, and wound up getting way on the short end of that stick. Some of the stories are no doubt exaggerated, but legendary just the same.

Andre was legendary among wrestlers for his capacity to drink. Stories of him drinking 50 beers and not having a buzz are legendary. How exaggerated they are is another story. One of the most famous stories was of him drinking 119 bottles of beer at one sitting and passing out in a hotel lobby. Since he was so huge, nobody could move him. They simply put a piano cover over him and let him sleep it off and acted like it was covering a large piece of furniture. There are dozens of stories just like them. Wrestlers joke about being out in bars in the mid-70s with Andre, and some local wanted to provoke a fight with the "normal sized" wrestlers to prove how tough he was or that they were fakes, and they'd laugh about it and signal for Andre, and the locals' face would turn eight shades of albino and he'd high-tail out of the pub. McMahon Sr. built a special trailer so Andre would be comfortable as he was driven from town-to-town, and always kept it stocked full so Andre could pass the time with his favorite pastime. Andre was a notorious eater with stories of him going into restaurants and ordering everything on the menu. There were also legendary stories about Andre's strength. Andre never lifted a weight, but he had the thickest bone structure and largest in condition torso that anyone had ever laid eyes on. With his big butt and huge legs, he looked physically like he could squat a ton. Andre was invited to the World's Strongest Man contest when CBS-TV sponsored the event, but declined and wrestling sent names like Billy Graham, Ken Patera, Ivan Putski and Jerry Blackwell (the latter as a practical joke by Patera) to compete. Stories of Andre being able to pick up and move big cars in his youth are legendary. But how strong was he really?

"When it comes to pulling power, he was enormously strong," remembered Graham. "Pushing power, he was nothing exceptional. Anything having to do with a pulling motion like pulling you around the ring, he could pull anything with the greatest of ease. Pushing he wasn't that strong, like in doing something like pressing guys overhead or something that would be like a bench press or military press motion."

As the years went by, Andre got older, and heavier. For a while he was billed as 7-5, but 7-4 become much more famous and a little less of an exaggeration. The weight went to 445, 485 and passed the 500 pound mark. At this point he was far from being solid muscle. Many have said that if Andre had taken care of himself physically, had gone to the gym, had drank less, that he could have been the most awesome specimen ever. But it never seemed to interest him, and really his fate was sealed at the time he was born anyway. As the years went by, the ever-smiling giant smiled less and less. Perhaps it was the pain of his incredible body turning against him. Perhaps it was the pain of the realization of his own inevitability.

"I remember the quantity he could drink," remembered Kowalski in an interview with the Montreal Gazette. "He used to drink to numb himself from the reality that he wouldn't live long in this world."

"I wrestled a lot of years for a lot of different promotions," remembered one of his most frequent foes, Big John Studd (John Minton), now 44, an interview with the Pittsburgh Post-Gazette. "Everywhere I went, everyone was glad to see Andre come. They knew the arenas would be full. I look around my house right now and I see a lot of things I wouldn't have if it wasn't for Andre the Giant.

This is a hard death for me. I had a lot of respect for Andre. This is a real loss, although I expected it because of his disease.

Andre was a real loner. The last time I saw him he was an angry man. I'd like to think the real Andre was the character he played in `The Princess Bride'--a nice, big gentle guy."

In the 1970s, when wrestlers never received any mainstream publicity--it was almost like there was a law against it--Andre was the lone exception. He appeared on the Tonight show and compared hand size with Joey Bishop, he did the Six Million Dollar Man, and had a lengthy feature article in Sports Illustrated about him. In 1974, many newspapers around the country aired photos of Andre talking about him getting a tryout with the NFL's Washington Redskins. Andre never took the tryout, which was mainly a publicity stunt, with the story being that he asked the Redskins for the same $400,000 he was earning as a wrestler which was almost unheard of in those days for an NFL player. When he first arrived in Quebec, the Montreal Alouettes had similar ideas about trying to make him a football player.

Around 1982, Hulk Hogan caught fire in Minneapolis and Japan and surpassed Andre as the leading draw in the business, and two years later took Andre's spot as the most popular and most famous wrestler on an international basis.

The first chink in the invincible armor came in 1981 when he woke up one day, got out of bed, and collapsed on the floor. His ankle had been badly broken. It was attributed to a match with Killer Khan, real name Masashi Ozawa, a 6-4, 280 pound Japanese star billed as the Mongolian giant, whose feud with Andre in 1981 after the legitimate injury was his main claim to fame in wrestling. Andre was already closing in on the 500 pound mark by this point. While his mobility was limited because of the weight, he still had enough left to have numerous genuinely exciting matches with Khan. Andre's peak as a worker was probably the late 70s, when he had picked up the ring psychology, his weight hadn't gotten too far out of control although he was no longer a physical specimen, and he still had his mobility and stamina. He had good matches in the United States, at least for what he was, even doing occasional 60:00 draws against Nick Bockwinkel and Race, but he excelled as a monster heel while in Japan. Perhaps his most entertaining matches were his cat-and-mouse encounters with the much smaller but gifted Tatsumi Fujinami, then a junior heavyweight champion, who worked a believable series of spots with Andre before finally getting caught and squashed at the end. Andre even let Fujinami, barely 200 pounds at the time, slam him.

Andre the Giant and Hulk Hogan wrestled for the first time around 1978 in Dothan, AL at the Houston Farm Center. Hogan was the newest big guy who could presumably be built into an attraction to give Andre a new opponent. Two years later, Andre participated in the angle which made Hogan a national star. On a WWF taping, Hogan, then a heel managed by Freddie Blassie, loaded his armpad and busted Andre's head with a lariat and left him laying. Just before the finish, Hogan lifted Andre up for a bodyslam. While Andre had been slammed before, surely no slam in the United States at least up to that point had been seen by so many people. Andre and Hogan took their feud to all the major arenas, and not just in the old WWF territory, but across the United States and Canada and into Japan. The first Andre-Hogan match in New York was at Shea Stadium on August 9, 1980, underneath the Bruno Sammartino vs. Larry Zbyszko cage match main event, which drew 35,771 paid and a then-record $541,730.

Unfortunately, Andre's most famous matches were also among his worst. The two Hogan matches, one setting the PPV and attendance record, and the other on NBC, both came when he was long past his physical prime and badly crippled from injuries. His matches with the likes of Warrior and Studd were even worse, since neither were Hogan's calibre when it came to charisma in hiding that Andre wasn't moving, or in working ability at carrying him. Few of his main events from the 70s in the U.S. were ever videotaped. With the exception of the Hogan matches, perhaps the most famous match of his career was in many ways one of the strangest matches ever. And could have been the most dangerous.

In April of 1986, Andre got into the ring with Akira Maeda. The circumstances behind what happened were never explained. Maeda was one of the leading stars for the first UWF in Japan in 1984-85, which worked matches in a so-called "shooting-style" and many of its wrestlers, particularly Maeda, decried pro wrestling for not being true sport and Maeda in his youth often had outbursts at fans, wrestlers and reporters regarding such a thing. The first UWF went out of business at the end of 1985, and Maeda, who was first trained in New Japan, was invited back to the fold. Apparently swallowing his pride because he needed to work and it was the only way to remain in the business, Maeda agreed, and actually turned into a phenomenal worker combing his submission style (which was the catalyst in changing the entire work style of Japanese wrestlers) moves with some pro spots. Maeda never did a job in the New Japan rings except to Yoshiaki Fujiwara, which was okay since Maeda acknowledged Fujiwara as a true wrestler. Maeda's statements about wrestling and American wrestlers in general often led to a lack of cooperation in those matches. It was well-known in those days that Maeda's matches would be phenomenal against the Japanese, but largely nothing with Americans. The two got into the ring and whatever spirit of cooperation he had with other Americans wasn't even there. Andre never sold any of Maeda's submissions, and was almost mocking his shooter gimmick. It appeared Andre kept going for Maeda's eyes, which would be scary when someone of that size makes a move in that direction. Soon, all cooperation was gone and the match had fallen apart and nearly turned into a real fight. Andre, as immobile as he was by this time, was still more than 500 pounds. Maeda started getting into a fighting stance and throwing wicked kicks at Andre's knee time after time. Andre just stood there, acting like he didn't feel a thing, and maybe he didn't. The few times Maeda got closer and went for a single-leg, Andre's lack of balance was evident as he went down easily like a redwood tree that had just been chopped through. Maeda never jumped on him, because strategically, if Andre snatched him, the size difference could prove embarrassing to the self-proclaimed super shooter. Andre would get to his feet, Maeda would kick the knee, go for the single-leg and Andre would go down. Andre, who wasn't in any kind of condition by this time in his career, after a few series, just decided to stay down and dare Maeda to jump on him. At this point Maeda asked one of the older wrestlers if he had permission to finish Andre off, but the wrestler shook his head no. Antonio Inoki, the promoter, finally jumped into the ring with no explanation and they broke the match up without an ending. Andre was furious and screamed to Frenchy Bernard, his traveling companion and the referee of the match, that he wanted Maeda back in the ring. Maeda threw his best kick of all after being ordered out, only the opponent was the guard rail.

Just a few weeks earlier, Andre won the most famous Battle Royal of his career, at Wrestlemania II in Chicago, a match which included a half-dozen NFL football players including William "Refrigerator" Perry, who was coming off a season where he was the most popular player in the league. Andre got some wire service coverage again because being around the 500 pound mark, he dwarfed the 6-3, 330 pound Fridge. Because the football players weren't workers, they did a dress rehearsal a few days earlier in secret. A few of the wrestlers and footballers were travelling back from the rehearsal when one of the football players, Ernie Holmes, a former all-pro with the Pittsburgh Steelers, was bragging about how tough he was. Everyone was getting tired of it but nobody said anything until suddenly Andre blurted out in that guttural voice, "You talk too much, you know what I mean" and Holmes didn't say another word the rest of the trip as apparently one of the wrestlers whispered to Holmes that you don't know what tough is until you get this guy mad.

It was hardly a stroke of genius to turn Andre heel and have him feud with Hogan, which led to Wrestlemania III. Andre had been a heel for 14 years in Japan. He knew what to do and when to do it as a heel, probably better than in his more familiar U.S. role as a face. He looked the part as well. Unfortunately, by the time his biggest money run was about to start, his physical condition had already badly deteriorated.

Andre's last run as a babyface came under a hood as Giant Machine. About one year earlier in Japan, as a gimmick that was largely decried and considered unsuccessful, manager Ichimasa Wakamatsu brought in Andre as The Giant Machine and teamed him with Super Machine (Bill Eadie) and Strong Machine (Junji Hirata, who still uses that name in New Japan) as the Machine Gun Army. Titan ran an angle where Andre was unjustly suspended by Jack Tunney, and he came back as Giant Machine, teaming with Super Machine against long-time nemesis Studd and massive King Kong Bundy (Chris Pallies, a 6-3, 440 pounder who once headlined a Wrestlemania against Hogan and retired in the mid-80s). Unlike most angles involving Andre, this one was not a success, and he quickly disappeared from the scene and headed to England to make "The Princess Bride," a movie where he played a loveable giant and got rave reviews. This led to a few commercials, most notably for Honeycombs cereal.

Andre's back and spine were already giving him major problems by this time. He walked with a major stoop and his long-time smiling face had a hard time making the smile. He became reclusive and was largely introverted except around his trusted friends, who were mainly wrestlers. In late 1986, Andre underwent major back surgery while in England. Because of his immense proportions, the operating crew had to build customized surgical equipment for the operation.

Andre went heel in January of 1987, leading to the most successful wrestling show of all-time. Nearly every wrestling attendance and gate record was shattered for the "first" Hogan-Andre match (Titan went to the extent of actually denying they had ever wrestled previously, let alone had a big money feud which spanned many territories). The Silverdome sold out two weeks in advance and it's no exaggeration to believe that if the building had been large enough, they could have put 125,000 people in the Silverdome that day. By this time, his physical condition was all but gone. Andre, who wore a backbrace underneath his long wrestling tights into the ring, was almost completely immobile. Legend has it that he had total numbness from his knees down when he was in the ring. He was largely kept out of the ring until the rematch on NBC, where he won the WWF title from Hogan with the famous twin Hebner referee finish and he immediately made the famed faux paus of selling "the world tag team title" to Ted DiBiase. He went back on the road working programs as a heel against Studd, Jake Roberts (where he faked a heart attack from fright the snake) and Ultimate Warrior (where he did the bulk of the total number of jobs of his entire career) and in his last run as a heel, held the tag team title with King Haku, winning and losing the titles to Demolition. He did very little walking by this point, except when in front of a crowd. Backstage he spent all his time sitting. He was often wheeled to and from his hotel to the car that would take him to the arenas. While in the ring he usually held onto the ropes to keep his balance. Andre disappeared again at that point.

He returned as a babyface and did his final U.S. angle being attacked from behind by Earthquake, since he was legitimately going to undergo knee surgery and this would be the wrestling cover reason. However, Andre never returned for his expected series with Earthquake. The closest he got was an appearance at Summer Slam where he came out as a cripple and the Legion of Doom kept Earthquake and Typhoon from attacking him so set up their tag program. He only made one more appearance on U.S. television, this past September in Atlanta for the 20th anniversary Clash of the Champions on TBS, walking with two canes.

In 1990, Seiji Sakaguchi and Giant Baba had a meeting. It's a famous story in that it marked two competing promotions, one asking its competition to use a major drawing card because they had so much respect for what the man had accomplished. Andre stopped touring for New Japan in 1986. The final submission job for Inoki was well-known as his last stand as athletically he just wasn't viable for a company so athletically based. Since Andre was able to earn so much money working for Titan over the next few years, there were apparently no significant inquiries back and forth about Andre returning. With Andre's career in the U.S. just about over, Sakaguchi asked Baba to bring Andre back to Japan. He'd always be able to draw money, but New Japan worked a very serious style and he had no place. All Japan always booked one pure comedy match per show, largely to give Baba a place on the tour, and the idea of Baba & Andre as a tag team would be a nice touch. Andre toured for All Japan three times per year from September 1990 until his final tour at the end of 1992. It was not a pretty sight. Each tour he grew progressively worse. However, out of loyalty, probably more than anything since his shows were doing sellout business without Andre and Andre's price tag (probably in the $15,000 per week range) was no doubt the heftiest ever for a wrestler working in the third match on a card, Baba continued to book him. This past year Baba didn't even put him as his partner in the tag team tournament as he had done in years past. Andre's last big match would have been the All Japan legends match on October 21, 1992 at Budokan Hall, teaming with Jumbo Tsuruta and Terry Gordy to beat Dory Funk and Baba and Hansen. The final match of his career came December 4 in the same building, teaming with Baba and Rusher Kimura against Haruka Eigen & Motoshi Okuma & Masa Fuchi. Ironically, Okuma also passed away less than a month later.

Andre never married. He was engaged once in the 70s, but reportedly got cold feet. He had one daughter, now 13, although he only saw her once or twice.

The World Wrestling Federation, at its cards over this past weekend and later on 2/1 on the USA network's Monday Night Raw announced the death of Andre and gave him a ten-bell salute. Fans chanted his name after it was over in some of the cities. All Japan, on its Sunday show in Tokyo's Korakuen Hall, did a similar ceremony.

Andre's death received major news coverage in Montreal, where it ran on page one of the newspaper, and the AP story hit many newspapers throughout the United States. Both CNN and ESPN covered it as part of their sportscast, as did many local news shows on Friday night. All the Japanese sports papers ran major stories as did many newspapers throughout Europe and Australia. Ironically, even though Andre did the bulk of his wrestling in the United States, his death received far more coverage internationally.

The Canadian Wire Services, which sent a far more in-depth story than the U.S. services, reported that there was an incredible demand for information regarding the life and death of Andre, with the biggest demand coming out of Europe.

Everyone that ever saw Andre the Giant will never forget him. He had that unique look and that unique presence. Probably everyone reading this, particularly those who saw him in the 1970s, can vividly remember the first time they saw him live. It's a moment you don't forget. Anyone who ever shook that gigantic hand will never forget it. Even the largest men in the world felt small in the grasp of the monster hand. Those memories only made the sight of him toward the end of his career that much sadder. But it can't be denied that Andre made his mark in his profession in a way that only a handful will ever be able to.

Thanks to Dave Stebbs/Montreal Gazette and Mark Madden/Pittsburgh Post-Gazette for help on this story

FEBRUARY 15

Andre the Giant update: Andre the Giant's body was flown to the United States from France this past week as they couldn't find a crematory that could handle a body so large. On Monday, his body was in Atlanta and was going to be transported to Ellerbe, NC and it was expected he'd be cremated, as per his wishes, on 2/9. A Memorial Service for Andre will be held on 2/24 at his 200-acre ranch on Highway 73 in Ellerbe, NC. News of Andre's death was heavily publicized in Mexico, and a moment of silence was held at the UWA's 18th anniversary show on 1/31 at El Toreo in Naucalpan. New Japan Pro Wrestling also rang the bell ten times in Andre's memory at its first show of the new tour on 2/1 in Tokyo with Antonio Inoki making a surprise appearance at the show holding up Andre's photo with Seiji Sakaguchi (Inoki and Sakaguchi are two of the very select group of wrestlers Andre ever cleanly put over). All Japan held a similar ceremony the previous day at its Tokyo show. News of Andre's death was covered prominently in every newspaper in Japan. Many U.S. newspapers reported a short wire story. Even the New York Times, which almost never acknowledges the existence of pro wrestling, and Sports Illustrated ran obit pieces. Ironically, both pieces gave as much ink to his role in the movie The Princess Bride as it did to his entire wrestling career. The Montreal Gazette, which ran the most lengthy mainstream obit, ran another article this past weekend from the referee of the 1972 Andre vs. Don Leo Jonathan match at the Montreal Forum talking about his memories of that match and of Andre in general. Frank Deford was scheduled to do a commentary on Andre this week on his Public Radio show. With the exception of the Miami Herald, every mainstream source used Andre's gimmicked height of 7-4. Award for best exaggeration goes to the Winnipeg Sun, which billed him at 7-4, 700 pounds. Weekly Pro Wrestling in Japan ran five pages of photos including showing him in January 1970 and May 1971 (in a photo with Karl Gotch and Billy Robinson where he really doesn't look all that much larger than Gotch) and shots vs. Chuck Wepner (1976), with Rene Goulet (winning New Japan's 1981 tag team tournament), vs. Inoki and Stan Hansen in his working prime of the late 70s and post-prime stints as Giant Machine, Inoki's partner and as Baba's partner. Andre looked barely 300 pounds in May of 1971 (and not more than 6-8 either), but easily 400 five years later. They had a few photos taken just before his death on his farm and he looked to be easily in excess of 550 pounds as we were told he was.

FEBRUARY 22

After being returned to the United States, Andre the Giant's body was cremated 2/11 in Southern Pines, NC. Funeral services are scheduled for his ranch on Highway 74 in Ellerbe, NC at 1 p.m. on 2/24 at which time his ashes will be scattered. New York magazine in its 2/15 issue had an article about his experiences working with Andre by actor William Goldman, who appeared in the movie "The Princess Bride" with him.

MARCH 8

Wrestlers and friends said their final good-byes to two of the biggest wrestling attractions of recent years, Andre "the Giant" Roussimoff and Kerry Adkisson, last week. Andre's long-time best friend and caretaker Frenchy Bernard put together a lavish ceremony in front of 200 to 250 guests on Andre's 200-acre ranch in Ellerbe, NC, a small town two hours North of Charlotte, on 2/24. There were actually very few wrestling personalities in attendance, the most notable of which were Hulk Hogan (who was one of seven who delivered a eulogy), Vince McMahon, Randy Savage, Brutus Beefcake, Rene Goulet, Pat Patterson, Wahoo McDaniel, Fabulous Moolah, Ivan Koloff and Rita Chatterton. Hogan broke down twice during the eulogy and was visibly moved from the moment he showed up, breaking kayfabe to an extent by saying how Andre let him slam him in the Pontiac Silverdome in order to take Hogan's career to a new plateau. "I bodyslammed him once because he let me do it. He said, `Slam me, boss.' I'll never forget how kind and how generous he was." Besides Hogan, Frenchy and Jackie Bernard, he was also eulogized by his personal doctor, a ranch hand, a cattleman he did business with and Dr. Terry Todd, a former champion powerlifter who became his good friend while writing a 1981 article on him for Sports Illustrated. Frenchy Bernard kept the ceremony low-key and made it clear that autograph seekers weren't welcome.

Getting Andre to his own funeral was just another in a series of unique stories that constituted Andre's existence both in life and in death. As mentioned here previously, Andre has asked to be cremated within 48 hours of his death, however there was no crematorium in Paris that could accompany his size (Andre was 555 pounds at death). A 300-pound custom-made oak casket was built for him, but plane flights had to be continually juggled because the cargo holds on many airplanes weren't large enough to hit the huge casket. When his remains arrived at the Charlotte Airport, the coffin wouldn't fit into a hearse. The funeral home had to bring in a forklift to get the 860 pounds of casket and body out of a friends truck, and needed the forklift to get him out of the casket because it was nearly impossible to pick up the 555 pounds of dead weight. A special mahogany case had to be built for his ashes, which themselves weighed 19 pounds, or about double that of a normal human being. Bernard, his wife, and five other riders concluded the ceremony by taking Andre's remains around the ranch for one last tour on a seven horse ceremony. Bernard kept the coffin and wants to donate it some day if there will ever be a wrestling Hall of Fame built. It should be noted that several newspapers eventually, including the Miami Herald, Montreal Gazette, Charlotte Observer and Los Angeles Times did print Andre's height at either 6-9 or 6-10, as opposed to the 7-4 figure that was printed in the wire services and carried in such periodicals of record including Sports Illustrated and the New York Times.

CHAPTER TWELVE

YOKOZUNA CONTROVERSY

FEBRUARY 15

KTTV (Ch. 13) in Los Angeles refused to air the Yokozuna vs. Jim Duggan match on Superstars this past weekend because of heavy protests from the Association of Asian Pacific American Artists (AAPAA), Japanese American Citizens League and Media Action Network for Asian Americans. A KTTV spokesman said the station refused to air the match because "We're not in the business of perpetuating stereotypes." (How self-righteous, because if that were the case, how could they even run WWF in the first place since stereotypical characters are what the company has always been built around?). When contacted, Steve Planamaneta of Titan claimed to have not seen the Duggan-Yokozuna match but said that it wasn't the company's intention to offend anyone. Wendy Fujihara Anderson of AAPAA saw a tape of the match and said the scenes and commentary promoted very negative images of Asians and promoted Japan-bashing. "They made it into an East-West type of thing," Anderson said in an article in a Japanese newspaper in Los Angeles. She complained about the comments about Fuji and Yokozuna being sneaky and underhanded. "It just perpetuates the hate. The general American population is being educated wrong on who we are." Planamenta said Yokozuna had been very well received by fans since he was brought in and defended his company saying the WWF has another Japanese wrestler, Tenryu, who is a good guy. KTTV said that future matches of Yokozuna will be monitored and decisions made as to whether to air them will be made on a case-by-case basis. When the show aired Saturday, it was interrupted by Lord Al Hayes who said because of the graphic nature of the match (as opposed to the real reason), it couldn't air and they put the Flair-Hennig loser leaves town match in its place. Duggan juiced from the mouth in that match and it was heavily pushed as U.S. vs. Japan and they are pushing that theme for the Wrestlemania main event with Bret Hart, which is ironic because Yokozuna and Fuji are both more American than Bret Hart.

FEBRUARY 22

The Chicago station also didn't air the Yokozuna-Duggan match last weekend due to the anti-Japanese match commentary. Phil Mushnick in the New York Post wrote a column on 2/15 critical of the angle and of the local New York station and USA Network for airing the match. The anti-Japanese rhetoric was toned down on this weekend's television.

MARCH 8

More news stemming from that Yokozuna angle. The Quincy Patriot-Ledger reported in its 2/25 issue that

Robert Burke, 54, filed a petition in U.S. District Court in Boston asking a judge to force the WWF to make a televised apology for mistreating the flag. Burke wrote a letter of complaint to Vince McMahon, which resulted in a phone call back from a WWF lawyer who said there would be no televised apology. Burke named five defendants--WWF, Yokozuna, Mr. Fuji, Duggan and McMahon saying they violated many provisions of federal law which prohibit using the flag as a costume or allowing it to touch anything beneath it such as the ground or floor and said it is illegal to use the flag in such a manner as to permit it to be easily torn, soiled or damaged. Don't expect anything to come out of that.

MARCH 22

The Superstars interview with Yokozuna where the jobber laid there and was splashed on again was actually a foul-up when it was taped live in Long Beach. The jobber got up and left the ring and was told to go back to the ring, so he went back to the ring, then laid down motionless, the interview started, and Yokozuna squashed him again. Through the magic of editing it was fine on television, but sure must have looked more than suspicious live.

SEPTEMBER 13

While ingenious, the start of this week's Superstars show showing what we are supposed to believe is a biased Japanese newscast reporting on SummerSlam, was also highly racist. It's one thing to pretend a certain individual is a villain, but another to try and portray it as an entire race of people is anti-American. It's not like it's anything new or a surprise, but it still in not very subliminal tones teaches the kids who watch that Japanese are prejudiced against Americans and it's cool to hate Japanese for that reason. I'm sure it does wonders for Japanese-American children watching. I could care less about it if we lived in a society that wasn't prejudiced, or if the audience was largely adults watching for humorous entertainment, but neither is the case here. Not that AAA is any better in that regard.

CHAPTER THIRTEEN

WWF INVADES USWA

FEBRUARY 22

The 2/8 show in Memphis with Doink the Clown and Howard Finkel drew about 1,100 fans, which is roughly what they've been drawing without outside help. Finkel's match with Downtown Bruno (Harvey Whippleman) saw Finkel work wearing his ring announcer tuxedo and it ended with Jerry Lawler pulling off his pants.

Lex Luger appeared on 2/13 in Nashville against Jerry Lawler and drew the largest crowd (estimated 2,000) for the USWA at the Fairgrounds in years. Ironically Luger was cheered like crazy, at least as heavy as Lawler, which shows Luger is over as a face to the rank and file USWA fans which says something about his impact as a heel to WWF fans and the remembrance that he left WCW as a heel since it appears he's still best-known for his stint as a face in WCW. Luger didn't sell most of the match, which was said to have not been very good. Finish saw Brian Christopher (who is turning into one of the best interviews in the business) throw in a chain, Luger used it and pinned Lawler to evidently win the USWA title. Eddie Marlin came out and reversed the decision however Luger wouldn't return the title belt. Marlin went to the heel dressing room (with a TV camera following him) and was beaten up by Christopher and Luger. When Lawler tried to save Marlin, he got similar treatment.

Luger was at the TV studio in Memphis that morning but didn't work the Monday night show after all since he had to be in Long Beach for the WWF tapings. Luger was neither a heel nor a face on TV although Christopher introduced him as his new friend and they aired a video from Royal Rumble where Bobby Heenan introduced him as the Narcissist. Luger in his interview flexed a bit and said he was in the USWA because it was filled with talented wrestlers and told Dave Brown that he was one of the best announcers around. Christopher wrestled Jeff Jarrett on TV with Luger at the desk and Luger never interfered. Mike Samples and Bert Prentice both interfered for the DQ.

MARCH 15

Sparked by the relationship with Titan Sports, the USWA promotion is doing its best business in years. The 3/2 show at the Mid South Coliseum in Memphis, with what appeared on paper as a weak line-up, still drew 2,800 fans and $15,000 (largest figures in more than one year) to see the debut of Giant Gonzales, who worked as a babyface managed by Downtown Bruno. The return of Randy Savage to his old stomping grounds after more than seven years on 3/6 in Nashville drew a sellout 1,800 fans and $13,000, the latter being the largest crowd in Nashville since 1987. The Savage-Jerry Lawler match, with Savage playing total heel but still being cheered heavily by the majority of those in attendance, ended in a double disqualification when Jeff Jarrett and Brian Christopher both interfered. The first Lawler-Savage match in Memphis since their famous loser leaves town match in 1985 that drew 11,000 fans to the Coliseum on 3/8, drew an estimated 1,500 for a show which saw the crowd split about 50-50 even though Savage played total heel, with the match ending with a double count out. After the match they did a role reversal from their Titan meetings the previous week, in that Savage left, Lawler challenged him to return, Jarrett met him in the aisle and threw him back in the ring, and while Savage and Jarrett argued, Lawler schoolboyed him while Jarrett counted the pin.

MARCH 22

Lawler vs. Randy Savage on 3/9 in Louisville drew an estimated 3,000 which would be the largest USWA crowd in that city since the mid-80s. Louisville usually draws 400-500, and even Lex Luger barely raised that figure.

MARCH 29

The USWA drew what was reported to me as its biggest crowd in several years on 3/16 in Louisville of a near sellout 4,000+ to see Undertaker vs. Giant Gonzales. Gonzales also drew the biggest Memphis gate in a few years some weeks earlier.

The WWF also did an impromptu Gonzales-Undertaker match on 3/19 in Utica, NY with Pat Patterson going to the show and watching intently. Gonzales did a walk-out finish in Louisville, which was the same finish they did in their first dry-run last week at the television tapings in Augusta, GA. In Utica the match ended with a DQ but him leaving Undertaker and Paul Bearer laying. It's pretty clear that with his size, that handled correctly, Gonzales can and will be a short-term draw. Gonzales was also put over big on 3/21 at Madison Square Garden, doing an in-hour angle with Rob Bartlett, and later in the show after the main event tag team match with Bret Hart & Mr. Perfect vs. Lex Luger & Razor Ramon, doing the choke slam on both Hart and Perfect and leaving both men laying.

The problem is that he can't work. The Undertaker matches have thus far been terrible, although give the WWF credit for getting the two in the ring for test runs before Wrestlemania because maybe they'll at least be able to practice their way into a watchable match. If they had gone out there live on PPV for the first time ever, it could have been really ugly. If one recalls, while WCW didn't use him right, he did make an impact at the beginning and caused curiosity and his matches with Ric Flair drew significantly better than WCW shows had been doing around that time period. However, after seeing him a few times, nobody had the desire to ever see him again. There is also the health problems (Gonzales is diabetic and has terrible knees) which have many WWFers saying that there is no way he can last the long haul on the road. Still, if protected and featured in a way that people see him actually lock up as little as possible, he can draw some houses before the fans catch on, and then he can be turned face and used as an occasional gimmick attraction as well.

APRIL 5

Shawn Michaels will have his first and only pre-WM match after his shoulder separation on 3/29 in Memphis defending the Intercontinental title against Jarrett. It'll be the first time a WWF title is at stake on a USWA show.

MAY 17

Papa Shango won the USWA title on 5/3 in Memphis from Jerry Lawler. Scotty Flamingo was at ringside distracting Lawler during the match. Lawler ended up throwing fire at Shango, who was hit but didn't sell it, which is a first, and then Shango's stick sprayed sparks into Lawler's eyes and he was pinned. They announced Lawler would only get one rematch, which took place 5/10, and ended in a double DQ.

Scotty Flamingo came out wearing a polo outfit (you know, the game associated with snobby rich people) and said he came out to reveal that his real name was Johnny Polo of the California Polos (see WWF section) and talked about having rich parents. The announcers still called him Scotty Flamingo for the rest of TV. He managed Shango who destroyed Jerry Lynn, who was making his return, in a squash.

MAY 24

Business has been pitiful the last two weeks which is the downside of using all the WWF talent on top. It gets fans to where when they aren't there (or when they are, but it's someone like Papa Shango who isn't a WWF star anymore) they don't want to come.

JUNE 21

The first appearance in Memphis of The Undertaker on a USWA show on 6/7 drew 1,750 and $10,100 which is about double the weekly average. Undertaker went to a double disqualification challenging Southern champ Brian Christopher in the main event. Clearly it was Undertaker responsible for the house since business everywhere else is pretty weak with lots of recent complaints from regular viewers about the quality of the current talent and stale booking not to mention continual talk of Lawler's New York character being inconsistent with his Memphis character and how it just makes all wrestling look like it's b.s. Since he was in New York for Raw, Jerry Lawler didn't work the show

JULY 5

Two title changes and a hot angle took place on 6/21 in Memphis, which drew an $11,000 house which is the largest house in recent months, largely once again due to the appearance of The Undertaker, who was disqualified against Brian Christopher in a Southern title match when Undertaker was caught with the chain Christopher brought in. In the title changes, Owen Hart won the USWA title in 7:39 from Papa Shango. Shango kept wanting Bert Prentice to give him his voodoo stick to use on Hart, but Prentice kept refusing. Finally as Shango argued with him, Prentice threw the stick to Hart who used it on Shango for the pin. The two embraced afterwards to signify Hart as a heel here. Afterwards, when Jerry Lawler was wrestling referee Paul Neighbors, Hart hit the ring and destroyed Lawler and left him laying on the ring steps in the same position Lawler left Bret Hart laying at King of the Ring. Also on the card, Rex King & Steve Doll lost the USWA tag team titles to New Jack (who is said to be terrible) & Home Boy (Mark Freer), and Jeff Jarrett beat Tony Falk in a hair vs. hair match. Doll & King are said to be headed to the WWF as heels Simply Devine.

JULY 19

The Jerry Lawler vs. Owen Hart USWA title main event on 7/5 drew more than 1,500 fans (nearly double the weekly average) to see Lawler regain the title. Finish saw Hart come off the top with Brass Knux, but ref Frank Morrell had been bumped and couldn't count the fall. Heel ref Paul Neighbors came in and counted the three count with Hart retaining the title. When Morrell got up, Neighbors told him he counted the three and Morrell got mad at Neighbors and said he was the referee of the match and he didn't accept that as the finish. Neighbors knocked down Morrell and then left the ring. As Hart argued with Morrell, Lawler snuck up from behind him and Morrell shoved Hart down, he tripped on Lawler and Lawler schoolboyed him for a fast three count.

AUGUST 9

No word on the house, but it was probably the largest in a while as the Saturday television did the best job of hyping a card in a long time with the Jerry Lawler vs. Bret Hart main event, which went 23:46 to a double disqualification. Most of the TV show consisted of airing one clip after another of angles involving Lawler and Hart, such as the King of the Ring angle, the Monday Night Raw angle and the syndicated match of Lawler vs. Owen Hart. Both did interviews with Hart playing a heel, although not a strong heel, and Lawler of course as the face here.

AUGUST 16

The 8/2 Jerry Lawler vs. Bret Hart match in Memphis which went to a double disqualification drew just under $17,000 (about 2,800 paid), which would be the biggest house in Memphis that I can recall since they had a USWA singles title tournament that Terry Funk won several years back. From what I was told, the match that stole the show was Chris Adams vs. Brian Christopher.

The 8/9 show was pushed as "The Perfect Night of Wrestling" with Lawler defending the USWA title against Mr. Perfect in the main event. This was really well promoted as well, with them both talking about their 1988 match that drew 8,000 fans when Lawler won the AWA title from Curt Hennig, which is a big change for a WWF wrestler to acknowledge a before-life. Hennig blamed his AWA title loss on Jackie Fargo being the referee. Actually Lawler and Hennig met several months back in Memphis when the USWA-WWF alliance had just started.

AUGUST 23

Jerry Lawler got to pin Mr. Perfect on 8/9 in Memphis which drew about a $10,000 house. The 8/16 show saw the house increase to $11,000 (about 1,850 paid) for Owen & Bret Hart beating Jerry Lawler & Jeff Jarrett in the main event. Bert Prentice interfered, throwing in his cane which Bret used on Lawler for the pin.

An interview was done on 8/18 in Lowell, MA in front of the fans with Lawler and Vince McMahon, which for the first time acknowledged the Memphis circuit and its happenings, building up to a match with Lawler against a referee (probably Paul Neighbors although the name was never mentioned) that cost him a victory in Memphis against Bret Hart (don't know if that's the 8/16 tag match or a singles match that has yet to take place) and that Lawler will have a match against the ref and if he doesn't put him in the hospital in an ambulance (boy, doesn't that sound familiar), he'll refund everyone's ticket money that night. McMahon said he'd be at ringside for that match because he wanted Lawler to refund him his money. McMahon was booed heavily when he came out. It would make sense for that to be the 8/23 show since it would make sense for McMahon to want to be there for the first Luger-Yokozuna match.

AUGUST 30

Vince McMahon got to live out his fantasy of being a heel at the Mid South Coliseum on 8/23. Although Lex Luger vs. Yokozuna was the main event, the big crowd came mainly because of Lawler's promise to refund money if he didn't put quasi-heel referee Paul Neighbors in the hospital. During the Lawler vs. Neighbors match, McMahon, who did a heel interview on television two days earlier, said he'd be in Neighbors' corner. Neighbors came out alone and Lawler grabbed the house mic and asked what happened to your big-shot friend. McMahon then came out with Pat Patterson and did a big-time heel anti-Southerner interview talking about how much nicer people were in New York and how in New York you don't have to lock the door at night because it doesn't have the kind of crime in Memphis, etc. and insincerely invited everyone from Memphis to come to New York to see how things were in a real city. Told the speech and facial expressions delivering it were tremendous, but that shouldn't be surprising because everyone all along has known Vince was one of the all-time great workers. He then introduced Patterson as one of the all-time great wrestler and told Lawler if he tried anything that Patterson would take care of him. During the match, Lawler would chase Neighbors, who would run away, and as Lawler ran after him, McMahon tripped him. When Lawler would go after McMahon, Patterson would get in between them. Finally Lawler threw Patterson into the ring and Pat took a few bumps for him. As Lawler went after McMahon, Patterson grabbed Lawler from behind in a fullnelson and McMahon punched Lawler and then he and Patterson walked out of the building together to a chorus of boos. Afterwards, Lawler ended up making his comeback and gave Neighbors six piledrivers before he did the stretcher job. While he was being carried out on a stretcher, Lawler threw a fireball at Neighbors.

SEPTEMBER 6

Jerry Lawler once again did the money-back guarantee gimmick on 8/29 in Memphis for a cage match with Bret Hart. The match, billed to settle the "King of Cages," saw Vince McMahon do a taped interview daring Lawler to put up his money-back guarantee against someone who wasn't a referee, like the real King Bret Hart. Lawler vowed to refund everyone's money if he didn't pin Hart in the middle of the ring, so of course, that's what happened. The show drew 2,100 fans and $13,000, which was down from $24,000 six days earlier when Lawler did the same gimmick with Paul Neighbors. The show also had a strong undercard with a Brian Christopher vs. Chris Adams loser leave town blow-off, which naturally Adams lost, a Southern title match with Jeff Jarrett beating Owen Hart, Dog Catchers keeping USWA tag title beating Moondogs and Giant Gonzalez beating Vampire Warrior. Everyone seems to expect Lawler to work against McMahon in the ring on the 9/4 show.

SEPTEMBER 13

The Lawler-Bret Hart match which took place on 8/29 in the cage with Lawler guaranteeing to refund everyone's money finished with Owen Hart attempting a run-in and Jeff Jarrett brawling with him. At that point Gonzalez went through the door, gave Hart a high-five and the two began pounding on Lawler. As Hart held Lawler, Gonzalez went for the clothesline, Lawler moved, Hart got the blow and was pinned. After the match Hart & Gonzalez beat up Lawler after and Hart put Lawler in the sharpshooter and refused to break it.

Vince McMahon didn't work yet this week, although it certainly appears they are building things up for the 1993 version of the Andy Kaufman-Jerry Lawler angle as McMahon did another interview on television Saturday hyping the Lawler vs. Giant Gonzalez match which took place 9/4. Crowd was way down as compared with the past month for the match, which ended when Lawler finally pulled down his strap and was making his comeback and the Dog Catchers hit the ring for the DQ.

None of the stuff involving McMahon is shown or even alluded to on the USWA syndicated television show. For those unfamiliar with how things are done here, USWA airs a 90 minute live show every Saturday morning from Memphis, and then edits it down to 60 minutes for airing the following Saturday in Louisville, Nashville, Evansville and the other markets. Everything involving McMahon is edited off the syndicated show. In fact, when they aired the clips of the Lawler-Neighbors stretcher match in syndication, everything involving McMahon and Pat Patterson was edited from the tape.

McMahon's heel interviews are so eerie they're incredible. It's the exact same McMahon, same voice pattern, same inflections as on Donahue, Larry King, etc. McMahon said that Memphis is the only city left in the country where the fans haven't seen through Lawler. Lawler, in his interview, blamed McMahon for talking Gonzalez into turning. Gonzalez had been a babyface in Memphis until 8/29.

SEPTEMBER 27

Latest word we get is that Vince McMahon will appear live at the Mid South Coliseum again on 10/4. I believe McMahon was to appear with Lex Luger on 9/20 originally, however with Luger still injured, it was postponed.

SEPTEMBER 29

Vince McMahon is playing the role of top heel "manager" cutting interviews every week bringing in wrestlers to feud with Jerry Lawler. This week McMahon said he's bringing in Tatanka, which should be the smallest crowd in a while. Both McMahon and Lex Luger were originally scheduled to be in Memphis on 9/20 so expect a loaded show next week. I don't believe McMahon will wrestle on that card, but eventually it looks like he will. Despite what was reported here, at least some of the stuff involving McMahon has aired on the USWA syndicated show.

Gonzalez, who was scheduled to be in for a month, gave notice his second day in and his last night in was 9/10. His appearances didn't increase crowds in any cities, even the smallest towns where you'd think the appeal of seeing a giant live would mean something. Gonzalez was said to be ready to return home to Argentina and fed up with pro wrestling completely by the end of the week, although some are trying to talk him into going back with Titan. Speaking of Gonzalez, he will be in the second episode of "Baywatch" this season in an episode called "Pelican Man." A song called "Pelican Man" penned by Jimmy Hart will be on that show.

OCTOBER 4

Because of the fair running this week in Memphis, there was no card at the Mid South Coliseum with the next date on 10/4. The television show didn't get too specific about that card, although Jerry Lawler did an interview challenging Vince McMahon to come to Memphis and hinted that if he did, he'd have a fireball waiting for him.

They did announce Randy Savage would be in Memphis for that show as well.

The 9/25 television show pretty well killed the cage match gimmick as several matches were held in a cage, all of which had outside interference. In the top match, Tommy Rich defended the USWA title against Jeff Jarrett. Finish saw Paul Neighbors use the key to get in (actually the storyline involving this one is pretty creative, they said that Neighbors when he was a referee used to take the cage from city-to-city whenever there was a cage match so obviously he had the key and had never returned it when he was fired as a ref and everyone simply forgot that minute detail when he was fired) after ref Frank Morrell was bumped. Neighbors threw in a chain, but Jarrett intercepted the pass and hit Rich. Morrell staggered up and counted the pin for an apparent title change. However Neighbors got in the ring and reversed the positions and Morrell then raised Rich's hand. Eddie Marlin then came out and told Morrell what happened and they held up the title pending rematches that will take place next week, which will be cage matches with Marlin as referee. The other major cage match was the Dog Catchers defending the tag titles against The Moondogs, and both Neighbors and Richard Lee interfered. This sets up six-mans with both manager but the tag titles will be at stake in the six-man matches.

Vince McMahon was scheduled to have an interview on television this week but Lawler claimed McMahon didn't have enough guts to send a tape after he had defeated Tonto (which is what he continually called Tatanka throughout his interview) and won back the title. Lawler did a great interview saying that obviously McMahon didn't send his interview federal express, because that's a Memphis-based company and they do their jobs correctly.

OCTOBER 11

Vince McMahon didn't appear on the card after all. Lawler during his interview on television Saturday once again challenged McMahon to come to Tennessee for a barbecue but it was never confirmed during the show that he would be there.

OCTOBER 18

Only details at press time of 10/11 in Memphis was that Randy Savage, with Vince McMahon as his manager, won the Unified title from Jerry Lawler, who was managed by Downtown Bruno (Harvey Whippleman) and that the show drew 850 fans and $5,000 which was a major league disappointment and makes four straight shows with disappointing crowds with Lawler against WWF babyface headliners playing heel roles. The 10/4 show with Lawler-Savage on top drew 1,200.

The title ended up being held up after the 10/4 match, which on the show Lawler won via DQ, as on television they ran the angle that McMahon's lawyers had gotten the title held up.

Doink the Clown (presumably Matt Borne) and Shawn Michaels start here next week and will be working the small spot towns as well.

NOVEMBER 29

Randy Savage was announced as being stripped of the USWA Unified title for failure to defend it within 30 days and a Battle Royal was held on 11/22 in Memphis. It came down to Lawler and Jarrett with Jarrett turning heel on Lawler and pinning him using the trunks to win the title. Earlier Buddy Landel won the USWA title from Jarrett, with Jeff still as a face in that match. Jarrett is heading full-time to WWF so after this week will only work spot dates in Memphis.

DECEMBER 6

Apparently Vince McMahon decreed about a week ago that there would be no more WWF wrestlers coming in, which is why they had to reverse the previously done switch with Crush as USWA champ and strip Randy Savage of the Unified belt, because neither would be coming in to drop the straps. Bret Hart was originally to face Lawler on this week's card which is why Lee is being brought in as a sub.

CHAPTER FOURTEEN

VADER LEGAL
ISSUES IN JAPAN

FEBRUARY 22

WCW champ Big Van Vader (Leon White) signed one of the most lucrative per-event contracts in pro wrestling history back on 1/30 with the UWFI. The contract announcement was made officially on 2/14 at the UWFI show at Tokyo's Budokan Hall. Lou Thesz, who along with Yoji Anjyo and Yuko Miyato were responsible for the deal being made, came to the ring and announced that Vader, the WCW world champion, was the first pro wrestling world champion to accept UWFI world heavyweight champion Nobuhiko Takada's challenge to unify the title. The fans were shocked at this announcement since Vader has in the past five years become almost synonymous with New Japan Pro Wrestling. While it was not announced, UWFI has a date on 5/6 at Budokan Hall and surely Vader will debut on that card, although they may hold off the inevitable Takada match until later in the year. Vader signed a $200,000 deal for eight shows over the next one year, plus received a $50,000 signing bonus. In addition, UWFI agreed to take care of any legal costs regarding any prior contractual obligations Vader had made with New Japan Pro Wrestling.

Vader's New Japan contract reportedly expires in February, 1994, although unlike American law, Japanese law provides for provisions where existing contracts can be broken provided the company whose contract is broken receives a monetary penalty as provided by law. However, Vader's situation is tricker since New Japan claims they created the name, the costume and the overall gimmick and claims all rights to the gimmick, and gave Vader the rights to use the gimmick in the U.S. for WCW. Because the contract is for just eight dates, Vader could still work just about a full-time schedule in the United States if he would so desire. Vader seems to have major leverage now when it comes to negotiations with WCW for his contract that expires on 3/4. Vader holds the title and there doesn't appear to be anything in the works to make a change in the near future, although with a new regime, that position is always open to change.

Vader has a guaranteed major income whether he works the U.S. or not, and has to work very few dates to get it, under his UWFI deal so he's really under little pressure to accept an offer he doesn't want. Vader hadn't worked with New Japan since canceling his appearance in the September tag team tournament because of his knee injury, a cancellation which caused at least a temporary split between the sides although there had been movement in the direction of rectifying it. It was not a secret that New Japan wanted a Hulk Hogan vs. Vader match on the 5/3 Fukuoka Dome show, which would have been extremely hard to put together politically in the first place, but this deal throws those plans out the window.

MARCH 15

WCW champion Big Van Vader (Leon White) reportedly signed an unprecedented four-year contract this past week which would tie him up through the first week of March of 1997. This, if the story is accurate, would be the longest-term deal in WCW history. While no figures are official and these numbers are prone to the normal exaggeration you can from unverified figures in wrestling, the figures I was given are that Vader's deal was for $2.5 million over four years ($625,000 per). Vader, 36, had just a few weeks earlier signed a $200,000 deal for eight dates with UWFI over the next year, plus received a reported substantial signing bonus with each deal which would make his March '93 to March '94 annual earnings at, based on our reports, $975,000. Keep in mind those figures may or may not be somewhat exaggerated. As far as guaranteed money in writing, Vader would be if these numbers are even close to accurate, the highest paid wrestler in the business. So much for WCW whittling away at the pay scale. Curt Hennig had been attempting to woo both Vader, whose WCW contract expired on 3/4, and Too Cold Scorpio, to the WWF to fill monster heel and acrobatic babyface roles.

MAY 3

New Japan is threatening legal action against UWFI over using Big Van Vader, who they claim is under contract until February of 1994 to them. UWFI claims that New Japan stopped booking Vader so the contract is void. UWFI is billing Leon White as Vader and as WCW heavyweight champion to set up a match against Nobuhiko Takada later this year. However, UWFI won't be using the Vader costume which New Japan came up with a trademarked.

MAY 10

It looks as though Leon White will be working the 5/6 UWFI card simply as "Vader" rather than Big Van Vader and with a new ring costume, although he will use the string mask, since New Japan went to court over its trademarking of the original gimmick.

MAY 17

The biggest out-of-the-ring news was also from Japan, but involved WCW's world champion, Big Van Vader, as he debuted for UWFI of Japan. Vader's first appearance, before a sellout crowd of 16,500 on 5/6 at Tokyo's Budokan Hall, saw him destroy Tatsuo Nakano in squash match fashion lasting just 3:35. Leon White was given the Vader name and gimmick by New Japan Pro Wrestling in December, 1987, which trademarked the name and the image. There were two major candidates for the role of Big Van Vader, who was going to be the monster foreign heel, one being White and the other being Jim Hellwig. Hellwig signed with Titan Sports and of course became The Ultimate Warrior just before the decision as to which one of the two was supposed to be Vader, although the original Vader drawings called for a large muscular man built more along with likes of Hellwig.

Although White started out as a huge, but very limited performer, over the years in New Japan he developed into the best worker for his size in the history of pro wrestling and became the first person ever to hold world titles on three continents (IWGP in Asia, UWA in North America and CWA in Europe) simultaneously before becoming a three-time WCW champ, although New Japan claimed it gave White the rights to use the name and gimmick in his European, Mexican and American forays. White wound up having a falling out with New Japan in 1992 after his knee injury caused him to miss the tag team tournament, but was still under a long-term contract with New Japan when he inked the UWFI deal at a reported $25,000 per match with an eight match guarantee per year plus a $50,000 signing bonus with UWFI agreeing to take care of all legal problems stemming from a possible breach of contract claim. New Japan filed a lawsuit based on that breach claim several weeks back.

In addition, on March 31, 1993, New Japan renewed its talent trading agreement with WCW for one year, and in the contract it specifically stipulated that New Japan have exclusive rights to the NWA and WCW champion in the Japan market. A second lawsuit by New Japan was filed against UWFI for using Vader and billing him in pre-card publicity as WCW world heavyweight champion on the day before the card. There was a lot of curiosity about whether or not Vader would bring the belt to the ring and be announced as WCW champion in the building, which would strengthen New Japan's claim. Photos were taken everywhere where it pertained to that and New Japan sent two major league lawyers to the show. On the scoreboard, White was listed as Big Van Vader and WCW world heavyweight champion for his match with Nakano. However, in the ring, he was introduced as the current WCW world heavyweight champion, "the man formerly known as Big Van Vader-- Super Vader. Vader was wearing the WCW title belt, and then threw the belt on the mat when the match started and Nakano kicked the belt out of the ring and Vader jumped him. Instead of working UWF style, Vader worked a New Japan style squash match and won in 3:35 with a stiff punch, a uranage (choke slam) and won via knockout when Nakano couldn't get back to his feet by the count.

MAY 24

Besides suing UWFI, New Japan also sued Big Van Vader, serving him at the UWFI Budokan show. Vader's defense seems to be that he hadn't received any New Japan bookings since canceling the tag team tournament in September because of the knee injury, and that New Japan hadn't paid for the operation which was suffered in Japan.

SEPTEMBER 13

Another semantic legal battle took place this past week in Japan involving WCW champion Big Van Vader. New Japan took Leon White to court, claiming creation of the name Big Van Vader and costuming, plus claimed a breach of contract when White, who was under a long-term deal with New Japan, signed and wrestled for UWFI. While we don't have complete details, it is believed the ruling, which may be appealed by New Japan to a higher court, went something like this. Since the name "Vader" was trademarked by movie producer George Lucas ("Darth Vader" of "Star Wars"), New Japan can't stop White from using the name "Vader," although he will no longer be allowed to use the name Big Van Vader since it was intellectual property of New Japan Pro Wrestling. White had already been using the name Super Vader on UWFI shows in Japan. I believe White will be allowed to continue to wear the same ring costuming, and the decision was ruled in favor of White in the breach of contract portion of the suit because New Japan had ceased booking White prior to his UWFI signing.

The legal battle comes at the same time as a potential contractual snag between White and WCW may come down. White and WCW agreed to a multi-year $625,000 per-year deal months back. The contract was never signed. Apparently WCW and White are having problems over the issue of White's working for UWFI, which originally WCW seemed unconcerned about when White first struck the deal. Since that time UWFI announced plans to broadcast PPV events in the United States starting on 10/5. Even though the UWFI PPV events should produce little in the way of buys, certainly at least at first, because of almost a complete lack of exposure of its product in this country, Vader would no doubt be the biggest and only initial drawing card. The 10/5 show, taped the previous night in Osaka, will feature Vader vs. Naoki Sano and Nobuhiko Takada vs. Billy Scott (the 190-pounder who scored a decision over then-World Cruiserweight boxing champ James Warring in December, 1991 on a UWFI show in a boxer vs. wrestler match). That show appears to set up a 12/5 card in Tokyo's outdoor Jingu Baseball Stadium (capacity 48,000) with Takada vs. Vader for the UWFI version of the world heavyweight title.

SEPTEMBER 27

New Japan is appealing the judges' decision in the lawsuit against Leon White for the name Big Van Vader, the costume, the breach of contract for signing with UWFI, etc. to a higher court.

CHAPTER FIFTEEN

JUMBO TSURUTA'S
HEALTH DECLINES

MARCH 8

On the other hand, two of the biggest names in recent Japanese wrestling history are on the shelf. Tomomi "Jumbo" Tsuruta, who turns 42 later this month, and has been out of action since 10/21 with an undisclosed illness believed to have been a severe liver problem, was hospitalized in the past few weeks with kidney failure. Tsuruta, who has been a main event superstar in Japan since his debut in 1973 coming out of the Olympic games, had been pushed as All Japan's top star for most of the past ten years. Word we get is that Tsuruta was in the hospital for two weeks, but was released over the past few days, and that an announcement will be made shortly of one of two things--either Tsuruta will announce his retirement from wrestling, or the promotion will acknowledge that Tsuruta will be out of action until sometime in 1994. As part of the in-ring story to try and fill the load left by Tsuruta's being absent, Toshiaki Kawada, the long-time partner of Mitsuharu Misawa, announced this past week that he would no longer team with Misawa after the current tour of advertised matches ends at the end of this week. Kawada said he wouldn't join up with either the old Tsuruta side (now headed by Akira Taue who is being pushed as a new Jumbo Tsuruta with similar haircut and attempted similar workstyle) or with Misawa's side in the traditional All Japan main event feud, but would try and work as an individual. Kawada feuding with Misawa and Kenta Kobashi is the spark All Japan has needed to break up the monotonous, although excellent inside the ring, series of main events the company has been running for the past three plus years.

MARCH 15

I believe the actual disease Jumbo Tsuruta is suffering from is Hepatitis B. He's going to have to be kept out of the ring probably until 1994 because it's very contagious and can be transmitted through spit or sweat.

JUNE 14

Jumbo Tsuruta was all over the news last week in Japan stemming from the newspaper article in Nikkan Sports announcing that Tsuruta's wrestling career was over. Tsuruta, 42, has been out of action since October 21, 1992.

Despite him being one of the true legends in Japanese wrestling history, his disappearance was largely ignored both by the office, and surprisingly on the surface, by the media as well, which led to many rumors about what really was going on with him. When Giant Baba switched Toshiaki Kawada from the side of Mitsuharu Misawa's, many believed that was a public acknowledgement that Tsuruta wasn't coming back, because Tsuruta, Kawada and Akira Taue as a trio would make one side "too strong" in comparison to the other in All Japan's typical six-man tag main event. The Nikkan Sports article interviewed Tsuruta's doctor, who said that there was no way Tsuruta would be able to come back to wrestling because his stamina and physical conditioning level were too far down after his lengthy hospital stay. The All Japan office was furious at the story, since it had made no public announcements regarding Tsuruta's condition and now it was being reported in a major daily that he was retired. Tsuruta did one major interview from the hospital with Weekly Pro Wrestling and was on the cover of both major weekly magazines. In the story, he denied the retirement and said he would return to action, although couldn't give a definitive time period but was hopeful of it being in the fall. The photos, the first published since his last match, showed him physically showing the effects of the illness as he was way down in weight. The story said that Tsuruta was suffering from Hepatitis C, not the Hepatitis B as we had originally reported, which was the first time any media source in Japan had even acknowledged any illness. Tsuruta said that he won't allow his career to end on this kind of a note, and said he'd be back, but wouldn't be back soon.

JUNE 21

Jumbo Tsuruta is scheduled to leave the hospital on 6/21 and in a later interview has tentatively scheduled his return to the ring for October. He'd better be in top shape when he returns or it'll be too noticeable with the style of wrestling they have here because he'll stand out otherwise in those main events

JULY 5

Jumbo Tsuruta left the hospital on 6/21 after a many month stay. Although no announcement has been made, it appears Tsuruta won't be returning until the December 3 show at Budokan Hall, the tag team tournament finals, which traditionally is All Japan's biggest show of the year.

JULY 12

It was announced that Jumbo Tsuruta would make an appearance at the 7/29 Budokan Hall show waving to the crowd. Tsuruta hasn't been seen since at an All Japan show since October.

CHAPTER SIXTEEN

DINO BRAVO MURDERED

MARCH 22

Montreal newspapers were speculating that dealings with contraband cigarettes were the reason for the apparent mob-style retaliation murder of long-time pro wrestling star Dino Bravo.

Bravo, 44, real name Adolfo Bresciano, was shot seven times, at least twice in the head, and killed sometime in the evening of 3/10 in his home in a luxurious section of Laval, Quebec, a city 20 minutes North of Montreal. Laval police found 17 shells from semi-automatic .22 and .380 calibre guns on the floor of Bravo's living room. Because there was no sign of a struggle or of forced entry, police believe Bravo knew his killers. Both Bravo's wife and 6-year-old daughter were out for the evening at the daughter's ballet class. Bravo's wife, Diane Rivest, last talked to her husband at 9 p.m. that evening. When she arrived home to their $850,000 house with her daughter at 12:20 a.m., she found her husband dead, sitting on his easy chair, with the television on. Because there were so many shots fired, including one which broke a window, and none of his neighbors heard a thing, caused speculation that the killers were professionals who may have used silencers. Police also found a "large sum" of money in his home.

Le Journal, a Montreal french language newspaper headlined Bravo's death in Friday's paper on the front page with a heading which translated into "Dino Bravo executed for trafficking in tobacco." A full-page story ran on page three of the newspaper in which police refused to confirm the story that their investigation was focusing on contraband cigarettes as a reason for his murder. However, by a Saturday follow-up quoted a Longueuil officer (a city 20 minutes South of Montreal where the Royal Canadian Mounted Police (RCMP) performed a major bust on 234 cases of cigarettes and 69 cases of tobacco worth $400,000 on the black market on 3/5) in regard to Bravo's death as saying, "A $400,000 loss of money in importing cigarettes is enough to justify an assassination." Another officer reported that the police believed "it was a settling of accounts." Laval police, who put 12 men on the case full-time, were tight-lipped saying they were looking in several different directions. RCMP investigators say they saw Bravo with well known traffickers but his role in the trafficking couldn't be proven, but they believed he was into it for a large sum of money and it was speculated he didn't cover his tracks well enough, which led to the major bust. The Friday story said that Bravo had become involved in smuggling cigarettes after he left pro wrestling full-time in 1991, although others trace his involvement back farther, and was operating his business on a significant scale. The RCMP confirmed Bravo's significant involvement in the operation and is currently investigating the network with which Bravo was believed to have been involved. The newspaper also reported that Bravo had confided to friends that he didn't think he had long left to live, although police wouldn't confirm that story. Gino Brito, a long-time friend, tag team partner and business partner of Bravo's did say in La Presse, another French paper that he had heard rumors Bravo's life had been threatened recently, although he admitted the two had kept their distance from one another in recent months. Bravo had also been involved in the local boxing scene since the end of his wrestling career.

La Presse also reported Bravo as having been an acquaintance of many who were arrested the previous week when the RCMP seized 477 kilos of cocaine smuggled into Montreal in tomato cans.

In Canada, the federal government has high duties and taxes on cigarettes manufactured in Canada. It has become a huge business, some say even more lucrative that hardcore drugs in some instances, to smuggle American cigarettes from the Northeast into Quebec and sell them at a much cheaper price than the domestic cigarettes from car trunks and fly-by-night warehouses. Police regularly raid Indian reservation and confiscate smuggled cigarettes. In addition, it is generally believed the American cigarettes are of superior quality, which along with price, is the reason for the black market supply and demand.

Within wrestling, Bravo's name had often been rumored linked to the Montreal underworld. His aunt Maria was the wife of Vic Cotroni, was had a reputation as being Montreal's leading mob godfather. Bravo often worked as chauffeur for Paul Cotroni, a relative of Vic's who was reported as being a member of the powerful underworld family. Rumors only got stronger several months back when Gino Brito, his long-time tag team partner and partner in several businesses over the years including the local regional wrestling office, was arrested as part of a loan sharking ring.

Bravo, began wrestling in his native Montreal in 1970. He began amateur wrestling at the age of 15 and was studying law at Sir George Williams College in Montreal when he became best friends with Yvon Robert Jr. His hero growing up was Yvon Robert, a former NWA champion who for years was the most popular wrestler in Montreal. He was trained at the Grand Prix Wrestling (name of Montreal's largest promotion at the time) training school by Carpentier, Luigi Macera and Brito and because of his strength, was pushed from the start as part of a young Italian babyface tag team combination with Brito, who was already a star wrestler at the time and was a childhood friend. Although the two were billed as cousins during their wrestling days, they actually weren't related, although the two were constantly being confused with one another because of their long-time association both in and out of the ring. After one year he was so high on the cards that he often joined Jean Ferre (Andre the Giant) and Carpentier on top in six-mans.

Bravo toured many of the American circuits during the 70s and early 80s, usually getting a strong babyface push and holding tag team titles, usually with another Italian wrestler like Dom DeNucci, Tony Parisi or Brito as an Italian connection tag team. In Southern California, which was his first major campaign after leaving Montreal, he held the tag team title with Victor Rivera. He often returned to Montreal, a bigger star on each return trip, then would venture to another American territory for a six-month campaign. When Eddie Einhorn's IWA bucked the established U.S. offices in its ill-fated 1970s promotion, Bravo and Brito were a mid-level tag team which was his first exposure in the Northeast. Soon after, Bravo was in the WWWF. He was initially was given a major singles push, but ended up teaming with DeNucci in 1978 and held the WWWF tag team title, winning the titles from Professor Tanaka & Mr. Fuji, and losing them to the Yukon Lumberjacks (Zarnoff LeBeouff of Montreal and the late Scott Irwin).

At about 240 pounds, Bravo combined the tag team flying maneuvers that young babyfaces were expected to use in the 70s, but was also known for his impressive strength, and was pushed as being able to bench press in excess of 500 pounds, which was an incredible figure during that time period.

When he returned full-time to Montreal around 1981. He, Brito, Tony Mule and Frank Valois joined forces to form International Wrestling, which became Quebec's major wrestling promotion. Since Carpentier had been moved from the top, the decision was made to go with Bravo as the group's top star along with Quebec City's Rick Martel. The group ran every Monday at Paul Sauve Arena in Montreal drawing respectable to very good crowds in the medium-sized building, during which time Bravo booked the shows and became something of a local sports hero. Bravo held the group's International title more often than not and brought in many of the biggest names in the business to challenge for the title and often drew crowds in excess of 10,000 for the major shows at the Montreal Forum. Among the top heel names Bravo brought in to challenge for his title included Abdullah the Butcher, probably his most frequent major adversary, The Road Warriors, Samu, Pat Patterson, Haku, Ric Flair, Rick Valentine (Kerry Brown) and Leo Burke.

International Wrestling was one of the many regional companies that folded when confronted with competition from the WWF, with the key blow being when the WWF signed the Rougeau Brothers. After that the other top local draws, Bravo and Martel wound up with the WWF and eventually Titan made Brito its local promoter, a position he held until he disappeared from the Montreal wrestling scene after his much publicized arrest.

Bravo first came to the WWF as a babyface in 1985 with a minimal push, although he always headlined the Montreal shows. He left the promotion in 1986 after a strange incident. A WWF show was held in the Forum on January 15, 1986, at a time Titan was running specialized shows in Montreal because of the widespread belief that to draw they needed to use local stars like Bravo and the Rougeaus in starring roles, rather than the run-of-the-mill circuit cards they would run everywhere else. The main event on the show was billed as having Hulk Hogan defend the title against Bravo, who was at the time the most popular local wrestling name. The show drew a sellout of near 20,000, but the card was re-arranged the night of the show with Hogan and Bravo each wrestling different opponents, apparently because WWF officials were worried at the time that Hogan would be perceived as the heel against the local French-speaking star. He returned in 1987, and became a bleached-blonde heel for the first time in his career and tag team partner of Greg Valentine. Later he teamed with Earthquake in 1990-91 as a top of the card heel working many main event tag team matches against Hulk Hogan and Tugboat, and getting occasional title shots at Hogan in what at the time seemed like one of the most curious main event pushes in wrestling.

On a national basis, Bravo is probably best remembered for his farcical attempt at breaking the world record in the bench press during the first Royal Rumble in January 1988 from Hamilton, Ontario. Bravo easily pressed weights billed from 450 to 660 pounds, although the weights themselves were gimmicked. He then attempted to what was billed as 710 pounds (the world record held at the time by Ted Arcidi, himself a one-time pro wrestler, was 705) but "failed" and needed help from spotter Jesse Ventura. After failing, Bravo was billed as Canada's strongest man in his heel role. According to several wrestlers, during that time period which was the height of the WWF's emphasis on the monsters, Bravo, even though he was already 39, was one of the two strongest (along with Warlord) when it came to bench pressing and realistically could max out in the 550-575 range, although local newspapers reported he could do an unrealistic 675 figure. While Bravo was considered a decent worker and fairly agile and acrobatic during the 70s, he gained about 20 pounds and had slowed down considerably in the ring during the period he gained the most fame, with his best work no doubt by that time coming in the weight room.

Bravo worked full-time with the WWF through Wrestlemania of 1991, where he ironically did the job for Kerry Von Erich, making him the third major WWF name of that era to die at a young age in a seven week period. After that, he worked some in Puerto Rico on top against Carlitos Colon, and did fill-in duty for the WWF and worked some shows in Montreal, working as a face in his home town once again. His final WWF action is believed to have been the April 1992 European tour. He was scheduled for a somewhat well publicized retirement match on December 4, 1992 at the Montreal Forum on the WWF show, but several weeks before the card, and in fact, as roughly the same time as Brito's arrest although there is no indication one had anything to do with the other, the WWF suddenly pulled Bravo from the card and announced it was postponing the retirement match. Bravo had told friends he hadn't been contacted by anyone in the WWF since being pulled from the show and was somewhat bitter about it. He told at least one person who had dealings with the office to inquire to Patterson about when he was going to get his big send-off but never called the office himself because he didn't want to come across like he was begging.

At the time of his death, Bravo owned two sporting goods businesses, "Dino Bravo Enterprises, Inc." and "Titan."

Bravo was the third resident of the high-rent district of Laval to be assassinated in the past nine months. The other two were also tied in with the Italian mafia, one as the accountant of another high-profile underworld figure and another who was heavily involved in cigarette trafficking.

His funeral was held on 3/15 in Montreal, although very few wrestling people were in attendance with the only name of note given to us as being Rene Goulet of Titan Sports.

MARCH 29

Among those in attendance at Dino Bravo's funeral on 3/15 were Rick Martel, Yvon Robert Jr., Rene Goulet, Gino Brito, Eddie Creachman (lead heel manager for International Wrestling during its heyday), Tony Mule and Lionel Robert. I believe Paul Bearer was also there out of character. According to newspaper stories, about 100 were in attendance and notable by their lack of attendance were anyone connected with the Catroni family, the Montreal underworld family Bravo was linked with although the limo used at the funeral was from Frank Catroni.

CHAPTER SEVENTEEN

ANTONIO INOKI
COMEBACK

MARCH 29

Antonio Inoki was at the card leading the crowd chants at the end and said that he was training for a return at the Fukuoka Dome. . .3/13 television show did a 6.0 rating headlined by Riki Choshu & Tatsumi Fujinami & Masa Chono & Muto vs. Axe Boulder & Scott Norton & TNT & Hercules.

APRIL 5

Antonio Inoki showed up at the card and sparred with two of the young lions to show everyone he had gotten into shape for the Fukuoka Dome show. He does look like he's in great condition for someone who just turned 50.

JULY 5

Although our details at press time are sketchy on this story, there is a major political scandal in Japan going on involving Antonio Inoki, the second most famous wrestler in Japanese history and currently a member of the Japanese senate and both the figure-head leader and often-times the real leader as well of New Japan Pro Wrestling since its inception more than 20 years ago. It started about six weeks ago when Inoki and long-time business manager Hisashi Shinma (who during the late 70s and early 80s ran New Japan Pro Wrestling, and recently has been in the pro wrestling news again by getting involved in running the re-birth of the new Universal office in September) split up. At about this time, Inoki fired a female secretary at his political office who apparently had been loyal to Shinma. The woman went public, many believe at the urging of Shinma, and wrote articles in a weekly magazine alleging Inoki with both district and federal income tax evasion going back ten years, talked about Inoki's involvement with Sagawa Express (a federal express type company that was his personal political sponsor and also bailed New Japan out of a financial crisis in 1987) both in his election campaign and also in sponsoring New Japan in 1987 as a way to get Inoki back in charge of the company after his 1983 debacle where he had to resign as company head to his allegations of financial improprieties. She also exposed that Inoki had nothing to do with getting Japanese hostages out of Iraq during the Persian Gulf war, and that he simply happened to be in the right place at the right time when a deal was made and took credit for it. The story has been a big deal in the mainstream Japanese media as well as the sports pages. Inoki went into seclusion when the story broke but made his first public appearance in more than one month on 6/29. Shinma also called a press conference on Tuesday and did what looked like a wrestling angle where he punched a male secretary who still worked for Inoki on a live television newscast, who was knocked out and carried off. New Japan president Seiji Sakaguchi amidst this crisis said that "Inoki's problems doesn't have anything to do with wrestling which is really successful right now." Many political media types in Japan have suggested that Inoki should resign from Japanese parliament.

This would not be the first time Inoki's name has been connected with financial impropriety. In the latter part of 1971, Inoki was kicked out of the Japanese Wrestling Association, the original major league promotion in Japan that Rikidozan founded, and charged with embezzlement. Inoki, who at the time was the No. 2 star in the old JWA behind Giant Baba, and it was well-known Inoki wanted to be No. 1 and was widely considered the better wrestler of the two, then formed the first incarnation of New Japan Pro Wrestling and began his several decade long feud and rivalry with Baba and his promotion. Inoki's second similar charge was made during the summer of 1983, when New Japan was in the midst of the biggest boom period in the promotion's history playing to 90 percent sellout houses over a one-year period and earning an annual profit of an estimated $9 million and its television show, which aired on Saturday nights from 8 to 9 p.m. was one of the five most highest rated shows in the country.

Several of the undercard wrestlers charged that Inoki had been embezzling their fight money to fund his losing outside business interests in Brazil. Several of the companies biggest drawing cards at the time, in particular the original Tiger Mask (Satoru Sayama) and Riki Choshu quit the promotion which in late 1983 in the wake of the scandals was actually perilously close to folding up completely. But the company survived and rebuilt to the point it is probably the No. 1 promotion as far as financial success in today's wrestling world. Although the last scandal nearly crippled what at the time was also the most financially successful wrestling company in the world, it doesn't appear that any of this negative publicity will affect New Japan. Although Inoki is still easily the most famous wrestler in the country, his face is no longer linked with New Japan's success and he only wrestles once or twice per year rather than being the entire foundation of the company as he was when he was a full-time active wrestler.

JULY 12

After a three-decade long run as one of the most popular sports personalities in his country, it appears the final story of Antonio Inoki is about to go down in disgrace.

After the business break-up of Inoki and long-time business manager Hisashi Shinma and the firing by Inoki of a political press secretary and confidante who was close to Shinma, the secretary went public in a major magazine with an eight-part story specifying allegations of illegal activities and misuse of funds by Inoki. Inoki, the second most famous wrestler ever in Japan and no doubt on a world-wide basis the second most famous wrestler in the world in the 70s (behind Andre the Giant), was voted into the Japanese Diet (equivalent to the U.S. Senate) in 1989 which signalled the end of his career as a full-time pro wrestler. There are two years remaining in the term.

The story grew even bigger this past week as Inoki broke his silence, holding a press conference on 6/30 which was carried live on all four Japanese television networks. During the press conference, Inoki once again tried to do the carny wrestling angle of blaming his accusers and denying across the board every accusation, without offering any evidence or substance for his claims. Inoki claimed everything written in the media about him was false and refused to resign from office, which political writers in the major newspapers had been suggesting and demanding as the stories by his former secretary continued to break. The main claims, besides ten years of tax fraud and tax evasion were a claim that Inoki received a huge payoff a few years back when he dropped out of the race for mayor of Tokyo and many instances listed where Inoki continually used public money or political sponsorship money in an attempt to put himself over as a babyface in tense world political situations where he had no actual involvement in but pretended he was a key player in. An example was getting the Japanese hostages out of Iraq during the Gulf War, which happened and he took credit for but he actually had no involvement in. Inoki went so far as to attempt to besmirch the reputation of his main accuser and the media outlets that reported the story. The secretary, an attractive 37-year-old career-minded woman, saw Inoki make implications about her "having relations" with Shinma and got stories into the media by "doing favors" for key editors. The story has been a main topic in all newspapers and a lead story all week in the Japanese network newscasts. The wrestling press itself is attempting to ignore the story as much as possible because of the fear it could hurt the wrestling business and on the New Japan television show, Inoki's name was never mentioned.

Thus far the way it has been explained to me, with older fans who link Antonio Inoki and New Japan as one, it has turned New Japan's reputation into one of a dirty business. Several mainstream media columnists are now snidely referring to Inoki as an actor-turned-politician rather than athlete. The real vs. fake issue hasn't even been an issue in Japan in so many years that nobody can remember when it ever was, even during the period when Satoru Sayama (the original Tiger Mask) was "exposing" the business in a book. Suddenly the Inoki story has caused some to talk about pro wrestling's predetermined nature as part of the story, which is a key part of the story because it explains how Inoki and Shinma have been able to manipulate Inoki into a national sports hero for the past two decades. Among younger fans, who have grown up in recent years with Inoki having little involvement with the current New Japan regime, they are easily able to separate the two, especially since at this point none of the charges against Inoki implicate the New Japan company. Both TV-Asahi (New Japan's network) and the wrestling magazines are refusing to release any photos or videotapes of Inoki for the mainstream press' stories. Inoki, who turned 50 in February, as a mainstream celebrity figure, is significantly larger in Japan than Hulk Hogan ever was in the United States, probably equivalent more to a James Bond level of popularity come-to-life in that basically everyone in the country of every age knows Inoki as the famous wrestler who "always wins."

The reporters covering Inoki's press conference where he denied all charges went after him strongly. Inoki couldn't come up with any substance other than accusing the accusers. This scenario in many ways is a repeat of the Hulk Hogan Arsenio Hall thing, only magnified by about 1,000 times in that the individual's sense of their own popularity was such that they believed they could pull the wrestling con in a mainstream situation and get away with it since that was how they achieved their success and it was simply the ways of the world they lived in. Even though Inoki's past was hardly pristine, he was always able to manipulate things to keep himself as a national hero after past indiscretions. However, at this point, Inoki's reputation has gone up in smoke, and is thought of by the public as the ultimate dirty politician like Richard Nixon of two decades ago rather than a sports hero. Inoki even brought religion into it, claiming his decision to fire Shinma was because he received word from God that after 26 years, he and Shinma had to go their separate ways and brought up God's will. He also claimed to be a misunderstood person and said that if people in Japan continue to misunderstand him, he hinted at leaving Japan and settling in another country. Shinma, the former figurehead president of the WWF and Chairman of the Board of New Japan in the early 80s during a major boom period when Inoki, Riki Choshu, Tiger Mask, Dynamite Kid, Hulk Hogan, Andre the Giant, Tatsumi Fujinami etc. drew TV ratings weekly in the 20 range, has also been all over the media. Shinma, who although he has his past as well, always linked with Inoki's including taking the fall in the 1983 New Japan embezzlement scandal which caused him to be expelled from the company he had built from a business standpoint, comes from a heavily religious upbringing. Shinma, the son of a Buddhist priest, countered Inoki's claim of religious intervention by saying it was funny how a man who never visited the grave of his daughter (Inoki's daughter died at a young age from cancer) or parents and never went to church or prayed, could all of a sudden use religion as his ally. Shinma said that Inoki simply got out of control and couldn't differentiate between the fantasy world he lived in and reality (THERE IS A MAJOR LESSON TO BE LEARNED HERE THAT EVERYONE WHO HAS ACHIEVED POWER IN WRESTLING NEEDS HEED BECAUSE MORE PERSONAL TRAGEDY IS THIS BUSINESS IS CAUSED BY THIS INABILITY THAN ANY OTHER REASON). Shinma, who will be the promoter of the new Universal office that opens in the fall, said that when Inoki was a wrestler, he (Shinma) was able to fix whatever trouble Inoki got himself into when his ego got out of control. But Inoki was in a world which was more heavily scrutinized and he continued to be blinded by the belief he was able to manipulate reality as if it were a wrestling angle. Shinma said after 26 years of being friends and business associates with Inoki, he finally gave up trying to cover for him.

It is uncertain how this will end up. Many still believe Inoki will come out of this and be able to rebuild his image, because he has been through similar instances, although all of a much smaller nature (of the Hogan Arsenio Hall denial level) throughout his career and has always come back stronger.

JULY 19

Antonio Inoki held a press conference on 7/7 for the wrestling media only and his outside of wrestling problems were never discussed or brought up. Inoki instead talked about wanting to return to wrestling and that he was going into heavy training to return in the fall and talked of a singles match against Genichiro Tenryu. Apparently Inoki wants to go back into the world he can manipulate to dig himself out of his problems in the world he can't manipulate so easily in.

AUGUST 16

At a post-Sumo Hall press conference, Antonio Inoki announced he was pulling out of his September dates on the tour with Hulk Hogan, etc. Inoki said he had suffered a leg injury while training for his latest comeback, but others are saying that due to his political position, New Japan didn't want to put him in the ring until his troubles have died down more. However, Inoki did get in the ring at the end of the final night's card to lead the crowd in the "Ishi-Ni-San-Da!" chant.

OCTOBER 5

Even more allegations thrown at a major pro wrestling name hit all the major newspapers in Japan on Tuesday morning. Antonio Inoki, the second most famous name in Japanese pro wrestling history and a member of the Japanese National Diet (equivalent to the United States Senate), was alleged to be part of a ring to smuggle in guns from the United States. George Domo, a famous martial arts fighter in Japan who lives in Los Angeles, was arrested on 2/8 at Narita Airport with 28 guns trying to smuggle them in. His trial started this past week and was still going on at press time. On 10/18, while on the stand, Domo claimed that Inoki was the one who asked him to smuggle the guns in. Japan has very strict laws when it comes to possession of firearms by citizens which is at least partially why the murder rate is almost non-existent there. This comes just a few months after Inoki's long-time business manager and former office assistant went public with allegations against Inoki that made news headlines for several weeks.

CHAPTER EIGHTEEN

JIM ROSS SIGNS FOR THE WWF

MARCH 22

Former WCW lead announcer Jim Ross was backstage at the WWF television taping on 3/9 in Augusta, GA and was introduced around to everyone as if he was going to be joining the company. Ross had expected to start with Titan as a television announcer, perhaps as early as 3/15, and was tentatively scheduled to debut at Wrestlemania, although there may be some hang-ups. Ross' deal with WCW upon resigning on 2/26 called for six months severance payment on his contract which is believed to be between $3,000 and $3,500 per week, and also called for him to not work for any competing wrestling organizations (read that Titan Sports) until the end of August. Ross was hoping to get a release from WCW, in which he'd give up his severance pay in exchange for getting the release to work with Titan. Officially, legally Titan wouldn't be allowed to even offer Ross a position until his release is signed because it would constitute tampering so from a technical standpoint Ross has yet to have been offered a position although reality is that he wouldn't be looking for a release and losing that kind of weekly income unless he thought the position was imminent. Whether or not Bill Shaw or Bob Dhue, who are the only parties in WCW authorized to give their approval to such a request, will release him to allow him join Titan is unknown at press time although we understand WCW is willing to give the release in exchange for Ross giving up the WSB radio show, which I'm presuming there's a good shot at that scenario taking place. As of press time Ross hadn't received his release since Shaw wasn't in the office during the end of the last week due to illness and Dhue was in Europe for the WCW tour. There are definitely factions within WCW who are opposed to Ross getting the release on the grounds it would look to the general public as if Titan had raided another key figure from WCW if Ross were to start this quickly. Ross had scheduled himself on Mike Tenay and John Arezzi's wrestling radio shows over the weekend, but canceled with Arezzi and was non-committal about anything with Tenay largely due to the delicate nature of everything. WCW pulled Ross from the hotline, which was going to take place in a few weeks anyway, after he went to Augusta. The speculation is that if Ross joins Titan, his WSB radio talk show deal on Sundays would have been history under any circumstances since WCW is the major sponsor of the show, and he would probably move from Atlanta to Connecticut. There will be an imminent vacancy in the WWF announcing team since Sean Mooney is leaving, and there has been talk of WCW getting him.

MARCH 29

The latest on Jim Ross' arrival is that nothing has changed since last week. Ross has yet to get a release from WCW as of 3/23, although he was definitely in Connecticut at some point this past week.

APRIL 5

Although he has yet to receive his release from WCW, Jim Ross tried to pull off an angle reminiscent of when Vince McMahon took over the TBS time slot nine years earlier. On Sunday, Ross announced on his radio show on WSB in Atlanta on Sunday night that he had joined the WWF broadcast team and had Vince McMahon, Bobby Heenan and Shawn Michaels as guests on a Wrestlemania preview on his radio slow that is sponsored by WCW. Actually Ross himself didn't make the announcement of his joining the WWF as an announcer, McMahon did. Ross also announced this coming Sunday on WSB his radio show (9 to 10 p.m. Eastern time) would simulcast the last hour of Wrestlemania (doing the broadcast feed of Gorilla Monsoon and Bobby Heenan live on radio), that he would be a part of, with an in-studio mystery host from Atlanta (another former WCW announcer).

The radio show had become the major bone of contention in working out the release between Ross and WCW. McMahon hyped Ross as the business' premier announcer, saying Christmas came early for the WWF this year because they've gotten Jim Ross aboard and called it equivalent to John Madden jumping from CBS to NBC. Psychologically, this must have done wonders for Ross' many enemies in WCW to hear Mania being hyped and that it would be broadcast next week and Ross being hyped even more as joining the WWF on a show the company is sponsoring.

Although it was well-known within the industry that Ross was WWF-bound as an announcer, Ross had been denying even negotiating with Titan because he had yet to receive his WCW release. It was well-known Ross had done try-out announcing with McMahon and Jerry Lawler at the WWF studios in Stamford a few weeks back and was in attendance at the television tapings a few weeks back in Augusta, GA. Ross, on the show Sunday night, was no longer denying going to the WWF, despite not receiving his release, and it is believed Ross is going to claim WCW removed him from the payroll as a legal loophole to enable him to start broadcasting with Titan on Sunday, and most likely on regular television starting the following weekend, without having obtained a contract release.

Evidently McMahon feels the case is strong enough since he went on the air with him to make the announcement. WCW was wanting Ross to sign a clause in order to get his release that would involve giving up the WSB show to WCW and signing a clause that he wouldn't do another wrestling radio show on the station for the next five years, which may have been the biggest hold-up in the release since it appears Ross is wanting to keep the show as a WWF show and that Titan would be willing to pick up the sponsorship. WCW had been wanting Ross to announce that Tony Schiavone was taking over the show. WSB will be bringing in a new program director in April, and there is some question as to the future status of the wrestling show in any form upon his arrival.

WCW has already met with the station about taking over the time slot, but thus far nothing is definite as to which company will control the show in the long-term future but both are seemingly wanting it. It appears it will be Ross and the WWF in the short-term. I've been told to expect some major fireworks to come out of this situation.

MAY 3

Nobody has told me this, but Jim Ross seems to have already gained enormous influence into what is going on. Witness: 1) Vince McMahon talking about Mr. Hughes' college football background on Superstars and the Steiners college degree. People all thought Vince would change Jim Ross' announcing style, when it looks like it's the other way around; 2) A tournament on television during sweeps; 3) Boni Blackstone getting a try-out to host stand-up interviews ala Raymond Rougeau and Events Centers; 4) Bruce Prichard getting a television role; 5) At least one upcoming angle that has Ross' fingerprints all over it; 6) The big push for Mr. Hughes, who

Ross has always been high on. While I don't know if Ross had anything to do with any of this, it doesn't seem coincidental.

AUGUST 16

Jim Ross is planning a two-hour WWF syndicated radio talk show every Saturday night for two hours, which would likely go head-to-head with Tenay's show. No definite starting time has been made, but it's expected to kick off in about two months.

CHAPTER NINETEEN

BUSINESS DOWN
ACROSS THE BOARD

MARCH 29

Hulk Hogan worked his first house show the same night. The advance for Lakeland was terrible, with them hoping for a crowd of 1,200 even with the Hart & Perfect vs. Luger & Ramon headliner that has drawn okay elsewhere. As a favor to promoter Gerald Brisco, Hogan agreed to work the show. They were only able to announce on television that Hogan & Beefcake would be there, but at the building they challenged anyone in the dressing room and did a dry-run against Money Inc., winning the non-title match. Crowd was about 2,400 and $31,000. Told Hart got a bigger reaction than either Hogan or Perfect.

None of the Florida dates over the weekend (West Palm Beach, Miami, Daytona Beach and Lakeland) drew well (all under 2,500), however Boston drew 6,000 and Madison Square Garden drew about 10,400 paid and $180,000 on 3/22, which is pretty close to the same house as they drew for Headlock on Hunger, the previous loaded up house show.

APRIL 26

World Championship Wrestling's return to New York and debut in Madison Square Garden on 4/14 turned out to be one of those nights the company would just as soon forget ever happened.

The show at the 4,500-seat Paramount Theater (part of the MSG complex) received unanimous negative reports, including by those within the company. The show got off to a bad start with the strange stopping of a hot Ron Simmons vs. Chris Benoit match and the announcement that Ric Flair (scheduled to do an interview segment) wouldn't appear due to a problem with his flight from Charlotte (which was legitimate in that the flight he was on had an engine problem and had to return to Charlotte). From that point, there were regular chants of "We Want Flair" and "We Want a Refund" which hampered the rest of the show, which from most reports, had no matches better than three stars and was compared unfavorably in most accounts to Wrestlemania.

Even worse was the inability to sell out the small venue after being out of the nation's largest market for approximately one year. The show drew about 2,900 paid (about 3,500 in the building) and a $47,000 house. While much larger than the typical WCW house show gate, those figures for New York can't be considered successful, especially with the track record of NWA/WCW over the years in the New York market which has shown significant drop every time in return business.

The show opened with Johnny B. Badd beating Tex Slashinger and Maxx Payne beating Steve Regal in a weak matches. Simmons-Benoit followed, opening with a hot two minutes which was largely described as the best action on the entire card, then shockingly ending at that point. The announcement was made that due to the two wrestlers violating WCW rules, that the match was being stopped and ruled as is it never took place. For reasons that nobody has made clear, one of the agents backstage ordered Nick Patrick to ringside to inform the local referee to stop the match immediately, which left a major sour note with the crowd that the show largely never recovered from. The match was booked to go about 9:00 with Simmons going over, so this problem was not one of bad booking but of a decision made backstage which nobody is taking credit for and there has been no real explanation for. Before that match came the announcement that Flair wasn't going to be there. After the hot but unfulfilling Simmons-Benoit moment came the Van Hammer vs. Vinnie Vegas match which was described as worse than their usual road match. It actually lasted 9:00 although some said it seemed like it was three hours and nearly everyone thought it was longer than 15:00 because of how ones perception of time is sometimes warped when having fun. Although the show got better from that point, the overall reaction to the show remained negative, closing with a Sting vs. Big Van Vader title match ending with the simple Harley Race interferes for the DQ finish which only added to the feeling of being ripped off by the high ($25, $19, $11) ticket prices. Many of the babyfaces were heavily booed, in particular Van Hammer and Marcus Bagwell. Most of the top company brass was at the show and seated with them was Verne Gagne, who might as well have been responsible for this lesson in how to not to put on a live show.

WCW also ran its first house show in years in Toronto at Sky Dome on 4/17. This was said to have been a really good show, capped off by the largest house in several months for an "ordinary" house show in the high $50,000s with all tickets $15 (just under 4,000 paid). Ironically, the Toronto date was a "sold show" which means WCW received a flat fee from the local promoters for providing the event rather than receiving the gate. From what I was told, the Sky Dome people did a great job of making the crowd size look good and not looking bad to hinder the show by the way the place was set up. 4,300 people in a 60,000 seat building is set up poorly can look disastrous and has been known to kill more than one show.

MAY 10

The first weekend of house shows since Mania by and large didn't draw well. The only big house reported to us was the 5/1 Nassau Coliseum which drew 8,400, which is below average for the building but nowadays any crowd of that size can't be considered unsuccessful. The rest were in the 1,500 to 3,100 range. Highlights of the "A" shows were Bret Hart beating Lex Luger via DQ when Razor Ramon interferes as Hart has Luger in the sharpshooter. After the match, Ramon holds Hart and Luger goes for the forearm but Hart ducks and Ramon gets knocked out. When Ramon finally gets up, they tease a brawl between him and Luger which seems to be building toward a Ramon face turn. Yokozuna and Jim Duggan are having horrible matches in the negative star range, although with all the TV behind Duggan's comeback, he's getting as big crowd reactions as ever. Mr. Fuji throws salt leading to Duggan getting counted out. The other big match is Shawn Michaels vs. Mr. Perfect which has largely been 20:00 draws, although they've done the Dusty finish with Perfect winning the title and then getting DQ'd after as well.

MAY 24

While a variety of reasons can be given as excuses, some valid, the weekend of 5/8 to 5/10 was the third lowest rated weekend when it comes to cable television ratings of pro wrestling in history. Topping the ratings was Monday Night Raw at a 2.5, which was its second lowest rating since its inception in January, although going head-to-head with an NBA playoff game on TNT didn't do it any favors. Sensing two straight weeks of falling ratings is probably in a small part responsible for the hot show on 5/17. WCW did a 2.0, Main Event a 1.6 (show started 33 minutes late due to the length of the Braves game), All-American a 1.5, and both Power Hour and WWF Mania did 1.1's. The average of all shows was 1.69, slightly above the all-time low of 1.62. Television ratings, just because of viewing patterns, will always rise in the winter and start going down as warm weather approaches. Overall comparing ratings on a month-by-month basis has predominately, with some exceptions, shown a continuing declining trend. This means the record lows set late last summer may be set to re-occur around August and September. What will be interesting to note is the ratings for next weekend because WCW is coming off a strong Saturday night show and WWF is coming off an even stronger Raw show. This past weekend shows that the upswing in ratings from the winter, and particularly in February when Hulk Hogan and Ric Flair re-appeared with WWF and WCW respectively, was more a combination of seasonal patterns and a very short-term revival rather than an indication of a business interest turnaround.

MAY 24

Slamboree would have been a great idea if this was baseball. Old-Timers day is traditionally one of the best drawing gimmicks for most teams. It would have been a great idea if this was basketball. The legends game is now a successful fixture of the all-star weekend. It would have worked in Japan. New Japan did it a few years ago and it worked. But in Japan, ex-wrestling legends like Lou Thesz, Karl Gotch, Lord James Blears and Billy Robinson are routinely brought in as either dignitaries or coaches to the current stars, and wrestling's history is well-preserved on both television and in magazines.

Was it a great idea for WCW? As of right now, it doesn't appear to be the case. As of late this week, less than 1,000 tickets had been sold for the live show on 5/23 at the Omni in Atlanta. WCW was both doing heavy giveaways and giving out a lot of 2-for-1 ticket coupons in the Atlanta suburbs in order to make the house at least look respectable on the PPV broadcast as opposed to being respectable when the cash is counted. A lot of people would ask why this is happening? As mentioned previously, bringing back the legends of the sport is a traditional draw in most sports and has worked with wrestling in Japan and in Mexico as well. In addition, the Slamboree control centers with Eric Bischoff and Gordon Solie have been some of the best produced segments WCW has done. Surely those segments should have given the event an aura that would make the viewer feel this event was something special and therefore worth attending or ordering. There can be nitpicking about certain individuals who should have been brought in that weren't (and in most cases, it was because the individual turned WCW down rather than a lack of an invitation) and there are certainly a few being brought in who it would be a stretch to call legends. There is even one, Barry Owen, son of long-time Portland promoter Don Owen, who to the best of my knowledge has never even wrestled but was plugged by Gordon Solie as a long-time top contender for the NWA junior heavyweight title, whose main claim to fame in front of the cameras is being a below average ring announcer and the son of a promoter unknown outside of Oregon and Washington. But putting a few names aside, this is an idea that "should" have worked. And barring a last week flood of interest, it also appears that it didn't work.

Why? Wrestling in the U.S. has ignored its own roots and history for so long, that when it tries to draw based on those roots, it is almost guaranteed to fail. There isn't a baseball fan in this country who hasn't heard of Babe Ruth and Ty Cobb, and they go back more than 60 years. Very few modern fans have heard of Lou Thesz, or even Johnny Valentine, and they were still active stars 20 years ago. To readers of this publication, Slamboree is a big deal. It's the chance to see the people who gave a lot of 20+ year fans memories from the past. In that way, this idea will satisfy long-time fans. But the live and die for the moment promotion of pro wrestling is such that most long-time fans burn out, and there just aren't enough who remain fans long enough to be interested in the stars of 20 or even 10 years ago. Even worse, is the names being brought in and largely either Florida/Georgia/Carolinas names from the 70s, or ex-AWA stars, which leaves a good portion of the nation in those days when stars were almost all regional, with little interest or knowledge of most of the names. In today's pro wrestling to the mass audience, the stars of "good old days" are not Johnny Valentine, Mad Dog Vachon, Harley Race, Dory Funk or Verne Gagne. Outside of parts of the Northeast and Southeast, they aren't even Blackjack Mulligan and Dusty Rhodes. They are George Steele, Roddy Piper, John Studd, Mr. T and Cyndi Lauper. As someone who has followed this business for more than 20 years, it seems somehow "wrong" to make that statement, but it is also undeniable truth.

About five years back, WCW promoted a show in San Francisco and one of the mid-card matches pitted Mike Rotunda against Dory Funk. This is the same Dory Funk who was NWA champion from 1969-73, which, even by the standards of that time period, was a fairly long title reign. Compare Funk's standing in the business to someone in another entertainment business, say, the movies, baseball, or football, that was the premier act in their field for a four year period and an international superstar for more than another decade. By and large the fans couldn't understand why Rotunda was having so many problems with "an old man." It wasn't until about 12:00 into the 15:00 match that the fans started getting into it a little with comments that "the old man can really wrestle." If there was any interest or knowledge among the audience purchasing tickets of things that happened in the past, it shouldn't have taken them 12:00 to figure it out that the old man could really wrestle. And Harley Race would mean one hell of a lot more as a manager today. Officially WCW announced two of the legends matches as Funk, with Gene Kiniski in his corner, against Nick Bockwinkel, with Verne Gagne in his corner, and a tag match with Bob Armstrong & Thunderbolt Patterson vs. Baron Von Raschke & Ivan Koloff. Because of the legit injuries suffered by Armstrong on 5/9 in Knoxville, it's questionable whether he'll be able to work, but either way that match sounds pretty bad. The six-man hasn't been announced, but no doubt it'll include Dusty Rhodes, Wahoo McDaniel and Blackjack Mulligan.

Putting all that aside, the real reason this show looks to be a tough-sell is all the emphasis on the legends has taken all the emphasis away from the wrestlers of today. Up to this point, little has been done for the line-up. Big Van Vader should be wrestling Cactus Jack if they could have capitalized on a rare angle that garnered interest rather than letting in slip away. There seems to be no reason for the company's supposed top draw, Sting, to be wrestling Scott Norton, at least this early in the game. Barry Windham and Arn Anderson have done a little to garner interest in their match, but more people are probably interested in seeing Windham against Ric Flair and Anderson and Flair challenge The Hollywood Blonds. Speaking of the Blonds, who are the surprise both in and out of the ring highlight of the entire promotion, based on this weekend's television, more people are curious to see them against Flair & Anderson then Rick Steamboat & Shane Douglas. And while the Dos Hombres idea was kind of funny and well executed, although hardly original to the long-time fans they seem to be gearing this show for, they have yet to do anything to give a logical reason for a cage match, or do anything that would get the cage stipulation over. Should be noted that the Maxx Payne vs. Van Hammer match was pulled from the show and instead Payne will do a guitar solo. Based on what I'm hearing, they will still be reintroducing the Four Horseman on the show, three of whom will be Flair, Anderson and Ole Anderson.

The Tully Blanchard deal is dead because the two sides couldn't reach a financial agreement and someone will be brought as a new Horseman, believed to be an ex-WWF mid-card performer who has never gotten a major push before, but has talent. The legends matches would be a real highlight for long-time fans and even newer fans if wrestling hadn't most often forgotten it's past the day after it occurs. But it won't be. I just hope the audience shows respect for these guys, at least some of whom were the real backbones of the profession in their day. I'm sure the 900 or so who bought the advanced tickets will. Just hope those who get in with the freebies and 2-for-1s can as well.

JUNE 7

Our reports indicate the buy rate for Slamboree at between 0.3 and 0.4 percent, which would make it the lowest buy rate for any PPV show from one of the two major companies in history. That would indicate WCW's share of the gross at around $800,000, which wouldn't be the lowest ever because of the $24.95 price tag as opposed to the $19.95 price tag on a few of the poor performing PPV shows of 1992.

Officially WCW has released information stating they will be cutting back from 300 to 200 house shows per year, and concentrate almost exclusively on the Southeastern United States. Largely this has been the case already for most of 1993. WCW has a schedule booked through June with a full schedule of bookings, and reportedly through July as well, although one report says that they are heavily laden with "B" town type cities during those months. While rumors abound about major changes they are as yet unconfirmed officially although everyone is expecting major changes in the company over the next few months. Despite reports from within the company to the contrary, there won't be an elimination of house shows in September, however the company is going to be run on a house show basis like an old territorial style promotion starting in September. It appears the original schedule of tapings in Orlando, FL have been cut back from 48 hours of television to 18 hours. They'll now be taping from 6/5 to 6/10, three hours per day. Don't know if that's 18 weeks of World Wide, nine weeks of World Wide and Pro or some other formula including Main Event or Power Hour which adds up to 18 hours total.

JUNE 28

King of the Ring did approximately a 1.1 to 1.2 buy rate, which would be the lowest of any WWF PPV event in history. If that figure is accurate, it would gross Titan Sports approximately $2.6 million from the show. While that figure amounts to a lot more revenue than would be garnered this summer if the house show business was successful, the proliferation of PPV events by sheer numbers makes them less and less special to the public as noted by the declining buy rates and revenue. The King show's orders were cut nearly in half from Wrestlemania. Mania, largely due to the reappearance of Hogan, did a far less severe year-to-year decline than any of the WWF PPV events during the period he was gone, showing Hogan's worth, at least for a specific one-time comeback, on casual fans pocketbooks. However, this number shows that most of those casual fans only wanted to pay and see Hogan once. Whether this is because Hogan is perceived as yesterday's news and drew at Mania based on "nostalgia," or fans saw his marked size difference at Mania and like Ultimate Warrior, someone whose main gimmick for success was freakish size lost a great deal of appeal when the size was no longer there, is something we can only speculate on. However, for short-term cash flow, running this show is going to generate a lot more money than running house shows all summer would alone. And given the precarious state of the industry on several fronts, short term has to take precedence over long term because by the time long term gets here, the entire landscape could change markedly and any long term plans wouldn't even be applicable.

The most sobering number of the week was the 2.6 rating that the Clash of the Champions did four days later. It was the lowest rated and least viewed Clash in history, drawing a 4.7 share and being viewed in 1,549,000 homes, or even less than most episodes of Monday Night Raw. Ric Flair's first live match drew fewer viewers than a December airing of his three-year-old match with Ricky Steamboat did which led to the TBS decision to bring him back because of the idea he'd have an impact on ratings. Although Flair will take the lions' share of blame by finger-pointers because the entire idea of keeping him out of action since February was based on the idea that his return would do a 3.5 to a 4.0 rating, the overall state of WCW right now is such that no matter who they debut and what match they put on, there simply is minimal interest in their product. Last month's house show statistics were more of an abomination than the Clash ratings. An even more sobering thought as it relates to Beach Blast is that for all real purposes, the main event at Beach Blast was given away as the semifinal on the Clash, and when it was available for free, nobody cared or watched. Now one month later they are going to try and sell basically that same match for $24.95 based on a promotional tape that is sure to turn more fans off than on. TBS is contracted to air two more Clash specials during 1993, at which point a new deal between TBS and WCW for Clashes can be negotiated. Considering the production and promotional expense of doing an undertaking such as a Clash, a rating in this ballpark doesn't justify the expenses and if the numbers don't show some life before the year is out, I'd say the entire idea of doing Clashes would logically be in jeopardy.

The Clash drew 6,000 fans to the Norfolk Scope, but about two-thirds of that number was paper and the house was in the $20,000 range. The crowd was all moved into one half of the 13,000-seat arena, so for television purposes, it gave the illusion of a hot packed house. The most important thing is the crowd, whether they didn't pay to get in or not, was one of the most vocal major show crowds in a long time, which is a major plus in a business largely based on illusion.

The first Ric Flair vs. Big Van Vader match took place on 6/19 in Charlotte. The house was up to $19,000, which is an increase over recent shows in the market, but still has to be considered terrible considering it was Flair's WCW return in his home town and had a lot of local media publicity. The two did a **** match despite Vader's injury, which should quell those who thought the two men's styles would conflict. Harley Race was more involved than usual and it seemed to be an older fan base in that they understood the history behind Flair and Race, which has never been explained on television. Race interfered for the DQ when Flair had Vader in the figure four. Same finish at the Clash. Same finish as they used for the television main event with Steamboat-Orndorff that same day.

JULY 19

As of the weekend, the Beach Blast show in Biloxi, MS had about 900 tickets sold. The building is set up for about 5,500 capacity and should look decent on television but it'll be largely paper in the house.

AUGUST 30

Pace Entertainment, a group which specializes in concert promotions, called off the 8/29 Alamo Dome date in San Antonio after all the local publicity we mentioned last week netted an advance five days before the show of only 400 tickets in a 45,000 seat building. WCW officials were really unhappy because they had been guaranteed $50,000 to do the show.

AUGUST 30

The United States wrestling business, mired in a state of almost continual decline over the past 15 months, began showing significant signs of recovery over the past ten days. This came during a time period in August when traditionally business is six to ten weeks away from its typical late fall seasonal increase. While some of the signs can be directly traced to the working agreements between the WWF, SMW and USWA being beneficial to each of the groups, others, like the comeback in WCW's cable ratings over the past two weeks, came as more of a surprise and are somewhat harder to explain. Among the positive signs:

The 8/18 Clash of the Champions posted a 3.8 rating and was viewed in 2.32 million homes, which caused a major league party at the WCW offices on Friday. It is the largest audience to watch any pro wrestling television show in the United States in 1993. More people saw the Big Van Vader vs. Davey Boy Smith on first-run than any United States match since the November 1992 Fox Network WWF special. It is also the highest rated Clash since the November 19, 1991 Clash from Savannah, GA did a 4.3 rating with a triple headliner of Lex Luger vs. Rick Steiner for the WCW title, Rick Steamboat & Dustin Rhodes winning the WCW tag titles from Arn Anderson & Larry Zbyszko and Rick Rude pinning Sting for the U.S. title. However, it should be noted that both the January and September 1992 Clashes did 3.7 ratings, neither of which at the time caused major celebrations. However the rating may have saved the Clash concept, which was in grave danger of going the way of Dinosaurs (you know, extinct) when the contract expired at the end of this year after the record low 2.6 rating that the June Clash, built around Ric Flair's first match back, earned. In addition, the 8/7 and 8/14 WCW Saturday Night shows did 2.5 and 2.6 ratings respectively, the best numbers for the show since the 3.1 in early March for Ric Flair's return to the promotion.

The WWF drew its largest crowd in the United States of 1993 for a regular house show on 8/22 at the new Duck Pond Arena in Anaheim, CA for a seven-match card headlined by Yokozuna vs. Bret Hart in a cage match. The cage match, by the way, was reported to us as being a ****1/2 match, and other cage matches between the two earlier in the week in California were reported in the ***1/2 range. A paid attendance of approximately 15,000 (although kids being reduced priced left the final gate at $155,000, not in the league with three of the Madison Square Garden houses, let alone PPV houses in Sacramento and Las Vegas or what the house on 8/30 in Auburn Hills, MI will likely turn out to be) beat out the Madison Square Garden show of just nine days earlier for the largest paid attendance for a U.S. house show this year. This came on the heels of the MSG show on 8/13 drawing 13,000 fans and approximately $225,000, which was the largest gate for a regular U.S. house show in 1993. Wrestlemania in Las Vegas drew 15,045 fans, although the freebie count was such that paid was almost surely higher for the Anaheim card. The Royal Rumble in Sacramento, which drew a legitimate sellout (something neither the Anaheim show or Wrestlemania did) had about 15,000 paid, or in the same ballpark.

Just six days after drawing its second biggest gate in its history, Smoky Mountain Wrestling shattered both its attendance and gate records for the "K-Town Showdown" on 8/20 in Knoxville, TN headlined by a Bob Armstrong vs. Jim Cornette lumberjack match in which Armstrong vowed to refund all the fans' ticket money should he fail to send Cornette to the hospital. A crowd of 2,780 fans paid $18,100--or more than double the previous biggest gate in the company's history in Knoxville.

The USWA, which drew its biggest gate in a few years (2,800 fans paying $16,800) on 8/2 in Memphis for the first Jerry Lawler vs. Bret Hart match, has been over $10,000 every week since that time. That mark was eclipsed on 8/23 for a Yokozuna vs. Lex Luger non-title match because of Lawler vow to return everyone's ticket money if he failed to put referee Paul Neighbors in the hospital and Vince McMahon vowing to be in Neighbors corner for the match. The crowd of 3,567 fans paying $23,826 was the biggest gate for a USWA show since the 1988 Jerry Lawler vs. Curt Hennig AWA title change match. The promotion expects another big gate on 8/29 for a rare Sunday night show (so as not to buck Summer Slam), headlined by Lawler vs. Bret Hart in a cage match and Jeff Jarrett vs. Owen Hart for the Southern title.

For cable television, the weekend of 8/14 to 8/16 was the most viewed weekend of 1993, although the pre-empting that weekend of Power Hour skewed that average and makes that statement partially misleading. The five cable shows averaged a 2.37 rating in about 1.43 million homes. In comparison, the low point of 1993 for television viewing in the final weekend of April, drew an average cable rating of 1.69.

Promoters of the 8/28 AAA show in Los Angeles are predicting one of the five largest gates in the United States. While the advance is somewhere between $60,000 and $75,000 six days in, the Mexican-style shows traditionally draw almost exclusively a walk-up audience. For example, the 5/16/92 card which drew nearly 6,000 fans, had about 150 tickets sold in advance and the show was in grave danger of being canceled almost until two days ahead of time. Whether the $200,000 figure prediction that has been thrown around is feasible or not, it appeared very conceivable the figure could top the Anaheim WWF show and with some luck rival the Summer Slam gate in Auburn Hills. Some feel the $12 to $30 ticket scaling aimed at predominately a lower-income audience will hurt walk-up, although the 7/4/92 Los Angeles show that did $119,000 was scaled similarly.

The same promotional group, headed by Ron Skoler, a New York attorney, and John Arezzi, the former New York wrestling talk show host, that is behind two of the three weekend AAA shows in California was also involved one of the biggest promotional financial debacles in recent memory on 8/21 at Fair Park Coliseum in Dallas. The group sold the promotional rights to an "International Wrestling All-Stars" show to Dee Gholdston-Hamilton for $35,000. Hamilton also spent an additional $12,000 on local radio and television advertising, and Arezzi, Sensational Sherri and Scott Putski were all over local radio in the two days before the event. This doesn't take into account other costs of running a show which put the break-even point at around $50,000. Running in a market in which the weekly Friday show is basically a freebie (the past few weeks the promotion has handed up coupons for 200,000 free tickets every week), and with two or three other weekly shows in the market that are established wound up with fewer than 200 fans paying an estimated $2,000 in a 9,000 seat arena. Making things worse for Hamilton was that Jake Roberts, thought to be the big draw for the show, moved to Dallas in recent weeks and has been working in the area including working the "free" Global show the previous night. The show was actually canceled at 7:50 p.m. that night, 20 minutes after the scheduled starting time, by Arezzi when Gholdston-Hamilton didn't have the second half of the deposit money on-hand (the first $17,500 was paid in advance). She later reconsidered and the show went on, starting at about 8:10 p.m. Even with the fiasco, all the wrestlers received their promised guarantees.

SEPTEMBER 29

In a statement that is somewhat misleading, the weekend of 9/4 was the lowest rated weekend in the history of pro wrestling on cable television. This came on the heels of several weeks of increased ratings for both WWF and WCW. The reason this statement is misleading is because the 9/6 edition of Monday Night Raw was pre-empted due to U.S. Open tennis coverage, so what almost surely would have been the highest rated show of the weekend, and hence upped the weekend average, didn't take place. All-American Wrestling was also pre-empted for the U.S. Open. The combination of a holiday weekend and shows competing against the first week of regular season pro football and college football didn't help matters. The WCW Saturday Night show, coming off the heels of four straight weeks above 2.5, fell to a 1.9 despite a loaded one-hour show that included the second Rude vs. Dustin Rhodes U.S. title match and a six-man with Flair & Sting & Davey Boy Smith vs. Sid Vicious & Harlem Heat, which has to be taken as a dangerous sign since the main event of the PPV show on 9/19 is largely the same participants and with the weakest PPV undercard in recent memory. The Sunday show dropped to a 1.7, while Power Hour did a 1.6 and WWF Mania did a 1.2. The ratings for this coming weekend will be a more accurate barometer of where interest stands in the wake of competition from football.

OCTOBER 11

While the WWF was setting records in ticket sales this past week, so was WCW, only its records were in futility of not selling tickets. The 10/3 card at the Omni in Atlanta drew just 800 paid fans and $8,000, which is believed to be the smallest crowd in the nearly 20 years it has housed pro wrestling. It was so bad that at the door, scalpers (if that's even the correct terminology) were unloading ringside seats for $1. This came just three days after WCW had to cancel a television taping in Anderson, SC because there were no fans, even in a town that was heavily papered. Depending upon which source one wants to believe, there were anywhere between 40 and 210 fans in the 3,900-seat arena when the decision was made to cancel the show, with the crew, truck and all the wrestlers already there and basically outnumbering the audience. The fiasco was blamed on bucking a major fair in town, but in reality the product has reached the depths where it has virtually no interest as far as a paid house show product. Now it has become difficult for the promotion to even draw a papered crowd in some cities. Reportedly this fiasco cost the company in the $50,000 range. The taping was re-scheduled for 10/13 in Gainesville, GA and it's being advertised that the first 1,800 fans who come to Gainesville will get into the show free.

NOVEMBER 8

Reports from the early part of the European tour based on crowds and show quality weren't good. Opening night in Cardiff, Wales drew about 3,000 fans although there was a lot of heat for the matches since WCW had never been in Wales before. After the incident later that night, the spirits of the wrestlers was way down and shows the next two nights were said to have been below par, as were the crowds. Ticket sales were hampered when one week before the tour, WWF, which is far more popular in England largely by default since the WCW had strong popularity not too long ago but lost it due to a television show that made no sense, announced UK dates for December.

NOVEMBER 15

From a business standpoint, the European tour, which ended 11/7, has to be considered a disappointment. The United Kingdom shows were 10/26 in Cardiff, Wales (3,000), 10/27 in Blackburn (1,900), 10/28 in Bournemouth (2,000), 10/29 in Birmingham (6,500) and a double shot on 10/30 in London, with the afternoon show drawing 1,200 and the evening show drawing a sellout 5,000. Most of the German shows did about 2,000, which is far less than Bob Ury's Universal Wrestling Superstars tours have done in the same country without any television exposure and using mainly recycled WWF wrestlers. The shows in the immediate days after the Vicious-Anderson incident were subpar, however the evening show at Royal Albert Hall in London had five good matches out of six topped off by a ***3/4 with the Hollywood Blonds against Flair & Steamboat.

DECEMBER 6

In the wake of all the wrestling news, both WWF and WCW attempted to run major PPV shows within four days or one another and the result, in each case, was the lowest buy rate in the history of the promotion. Although many thought Battle Bowl was the worst major PPV ever, it is almost like it didn't even exist. The responses to our poll were barely half of what we would get for a normal PPV show, and the buy rate indicates

Observer readers weren't much different from the public at large. Early estimates are that Battle Bowl was ordered in 60,000 homes, or an 0.27 buy rate, which is believed to be the first major office PPV show that may not even show a profit. Royal Rumble did much better than Battle Bowl of course, with preliminary estimates showing 185,000 buys, which is still only an 0.82 buy rate. It would be the first WWF PPV show to fall below the one percent buy rate. The combined estimated company revenue of both Battle Bowl and Survivors combined would fall about $130,000 to $150,000 short of what Survivor Series itself did last November, and roughly $1 million short of the 1991 Survivor Series. When it comes to Survivor Series, it was pretty well expected going in this would be the case so the lowest buy rate ever doubtfully shocked anyone. It did cause some in WWF to re-evaluate the Survivor Series formula, as it did a few years back in taking it from a show of elimination matches to simply a regular card of matches last year. The elimination series worked well both in public interest and in the ring when the company had a lot more depth in the late 80s. As with Battle Bowl, both companies overall talent depth is at such a low point that the strongest PPV shows are the ones where they present the fewest number of wrestlers.

CHAPTER TWENTY

THE FADING INFLUENCE
OF THE NWA

APRIL 5

SMW has applied for membership in the National Wrestling Alliance, for whatever that is worth these days. In theory it gives them the availability on dates with the NWA champ, although Dennis Coraluzzo joined the NWA last year and hasn't gotten any dates of the champion thus far.

JULY 5

Expect some dispute to be arisen at some point over the NWA singles title. The NWA name is controlled by Bill Watts, Seiji Sakaguchi and Steve Rickard, none of whom are involved with WCW. There are also independent promoters out there, most notably Dennis Coraluzzo in New Jersey, Jim Cornette and Jim Crockett, who will be promoting once again in the fall, who are members of the NWA, thus by the bylaws have the rights to get dates on the champion. Coraluzzo has been attempting to get dates as is his right under the bylaws but WCW has ignored the requests. Unless a compromise is worked out, it wouldn't surprise me to see the NWA not allow WCW to use the name for the title or to see WCW simply let the belt evaporate into never-never land, which really isn't the worst idea because having two world champions in one promotion for this long a period is ludicrous.

JULY 12

Expect some fireworks regarding the NWA title. Several promoters who are members of the NWA, most notably Dennis Coraluzzo from New Jersey, are requesting dates of the NWA champion as part of the NWA bylaws, and of course the requests are falling on deaf ears. The NWA may have to take action which may result in WCW simply dropping the title. At the last convention, the key power in deciding the title legally was given to Bill Watts, Steve Rickard and Seiji Sakaguchi. Watts hasn't been in contact with the NWA lawyers and they don't even know where to contact him, and Sakaguchi seemingly has washed his hands of the title ever since Muta lost since Barry Windham means nothing in Japan and they had no intention of using him as champion. Coraluzzo has already sent a letter threatening a lawsuit against both WCW and NWA if he can't get dates on the champion.

AUGUST 2

In what could be a related note, the National Wrestling Alliance will be holding its annual convention on 9/3 in Las Vegas. Probably the most important topic that will be under consideration is the status of the NWA world title. Even though a legal letter was sent by the NWA to WCW regarding the unauthorized changing of the NWA title at Beach Blast, nothing will come of it largely because Barry Windham isn't going to be wrestling anyway and most NWA members like the idea of Ric Flair as champion once again. This is where it gets sticky. I'd surmise that many, if not most of the non-WCW members of the NWA would rather for many reasons have Flair as champion instead of Rick Rude, which WCW wants, because if they were to get dates on the champion, Flair would mean more on a one shot deal than Rude. According to bylaws, the NWA title recognition is in the hands of the Board of Directors, which is now a two-man board of Steve Rickard (New Zealand) and Seiji Sakaguchi (Japan). Bill Watts, who was the third member of the board, resigned his post about one week ago, which I guess says that he's fed up with wrestling completely. Currently the NWA consists of WCW, New Japan Pro Wrestling, Jim Crockett, Larry O'Dea, Rickard, Excalibur Promotions (Dennis Coraluzzo) and Gary luster and possibly one or two others. There has been a lot of talk of late that Jim Cornette and SMW were going to join the NWA but as of yet they haven't applied. Main stipulations for a promoter to become a member are a $500 entrance fee and proof that the promoter has been in business for more than one year. Since WCW is planning on changing the title to Rude on 9/19, this meeting may be an interesting political football game and conceivably could wind up with WCW losing power in the NWA and the title change not being recognized, which of course will make the previously taped television with Rude as champion a mess.

AUGUST 16

Todd Gordon, who has applied for membership in the NWA which could and probably will turn into a major political fight come the convention on 9/3 in Las Vegas. By the way, a correction to what was previously reported here, the Barry Windham-to-Ric Flair NWA title switch at Beach Blast was approved beforehand by the NWA. After NWA lawyers sent a letter to Ole Anderson saying they needed NWA approval or they couldn't switch the title, WCW went through the channels to get the approval before the Biloxi match.

SEPTEMBER 6

WCW has sent word to cable systems that the Flair-Rude match is to be only advertised as for the "World heavyweight title" rather than the NWA heavyweight title. On 8/17, the day before the Clash, WCW sent faxes to cable operators to replace Road Warrior Hawk with Road Warrior Animal in all advertising for the War Games match, which is funny because by that time most everyone in the organization knew that it was going to be Fred Ottman in the match (but they may have not decided upon the name by that time, and they ended up switching the name anyway). At the same time, everyone knew Animal wasn't going to work because of his insurance settlement so it appears to be a company knowingly false advertising.

SEPTEMBER 6

SMW has applied for membership in the NWA. The convention is this coming weekend and if the votes are there and it looks like they are, the NWA promoters are going to attempt to get a deal that they'll allow Rick Rude to win the title since the TV has already been taped, but only if WCW agrees to have Ric Flair regain the title from Rude at a house show promoted by a non-WCW NWA affiliated promoter.

SEPTEMBER 13

A question of semantics and public perception seems to be the main issue that came out of the National Wrestling Alliance convention held on 9/3 in Las Vegas. The convention was the first NWA convention involving largely unaffiliated promoters struggling to rebuild what was once the dominant wrestling organization in the world since the sale of Jim Crockett's wrestling company to Turner Broadcasting in 1988.

While the NWA has continued to exist, largely as a paper organization, in the summer of 1991 its name was largely done away with in pro wrestling circles with the departure of then-champion Ric Flair from WCW to the WWF. From its inception in 1948 through the mid-80s, the NWA was the largest wrestling organization in the world, comprised at one point of 26 different regional promotions, and its champion was the most recognized champ in the world until the WWF's national expansion combined with almost all the regional promotions going out of business all but destroyed the organization, which continued to exist in the late 80s as a euphemism for Jim Crockett Promotions. For the most part, the world title Flair held, for his final reign was generally called WCW champ rather than NWA champ although it was generally considered that the two were one and the same as it was the lineal title descent and same championship belt that the NWA champion had used. The "NWA" name was downplayed and eventually dropped in order for WCW to not have to pay a booking fee to the NWA for the right to use the name. After Flair was fired by then-WCW Executive Vice President Jim Herd, the NWA, which at the time was totally a paper organization, continued to recognize Flair as champion for the next three months until he joined the WWF, at which point no champion existed for approximately one year. When Kip Frey took over from Herd as WCW's Executive Vice President, he and New Japan President Seiji Sakaguchi came up with the plan to revive both the NWA singles and tag team titles with tournaments, one in the United States and the other in Japan, as international titles to be recognized by both New Japan Pro Wrestling and WCW. Both tournaments were held in 1992, although by the time they were held, Frey had been replaced by Bill Watts.

During this past year, Dennis Coraluzzo, an independent promoter of the New Jersey-based WWA, joined the NWA and began making noises about wanting dates on the champion. As the annual convention approached, with long-time member Jim Crockett no longer being affiliated with WCW in any way but a paper contract and well-known to be planning on starting his own promotion as soon as he was legally allowed (upon making the sale in November 1988, Crockett had signed a five-year no compete clause), there was a lot of talk about a nasty fight for control of the name and the title. In the weeks before the convention, both Tod Gordon (Eastern Championship Wrestling based in Philadelphia) and Jim Cornette (Smoky Mountain Wrestling) applied for membership. The week before the convention, World Champion Wrestling and Keystone Promotions (Gary Juster), both resigned from the group. In addition, the other WCW-affiliated vote, Joe Murnick Inc. (Elliot Murnick) didn't send membership dues, in effect, resigning as well. The fact that WCW was preparing for all this for months was obvious, as at the Disney tapings, for the shows to be held after the 9/19 PPV, when Rick Rude held the belt that signified being NWA champion, he was only referred to as "World heavyweight champion" with the initials NWA no longer being used. Sakaguchi, who was named NWA President at the 1992 Convention, also failed to send membership dues, effectively ending New Japan's involvement. Steve Rickard of New Zealand, Tony Rickard of New Zealand and Larry O'Dea of Australia, all names dating back to the glory days of the NWA's power, retained their membership. New Japan had decided to wash its hands of the NWA back in February when WCW made the decision to go with Barry Windham, who New Japan had no interest in using as a world champion, as the holder of the belt.

The convention itself only consisted of five people, Crockett, Coraluzzo, Steve Rickard (who brought with him voting proxies of Tony Rickard and O'Dea), Bob Trobich, a Charlotte attorney who is the NWA's legal counsel, and Paul Heyman (Paul E. Dangerously), as a representative of Crockett. Most of the discussion concerned the future of the NWA world heavyweight title, the power structure of the new NWA and discussion of approving the applications of Gordon and Cornette. No new President was named, with the power being in the hands of a three-person board of directors consisting of Crockett, Coraluzzo and Rickard. While the tag team title was brought up at one point, the subject was dropped quickly without any real decisions made. Gordon's application was accepted, while Cornette's application was tabled because the members wanted assurance that Cornette's promotion would recognize the NWA champ, since he's in the unique position of managing the current WWF champion. Word we get is that Cornette is going to accept that stipulation so it is expected his application will be approved shortly. It is also believed that a promoter in England will be sending in an application as well.

The biggest concern going into the convention and coming out is the status of the NWA heavyweight title, currently held by Ric Flair, although scheduled to be switched to Rick Rude on 9/19. It is expected that Trobich will be contacting WCW this week with a plan to switch control of the title from WCW to the members of the NWA. While unconfirmed, it is believed this plan suggested by the NWA will be to approve of Flair losing to Rude, provided WCW agrees to allow Rude to lose the title shortly thereafter to a person of the NWA board's choosing on a house show promoted by an NWA promoter. Since, at press time, WCW had not yet even received a proposal, let alone this specific one, what its response will be is unknown. I believe there is a good chance this proposal won't be accepted and WCW will continue to bill Rude or whomever of its choosing as World heavyweight champion without the NWA name. This is made clear by WCW sending a fax to cable operators asking them to not bill the Flair-Rude match on 9/19 as an NWA title match, but instead simply a world heavyweight title match. At this point, this could turn into a bizarre legal battle, since the wrestling public will consider Rude, or whomever he loses it to later, as the NWA world heavyweight champion whether the initials are used on television or not, since the initials had been used on television for that specific title and physical belt going back many years. WCW does own the physical title belt itself, as Sakaguchi, as NWA president authorized the sale of the belt to WCW when Windham became champion. This may speed up the inevitable process of unifying the two title belts in WCW, and simply having the eventual winner, with Dustin Rhodes name being touted the loudest as being groomed for the spot, be referred to as simply WCW champ or undisputed world champ, which fans will accept as also being the "real" NWA champ just as the same situation occurred in 1991 when the NWA champion legally ceased to be the WCW champion but that issue wasn't made clear on television to wrestling fans so virtually all assumed they were one and the same. The names bandied about the most as far as future NWA champion were Road Warrior Hawk, Terry Funk and Ted DiBiase. A contract, with guarantees and house show percentages, was drawn up which will be offered to whomever is decided upon to be the new champion.

SEPTEMBER 29

Yet another legal issue, this time of a more imminent regard, takes center stage in this week's news. Coming out of the NWA convention on 9/3 in Las Vegas, which took place just days after WCW's withdrawal from the organization, the alliance alerted WCW that it wanted to arrange for a smooth transfer of the NWA title (held at press time by Ric Flair, but scheduled to be dropped to Rick Rude on 9/19 in Houston) to a wrestler of its choosing, and that the NWA doesn't authorize the Flair-Rude match to take place involving a transferring of the title. A letter from NWA legal counsel Robert Trobich to WCW on 9/8 indicated an attempt to reach a negotiated settlement as to the transfer of the belt by the close of business on 9/10. It was the position of the NWA coming out of the convention that simply no longer using the words "NWA" in front of the phrase World heavyweight championship in advertising, as WCW has attempted to do on television the past few weeks (although the match was still advertised the weekend of 9/4 as for the NWA world heavyweight championship, and in syndication that aired the weekend of 9/11, Flair was still referred to as "NWA world heavyweight champion") was not acceptable to the membership because most fans viewing would be misled, because of so much prior television time emphasizing the belt and championship, that without a disclaimer, most fans would believe whether the term NWA was used or not, that it was the NWA world heavyweight title at stake. It is believed the NWA would have authorized the planned title switch to Rude only if WCW had agreed to allow Rude to appear on an NWA show and drop the belt, although in reality this scenario was never even discussed since nobody from WCW responded to the letter with any negotiations. As of press time, the NWA has scheduled a hearing in an attempt to get a preliminary restraining order on 9/15 to ask that the Flair-Rude match not be referred to as for any kind of a championship on the PPV and that any television references to it being for any kind of championship that were pre-taped be erased from future broadcast.

In other news involving the NWA name and group of promoters, despite how it was worded here last week, Jim Cornette and Smoky Mountain Wrestling's application to join the NWA was tabled and doesn't appear to be set for imminent approval. At least some of those at the meeting felt that, as was the case with the old NWA, that promoters involved should recognize the NWA champion as the world heavyweight champion, and believe

Cornette managing WWF champion Yokozuna is a conflict with that. From what I'm told, Cornette and SMW's check to join was neither returned nor cashed, and that Cornette will be accepted when his tenure in the WWF is over.

OCTOBER 4

At the house shows this week, the main events were Ric Flair vs. Rick Rude, with no announcement made regarding the title. When Flair gets the clean win, fans thought the title had changed and no announcement was made but no presentation of the belt and people left unhappy.

OCTOBER 11

A story on the NWA/WCW court-fight which originally appeared in the Charlotte Observer on 10/1, went national on the Knight-Ridder wires the next day. Right now there is no news on the case other than some of the NWA promoters are talking of raising funds to sue over the validity of the document signed by Seiji Sakaguchi giving WCW rights to use the NWA title belt and name.

CHAPTER TWENTY ONE

WRESTLING IN OREGON

APRIL 5

The legislature in the state of Oregon has introduced two bills regarding regulation and pro wrestling. Because of state budget deficits, the future of the Oregon Boxing and Wrestling Commission, probably the most high-profile of its kind in the country in that they've actually attempted to enforce some regulations, is in doubt. Senate Bill 525 is proposing that if there is no regulatory body that both pro boxing and pro wrestling events would become illegal in Oregon. Bruce Anderson, who is the head of the commission, made statements along the same line some months back when there was talk of eliminating his commission, saying that the activities should be banned without regulation. Another bill, House Bill 2125, would add a tax on PPV boxing and wrestling events to fund the commission, and would stipulate that no taxpayer money would go toward supporting the commission. The Oregonian, the Portland daily, ran a column by Margie Boule this past week in support of HB 2125, and of regulation of pro wrestling. The article cited in a favorable manner that the commission wouldn't let Art Barr wrestle (this is the same columnist that wrote numerous stories regarding Barr's sexual assault guilty plea), that a commission exam caught cancer in its early stages on a boxer, that the emergency procedures and regulations regarding promoters carrying insurance for all participants in boxing and wrestling events in 1992 provided for immediate surgery from a brain hemorrhage a boxer suffered in the ring and that an insurance company rather than the taxpayers paid the bill, and that it banned blading, because of the threat of AIDS and hepatitis. The article also noted that the commission instituted AIDS and drug testing of boxers and wrestlers (although not for steroids). Another major story involving wrestling in Oregon. Don Owen sold the Portland Sports Arena to a church group. When the group went to the building (they bought in sight unseen from realtor Anthony Osborne aka Doink the Clown Sr.), several of the wrestlers chased them away. The church group then demanded immediate eviction of the place by the Portland wrestling office, however Tough Tony smoothed things over telling the church group that until they took over they couldn't keep Owen from losing his regular rent from Batt's wrestling office. Escrow will end on February 25, 1994, so the group has until that time to run weekly shows in the Sports Arena but at that point they're done. Owen is removing anything worth anything from the building which includes both the heating and air conditioning so during the hot and cold season, there are going to be some uncomfortable nights in the final season of wrestling at the Sports Arena.

MAY 17

Newsletter Ring Around the Northwest (50 cents, 2740 SE Lewellyn, Troutdale, OR 97060) did an interesting issue covering the goings on in regard to the two bills in the Oregon state legislature regarding pro wrestling.

Rogers sent letters to various legislators and his letters and their responses are in the issue, along with two newspaper articles on the subject. The two bills in question are a bill that would require a six percent tax on boxing and wrestling PPV events along with continuing the current six percent live event tax to fund a boxing and wrestling commission. The second bill proposed is that if the commission is abolished, and because without the proposed taxes it wouldn't be economically feasible for it to continue, then both pro boxing and pro wrestling would be banned. Right now both bills are still in the discussion stage. According to a column from the Oregonian by Michael Burgess, word has it that the bill to tax the PPV events is a dead duck. The paper also printed an editorial on the subject which read: "The Oregon State Boxing and Wrestling Commission, created by the Legislature in 1987, has done such a good job in regulating those violent and sometimes corrupt sports that the commission's revenues are drying up. By cracking down on many shady, marginal boxing and wrestling operations, such as the so-called "tough-guy" fights, the commission over the past two years has chased away some of the undesirable events. And, with them, some needed revenue. The commission's budget, about $175,000 per biennium, is funded primarily by a six percent gross receipts tax levied on all professional boxing and wrestling events, including live, local closed-circuit telecasts. In the past two years, fewer boxing and wrestling events have been held in Oregon, so tax revenue is down. The Legislature should instruct the commission to increase its license fees and taxes on local promoters. If doing so prices professional boxing and wrestling programs out of the Oregon market for eternity, so be it. The Legislature's choices are to find additional funds for the commission, let it starve or abolish it and hope that the sleazy operations it has cleaned up won't return. A fourth option, favored by House Speaker Larry Campbell, R-Eugene, is to abolish the commission and ban boxing and wrestling in Oregon altogether. That's too extreme. The governor wants to pay for the commission's staying in business by expanding the six percent gross-receipts tax to include the distributors of pay-per-view boxing and wrestling telecasts in Oregon (HB 2125). This would be a tax on organizations such as Top Rank Boxing and Don King Enterprises, not on local cable companies or subscribers. Florida, Pennsylvania and Missouri finance their boxing commissions this way, and many more states are proposing to do the same. But a six percent tax on receipts from pay-per-view events originating outside the state is a poor substitute for going directly to the source; the local boxing and wrestling promoters and performers. They are the people regulated by the state. They should be the ones to pay the true costs of their own regulation." It's a sticky situation because live wrestling events in Oregon are operated on such a thin budget that a major increase could conceivably eliminate all but the rare WWF Portland house show.

AUGUST 23

Oregon passed a bill keeping the commission intact through funding from taxing wrestling and boxing PPV revenue. Sandy Barr, the Portland promoter, who expected the commission to be abolished and bounced his $58 license check, may find himself subject to disciplinary action. Barr's Saturday night cards in Portland are drawing around 150 to 200 per week, so the audience is staying steady using mainly students of his wrestling school. I'm not sure the fairness of WWF and WCW, neither of whom run shows in Oregon that have to be regulated, being the ones paying the freight for a commission to regulate local shows.

SEPTEMBER 6

The feud between Oregon commissioner Bruce Anderson and promoter Sandy Barr continues. Barr expected the commission to be abolished, but a bill passed to continue it. Barr's license check to the commission (which was only $58) bounced so he technically doesn't have a promoters license but is still running shows. Anderson sent him a letter saying he must pay the six percent tax on every show since 7/1, a convicted pedophile will not be allowed to work security, more railings must be set up to keep fans and wrestlers apart and no further wrestling shows can be held until all these matters are cleared up. Barr responded with a letter to the state attorney general saying he's not promoting wrestling matches, just workouts and since he isn't charging admission (getting around it by charging for parking), he shouldn't be under commission jurisdiction. In addition C.W. Bergstrom returned and is wrestling without a license.

DECEMBER 20

Hearings regarding the future of Sandy Barr's wrestling promotion in Oregon began on 12/3, with the state athletic commission, which requested the hearing to shut Barr down due to numerous violations. According to Mike Rodgers of the newsletter Ring Around the Northwest, the beginning was like a terribly one-sided squash match with the commission prepared and loaded with evidence and Barr and his lawyer having virtually no defense. Barr had been running weekly shows without commission approval, claiming to be running public workouts rather than pro wrestling exhibitions, and charging for parking rather than for admission. Barr had claimed that they weren't pro wrestling shows because he wasn't paying the wrestlers. Barr claimed he was just giving wrestlers expense money to get to the building. During the hearing it came out that the normal pay for a wrestler to work Barr's Saturday night shows before July 1 (when he was promoting pro wrestling matches) was $50 per night. The normal expense fees the wrestlers were getting when Barr claimed he was promoting public workouts was, you got it, $50 per night. On 12/6, the hearings were re-started. The way the process goes, the hearing officer will at the end make a recommendation. Should Barr lose this round, and from our reports he appeared to be losing badly, he could still appeal and stay in business until his appeal. What gets more bizarre is what happened between the Friday and Monday hearings. Before the show started Barr apparently said in the dressing room according to RATW that one of the wrestlers was a stooge for the commission and he was going to find out who it was. Later in the show, Love Machine (Sandy's son Art, same wrestler who is the major star for AAA in Mexico), was in town for a rare weekend appearance and faced John Rambo. Reportedly there was a spot where Rambo was to duck a clothesline, but instead Machine punched him in the face twice and blood was flying everywhere. The two began fighting in the ring with Rambo reportedly starting to get the upper hand, Rambo quickly called for the finish, in which he was supposed to go down, which he did. After the pin, Machine got out of the ring and Sandy Barr hit the ring and grabbed the mic in front of the fans and said that 15 minutes ago he found out John Rambo was a stooge for the wrestling commission and told Rambo to get back in the ring so I (apparently meaning Sandy, who has to be in his late 50s by now) "can beat the shit out of you." Rambo reportedly grabbed the mic and said, "Sandy, I don't know what you're talking about. These people don't know what you're talking about. I've never stooged. I'm just here to do my job." Reportedly later that evening Love Machine and Rambo got into it backstage when the other wrestlers broke it up. Rambo suffered a broken nose and several broken bones in his face and the nose was damaged so much that he was unable to breath out of it and was scheduled for surgery later in the week.

CHAPTER TWENTY TWO

WALLY KARBO
PASSES AWAY

APRIL 5

One of the original founding fathers of both the National Wrestling Alliance and the American Wrestling Association, Wally Karbo, passed away Thursday afternoon. He was having lunch with a friend in Bloomington, MN when he suffered a heart attack, and was pronounced dead on arrival at Fairview Southdale Hospital in Edina. Newspapers listed Karbo as 77 although friends said they believed his real age to be 79. Karbo was a well-known figure over the past two decades in many cities where the AWA promoted, known more for his often-imitated stuttering voice and mannerisms when announcing he was levying the biggest fines and suspensions after a notorious angle was shot in the TV studio at the AWA tapings. He was particularly well-known in Minneapolis and Winnipeg as the long-time person known as the promoter in both cities.

Karbo, who lived his entire life in the Twin Cities area, was offered a basketball scholarship to Notre Dame in the early 30s, wound up as a boxer for a short spell for boxing/wrestling promoter Pinky George of Des Moines. The connection brought him to Tony Stecher, the boxing/wrestling czar of the Twin Cities and he worked as an office boy and referee for many years, starting around 1936. Karbo carried finishes and helped book out-of-town shows for Stecher in the Midwest and became more powerful within the office. By the 1940s, Karbo in many ways was running the wrestling end of Stecher's operations. In those days, the Minneapolis office would traditionally shut down the wrestling every, and Karbo would spend the summers in Toronto helping the late Frank Tunney in the office.

Although Karbo is not listed among the six promoters who got together and formed the National Wrestling Alliance at a 1948 meeting, his was actually in attendance at the meeting as Stecher representative along with Sam Muchnick of St. Louis (the lone founder still alive), George, Frankie Talaber, Al Haft and Orville Brown. When Stecher died in 1954, Karbo and brother Dennis Stecher became co-owners of the Minneapolis Boxing and Wrestling Club, which was the forerunner of the AWA, and worked with Fred Kohler as a talent supplier for his nationally televised broadcasts from Chicago on the old Dumont Network. Karbo was instrumental in several top football players from the University of Minnesota getting into pro wrestling, the most notable of whom was Verne Gagne. Others included Butch Levy, Cliff Gustafson, Bronko Nagurski, Leo Nomellini and his long-time promotional assistant Bill Kuusisto.

Several years later, Karbo and Gagne together bought out Dennis Stecher's piece of the office, and created the American Wrestling Association as a promotional vehicle for Gagne to claim the world heavyweight title. Karbo and Gagne worked together for the next 26 years, climaxing in the early 80s with Hulk Hogan when the company had its most profitable run ever, including consistent monthly sellouts at the 18,000 seat St. Paul Civic Center. After Hogan left and the WWF started expanding, which included raiding much of Gagne's office, Karbo and Verne had their bitter falling out in 1985. Many say spelled that spelled the beginning of the end of the AWA because Karbo got along well with most of the wrestlers while Gagne didn't, and the AWA started losing its wrestlers at a rapid pace from that point forward. He worked for a brief time as the WWF promoter in Winnipeg, but eventually signed a non-compete pact with Gagne as part of the settlement when Gagne bought out Karbo's share in the company. In recent years, Karbo had worked with the LPWA.

Karbo was fondly remembered by most wrestlers in the Twin Cities area, and was particularly well-known as well-imitated for his distinct voice. In the mid-80s, after an arrest for being a "fence," (selling off stolen goods) Karbo was regularly heckled at the matches. As a television personality, Karbo came off as a slow thinking man, although those in wrestling, including the key promoters of the 70s, always considered that as a front because Karbo was well respected for his promotion's success. He was scheduled to be honored for his 50 plus years in wrestling on 4/17 at an independent show in Minneapolis promoted by Dennis Coraluzzo, his long-time friend Ed Sharkey (Pro Wrestling America promoter) and Sean Waltman (Lightning Kid). Sharkey talked of doing a annual show in Karbo's name, but was afraid because of how the Von Erichs used deaths to sell tickets that doing a show honoring someone may be taken the wrong way within the wrestling world. Karbo's funeral took place on 3/29 with Nick Bockwinkel delivering the eulogy.

CHAPTER TWENTY THREE

SMW THRIVING

AUGUST 23

Smoky Mountain Wrestling is seen as a lot of different things by different people. Some long-time fans see the group as a glimmer of hope that the future of wrestling will be the same as the past, but completely different from the present. Some see it as the only American wrestling show worth getting tapes of on a weekly basis. Fans in the cities where SMW promotes regularly probably see it more as simply the latest incarnation of local wrestling promotions that have come and gone for decades. Some wrestlers are using it as a chance to stay in wrestling and still be big fish, albeit in a smaller pond than they used to play in. Others are using it, and have used it, as a place to gain experience and a potential springboard to hit major promotions. And a few are just happy to be there and have no aspirations to work for anyone else in the United States, even though they could if they wanted to.

After being around for more than 18 months, Smoky Mountain Wrestling has established a legitimate foundation of fans in its core cities and can be viewed as one of only four legitimate full-time wrestling circuits left in the United States. But it is completely different than the other three.

The WWF is the established No. 1 promotion, still national in scope, suffering in recent months at the box office, but showing legitimate signs of revitalization. For the most part its product quality has taken a major turn for the better in recent months. But only those living in denial of the obvious can't recognize it has potentially the biggest cloud over its head in terms of if there is a fallout coming from the Justice Department investigation. Any long-term analysis of its situation by examining traditional wrestling factors or worrying about product quality, gates, angles, television ratings, etc. looks murky, but may not even be germane.

WCW is the laughing stock of the industry. Those at SMW are quick to point out that they largely outdraw WCW in head-to-head competition within their territory. In fact, based on average attendance, SMW doesn't trail far behind WCW. And that's with a company in which the salaries of the entire crew combined for one year is less than half of what either Sting, Sid Vicious or Big Van Vader will earn this year. While the life support systems of the remnants of the traditional National Wrestling Alliance of the 60s and 70s are waiting to be pulled, one factor can't be overlooked. WCW has the largest money conglomerate ever backing a wrestling promotion in this country. Major losses, the size of which would have killed every wrestling promotion in history in this country may be nothing more than annoying headaches for bookkeepers at Turner Broadcasting. Any traditional analysis of this company looks worse than bleak, but it, too, can't be judged by traditional wrestling standards. As long as TBS wishes to support the company, it can ride out any financial storm.

The only other group left is Jarrett Promotions, the final leftover of the territorial days. Jarrett is the lone survivor of the deaths of the territories caused by a number of factors, the biggest of which is the inability of the others, most of which were long-time monopoly businesses, to stay competitive against more financially strong and usually much smarter competition.

Smoky Mountain has almost risen from the ashes of the corpse of the wrestling business. But over the past nine months, even though from a business standpoint the group is largely in the same basic situation it was in, the look and face of the promotion are completely different. The Smoky Mountain Wrestling office of November, 1992, the last time we made the trip there, was new in almost no way except name. It was largely a conglomeration of veteran talent, most of which had worked before in previous Knoxville-based circuits and had seen its best days. Most of the wrestlers were knowledgeable in that they knew what to do to get a reaction, and could still do enough of it to get by and keep the audience riled up. It was obvious at that time from attending the shows that fans put up with, laughed with and at, and got a little heated during a series of prelim matches. The crowd basically waited for the real celebrities of the promotion, The Rock & Roll Express vs. The Heavenly Bodies with Jim Cornette, to tear down the house, which they did often enough to slowly build up a following at a time much of the rest of the business was sinking in a quicksand of red ink. While the newest office in the country, it also was the oldest in terms of age of its wrestlers. Gradually, more by the process of coincidence than any long-term plan, the August 1993 version of Smoky Mountain Wrestling looks completely different.

One thing is still the same. Those brief spots in matches with wrestlers who are either a little too green or just not talented enough that make a fan groan, still rarely exist. There are no Van Hammers or Erik Watts' being shoved down the fans' throat without much of a clue as to what to do. From the top of the show to the bottom, you rarely see a bad match, which is something none of the four major multi-million dollar companies in the world can boast of.

In the past nine months, Smoky Mountain Wrestling has established staying power. While artistically they are a success, financially it is most likely they are still just hanging in there. I've been told a normal spot show needs 400 to 500 fans to break even. Back in May and June, they weren't coming close to that, and even now, they hover around that figure most nights. Knoxville, the largest city on the circuit, has been a break-even proposition most shows because of the higher costs of renting and working at the auditorium. It's not an exaggeration to say that every penny is pinched. For example, tickets in Knoxville only go on sale a week or two before the event to save the $50 per day ticket charge the building box office has. Television production has been cut back as compared with months before. Still, the company keeps chugging along, fueled by a crew of wrestlers and other assorted personnel largely consumed by wrestling rather than people driving from towns to get a payday. There are spiritual uplifts, such as being the first promotion ever to be mentioned on television by the WWF, and in a positive light, something that even two months ago would have seemed mind-boggling. And there are the financial successes, a near-$10,000 house, the second largest in the history of the promotion, this past Saturday night in Johnson City, TN.

But for all the romanticizing people do about SMW, and for all the talk about the quality of its television show, the booking, the interviews, and the workrate, this is still more a story of an ability to survive and perhaps even a constant battle to survive.

On the positive side, no promotion in the country has as high a percentage of good workers. The television, despite having virtual no production budget as compared with the big boys, as is good as any around. No promotion can touch SMW for the quality of interviews from top-to-bottom. And at least based on three shows this past week that I attended, from top-to-bottom SMW puts on the best consistent house shows in the country. A Friday night show at an old red brick high school gym in Morristown, TN was, for heat and match quality, as consistently good quality as any PPV show thus far in 1993 besides the WCW SuperBrawl. A Monday night television held at a middle school in a coal mining town somewhere in the hills of Virginia before 300 fans was more entertaining than any WWF taping held in the Bay Area in the past eight years. From a spectator standpoint, the wrestling ring they work in is the best in the country, and leaves one confused as to why WWF and WCW can't or don't build a comparable ring. The key seems to be the amplified noise level that impresses the audience with every bump. On the negative side, fans watching the first hour of the taping were hit with so many angles that few were able to remember them all. The promotion also uses more groin shots per capita than any promotion I've ever seen. Without exaggeration, there must have been close to two dozen on Saturday night in Johnson City, TN.

SMW wrestlers work anywhere from two to five nights per week, generally earning $100 to $200 per shot, that's income before expenses. The babyfaces augment their income by selling photos, t-shirts, buttons, etc. of themselves that they autograph before the show and during intermission, but nobody is going to get rich working this territory, nor are they going to starve to death for the privilege and fringe benefits of being called pro wrestlers. It's funny because almost to a man, everyone who worked WCW that is with this group will complain about the guaranteed contracts in that group creating unmotivated talent and that the old system of being paid on the house was superior. Yet, albiet on a much smaller scane, the wrestlers here work on a certain amount per shot, rather than a varying pay determined by the house. The overall attitude of the performers is tons better than those making a lot more in WCW, and there isn't the constant jealousy that's so prevalent in the WWF and USWA. The face crew is led by Bob Armstrong. Now in his mid-50s, Bob looks in good shape considering his age, but everyone knows his age since he's got four sons who are active wrestlers, and can only work in short spurts. Correctly used, he's been an effective draw since the angle that subsequent moving from "commissioner" to active wrestler. Over the long haul he's better suited for the commissioner role, but there's still a little mileage left for his as an active wrestler. His son Steve is a very good worker, but somewhat lacking in charisma. His son Scott is adequate in the ring, but smaller than everyone else on the circuit. His son Brian, who also works as TV jobber The Dark Secret, has the most size, but is short on experience and doesn't have the "look" of a star.

The top singles babyface is Tracy Smothers, who has been a good worker for years but is now on the borderline of being great, with those who traveled to SMW this weekend seemingly feel he was the best worker in the promotion. He may be the most improved wrestler in the world this year. But it's questionable how long he'll keep that spot since it seems he's going to become a regular traveler to All Japan, and the promotion can't continually "injure" its lead face as it did this past week to enable him to leave for a month. Smothers, who fashions himself and the wrestlers in the promotion as the L.A. Raiders of wrestling, has a most interesting role with his gimmick of waving the Confederate flag as the Wild Eyed Southern Boy. After an angle where the flag was burned by Dirty White Boy, an obvious Southerner who gets heat by pretending to be from New York, the flag became an even more focal part of is appeal. It was ironic that the first day in Tennessee, on the front page of the Knoxville newspaper was a story about the local controversy surrounding the flag and how most blacks and some whites find it offensive as if it somehow represents slavery and/or racist viewpoints. For better or worse, blacks don't attend SMW shows, either. The most popular act on the promotion, after all these years, is the Rock & Roll Express, who, along with the original Heavenly Bodies and Jim Cornette, largely rebuilt the territory. Ricky Morton is still very good and Robert, as always, is just good enough not to hurt the team. They must like working here since they turned down an offer to be the top face tag team in WCW a few months back. Underneath are Tim Horner, a solid worker who lacks charisma, but has some appeal as a hometown boy, and Bobby Blaze, a jobber who has the "never quit" gimmick and shows a lot of potential.

The heel side isn't quite as strong, although Jim Cornette is far and away the best manager around. Jimmy Del Rey is technically very good, but doesn't look like a star like Stan Lane did. Tom Prichard has everything but the size to be comparable or superior with most of the top stars in the major groups. Brian Lee has the size, and is much better in the heel role than he was as a face. Inside the ring he's not the quality worker of the rest of the crew, but working with Smothers put on great matches. Dirty White Boy, who will be a face probably in about two months, is a great worker, especially for the brawling style the promotion is built around. Kevin Sullivan is limited in the ring, but during his matches he spends very little time in the ring. His unique character is effective because he's so different and more so because he's an excellent interview. Sullivan could be focused on stronger, but he's only a part-timer working in between overseas tours. The Bruise Brothers aren't smooth workers, but are athletic enough and fast enough to be impressive with the Rock & Roll Express. In a territory with so many guys who are 5-9 and 5-10, a pair of 6-8 twins surrounded by guys so much smaller has an intimidating appeal.

Chris Candido, who is only 21 and getting his first real chance at a real territory (he worked Memphis last year but was never given a chance there) and has both the attitude and aptitude to be a superstar in time, with his only drawback being his lack of height. Ironically the strength of his work style, doing a lot of hot moves, would be most applicable to New Japan and isn't really necessary and sometimes doesn't even fit his crybaby heel role here. But he's been very good doing the crybaby gimmick, and throws in hot moves from time-to-time perhaps as much for his own enjoyment. Tammy Fytch, doing a college brat gimmick as Lee's manager, is going to be a major star in this business.

CHAPTER TWENTY FOUR

AJW ON FIRE

APRIL 19

The All Japan women All-Star Dream Slam II on 4/11 in Osaka, just nine days after what was easily the most highly publicized and financially successful women's wrestling show in history, failed to pack the 7,000 seat Prefectural Hall. The show, which was announced as drawing a sellout 7,500, actually drew about 6,500 fans paying from $26 to $177 for the four-and-a-half hour long nine match show featuring All Japan Women against the women from three other Japanese promotions. The non-sellout can be explained partially by the fact that the card was flanked by UWFI (which did sellout plus standing room) and All Japan (which ran on Monday night which we don't have a report on at press time but probably sold out as well) house shows in the same building the day before and the day after. In addition, many of the hardcore Tokyo fans who travel to the major shows probably had their fill of women's wrestling with the six-hour long house show the previous weekend.

Either way, it was no doubt the largest women's wrestling gate ever in Osaka, but it wasn't the largest crowd (a 1985 Chigusa Nagayo vs. Dump Matsumoto hair match drew 12,500, and the same two had a return hair match in 1986 that drew 9,500, but with lower ticket prices). The Lucha Libre match was canceled because Ultima Tigrita (Esther Moreno) apparently suffered a pretty severe leg injury. The highlight and main event of the show was the return match from last year's Match of the year as voted by the promotion with Dynamite Kansai & Mayumi Ozaki of the JWP office winning the WWWA tag team titles from Manami Toyota & Toshiyo Yamada in a best-of-three fall match that went just over 30:00 and I'm told was five stars plus, similar to their to last year's match. The two teams will be rematched with the belts at stake on 6/2 in Sapporo. The semifinal saw Akira Hokuto and Shinobu Kandori matched up again in a tag match with Hokuto & Aja Kong vs. Kandori & Eagle Sawai. Kandori caught Hokuto in a submission hold and the referee stopped the match because it was ruled inescapable, although Hokuto didn't submit and it was announced Hokuto suffered a shoulder injury from the hold. This is to build up a Kong vs. Kandori match before Hokuto-Kandori in August. Chigusa Nagayo did a second job, this time to Bull Nakano, in one of the other highlight matches. Nagayo did a magazine interview pretty much saying that she's trying to peak for the 8/25 show and by then she should be 100 percent after taking four years off to be an actress.

Told that seven of the nine matches on this card were ***1/2 or better, and that on the 4/2 show, that eight of the 11 matches were ***1/2 or better with the Hokuto vs. Kandori match being ***** and the magazines wrote it up as a match of the year and those who have already seen the video in this country have given me similar comments. I was told that the Yokohama card was the better of the two in that it was one of the best wrestling shows ever in Japan. The Yokohama three-tape videotape collection will be released on 4/25 (selling price is $177) while the Osaka two-tape collection comes out on 5/8 ($158). I wonder how many people actually pay those kind of prices for the tapes, although the tapes of both of these shows are going to become collectors items.

APRIL 26

I had the chance to see the Dream Slam I show on a hand held video. It was definitely one of the greatest wrestling shows ever. The only drawback is maybe there was too much for one show, as six hours may be overkill. Instead of producing it as a show to fit a time limit, it seemed like in eight of the 11 matches, everyone was out there trying to have the best match of their career since it was the biggest crowd any of them had ever worked in front of, with time restraints be damned. That was largely the case as it had more great matches than any Starrcade and was easily superior as an overall show to the 1989 Baltimore Bash and Music City Showdown that are largely remembered as the best major U.S. big shows of the past five years. They also did what WCW should (and no doubt won't) do for the legends. They had 21 of the most famous retired wrestlers in the 25-year history of the company come out, to their original entrance music, walk down the aisle while a tape is playing on the big screen of the finish of the match with them winning a major title (or in the case of Dump Matsumoto, making a spectacular ring entrance). So you see them walking down the aisle today superimposed on the big screen of them in their prime in the ring.

MAY 17

The All Japan women's promotion is riding the wave of a new boom in popularity coming off the two big shows in April. The 4/2 All-Star Dream Slam I show selling out Yokohama Arena and being such a spectacular card and gaining so much publicity saw several of the biggest weekly news magazines (Newsweek, People, Business Week, Esquire types) commission features on the promotion, in particular focusing around Aja Kong, Bull Nakano and Akira Hokuto (who seems to have benefitted most in popularity from the big shows and is now the hottest wrestler in the promotion). Three major magazines in particular were at the 5/8 Korakuen Hall show "discovering" this "new" phenomenon. The show drew the usual sellout of 2,200, but the most incredible number, and this is almost surely a record for any kind of wrestling promotion, was that they did $36,000 alone in sales of the Dream Slam I videotape at the show. All 200 tapes the office brought to Korakuen at $180 per head sold out almost instantaneously. There is a good chance this group will run a show at Tokyo's Sumo Hall in December.

The line-up on paper was nothing special, headlined by a special tag team match in which Manami Toyota and Toshiyo Yamada worked on opposing teams as Toyota & Yumiko Hotta beat Hokuto & Yamada in 21:49 when Toyota pinned Yamada with the Japanese Ocean Cyclone suplex in what was said to have been a great match. They ran an angle after the show to build up LLPW's house show in the same building on 5/11. Rumi Kazama (LLPW's president and also a wrestler) grabbed the house mic after the main event and jawed off with Hokuto, ending with Hokuto saying she'd be at the LLPW card. The semifinal was an interpromotion match with Takako Inoue going to a 30:00 draw with LLPW's Harley Saito in a match with a ton of heat. On the downside, the schedule of running about 250 house shows per year with the great workrate every night is more than taking its toll on the crew. The regular spot shows these days are going with almost a skeleton crew, which only makes things worse as those who aren't hurt have to work longer matches every night, which only increases their injury odds. As mentioned before, all the foreign regulars (Debbie Malenko, Esther Moreno and Terri Power) will be out several months due to serious injuries. Bat Yoshinaga is out of action with a disc problem in her neck which required surgery. Sakie Hasegawa, who just returned from knee surgery, has a pinched nerve in her neck which has left her right arm numb, but she's still working. Mariko Yoshida has been out of action for several months with a herniated disc in her neck which required surgery.

In addition, Bull Nakano is only working major shows which apparently is a concession the office made with her to keep her from retiring, and will only wants to work mid-card matches with no major program so she can have "ordinary" matches which aren't as physically punishing. By the time they get to the big show at Budokan

Hall on 8/25, one wonders how many more will drop. There is talk about dropping from 20 to 25 shows per month to about 15, but pushing those shows harder by making them more important, which is the formula New Japan seems to be using successfully, although there is resistance by those in management who simply believe wrestlers should be working every night because that's how it has always been in the past.

Speaking of this group, the newsletter International Wrestling News out of New Zealand published a list of the largest crowds in history for women's wrestling shows. The Dream Slam show was second largest crowd ever on the all-time list, which is headed by a crowd of 18,000 in 1941 for a match between Mildred Burke and Elvira Snodgrass. In third was a crowd of 14,000 at the Boston Gardens in 1948 for Burke vs. June Byers and a crowd of 14,000 in Monterrey, Mexico in 1939 for Burke vs. Lupe Acosta. Next on the list were the 13,000 for the 1985 Lioness Asuka vs. Jaguar Yokota match, and the 12,500 for the 1985 Chigusa Nagayo vs. Dump Matsumoto match and also for the 1989 Chigusa Nagayo retirement show.

AUGUST 23

All Japan women have its first show at Budokan Hall in many years on 8/25. Because of the problems associated with the Yokohama Arena Dream Slam I card, which didn't end until 12:30 a.m. (last train left at 12:05 a.m. so the problem with getting taxis for about 16,000, largely getting back to Tokyo which is an hour away, was enormous). Budokan officials have apparently put a 10 p.m. curfew on the show, so the starting time was moved up to 5 p.m. on a Wednesday night, so the majority of fans will still be at work when the opening bell sounds.

SEPTEMBER 6

Despite having a 5 p.m. starting time on a Wednesday night, the All Japan women's "Budokan Legacy of Queens" show drew an announced 14,500 fans, or about 2,000 shy of a sellout. The show, headlined by WWWA (All Japan women) champ Aja Kong defending her title against JWP champion Dynamite Kansai, was the third largest recorded crowd in history for a women's pro wrestling show and certainly the second largest gate ever, trailing only a 1941 match in Louisville, KY between Mildred Burke and Elvira Snodgrass which drew 18,000 and the Dream Slam I show on 4/2/93 at the Yokohama Arena which drew 16,500 as far as attendance. In some ways, this crowd was more impressive than Dream Slam I for a number of reasons. First, Dream Slam I was the first show filled with interpromotional matches, and the first show with a gimmick such as that should draw better than subsequent shows. In addition, Dream Slam I featured the return to the ring of Chigusa Nagayo, who didn't work this card. The early starting time of a weekday couldn't have helped, either. As far as gate, it almost surely only trailed Dream Slam I and may have been the second million dollar house in the history of women's wrestling.

SEPTEMBER 13

AJW ran Korakuen Hall on 9/5 drawing a sellout 2,300 fans with the main event being a match to decide the new UWA (Mexico) womens tag team champions as Yumiko Hotta & Takako Inoue beat Suzuka Minami & Akira Hokuto in 24:55 when Hotta pinned Hokuto. The last champs were Manami Toyota & Toshiyo Yamada, who vacated the titles. The big news was after the main event, when LLPW President Rumi Kazama came to the ring area and challenged Hokuto to a hair vs. hair match on the LLPW's biggest card of the year on 11/9 in Tokyo. Hokuto said she'd announce on 9/29 in Nagoya as to whether or not she'll accept the challenge. Hokuto has been working every night with a blown out knee suffered the first week of August, and then on 8/21, broke a bone in her back, but still has worked almost every night. She'll be getting a knee operation on 9/17. While this has yet to be announced, I believe the ultimate hair vs. hair Hokuto vs. Shinobu Kandori match will take place on 12/6 at Tokyo Sumo Hall.

The next major show will be 9/29 in Nagoya which will be composed of mainly All Japan women vs. LLPW matches with Kandori vs. Hotta, Aja Kong & Kyoko Inoue vs. Eagle Sawai & Midori Saito, Toyota & Yamada vs. Harley Saito & Miki Handa, Bull Nakano vs. Noriyo Tateno, Takako Inoue vs. Yasha Kurenai, Suzuka Minami vs. Otaku Hozumi, Sakie Hasegawa & Kaoru Ito defending the Japanese tag team titles against Mikiko Futagami

& Leo Kitamura, Etsuko Mita & Mima Shimoda vs. Bat Yoshinaga & Tomoko Watanabe to determine the No. 1 contenders for the Japanese tag title and Numatchi defending the Japanese jr. title against Mitsuki Endo.

An even bigger combined show was announced for 10/9 at Tokyo Bay NK Hall with Kong vs. Hokuto for the WWWA world title, Yamada vs. Dynamite Kansai, Toyota vs. Mayumi Ozaki, Kyoko Inoue vs. Devil Masami, Bull & mystery partner vs. Hotta & Minami, Takako Inoue & Yoshinaga vs. Kandori & Kurenai, Shimoda & Ito & Chikako Shiratori & Asari vs. Cutie Suzuki & Plum Mariko & Hikari Fukuoka & Boirshoi Kid, Hasegawa vs. Candy Okutsu and Mita & Watanabe & Numatchi vs. Futagami & Endo & Midori Saito.

OCTOBER 18

All Japan women's Wrestlemarinpiad '93 sold out Tokyo Bay NK Hall with 6,700 fans on 10/9. The main event was scheduled as a WWWA title match with Aja Kong defending against Akira Hokuto. Before the match, Hokuto said she wanted it to be a non-title match, which is a switch. Hokuto said that since she had the knee operation (she was on crutches as late as the day of the match but still worked) that it cheapens the title for someone who is injured to be a challenger. Hokuto worked the match, but was obviously nowhere close to ready so it wasn't the great match you'd expect from those two, and eventually Hokuto was pinned. The two best matches on the show were said to have been Manami Toyota pinning Mayumi Ozaki of JWP and an eight-women captains fall tag team bout with Team JWP of Cutie Suzuki & Plum Mariko & Hikari Fukuoka & Commando Boirshoi beating Mima Shimoda & Kaoru Ito & Chikako Shiratori & Asari. A captains fall match means that each team picks a captain and the only way the match can end is when the captain of one team pins the captain of the other. In this case the captains were Mariko and Shimoda. The show airs on television this coming week. All Japan women sold out Korakuen Hall the next night for the beginning of their tag team tournament. In tourney bouts, Sawai & Kurenai beat Shimoda & Etsuko Mita, Yumiko Hotta & Takako Inoue upset Bull Nakano & Suzuka Minami when Hotta pinned Bull and Aja Kong & Sakie Hasegawa beat tournament favorites Kyoko Inoue & Toshiyo Yamada.

DECEMBER 6

All Japan women attempted another major cross-promotional undertaking on 11/28 in Osaka Castle Hall, drawing 9,600 fans in the 15,000 seat building. The show was described to me by several as being not as good as either Dream Slam I or II or the August Budokan show, but still a very good show. A few negative notes. Osaka is the second largest city in Japan behind Tokyo, and the relationship between the two cities from the Osaka residents eyes is often one of jealousy because Tokyo gets all the great concerts, all the great sports events, etc. and with the exception of New Japan, all of the wrestling companies specifically cater to the Tokyo audience and run their major shows there. All Japan women announced both this card and the 12/6 Tokyo Sumo Hall card simultaneously, and there was a strong feeling even among those who attended that Tokyo was getting the "real" blow-out show, which from the line-up, does appear to be the case. Hence the show came nowhere close to selling out. In addition, the rep from the Dream Slam cards carried over. This card lasted four hours, 40 minutes (started 3 p.m. Sunday afternoon, ended 7:40 p.m.). While the super hardcore fans love the five and six hour marathons of four and five star matches like Dream Slam I & II, it is hard for most people to sit still for that long no matter how exciting the action is in front of them. Lots of fans for that reason didn't even show up until 4:30 p.m. to 5 p.m.

Most reports are the best match was a Captains fall Survival Elimination match with All Japan vs. JWP, won by JWP three to two. Captains fall rules in Japan are that in six, eight or ten mans, each team picks a captain and the match can only end when one captain pins the other. This had a twist with the elimination rules, however it also had rules that the first team to win three falls could also win the match, which apparently was done to allow JWP to win without Akira Hokuto having to do a job on the show, since she's in such a major match this week with Shinobu Kandori. Toshiyo Yamada pinned Manami Toyota in 30:47 with a reverse Gori (Guerrero, famous Mexican wrestler of the 50s) especial in a match to determine the vacated All-Pacific title (the second ranking belt behind the world title in the promotion). Both women debuted dozens of high spots in this match. Told this will be sensational on video, but it wasn't as good live because neither woman played to the crowd at all, just were doing the match to provide for their own personal self satisfaction which is often the knock on Toyota that she does spots to get the rookies at ringside to pop and for her own self more than she tries to work the crowd. The finale of Takako Inoue & Yumiko Hotta keeping the UWA tag titles beating the LLPW team of Kandori & Miki Handa, who looked like the weak link going in, going down, in a double juice match.

DECEMBER 20

All Japan women finished off its most successful big show year ever by selling out the 11,500-seat Tokyo Sumo Hall for a card billed as St. Battle Final on 12/6. The five-hour marathon show was headlined by rematches of the most remembered match from both Dream Slam I and Dream Slam II in April, in both cases with the losers from Dream Slam prevailing. Shinobu Kandori beat Akira Hokuto in the main event. The original plan was for this to be a hair vs. hair match, but tickets were selling so well promoters decided there was no need to put the stipulation in that would require Hokuto to lose her hair at the end when the show was going to sellout anyway. In the other, Manami Toyota & Toshiyo Yamada regained the WWWA tag team titles beating Dynamite Kansai & Mayumi Ozaki in 25:33, while Aja Kong retained her WWWA title beating FMW's top woman wrestler, Megumi Kudo in 22:34. Judging from photos, it appeared the top two matches were excellent, although live reports didn't indicate either match was the calibre of their previous classic matches. Two titles changed hands in the undercard to keep the promotion vs. promotion feud alive as All Japan women dropped titles to wrestlers from other groups. Japanese Jr. champ Chapparita Asari lost her title to JWP's Candy Okutsu, while Japanese tag champs Sakie Hasegawa & Kaoru Ito lost their titles to LLPW's Miki Handa & Yasha Kurenai.

A few days before the show an even bigger announcement was made in that the group has booked the Tokyo Dome for November 20, 1994, which is a huge risk. All Japan women with tons of publicity and months of hype legitimately sold out Yokohama Arena (16,500 seats) but that was with the return of every major star in the history of the promotion for cameos and the return to the ring of Chigusa Nagayo, who was the biggest superstar in the history of Japanese women's wrestling. Even that Dream Slam I, which may go down in history as the greatest wrestling show of all-time, needed a huge walk-up to sellout. The ability to come back and easily sellout Sumo Hall with a killer line-up after some of the other big shows that followed failed to sellout with weaker line-ups shows the potential with the right line-up to still draw 10,000+ with high ticket prices. It's quite another thing to go into a 60,000 seat building and run a profitable show, although just going into the Dome and attempting such an undertaking will bring with it a lot of mainstream publicity. It's also well-known that the Dome is the absolute worst building in the world to watch pro wrestling and the women's appeal more than any other group in Japan is based on the ability to view incredible live matches. New Japan's annual sellouts are largely due to the show now being traditional rather than fans going and expecting the greatest wrestling show they've ever seen.

CHAPTER TWENTY FIVE

VIOLENCE LEVELS IN WRESTLING INCREASE

APRIL 19

The Cactus Jack vs. Big Van Vader brutality feast airs this coming Saturday (4/17) on TBS. Don't know how much, if any, will be edited, but it probably was the most brutal U.S. match in a long time. Too brutal actually, since Jack was hospitalized after it was taped, and needed 24 stitches, 17 above the eye, seven below, suffered a broken nose, dislocated jaw and a concussion. There is a lot to admire about Cactus Jack as far as the lengths he'll go to put on a good performance and making the most out of his somewhat limited physical talents. Still, sometimes the limits he's willing to exceed are way past the point of what's good for him. As banged up as he was, he still worked all his scheduled dates over the weekend and had good matches to boot.

APRIL 26

The Cactus Jack vs. Big Van Vader match aired this past Saturday, edited so that none of the blood was visible on television. It was beyond brutal in what Vader did to Jack, but I'm not sure the effect of the brutality got across to the average fan at home. The surprise win by Cactus and Vader's incredible post-match performance made the thing the most "believable" thing on a major promotion television show in a long time. Rematch will be taped 4/21 and air this coming Saturday. Cactus, despite the concussion, 24 stitches and dislocated jaw, didn't even miss one booking.

MAY 3

WCW ran on television 4/24 what appeared to be its best angle in years involving Big Van Vader and Cactus Jack, but it largely wasn't an angle at all. In what was easily the best television show, at least in terms of production, since the new regime took over, the return match from the brutal encounter that aired 4/17 was the highlight. It was another very good match, in many ways better than their first match even though Jack was working when logic said he shouldn't. The match wasn't anywhere near the over-the-limit brutality of the first meeting where Jack suffered numerous facial injuries and a concussion from Vader's punches. Jack, for reasons he himself probably only truly understands, wanted in that way to create a memorable match and in that way, he did succeed, although one questions if the injuries are worth it. The rematch was even more memorable for reasons that make one ask the same questions. After missing a somersault bodyblock off the ring apron, Harley Race pulled off the mats covering the floor and Vader power-bombed Jack. The drama of this was increased to the nth degree when Vader lifted Jack up for the move and Tony Schiavone said, "If he power bombs him on the floor, he may kill him." That was supposed to be an angle where Jack would be "injured" enabling him to take four months off to recuperate from the injuries he'd already suffered and has been working nightly on. As it turned out, even with Vader attempting to protect him on the move, Jack's head apparently hit the floor hard on the power bomb (a sickening thud was heard on the landing, although Jack has taken numerous more spectacular and theoretically more dangerous bumps on the floor with sickening thuds before). Jack was knocked out and lost feeling in various extremities, which resulted in him being immobilized and rushed to the hospital in an ambulance, all of which aired on television. On television, it almost appeared to be a legitimate career ending or even life threatening situation. In the building, there was legitimate fear that he had broken his neck.

At press time, the nature of Jack's injuries weren't completely known other than he suffered a severe concussion which was made even more dangerous by the closeness in time to his previous concussion just 16 days earlier. There were no broken bones. The numbness in his hands hadn't gone away which could be an indication of nerve damage, which would be the most serious of the injuries in that it could keep him out of the ring for an extended period. There is really no way of saying when he'll return, but nobody expects even in a best-case scenario of him being back for at least a month, but barring unforeseen developments based on further examinations by a neurologist, it doesn't appear it's a career-ending situation.

MAY 3

Between the injuries to Cactus Jack and the great extremes certain gimmick matches are going brings up a scary subject of where this is all leading to. Next Wednesday in Japan, with both the explosive barbed wire death match and a ring surrounded by a bed of nails match for competing offices on 5/5 brings up how extreme the gimmicks are going. And we'd be remiss in not bringing up what may be the most dangerous situations of all, the weekly "can you top this" approach to dives of the younger wrestlers each week on AAA. In addition, the level of legitimate brutality, similar to the first Vader vs. Jack match in the recent All Japan main events and even in some of the women's matches, not to mention dangerous gimmickry to the extreme like people taking DDTs on baseball bats with nails stuck in them with W*ING. At some point several of these offices need to draw the line between the daredevil mentality which in many promotions the realities of the business is always going to breed, and safety. Where are we going when it comes to these extremes? Where do we go after this? How powerful can we make the explosives before someone gets hurt? We've already had a ring of fire match last year which wasn't well planned enough and the heat inside the ring was such that everyone had to run for their lives and it nearly ended it all for The Sheik. And what are the ramifications going to be before somebody tries to go one gimmick too far and goes over the edge in an attempt to draw money?

This is completely different from the bad taste to draw money arguments of the past. There is a difference between exploiting situations and going one step over the line when it comes to testing the real limits of dangerous situations. There are always going to be certain individuals who are willing to do things far beyond rational thought. Pro wrestling in some ways caters to these types. Fans by and large love it. And even if they don't know what it is or love it, they remember it. Every wrestler worth his salt's goal is to make a lasting impression. Some have types of ability and charisma that they don't even have to even dream of going to the ultra-dangerous extremes to make an impression. But those types will always be the fortunate minority. Others who don't have those gifts and are willing to accept it and make a living. But there will always be those people with an uncontrollable inner drive who are aren't willing to accept the limitations of a human body.

Obviously pro wrestling has to give the illusion of violence or it can't exist. But the point should be that while some level of danger has to exist, the most dangerous situations should be illusion and not reality. The ability to make the people believe you are hurt or you took a fall so bad you need to go out on a stretcher is okay, and to do it you don't have to really suffer the kind of injuries that the daredevils of this business seem to be suffering on too regular a basis. Just this past week or two, besides Cactus Jack, we've heard about Esther Moreno breaking her leg doing an Asai-moonsault on a spot show in Japan, Psicosis cracking his ribs doing a Liger-dive, and with the standards seemingly getting rougher and rougher and gimmick matches going to more extremes, the injury rate is only going to increase. Injuries, stiff blows, bloody noses and fat lips from occasional accidental potatoes, bad falls resulting in a knee going out and lower back damage from bumps are always going to be a part of this business. That has to be accepted and I don't think anything can be done to change that. But taking a quick path to physical destruction shouldn't be a part of it.

There is a Japanese wrestler named Akira "Tiger" Katayama. Nobody speaks his name anymore. Nobody knows his fate. The last wrestling fans in Japan heard of him was about a year ago. They knew he suffered a serious injury and was carted out of Korakuen Hall in am ambulance after missing a dive out of the ring. Katayama landed on his head on the missed move, and broke his neck. He's now a quadriplegic in a wheelchair. The only part of his body he has any movement is his tongue, which he has to use to operate his wheelchair. He will never escape from his wheelchair. There are two more sad points when you think about him. One is, in reality there is no turning back in sports. The second is, because of that, there will eventually be another like Katayama. It's something that needs to be considered the next time you hear about people doing dives off the balcony or triple somersault splashes to the floor.

MAY 17

This week's wrestling recipe:

Take one crazy person. Put him in the ring with the person with his mentor, the person who taught him most of what he's learned about being crazy. Surround the ring with barbed wire laced with explosives. And 15:00 into the match, blow the entire ring up.

The end results? Two men drenched in blood hugging each other. One going to the hospital needing 72 stitches in his back and upper stomach. The other had his nose nearly shredded from the barbed wire. And a packed house of 41,000 fans (approximately 32,000 paid) paying $1.8 million gate made it the biggest and most successful financially over-the-edge wrestling show in history.

Wednesday night's (5/5) Atsushi Onita vs. Terry Funk match at the Kawasaki Baseball Stadium was the latest step in the world of "Can you top this?" wrestling gimmickry. By the results at the gate, it will only signal more of the same but going farther over the edge for both Frontier Martial Arts-Wrestling, and its imitators. These new levels of risk-taking to be labeled as pro wrestling will no doubt go unchecked until serious injury, or worse, results.

Fortunately nobody was hurt this time. Well, hurt badly, that is. And a lot of money was made. From this and his other outdoor shows, not to mention the solid nightly business of his office, Onita's place in wrestling history needs to be acknowledged. He has to be ranked as one of the biggest drawing cards in the history of the pro wrestling business. If you're skeptical of that label, think of how many people have drawn 32,000 paid or $1.8 million for what was promoted as a one match show, but also drew over a consistent basis of several years as this show was not a one-time fluke? A few, all of whom's place in wrestling history is safe. And Onita is probably the most unlikely of those that would be grouped in with him in that category. He's bled a lot worse, taken just as many stitches and the hospital visits for a lot less of a financial payoff at the end than this. And until the day he retires, which may not be far off in the future as he admitted at Korakuen Hall in January, he'll no doubt continue to do so.

Starting his pro career at the age of 15, Onita worked for several years in the United States, mainly in Texas and Tennessee learning the brawling style that made him a celebrity a some 15 years later. He was pushed as a bright young junior heavyweight star in All Japan, kind of All Japan's answer to Tiger Mask (Satoru Sayama) when he returned home as NWA International junior heavyweight champion having beaten Chavo Guerrero in a memorable match in Charlotte, N.C. in 1982. His manager for that match? Terry Funk. But that stage of Onita's career didn't go as expected. Onita was one of the first in Japan to consistently do dives, or topes, out of the ring. His topes were more reckless and out of control than others, not so much in terms of degree of difficulty, especially when compared with the moves today, but in his own timing and proficiency since the art form was very primitive at the time. He frequently misjudged his target which resulted in some serious landings. He suffered a devastating knee injury in a 1983 match against Hector Guerrero that kept him out of action for nearly one year. In 1984, after attempting a comeback, his knees were so bad that he announced his retirement at the end of the year. It wasn't until four years later that the name Atsushi Onita resurfaced in a bloody independent match against karate star Masashi Aoyagi (who is now a member of New Japan's Skinheads). The success of that show was a predecessor to Onita forming his own promotion, Frontier Martial Arts-Wrestling. By the end of its first year, the group was already a small-time hit in Tokyo drawing enthusiastic sellout crowds monthly to Korakuen Hall with Onita gaining cult appeal for his bleeding and his post-match crying interviews. Popularizing street fight matches, barbed wire matches, and nightly bloodbaths, some to the point of being grotesque, Onita and FMW took Japanese pro wrestling in a new and bizarre direction.

Four-and-a-half years after his bloodbath with Aoyagi signalled his return to the pro wrestling world, he was covering Funk as eight explosives went off like the finale of the July 4th fireworks show. The ring was engulfed for 20 seconds in a cloud reminiscent of bombs going off in war footage. In reality, the explosion wasn't nearly as impressive or as devastating as the test explosion a few weeks earlier in the same stadium, which was empty, for the press photo coverage of the test explosions to hype ticket sales for the show. But the climax of the match was still visual enough to be reproduced in living color not only on the front page of the major sports daily newspapers in Japan, but also in many mainstream non-sports newspapers that usually don't cover pro wrestling shows.

While this wasn't actually the largest crowd in FMW history, the previous record (48,300) was set in conjunction with a major rock concert in which the music was more of a draw than the wrestling. For just wrestling, the FMW major annual outdoor spectaculars the past two years, headlined by Onita doing electrified barbed wire matches against Tarzan Goto and Tiger Jeet Singh respectively, have drawn in the 20,000 to 25,000 paid range. Onita, who has become a mainstream celebrity with his frequent appearances on talk shows, game shows and television commercials, was going from media outlet to media outlet in the days leading up to the show hyping his match with his teacher, and the card drew incredible walk-up business. The success of this show was such that in the days following the event, FMW announced follow-up outdoor stadium shows on 7/24 in Fukuoka and 8/22 at the Osaka Baseball Stadium.

Although this was a ten-match show which provided a literal smorgasbord of wrestling styles, from a promotional and drawing standpoint, it was a one match show. Onita, a strange cult celebrity figure for his propensity for self destruction, and Funk, who taught him wrestling in Amarillo when he was in his mid-teens back in 1973. While this was definitely student vs. teacher in hype, there was no babyface/heel here, as both men are enormously popular in Japan. This match gave Funk, one of the first of the foreign babyfaces to achieve mainstream popularity in Japan in the 70s, a career rebirth in the country he gained the most fame in. The match itself was said to have been a spectacular performance by Funk, in a building packed with kids who weren't even old enough to turn on a television set by themselves when the Funks had their famous match with The Sheik & Abdullah the Butcher that really was the phase one stage in what has evolved into what Onita has taken and turned into a shockingly, no pun intended, profitable business. Some said Funk's performance was so good that he made this match was Onita's finest hour.

The rules and stipulations of the match went something like this. The ring ropes were taken down and the ring was surrounded by barbed wire. If a wrestler was caught in the barbed wire, a small kaboom would go off, a minor explosion would take place and sparks would fly everywhere. At the 15:00 mark, the eight bombs that surrounded the ring would go off. Both men vowed they would be the last one left in the ring. For the record, Onita pinned Funk in the match's only fall at 12:14 after a DDT. Onita then left the ring and went to the dressing room while Funk laid motionless. As the fans began the countdown for the big boom, Onita showed up at ringside. As the announcer gave the ten second call, the fans started counting down 10-9-8-7-6, etc., all of a sudden Onita ran back into the ring and with just a few seconds before the explosion, he covered Funk as if to protect him and sacrifice himself, taking the brunt of the explosion for his teacher. The bombs went off and the ring filled with smoke and surrounded by fire. There was enough smoke that momentarily, the fans at ringside had a hard time breathing, and it was even worse for the two in the ring. But it was only momentary. As the smoke cleared about 20 seconds later, both wrestlers were laying on the mat as if they were dead. The crowd shrieked and pleaded chanting "Onita" and "Terry" as they slowly held onto each other as they rose to their feet.

The show was described as a good card overall, with the many different variety of matches taking place. One observer described it as like going to a sports event and seeing tennis, baseball, volleyball and soccer games one after the other. The only similarity was that they all have a ball. In this case, maybe the only thing all the matches had in common is that they were all worked inside of a pro wrestling ring.

NOVEMBER 1

The Vader-Cactus Jack main event exemplified what is beginning to turn into a dangerous trend in this business. Not disturbing to fans because many love matches such as this. It's disturbing because the element of risk and injury is being flirted with much too closely when matches get as stiff and legitimately brutal as this and other recent matches have turned out to be. I was actually planning on writing this before the Havoc show, with the main emphasis being on the plight of the All Japan women's wrestling promotion in 1993 and the daredevil tactics of Sabu, but Jack and Vader then put on a match that was one of the best of the year, and in many ways defines the problem.

Violence on television has become a major political issue in recent weeks. Luckily for pro wrestling, "nobody cares" enough about it to where any possible ramifications of senate hearings aren't going to be applied to its product mix. Besides, any serious wrestling fan shouldn't be nearly as offended by what's fake about the product, as by what's real. Without violence, whether fake or real, there would be no pro wrestling. That's the lure. Going overboard can and is a turn-off to the general audience, although there is a small hardcore that even going way overboard appeals to. But total elimination of both fake and real violence in the long run would mean the total elimination of pro wrestling as an entertainment form.

Most pro wrestlers matches aren't as brutal, dangerous or legitimately violent as many other pro sports, boxing being the first that comes to mind. That's a necessity because the top pro wrestlers have to work anywhere from 150 to 250 times per year. In a UWF-style promotion, where there is more legitimate violence, the wrestlers have the benefit of generally working once every four weeks or so.

There is always going to be a "can you top this" mentality to pro wrestling. Younger wrestlers are constantly learning from and imitating those who have stretched the boundaries of their imagination when it comes to brutality and acrobatics. Because of that, and despite the cries that this isn't so from old-timers, the actual in-ring product constantly evolves and constantly improves unless it's stifled by those who can't bear to let go of the past.

But with improvements, if the new ways include either stiffer and more realistically brutal blows, as in Japan, or higher risk acrobatics, as in Mexico, comes an increase in the dangers. At what point do the risks exceed the potential rewards?

Time can't be turned back, but if you want to see where this trend is going to lead with men's wrestling in the future, you have to look at the group that is years ahead of all others when it comes to the in-ring product, the All Japan women. All Japan women had its most successful year since the mid-80s at the gate and achieved its highest level of mainstream popularity in many years. Two of its shows, the 4/2 Dream Slam I card and the 8/25 Budokan Hall show, were among the five largest crowds in history for all-women's wrestling shows and most likely far-and-away the two largest gates, with each most likely topping $1 million (previous record before this year was about $500,000). Dream Slam I was, if one can make a totally subjective statement as fact, the single greatest collection of matches on any card in history and in the opinion of many, the greatest wrestling card of all-time. Dream Slam II wasn't far behind. When it comes to moves, speed and execution, they've taken the art form to a new level. Even though they are women, when it comes to legitimate brutality, working with pain and overall guts, they are second to none. The result of this has been a very successful year for the promotion. But is it worth the human cost?

Virtually every wrestler in the group works with varying degrees of serious injury and pain. Pain is a part of life of any wrestler. It goes with the territory. So is doing risky moves. Many injuries have and will always occur on basic moves that aren't even all that dangerous, but either the landing is a little off and a body part blows out, or a body part simply gives out from the constant wear and tear. But when a wrestler, like Akira Hokuto, comes back too fast after a knee operation and after a broken back to appear on a major show, is it guts, or is it insanity? When a wrestler stands there and lets another man swing a chair as hard as he can to his head without putting up his hands to block or cushion the blow, is it guts, or is it insanity? When a wrestler dives out of control from the ring to a concrete floor without the fluidity and experience to protect himself and then literally has to be scraped off the concrete, is it guts or insanity? Anyone who saw the second back suplex that Steve Williams gave Kenta Kobashi a few weeks back was in awe of the move, but the truth of the matter is that Kobashi, the most talented performer in the business, literally risked a serious chance at a broken neck that could have ended his career to make a finish look like nothing ever seen before. People like Cactus Jack, Sabu, Psicosis, Rey Misterio Jr., Tsuyoshi Kikuchi and countless others are either beginning to or already have taken the limitations of insanity and stretched them to insane levels. It's scary to think of the condition their hips, back and joints will be in when they reach the age of 30 (Sabu, who didn't achieve stardom in this business or work a full-time schedule until recent years is about 30, Jack is 28), let alone in old age. The crazy moves of Dynamite Kid, who had the advantage of being an incredible athlete to boot, paled in comparison with these men, and yet Kid was nearly a cripple by the age of 30 and now, at 34, is a forgotten man in the profession where ten years ago, before his 25th birthday, he was revered by many as being its best worker. There are Japanese and Mexican wrestlers that have become quadraplegics from missing dives outside the ring. The fact that the nature of this business is such that taking care of those who have given isn't one of its strong suits only makes the long-term stories of these men even more precarious, even as their peers and fans applaud them for their courage, imagination and guts. In their cases, it is no longer working a style with an element of risk, it is working a style with a certainty of both risk and of long-term serious damage. Anyone who has been around older wrestlers who have put 20 years in knows that while some wind up in old age as the pictures of health, the bumps aren't so kind in the long run to others. But the daredevils of today put their bodies through more punishment in a few years than some crippled ex-wrestlers did in 20 year careers.

The All Japan women's group has just enough wrestlers left standing to put on cards. Virtually all are hurting in some way or another. It is not unheard of for young women to come to the building with knees and ankles so blown out that it hurts to walk, and then do topes onto the floor to further damage those joints. The casualty list for 1993 is scary. Hokuto, who came back from a broken neck suffered years ago from a tombstone piledriver off the top rope (a move that, because of its risk, hasn't been repeated that I know of since), has gone from one major injury to another in what will probably be her final year as a wrestler. Terri Power practically destroyed both one knee and one side of her upper body learning the ropes in Japan, and hasn't been able to wrestle since April. The two other non-natives that were regulars, Debbie Malenko and Esther Moreno, both have been out of action for more than six months after suffering broken legs. Mariko Yoshida, who one year ago was thought to be potentially the best of all the younger girls, broke her neck and missed virtually the entire year. This past week alone, nine of the 24 wrestlers who started the year were out of action due to various injuries. Sakie Hasegawa's back and knees have led to constant recurring injuries. Most of the remaining "healthy" ones, besides working on damaged joints, are performing a style where the risk of serious injury is so high that it's almost a certainty. The upside is these women, as a group, are the best in-ring performers this business has and when enough of the top women are healthy at any one period, they have the ability to put on the best shows this business has ever seen. They also go from being inexperienced rookies to superior workers on average many times faster than performers in any other group. But when the chance of injury increases from the risk that the nature of this business demands to a certainty, it may be time to try and get things under control. How can that be done? First, increasing the amount of submission holds that are over allows less bumps to be taken and less crazy moves to have to be done during the climax of the matches. Second, if the style demands high-risk maneuvers, keep the schedule manageable enough to at least try and minimize certain risks. Any promotion that works a serious hard style nightly (none in the U.S. qualify in this category) is insane to work guys 200 dates per year, or else their best young talent will never reach its prime in one piece. While many are waiting for the day American wrestling reaches that level of proficiency, if it does without learning safeguards, there is a serious downside to progress.

CHAPTER TWENTY SIX

THE EARLY
DAYS OF ECW

MAY 3

Paul E. Dangerously was on John Arezzi's radio show 4/24 talking about his full involvement in a new promotion run by Jim Hudson of Austin, Texas. The group is starting in June and talked about taping television for High Density television (which is being experimented with in Japan, but is currently a good five years away from being television technology in the U.S.).

MAY 10

Paul E. Dangerously (Paul Heyman) has been on a few radio shows over the past two weeks talking about the new promotion he's involved with. All that he spoke of was the group was holding its first television taping on 6/11 in Fort Hood, TX and names mentioned as appearing were Road Warrior Hawk, Pat Tanaka and Paul Diamond (Max Moon). Jim Hudson is listed as the promoter and the show is being taped for High Density television, which is superior picture images to the current system. Hudson believes will be the big thing world wide in the next few years although it won't spread to the U.S. until several years later. The taping will be a pilot that they'll be trying to sell in syndication during the fall season when the new TV schedules are made. The only other thing we've been able to learn is that Dangerously will be the booker and he'll largely be building around trying to get over new talent to U.S. fans, among whom will be Konnan, Eddy Guerrero and Crash the Terminator.

MAY 24

Even though there were only about 300 fans at the shows each night, there has been a ton of talk stemming from the Eastern Championship Wrestling television tapings on 5/14 and 5/15 in South Philadelphia. Among the names who worked the shows were Road Warrior Hawk, Terry Funk, Paul E. Dangerously, Don Muraco and Jimmy Snuka for booker Eddie Gilbert. However, the most talked about incident took place the first night, and it wasn't Eddie Gilbert throwing fire in the face of Hawk, although that happened also. It was during a match with J.T. Smith and Dark Patriot (Doug Gilbert) which wound up in a brawl and they were fighting on a television interview platform. Patriot knocked Smith off the platform and Smith landed on the floor some 14 to 18 feet below, which is an awful lot of punishment on one's knees trying to land. I guess the original plan was for Smith to take the bump while hanging down, which would take seven feet away from it. One report we got was that Smith injured his knees badly on the bump, although he worked the next night. Patriot then flew off the platform with a double sledge onto Smith. Both were limping at television the next night. The taping was loaded with outside interference and wild Memphis type brawls at the end of almost every hour, including the finale on the second night with Funk vs. Snuka where every wrestler on the card ended up brawling all over the Sportatorium-like building.

JULY 5

The ECW show on 6/19 in Philadelphia headlined by Eddie Gilbert vs. Terry Funk drew a $10,500 house, which is more than most WCW houses have done of late and rival some of the smaller-town WWF gates as well. Lots of complaints continued last week regarding the leaving of the woman bare breasted in the ring, including promoter Tod Gordon denying knowledge of it beforehand and decrying the incident saying that his wife and kids were watching the show as well.

JULY 26

Eddie Gilbert is now 49 percent owner of ECW after a deal was closed with majority owner Tod Gordon this past week. Gilbert is negotiating with Tito Santana and Koko Ware and is hoping to bring in Stan Lane for the 8/7 and 8/8 TV tapings and Big Bossman and Sensational Sherri in the fall. Abdullah the Butcher, Stan Hansen, Shane Douglas and a few wrestlers from W*ING are all already committed. Douglas may be brought in as a heel to team with Gilbert. Stevie Wonderful (heel manager), Rockin Rebel (Chuck Jones aka Chuck Williams), Johnny Hot Body and Renesto Benefico are all finito. Although the W*ING wrestlers canceled the SMW bookings, they are going to come in for the TV tapings and again for a 9/18 house show in Philadelphia billed as "Ultraclash '93" with a main event probably being Abdullah & Gilbert vs. Hansen & ? with attempts being made for ? to wind up as Terry Funk.

AUGUST 16

With no WWF shows being run over the weekend and WCW just in small Georgia towns, the most talked about shows over the weekend were the TV tapings on 8/7 and 8/8 at the ECW Arena. Stan Hansen and Tito Santana debuted as babyfaces, Shane Douglas (as a member of Gilbert's First Family, who could barely work because his shoulder is nowhere close to being healed) and Ivan & Vladimir Koloff debuted as heels, and Victor Quinones brought in The Head Hunters, Masayoshi Motegi, Mitsuhiro Matsunaga (who worked the first night as Mr. Danger and the second as Matsunaga) and Miguelito Perez. Of the group, The Head Hunters, two identical 380 pound 24-year-old twins named Victor & Manuel Santiago who were born in the Bronx but are citizens of the Dominican Republic, were by far the most impressive doing numerous moves off the top rope including moonsaults. Motegi looked green, but with potential and the crowd cheered him a lot after his face vs. face match with J.T. Smith, while Matsunaga didn't look impressive.

SEPTEMBER 6

Eddie Gilbert continues to run down Jerry Lawler in interviews on the ECW television show. Speaking of ECW, it'll be opening a pro wrestling school on 10/1. Tito Santana will lose the title on a fictitious title change since he's unavailable for future dates. Expect heel Shane Douglas to be announced as champ soon. Complete line-up for the 9/18 Ultraclash I at ECW Arena is Gilbert & Abdullah vs. Terry Funk & Stan Hansen in a Tornado bunkhouse match, Head Hunters vs. Miguelito Perez & mystery partner in a barbed wire baseball bat match, A mixed gender Battle Royal with women wrestlers, valets and managers, Dark Patriot vs. J.T. Smith in a scaffold match, Tommy Cairo vs. Tony Stetson for Pennsylvania state title, Shane Douglas vs. Sandman, Sal Bellomo vs. Richard Michaels and mask vs. mask with Super Destroyer #1 vs. Super Destroyer #2. Next TV tapings are 10/1 and 10/2 and already booked are Funk, Abdullah and Paul E. Dangerously.

SEPTEMBER 27

The most-talked about independent show in this country in several months was Tod Gordon's Eastern Championship Wrestling's 9/18 show at the ECW Arena in Philadelphia. The figures reported to us were an SRO attendance of 1,131 fans (960 capacity in ECW Arena) and a $16,147 gate. Many have disputed those numbers claiming 780 as the accurate attendance figure and less than that as paid. Either way it was the largest show in the company's short history and one of the wildest shows in recent memory in the United States. We received several reports, with some calling it the best house show they had ever seen and others saying it was the best show they'd seen in months or even a few years, and others who were more critical saying the show had the same excesses (12 guys juicing) that led to the demise of Joel Goodhart's promotion. Still, the basic agreement was the main event, while scheduled as a barbed wire baseball bat match between The Head Hunters vs. Crash the Terminator & Miguelito Perez stole the show, even though the announced stipulation never took place. It was announced there would be no barbed wire baseball bat match due to the commission stopping the match, but they did have a baseball bat that was used throughout the match, just without any barbed wire wrapped around it. I believe actually nobody brought the barbed wire, although all four wrestlers were willing to do the match. The two teams brawled for 8:38, pounding on each other with the bat and brawling all over the building. The highlight of the match with quadruple juice came when Perez whipped one of the Head Hunters into the wall of the building and dry wall flew everywhere and a big crack broke in the wall. A second whip into the wall saw the Head Hunter go right through the wall into the street. Finish came when Crash (280+) missed a moonsault and one of the Hunters (380 ish) hit a perfect moonsault for the pin. We had ratings varying from ***3/4 to ***** on the match. The semifinal was a bunkhouse match with Terry Funk & Stan Hansen vs. Kevin Sullivan & Abdullah the Butcher, which ended with a DQ finish when Eddie Gilbert attacked Funk, even though it was a no DQ match. Everyone but Hansen juiced in this match, which was rated *** to ****, with many crediting it largely to Funk's antics. After the match, Gilbert, who had been dumped as booker two weeks before the show (new booker is Paul Heyman/Dangerously), did a speech that nobody knew he was going to do, turning himself babyface, saying how much he loved Philadelphia and telling fans to continue to support the promotion and saying that it was simply that he and Tod Gordon couldn't come to a new contractual agreement. Earlier in the show Gordon announced that ECW would be a part of the NWA.

SEPTEMBER 29

Just one week before the company's biggest show to date, Eastern Championship Wrestling owner Tod Gordon and booker Eddie Gilbert have severed ties. Largely the split-up, described by Gordon as amicable, is because it appears Gordon is likely to become the Northeastern regional promoter if/when Jim Crockett Jr. starts up a promotion after his no-compete clause with WCW expires. Gilbert is expected to return home to Tennessee and get involved in state politics. Gordon has yet to decide whether or not he'll simply promote a Crockett product which may or may not go by the World Wrestling Network (WWN) name, or he'll promote in conjunction, doing a split television show which, for instance, may include him adding 15 minutes of locally produced matches/interviews/angles and continuing the ECW to a national show. The 9/18 show in South Philadelphia billed as "Ultraclash," headlined by a bunkhouse match with Terry Funk & Stan Hansen vs. Kevin Sullivan (replacing Gilbert) & Abdullah the Butcher and a barbed wire baseball bat match with W*ING wrestlers The Head Hunters vs. Crash the Terminator & Miguelito Perez had a $4,500 advance as of the weekend, which is the largest in the company's short history, in a building set up for about 1,000 capacity.

OCTOBER 4

Word from WWN is that they're saying the report here last week about a dispute among the factions was incorrect. Word we are being given is that Jim Hudson and Jim Crockett aren't affiliated and whatever Hudson is doing right now is being kept close to the vest. Crockett and Paul Heyman (Dangerously) are in the planning stages of opening the WWN company and Tod Gordon in Philadelphia is affiliated with them. Eddie Gilbert and Gordon's split, which was largely amicable, came because Gilbert didn't like the idea of Gordon being affiliated with Crockett and resulted in a lot of heat between Gilbert and Heyman. Gilbert moved from Philadelphia back to Tennessee this past week. At the last ECW card, Gilbert's run-in during the tag match was planned, however his interview where he announced his retirement, turned face and started selling his gear wasn't expected by anyone. Heyman put together his first TV show that aired this past Tuesday. On the show scheduled to air this week, they will announce that by calling the hotline you'll get information on which matches will air on which nights for the 10/1 and 10/2 TV tapings at the ECW Arena. Originally it wasn't announced which main event matches would air on which night for this weekend's shows.

OCTOBER 11

The weekend television tapings on 10/1 and 10/2 in South Philadelphia drew about 250 and 400 respectively with Sabu coming out of it as the star of both shows and the promotion. Sabu debuted the first night beating Tazmaniac. He chased fans all over the building and was so scary that supposedly some of the children attending had nightmares about him. He did a moonsault off the top rope and landed on chairs in the front row and was chasing fans and throwing chairs all over the building. Then he put a table into the ring and started coming off the top rope with moonsaults on it until the table broke. There are guys who do high-risk moves, and there are guys who do insane moves and are going to be injured very badly before their careers last too long. Cactus Jack was the guy most would associate with the latter category, but Sabu is in another league from even Cactus Jack. For those who like his work, my advice is to enjoy it while you can because he's not going to be able to physically continue doing the things he does for a long period of time. He showed up the second night strapped to a horizontal stretcher with chains and when let loose, did a Hannibal Lecter gimmick. On the second night, Paul E. Dangerously brought out ECW champ Shane Douglas and wound up getting into an argument with Sensational Sherri and Sabu got involved. The idea was to keep Douglas and Sherri a heel combination, but make sure Sabu, who everyone wanted to cheer, would stay heel by making Dangerously his manager. Told everyone cheered Sabu anyway, as he won the title with a moonsault in the middle. They announced an 11/13 show at the ECW Arena and brought out Sabu and Terry Funk and said that each could pick any partner of their choosing for the match. Sabu picked Hawk, but before Funk could pick a partner, he was attacked. The 11/13 date is right in the middle of the WCW tapings in Orlando which Hawk was originally booked for, but apparently he gave the okay that he'd be in Philadelphia for the show.

NOVEMBER 15

On the ECW television show that aired on 11/2, announcer Joey Styles opened the show "caught offguard" reading the Newsday story with the giant headline "Steroids: WWF Boss may be pinned" visible to the camera. That television show is definitely different. They've been plugging a main event for 11/13 with Hawk & Sabu vs. Terry Funk & mystery partner. They did a segment where local promoter Tod Gordon tells Paul E. Dangerously (who puts this TV together and is Sabu's manager) that the identity of the partner is no mystery and shows Paul the name, and he freaks out. Then Tod goes to tell the name to the fans and right before he says the name, a test pattern appears on the screen. They also announced that is Hawk & Sabu lose, then Sabu loses his ECW title, and if Funk & partner lose, Funk loses his TV title. They are also doing a campy segment with Jason Knight as a manager doing a Rick Martel gimmick but taking it farther than Martel ever did.

NOVEMBER 22

The "November to Remember" on 11/13 in Philadelphia drew 1,492 fans which is the group's largest crowd and gate to date. Most reports are it was an average-to-good show overall. King Kong Bundy, who hasn't wrestled in about six years, turned out to be Terry Funk's mystery partner against Hawk & Sabu. Bundy looked to weigh in the 350-380 range. With Hawk's knee being out, they did a gimmick where he was handcuffed to the post immediately making Sabu the face in a 1-on-2 situation. Hawk juiced heavily. It wound up with Bundy turning on Funk and Sabu pinning Funk. Sabu had put his ECW title up in the match and Funk put his TV title up so Sabu is now a double champion. The result of Sabu pinning a legend like Funk has upped Sabu's rep in Japan already. It looks as though they are building the next major show to a Funk vs. Sabu singles match. The Sensational Sherri vs. Madusa match never took place as Madusa sent word a few days ahead she couldn't work the show and Malia Hosaka took her place. The match itself was said to have been terrible. Sherri ended up disqualified for hitting everyone in sight with a chair and wound up with valet Angel, Don E. Allen and the referee all juicing. They announced that Madusa wasn't there because she had signed a WWF contract and Vince McMahon had told her not to work the ECW show, although Madusa did work an indie in Baltimore the same night and one the next night in the same area. Johnny Gunn & Tommy Dreamer won the ECW tag titles from Johnny Hot Body & Tony Stetson. Stetson & Hot Body had just beaten Ian & Axl Rotten and were challenged by Gunn & Dreamer impromptu for the belts ala Hulk-Yokozuna and the faces won in 20 seconds. The "shoot fight" with Kevin Sullivan vs. Tommy Cairo was a mess as they announced you couldn't win by pinfall, only knockout or submission, and Kevin won hitting Cairo with a chair and pinning him in 3:00 of a match that included nothing of the "shoot fight" style.

CHAPTER TWENTY SEVEN

AAA SURPASSES
ALL EXPECTATIONS

MAY 3

On 4/30, a promotion that didn't even exist one year ago, may draw the largest paid crowd for a pro wrestling show in North America in more than three years.

The Mexico City-based Asestencia Asesoria y Administracion (AAA), or Triple-A as it is called, is running its first major spectacular, billed as "Triple Mania," on 4/30 at the Plaza de Toros in Mexico City. Reports from those within the promotion indicate that a crowd of approximately 50,000 paid is expected for the show. This would most likely be the highest paid attendance for pro wrestling in North America since the 1990 Wrestlemania Hulk Hogan vs. Ultimate Warrior match in Toronto's Sky Dome drew 64,287. The actual paid attendance for the Hogan vs. Sid Justice Wrestlemania match at the Hoosier Dome in Indianapolis in 1992 is unclear since there were 62,167 in the building, but it was well known the show was heavily papered and the paid figure was told to us by various WWF sources as anywhere from 37,000 to 54,000.

The rise of AAA has been the biggest promotional success story in North America since the WWF's national rise in 1984. Although the background of the rise is different, the brains behind AAA, Antonio Pena, largely studied the WWF's initial success and worked it into his own marketing plan that has resulted in the most consistently successful drawing house show promotion on the continent. Taking on a promotion that was nearly 60-years-old (EMLL), a company which at the time drew more fans, ran more shows and employed more wrestlers than any other wrestling company in the world, plus with the political ties being No. 1 in the country has, was not without its initial headaches. The seeds were planned actually for more than one year before the initials AAA were known to everyone, as those in the know in Mexico City knew about Pena, at the time the EMLL booker who created several new characters like the midgets and Octagon that had caught fire and saw EMLL overtake UWA as the country's top group. Pena resigned as booker on May 4, 1992, the same day Konnan El Barbaro, the most Americanized of the top Mexican wrestlers, also announced his resignation from EMLL. Pena announced the formation of the new promotion three days later. Pena lured many of the top drawing cards of the two established groups like Perro Aguayo, El Hijo del Santo, Cien Caras, Blue Panther and Fishman to work on top while using the undercards to showcase largely unknown or formerly unpushed great workers, some of whom had never even worked in Mexico City, and giving them new gimmicks, new identities and major pushes. This new breed of wrestlers like Rey Misterio Jr., Heavy Metal, Psicosis, Winners and La Parca has been responsible for taking the ring work to a completely new frontier, making the established promotions look old and outdated, and have been responsible for some of the best matches ever seen in the country.

AAA's first year hasn't been without some major stumbling blocks. Early in the game, EMLL managed to temporarily deport one of AAA's biggest drawing cards, Konnan El Barbaro, a Cuban who grew up in Miami and is a naturalized American citizen, back to the United States after he jumped. Even more disruptive, was EMLL and UWA, two promotions which had feuded back-and-forth for 17 years, banding together to take on the new office and being able to keep them out of most of the major arenas in Mexico, including out of any major facilities in Mexico City for several months. In some ways this turned into a blessing in disguise since they ran major shows in cities that for years had to be satisfied with "Mexico City leftovers" from the big groups and had never seen such spectacular house shows, they played before hot crowds in largely packed arenas weekly while the Mexico City fans had to wait to see the group live. It also created new stars televised into Mexico City that had never appeared there, whetting the appetite for the new promotion in that city that have led to the success the last three months. Also early in the game, AAA ran a few shows in Los Angeles, including a television taping that drew a whopping $120,000 (the largest house ever drawn by either by a foreign-based or an "off-brand" promotion in the United States and a larger house than WCW has drawn for any house show since the 1990 Great American Bash) on 7/4/92. After a dispute about who got what share of the big gate, the AAA wrestlers have never returned to the United States. At least two other attempts to promote in the United States, one in conjunction with Titan Sports, appear to have also fallen through. Indeed, Pena's group, even though loaded with great workers, has no talent trading agreement in Japan. Similar to the early WWF, this is a group that seems to have no working agreement with any other promotion in the world and is beginning to gain a reputation as being hard to work with.

The concept in taking on, and, to this point, whipping the established EMLL consisted largely of taking advantage of the potential of television. With the backing of Televisa, Mexico's largest television network, having the superior time slot on the strongest station in the country is the key advantage point. Like the WWF's rise in 1984, Pena raided the two existing offices of the top babyface talent. On 1/19, AAA finally got its break after several announcements and forced cancellations due to problems bucking the existing offices and union that tied them together, and announced its first Mexico City show, for just three days later, at the 10,600-seat Juan de la Barrera Gym. The opposition breathed a sigh of relief when the show drew only 5,000, although in hindsight it was simply because three days wasn't enough time to get the word out. The group's second show on 1/29 sold out, and since that time, they've run every Friday night but one at the Gym, with just one other of the Mexico City shows failing to sellout to the tune of about $80,000 per weekly show. During the same period, the EMLL's traditional Friday night shows in Mexico City at Arena Coliseo and Arena Mexico have drawn their poorest crowds in many years. The crowd had dropped to well under 1,000 on 4/23. Like Titan Sports in 1984, AAA has brought major celebrities such as famous actors, actresses, rock stars and television personalities and shown them on television at ringside at the shows. From a live show standpoint, the production values of the Friday night cards are unequalled anywhere in the world, with only WWF television tapings coming close. The packed gym has spectacular lighting, although not at WWF level. But the dry ice spectacular ring entrances for every match with the wrestlers, models, sidekicks, and gimmicks are so elaborate to the point they may even be too elaborate (and probably are too lengthy in many cases). For every match on a regular house show, the ring entrances are even more spectacular than the most elaborate ring entrances on the biggest New Japan, WCW and WWF mega-events. The top wrestlers have appeared on the most popular talk shows in the country building up the major feuds, in particular Konnan vs. Cien Caras, the current top babyface and top heel in the group, in the 2-of-3 fall loser must retire match that headlines on 4/30.

The next step is going to be to see how the public responds to Friday's show. The card is being billed as "Triple Mania," both because of the name of the promotion combined with Wrestlemania, and because the card is being built around a triple main event. The other two headline matches are Perro Aguayo putting up his hair against Mascara Ano 2000's mask in 2-of-3 falls and Lizmark defending the Mexican light heavyweight title against La Parca in a very rare for Mexico one fall title match. The undercard, all one fall matches, from the opener down, will have Lola Gonzales & Vicki Caranza & Reyna Gallegos vs. Martha Villalobos & Wendy & Pantera Surena, Rudy Reyna & May Flowers & Baby Sharon vs. Winners & Super Calo & El Salsero (a newcomer making his debut), Misterioso & Volador & Rey Misterio Jr. vs. Tony Arce & Vulcano & Rocco Valente, Fuerza Guerrera & Heavy Metal & Rambo vs. Octagon & El Hijo del Santo & Villano III and a mixed match with Mascara Sagrada & Mascarita Sagrada & Love Machine vs. Jerry Estrada & Jerrito Estrada & Blue Panther. The show will air on Galavision in the United States on 5/9. However, the concentration of the hype has been around a loser must retire match in which it doesn't appear that anybody is really going to retire. How that will affect the company's credibility, if at all, when it plans future major shows is something that is already being questioned. There is considerable talk that the angle coming out of the main event retirement match being planned for a blow-off on an even bigger show months down the line at the 130,000 seat Azteca Stadium. Yet there are many problems that could keep that angle from even taking place, which, if it does or doesn't, will probably be the biggest story to come out of the show. There has already been open talk about the potential of breaking the current verified world record for wrestling attendance set at the Pontiac Silverdome by Hogan and Andre in 1987. Whether booking such a large venue as Azteca Stadium for the future is viable is something that will have to be proven by a sellout on Friday.

AUGUST 23

The AAA show in California on 8/28 looks like it'll draw one of the biggest houses of the year in the United States. The advance, money-wise, at press time, is significantly larger than any WCW gate of the year (in the $50,000 range more than two weeks out) and Lucha shows generally do 90 percent of their business walk-up. The largest Lucha gate ever in the United States was the $119,000 on July 4, 1992 in Los Angeles, which was also the largest gate in history for an independent wrestling show, and this could break that mark because it's a larger building with a stronger line-up and the television involving these wrestlers has been more focused.

SEPTEMBER 6

A promotional company whose name is largely unknown to even the most ardent wrestling fans in the United States, in space of one weekend, has become a serious threat to become the No. 1 promotion in terms of arena attendance in the nation's most populous state, and is already the second most successful house show promotion in the country.

Virtually no wrestling fans in the United States have even heard of the name Asestencia Asesoria y Administracion. Only a small percentage of wrestling fans even know its initials, AAA, or the term "Triple-A," as anything more than the designation of the top rung of baseball minor leagues. But in one weekend in the United States, the Mexico City-based AAA drew a total of $384,000. The biggest show of the three, on 8/28 at the Los Angeles Sports Arena, has to rank as one of the five best live cards I've ever seen in 23 years of regularly attending house shows and the single best card I can recall seeing in the United States, which takes a lot of Starrcades, 1989 Music City Showdown and Bash, etc. into consideration. There are a shows that had one or even two top matches that I'd rank ahead of anything on the Los Angeles show. There are a few shows that could top it purely for in the ring action, but for heat from the beginning of a show until the end of a show and overall work quality, the only card I can compare it with that I've seen either live or on PPV would be the finals of the 1984 All Japan tag team tournament. But Asestencia Asesoria y Administracion wasn't the only promotion that drew impressive numbers this past weekend.

SEPTEMBER 29

Two weeks ago, AAA out of Mexico City literally stunned everyone within pro wrestling with its success in running house shows in San Jose and Los Angeles, particularly the latter, which was only the second major arena (10,000+ capacity) wrestling card in the United States to draw a legitimate sellout (the other being the WWF

Royal Rumble in Sacramento) in 1993 and the largest crowd up to that point this year to attend a pro wrestling event in this country. San Jose was impressive in that while Galavision is on the cable in San Jose and Campbell, virtually all surrounding areas, including some with large spanish-speaking population don't even get the station on cable. A show in San Diego, while still drawing a larger gate than WWF has drawn in that city in more than one year, was not a financial success due to heavy advertising costs and the costs involved in putting together shows of this calibre with all the special effects. Unlike in the United States, in Mexico, cards are literally put together about a week ahead of time. Most of the house show line-ups for the big weekend events usually aren't released publicly until the Monday prior to the event yet by tradition they still draw mainly a walk-up crowd. The audience that attended in California reacted similarly, as there were about 10,000 tickets in Los Angeles sold the day of the show and an estimated 8,000 more turned away. I can't ever recall a U.S. card which did an 18,000 person "walk-up." This tradition stems from running most arenas on a weekly basis, and some arenas in Mexico City run as many as three house shows every week. With that kind of promotional schedule, it is counterproductive in Mexico to announce line-ups more than a week or so in advance as it only confuses the issues. So in that way, it is no surprise that the next AAA tour of the United States, in conjunction with the New York-based International Wrestling Conference (which helped promote Los Angeles and San Diego, but had no involvement in San Jose), scheduled for November, has little officially on the table except for an 11/12 date at the Los Angeles Sports Arena. The only thing known about that show is the ticket prices will be raised from $30-$15-$12 to $30-$20-$15, or scaled for about a $300,000 capacity house.

The main event is expected to be a trios match with Konnan El Barbaro & Perro Aguayo & Cien Caras vs. Jake Roberts and two others Americans (Terry Funk, Diamond Dallas Page and/or Love Machine) stemming from the main event angle on 8/28. Traditional economic law of supply and demand does indicate that debuting with a sellout and turning away thousands and producing a show that seemingly left everyone both pleased and hot justifies an ability to raise prices, but wrestling doesn't go by traditional economic laws and it may be smart to sit tight and not make long-term decisions until after the second show. The shows last summer at Cal State-Los Angeles gym did show that the crowds will maintain at high levels provided there are top Mexico City drawing cards, and as shown by Canadian Vampire Casanova drawing when EMLL wasn't on television, they needn't necessarily be on television to draw. The crowds plummeted last year in the same building after the local promoters and Antonio Pena (AAA President) had their split, even with good action, when the shows didn't have the top drawing cards. There will be most likely two other dates booked during that weekend with San Jose and San Antonio being the cities mentioned the most, but neither city has even been booked.

There is also a good chance that TripleMania II, scheduled for April 30, 1994, will take place at either the Los Angeles Sports Arena, or outdoors at the Los Angeles Coliseum (original site of 1991 Wrestlemania before it was moved indoors because of a lack of ticket sales) if the Los Angeles crowds hold up and these promotional ties don't break down. As of right now it appears the show will either take place at Plaza de Toros, a 48,000-seat bullfighting arena in Mexico City where the first TripleMania took place, Rio Nilo Coliseum, a 21,000-seat arena in suburban Guadalajara which AAA has packed twice in recent months, or in Los Angeles. The advantage of Los Angeles is the ability to charge higher ticket prices and thus draw the most money. In addition, if things continue on course with Jake Roberts and the main event involves a blow-off with him, Los Angeles is the only city the match can take place as the commission banned him for life from Mexico because of the TripleMania I angle. The risk is nobody knows for sure how well the product will hold up in Los Angeles after running regular house shows for a while, while in Mexico City it's largely a given the group will maintain a strong level of popularity.

Ron Skoler, who heads the IWC which currently has all U.S. promotional rights to AAA shows, wants the IWC to have a separate identity from AAA. He also wants to use more and more non-AAA names on the show, maybe 50 percent of the card as opposed to everyone in the top matches sans Jake Roberts. The problem is the Hispanic audience won't pay to see American wrestlers as a rule in the drawing positions. They're okay in preliminary matches as was the case in Los Angeles, and they're okay if they're part of the storyline as Roberts and Love Machine are. But the 1987 promotion that ran the Olympic Auditorium saw crowds dwindle when it started using local Americans on top to save trans from Mexico and because the promoters, who themselves were American, thought using Americans would expand the audience base when the opposite proved to be the case. At the same time, in attempting to establish a promotion, relying 100 percent on Pena has the potential downside of being left with nothing should a split occur, as happened with the Los Angeles promoters last summer after the July 4th show.

Galavision, the spanish cable network which broadcasts AAA, has gone through a time slot and schedule change as of this past weekend. The AAA show, which formerly appeared on Sunday nights, was moved to Saturday at 7:30 p.m. Rival EMLL is back on in the United States from 10 p.m. to midnight on Sundays airing the show taped nine days earlier, while one hour of AAA follows at midnight (all times Eastern, Pacific time is three hours earlier). Satellite guides also list a special wrestling show on 9/16 at 1 a.m. Eastern and another on 9/18 at 7 p.m. However, our local TV guide lists the same shows as starting two hours earlier. The Sunday show in the local TV Guides was listed as having a 5 p.m. Pacific start but in fact started two hours later. The reason for all these changes is largely unknown and confusing and it's quite surprising to see EMLL back on. The only word we've received is that EMLL won't be on for long in the United States. I believe the Los Angeles card aired in Mexico City this past weekend which means it'll probably air on the Saturday night time slot on 9/18. In response to requests from dish owners, the shows that air in this country air one week earlier in Mexico City and can be picked up via a dish. The schedule as of last week was that EMLL aired from 11 a.m. to 1 p.m. on Sundays on M1, Ch. 14; AAA aired on Sundays on M2, Ch. 8 from 9 to 11 a.m. and again on M1, Ch. 14 from 1 to 2 p.m immediately after EMLL.

OCTOBER 11

People who stereotype a pro wrestling audience and pro wrestling itself as fitting into some narrow mold should probably (if they live in California and have the chance) attend both a WWF show and a Lucha Libre show in the same market. It's two different worlds.

On 10/1 here in San Jose, WWF broke the cities all-time gate record set five weeks earlier by AAA drawing approximately 7,500 fans and $97,000 to the new 20,000-seat San Jose Arena. WWF crowds in general have increased since the loading up single shows concept took effect in mid-August. However, this crowd was largely due to it being the debut card in a newly-opened arena combined with a heavy advertising budget, with ads all over several area radio stations and large ads in the sports section of the local newspaper nearly every day during the ten days prior to the event. The radio ads up until the final day listed the Steiners and Michaels as appearing but the newspaper ads from the beginning had the card that materialized. I hadn't heard so much reaction ever in this city, particularly among people I barely knew that weren't wrestling fans, to a wrestling show in this area. I think this was more to the heavy advertising than the debut in the new arena. Because of that, I actually expected a lot bigger crowd. I heard absolutely nothing about the AAA show except for a few television ads, which didn't even mention the line-up, on the station that broadcasts AAA, and was astounded walking into the building and seeing a nearly full house. What was most interesting is the make-up of the San Jose Arena crowd was completely different than the make-up of the crowd at the WWF television taping in February, about two miles away at the San Jose State University gym.

Attempting to label a large gathering of people and making blanket statements about them and their make-up is often ignorant. However, the ignorant viewpoint is that this was a crowd largely of first-time fans, very much the family audience that WWF likes to pretend is its main audience but in most markets, hasn't been the case at the house shows, at least in the San Francisco Bay Area, in years. Aside from the regular hardcores at ringside, the audience seemed largely early 30s parents bringing two very young children, and suburbanites making their first visit into the highly-publicized new arena. The crowd was almost exclusively white. There were a few blacks, but virtually no Hispanics. At the WWF taping, the crowd seemed to 30 to 40 percent spanish and the AAA crowd was probably 95 percent spanish, with the rest being a few college students, non-Hispanic girls on dates and very few Observer readers sprinkled in. AAA drew a better dressed audience, with lots of teenagers and young adults of dating age, the kind that seemed to want to show off that it wasn't poor, rather than suburbanites who wouldn't dress up to attend pro wrestling nor most likely attend it on any kind of a regular basis, if ever again. The AAA audience in San Jose was a different mix than the AAA show in Los Angeles drew (heavily male young adults pouring always on the verge of going out of control) except consistent in ethnic make-up. In fact, I couldn't find even one person who I saw at the AAA show that was at the WWF show, even among readers. Of course the product difference was night-and-day. I think it would be difficult for the fans of one product to enjoy the other because you have to go into each product with a different frame of mind. AAA, while far more action-packed, acrobatic and despite a reputation to the contrary, probably more realistic in work style as well, still would turn off a typical WWF fan simply due to unfamiliarity and something as simple as all the announcements being made in Spanish, unless one were to go in with a mindset of wanting to learn something different. This isn't a typical mindset one goes to wrestling matches with. It would be difficult for someone seeing an AAA show to sit through a WWF show afterward, because it would seem too slow, and totally lacking in heat and intensity. There are the similarities in that both groups rely heavily on characterizations rather than people with real names, and have elaborate well choreographed ring entrances which are to many the highlight of the show. Both groups have a certain amount of jingoism built into the story lines, although at the AAA show, the crowd was vehement in its "Mexico, Mexico" chants at Love Machine and flag waving, while Lex Luger's attempts to get "USA, USA" chants received only a smattering of a response that quickly died out. The faces at both shows were cheered equally upon the introduction, although that similarity ended once the match started. The AAA heels were loudly booed while the WWF heels got only mild reactions, although both groups seemed to have about the same percentage of heel fans. AAA had intense heat from start-to-finish while WWF had little heat except for the main event, and even that had less heat than the AAA opener.

It doesn't appear the two groups are in competition for the same audience at all. But as far as being the No. 1 pro wrestling promotion in the market, and the leverage that entails as far as building availability and acquiring good dates, it is already very competitive. WWF drew more fans, and slightly more money, but spent far more on advertising. The costs of running the new larger building is much higher than the smaller building, so the AAA show surely was more profitable, which is the bottom line. There are still many questions unanswered about AAA's ability to maintain crowds at the level of the first tour, which the follow-up show should do a great deal toward answering. WWF had the advantage of booking a show during the building's opening "hot" period. It's doubtful it could consistently draw anywhere near this level on a consistent basis, nor does one expect they'd even run more than three shows a year here. WWF returned to the Los Angeles Sports Arena two nights later with its first show since the big AAA show, and did a respectable 7,000 fans and $111,000, but still less than half of what the AAA did in the same building on 8/28. While a comparison of figures on the surface may not seem germane because it is largely drawing from different audiences, it is a major competitive point. As long as AAA can draw better, or even in the same ballpark as WWF in the same building, it'll be able to continue booking the building and getting good weekend dates, unlike a WCW which found itself unable to book the key buildings in most major markets because of WWF's ability to lock them out because of consistently much stronger attendance. It's ridiculous to think any promotion can draw consistent sellouts at a building as large as the Sports Arena in this day and age, although I seem to be the only person following the subject who thinks a sellout for the 11/12 AAA show isn't an automatic. One thing that was painfully obvious is that even loading up the shows, with the loss of Shawn Michaels and the Steiners being pulled from the show, plus Bret Hart having the weekend off, even a loaded WWF show from a match quality standard wasn't as good as the split shows of the summer when the tour came here.

NOVEMBER 22

AAA made its second trip to the United States of 1993 and like the first, it was an overwhelming financial success. The 11/12 show at the Los Angeles Sports Arena drew 11,600 paid and $195,000, while the 11/13 show in San Jose drew 5,200 fans and a gate in the $100,000 range. The quality of the shows wasn't quite of the level of their August shows in both cities, although Los Angeles, which started slow, turned out to be a very good show, about the quality of a mid-1980s NWA loaded house show in a Greensboro/Charlotte when it comes to match quality on top and atmosphere. San Jose, which drew just a few hundred shy of capacity despite having no advertising during the local AAA television show, even on the show that aired the afternoon of the card, was a good show as well, although not the level in the ring of the debut show in August. San Jose would have easily turned away many had the show been advertised during the local TV show and even without the ads if the box office hadn't opened until 7 p.m. the night of the show (since an estimated 4,400 walked up as Lucha Libre traditionally draws almost exclusively walk-up business), because the walk-up lines were so intimidating it caused many to give up. The next AAA show in the United States is slated for January 8 in New York, which is a lot more of an iffy drawing proposition than the California shows since the shows appeal almost exclusively to a Mexican-American crowd. The next Los Angeles Sports Arena date is March 12, with most likely a San Jose card that same weekend. Unlike the first round of shows in Los Angeles and San Jose, which were such an unbelievable success that everything was done correctly, this time around the shows had flaws. Los Angeles ended at 11:50 p.m., although virtually nobody left early. San Jose's show, which featured five matches in excess of 20:00, didn't end until 12:05 a.m. and many fans left after the "world" title match where Cien Caras became the first IWC heavyweight champion and before the start of the trios main event, which was marred by the crowd having already been burned out because of the late hour.

Both nights started weak, and then nearly went into the toilet during the trios match featuring Los Exoticos (Rudy Reyna & May Flowers & Baby Sharon who do a middle-aged La Cage Aux Folles gimmick) which went entirely too long both nights. From there, both shows were hot, with Los Angeles having incredible heat particularly when you consider the final two matches took place after 11 p.m. and the audience was a family audience with lots of very young children (even more so than WWF crowds). Both shows featured two major full turns, with Heavy Metal going face and Blue Panther going heel. The Metal face turn in Los Angeles was one of the best executed and easily the best responded to based on crowd reaction turn I've seen in years. The heat for Metal vs. Fuerza Guerrera was such that a match with those two would be major ticket seller as a semifinal on a return show. The Panther turn in Los Angeles was the exact opposite. It was similar to the Survivor Series double turn years back with Powers of Pain and Demolition in that the idea didn't get across, only ten times more magnified in that the wrong idea got across so well that Konnan El Barbaro and Perro Aguayo, the company's top two faces, turned into major heels, and Cien Caras and Panther, the heels, turned into faces, although after much flag-kissing the fans finally cheered Konnan and Perro at the end. In San Jose, the Panther turn, done completely different, was the highlight of the show. The Metal turn was done very well in San Jose but didn't take place until midnight and many fans had already gone home, so it totally paled in comparison to the "magic" in Los Angeles.

The San Jose semifinal was the first Konnan vs. Cien Caras singles match since TripleMania, for the newly created IWC world heavyweight title. It was the Dusty finish all over again, which hopefully for the promotion won't bring the same end result (nobody going to house shows) that happened when the Master did it. At the same time, that finish is excellent--the first time you see it if you don't see it again in a city for several years. It appeared to me that a miscalculation was made in that much of the crowd seemingly had seen the Clash because the reaction to the finish wasn't one of anger or surprise at the reversal of the decision, but almost of a "Didn't we just see this on Wednesday" reaction. Konnan won the first fall with a ziplock. It was almost funny watching the first fall because Konnan is juiced up to the point you expect him to be a guy who does the strongman style of standing there like his feet are loaded down with cement blocks and instead spent the entire fall on the mat doing great submission maneuvers that got over with the crowd. Whenever he'd have Caras in a submission, new heel Panther, who came out as Caras' second, continually interfered. In the second fall, Panther kept interfering behind the conveniently turned heel ref Tirantes' head when Konnan would get a submission hold on and finally Volador jumped in and began brawling with Panther. Tirantes called for a DQ giving Caras the fall for Volador's interference even though he never touched Caras and Panther was also in the ring. Tirantes then ordered Volador banned from ringside as Panther kept laughing. Antonio Pena then came out and called for a time-out (really) early in the third fall. He then kicked Panther out of ringside and threw Tirantes out as ref and put Pepe "Tropi" Casas in. The place was going nuts at this point. Immediately Casas was shoulderblocked out of the ring by accident by Konnan and had to be carried out. The two kept wrestling with no ref until finally Tirantes returned. Tirantes started shoving Konnan, who responded by shoving Tirantes who flew out of the ring. Konnan then got the ziplock on Caras but Tirantes got back in, called for the whistle (as opposed to the bell), Konnan celebrated, and he then raised Caras' hand on the DQ making Caras AAA's first recognized world heavyweight champion. As far as match quality goes, the first fall-and-a-half, all Konnan doing unique mat holds, was pretty good. The booking carried it to a 24:10 length match since when it comes to high spots, there is very little these two can do with each other, but the finish itself would have been a lot more effective in Mexico where people haven't seen it so much before.

"La Lucha Del Honor," was the name of AAA/IWC's second card at the Los Angeles Sports Arena, which drew the second largest non-WWF paid crowd in the United States since 1989, second largest live gate since 1987 and second largest non-WWF gate in California wrestling history (trailing only the August 28 AAA debut show at the Sports Arena in both cases) which was actually a disappointment to some because it was still 4,000 shy of capacity.

The success of AAA in California has created one of the more controversial issues of the year regarding wrestling magazines, and to some extent, newsletters and radio shows. With the exception of the Observer, which doesn't really factor into this controversy because it has always covered everything worldwide in wrestling to begin with rather than being national in scope as virtually all the rest of the American wrestling media, and some coverage in Torch and even less in PWI Weekly (which actually gave decent superfluous coverage to the first Los Angeles show), coverage of this phenomenon has been non-existent. John Arezzi, one of the promoters of the show, blasted the wrestling media, particularly the magazines, on his New York radio show the morning after this card for living in the 70s (which is actually the opposite because during that time period these shows would have received tons of coverage) and ignoring a group that draws such large crowd in the U.S., has the best stable of workers in this country and draws the most heat at its matches. The comments no doubt came at the frustration of being part of one of the most successful house shows of the year in the United States, and having numerous photographers at ringside, but all of them were either for Mexican or Japanese publications. The funny thing is, in the 70s, all the wrestling mags covered the Los Angeles promotion, which, like AAA, drew a predominately Mexican-American audience and Mil Mascaras was almost treated as a God in wrestling mags during that time frame and the rest of the crew was covered as a major promotion. AAA right now is the No. 2 house show promotion in this country (largely by default admittedly), even though it runs few events, and is possibly No. 1 in this country's most populous state. When it comes to television viewership in the United States, AAA is the 15th highest rated alternative language television show of any kind. I'm sure that doesn't add up to more viewers than WWF or even WCW, but it certainly adds up to tons more television viewership nationwide in this country than any other U.S.-based promotion and in the country's No. 2 market (Los Angeles), it is clearly the No. 1 house show promotion and one can only speculate where it is as far as television viewership but logic says it has to be very strong. Obviously the argument against coverage, aside from the specious reasoning that the phenomenon caught those in charge of the magazines, radio shows and newsletters by surprise and they aren't educated to the different wrestlers and style, which is true but not a valid argument, is that the audience is virtually entirely Mexican-American. But as noted, that isn't all that different from the Los Angeles wrestling from the early 70s that was very successful and received lots of coverage, or the Los Angeles wrestling of the late 70s that received decent magazine coverage even though it was dying at the gate and its work quality was abysmal. Arguments against coverage because the workers themselves aren't American, while arguable as even being valid if true, aren't even true to begin with since 15 of the 34 wrestlers on the Los Angeles show are Americans. Arguments that the specific readers and listeners aren't familiar with the product, the most potentially valid argument of all, would only be valid if the rest of the media ignored non WWF and WCW wrestling because the vast majority of readers and listeners wouldn't be familiar with the names of wrestlers in all other American companies either.

CHAPTER TWENTY EIGHT

VINCE MCMAHON RESIGNS AS HEAD OF WWF

JUNE 7

Vince McMahon resigned as President of Titan Sports approximately two weeks ago in a major news item that has been largely kept hush-hush. McMahon, who was both President and Chief Executive Officer of the largest wrestling company in the United States, apparently had company control transferred to wife Linda McMahon a few weeks ago, either on or just before 5/14. Vince McMahon remains CEO of Titan Sports and will remain as a television personality. Titan has not publicly released this information in press release fashion, although several sources within the organization have admitted it was true and the public relations department has confirmed the story. Aside from the obvious speculation regarding this somehow being tied to the ongoing federal investigation, no other details or significance is known. It was already reported elsewhere that on 5/24 in Halifax, Nova Scotia, there was a production meeting in which Vince McMahon, who has been President of the company since taking over for his father in 1982, told employees that Linda was now in charge of the company and also acknowledged the federal investigation. However, from the outside, there doesn't seem to be any significant change in the operation of the company and many employees of the company weren't even aware of the switch in the company presidency as late as press time. The only attempt at press coverage regarding this was a press release item by Titan sent on the New York Times Wire Services that to the best of our knowledge, didn't run in any newspapers, which didn't mention any change in the organizational presidency, but focused largely on Linda McMahon, with mentions of the couple's son, Shane, and daughter, Stephanie. Linda, whose title as Executive Vice President of Titan Sports before this change in title, was, according to one Titan source, theoretically on an equal power footing as the other company Vice Presidents and this put her unequivocally as more powerful. Linda McMahon, according to the wire story, was credited with putting in a day care center at the Titan offices with toys with wrestling themes, developed community relations programs and credited her with the Headlock on Hunger campaign and being on the committee for the 1995 Special Olympics.

JUNE 14

With just days before its inaugural "King of the Ring" pay-per-view show, it is things having little to do with wrestling storylines that top both the news and speculation from Titan Sports. The resignation, or transfer of titles, or whatever the correct terminology regarding the presidency of the nation's biggest wrestling company from Vince McMahon to wife Linda has caused rampant speculation, especially with the timing of the change in regard to ongoing Grand Jury testimony and activities. Titan spokesman Steve Planamenta called the change more of a transfer of titles, not a resignation, and tried to downplay the changes. "It's not as big a deal as people are making it out to be," he said. "People are reading things into this that aren't there." Planamenta described the activities of Vince and Linda McMahon as that Linda has largely been running the business end of the company and Vince has been in control of the creative end. Hence, the title switch simply formalizes what has been the case all along. There is a large measure of truth to this definition of Linda McMahon's background. Linda McMahon, whose official title was Executive Vice President of Titan Sports, has always been a key party on the business and legal end and her involvement in Titan Sports goes far beyond simply being the wife of the President of the company. However, the timing of this title switch given what appears to be going on in the legal front makes it hard to believe the two items just coincidentally are taking place at the same time and are unrelated. Apparently Vince McMahon, at the production meeting in Halifax on 5/24 when announcing the change, made a comment about it being the year of the woman, and when acknowledging the investigation, said that he knew he was under investigation but had no idea why. Vince McMahon also gave the impression that son Shane, who is 22 or 23 and has long been groomed as the heir apparent to run the company, will be taking a more prominent role in the company's hierarchy.

JUNE 28

The Chicago Sun-Times ran an article on Linda McMahon in the 6/22 issue saying that "Linda McMahon, mother of two, is trying to project a new, wholesome image for the WWF." The story went through the scandals and acknowledged attendance has dropped. It said WWF shows at the Horizon draw between 4,000 and 9,000 (2,400 to 6,500 has been the recent range) currently, which is a bit of a stretch, although Friday's show with Hogan vs. Yokozuna on top should drew the best house in a while. It also said WWF PPV shows are all ordered by more than 1,000,000 per event which is more of a stretch (230,000 to 450,000 has been the recent range). McMahon, described as the WWF's newly appointed President and chief operating officer (I believe Vince would still be chief operating officer unless things have changed again) talked about changes like the face-to-face segments, participating in charity events, talked of attempts to increase local retail tie-ins. Her comments regarding steroid use were: "The harmful effects of steroids are just now really being looked at. Steroid use was not encouraged in the WWF, but in the past some of our wrestlers did use prescribed steroids." . . WWF record album will be released 7/27.

JULY 5

Linda McMahon did the first of a two-part interview in the Charleston Post-Courier that ran on 6/20. She said that she assumed the presidency of Titan Sports to deflect negative publicity as "almost laughable. If you're a good manager or a good administrator, you take a look at the company and decide if you are running all the departments in the most efficient way. Sometimes there are steps you need to take to make it better. It has absolutely nothing to do with any kind of investigation." She was also critical of Phil Mushnick but didn't specifically address any of Mushnick's major allegations in his stories.

JULY 12

Titan President Linda McMahon, in a lengthy article by Mike Mooneyham in the 6/27 Charleston Post-Courier, addressed several of the stories and individuals in a manner that one would expect to be similar to the upcoming house organ magazine articles.

On Tom Cole, whose story that broke in early 1992 in many ways took the media focus from the steroid issue and into much seedier grounds, and who filed a $1.6 million lawsuit against Titan, Pat Patterson, Terry Garvin and Mel Phillips recently, Mrs. McMahon, who herself has a legal background, said she now doubts Cole was ever sexually abused.

"As I have found out now, no, I don't. I think he's very confused. He comes from a very large family. I've met a sister who is very nice woman and gave her the same response that I had given Tom, that he would have every opportunity to succeed provided that he help himself. But when he stopped helping himself, then I would have done all I could to help him. So we spent over a year trying to help him in every way we could."

As noted here previously, the lawsuit Cole filed did not detail any instances of sexual abuse on him personally, but did list an incident where Cole alleges he was originally fired by the WWF in 1989 after turning down a homosexual advance. Cole's original complaint, which was never filed because of the settlement agreement reached between the two parties, and an interview that didn't air on the television show "Now It Can Be Told," saw Cole specify instances of sexual abuse between the ages of 13 and 16. During that same time period, Patterson (booker), Garvin (assistant booker) and Phillips (head of ring crew and ring announcer) all resigned from TitanSports, before any of their names had surfaces in any newspaper stories. There have been claims that Cole, as part of the settlement was promised that none of the three would be brought back, however the settlement agreement between Cole and Titan only mentioned Garvin and Phillips by name, neither of whom returned to the company. Patterson officially returned as booker about six months later.

McMahon went into a lengthy discussion of Cole's tenure with the WWF prior to the filing of the recent lawsuit: "I think Tom is a very confused young man. Just about a year and a half ago, we heard stories from some of the wrestling newsletters and from the New York Post that a `ring boy,' as he was categorized at that time, was going to file a lawsuit against the WWF. None of that had ever been brought to our attention. We didn't know who they were talking about. And we literally spent three weeks trying to get to the bottom of it. We finally found out who Tom Cole was. We made contact with his attorney. The day I called his attorney to talk to him, by the time I talked to him that afternoon, he told me he had been fired. A new attorney had been hired in New York City. But our attorney, and Vince (McMahon) and I, met with Tom Cole and his attorney in New York to find what grievance Tom had. We addressed the grievance. Basically from all understanding we could get form him, all he wanted was his job back. He wanted to work for the WWF--that's all he ever wanted to do his whole life. And he's a young fellow and we had compassion towards him. We didn't know at the time, but we thought he was confused, and we did not know if he had suffered some kind of abuse, and we wanted to find out. But at the same time we wanted to do right by him. So we offered to repay him all of the back wages he would have earned had he not been fired by the company, and to give him his job back, with no promises other than he would be treated like anyone else and would be given the opportunity to succeed and to grow within the company. The ball was in his court. Tom then came to work for us and said that when he went back on the road again as part of the ring crew, that people started making jokes and doing catcalls at him from the arena, and he came to me and said he was very uncomfortable and just couldn't be on the road again. He wanted to know if there was a job he could have here at the company. He said he'd scrub the floors, do anything. Well, we just didn't have a job here for him. But he also indicated to me that he wanted to further his education and I said, `Tom, if you want an opportunity to grow, this is what we'll do for you. We will pay your salary that you're earning now, and we'll pay for you to go to school. So he enrolled in Westchester County Community College, and this is after a whole series of things in between. We tried to get him to see a psychologist, and I set him up with that, but he never made the appointment. He registered at Westchester to get his associate degree in criminal justice. I talked to this young man as I would my son, and told him how supportive of him we would be. But I did tell him, `Tom, I've tried everything I know to try with you,' and I had a document for him to sign, and I said but if you fail in college, that's all I can do for you. So he signed the letter. A little ways into the semester, he called and said he was having trouble with the course. I told him we could arrange for some special help, and if I get a report that you're in class and really trying, we'll take that into consideration. So the semester ended and I got his grades and his attendance report. He failed every subject, and he never went to class. So I just felt he let a golden opportunity slip right through his fingers. The day before we got his grades, we were notified by the Utica Dispatch that he had filed a suit against us. The suit is ludicrous. The allegations that are made in it are just totally unfounded. And Tom Cole has been and continues to be manipulated by his brother Lee Cole. And it's a tragedy. It's really a tragedy."

The main claim in the breach of contract aspect of the suit Cole filed was his failure to be given a try-out as a ring announcer, which was part of the original settlement agreement averting the what likely would have been the original lawsuit. Linda McMahon claimed Cole was given the opportunity to be a ring announcer on two or three occasions.

"Our agents gave him the opportunity aid a match and to rehearse in the arena, which is what he had asked to do. We have him that opportunity, but after that he said he didn't want to be on the road anymore. He just couldn't be exposed to the fans, and he said some of the wrestlers gave him a hard time, and we said fine, we'll take you out of that environment."

On the Jim Hellwig (Ultimate Warrior) lawsuit against Titan, which was since dropped: "We pointed out to Mr. Hellwig's lawyer the absolute inaccuracy of the claim that was filed and the misrepresentation that Jim Hellwig made to his attorney. His attorney withdrew the suit. That's why it went away. It was withdrawn."

On the Kevin Wacholz (Nailz) situation, where Wacholz attacked and was choking Vince McMahon after an argument, and where Wacholz then called the police and claimed he was retaliated from an alleged sexual assault, which has since resulted in a lawsuit and a countersuit: "We sued him and depositions will be going forward during the month of July. I have no idea why he acted that way. He acted like someone who had just gone off the deep end. I'm not quite sure what the motivation was, or what happened, but I can tell you there were several witnesses who saw and heard the attack and know the lack of truthfulness that Kevin reported, and that testimony will be made very clear."

CHAPTER TWENTY NINE

ISSUES WITH WCW
TAPING IN ADVANCE

JUNE 14

The WCW television tapings in Orlando, FL have been cut back once again. In what appears to be the final word, the group will tape four consecutive days (July 6-9) at Disney World, taping three television shows each day, all for World Wide Wrestling, totalling 12 shows, or three months worth. The shows would run weekly through mid-October, which leads to the obvious storyline problems regarding unforseen happenings that always seem to happen in wrestling such as wrestlers getting injured or otherwise leaving the promotion. About 10 minutes of each show will be left open for an update segment that will no doubt be taped a lot closer to air date which would fill in the gaps, wherever they should pop up. The idea espoused is that the syndicated show would have a fresher atmosphere being taped before a largely fresh-faced younger crowd that hasn't seen so much wrestling and thus may be easier to get strong reactions from, and thus give the illusion to those watching on television, and more importantly to television station managers, that the product is "hot" and kids love the WCW product.

JULY 19

World Championship Wrestling broke new ground this past week in not only exposing long-term booking plans but also in trapping themselves with those plans. Tapings from 7/7 to 7/10 at MGM Studios as DisneyWorld in Orlando, for among other things, all episodes of the syndicated World Wide Wrestling shows that will air from 8/27 through 11/20, revealed the following:

On 8/27, the NWA heavyweight champion will be Ric Flair, the unified tag team champions will be Arn Anderson & Paul Roma and the WCW television champion will by Ricky Steamboat. There was no acknowledgement of a U.S. champion during the entire period, although both Rick Rude and Dustin Rhodes made numerous appearances. Obviously this means that Flair will be beating Barry Windham (who never appeared nor was acknowledged during the entire taping period, so it appears there are no plans for him to be used in any capacity in front of the camera after the 7/18 Beach Blast PPV show) for the NWA title. A monkey wrench of sorts may have been thrown into that because during this past week, the NWA legal representatives sent a letter to WCW saying that they have no right to change the title without first getting confirmation by the NWA board of directors (which, by NWA bylaws, controls the NWA title belt). The NWA board consists of Seiji Sakaguchi, Steve Rickard and Bill Watts, none of whom had at press time given the okay for the title switch. The NWA threatened to sue WCW if they did the switch this coming Sunday without permission, or advertised Flair as NWA champion without authorization of the NWA board. WCW was attempting to rectify the situation before Sunday. Anderson & Roma will obviously be beating the Hollywood Blonds (Brian Pillman & Steve Austin) for the tag team title, likely at Beach Blast, while sometime over the next six weeks, Steamboat will win the TV title from Paul Orndorff, perhaps at the 8/18 Clash of the Champions.

WCW heavyweight champion Big Van Vader was in Florida, but never appeared on camera. Original word we received was that Vader didn't have doctor's clearance to work and was sent home, which makes no sense to send him home unless the doctor's believed his back injury also prevented him from doing interviews

On the television show that airs 9/18, The Nasty Boys, as heels without Missy Hyatt (who doesn't show up as their manager until mid-October), come out for an interview announced as World tag team champions and holding the belts

On the television show that airs 9/25, Lord Steven Regal comes out as new WCW television champion

On the television show that airs 10/8, Rick Rude comes out with the NWA heavyweight title belt announced as the new champion

In tapings in November, Rude still came out with the NWA belt but was announced by the ring announcer as "world heavyweight champion" as opposed to NWA champion

At one point, the Nasty Boys and Hollywood Blonds join forces for a match against The Four Horsemen, whomever they may be, that wasn't taped, but by November the two teams were seemingly building up for a feud with one another, with the Blonds seemingly as the babyfaces although that wasn't made clear. There seemed to be no evidence of any other major turns during the time period except for possibly Chris Benoit

Newcomers who received pushes were Yoshi Kwan (Chris Champion aka David Ashford-Smith) managed by Harley Race, The Colossal Kongs (Awesome Kong & King Kong from Dallas), also managed by Race, Indian Charlie Norris as a face, and a muscular newcomer called Ice Train (Harold Rains), making his pro debut to a megapush throughout the tapings, managed by Thunderbolt Patterson, The Equalizer managed by Paul Orndorff, and the tag team of Thunder & Lightning as faces. With the exception of Kwan, all the newcomers were very unimpressive. I was told Train had potential, but was nowhere near ready for what they were pushing him for.

Cactus Jack did interviews at the taping for a PPV main event match with Vader, showing no signs of the amnesia gimmick that he is playing on current television

It had been rumored beforehand that Dusty Rhodes and The Assassin would continue their bizarre feud (in which they continue to give each man ample television time for interviews that never actually build to anything), but neither appeared in front of the camera during the entire set of tapings, however their names were all over the rundown sheets, so they may have done their interviews backstage

Road Warrior Hawk will debut on 8/18 as Dustin Rhodes' mystery partner in a tag match at the Clash against Rude & The Equalizer. Sid Vicious did an interview where he did the freaked out bit when he was informed that "the Road Warriors" are coming in. No word on what this means, although Animal, because he is collecting a reported $20,000 per month in a Lloyd's of London policy due to a back injury, may come in but won't ever be involved in any physical conflict inside the ring

Yet another pay-per-view show was added for 11/21, just three days before the WWF's Survivor Series is scheduled, the first time the two companies will run PPV shows in such proximity of one another, which isn't going to help the buy rate of either show. WCW now will run PPV shows in September, October, November and December. While there is no doubt for short-term income, the company will make more money this year doing monthly PPV shows, over the long haul this will rapidly burn-out and already burning out the company's main source of revenue. Whatever income is made this year, the company will have to pay dividends on in lessened interest in future PPV events if it survives into 1994. If the company is on the verge of shutting down, running like this trying to make as much quick money as possible does make sense

The Halloween Havoc PPV show, which takes place 10/24 in Orlando, will be headlined by Vader vs. Cactus Jack in a spin the wheel, make the deal match, plus Sting vs. Sid Vicious and Nasty Boys defending the tag team titles against Flair & Roma

Another set of tapings was announced for early November at the same location, where tapings that will air through the end of February will take place, so storylines will again be made public months ahead, that is, if there is even still a company by that point

During the fall, another Jesse the Body strongest arm contest will be taking place seemingly with Ice Train and Equalizer as the focal points

Nearly everyone within pro wrestling was shocked that WCW would trot out in front of a live audience wrestlers wearing belts and announced as being champions that they are months away from winning. Apparently even within the company there were a ton of private reservations about this. Long-time wrestling veterans, who had it drummed in their heads from the first time they laced on boots that exposing the business equals death of the business were mortified at the happenings this past week, although it should be noted that the WWF has done similar things such as give away upcoming title changes before they happened at television tapings. The WWF never did so overtly as in having the ring announcer announce someone as champion before they had won the title. Certainly they had never given away storylines this many months in advance, partially because it leaves no room for editing if something doesn't go right or if something needs to be changed. Jarrett Promotions has been doing the same thing on a smaller scale with its titles for decades (wrestlers who lose the title belts on Mondays in Memphis still hold the belts and lose them again a week later in Nashville, Louisville and Evansville).

From a production standpoint, these shows were said to have been near-WWF quality, including the big screens in the background ala WWF and easy, rabid fans. The shows were held in a 628-seat building, packed for every taping with DisneyWorld guests, with admission free to anyone who was at DisneyWorld on the days of the taping. The crowd was composed of largely non-wrestling fans, who were shown a videotape telling them who to cheer for and who to boo, and they had signals given to them when to cheer and boo during the tapings as well. Those at WCW, who are apparently embarrassed at their own fan base, largely wanted it this way, since the tapings were never advertised to wrestling fans, figuring guests at an expensive amusement park are going to be cleaner, better dressed and more upscale looking than wrestling fans, thus enabling television programmers to be more comfortable with the product. As mentioned last week, WCW didn't want wrestling fans at the show, since it never mentioned the tapings on its Orlando syndicated television shows and there was no advertising either by WCW or Disney that tapings would be held at the park beforehand.

Where the utter stupidity comes in, and no matter what the future of the company is, these tapings in the long-run are almost certain to be viewed in hindsight in November as an exercise in stupidity, is what if--What if a key wrestler who is being planned for and has already been taped in either a key angle or with a major title either a) Gets injured; b) Jumps to another promotion; c) Holds the company up for money; d) The wrestler planned for the push just doesn't get over or a scenario simply isn't working. That wrestler will appear with a title belt on syndicated television for months afterwards. In the mid-1970s this very same taping idea was tried by Eddie Einhorn when forming the ill-fated IWA, and all of those things happened before key events that were taped aired on television with talent no longer with the organization. The odds are great, being the type of business this is, that someone in a key position will get injured. It happens all the time. Almost surely people will be jumping from this sinking ship if they can find a life raft. As for holding the company up for money, this may also be tried, but given the way the company is going, that may not be a wise idea for a wrestler because this company seems like it'll just let them go and continue to air their scenarios on television. And this isn't even getting into the fact that what appeared to be the most logical and most profitable match-up the company could run over the short-haul (Flair vs. Vader unification match for the both world titles at Starrcade) is clearly out the window with Flair not only dropping the NWA strap, but used as a tag team wrestler from that point forward. And there is no indication whatsoever that Regal deserves a serious push which they are now locked into giving him. Using a modern example of what if, If four months back, the WWF put itself in this kind of a position, it would have already "written" scripts for Hogan to bodyslam Yokozuna on 7/4 and win the title on 8/30, and the company would literally be forced into using Hogan on top under whatever demands he would make, because television that had been written wouldn't allow for a Lex Luger turn to fill in the emergency gap as needed to have been done, ditto for the Curt Hennig turn last year when Ultimate Warrior and Davey Boy Smith departed. Situations like this happen with enough frequency in wrestling that the odds are better than 50-50 that something will happen that will make WCW look foolish by taping this far in advance well before November. This also almost guarantees, both by the choice of new talent (and the wording of the steroid policy was that all new talent must pass a steroid test before they could be signed, and while I don't know this as a fact, I'd be surprised if any of the new talent was even tested before being put on television) and being locked into key scenarios, that the steroid policy is a complete fraud because the company has already taped things with key individuals that they full well know are on the juice and can't afford to suspend them with television already taped and PPV shows already announced.

Maybe the key point from having done all this which hasn't been brought up is that it effectively solidifies the managerial positions of the key decision-makers, Ole Anderson, Dusty Rhodes, Sharon Sedello, Eric Bischoff, etc. Despite the company setting a new low in attendance in May and completely botching up the return of Ric Flair to the arenas in June, and producing perhaps its worst run of television ever including its all-time lowest ratings sweeps period in May, a change in leadership really doesn't matter at this point. If someone new was brought in to replace Anderson or Rhodes, it wouldn't be until November that they could bring in any new talent, get rid of any talent, change the direction, etc. because everything is locked in place. There is little point now in changing upper management until November.

The line-up for the 8/18 Clash of the Champions from Daytona Beach will be Vader vs. Davey Boy Smith in a no DQ match for the WCW title, Sting vs. Awesome Kong, Rhodes & Hawk vs. Rude & Equalizer, Anderson & Roma vs. Pillman & Austin for the tag team titles, Johnny B. Badd vs. Maxx Payne, Orndorff vs. Steamboat for the TV title (looks like this will be the title switch) and Too Cold Scorpio vs. Regal.

AUGUST 16

What appears to be the first casualty of taping months ahead became apparent to World Championship Wrestling this past week. Road Warrior Hawk pulled out of his scheduled matches on the 8/18 Clash of the Champions and the 9/18 Wrestle War PPV show. Hawk was to be Dustin Rhodes' mystery partner against Rick Rude & The Equalizer on the Clash, and be in the War Games on 9/18 teaming with Rhodes, Sting and Davey Boy Smith against Sid Vicious, Harlem Heat and Big Van Vader. On this past weekend's television, WCW began teasing that either Hawk or Animal were to be Rhodes' partner at the Clash with Rhodes' tape of the announcement of his partner scheduled on the television show that airs 8/14. The mystery partner angle has been the focal point of the build-up for the Clash. We've been told there will be one more conversation between Hawk and WCW when Hawk returns from Japan after press time so there is a possibility the deal could be saved and Hawk may still work the Clash, but not the PPV. There has been some criticism about WCW putting all this time on television into pushing the return of Hawk when they had yet to sign him to appear on the two shows. Rhodes did a taped interview talking about a different mystery partner (inaudible to the live audience) that may air this coming weekend provided the deal with Hawk isn't straightened out. The mystery partner will be Fred "Typhoon" Ottman, using another ring name. We do know WCW has already begun going through the various pre-taped shows to edit out references and interviews where Hawk's name is used, which would be a-plenty leading up to the War Games. The name that would make the most sense as a replacement would be Dusty Rhodes, however management has seemingly stopped every attempt Rhodes has made to put himself back in the spotlight in the ring. It would be a miracle if this was the only casualty that will result of taping so many months in advance.

AUGUST 16

The first Disney tapes aired 8/7 on WCW Saturday Night, which is the only Saturday show taped at Disney.

Visually the show looked better than ever, with special effects and the like, and in some ways it even looked superior to WWF broadcasts and certainly way superior to the "look" of the Raw shows. However, content-wise, the show, had little, although upcoming WCW Saturday shows are much improved in that regard with Flair and Sting being all over every Saturday night main event. While the crowd was up, it was downright embarrassing to hear the crowd cheer for Rick Rude and clap for his music and see the guy leading the crowd point his thumbs down on camera and then have everyone start booing. It came off like you were watching a game show that wrestlers were performing on and that all the wrestlers were interchangeable, because they all got the same amount of reaction and armlocks got the same reaction as finishing holds. There was some good to this, as far as the look of the show which is more important in selling the show to syndicated stations than having strong quality matches, but it's questionable whether it's more effective in getting ratings or garnering viewer interest to pay money to see PPVs. The crowd as it was is impossible to gain any real intensity or real heat, which in theory is what causes the impulse ticket buys that wrestling crowds have long been built on.

NOVEMBER 22

World Championship Wrestling's quarterly Orlando World Wide tapings once again gave away many future story lines and occurrences, although not nearly to the extent of the first set. The entire Starrcade card on 12/27 in Charlotte (tickets go on sale 11/22 in Charlotte) was released, headlined by Vader vs. Ric Flair for the WCW title with Flair vowing to retire if he doesn't win the title (more on that later), Rick Rude vs. Davey Boy Smith for what is being called this week the WCW International World title, Nasty Boys vs. Hawk & Sting in a 2/3 fall match for the WCW tag titles, Steve Regal vs. Rick Steamboat for the WCW TV title, Dustin Rhodes vs. Steve Austin for the U.S. title, Paul Roma & Paul Orndorff vs. Marcus Bagwell & Too Cold Scorpio, Shock Master vs. Awesome Kong and The Equalizer vs. Terry Taylor. The originally booked card was Vader vs. Sid Vicious, Rude vs. Sting, Nasty Boys vs. Flair & Steamboat and Arn Anderson vs. Roma.

The elimination of both Anderson and Vicious from the card, plus the lack of mention of both men during the tapings for four months in advance gives one the impression that there are no plans for either man. As of Monday, the company's official word was that both men were still with the company but that a decision was expected to be made regarding their status stemming from the brawl in England by the end of this week. However, on a wrestling radio show this past weekend, Gene Okerlund was interviewed and said that both men had been fired, which I know for certain comes as news to them. If that's the case, it makes the Clash on Wednesday mind-boggling because the second most-pushed person on the card (behind Okerlund) was Vicious. The reasoning behind it seems to be that they wanted to push him hard in order to use his name to draw a rating for a previously taped match that would air the following Saturday, but it's almost mind-boggling with two PPV coming in such a short period of time to spend so much energy and focus of a Clash to build up a Saturday television rating. In the Clash hard-sell segment with Okerlund, Vicious was prominently mentioned as appearing on the 11/20 Battle Bowl PPV show even though the company had known for two weeks that his injuries wouldn't allow him to appear for that show even if he was retained, which is yet another example of consumer fraud. However, on the television show that aired on Saturday, they showed a main event with Vicious & Flair vs. Vader & Austin where The Kongs attacked Vicious before the match and ironically Anderson helped Vicious out and teamed with Flair. The original finish of the match was Flair about to be squashed by Vader when Vicious comes in for the save. However, with Flair getting the title shot instead of Vicious, it made no business sense to show him in that vulnerable of a position (not that WCW has any business sense) at the hands of Vader. Instead, they went off the air with the match in progress, saying they'd show the finish on television the next day. However, on the Sunday Main Event show, the match and finish were never even acknowledged. When they aired the spot of Vicious being injured, Jesse Ventura made a remark that it seemed to be a career ending injury so it looks like this is how Vicious will be written out of the script for now.

CHAPTER THIRTY

THE DESTROYER RETIRES

AUGUST 9

The Sensational Intelligent Destroyer, one of the biggest names worldwide in pro wrestling during the 60s and 70s, retired this past Thursday night amidst a major ceremony at Tokyo's Budokan Hall. Destroyer, real name Dick Beyer, during his 39-year career held major versions of the world heavyweight title on four occasions. Beyer, who turned 63 less than three weeks before his final match teamed with Giant Baba and son Kurt Beyer to defeat Masao Inoue & Haruka Eigen & Masa Fuchi when Destroyer put the figure four leglock on Inoue while at the same time Baba had Fuchi in the abdominal stretch and Kurt had Eigen in the figure four. Destroyer's retirement was major enough news in Japan that Nippon TV (one of the major networks) covered it on its night World News program. After the match Beyer held a press conference, and unmasked before the cameras, and gave his mask to his son, who when he returns to Japan will become The Destroyer Jr. Besides several family members at the show, also at the Budokan show was Don Manoukian, a former college and pro football star during the 60s who held the California version of the world tag team title with Destroyer.

Dick Beyer was a football and wrestling standout at Syracuse University in the early 50s. He placed in the NCAA tournament in wrestling and played in the Orange Bowl in football. During that era, it was far more common than today for top-flight amateur wrestlers to make the transition to pro. He started pro in 1954 and was named "Rookie of the year" by at least one national magazine, but his wrestling career largely went nowhere, partially because he mainly worked during the summer and coached football at Syracuse during the year.

In 1962, he was brought into the Los Angeles territory by then-promoter Jules Strongbow, and put under the hood as The Destroyer, an idea he originally didn't like. But the mask almost immediately put him on the map as a wrestler offering "$5,000" to anyone who could remove his mask or break his figure four leglock, and he later refused when Strongbow decided it was time for him to lose his mask. He quickly won the old Western Wrestling Alliance version of the world title (recognized in California and Japan) from Fred Blassie on July 27, 1962 in San Diego, and held it for a ten-month run before losing it back to Blassie. During that time frame, he went to Japan and had legendary matches with Rikidozan, including what I believe was the final job Rikidozan did before his death, and the rematch from that is believed to be the largest television rating for any pro wrestling show in the Orient. Destroyer, who regularly toured Japan while being based in Los Angeles for the next few years, had two more runs as WWA champion, beating Dick the Bruiser on July 22, 1964 at the Olympic Auditorium in Los Angeles, and losing it two months later to Cowboy Bob Ellis. Destroyer regained the belt once again September 19, 1964 from Ellis, and lost the belt on December 4, 1964 in Tokyo to Toyonobori, but the switch wasn't recognized in California and he was recognized as champion until March 12, 1965 when he lost the title to Pedro Morales. During that time period he also had at least three runs as WWA world tag team champion with partners Hard Boiled Haggerty and Manoukian. At that point Destroyer left for the AWA, where he worked back-and-forth with in Japan for many years. In 1967, he dropped The Destroyer gimmick and came back as Dr. X, and held the AWA title for two weeks in 1968, winning from and losing to Verne Gagne.

In the early 70s, Dr. X was "injured" by Ray Stevens in the AWA so The Destroyer could tour Japan. When he returned to the AWA, it was as a babyface. In 1973, a major singles match for the International title was held in Japan with champion Giant Baba vs. The Destroyer, with Destroyer, doing an anti-Japanese gimmick at the time, promising "to live" in Japan if he lost. The decision of course was made well before than that Destroyer would become one of the first foreigners to work "as a Japanese" in the days of strict division of Japanese and foreigners on Japanese cards. Destroyer became a regular tag partner of Giant Baba and Jumbo Tsuruta for All Japan Pro Wrestling during its infancy, and held a title known as the World Masked Man championship for several years with his major opponent being Mil Mascaras. During this time period, Destroyer became a mainstream celebrity. Japan was developing its own copy of an American TV hit from years earlier known as "Rowan and Martin's Laugh-in," which was the hottest show on American television in the late 60s. The Destroyer became a weekly regular on Japan's new comedy ensemble show which for years was one of the five most popular shows in the country. Occasionally the program was used as a backdrop for wrestling angles, such as the time Destroyer was doing a sketch when Abdullah the Butcher came out of the audiences and attacked him and left him bloody. After six years living in Japan wearing the mask full-time in public, in 1978 Beyer returned to Akron, New York and stopped wrestling full-time. He was a high school football and swimming coach for the past decade, doing some indies in the area and touring Japan every summer. His role as a serious performer in All Japan ended in the early 80s, but his July tours continued through this year, with him working against young wrestlers or prelim wrestlers in the first or second match every night and beating them with his figure four leglock.

CHAPTER THIRTY ONE

NEW JAPAN DOING BIG
BUSINESS AT THE BOX OFFICE

AUGUST 16

New Japan Pro Wrestling, the most successful at the box office and considered by many to be the "model" pro wrestling company in the world today, finished its most ambitious undertaking to date on Sunday night. The company attempted to run seven consecutive major shows in the same building on successive nights.

Trying to bring fans back seven straight nights, even with an 11,500-seat capacity arena (Tokyo Sumo Hall), seemed a tougher undertaking than attempts and successes in the past by different major promotions in filling up large baseball/football stadiums for a singular big event. Some predicted going in that they would draw seven sellouts in a row, but that wasn't the case. After the second night, which drew an estimated 7,500 fans, or the lowest Sumo Hall crowd for New Japan since 1987, it looked like this idea was a little too ambitious. But by the time the week was up, four of the seven shows sold out and approximately 71,000 tickets were sold for total box office revenue estimated in the $3 to $4 million range. It was likely the biggest week, dollar equivalent wise, for any promotion at any time in history, based on box office receipts, that didn't include a major stadium show. In a post-show company party after the final card on 8/8, New Japan President Seiji Sakaguchi called the event a success and announced that it would be duplicated in 1994 with seven consecutive shows at Sumo Hall during the first week of August.

Tatsumi Fujinami won the third annual Grade One (G-1) Climax tournament, making Hiroshi Hase submit to a scorpion deathlock in the championship match on 8/7. Most of the tournament went as expected the first three nights, with the only major upset being Hase pinning Shinya Hashimoto on 8/3. However, the semifinals on 8/6 saw two upsets, as Fujinami made IWGP world heavyweight champ Keiji Muto submit to the dragon sleeper in 24:26 in what would have to be tabbed only a mild upset due to Fujinami's seniority, and Hase made Masa Chono submit in 26:46 by becoming the first wrestler ever to reverse the STF into his own submission maneuver. Chono had won the two previous G-1 Climax tournaments held at Sumo Hall in August. In the 1991 tournament, which was one of the greatest singles tournaments in pro wrestling history, he pinned Muto in the finals which was designed not only to singularly established this event as an annual tradition but to put Muto, Chono and Hashimoto over the top as superstars in Japan as they outlasted the traditional superstars Fujinami and Riki Choshu and Americans Big Van Vader, Bam Bam Bigelow and Scott Norton. The 1992 tournament, which doubled as a tournament to decide the NWA world heavyweight title, saw Chono pin Rick Rude in an excellent final match, although the tournament overall couldn't compare with the previous year. This year's tournament was a major letdown on paper, with 16 wrestlers entered, all Japanese, but with the two biggest "name" wrestlers working for the company, Choshu (injured) and Genichiro Tenryu not entered and guys like Michiyoshi Ohara (although there was a reason), Takashi Ishikawa, Super Strong Machine, Great Kabuki, Hiromichi Fuyuki, Osamu Kido and Takayuki Iizuka involved. The weak overall line-up was blamed for the non-sellouts on 8/3 and 8/5. The 8/4 show, with a Fujinami vs. Yoshiaki Fujiwara and Muto vs. Kabuki double main event did fill the hall. The purpose of the final seems to be to try and establish Fujinami as a major player once again for a potential first-ever singles match with Tenryu, and to go with Hase in the finals since he's the best worker in the promotion so had the best chance to carry Fujinami into a classic match. Hase, who had done jobs in most of his key matches this year (his last big singles win was a non-title match from then-NWA champ Chono in December), was attempted to put on an equal footing with the top guys in the promotion this week with his spot in the finals, followed by a clean pinfall win over Fujiwara on 8/8.

The Jurassic Powers, Scott Norton & Hercules, became the first team to "Stop the Hell Raisers" (the three primary themes in television advertising for the seven days were 1) G-1 tournament; 2) "Stop the Hell Raisers" with various teams brought in to challenge for the IWGP tag title: and 3) Seven singles matches for Tiger Mask. In doing so, Hawk did his first clean final job in nine years of wrestling in Japan (in 1985 during a 2/3 fall tag match, Hawk was pinned in a fall by Jumbo Tsuruta however the Road Warriors lost that match via DQ in the third fall) when Norton pinned him after a powerslam in 13:36. I believe the match storyline was that Power Warrior (Kensuke Sasaki) was "injured" early so Hawk had to stay in against both men in and was worn down and finally pinned. Nevertheless, the fans were really shocked to see the Hell Raisers lose the title and Hawk, in particular, do a clean job. A rematch for the title on 8/8 saw the Hell Raisers get disqualified (the only DQ finish in seven days) when they used Hercules' chain on him. This established the Jurassic Powers as legitimate opponents for the Hell Raisers, who badly needed a team of this type to challenge them (although admittedly Hercules isn't the greatest person to be put in this position for Japan) since Rick & Scott Steiner went to the WWF.

The seven match challenge for the newest Tiger Mask, Koji Kanemoto never materialized. Kanemoto was scheduled for him to wrestle Shinjiro Otani, Eddy Guerrero, Wild Pegasus (Chris Benoit under a mask with a new ring name, last week's listing of his ring name as White Kid was incorrect), Jushin Liger, El Samurai, Negro Casas and El Engendro. However, he suffered a shoulder separation on the first night. He tried to wrestle Pegasus on the second night but the referee had to stop the match after just 4:00. Otani took his place in singles matches the rest of the tour. Guerrero seemed to be the prime beneficiary of the week, as put in the spotlight several nights during the week in front of the hardcore Tokyo fans turned him into a new superstar in Japan.

Another new junior heavyweight contender was born during the week in the form of a wrestler called Black Tiger, who most likely was brought in to feud with Tiger Mask. Tiger Mask was a famous animated television cartoon character in Japan in the 1970s whose main villain rival was his real-life brother called Black Tiger. When the original Tiger Mask (Satoru Sayama) became a wrestler in 1981, his biggest early rival was Black Tiger (Mark Rocco of England). So a new Black Tiger, identity of whom I don't know, was brought in most likely for the new generation of Tiger Mask. With Tiger Mask out of the picture, his debut came in an Americanized angle. On 8/8, Jushin Liger was defending the IWGP jr. heavyweight title against Pegasus, who had captured the Top of the Super Junior tournament in June to earn the shot. Pegasus unmasked before the match started (what the purpose was of him returning as a masked wrestler when one week later he was removing the mask voluntarily and everyone knew who he was beforehand is a mystery to me). After their usual great match, Liger pinned Pegasus after a uranage (Soviet suplex). At that point the new Black Tiger hit the ring and he and Pegasus attacked Liger and destroyed him, and Black Tiger pulled off his mask and left him laying in the middle of the ring.

The other major storyline of the week involved Michiyoshi Ohara. Ohara had been getting a minor push of late as regular tag team partner of Shinya Hashimoto in feud matches with the Skinheads. On the 8/4 show, he had a first round G-1 tournament match against Kengo Kimura. Even though everyone "knew" Kimura would win, they teased a 30:00 draw as Ohara kept kicking one of near falls which caused the crowd to go crazy. Finally Kimura won in 26:44. After the match Kimura told Ohara how impressed he was by him and asked him to join the Skinheads group. Ohara refused. On 8/8, they had a ten-man tag match with the Skinheads vs. the New Japan quintet of Ohara & Takayuki Iizuka & Muto & Chono & Fujinami. Before the match, Shiro Koshinaka and Kimura once again asked Ohara to join the Skinheads. This time Ohara seemingly ignored the comments. During the match, the first time Ohara was tagged in, he did a quick bodyslam on Koshinaka and tagged out immediately. He then kept being in the wrong spot when one of his teammates went to tag him. Finally Ohara turned on Chono and held him as Koshinaka used his butt-bump finisher on Chono, who was pinned. The fans really booed Ohara as a new heel when he grabbed the house mic after the match and announced his joining the Skinheads and that he'll beat all the New Japan wrestlers.

SEPTEMBER 27

New Japan opened what should be an even bigger week dollar-wise than the seven nights at Sumo Hall in August with a week's worth of major shows with inflated ticket prices that started 9/20 in Nagoya. The Nagoya show drew a legit turn-away crowd of 11,500, which based on ticket prices would have been a gate of near $700,000, although usually there is an element of discounted tickets at these big shows so the gate was probably a little less than that. In the headline match, Shinya Hashimoto won the IWGP world heavyweight title from Great Muta with a DDT after Hashimoto caught Muta with a kick to the ribs as he tried a moonsault. After the match Hashimoto issued challenges to Genichiro Tenryu (who has pinned him twice in singles matches this year), Tatsumi Fujinami and Riki Choshu for title matches and said he wants his first title defense to be against Tenryu. Muta pretty much had to lose the title, as doing two non-title jobs for Hulk Hogan and never getting to beat him would hurt the belt's credibility as a world title. In addition, New Japan attempts to keep a form of parity with all its top stars (anyone of the top guys can beat any other of the top guys) and since Hashimoto did two jobs for Tenryu and was eliminated by Hiroshi Hase in the first round of the G-1 tournament, he needed a big win to maintain his position. Gates for 9/23 at the Yokohama Arena and 9/26 at Osaka Castle Hall are both scaled for $1.5 million capacity.

Tickets for the January 4, 1994 card at the Tokyo Egg Dome go on sale 10/9. The only thing New Japan has announced is that Tenryu, Choshu, Hulk Hogan and Antonio Inoki will all wrestle on the card and the newspapers this past week were hinting Inoki vs. Tenryu will be the main event. Inoki just returned from Minneapolis where he had knee surgery.

OCTOBER 4

New Japan Pro Wrestling did what was most likely an all-time record for the biggest house show week, dollars-wise, in history between 9/20 and 9/26. While we don't have official figures, and it's hard to estimate money revenue accurately in Japan because tickets are often discounted if the advance is slow, the five shows drew approximately 54,500 fans. While that is less than the seven straight nights in Sumo Hall in early August, which drew 70,000 fans, tickets for the two main shows, 9/23 at the Yokohama Arena and 9/26 at Osaka Castle Hall, were priced considerably higher than the Sumo Hall tickets and the gate for the entire week was likely in the $4 million range, which would be the biggest week I've ever heard of for house show business.

The week wasn't as big as the Sumo Hall week as far as in-ring wrestling news. The biggest stories coming out of the week were the IWGP heavyweight title change from Great Muta to Shinya Hashimoto as reported last week and an apparent angle to set up a Hulk Hogan vs. Antonio Inoki match. The climax show of the week in Osaka was headlined by the first Tatsumi Fujinami vs. Genichiro Tenryu match, which, combined with a loaded undercard, resulted in packing a record 16,000 fans into Castle Hall. For most of the decade of the 80s, Fujinami held the No. 2 spot with New Japan Pro Wrestling behind Antonio Inoki, and was considered by many as the all-around best worker in the country before back injuries pretty much curtailed him and nearly ended his career. Tenryu, who was a big name in sumo before joining pro wrestling in the late 70s, because of his sumo name was always pushed with All Japan Pro Wrestling, and for most of the 80s dueled with Jumbo

Tsuruta for the top spot in the company before he quit to be the top star with the now-defunct SWS promotion. Because they had worked their entire careers for rival groups, the two had never wrestled before in singles matches, although they had worked against one another in tag matches a few times this year. In typical New Japan fashion of trying to keep parity among the top names, Fujinami scored the "upset" win in 9:32 with an abdominal stretch dropped into a cradle. Of the "top-level" older wrestlers that work for New Japan and its sister WAR promotion (Choshu, Tenryu and Fujinami), Fujinami is the least over so he's usually given the wins in these kind of matches. Hogan worked both in Osaka, pinning Keiji Muto with the axe bomber (lariat) in 9:55, and in Yokohama on 9/23, where he and Muta beat The Hell Raisers in 15:29 when Hogan pinned Power Warrior (Kensuke Sasaki) with the axe bomber. After the tag match, Hogan refused to shake hands with Muta afterwards to build some heat for the singles match three days later, and then pushed and shoved Inoki, who was sitting at ringside. When Inoki jumped into the ring, Hogan got out. After the Osaka match, Hogan and Muto posed together in the ring. It was only the second job the Hell Raisers had done as a team since forming late last year and being pushed most of this year as New Japan's top team, the other being to the Jurassic Powers (Hercules & Scott Norton) in August, but that was largely for the purpose of creating a rival team after they'd beaten everyone else in the promotion, and being put back in the "chaser" position in regard to the IWGP tag team titles. The Hell Raisers won all their other matches during the week, as did the Jurassic Powers, to set up a title rematch later this year. With the exception of doing the job for Hogan, Muto was put over strong all week with singles wins in main events on 9/21 in Shizuoka over Masa Chono and 9/24 in Miyagi over Hiroshi Hase. Hase, the New Japan acting booker on the road with Riki Choshu out of action with an injury, largely sacrificed himself after being pushed so heavily in August. In other words, with his upset wins over Chono, Yoshiaki Fujiwara and Hashimoto in August, Hase had been made into a main eventer capable of beating anyone. During this tour Hase not only put Muto over in a singles main event, but also put over Tenryu in Yokohama and Hashimoto in Osaka.

In the junior heavyweight division, the big push in creating a new top star went to Black Tiger (Eddy Guerrero). Tiger scored clean pins over both Tiger Mask (Koji Kanemoto) and Jushin Liger (in a non-title match in Osaka), to set himself up for a shot at Liger later this year. Liger himself was protected otherwise by pinning Tiger Mask, who had beaten him at the Fukuoka Dome, and WAR's Masao Orihara in a title match in Yokohama. Orihara upset Tiger Mask in Osaka.

This concept of all the top guys in each different "class" exchanging top wins with clean finishes may be a large factor in New Japan not only having the most-widely viewed wrestling television show in any country but also in being the most successful pro wrestling company of this year. It's interesting that this is coming during a year when the New Japan in-ring product is nowhere near the calibre of years past.

Although the company has been very successful for years, this year's success can largely be traced by the working of a promotion feud with WAR, a promotion which seemed to be on its last legs at this time last year and has benefitted tremendously from the exposure and the feud going from a nearly dead promotion to a somewhat hot office that has drawn several huge houses this year as well. Tenryu, WAR's top star and only wrestler with any real box office power, stared by feuding with old rival Riki Choshu, before saving his "first ever" meetings with Fujinami and the Three Musketeers (Muto, Chono and Hashimoto) for later in the year, and Hase was pushed enough as a single wrestler to where his match with Tenryu meant big box office as well, and Yoshiaki Fujiwara, who returned to New Japan after for years of being with the old UWF and his own promotion, is waiting on deck for his first-ever singles match with Tenryu as well. While these matches themselves are generally not classics, since Tenryu, Choshu and Fujinami are in the 40-age bracket and have been through plenty of stiff injury-producing wars during that period, they are "dream matches" in many cases. The first Tenryu-Hashimoto match, which was never televised, has been written up as if it were a match of the year level bout, although that hasn't been the case with any of the others. The promotional concept with the parity and trading wins with clean finishes is simple and uncreative by pro wrestling standards, but it's also neither confusing nor insulting to its audience and the results can't be argued with.

OCTOBER 5

First-day ticket sales for the January 4, 1994 Battlefield in Tokyo Dome totalled $1,488,650, which is the second largest first day ticket sales in Japanese history, trailing only the $2 million done for the UWF show at the Tokyo Dome on November 29, 1989, although the UWF figure was for 40,000 tickets and this figure was for only 12,684 tickets

At press time, Shiro Koshinaka & Michiyoshi Ohara were in first place in the tag tourney with eight points, with Hell Raisers in second place with six. All three of the tourney matches on 10/15 at Korakuen Hall ended with upsets. Jushin Liger & Wild Pegasus beating IWGP champ Shinya Hashimoto & Masa Chono when Liger pinned Chono; Ohara & Koshinaka beat Hiroshi Hase & Keiji Muto when Koshinaka pinned Hase and Akira Nogami & Takayuki Iizuka beat The Barbarian & Masa Saito when Saito did the job for Nogami for the first time ever.

CHAPTER THIRTY TWO

MEAN GENE OKERLUND LEAVES WWF FOR WCW

AUGUST 30

Gene Okerlund, who came along with Hulk Hogan and David Shults in the first Vince McMahon "talent raid" of the AWA in late 1983, appears to be severing ties with the group after nearly ten years of on-again off-again employment. Okerlund, who began announcing for Verne Gagne's AWA in the late 1970s as a replacement host during an on-air television talent strike in the Twin Cities, apparently will finish his WWF tenure with the SummerSlam PPV show and start with WCW doing Events Centers and Magazine segments on television and taking over control of the 900 number in early September. Originally Okerlund and Bobby Heenan had talked of trying to negotiate as a package deal with WCW, but Heenan apparently backed out before any serious negotiations took place. No other details are available other than word reaching us that Okerlund was unhappy with his new deal offered by the WWF which may have included having to move full-time to Connecticut. His WCW deal was reportedly for $250,000 per year plus 35 percent of the 900 number.

SEPTEMBER 6

Gene Okerlund is scheduled to start on 9/10, and will probably co-host the second hour on TBS. Speaking of Okerlund, a basketball insider newsletter printed that he was going to be offered the job as commission of the Continental Basketball Association. Terry Taylor looks like he'll be hosting the Sunday Main Event, so Michael Hayes will be back in the ring again.

SEPTEMBER 27

Last word we've got is that Gene Okerlund will start working here in less than six months, but won't be in front of the camera. Jesse Ventura acknowledged a "Welcome Mean Gene" sign in Houston saying that "he's on his way."

SEPTEMBER 29

Gene Okerlund won't be coming in that quickly as reportedly Titan is going to enforce a non-competition clause in his contract.

OCTOBER 11

The new WWF Magazine came out with no story or even mention of the "Now It's Our Turn" segment. They had a brief item of Gene Okerlund leaving, trying to claim it was their decision. The idea of someone leaving the organization because of a bigger money offer elsewhere seems hard to acknowledge. The story said that Okerlund had become one of the most visible characters in the WWF but the company had decided it was time to move in a new direction and that Okerlund's contract wasn't renewed.

NOVEMBER 15

The main focus of the 11/6 TBS show was the debut of Gene Okerlund. Tony Schiavone plugged the previous week how there was a huge surprise for Jesse Ventura. Despite the fact Ventura acknowledged Okerlund's arrival two months back on a PPV show, that it was plugged all week on the WCW Hotline and on the morning Power Hour, they still had Jesse act shocked when Okerlund arrived. Larry King even did a promo building up Okerlund's debut like he was Walter Cronkite. After all these years they finally get some cooperation from TBS to get a CNN celebrity on their wrestling show and they waste it by having him plug someone who can't draw them any money. It's interesting to see that when wrestlers run wrestling companies, everyone who isn't in a wrestling position or never wrestled gets treated like they aren't important. Now that they have TV announcers running the company, all the focus is on hyping the announcing team rather than the wrestling product.

NOVEMBER 15

Okerlund made comments on his Hotline debut that really ruffled some feathers in Titan Sports. Okerlund categorized himself as the anchor announcer for the WWF for the past ten years and said that he had philosophical and intellectual differences with Vince McMahon and that for the past three years the two were barely on speaking terms. He then criticized Titan's recent hirings, mentioning by name Jim Ross, Boni Blackstone (who is no longer with the company), Jim Cornette, "Bruce Prichard's brother" and Todd Pettingill and noted WWF TV ratings have declined over the past three years. At this point Gene fell into fiction claiming when he hosted All-American Wrestling that they got no production budget but the ratings were excellent, and that Vince used the money that should have been spent on All-American for Vince's Monday Night Raw show, which Gene claimed has struggled in the ratings. The comment that struck the nerves was when he called the WWF a cottage industry and called TBS a multi-billion dollar conglomerate. Cottage industry is a term Vince McMahon has used for years as a derisive term for everyone else in the wrestling business.

DECEMBER 6

Gene Okerlund on the Hotline called Anthony Valenti and Sean O'Shea (the government prosecutors in the Titan investigation) "clowns" and "government henchmen," which seems a wise move given the company he's working for is a sitting duck for the same kind of investigation. He said he'd love to be a character witness for Vince and that Vince was completely innocent of everything and that the government has no case. The last time I remember Gene as a character witness it was for Ken Patera and it sure did Patera a lot of good. Then he said that Vince's ego is way out of control for not taking himself off television until the case is settled. Gene also regularly talks about Hulk Hogan on his way in as well, which is all just a way to increase calls to the hotline and not a scoop with any semblance of reality.

CHAPTER THIRTY THREE

SHAWN MICHAELS QUITS WWF

SEPTEMBER 27

A considerable bit of talent turmoil hit the World Wrestling Federation this past weekend, including the first time in more than a decade that a champion left the promotion before losing his belt. Intercontinental champion Shawn Michaels (Michael Hickenbottom), 28, considered by many as the best worker in the country, quit the company early last week, before a match could take place where he would lose his title. While this was not confirmed, at press time it was believed that there would be a 20-man tournament for the vacant title held on 9/27 at the television tapings in New Haven, CT.

Three other top-name wrestlers were also removed temporarily from the booking sheets, Matt "Doink the Clown" Osborne, and Rick & Scott Steiner (Rob & Scott Rechsteiner). Osborne, 36, was removed from all house shows for eight weeks, however he is scheduled to return at that point. His absence will be the one of the four that will largely go unnoticed because Steve Lombardi (Brooklyn Brawler) started taking all his bookings on 9/17 in North Charleston, SC, wrestling as Doink the Clown. The original Doink the Clown II, Steve "Skinner" Keirn, is no longer with the WWF. In addition, since his Doink character was in the midst of a babyface turn, Osborne, at press time, was still scheduled to portray Doink at all television tapings held during that eight-week period. The Steiners, who lost the WWF tag team titles on 9/13 on Monday Night Raw from the Manhattan Center to the Quebecers, which appears now to have been a decision made largely because of things happening behind-the-scenes rather than a booking decision based on drawing dollars to the gate, were also removed from all scheduled bookings for an eight-week period beginning with the 9/24 card at the Rosemont Horizon. It is believed that this is due to a suspension of Scott, and includes television appearances. All three should be available to start back right around the Survivor Series (11/24 in Boston) in which the Steiners were originally scheduled as part of the main event. Word we are getting is that the Steiners are still going to make their scheduled 10/7 to 10/10 dates with Smoky Mountain Wrestling, but are uncertain about whether they'll be returning to the WWF. While there is no confirmation of any negotiations going on, the logical assumption is the Steiners would leave Titan is that they would resurface with New Japan Pro Wrestling. The Steiners will be replaced on all WWF house shows during that period by The Quebecers (Jacques Rougeau Jr. & Pierre Oulette), who will be defending their newly won tag team titles largely against Adam Bomb & Bam Bam Bigelow, at least during the early period of these dates being changed. No word when that change, and the change regarding

Michaels will be announced on television, but it is believed some sort of a storyline involving Michaels will be on television this coming weekend. The Quebecers vs. Bomb & Bigelow creates an interesting situation since Johnny Polo manages both Bomb and The Quebecers, although the assumption is that Polo will be in the Quebecers corner for those matches. In matches this past weekend, Michaels was replaced in his scheduled Intercontinental title defenses against 1-2-3 Kid by Bastion Booger.

The situation with Michaels marks the first time in the modern (post-1984) history of the WWF that a champion has left the promotion without losing the title. The most recent example of this in WWF history would be in 1981, when The Moondogs (Sailor White & Randy Culley were that incarnation of Moondogs) held the tag team titles and Moondog King (White) was detained at the border from Canada to the United States and no longer allowed in the country, presumably due to drug charges. That situation was rather easily dealt with as Larry Booker was brought in as Moondog Spot to replace him in the championship team. The last time a champion quit the promotion was in 1975, when the tag team title was held by Domenic DeNucci & Victor Rivera, and Rivera quit the WWWF to join the then-rival Eddie Einhorn's International Wrestling Association. Pat Barrett was brought in as DeNucci's partner on the tag team championship team.

While no confirmation is available from either side, a source close to Michaels said that he had been unhappy with the promotion which had caused him to gain weight (he was up to about 240 legit, and that's an off-steroids 240, with a noticeable belly for the first time in his career) and get out of shape. There are many reports that contradict one another as to the reason for Michaels leaving, none of which we've been able to confirm. As of press time, negotiations were still going on between both parties, largely because apparently Titan had refused to give Michaels the contract release which would allow him to begin negotiating with other promotions.

Problems between Titan and the Steiners had been rumored going back several weeks, and quite frankly, were expected by many within wrestling before the Steiners decided to go to the WWF in mid-December of 1992. The money, even as tag team champions in the WWF, was presumably nowhere close to what they had gotten used to earning in WCW (reportedly $6,000 per week apiece), where they left after a contract dispute with then-Vice President Bill Watts, who wanted to break them up as a team with Scott being turned into a heel after apparently Scott was told earlier that his apparent heel turn with Rick Steamboat was just an angle that was to keep people guessing, at which point he knew people were being less than honest with him and resulted in him blowing up at Watts in the dressing room one day. In addition, Titan remains under the gun in regard to pressure from federal authorities regarding steroid use and has in place a much-publicized testing policy. New Japan, the Steiners' other option, besides the possibility of negotiating a return to WCW, has no steroid testing program. It is unknown what the contractual situation is with the brothers, but it is believed they inked a Titan deal on or around December 16, 1992. Generally these initial deals run for two years, although there have been those who have said the Steiners only signed a one-year deal. Either way, they wouldn't be legally allowed to work for anyone without a Titan release or Titan approval until possibly December 1994, and at the earliest this coming December. Titan could conceivably not block their path if it came to a deal with New Japan, but they almost surely would enforce the contract if it came to any attempts to negotiate with WCW. New Japan would only book the Steiners for a certain number of weeks per year, likely ten or less, and the WWF does have a certain lure to it about being the big-time in the United States. Even though the per-week money would be expected to be much higher with New Japan than the WWF, the WWF booking them on a year-round schedule would add up to more money.

OCTOBER 4

Razor Ramon (Scott Hall) became the new WWF Intercontinental champion by beating Rick Martel in the 9/27 match in New Haven, CT to fill the title vacated by the departure of Shawn Michaels. While rumors have continued to persist as to the reason Michaels quit the WWF, nothing has been able to be confirmed. The storyline reason given was that Jack Tunney suspended Michaels and stripped him of the title for failure to complete his contractual obligations, which sounds like a pretty honest reason. Michaels' departure was first announced on the 9/27 edition of Monday Night Raw, which aired live from New Haven. It was announced on that show that a 20-man Battle Royal would take place on television 10/4, and that the final two men left in the Battle Royal would meet in a singles match to determine the champion in a match that airs 10/11. Both matches were taped 9/27. The Battle Royal went 19:24 and was rated **1/4, or better than a typical Battle Royal. Order of elimination went Giant Gonzalez, Mabel, IRS, 1-2-3 Kid, Diesel, Bob Backlund, Jimmy Snuka, Mr. Perfect, Marty Janetty, Tatanka, Bastion Booger, Bam Bam Bigelow, The MVP (Steve Lombardi) and Owen Hart. This left The Quebecers, Martel, Ramon, Randy Savage and Adam Bomb. Savage and Bomb then went out together leaving Ramon with three heels for several minutes. Jacques held Ramon for Pierre's clothesline, but Ramon ducked and Jacques went out, and Ramon quickly dumped Pierre, leaving he and Martel. Their match took place a few hours later, lasting 12:29 with Ramon winning with the Razor's edge in a match given *1/2 with little action until after the 10:00 mark when it picked up.

OCTOBER 5

They also did a segment where fans could vote on whether Shawn Michaels would be reinstated. Although fans voted not to reinstate him, this is a prelude to an angle where Michaels will be brought back

OCTOBER 18

It appears the situation with Shawn Michaels has been resolved and expect him to make a "surprise" return shortly the same way Marty Janetty always does when he's let go and comes back. Michaels will be working USWA starting 10/21.

NOVEMBER 22

Shawn Michaels returned with the old Intercontinental belt at the 10/9 tapings in Carbondale, IL to start a feud with Razor Ramon over who is the real IC champ. Best bet is they'll have a belt vs. belt match at Royal Rumble.

CHAPTER THIRTY FOUR

LAUNCH OF THE UWFI

SEPTEMBER 27

The next PPV show in the United States will be the UWFI's "Shootwrestling--It's real" card which airs 10/5 and will be a two-hour show taped the previous night in Osaka, Japan. According to Joe Hand, a pioneer of promoting boxing on closed-circuit television, his Front Row Entertainment will come back with a second UWFI PPV show just three weeks later on 10/25, or just one day after the WCW Halloween Havoc show. Hand said that as of right now there were no plans to PPV the December UWFI show from Tokyo's Jingu Baseball Stadium (Nobuhiko Takada vs. Vader was announced officially this past week as the main event on that show billed as a battle to recognize the real world champion with Takada's UWFI title at stake and Vader being WCW champion, although he may not be by December if Dusty Rhodes has his way) because he felt early December would be a tough time to sell a PPV event based on past experience. Both cards will be priced at $14.95, as opposed to the $24.95 that WCW is pricing its now-monthly PPV events at or the $27.50 WWF is pricing most of its five-per year events at (with Wrestlemania going at $29.95).

Forgetting arguments about differences in quality or style of product, the UWFI show goes in with the insurmountable disadvantage of being a product unfamiliar to the U.S. audience, having no television of any kind in this country to sell the style and wrestlers. Its style and competitors are only known to the most ardent tape traders and Observer readers in the United States, which is a very small base to draw from. From an economic standpoint, Hand's company is budgeting $895,000 as costs of putting this show together, of which $285,000 will be his advertising budget, largely consisting of buying spots on Major League Baseball games during the final week of the season and one $75,000 spot on the Monday Night Football game on 10/4. These commercials won't attempt to sell the names or abilities of any of the participants, but instead try to sell the violence and the idea that it is pro wrestling that is real, which it isn't entirely true although it certainly looks far more realistic and is based more on realistic moves than any other pro wrestling promotion in the world with the possible exception of RINGS. "This is not for children," said Hand, who was vehement about this show being a success. "I don't want to see Takada as the next Hulk Hogan."

Hand claimed PPV analysts have told him to expect a 1.0 to 1.5 buy rate for the event, which sounds ridiculous on the surface since that would be equal to SummerSlam, although at an 0.5 buy rate, his company would make a $228,385 profit and there have been Tough Man tournaments that have done 0.5 buy rates as late as this year and they don't have any television show building up their product nor are the competitors names and personalities well known, which is Hand's argument in saying this will be a successful and profitable promotion. Of course WCW's recent PPV shows have hovered in that area, and that is with years of history (which admittedly is a negative in many instances), several names with significant name recognition among wrestling fans and hours of both cable and syndicated television to sell the events. Hand said his company's plan is to do two or three PPV events from Japan on a one-day taped delay over the next few months before trying to promote a live PPV event from the United States.

The Osaka card is scheduled to have a double main event of Takada vs. Billy Scott and Super Vader vs. Naoki Sano, however in press information given out by Hand's company, the Vader match is not listed on the PPV. This may be due to WCW believing it has the exclusive rights to promote PPV and house show events with Vader in the United States, since Vader is definitely going to appear on the Osaka show itself. However, if this is even in Vader's contract, that should be a moot point because Vader and WCW at press time have not signed a contract although they may work out the deal before you are reading this. Matches listed in a press release by Hand's Front Row Entertainment for the first show are Takada vs. Scott, a tag match of U.S. vs. Russia with Gary Albright & Dan Severn vs. Salman Hashimikov & Vladimir Berkovich, Dennis Koslowski vs. either Kazuo Yamazaki or Yoji Anjyo, and other matches not advertised. However, in Japan advertising for the card, which I would assume to be more reliable, the tag match has the Russians against Severn & Koslowski. Probably the most important element in being able to get this show "over" to those who do buy it would be the announcers, and we've been unable to find out who they will be.

OCTOBER 4

The complete line-up, which differs from what is being listed in U.S. press releases (I'd say different from what is being advertised but the matches themselves aren't being advertised) for the 10/4 UWFI show at the Osaka Furitsu Gym that will comprise the 10/5 PPV show, is Super Vader vs. Naoki Sano, Nobuhiko Takada vs. Billy Scott, Salman Hashimikov & Vladimir Berkovich vs. Dennis Koslowski & Dan Severn, Kazuo Yamazaki vs. Badnews Allen, Kiyoshi Tamura vs. Yuko Miyato, Tatsuo Nakano vs. Yoji Anjyo, Mark Silver vs. Masato Kakihara, Gene Lydig vs. Greg Bobchick, Tom Burton vs. Yoshihiro Takayama, Tommy Cairo vs. Hiromitsu Kanehara and Ray Lloyd vs. ?. The show will be edited down to two hours with Takada-Scott, the tag match, and Yamazaki-Allen all definitely airing. Vader-Sano won't air on the PPV show. Even though Vader didn't have a signed contract with WCW as of press time, he has signed a paper that is an agreement in principal to the four-year contract which gives WCW all rights to market and promote him everywhere but Japan. Even though this PPV emanates from Japan, it airs in the U.S. where WCW controls his rights and doesn't want him appearing on the show. This also will block the upcoming Takada-Vader match from airing on PPV in the United States, which thus explains why there is no plan to PPV the 12/5 stadium show. We'll be doing a thumbs up/thumbs down poll on the 10/5 show.

OCTOBER 11

While the UWFI's first PPV show in the United States aired after our deadline, we did get the results of the show which took place 10/4 at the Osaka Furitsu Gym. The show drew about 5,900 fans, which wasn't a sellout (about 85% full). The inability to sell the show out was a pretty big deal. The key results went as expected. Super Vader defeated Naoki Sano in 6:20 after the match was stopped due to the five knockdown rule; Nobuhiko Takada made Billy Scott submit to a cross-arm lock in 13:00; Salman Hashimikov & Vladimir Berkovich beat Gary Albright & Dan Severn when Hashimikov made Severn submit to a cross-arm lock in 13:09; Kazuo Yamazaki made Badnews Allen submit to a half crab in 13:34; Kiyoshi Tamura made Yuko Miyato submit to an armlock in 8:19; Dennis Koslowski made Masato Kakihara submit to a full boston crab in 8:55; Yoji Anjyo beat Tatsuo Nakano in 9:22 with a sleeper; Gene Lydig beat Greg Bobchick with a cross-armlock in 7:37; Yoshihiro Takayama beat Tom Burton with a chicken-wing in 11:12; Tsunemitsu Kanehara knocked out Tommy Cairo in 3:49; and Mark Silver beat Sakuraba with a sleeper in 7:14. The adding of Albright to the show in the tag match, as actually was announced in the U.S. before in Japan, was made public in Japan the Tuesday before the show. We'll details next week on at least the matches that air on the PPV and how the show was organized and came across. The commercials in the United States, which aired heavily in the final week on baseball games and on Monday Night Football, caused a surprising amount of curiosity in the days leading up to the event over the idea of pro wrestling sold as "being real" and "looking" real since the first word the U.S. sports public (which the show was advertised to rather than on wrestling broadcasts to the wrestling fans) associates with pro wrestling is fake. Whether that curiosity will result in PPV buys is another story. On the surface, a lot of buys would seem unlikely due to this style's lack of exposure in this country.

The reason given for the show being unable to sellout is that Takada and UWFI are right now pretty hot in Tokyo, which is the hardcore wrestling fans capital of the world. However they don't have television in Japan. Most of their publicity for outside Tokyo shows comes from the magazines and newspapers. UWFI has a reputation with the press of non-cooperation when it comes to interviews and the like. In the Japanese magazines, with the exception of Weekly Pro, nobody goes out of their way to do favors for the group so it isn't treated as if it's as big a deal as its Tokyo attendance figures suggest it should be. Hence, outside of Tokyo, this becomes not as big a deal as some of the other groups. Tokyo is its own world in Japan and there are Takada posters in the subway stations so he's kind of a celebrity there so this shouldn't have an effect on attendance for 12/5. All that reasoning may simply obfuscate the most simple fact when it comes to creating interest. Everybody knew who would win both main events and neither on paper looked to be very competitive.

NOVEMBER 8

Based on further cable industry reports, it seems the reported 0.5 buy rate for the UWFI PPV show looks to be unrealistic. We've been unable to get any independent national buy rate estimate, although several regional estimates we've received were much lower than 0.5. Reports are that Joe Hand Promotions is still going ahead with plans for four UWFI PPV shows in 1994.

NOVEMBER 22

Choose which source you want to believe department. Buy Rate magazine, which traditionally seems to have been the most accurate trade journal covering PPV, listed the UWFI PPV show as doing 108,000 buys, which would be more than most of the recent WCW shows. However, other sources claim the figure is nowhere near that amount. The next UWFI PPV show has tentatively been pushed back to March.

NOVEMBER 29

UWFI is remaining strong in Japan as the 12/5 Takada vs. Vader show has a huge advance. However, Rings is taking some lumps, as it was unable to come close to selling out Sumo Hall on 11/18, because of the popularity of Pancrase. From what I'm told, in Japan, most fans saw UWFI as a more realistic looking New Japan style promotion with angles, where as Rings was a hardcore thing that expected to be real. Unfortunately, Pancrase, by its style, has shown what a shoot really looks like and Rings fans aren't the kind who largely want to see stiff realistic working matches like UWFI fans. Maeda's matches have pro wrestling psychology (Maeda gets beat up and twisted around for several minutes, but makes a comeback to dramatically win) and Pancrase has no psychology since a shoot can't.

DECEMBER 20

The fourth largest crowd to attend pro wrestling in the world in 1993 (trailing New Japan cards at both the Tokyo Dome, 63,500, and Fukuoka Dome, 55,000 and AAA's TripleMania in Mexico City, 48,000, saw a battle of World champions at UWFI champ Nobuhiko Takada faced WCW champ Super Vader (as he's billed in UWFI rings) on 12/5 at Jingu Stadium. Despite freezing weather conditions at the outdoor baseball stadium, a turnaway crowd of 46,168 (approximately 45,000 paid) paid what would have to be one of the largest gates in the history of pro wrestling (we haven't received a reliable figure at press time although it can be estimated as well in excess of $2.5 million) for the match which ended with Takada winning via submission with the short arm scissors in 14:23 after continual kicks to Vader's arm in a match described as brutal. What made the sellout even more amazing was that it was held during a six day period in which there were four different major shows from four different offices within the Tokyo city limits. The four shows (others being All Japan, FMW and All Japan women) all sold out and drew a total of about 86,500 fans. There was a lot of consternation in WCW, apparently by those who don't realize that this business is a work, about their champion doing a clean job to another world champion. Maybe the size of the crowd will make them realize that it's those clean jobs and the knowledge by the fans that they won't be screwed in the end is one of the reasons crowds like this exist elsewhere in the world. Apparently there were pretty stern warnings about Vader's future should he do the job, which is hilarious since WCW five days later had its world tag team champions (Nasty Boys, as if anyone even cares) do a clean job in New Japan rings for New Japan's tag champs (Jurassic Powers) on a major show in Nagoya, and I'll bet nobody in the office was even aware of concerned about that, nor should they have been.

It was pretty much exclusively the Vader-Takada match that drew the crowd, as the next two matches from the top on the show were a rematch from the PPV show with Salman Hashimikov & Vladimir Berkovich once again beating Gary Albright & Dan Severn when Hashimikov made Severn submit inn 17:14 and Kiyoshi Tamura made Dennis Koslowski submit in 12:49. UWFI has some minor shows booked in December at Korakuen Hall, but is planning major shows at Budokan Hall in Tokyo in February and Castle Hall in Osaka for March. Actually there was a lot of talk in wrestling that the result wasn't the "correct" result since the size of the crowd was such that Vader winning cleanly would make more sense to build to a rematch which would do similar business. However, the long-term of Vader with UWFI is in question, even with his hefty $25,000 per match deal, so there was no guarantee he'd be around for the rematch. Apparently when Eric Bischoff a few weeks back met with New Japan, New Japan was only interested in four or five WCW wrestlers, the two main ones being Vader and Sting so for Bischoff to put the deal together, it may not be imperative but it would definitely be very helpful for Vader to be part of the deal since New Japan is desperately lacking in foreign main event talent.

CHAPTER THIRTY FIVE

RANDY SAVAGE
BLASTS HULK HOGAN

OCTOBER 5

Randy Savage blasted Hulk Hogan in a lengthy interview on Jim Ross' "Radio WWF" show on 10/16 with comments regarding Hogan's lying on the Arsenio Hall show to subtle and not-so-subtle comments on Hogan and Hogan's wife's role during the period when Savage and wife Elizabeth broke up. As of press time, neither Hogan nor any of his close associates had commented on the interview.

It should be noted that it was pretty obvious the way Savage, Jim Ross and Johnny Polo (who co-hosts the radio show) were interacting during the segment that all three knew what was about to be said. Ross, before bringing Savage on as a guest noted that he would be saying things that you won't believe and later made comments that some of the things he would be saying you will be reading tomorrow morning in the sports pages of your newspaper, although at press time no newspaper had acknowledged the interview although I suspect the comments to make the wrestling columns in the few newspapers that have them. It's clear from the television promotion of the show that Ross is working very hard to garner publicity for his radio vehicle. A few weeks back Ross was able to get the green light from Vince McMahon to be more controversial on the show and talk about other promotions. The question begging to be asked is Vince McMahon's role in the decision making process of this specific interview, if it wasn't an angle arranged ahead of time with Hogan's permission. It is well-known within wrestling that what Savage said on the show echo things he's been saying in the dressing room dating back to the period shortly after his divorce in the summer of 1992. It is also obvious Ross is trying to earn a niche for the radio show as being something other than an extension of weekly WWF television. Nevertheless, it is very difficult for me to believe that either would go public in that nature without the okay from McMahon. Hogan was very protective of McMahon whenever the subject came up in his publicity tour for "Mr. Nanny." However, an item in the New York Daily News gossip section last week said that Hogan would be meeting shortly with Ted Turner about starting up a new wrestling company and it is believed the item wasn't planted by Hogan's side. How WWF officials reacted to reading the item is cause for a lot of speculation. While the details of what the meeting is supposed to be about can't be confirmed, other sources confirm a meeting is scheduled shortly between the two although it is believed that it concerns Hogan and WCW and not starting up of a new company. Hogan did turn down an invitation to appear on WCW to plug his movie. Hogan, in other interviews doing publicity for Mr. Nanny (which received generally horrible reviews and did $921,000 of business during its second week, finishing 16th for the weekend with a $3.4 million two week total), claimed to have been besieged with wrestling offers outside of the WWF mentioning New Japan, Turner and overseas tours.

Savage's comments started with: "Have you ever heard the name Hulk Hogan? The five-time World Wrestling Federation champion. Hulk Hogan became at one time the biggest superstar in the history of professional wrestling. I personally used to look up to Hulk Hogan. But that was a big mistake. I really thought he was a friend. But he's definitely not. He's the worst prima donna I've ever met in my life

Hulk Hogan's ego went so far out of control that Hulk Hogan consumed Terry Bollea, which is his real name

Let's just say I've lost a lot of respect for Hulk Hogan aka Terry Bollea, both as a man and a human being. That's an extreme understatement that I'm saying right there. A lot of people out there might be thinking it's professional jealousy. But putting professional jealousy aside, if there is any, which I'm not saying there is, I lost respect for Hulk Hogan big time. Number one, when he completely lied on Arsenio Hall, denying the use of anabolic steroids except for rehabilitation for an injury."

At this point Ross asked Savage if he had ever used steroids. "Yes I have. I used anabolic steroids and when I was on Arsenio Hall, I told the people I did, when they were legal. But it's like putting poison in your body." Ross then asked Savage if he currently uses them. "No, I sure don't. Nobody does in the WWF. But at the same time I was asked about it, I told the truth. It was prevalent at the time, not just in wrestling, but in all sports, baseball, basketball, football, you name it, it was there. It was in the gyms. It was legal at the time. But at the same time, if Hulk Hogan is the guy he says that he is, if he's leading the Hulkamaniacs down that tunnel where there's light at the end of the tunnel, and he's showing them the way, hey, the children are our future and if you're lying to them, if you're lying to me, you're lying to everybody, brother because that's just not the way it's happening. I remember being in the car with him the day before he went on Arsenio Hall in St. Louis, Missouri and I begged him for three hours not to go on and do that."

At this point Ross, attempting to act surprised by the last statement, said, "You knew he was going to go on there and lie?" Savage responded, "Exactly. I knew that he was going to do it and lie about using anabolic steroids. I told him he could be a leader among men if he would tell the truth. But he was worried about the image of the character of Hulk Hogan aka Terry Bollea. I said, `brother, listen, we all make mistakes. Be honest. The world is more forgiving than you think.' Steroids were legal then. But he said, `Not a chance.' He went on Arsenio Hall and lied. He lied big-time. He hurt himself. I'm not worried about him hurting himself. But he hurt all of the World Wrestling Federation, because like I said before, he was a leader. He was a big-time, five-time World Wrestling Federation champion. When he talks, people listen

Yeah, but when we went on Arsenio Hall and lied and then everything came down after that. You realize that he hurt himself. That he cared about. But I guarantee you from heart-to-heart right now, he couldn't care less about hurting any of us at the World Wrestling Federation."

At this point Ross interjects, "Are you saying he's selfish?" Savage said, "Selfish to the umpteenth degree. And I'm not perfect. No doubt about it. This guy is really not even perfect, though he wants you to believe it."

Ross then brought up his celebrated marriage and divorce with Liz Huelette (Elizabeth). Savage's comments were: "There was a time I fell in love. I got engaged and got married, and it was to Elizabeth. Then it got to a point that some of the kids out there can relate to. Maybe it happened to their mother and father or uncle and aunt. Sometimes it just doesn't go forever. Elizabeth and I were married, but we were having problems. It happens that at the time Elizabeth and Hulk Hogan's wife were very, very, very best friends. And they were running around together. I didn't think it was healthy for our relationship, but whatever's whatever. A lot of people can have different kinds of friends. But there was a time when I was wrestling on the road while we were having problems and I would call home and Elizabeth wouldn't be there. During a certain segment of time, I would just get another phone call. Being the master of the phone that I am and I would have conversations with Hulk Hogan. And he would give me swerves and curves, but never tell that Liz was over there

She was either out with his wife Linda or hiding out at their house. Later on, while I was wrestling on the road, basically when I would call home and there was no answer for four days and Elizabeth was MIA, missing in action for four days, I was worried about my wife then, and I still am now. I can't help that. Because in my heart I'll always love her. It's very hard to let go. But you've got to let go. That's for those people out there who have situations like that. But no doubt about it, being honest, four days went by and Liz called me and told me to get a lawyer because she wanted a divorce. That was end of story right there."

Ross then asked Savage if he thought Hogan knew about the divorce and what was going on at that time. Savage responded, "Like, Hogan and his wife were in Miami making that movie that bombed," at which point Ross asked him which one that bombed and Savage responded, "Mr. Nanny. He's a three-time loser. He started out with No Holds Barred that did about $10 million. Then Suburban Commando did less. Then he broke his own record for doing less than that with Mr. Nanny. Not to say there's anything personal right here. It's kind of like Crush. A Hulk Hogan situation. I was making calls and going completely out of my mind because I didn't know where she was and couldn't even talk to her about it because she wanted the lawyers and all, but he gave me curves and swerves again saying he didn't know where she was but said, `Brother, if I hear anything, I'll let you know.' But in desperation, I flew to Miami at the jockey club where Hogan was staying and where they were filming the movie Mr. Nanny and there I found Liz, shockingly (the word shockingly was said sarcastically). Obviously by this time, only half-shocked, ya dig

Honestly and friendship between Hulk Hogan aka Terry Bollea and the Macho Man Randy Savage aka Randy Poffo, brother I'm out there in front of you. Hit me with your best shot. The honestly and friendship wasn't there and possibly it was never was. And right now, talking on Radio WWF, I would tell you it was never there. I was fooled. I didn't know it and Liz didn't know it either. She thought she had a best friend with Hulk Hogan's wife. But now we both know. Separately, of course, because we are legally divorced. Can you believe the fact that Hulk Hogan's wife and Liz don't talk now? So what kind of friends do you think they were? It's almost like they got the job done. This is a worst case scenario, broke us up, did whatever they had to do. They're not even friends now. I think Liz realizes a lot because as time goes by, you know what I mean, and I wish the best for her. But a lot's changed and the trust is broke

I've changed a lot in my lifetime

A WWF match, if Hogan didn't like what I said over the airwaves and wanted to do that in front of the WWF in an arena near by or in a garage of his choice, that would be cool for the Macho Man Randy Savage, because you can beat me, but not eat me. And I don't think you could beat me."

Obviously those last comments, where Savage was sounding like he was doing a promo, almost would make one believe that this is simply the start of an Antonio Inoki/New Japan-like shoot-angle for a Hogan-Savage match at Wrestlemania. Part of it, at least when it comes to where the interview was done and the timing, can be labeled as a hot-shot angle to get the radio show over, which should at least partially succeed. Equivocating the Hogan thing with Crush would lend credence to that idea and many within wrestling seem to believe it to be an angle, which, based on follow-up comments on Monday Night Raw make me think that way as well. It is well-known throughout the business that there is, or at least was, major legit heat between Hogan and Savage stemming over the incidents he talked about on the show. But this is the type of angle Jerry Jarrett would come up with and that Randy Savage had done and even specialized in earlier in his career. It should be noted during the 1987 Maeda-shoot kick non-angle with Riki Choshu, that several of the American wrestlers on the New Japan tour and virtually all on the simultaneous All Japan tour believed it to be nothing more than an angle, suspension, injury and all, even though it wasn't, and the belief it was an angle by some of those wrestlers continued up until the point Maeda started the new company rendering throwing those beliefs out the window. The fact that the WWF of the past would never consider doing anything of this type means nothing because all the rules are different now. That this is simply stage one of an attempt at an elaborate angle between the two best-known living pro wrestlers in the country for Wrestlemania can't be ruled out, although if that was the case then Hogan would have to be in on it and agree to allow Savage to make all these statements beforehand. The portrayal of Hogan in such a light, considering the timing, prevalence within wrestling of rumors of him talking with other groups or starting his own group makes it also a possibility that this may be stage one of WWF attempting to counter any business competition from the most powerful force the company has created. Or maybe it's simply an attempt to shield itself from whatever potential bad publicity may be forthcoming by confusing the issue and trying to portray Hogan as the bad guy and his much-publicized interview on Arsenio Hall as a reason for all the negative publicity, thus diverting attention from charges aimed at the company and making the company seem like innocent victims of an ego of its top star that went out of control.

NOVEMBER 1

A few notes on the fallout of the Randy Savage interview regarding Hulk Hogan on the WWF Radio show on 10/16. First, this was not an angle as was believed at the time last week's Observer went to press. The most intriguing aspect of all this is that Hogan was asked a few days earlier to appear on the show although never informed that Savage would be on or what subject matter was being planned for the show. Apparently there was a well laid out plan to "ambush" an unknowing Hogan with Savage's comments in a public forum. Hogan, who had done the same radio show two weeks earlier, apparently had a premonition something was up since it was awfully quick to be asked back to do a radio show for a company he was no longer working for, or simply was busy and "lucked into" not being in a potentially embarrassing position. Even as the show was going on, neither Jim Ross nor Randy Savage knew for certain whether or not Hogan was going to call in as reportedly he never either confirmed or non-confirmed the request to appear. While many were furious with some remarks Savage made, Hogan is publicly taking the "ignore it and it'll go away position" and isn't expected to publicly acknowledge any of this ever happened. Hogan, who spent most of this past week at Disney Studios in Orlando filming "Circus of the Stars," which he's hosting with MTV's Adam Curry for CBS-TV, supposedly wasn't even aware of the comments on either television or radio until Tuesday. There is a good case to be made for taking this position since if Hogan were to get into a public pissing contest, he'd end up having his name soiled even more, particularly since any attempt at defending himself on the charge of lying on Arsenio is going to be tough to pull off. At the same time, this "ignore it and it'll go away" position when it comes to same repeated criticism for lying on Arsenio Hall in July 1991, has ended up being extremely damaging to Hogan. While he's attempted to ignore it and pretend it has gone away for two-and-a-half years, it has constantly resurfaced since that time and has resulted in severe damaged to his image both as a wrestling drawing card and in many public arenas and much private criticism within his profession. If not the idea itself, almost surely the approval of the idea, to have Savage go on radio and make those comments had to come from Vince McMahon. Because of that, the relationship between the WWF and Hogan, the name synonymous with the organization for the past ten years, has to be strained more now than ever before and many close to the situation believe it is now strained beyond repair. Nobody has come up with any reasons, just speculation, for why this plan, which in hindsight appears to have been a dramatic way of making a statement against Hogan was implemented. But if you're anxiously waiting for more interviews of this nature to build to a Hogan-Savage match at Wrestlemania, the odds are extremely long against anything more being said or the match happening.

I didn't want to make many comments about the actual remarks Savage made since at the time of last week's issue, I was under the impression it was a unique beginning of a Wrestlemania angle. First, while this is hardly saying anything that hasn't been said to death, it's hypocritical in this position to knock someone for telling the truth. Savage's comments regarding Hogan's Arsenio interview have been said by others both publicly and privately for two-and-a-half years. One can knock Savage or Titan Sports itself, since Savage was acting in some ways as a company mouthpiece in this interview, for saying the same thing the company had been so outraged about when others went public with identical statements years earlier. But truth is truth. Among the many within wrestling that have privately commented to me on this situation the consensus of opinion is that if Hogan lied on Arsenio regarding steroids, then at best, Savage's appearance when he addressed the same subject many months later was only slightly more honest. Savage did the show after much outcry claiming Hogan lied had already gone public and could learn from the mistake he made. Savage at best addressed the steroid subject as a way to get off a pre-planned joke when he categorized his own use as "experimenting when it was legal" but he quit when they gave him P.M.S. Savage didn't lie and deny use, but hardly can be congratulated for setting an example and coming clean on his personal use, exactly what he criticized Hogan for not doing. The term experimenting would lead to the public to believe very minimal use over a short period of time. Statements about legality of steroid use are in some cases questionable depending upon time frame used, how they were obtained and where they were used and obtained as laws varied from state-to-state and from year-to-year. Many comments by wrestlers regarding use when legal have turned out to be incorrect. Grand jury evidence have shown Federal Express packages from convicted steroid dealer Dr. George Zahorian to Randy Poffo between 1987-89 totalled nine pounds, roughly the same quantity during the same time period as of packages sent to Terry Bollea. It can't be confirmed that these packages contained exclusively steroids or even steroids at all since Zahorian was convicted of distributing illegal drugs other than steroids and also distributed "vitamins" and other "medications" to wrestlers based on trial testimony. As far as Hogan and his wife's role during the period of Savage's separation from his wife, many feel it was a cheap shot by Savage, particularly in bringing Hogan's wife into it. I'm in no position to judge any statements on that subject. My feeling is you can't knock someone for saying something if it's the truth but what the actual truth was of that situation is something that only a few people know.

CHAPTER THIRTY SIX

EMLL 60TH ANNIVERSARY

OCTOBER 11

EMLL, the first Mexico-based pro wrestling promotion, which ran its first show on September 21, 1933, celebrated its 60th anniversary on 10/1 at Arena Mexico. The show drew a sellout of about 18,000 fans--the largest crowd to witness an EMLL show in about 18 months and the largest crowd in the Mexico City area for wrestling since AAA's TripleMania on 4/30. It's unknown if this was a gate record, because ticket prices were raised for the card, however kids were allowed in free. The anniversary show was originally announced for 9/17, and then 9/24, but postponed twice in order to "confuse" rival AAA, which was making plans for a blow-out show of its own across town at Juan de la Barrera Gym to counter. AAA exhausted its three major pushed stipulation matches that were being built up as opposition. Lizmark vs. El Satanico for the light heavyweight title took place on 9/17, Villano III vs. Rambo mask vs. hair on 9/24, and Mocho Cota vs. Latin Lover hair vs. hair--built up to headline against the anniversary show all along, never took place because Cota jumped to EMLL just before he was scheduled to lose his hair. We've received mixed reports on the show, which had a triple headliner, ranging from it being called fair-to-very good, but the general consensus was it was disappointing considering what the line-up promised. During the television broadcast of the show on 10/3, they shows clips of highlights of the past 60 years of EMLL. The main event was a mask vs. mask match with Atlantis vs. Mano Negra, which was largely a letdown from most reports after months of build-up, with Atlantis winning the final fall in six seconds and Negra being revealed as Jesus Rosales. There were a lot of people who felt after going so long with small crowds, that when they finally got the big house in, they shouldn't have done a six second final fall in the main event. Negro Casas beat La Fiera in a hair vs. hair semifinal which received very mixed reviews (some saying excellent, others being disappointed since it was a brawling match with no topes) and the main trios match had three foreign babyfaces King Haku (Tonga) & Canadians Vampiro Casanova & Pegasus Kid (Chris Benoit) beating Black Magic & Pierroth Jr. (who turned back heel on Vampire the previous week) & Cota via DQ when Sangre Chicana interfered. Rayo de Jalisco Jr., who had just jumped back from AAA, made his "surprise" return making the save for the foreign trio. Rayo has since said in the newspapers that jumping to AAA was the biggest mistake of his career. Expect some AAA wrestlers to publicly have some choice words about Rayo this week. AAA drew about 6,000 in opposition at Juan de la Barrera Gym for a triangular mask vs. hair vs. hair with Misterioso, Huichol and Vulcano, which ended with Vulcano getting his head shaved.

It really does say something in a world as cutthroat as pro wrestling that one wrestling company could survive for 60 years. Probably the only other example I could come up with of a promotion that survived for that long was the generation of Owen family members in Oregon that lasted just over 60 years before Don called it quits a few years back. That one company could not only survive, but maintain its position as the No. 1 promotion in a wrestling-mad country for almost that entire period is even more impressive. EMLL, founded by Salvador Lutteroth, was pro wrestling in Mexico from its inception. From the 50s through the 70s, EMLL was also a member of the old National Wrestling Alliance and controlled the NWA light heavyweight championship (that title still exists in Mexico but has had no connection with the NWA since the late 70s). Since that time the company has always been controlled by the Lutteroth family. There were challenges along the way, but none of a serious nature until around 1975 when several of the biggest drawing wrestlers from EMLL banded together and formed UWA. UWA, built around Canek and having strong ties with New Japan Pro Wrestling, became the country's top promotion quickly. The UWA's downfall in many ways parallels the United States WWF vs. NWA war of the late 1980s. UWA, then established as the top promotion, continued to push the same storylines and same names on top with the same inconclusive finishes and repeated storylines that eventually turned off all but the hardcore following. EMLL then rebounded when Antonio Pena became booker, using television to its advantage, creating new gimmick characters and building around younger stars and doing fresher finishes. By the late 80s, EMLL, now run by Lutteroth's nephew Paco Alonso, was back on top again. AAA, which is now the country's top promotion, copied the WWF formula of 1984 with its own ramifications and tailored to its own culture, to buck EMLL from its top spot. However, judging from this sellout and the public perception when people start jumping back, some of the momentum of the recent AAA vs. EMLL rivalry has started to change.

CHAPTER THIRTY SEVEN

900 NUMBERS AND CONSUMER FRAUD

NOVEMBER 1

The way that 900 number thing to vote on whether Shawn Michaels could return when it had no bearing on the decision whatsoever was done was a total fraud. I realize what pro wrestling is and I'm not sure what the law is, but there is something really sleazy about the way this was handled.

NOVEMBER 22

This has not been an easy last few weeks to cover the wrestling industry and the consensus belief right now is that things are going to get worse before they get better. I don't believe there has ever been a period in the recent history of wrestling where simultaneously so many different promotions are facing grave public relations problems significant enough that their long-term prognosis is so cloudy. There have always been promotions in trouble, but a lot of the trouble in most of the cases currently has to do with things having nothing to do with the ability to sell tickets to matches, produce entertaining television and create strong angles. Pro wrestling will always be around in some form. And more and more I've come to the conclusion that in some ways the industry would be stronger if much of the current hierarchy that created all these messes and scandals were to disappear and be replaced by a new crew that will take an honest look at what created these problems and learn from these problems to create a stronger business.

The problem is, my truthful belief is that it wouldn't be stronger because the replacements in the same position won't learn from the mistakes, would have to avoid producing Monkey See Monkey Do wrestling and even more importantly "It's always been this way" style of management because unfortunately each and every week we are seeing the end result of both of those attitudes. And newcomers in charge in most cases won't have the background in studying the business and have learn from years of experience and from mistakes of the past in regard to product and booking decisions. There are far too few people working in this industry and far too much that has gone public and even more that may be going public in the near future for the various stories that have come out recently to be excused as isolated incidents. Let's look at the current scene. We've had a brawl that could have conceivably with a little bad luck resulted in a fatality, and a company that in response has seemingly spent more time and energy in trying to cover up the incident as opposed to trying to get to the real root of the problem because of fear where an honest appraisal of the situation will lead the ultimate finger of blame pointing at. We have an 18-month long Justice Department investigation into the country's leading office that is apparently in its final stages with an entire industry bracing itself for the results. We've had one of the leading stars indicted on sex charges. We've had allegations made concerning drug distribution linked to other stars. We may have had an attempted suicide. We've had definite repeated cases of consumer fraud. And we've had continuing pushes of top names based largely on physique, which continues from the top the encouragement of illegal drugs which have been largely ignored in one company despite more warning lights than one could shake a stick at. That's all in the past few weeks.

Consumer fraud is nothing new to this business. Promotions advertising talent they know in advance won't be appearing has been done in some promotions with regularity. Largely, since some embarrassing situations went public in 1991 and 1992, the WWF has cleaned up its act regarding false advertising. As with most issues, WCW just ignores it while seeing its house show attendance dwindle to nothing. The latest type of fraud has been in the 900 number category.

Expect to see far more hype and for the WCW 900 line on its various television shows, since its most pushed television commodity, Gene Okerlund, heads the division and has a contract that calls for a percentage of the income. While 900 lines seem to be a business that is here to stay, and many in other industries that advertise late night are far more sleazy than WCW could ever be, it appears that nothing WCW uses the 900 line for falls under the category of consumer fraud.

That can't be said about the WWF, with its more limited use of 900 lines. In 1992, the WWF did a 900 line poll where fans were asked to vote for who they thought deserved a title shot at Wrestlemania against Ric Flair and given a few names to pick from. The actual come-on was that Jack Tunney would consider the results of the poll when making his decision on who got the title shot. It was never said the results of the poll were in any way binding. This probably is the loophole that possibly would make the distinction between misleading and outright fraud. This poll was being pushed to fans even though the storyline, where Tunney would pick Hogan, the late Sid Justice would turn on Hogan, Hogan would pull himself out of the match with Flair to fight Justice, and Randy Savage would get the title shot, was already laid out in the office before the promotion asked fans to spend 99 cents to vote.

In recent weeks there have been two more blatant examples that undeniably crossed the line of fraud, to the point where after the subject was brought up (by myself in an editorial on Friday on a 900 line of all places), the next day the WWF quickly responded. Several weeks back on a Monday Night Raw show, the WWF advertised a 900 line vote, which it indicated the results of which would be binding, to determine whether or not "suspended" Shawn Michaels would be "reinstated." This was done after the WWF and Michaels had already reached a deal and he'd been given a return date. During the show, there were many interviews and come-ons trying to get fans to call the number and lead them strongly into voting against Michaels return, ironically, the exact opposite of a decision that was already made. As the show aired live in most of the country, percentages were given during the show, and at the conclusion of the show, it was announced that 64 percent of the fans voted against allowing Michaels back. Two hours after that announcement, the show aired in the Pacific time zone. Despite the inherent fraud in the premise to begin with, this case of trying to get viewers in other time zones to vote after an announcement was made of the results was undefendable. Virtually the same scenario was repeated on 11/8, when fans were told they could vote for Pierre's opponent on the 11/15 Raw main event. During the entire show, the voting was hyped and interviews were done to encourage votes for Lex Luger. This was done despite there almost surely having been a production meeting, and booking meetings done well in advance of any poll where the angle was decided upon for Luger to injure Pierre leading to Crush to take his place at Survivor Series. At the end of the show, the announcement was made that Luger was the leading vote getter and the match would take place. Two hours later, actually after the Luger-Pierre match and angle had already taken place, Titan was calling for votes in the Pacific zone to determine who Pierre would wrestle next week. Titan has since made the decision that all revenue from the Mountain and Pacific time zones for both the Michaels poll and the Luger poll will be refunded. The response is that the company simply didn't consider the time zone change and staggered schedule of the USA network (as opposed to TBS which airs shows at the same time nationwide). It's the best, and only excuse possible, and could even be believable except that it doesn't explain how originally when the decision was made to do these polls that the phone lines were kept open for all those hours after the results had been announced to Eastern and Central viewers if the time zone differences hadn't been considered from the start. And it also is questionable as to billing that decisions will be made based on fans voting with the votes as a revenue source when those decisions had actually already been made beforehand.

DECEMBER 27

They also seem to be doing a "900 line scam of the week." Last week they asked fans to vote where Randy Savage should be allowed back as a broadcaster, which set up him co-hosting WWF Mania. This week they were asking fans to vote to give Jack Tunney input on whether or not Lex Luger should be allowed in the Royal Rumble, which is a total scam since that decision was made in the office months ago.

CHAPTER THIRTY EIGHT

SID STABS
ARN ANDERSON

NOVEMBER 8

A vicious hotel street fight in England between Sid Vicious (Sid Eudy) and Arn Anderson (Marty Lunde) resulted in both men receiving numerous stab wounds. Not only are Vicious and Anderson's future in World Championship Wrestling in question at press time, but WCW management faces some major scrutiny because of rumors of hypocritical and double-standard decisions that many believe could have set the tone for the incident. As of press time, WCW officials have only responded to questions regarding the futures of both wrestlers with comments that the incident is under investigation, and have avoided answering several serious questions the incident raised regarding the company's drug testing policy and booking and contract decisions that have been made in recent weeks by a company desperately pretending to ignore the obvious.

The Vicious-Anderson brawl took place at approximately 2 a.m. the evening of the 26th at the Moat House Hotel in Blackburn, Lancashire, England. The two were part of the WCW troupe that began touring Europe, with its first show having taken place hours earlier in Cardiff, Wales. After a lengthy plane ride to England, followed by a show and a three-hour bus ride to the hotel in Blackburn, trouble started between the two at the hotel bar.

According to numerous reports, most of which were, with the exception of minor details, remarkably similar, the first stages of trouble started when Vicious started bragging about how he just held the company up for a major contract raise (reportedly up to $600,000 per year) to agree to do the job for Sting at the Halloween Havoc PPV show a few days earlier. Both men had been drinking and Vicious was apparently ribbing Anderson over the fact that he had just received a $100,000 per year raise, while Anderson had received a $100,000 pay cut (under Bill Watts, Anderson's 1992 contract of $250,000 per year was cut to a 1993 deal of $750 per night deal which should result in roughly a $100,000 pay cut). Vicious was reportedly bragging about how the company was going to be built around him and it was time for Sting to step out of the spotlight as the company's main character, apparently taking the "franchise" angle from the PPV match seriously, and said that it was time for Anderson and the other old man (in reference to Ric Flair) to retire so the company could start being successful. Those close to Vicious confirm a similar argument story with Vicious claiming Flair was repetitive and washed up and should retire for the good of the company and Anderson defending his friend. Anderson responded something to the effect that Vicious couldn't work and had never proven to be able to draw money. Anderson got in Vicious' face and perhaps some of the guys were egging them on. At one point Anderson challenged Vicious to step outside and Vicious backed down, but at about that point, WCW security chief Doug Dillinger separated the two and ordered both to go to their hotel rooms and cool off.

Anderson was taken back to his room by Dillinger and Vicious, who trailed behind, went back to his. Just before Anderson shut the door, the two had words again as Dillinger threw Anderson in his room and locked the door. Some time shortly thereafter, Vicious came down to Anderson's room and brought a broken off piece of either a chair or table from his hotel room with him. Stories get dissimilar at this point. The version attributed to Anderson is that someone tried to kick down his door and the kicks were so powerful the door was practically coming off its hinges. As he looked through the peep hole, he saw nothing and the kicks stopped. He opened the door and nobody was there. As he stuck his head out the door, he was blindsided with a baseball bat swing like blow from the weapon and knocked out. The other version was that Vicious asked Anderson to talk things out because they had a long tour ahead of them, and Anderson responded he was going to cut him up and chased him with scissors and Vicious was defending himself with the chair shot.

At this point Vicious allegedly jumped on him and the two started brawling. Anderson reportedly told friends that the first blow with the weapon knocked him out for a few minutes and when he started regaining his senses, Vicious was on top of him beating his face into oblivion. Somehow Anderson got loose and grabbed a pair of scissors with a dull tip rather than a spike-like tip and stabbed Vicious in the stomach with them, opening him up. At this point Vicious retreated and went into the hall, where Anderson jumped on him again. Vicious was stabbed with the scissors at least three more times, with most reports saying they were in the stomach but those close to Vicious saying two shots were in the face and one in the hand. Vicious somehow got the scissors away, with reports ranging from Anderson dropping them while wrestling with him in the hotel hallway and Vicious picking them up, to Vicious punching Anderson in the eye and grabbing them from the ground. At any rate, Vicious allegedly began stabbing Anderson over-and-over, with Anderson receiving a total of 20 stab wounds, most in the shoulders and back but at least one that was one-inch below his eye that there is belief was aimed at the eye (wrestlers are always taught in street-fight situations to go for the eye) and another in the throat and was covered in blood from head-to-toe by the time Too Cold Scorpio heard the struggle and broke things up, which may have saved Anderson's life. Vicious apparently claimed to have blacked out and not remembered anything other than regaining his senses while on top of a bloody Anderson. Most of the gashes were about one-half inch deep, but the gash in the throat was five inches long. By the time separate ambulances arrived, they found Vicious waiting in a reception area and Anderson in bad shape in his hotel room. At some point in the struggle a hotel window was shattered as well, because the hotel hall the next morning was covered with both men's blood, broken glass, police and newspaper reporters and reportedly WCW had to make major amends to the hotel to settle the situation.

Both men were rushed to the nearby Blackburn Royal Infirmary hospital. Vicious, whose eye reportedly was swollen up like a tennis ball, had exploratory surgery done on Wednesday and was released from the hospital and returned home by the end of the week. Anderson, who was weakened by losing approximately a pint-and-a-half of blood and whose eye was totally swollen shut, was also released from the hospital and returned home by the weekend but was still in a very weakened state a week later. Doctors reportedly told Anderson that if he had lost much more blood that the damage could have been life threatening, that if the scissors had a sharp edge that it is questionable if he could have survived the attack, and if the gash near the eye was an inch in another direction he'd have lost the eye. Initially both men filed complaints against one another but withdrew their complaints largely because they would have had to remain in the country for 90 days to get the complaints prosecuted on and the police didn't file charges likely because both were immediately going to leave the country.

Although the story received banner headlines in both London and Lancashire, England tabloids, because of the manner of which the stories were written and the reputation of pro wrestling in the country, our reports are that most British wrestling fans simply felt it was an angle to hype ticket sales for a disappointing tour. Reuters News Service sent the story on its international wire, although it received only minimal coverage in the U.S., and a little more in Canada, including a brief item in Thursday's USA Today. Most of the North American reports noted both men as being stabbed, although gave the indication it wasn't the result of a fight between the two but from outside parties, and listed both men as "WWF wrestlers," as did most of the British radio and television media when covering the story. WCW p.r. head Mike Weber, who was on tour in England, tried to use the fight as a means of hyping pro wrestling as real, with his quote in the London Sun saying, "It just shows that what you see in the ring is what you see in real life. These two haven't fought each other for several years and obviously don't get along. I don't know what the disagreement was about." Actually, according to those close to the situation, while the two were not friends, they were co-workers on-and-off for many years and not enemies prior to this incident. Vicious attempted to call Anderson on Monday to apologize. On the WCW hotline this week and on its television shows over the weekend, there was no acknowledgement of any incident having taken place except by Missy Hyatt. Hyatt talked of the incident on Sunday on the hotline, placing the blame on Vicious and saying that he was fired because of it, which may have been jumping the gun because the company has officially not made any announcement of such.

As of our latest reports, Vicious was going to see a doctor early in the week to determine how long it would be before he physically would be able to return to the ring, if he still had a place to work. The estimates as to when Anderson would be able to return were between one and two months, but there was no word on his employment status although it is now believed he'll be retained. By Thursday, WCW officials gave word to the production staff to remove Vicious and Anderson from all pre-taped television shows that would begin airing this coming weekend, which led to wide-spread belief within the production and announcing crew of the company that both had been or were going to be fired. Reportedly all promotion for the Starrcade PPV show where Vicious was initially scheduled to win the WCW title from Vader, has been changed to pushing Vader defending against Flair as the main event. That was actually the second choice as steps were taken to put together a different main event bringing in a wrestler from outside whose name can't be confirmed, but that deal quickly fell apart. The decision was made that it was too late to re-edit the TBS shows over Halloween weekend, one of which included a heavily pushed Vicious vs. Ric Flair match to determine who would meet Vader at the 11/10 Clash (Flair winning on DQ leading to Vicious' babyface turn).

Both men had been prominently featured on TBS Saturday Night shows taped through the end of November. On the 11/6 show, Vicious was the person being interviewed when Gene Okerlund makes his WCW debut. On 11/13, Anderson & Paul Roma were in a key television match against Paul Orndorff & Yoshi Kwan. On 11/20, the television main event was Vader & Steve Austin scheduled against Flair & Vicious where the Kongs destroy Vicious before the match and, ironically, Anderson replaces him in a 30:00 match which ends with Vicious doing a run-in to save Flair & Anderson. At some point in November, an angle was scheduled to be shot where Roma would turn heel on Anderson, leading to a Starrcade match on 12/27 in Charlotte. It is well known the original plan was for Vicious to win the WCW title from Vader at the same card, then win the other world title from Rick Rude in early 1993 to finally unify the belts, and pushed as the focal point of the company. And therein lies a problem that WCW management at press time is desperately avoiding addressing and the crux of the problem the WWF has spent years trying to circumvent.

Steroids. Lies about steroids. Steroid tests. Hypocrisy about steroids. More lies about steroids. Double-standards when it comes to steroids. Lies about steroid tests. For years it has almost become a subject of weekly discussion within these pages. And it has all come to a head once again between this incident, a front-page article on 10/30 in the Long Island daily newspaper Newsday on the WWF, Vince McMahon, the federal investigation and the Zahorian trial that went on the national wires and a spoof on the subject that evening on NBC's "Saturday Night Live." It's a story that will never go away because of wrestling management that can never address it or deal with it in an honest manner and promoters who can't resist the temptations of pushing freakishly muscular individuals because of the belief, founded in some cases and not in others, that they are what the public wants to see and thus going to draw them money. These promoters either figure they can either fool the public, or perhaps delude themselves that said wrestlers aren't using artificial physique enhancers when deep down they can't be so blind as not to know, and hide behind the words "we test" when the inevitable heat comes down.

The term "roid rage" has been used endlessly in the past week by wrestlers and other officials within wrestling and those following wrestling in reference to the Anderson-Vicious brawl. The medical profession can debate itself endlessly over whether it's even a viable term. There are many people in this world who have used steroids and only a minute percentage have ever had any behavior of this manner, although many on steroids have claimed while on the drugs their tempers shorten. The vast majority of wrestlers have used steroids at one time or another in their lives and incidents of this type virtually never happen, so pointing the finger of blame at steroids, while it might be as a defense used in court if this case happened in the United States, doesn't seem to be in and of itself a valid explanation. If the term is viable, there is always the question as if it's applicable in this case. Either way, enough people are calling this a classic example of "roid rage," maybe even multiplied by the effects of alcohol, despite no concrete evidence except visual of any steroid use. If that term is correct, the fingers all point straight at WCW management. If that term isn't, the fingers of question still have to point in that same direction.

Some people are going to read this as an indictment of Sid Eudy. While that conclusion based what happened is justified, the real crux of this problem is not Sid Eudy at all. It is the environment that created Sid Eudy. If this reads like a liberal viewpoint that blames society for criminal actions, it is not. It is a realistic viewpoint that blames management of both major promotions in the United States for creating a double-standard of on one hand professing to be anti-steroid/illegal physique enhancing drugs and on the other hand rewarding past, and perhaps present, users with the biggest pushes, the title belts and most importantly, both preferential treatment and the most money, trying to hide behind the words "we test" as a defense mechanism to avoid blame and liability despite numerous people in key positions who readily, anonymously, admit what reality is. It is a system that has continued through a federal trial, much negative media publicity and through a nearly two-year long federal investigation. And it is a hypocritical system which few have thrived in and perhaps none have made a mockery of more than Sid Eudy. If it wasn't for the fact that he's almost universally disliked by those within his profession, he would deserve much commendation from wrestlers and the wrestling press as the man who is the proof of what everyone assumes all along but can't prove tangibly, that those who use the magic words "we test" the most are the biggest hypocrites and provably do have a double standard.

Sid Eudy, in all his muscular glory, signed a $250,000 per year deal with World Championship Wrestling in 1989, based on anything but his wrestling ability and almost exclusively based on his size and muscularity. A few months into that deal, he suffered a collapsed lung, which most attribute to taking a bad bump in a match against the Steiners. He continued to receive his $5,000 per week while recuperating, as well he should have despite claims of others, because the injury was suffered on the job. Several months later, WCW was running a string of major house shows and even though Eudy hadn't been cleared for wrestling, they wanted him to be in the corner as a second so at least whatever name value he had could be used to sell tickets. Sid Vicious was advertised on about a months worth of house shows as being in the corner of various heel main eventers, but Sid Eudy missed the entire run. The story from WCW management privately was that he missed the shows because he stayed home to play softball. Was Sid Eudy suspended without pay for his no-shows? Was he fired because they believed he stayed home to play softball rather than go to work, even though his appearances were booked so he was being kept out of physical contact because he hadn't recovered from his injury? No. Eventually he came back to the ring, was pushed like crazy, got over, and stunk up main event matches because while his look was an A+ at the time, his ability was still a D-. He still was pushed to the top, and was even rewarded with a $25,000 bonus for holding the company up before doing a job with one of the world's most screwed up finishes ever to Sting on the 1990 Halloween Havoc PPV show. Was it his fault for holding out for a bonus to do a job, even though most other wrestlers do them as an every day thing? No. The same rules that apply to mere wrestlers don't apply to Sid Eudy. Is that saying Sid's ego was out of control? No. Management once again gave him the bonus. Sid was right. The same rules didn't apply. Most wrestlers, as Scott Norton and many others have found out, would be given the heave-ho pronto for trying to stunt like that. Sid Eudy received a bonus. About a year later, with about one year remaining on his contract, Eudy held out for more money. At the time he had gotten an offer from Vince McMahon and believed he'd be the next Hulk Hogan and believed he was promised the Wrestlemania 1992 main event. Despite being offered a huge raise by Jim Herd, and at one point accepting the deal, he decided to jump a valid contract to join the WWF. In between these two things there was a minor item of a loser gets carried out on a stretcher match on a PPV with El Gigante (now Giant Gonzalez). In putting on a performance that epitomized the term not showing up to work, Vicious did the job, got right back up, and walked back to the dressing room leaving the stretcher job for someone else. Was that his fault? No. Management booked someone else to do his stretcher job for him even though it was his final appearance with the company. They didn't force him to do it, or even hold his release up unless he agreed to. The same management then gave him his release on a valid contract to work for the opposition, despite instances when the situation was reversed and the opposition was hardly so obliging. So Sid Eudy learned that a valid contract means nothing, pre-booked match stipulations don't apply to him, and he could do basically whatever he wanted and not suffer the same consequences as would face virtually all others.

Soon after came the Zahorian trial, Arsenio Hall, and the announcement of the world's first unbeatable steroid test by the WWF, a test later exposed by its own second doctor-in-charge as being precisely the same beatable testing every other sports organization was doing at the time. Eudy was immediately pushed to the moon by the WWF in spite of its public anti-drug stance, and why shouldn't they have? Sid had still never failed a steroid test so how could anyone have had a clue he had ever used the stuff. By the time the testing started, Sid was on the sidelines with a torn bicep. So during the exact same period that Vince McMahon was on Larry King proclaiming that nobody in the WWF was using steroids, bragging about unbeatable drug tests, and taking issue with people who claimed his organization promoted use, here was Sid Eudy, still devoid of wrestling ability, being pushed for the main event at Wrestlemania. There was a little matter of steroid testing to get around. There have been many stories that Sid wasn't the only one using Visine bottles, or sleight-of-hand, or whatever it was that was done to substitute someone else's urine, but at one point, just one week before Wrestlemania, he was caught. WWF steroid policy specifically states cheating on a test is an automatic positive, six weeks suspension. Wasn't it ironic that this took place just days before Dr. Mauro DiPasquale, North America's leading expert on how to circumvent steroid tests (well known by world class powerlifters as "the man to call" for advice on beating that sports' tests), was announced at a seminar as the new man to administer the new greatest most comprehensive and second first unbeatable testing program. Dr. D, in an interview with me on March 25, just days before Mania, talked of how serious both he McMahon were about testing and that if a headliner tested positive right before a PPV and wasn't suspended, how he'd quit the program. Luckily the incident with Sid took place three days too early for Dr. D to find out what McMahon would have done. In McMahon's defense, there is no question he was serious about getting rid of steroids because of the p.r., not to mention legal problem, but he couldn't resist the temptation of still pushing the muscular bodytypes and using "drug test" as his defense when it came to a guy who looked like Sid Eudy. But when push came to shove before Wrestlemania, there was no suspension when it would have meant changing a PPV main event. There would have been hell to pay with all the publicity out, and few believe any wrestling promoter in the world would have suspended someone in the same position. The problem was that after Wrestlemania, there was still no suspension. After a European tour, with Sid main eventing every night, they opened the new U.S. post-Mania season and within a few days, Sid walked out. Then he was suspended. After having to sit out for nearly one full year because McMahon wasn't as "generous" as Jim Herd about releasing someone with a valid contract to work for his opposition, Sid Eudy, as big as ever, returned to WCW for yet another big money deal and huge promises of a push to the top.

A few months back, after one WCW wrestler after another was being brought in by federal agents in investigating steroid use within TitanSports during the period those same wrestlers worked there, an organization that largely, although despite claims to the contrary, not entirely, had rid itself of steroid use, WCW had become the new haven for certain wayward steroid users. This was despite a verbal anti-steroid stance by management going back to January 1992 when Kip Frey authored the most unique steroid policy in sports, that was released with major hullabaloo, and quickly ignored when Frey was replaced by another vocal anti-steroid hypocrite named Bill Watts. Wrestlers within the company estimated use at 50 to 70 percent (50 percent was probably closer to accurate at the time), nowhere near the level wrestlers had claimed Titan was at its peak, but certainly significant since the use was strongest at the top of the cards and there was no semantic questions of the drugs legality in any form or fashion by this time or that a wrestling company was flirting with disaster in continuing to ignore the issue. It was already proven fact that a company could take a major hit from a steroid scandal, not to mention potential serious legal ramifications as well, as anyone with two ears and eyes in the business should have been well aware of. So one day an announcement was made about yet another new steroid policy, released to the wrestlers in a lengthy memo, saying that all wrestlers signing new contracts had to be tested and pass the tests before they could receive their new deal, and that there would be both regular testing of everyone, and also more extensive testing of those displaying symptoms that would be suspicious. Now, whose photo is in the encyclopedia when they talk about "those displaying symptoms?" Right about the same time, WCW held a try-out to bring in new talent in Florida. When wrestlers like Thunder & Lightning pass the try-out and are brought in, and someone the calibre of Jimmy Richland (SMW's Jimmy Del Rey) is turned down, it makes yet another mockery out of those pronouncements. Eventually, after being told ahead of time, all WCW wrestlers were supposed to go in one afternoon before a taping to be steroid tested. The results or lack thereof of such have turned into only the latest in a long series of laughing stocks when it comes to the subject since either failure didn't result in suspension as the existing policy stated, or nobody failed, which even the thought of was preposterous even given the beatable nature of tests and lackluster monitoring of them. The one thing we know for sure is that Sid Eudy didn't fail that test. He missed the test. He had a valid reason. The company booked him for a public appearance the day before and he couldn't get back in time. Eventually according to several reports he was asked to take the test at a television taping a few weeks later and walked out. By company policy, that would mean an automatic six week suspension and no reinstatement until he was able to pass a new test. The next day, everything was smoothed out. It is the belief of many wrestlers but unable to be confirmed at press time that Eudy never took the test, and may have even refused again on a later occasion or even on two later occasions, a statement TBS and WCW management had refused comment on despite several media requests early this week in the wake of the latest incident. If this is true, and if is the key word because nothing is confirmed, then here is the crux of this entire situation.

How can a company give a huge raise and make the decision to make someone world champion and build the company around someone with a track record like this? Easy, because of how the man looks. Rules that apply to most wrestlers don't apply to someone who is 6-8, 300 pounds with little bodyfat and freakish muscularity, even though people who look like that are the exact reason wrestling companies have been pressured into making those rules to begin with. If Sid Eudy walked out on a test and wasn't suspended right then and there, the management of WCW needs to answer the question as to why its written policy wasn't enforced. If Sid Eudy did this more than once and wasn't fired after the second occurrence, more questions need to be answered, and those who let him slide need to be called on the carpet and severely reprimanded for creating the double-standard. If those officials didn't immediately follow up by insisting on changing the planned storyline of Sid Vicious becoming the next world champion at that point, there is strong question as to whether they should be allowed to continue in their positions. If he did this a third time, those who allowed it and continued to allow the story lines to go unchecked in the direction of making him world champion while possessing knowledge of this, need to be fired, not to mention the legal liability they should have to answer for because of the end result of all this. If he walked out on a steroid test and was subsequently given a raise, or a bonus to do a job, or however it is worded, the people responsible for making the decisions to give him that raise and still give him the world title should be fired along with if not ahead of Sid Eudy. Even if steroids are not applicable to this story and none of the items regarding walking out on tests are true, there is still no way WCW can justify Sid Eudy remaining part of the company.

NOVEMBER 15

As of press time, some two weeks after the incident between Sid Vicious and Arn Anderson took place, WCW officials have still not commented on the incident nor on the many questions regarding management of the company that the incident raised.

While no official disciplinary action has been announced, it is believed by several within the company that Vicious, believed by many to be the instigator of the physical aspect of the incident, will be fired and that Anderson will be retained. Vicious has denied to friends that he started the fight, and claimed Anderson threw a beer mug at his head earlier in the evening while they were arguing at the bar. We've been told current plans are that there are no plans in the cards for Vicious and that Anderson's name was listed on new booking sheets. WCW on Tuesday said that neither man would appear at the Clash, the Disney tapings, or the 11/20 PPV show, although neither would be physically ready to wrestle by those dates to begin with. If there are no plans for Vicious, nobody has told him as Vicious was given the indication from WCW President Bill Shaw that he was still with the company and that Shaw believed his version that he wasn't the instigator. Reports we get are to expect something concrete from the company this week since all the witnesses involved in the early aspect returned from Europe on Monday. All pre-taped material with Vicious on WCW Saturday Night shows that air from 11/20 on have been edited from the show. On the show that airs this coming week, an angle was shot where the Kongs beat up Vicious before a scheduled Ric Flair & Vicious vs. Vader & Steve Austin match. Vicious made a big comeback for the finish. If his comeback doesn't air, the injury would likely be the "writing him out of the script."

Because Vicious' stab wounds in his stomach and swollen face from punches thrown are still noticeable and overall he wasn't recovered from the brawl, Vicious, if he remains with the company wouldn't be appearing at the Orlando television tapings in which four months worth of syndicated World Wide shows will be taped. Anderson's injuries were severe enough that he would also be missing the Clash if he'd been booked on the show, and the Orlando tapings, which he was booked on. If Vicious, who had reached a verbal agreement before Halloween Havoc with WCW management on a $2.4 million four-year contract (and that money figure reportedly didn't include either merchandising or PPV bonuses) will return WCW, it would likely be by early December, although in either case it is believed his PPV main event title match against Vader scheduled for Starrcade will be changed to Vader vs. Ric Flair as a Clash rematch.

Given Sid Eudy's track record since 1989, it is simply mind-boggling WCW would agree to such a lengthy time frame for a guaranteed money deal with him. But no wrestler deserves any heat for accepting a deal that a company agrees to give him.

There have been no confirmation whether the stories regarding whether or not Eudy had been steroid tested before leaving on the tour are true since WCW has avoided returning phone calls to those who asked. The very fact of that has only fueled further rampant rumors. While there may be no tangible evidence of steroid use by Sid Eudy that would hold up in a court of law, the incident has largely raised the steroid issue once again among both wrestlers and those covering wrestling.

It is believed that several WCW wrestlers who did take the recent drug test failed the test and are being required to attend a one-day seminar on the evils of steroids and other illegal drugs. Whatever evils there may be, a question that has to be asked by all wrestlers is if those evils override the potential benefits--a significant advantage in obtaining a job and an ability to earn a more lucrative contract with more job security than far more talented counterparts. No suspensions were levied. This may have been because the company would have had a hard time even fielding a line-up for the European tour and all these major shows if the written rules regarding six-week suspensions for first offense and no reinstatement until able to pass a subsequent test had been enforced. The belief of at least some wrestlers is that the company is serious about the steroid subject at least to the level of wanting everyone to be able to pass tests, which to this point are given with advance warning (which makes them the easiest to beat) when it pertains to the rank-and-file wrestlers. It has appeared obvious that many wrestlers that had been using steroids two months back are now off the stuff. But to suggest that is uniform throughout the company or that use is at the same level as the current WWF, which has a far more strict testing system in place, would be ridiculous. Whether the company would seriously enforce its rules should a main eventer fail a second test during a key time period such as just before a PPV or Clash, or test regularly those who show signs of use as its written policy states is at best a matter of conjecture.

The WCW television shows over this past weekend never acknowledged the incident, nor were any aspects of the previously-taped shows edited, so both men appeared on television over the weekend, even though some voice-over work on shows that aired this weekend was done after the incident. It was actually almost eerie to see Vicious refer to himself as "Psycho Sid," them talk about Rob Parker getting a court order to keep him more than 50 feet away from him and Vicious during an interview plugging the Clash and taped weeks before the British tour say that he could be 5,000 miles away and Parker wouldn't be safe. They left everyone with the impression Vicious would be at the Clash, although not wrestling, and that both men would be on the next PPV show. The entire lack of reaction to this incident combined with the actions by the company that led to the atmosphere that created the incident speaks volumes about the company's current management even more negatively than its monthly business statements.

NOVEMBER 29

Sid Vicious and Arn Anderson are each suspended without pay. The company has publicly yet to acknowledge this, and is still advertising them as appearing on upcoming house shows on television shows that aired as late as this past weekend.

DECEMBER 6

Speaking of Vicious and Anderson, as of press time both were suspended without pay but no final decision was made on the incident. Unofficially, here is the story. There really will be a ruling made at some point, but for reasons that nobody can publicly say, it is a much more complicated issue than it appears but anyone believing a decision has been made already is and that it is a given Sid will never be back appears to be ahead of reality, even though at least most of the wrestlers seem to have been given the impression Sid won't be back.

DECEMBER 20

Sid Vicious was fired. Vicious, who had agreed verbally with WCW officials to a four-year $2.4 million contract just before the 10/26 incident in Blackburne, England where he and Arn Anderson stabbed one another in a fight that got out of control, technically wasn't fired over the incident with Arn Anderson because of legal reasons, but for what was termed overall volatile behavior. Because of WCW officials apparently letting Vicious slide on steroid tests, there is a very messy can of worms that still has to be dealt with so any decision being absolute may not wind up being the case in the long-run, but for now, Vicious has been fired. Arn Anderson, who had been suspended since the incident, will be re-instated on or around 12/28. It's been ironic since television is not taped months in advance to see Anderson doing interviews that were taped in September and October talking about being stabbed in the back.

DECEMBER 27

Sid Vicious was in the office on Thursday and was told by a high-ranking official that they'd like him back as soon as possible but put the heat on the other wrestlers for not wanting him back and saying they'd bring him back but they'd have to wait for the wrestlers to cool down. This came two weeks after WCW informed Vicious' lawyers that he was terminated and the four-year contract for $2.4 million that both sides had agreed to wasn't going to be honored due to his volatile nature.

CHAPTER THIRTY NINE

ORO DIES
IN THE RING

NOVEMBER 8

Oro, the wrestler being groomed to be the future top star of the EMLL promotion, passed away during a match on 10/26 at Arena Coliseo in Mexico City. He was two months shy of his 22nd birthday. Oro's real name was unknown at press time, although he is the son of former wrestler Calavera II and brother of EMLL wrestler Plata (not to be confused with EMLL wrestlers Brazo de Oro and CMLL world heavyweight champion Brazo de Plata). Because of Oro's daredevil tactics, second in the world to AAA's Rey Misterio Jr. in degree of dangerous and innovative flying moves and said to be comparable to only La Fiera in his youth as being willing to do spectacular topes with his foe moving and being willing to crash onto the floor for finishes when he was scheduled to lose a match, the idea that he would wind up with a serious injury from wrestling would not have been a surprise. At 5-10 and 195 pounds, he was much larger than Misterio Jr., which is why it was felt his potential was such that he was ultimately going to be EMLL's top native star within a few years. He was taken out of his trio of "Los Metalicos" in the past year in order to groom him as an individual.

Ironically, his death came after a simple chop during the six-man tag team semi main event pitting himself, La Fiera & Brazo de Plata against Dr. Wagner Jr. & Kahos I & Jaque Mate. The match aired on the EMLL's television show in Mexico City on Sunday. In the first fall, Kahos chopped Oro, who apparently tried to take what was described as "the Kenta Kobashi bump" (in reference to the two back suplexes Kobashi took in a recent match with Steve Williams that it looked to be a miracle didn't break his neck) spinning and landing on his head from the chop. Kahos tried to pick Oro up for the next spot but he was already limp. He collapsed in the corner and his pulse got low and he was screaming to take his boots and ring outfit off and for the wrestlers to not let him lapse into a coma. It is a longstanding Mexican tradition because there have probably been more deaths in the ring there than anywhere else that you can't die when you are conscious and those fearful always scream at the others in the ring to slap them around to keep them from going out. Eventually he was stretchered out early in the second fall but by the time he was in the ambulance to be taken to the hospital, he was already dead. The incident reminded many of an incident in the same building on December 25, 1979 when 23-year-old Sangre India missed a dangerous tope, suffered a broken back, went into shock, and died in front of the fans.

No autopsy was performed on Oro at the families request, however those in Mexico claimed he never used drugs and was in perfect health. It is believed he died of a brain aneurism. Oro was the kind of wrestler who insisted on doing at least one high-risk move in every match and was very competitive with his flying moves. If someone did a spectacular move lower on the card, Oro felt it was his duty being a young wrestler higher on the card, to top the move. Because of the death, there has been a clamor for doctors to be more cautious when wrestlers take major bumps or seem to be in a bad way. A lot of fans have freaked out in recent days when certain wrestlers have taken big bumps or collapsed out of the ring, including a few days later a lot of women crying hysterically when Vampiro collapsed on the floor after a match with Black Magic at Arena Mexico. Even the rival AAA on its television show taped three nights later had a three minutes tribute to Oro with many fans in tears.

Oro, which translated into English simply means Gold, was born December 24, 1971 in Guadalajara. He debuted one month before his 19th birthday, on November 24, 1990 as part of a trio called Los Metalicos with older brother Plata and non-relative Platino (who was later replaced by Bronce on the trio before Plata & Platino & Bronce became the trio when Oro started being pushed as a single). He & Plata captured the Mexican tag team titles on December 4, 1991 in Acapulco before losing them back on December 17, 1991 at the same Arena Coliseo. He was a big hit in his Japanese debut for the Universal promotion in April, 1992 with his spectacular flying moves, and was scheduled for his next tour as part of the debut of FULL in mid-December. His hardcore reputation in Japan was such that a few months back when he teamed up in Mexico City with Mil Mascaras & Ultimo Dragon, the magazines billed it as a team of the best flier of the 70s, 80s and 90s. He was given his first world singles championship on May 23, 1993 when he defeated Mano Negra for the NWA middleweight title in Guadalajara, but lost the title back on June 15 in Puebla to Negra.

NOVEMBER 15

Since last week's issue we've received several additional notes on the death of 21-year-old EMLL wrestler Oro, whose real name was Jesus Javier Hernandez Silva, known as Javier Hernandez to his friends. According to a magazine interview with Kahos, the wrestler who delivered the chop to the chest in the match on 10/26 at Arena Coliseo in Mexico City which Oro passed out from, he believed something was wrong prior to the chop. Kahos said that he gave Oro a dropkick, which was the previous move, and that Oro's eyes rolled back in his head. In looking back, he realized that something was wrong. Initially, after the chop, when he collapsed, the wrestlers thought he was selling until they realized something was wrong and the commissioner quickly called for the stretcher. By the time he was placed in an ambulance, he was already dead. When he was examined that night the cause of death was listed as cerebral hemorrhaging caused by a brain aneurism. His funeral took place on 10/28 in his home town of Guadalajara.

While Oro's debut was listed as November 24, 1990 in last week's issue, that was actually his debut under that ring name. He had started wrestling a few months earlier in 1990 in his native Guadalajara under the name Spiderman. Since the death, Oro's older brother who wrestled for EMLL as sometime tag team partner Plata (Estevan Hernandez), announced his retirement. Plata, 32, was never as gung-ho about wrestling as his younger and more talented brother, but started wrestling regularly in 1990 largely to be a partner with his brother. Kahos was immediately pulled from all bookings for several days because he was so shook up about what happened, and since his return (after the weekend shows that had been previously booked) he has only been booked in heel vs. heel matches in something of a face role in order to quell the heat by some fans who might somehow in their own minds be led to believe he killed Oro.

On rival AAA's television show that aired 11/6 in the United States (taped 10/29), before the Heavy Metal vs. El Hijo del Santo title vs. title main event, they brought out Oro's father, who wrestled as Calavera II, a big star years back in his native Guadalajara, and made an announcement of Oro's death and asked fans to give him one last cheer. They superimposed a photo of Oro over the cheering and crying crowd during a 75 second-long standing ovation. Even heels Metal (who had his head down so the fans couldn't see him crying) and second Love Machine were clapping during the ceremony. Similar ceremonies were held at most arenas throughout the country, regardless of promotion, during the week after the incident.

DECEMBER 6

The match where Oro died aired last weekend in Los Angeles. The actual match circumstances went like this. Oro missed a dropkick, which is where his opponent Kahos I later said he noticed things being weird. Kahos gave him a chop and Oro took a strange bump since apparently either the missed dropkick or chop caused his congenital brain aneurism to burst. Oro did try to finish his sequence before he collapsed in the corner and by the time they figured out he was doing more than selling big and got an ambulance into the building and carried him from the ring, he was already dead. Although Oro was a daredevil, this death had nothing to do with either a risky move or a risky bump. By the way, aside from Plata, Oro had two other brothers who were wrestlers, Guadalajara boys who worked as Excaliburs I & II. II also now wants to retire as Plata has done although the other brother wants to continue.

CHAPTER FORTY

TEXAS WRESTLING
TURNS BACK THE CLOCK

NOVEMBER 8

In 1947, Dory Funk Sr. arrived in Amarillo, TX and became a prominent star in a territory he would later own, that would result in the beginnings of the careers of some of the biggest stars the business would ever see many decades later. Some 46 years later, his son and namesake, who was five-years-old at the time, returned for the first wrestling match in the city where he grew up in 11 years. When he arrived, an elderly female fan showed him an autograph, in pencil, that his father signed during his first year in Texas.

To a pro wrestling fan of the 1970s and early 1980s, West Texas State University, in the Amarillo suburb of Canyon, TX, would have to be thought of as similar to Notre Dame to fans of pro football. While it is logical, being that the college was based in the same city as a regional wrestling office known for breaking in new talent, and that the sons of the promoter played football at the school, that many from the school would get started. What is staggering is the percentage of those who got started in that manner that achieved so much success. There were 14 football players from the school between the mid-60s and mid-70s that went into pro wrestling. Of them, two, Lee Miller and Mark Allen, were around for such a short period of time that virtually nobody would even remember the names. One other, Kelly Kiniski, lasted a few years and worked several territories but never broke out of the preliminary mold. Of the remaining 11, you had three that were genuine national stars--Tito Santana, Bobby Duncum and Manny Fernandez; three more that ranked right at the top of the list of the best workers of the 1980s--Tully Blanchard, Ted DiBiase and Barry Windham, and five that are unquestionably legends of the business--Dory Jr. & Terry Funk, Bruiser Brody, Stan Hansen and Dusty Rhodes. One more wrestler, Dick Murdoch, who was a superstar for two decades, grew up in the same environment and started in the same manner. Although Murdoch was always billed during his career as having played football at the school, he actually never did.

There is no West Texas State University anymore. It's now called West Texas A & M. Despite the success of its football players in pro wrestling, the school was never what would be called a football power. Probably the only players who achieved any notable success in pro football were Mercury Morris, a star running back with the Miami Dolphins in the early 70s who played at about the same time as Rhodes and Brody, Duane Thomas, a star running back with the Dallas Cowboys at about the same time, and years later, John Ayres, an offensive lineman for the San Francisco 49ers team of the decade in the 1980s who played in college with DiBiase, Blanchard, Santana, Fernandez and Kiniski.

There is no Amarillo wrestling circuit either. It died out a few years before Vince McMahon's national expansion killed most of the territories, around 1980, amidst financial ruin with the death of M & M (Murdoch & Mulligan) promotions. Mulligan & Murdoch had bought the territory a few years earlier from the Funk Brothers, who inherited it from their father. Dory Funk Sr., a former college wrestler and top-rated junior heavyweight, was still active as a top star in pro wrestling and known as "King of the Texas death matches," passed away from a heart attack in 1973 at the age of 54 shortly after winning a side bet at a barbecue with another "shooter" who bragged Sr. couldn't hold him in a front facelock.

On Thursday night, for one brief moment, wrestling turned back the clock. Amarillo was a wrestling capital once again. Dory and Terry Funk, Dick Murdoch and Ted DiBiase were local kids who made good, as older fans reminisced about the night when Dory's father and Ted's father had a Texas death match in 1969 that went something like 27 falls and lasted nearly three hours that started on a Thursday night and ended sometime Friday morning at the old Amarillo Sports Arena.

The "High Country Chevy Free-for-all" on 10/28 was a show put together by Terry Funk in conjunction with 19 local Chevy dealerships. Funk did their television commercials, and in exchange they financed a live wrestling show and gave the tickets away for free at their various locations. Whatever proceeds, basically selling of souvenirs, programs, t-shirts and a collection bottle using several members of the local college football team as collectors went to benefit Ayres, Terry's long-time friend who, at 40, is battling liver cancer. Having been at this show and seeing how this was handled, the difference between this and every other "charity" type collection deal I've seen associated with wrestling in recent years was so marked that it only made clear just what the motives in so many other cases really are. 7,200 tickets were given away, enough to fill the Civic Center. About 5,500 showed up, a surprising amount of whom were certainly old enough to remember the weekly Thursday night cards from the 60s and 70s, and many of whom were kids who came largely to see the Big Bossman of WWF television fame.

CHAPTER FORTY ONE

JERRY LAWLER INDICTED

Jerry Lawler, long-time co-owner of the United States Wrestling Association and one of the most enduring regional headliners in the history of pro wrestling, was indicted on 11/12 of one count of second-degree rape, three counts of second-degree sodomy and one count of harassing a witness.

Lawler, who is scheduled to be arraigned in Louisville on 11/22, was charged by a Jefferson County, KY grand jury of the five counts in reference to an alleged encounter with a 13-year-old Louisville girl. He is also being investigated for criminal allegations in Southern Indiana on what are allegedly similar circumstances.

Lawler, who turns 44 on 11/29, was the biggest drawing card in Memphis and its surrounding area for most of his 23-year career and has held numerous versions of world heavyweight titles. His reputation within pro wrestling is of being one of the greatest interviews in the history of the business, an ability which is more than any other responsible for his long-term success. In the late 70s he became a partner with Jerry Jarrett in the regional wrestling company which promotes in Tennessee, Kentucky, and parts of Mississippi, Arkansas and Indiana, a company of which he and Jarrett each currently own 50 percent interest in. Over the past year, Lawler achieved his biggest national and financial success in his lengthy career by parlaying his color commentary role on WWF Superstars into becoming the hottest heel in the United States, and in recent weeks, the country's biggest drawing card on a national basis. His ongoing feud with Bret Hart was the biggest drawing match in the United States at the time of the indictment.

The World Wrestling Federation, faced with its own image problem over many printed allegations of sexually deviant behavior among two of its former employees, a steroid scandal and a nearly two-year long Justice Department investigation which went public in the New York mainstream media with a front page Newsday story less than two weeks earlier, immediately suspended Lawler without pay upon receiving word Friday of the indictment, even though he was the company's hottest heel. His match on the 11/24 Survivor Series PPV, where he was to team with three unknown Masked Knights against Bret & Owen & Keith & Bruce Hart was considered by most as the top drawing match on the show even though it was positioned by the company as second from the top. Company officials announced the next evening on its Radio WWF show that Lawler had been indicted on five charges in Louisville and put on immediate hiatus from the WWF pending clearing up his legal situation. The company on the same show announced Shawn Michaels would be replacing Lawler in the Survivor Series. Michaels is expected to be Lawler's replacement in many of the already advertised house show matches with Bret Hart in the upcoming weeks in some markets. Jeff Jarrett will be replacing Lawler in matches against Hart in other markets including the early December California shows. On Monday Night Raw, the situation was acknowledged in passing that Michaels had been reinstated and that he'd replace Lawler at the Survivor Series because Lawler has had legal problems. If or when Lawler is cleared from these charges, he will be brought back by the WWF.

Lawler was heavily pushed on WWF television shows that are already taped ahead for approximately four more weeks. The decision was made Friday to edit out all business-related references to Lawler and anything featuring or related to Lawler from the already-taped shows effective immediately. Company officials were still unsure of how the two-hour Survivor Series preview show, scheduled to air on 11/21 on the USA network, which was taped 11/10 in Delhi, NY would be put together since situations involving Lawler were critical to the entire flow and storyline of two key matches and the beginnings of what appeared to be a brother vs. brother feud with Bret and Owen. There is some talk WWF may have to do an emergency taping this week at a house show in either Niagara Falls or Syracuse to create a new Survivor Series showdown special for Sunday. Lawler's role as co-host on WWF Superstars as of this coming weekend will be taken by Bruce Prichard, who will use the television name Rio Rogers, doing a heel character designed as a parody of WCW booker Dusty Rhodes.

Lawler will continue to wrestle for the USWA in Memphis and at this point in the rest of the territory with the exception of Louisville, where the alleged incident took place. Both Lawler and the girl, a front-row regular at the matches described by both Lawler and others as a groupie, that the indictments are related to, had been banned by the management of the Louisville Gardens from the building for at least the past several weeks when police informed building management of the investigation and potential charges. Lawler had traditionally headlined approximately one show per month in Louisville since many years back he had stopped travelling the entire circuit each week. The USWA, which traditionally runs wrestling shows every Tuesday night in Louisville, has pulled out of the city for the next few weeks in the wake of the negative local publicity.

However, the indictment has led to rampant speculation throughout the wrestling industry about the future of Lawler and Jarrett's USWA, the last surviving regional office from the days of regional wrestling territories. On October 30, Jarrett, who is now heavily involved in the booking of the WWF and has rented a place in Connecticut, offered his 50 percent of the USWA company to Indianapolis real estate broker Jeffrey Cohen, who promotes weekly house shows in his home town. Cohen, who admits to having his eyes on someday running regularly in Louisville and Evansville, two weekly USWA stops, had already known of the background of the investigations against Lawler in both Indiana and Kentucky. He turned down the offer before a price was even discussed. Jarrett's Hendersonville, TN home is also reportedly for sale, but that has been the case for some time now and is believed to have preceded his getting the WWF job and whenever he became appraised of the potential problems involving his partner doesn't appear to be related. Jarrett was unable to be reached for comment at press time.

In addition, there has been heavy speculation as to the status in 1994 of the weekly tapings and 90 minute live show at the WMC-TV studios in Memphis due to the station going under new ownership that reportedly wasn't thrilled by the weekly fee the station was paying Lawler and Jarrett for the show and the station's image in carrying the show. This is in spite of the fact the show has been an incredible ratings success on the station for 15 years. Jarrett and Lawler, because of the shows long-term ratings history, should have little trouble under normal circumstances finding a new station in the Memphis market if WMC management dictates changes, although this situation has the potential to complicate matters. At one point in the early 1980s the 90 minute wrestling show garnered a 23 rating and a 70 share and trailed only "Dallas," (the night-time soap that was the most popular show in the world during that time period) as the most watched show in the market. In the late 70s, there was a one-year period when the promotion was at its all-time peak with Lawler on top as a babyface that it averaged 8,000 paying customers each Monday night, making it the hottest wrestling city in the country at the time.

The second-degree rape charge, which is a statutory rather than forced rape charge, along with the three second-degree sodomy (oral sex) charges are felonies and carry possible prison sentences of five to ten years apiece. The harassment of a witness charge is a misdemeanor with a maximum sentence of one year in prison and a $500 fine.

The Grand Jury indictments on the four felony charges are related to alleged encounters in Louisville hotel rooms on June 6 and July 7 of this year. The harassment charge alleged that on October 4, Lawler "engaged in misleading or unlawful conduct intended to dissuade a person who he believes may be called as a witness from causing a criminal prosecution to be sought or instituted," according to a story in Saturday's Louisville Courier-Journal. The charge is not related to the alleged victim of the sex crimes Lawler has been indicted for, but related to a 14-year-old girl who may have been the first person to go to the authorities related to these charges.

Detective Mike Redmond of the city-county Crimes Against Children Unit said no force was used, but the charges were brought because of the girl's age. The age of consent in Kentucky is 16, unlike 18 in much of the rest of the country.

According to a television news report by Mark Grimm on WLKY-TV, the CBS affiliate in Louisville on Friday night, testimony to the Grand Jury on Friday centered around the two alleged incidents in Louisville on June 6 and July 7 and a third alleged incident on May 26 in Selersburg, IN, which is a town across the river and the state border that wrestlers often stay at when wrestling in Louisville. The television report focused on the testimony of one of the two girls who reportedly told the grand jury, "As soon as we walked into Lawler's room, he said, `Let's get naked." We took off our clothes and all three got onto the bed. We had sex while we were watching cartoons." According to the testimony, after the alleged encounter, Lawler took the two girls to Value City and Taco Bell.

A total of 17 people, including Lawler, were called to testify in the Friday hearing that led to the five indictments, which took the Grand Jury just ten minutes to vote on. According to Grimm's report, a second wrestler, Bill Martin, who formerly worked for the USWA as Young Stallion Bill Marino, was also linked to the case in testimony but wasn't indicted.

Outside the courtroom on Friday, Lawler was interviewed by the station saying, "The King is fighting back. The King is not going to take this lying down. The girls are lying." Lawler has told reporters he has a taped telephone conversation which he says will exonerate him. The station had phoned WMC-TV in Memphis, the flagship station where the weekly USWA shows have been taped for nearly 15 years, for footage of Lawler, which the station refused to release.

The only other statements to the press Lawler is known to have made were on the WMC-TV news on Saturday and in a phone conversation initiated by Lawler to Wade Keller of the Pro Wrestling Torch on Sunday. Lawler said on WMC-TV that, "This was a situation where a couple of young wrestling groupies were bragging about some supposed sexual conquests of theirs to some friends...and, uh...it snowballed and was related from one person to another. And my name was dropped in, among other names, as having been with these girls." Lawler told Keller that, "Each and every one of the allegations are false. They'll be proven false if need be in a court of law. This is a case of a couple of girls who are wrestling groupies who told another party about a supposed sexual conquest. This party went to authorities. The authorities then came to me. I volunteered to tell my side of the story to a Grand Jury but when I was in front of the Grand Jury, I didn't get to tell my side of the story and what I know about the situation."

Lawler also acknowledged the situation on the live Saturday morning Memphis wrestling television show. In the middle of his interview talking about a Monday night match with himself and son Brian Christopher (not acknowledged as his son even with Christopher's recent face turn which was done to groom him to carry the promotion as lead face while Lawler and Jeff Jarrett were going to work regularly for the WWF) against Rex Hargrove and Koko Ware, Lawler said "I've got a lot of friends and family here in this town, and I want you to know that in the next couple of days, you're going to be hearing some stories or seeing some stories on some allegations made about me. And I just want to say right now that each and every one of these are totally false, and I guarantee you that I will prove that, if I have to, in a court of law. That's all I'm going to say about that."

Lawler used the manner of speech and inflections in addressing the charges that he would use when doing a typical wrestling promo, as his voice rose to raise the excitement level that encouraged the live crowd cheered him on, which it did, but also made it come off as tacky, and after he finished, went back to talking about his Monday night match.

Lawler is currently single and has had two previous marriages. Besides Brian, he has a second son, Kevin, both from his first marriage, who referees for the USWA and wrestles independently under the name Kevin Christian.

The AP story on the indictments received heavy play on Saturday throughout the Tennessee media, including page one stories in the newspaper in Memphis and Jackson, TN (where it was the lead story on page one). The Memphis Commercial-Appeal also ran a second-day story on Sunday, printing Lawler's remarks made on the wrestling television show the day before and quoting a fan and wrestler Reggie B. Fine, interviewed at the studio, as saying they didn't believe the charges were true. Ironically, in the AP story, which ran in several newspapers around the country, Lawler's status as the leading regional draw in that part of the country for more than two decades, his 50 percent ownership in the promotion and his current status with the WWF were not acknowledged. The story said Lawler may be best known for his 1982 wrestling angle with the late comedian Andy Kaufman of "Taxi" fame. The stories treated the encounter as if it was a shoot and that Kaufman was really injured. This led to Lawler's memorable appearance on the David Letterman show which resulted in Kaufman throwing coffee on him after Lawler slapped Kaufman.

NOVEMBER 22

Lawler did a hilarious King's Court that will never air where Johnny Polo pretended to be Stu Hart and Harvey Whippleman pretended to be Helen Hart. Polo then faked having a heart attack and died but Harvey revived him with mouth-to-mouth.

NOVEMBER 22

Titan deserves credit for handling the problems with Lawler with such expediency and doing the extra round-the-clock work in editing out previously taped television shows. This is a stark opposite with WCW when it had its problems with Sid Vicious and it did exactly the opposite.

NOVEMBER 29

The case against Jerry Lawler on statutory rape, sodomy and harassing a witness charges took a bizarre series of turns this past week.

Lawler's attorney William Massey told numerous media outlets in the Memphis area, and the Associated Press, that he had a four-page written affidavit from the 13-year-old Louisville girl who was listed as the victim in the rape and sodomy aspect of the case, and her mother, recanting their story and saying none of the incidents took place. Both Massey and Lawler spent the weekend telling the media and friends that all charges would be dropped at the arraignment that was scheduled to take place on Monday, 11/22. Massey, in an interview before the arraignment said he'd accept nothing less than a complete dismissal.

After the arraignment, where Lawler plead "not guilty" to all five charges, none of the charges were dropped. Lawler, was freed on a $1,000 bond. Lawler returned to Memphis for largely positive press on Monday night's news shows, saying the procedure didn't allow for the admitting of the affidavit as evidence until a December 6 discovery meeting. Lawler said in an interview with Pro Wrestling Torch later that afternoon that the lengthy article which practically absolved him of all guilt in the previous day's Memphis newspaper was mistaken in its reporting that Massey said he expected charges to be dropped the next day, although Massey was quoted in other media outlets as saying the same thing. Lawler himself had gone on the Memphis television wrestling show on Saturday saying he expected the whole situation to be over very soon.

WWF officials had decided that Lawler would return to both his wrestling and announcing duties with the group if or when he was absolved of all charges, but with word throughout wrestling on Sunday that Lawler had been cleared, talk was that he may be back for Survivor Series after all, although there is no confirmation of anything of the like.

Earlier in the week, the Nashville Tennessean had run an editorial critical of Lawler claiming his public explanation of the indictments as exaggerated girl talk didn't come off as plausible.

Lawler's only major wrestling appearance during the week he was under suspicion was the 11/15 card in his home town of Memphis. The show drew approximately 1,250 fans and $8,600, an increase from the previous weeks 1,100 and $6,600 (there was a $1 increase in prices). The debut of Crush in the main event may have been a factor as well as the local publicity regarding Lawler. Lawler received one of the loudest and most sustained cheers for his ring introduction at the show in recent memory.

In an article in the 11/21 Memphis Commercial-Appeal, Massey was quoted as saying he expected all charges to be dropped at the scheduled arraignment in Louisville.

In the article by Michael Kelley, Massey said he met with the girl and her mother "at their request" in Louisville last week and obtained a statement completely exonerating Lawler.

"The young lady says this never happened," Massey said. "It just got blown out of proportion. And when she tried to stop (the prosecution), the authorities did not want to. They didn't want to hear the truth."

At press time, a Louisville station had already taped an interview with the older brother of the alleged victim, which the station was taking to lawyers to decide whether to air since the older brother was still under 18, which sources say may paint a new portrait of the entire proceedings.

Massey said Lawler has given the girl and her mother nothing in exchange for the statement, that no civil suits have been filed in either direction and that there was no monetary settlement.

Massey claimed the situation stemmed from a dispute with the girl in question and a family friend that Lawler had no part of.

"They have a family friend...who almost sees himself as a fatherly figure to this young lady," Massey said in the newspaper article. "He will constantly probe into where she's going and what she's doing, and he questions her, even accuses her, of going out with people constantly. This gentleman was accusing her at one time--I think it was in September--and he just kept on and kept on, and he was saying, `Who else have you been with?' Just to spite this man and to make him leave her alone, to make him back off of her, (she said), `If it will make you happy, I've been with Jerry Lawler,' and named a few others. This man went to the police and that's where it got started."

Massey said the statement also cleared Lawler of alleged wrongdoings in the Indiana investigation, where charges had not been filed. He said the grand jury indictments came without either Lawler or the girl being put on the stand, which seems to make erroneous the report on the WLKY-TV news that was reported here and elsewhere last week quoting detailed testimony from an alleged victim, although many aspects of this story at this point don't seem to make sense.

"Mr. Lawler sees this young lady as more or less a victim of the system herself--her and her family," Massey continued in the article. "This just got blown out of proportion, and that happens sometimes with major celebrity figures.

Massey said that Lawler admitted to meeting the girl when she came to his hotel room at one time and they talked for 30 minutes, but that was the extent of it.

DECEMBER 6

The state of Indiana has dropped its investigation, which never resulted in charges being filed, of Jerry Lawler in the wake of the girl in question changing her story. The Kentucky authorities have not dropped the charges, although it seems impossible to believe they can continue prosecution with the girl changing her story. In the wake of these charges, Lawler is trying to turn the television show into his personal public relations campaign to show what a great guy he is ala WWC with Jose Gonzales in 1988, only to a far great extent than WWC did with Gonzales. On the Saturday television show, Lawler talked about his ordeal as having been an unbelievable nightmare and said that hopefully the end was in sight and thanked everyone for their support. He then showed clips of him doing benefit work in the Memphis area (one of which appeared to be about eight years old), and had local musician and friend Tom Nunnery go on television and say what a great guy he was.

CHAPTER FORTY TWO

BOBBY HEENAN LEAVES THE WWF

DECEMBER 6

The biggest news backstage at the show was the idea that this may be Bobby Heenan's final PPV show as a broadcaster. Heenan, who is far and away the best man in wrestling in his field, co-hosts all major WWF events and three weekly shows, Challenge, Raw and All-American. His contract expires in mid-December and according to several sources within the company, it is considered to be less than a 50 percent chance that he and McMahon will come to terms. It is expected that when Heenan's contract expires in a few weeks, if a new deal isn't reached, that he'll leave the company immediately leaving a huge hole to fill. No names have been speculated to me as to who may fill that hole, although Bruce Prichard as Rio Rogers was almost universally described as the flop of the century and was replaced on Superstars as co-host with Stan Lane after just one week. The biggest stumbling block may be that McMahon wants all announcers to move to Connecticut so the company can save on travel expenses for Heenan's several times weekly flights in from Florida. At this point in his life with a family, Heenan, who is 50 and has been in the wrestling business for 27 consecutive years, apparently doesn't want to make the move. This is largely the same reason Gene Okerlund wound up leaving WWF for WCW. Although I don't know this for certain, it appears they are building up to a confrontation in the next week or two between Heenan and Gorilla Monsoon which will result in Heenan being "injured," and be the storyline reason for Heenan no longer being around.

DECEMBER 20

Bobby Heenan's official departure from WWF came on the 12/6 edition of Monday Night Raw, and he'll be starting with WCW according to several sources in January, although that hasn't been confirmed by the company. Heenan over the past year or two had taken his already strong rep as a color man to new levels with his work on Raw and on some of the PPV shows. Heenan coming to WCW may spell the end for Jesse Ventura, although nothing is official on that. Ventura's contract, which reportedly is in the $500,000 annual range. expires in the next few weeks and it seems unlikely WCW would be wanting to renew him at that kind of a salary figure. Ventura himself on his WCW Hotline role brought up that his contract was running out and that he didn't know what his role would be long-term. It seems unlikely, but not impossible, that WCW would keep Gene Okerlund, Heenan and Ventura because of the huge payroll, and obviously of the three, Okerlund and Heenan are solid. Mr. Perfect has also left the WWF. He's also contacted independent promoters about being available for dates, and has reportedly negotiated with WCW, but the most likely scenario is that he'll be returning to the WWF in the spring or summer. The loss of Heenan, who apparently had a money figure given to him and then taken back which largely, along with the directive of wanting him to move to Connecticut, spelled the end of his nine-plus year relationship with Titan, is one of the first major signs to the general public that from a business standpoint, things in the WWF have never been shakier, and his following Okerlund to WCW will for the first time in a long time create the public perception that people are leaving WWF for WCW and give people the idea that somehow WCW is turning things around, even though there is really no evidence of it happening. WWF will apparently use Gorilla Monsoon in the color role on Wrestling Challenge, and it is uncertain who will fill the role on Monday Night Raw. Jim Cornette filled the role this past week and was said to have been excellent with rapid-fire jokes, but didn't blend in well with Vince McMahon who seems for obvious reasons more and more pre-occupied while on television and really needs to get himself off television until his situation is settled. However, Cornette is not the long-term answer because he's not about to move to Connecticut full-time either and he's already trying to accomplish too many things for one human being at one time without adding more responsibilities.

CHAPTER FORTY THREE

BRITISH BULLDOG
FIRED BY WCW

DECEMBER 20

Davey Boy Smith was fired this past week, reportedly to set an example about too many no-shows. Despite what is being heavily rumored and reported, WCW is not getting out of the house show business (at least based on who is in power this week, as things could change at the drop of a hat) although there are only four non-TV tapings house shows scheduled for January, but the scheduled is a lot fuller come February and March reportedly. WCW management has finally acknowledged that one of the biggest problems that has absolutely destroyed their house show business is the consistent going into cities and not delivering the advertised product due to no-shows and apparently they are making Smith the well-paid example. Reportedly Smith has already contacted Titan about returning and has definitely contacted independent promoters about being available for dates. WCW did a major burial job on Smith on television that will air probably before you read this. On the television show that was to air this weekend, Smith was going to beat Rick Rude in a non-title match (taped back on 11/30) to set up their match for whatever Rude's title is called this week at Starrcade. Instead, a re-taping was done on 12/13 at Center Stage where Smith's music plays for a match with Rude and he isn't there and I guess is pretty well buried as a chicken who no-showed a contracted match, violated his contract, and is pretty well said to be history. At this point, "The Boss" (formerly Big Bossman) showed up and promptly defeated Rude in a non-title match to set up a PPV match between the two. Roddy Piper was originally talked about for the replacement role but apparently that didn't happen. Bossman was scheduled to return full-time to WWF early in 1994, and as recently as the past week had worked on WWF shows in California, so his appearance was a big surprise on the WCW taping. WWF officials who apparently have Bossman under a contract reportedly are going to attempt to take legal action preventing his jumping.

DECEMBER 27

In the case of Davey Boy Smith, who was the subject to something of a burial that at least bordered on being a cheap shot on television Saturday, the story goes something like this. Smith negotiated a deal with Bill Watts for a certain amount (presumably $1,000 although I don't know this to be an accurate figure) per match. Smith was under the impression that on dates he wasn't working for WCW, he was free to work independent shows, which is consistent with what Watts had said about the contracts he was signing people up with during that time period. Watts also agreed to allow him to tour Japan since he had a deal already with Giant Baba before he negotiated with WCW, provided he give WCW two months notice before tours. Smith also claimed that Watts agreed to pay him a higher amount per match for European matches, since Smith was going to be the company's top draw there because of his existing popularity there from his WWF exposure and because of being a British native. Smith received the same amount from the recent (late October/early November) European tour as if the matches had been held in the U.S. He complained about the money and it wound up with him saying he wouldn't be going to the house shows unless he got what he felt was due him for the European tours. Apparently nobody at WCW contacted him to sort all this out, with the claim being they didn't know his new phone number for the communications problem.

On 11/30 he taped the angle where he beat Rick Rude to set up their planned match at Starrcade. He then missed a TV taping in Dalton, GA and quit unless the European money was made good. WCW then "fired" him citing the missed show. This of course led to the angle that aired on television this past week where they re-taped the match with Rude, this time with Smith not showing up and largely buried as a coward on television, and with The Boss (Ray "Bossman" Traylor) beating Rude in the non-title match to set up a Starrcade match.

Communication between Smith and WCW was still alive as late as the Monday after the television show aired which makes one think there's a possibility it could still be worked out, although Smith was buried again by Gene Okerlund on the hotline two days earlier. WCW was also mad about Smith working an indie show for his brother-in-law Jim Neidhart in Gate City, FL and demanding 60 percent of his pay for the show, with Smith believing his deal with Watts allowed him to work indies and WCW basically with the idea that anything Watts agreed to doesn't count because Watts isn't around, and Smith claiming he worked the show free since it was a family deal.

Smith had also agreed to two All Japan tours this year, both of which WCW wouldn't let him go on because they had PPV shows that coincided with the tours. At this point All Japan lost interest in him, but New Japan then wanted him for the recently completed tour. He asked to go on that and WCW wouldn't let him because he was told they had big plans involving him for the Battle Bowl PPV show. As it turned out, the Nasty Boys, who were billed on all the house shows that followed Battle Bowl in the U.S., worked Battle Bowl, missing the first few days of the New Japan tour and worked the rest of the New Japan tour with the blessing of the office. Quite frankly, a trained chimpanzee could have done the same job Smith was required to do at Battle Bowl to begin with. Word we get is that Smith will be headed to England in mid-January to work for Max Crabtree, who has promoted the local wrestling in England for decades, and will also attempt to merchandise himself including putting out a bodybuilding video aimed at the British market.

CHAPTER FORTY FOUR

BITS AND PIECES

MOTOSHI OKUMA PASSES AWAY

(JANUARY 4) Saddest news of the past week is the passing away of veteran All Japan prelim wrestler Motoshi Okuma, who passed away 12/27 at his home in Soka, Japan of a heart attack just nine days after his 51st birthday. Okuma was a member of the Wild Bunch trio with Haruka Eigen and Masa Fuchi, generally working in either comedy tag teams or six-man matches against Giant Baba & Rusher Kimura and a third partner. With the exception of Baba and Kimura, Okuma was the oldest active wrestler working full-time with a major office. According to the reports we received, Okuma was one of many who passed away as Japan suffered its coldest weather in many years over the past week. Okuma, a squatty 5-8, 250 pound ex-sumo wrestler, made his debut back in 1962. He was a prelim wrestler the majority of his career, working in the 70s with the late Masio Koma (who, if I recall, died at the same time of the year about 15 years ago while still an active wrestler), and later as a tag partner of the now-retired Shinya "Great" Kojika. Kojika & Okuma held the Asian tag team titles on many occasions during the 70s. Okuma remained a "serious" wrestler through the mid-80s and on occasion worked in main events in tag team matches, generally to drop the fall. By the late 80s, when Baba removed himself from the top as a serious wrestler, he worked the same patterned comedy spot matches and used Okuma, Eigen and Fuchi as his foils. Okuma had appeared to really age physically this past year, dropping some weight, although nothing that wouldn't be expected of someone his age.

STING MISSES DATES

(JANUARY 4) Sting missed both Fort Myers and Charlotte because he has a specific amount of dates per year that he has to work in his contract that they booked him in more than that number of dates, so he skipped the afternoon of the two double-shots. In the company's defense, they probably didn't know about this in time to change the advertising, and in Sting's defense, considering Bill Watts' comments and actions, I don't know he should feel any moral obligation to do anything not specified in his contract. But the fans got screwed as well in both cities when the company's top star doesn't appear as advertised. Actually it was worse since Rude was injured, although he appeared at all the shows but couldn't work. In Charlotte, Simmons and Armstrong both missed the card as well since they missed their flight out of Florida. It was announced in the building that it was transportation problems because of the bad weather, and the weather was bad enough that the fans bought it as the reason for Simmons and Sting not being there even though it wasn't the reason.

WRESTLEMANIA IX PLANS AND BEYOND

(JANUARY 15) A sign in from of Caesar's Palace in Las Vegas for Wrestlemania lists Brutus Beefcake, LOD Animal, Paul Ellering and Jake Roberts as among those appearing at Wrestlemania.

(MARCH 29) Post-WM house show marriages will be Bret Hart vs. Bam Bam Bigelow, Yokozuna vs. Jim Duggan, Lex Luger vs. Mr. Perfect, Undertaker vs. Giant Gonzales, Money Inc. vs. Steiners, Shawn Michaels vs. Brutus Beefcake, Tatanka vs. Papa Shango, Nasty Boys vs. Head Shrinkers, Crush vs. Doink, Bob Backlund vs. Damian Demento, Tito Santana vs. Razor Ramon, Kimala vs. Skinner, Owen Hart (when he starts back after the WM break) vs. Terry Taylor (no imminent starting date as an announcer if that even does ever materialize) and Bushwhackers vs. Beverly Brothers.

TSUNEMITSU NAOI KILLED IN CAR CRASH

(JANUARY 15) Tragic news from Japan. Tsunemitsu Naoi, a 26-year-old rookie wrestler for Kazuo Sakurada's Network of Wrestling (NOW) promotion in Japan, passed away on 1/8 in an automobile accident. Naoi was driving back to Tokyo from Fukui, where the promotion had a show, driving the truck with the ring. Apparently he fell asleep at the wheel and got into a major accident. The only passenger in the truck, another rookie wrestler Hikaru Kawabata, was also injured in the accident but he's expected to make a full recovery and to be back in wrestling by the end of February. Naoi just started wrestling four months ago and generally worked the opening matches. On 1/3 at Tokyo's Korakuen Hall, he was put over in a Battle Royal and received some of the most enthusiastic cheers of anyone on the show, although that was partially due to a cheering section of family and friends from high school.

RICK RUDE

(JANUARY 20) The biggest story has to do with Rick Rude. Rude will be out until around the first of March because of the bulging disc problem in his neck. Apparently WCW is refusing to pay him because he's not working, despite this injury occurring in the ring. Watts reportedly wanted Rude to go on workmen's comp. Rude does have an insurance policy with Lloyd's of London as part of his contract, paying him in the neighborhood of $20,000 per month if he can't work, however the policy doesn't go into effect unless Rude misses three months, when, as it was explained to me, it's pro-rated to include the first three months and the company would be paid back his salary laid out during the injury only if he misses three months. I've heard conflicting views as to the nature of Rude's contract as to whether or not it is guaranteed in case of injury and what time frame, but it was a deal put together by Kip Frey which means one would suspect it isn't as heartless when it comes to injuries as deals put together after Frey was gone. Needless to say, there is tremendous heat right now regarding this situation. On the television show that aired 1/16 (taped 1/11), Bill Watts cut a promo about Rude refusing to return the U.S. title belt, which is a shoot, based on the dispute.

(JANUARY 25) There is also continuing controversy regarding the status of Rick Rude. The situation is between TBS attorney Ginger McRae and Rude's attorney and the discrepancy involves an interpretation of the contract Rude signed with Frey last year. While I'm not aware of the specifics, I believe part of Rude's contract included provisions for a Lloyd's of London disability insurance policy (similar to the one Mr. Perfect, Road Warrior Animal, etc. are/were under). I believe Rude's contract called for WCW to take care of the insurance premiums, although I don't know that to be a fact. The insurance payments if Rude would be out of action with a disabling injury are in the $20,000 per month range and kick in during either the third or fourth month off work. Most estimates are that Rude will be back in action on or around 3/1, so his neck injury will keep him out approximately ten weeks, so the insurance policy will likely not be covering the injury. WCW isn't paying Rude his contract money while he's missing dates, and reportedly Watts asked Rude to contact workmen's comp to get income until he returns to action. The question the lawyers are haggling over is whether or not his contract calls for him to receive his regular salary during the first two months of an injury, or during the period prior to the insurance policy kicking into effect. Rude has yet to return the U.S. title belt to WCW as of press time because he's reportedly unhappy with how this situation is evolving.

THE ULTIMATE WARRIOR

(JANUARY 20) Formerly known as The Ultimate Warrior made his first post-WWF wrestling appearance on 1/8 in Billerica, MA pinning Hercules. Formerly known worked as simply The Warrior, drawing 500 fans to the show. Don't know how many promoters that draw 500 fans are going to be able to afford his asking price.

(FEBRUARY 1) Wendell Weatherbee, who promoted the 1/8 show in Billerica, MA using formerly known as Ultimate Warrior as his headliner noted the paid attendance for the show was a sellout 1,000. We had reported the crowd at 500. He also said the correct attendance for a 12/5 show he promoted was 3,000. Hellwig also worked a show on 1/9 in Hanover, MA which drew 1,300, as a last minute replacement for Honkytonk Man after he and the promoter had a problem. Anyone wishing to book Jim Hellwig for personal appearances can go through Weatherbee. Hellwig was telling people over the weekend that he's interested in movie roles and personal appearances but didn't seem to be interested in doing any wrestling saying he went as far as he could go in that endeavor.

(FEBRUARY 8) Formerly known as Ultimate Warrior is telling people he doesn't want to wrestle any longer, and is working on martial arts, martial arts weaponry and horseback riding because he's looking to break into action movies. Warrior's agent was asking $5,000 plus first class airfare for a card show, so that appears to be his appearance price for autograph shows. We'll see how serious he is because I expect he'll be receiving some big money offers to work Europe.

(MAY 3) The Warrior (Jim Hellwig) headed up a tour of Germany promoted by Bob Ury's Wrestling World Superstars group. Warrior defended his WWS title against Hercules Hernandez in the main event of the shows. I believe a show in Munich drew 8,000 fans and most of the other shows drew well. Also on the tour were Jake Roberts, Greg Valentine managed by Madusa, Warlord, Butch Reed and The Youngbloods.

(MAY 10) Bob Ury's Wrestling World Superstars finished a very successful tour of Europe headlined by Jim Hellwig. Ury didn't finish the tour, as he was sent home by the European promoters four days into it. Supposedly Hellwig received something in the neighborhood of $120,000 for the two-week tour, which is a guaranteed figure the likes of which would be pretty much unheard of previously, although I figure Hulk Hogan earned at least $100,000 for Fukuoka Dome. Apparently Warrior and Jake Roberts got their money in advance but some of the undercard guys were in the process of being screwed when Warrior took control and got the guys together and refused to go on one hour before one of the sold out shows unless things were done right for everyone. All the cards were headlined by Warrior vs. Hercules and Roberts (babyface) vs. Greg Valentine managed by Madusa. Work rate wasn't good by and large, in particular in those matches, but crowd reactions to both Warrior and Roberts were exceptional. In Vienna on 4/27, the final night of the tour, they drew a sellout 8,000 with tickets $25 to $75.

(MAY 17) Negotiations were going on to headline the WCW Beach Blast PPV (7/11 in Gulfport, MS) with The Warrior & Sting vs. Sid Vicious & Big Van Vader, but they've apparently fallen through as Warrior will be working a tour of the Far East at that time. So at this point the main event planned is Sting & Davey Boy Smith vs. Sid & Vader.

(MAY 24) There may be some serious legal repercussions stemming from the WWS tour of Europe that included Jim Hellwig and others. Bob Ury, who put together the tour, was furious with the behavior of certain wrestlers which included him leaving the tour and going home after the fourth stop of a ten city tour. He claimed that his company will be pursuing both civil and criminal charges against two wrestlers including claiming that one wrestler (not Hellwig) physically extorted money. Ury claimed that Hellwig, despite his huge price tag, was not a draw, although several of the stops drew big money. Hellwig had to be the biggest draw because the only other wrestler who could have possibly been a draw on the tour was Jake Roberts. Hellwig was contracted for $135,000 for 18 shows over a three week period, although Ury claimed Hellwig ended up receiving $144,500 for 10 shows because he held up local promoters. Hellwig demanded and received $67,500 before he would get on the plane to Europe and another $35,000 upon arrival in Munich before he'd do the first show, then got $22,500 and $20,000 at two other stops on tour before going into the ring. Hellwig was also scheduled for an early July tour of the Far East, but was fired from the tour this past week because he kept changing and trying to continually up what the promoters claimed was an agreed upon deal for $50,000 for a two-week tour. Hellwig's attorney on Monday tried to get the deal put back together but at press time it looks like it won't be happening. That would free Hellwig to be available for the 7/11 WCW PPV show, but don't know if talks have re-opened regarding that or not.

(MAY 31) AAA wants to bring in Ultimate Warrior as a heel, but that is a whole lot easier said than done.

CONTROVERSY OVER CRUSH AND DOINK ANGLE

(FEBRUARY 1) Some negative mainstream press regarding the Doink/Crush angle in at least two newspapers this past week. The New York Daily News in a column by TV writer Bob Raissman wrote: "On the flip side of credibility, you have the kind of sleaze only the World Wrestling Federation is capable of generating. The toilet bowl Vince "Sir Swill" McMahon operates has no bottom. On Saturday's show, seen on Ch. 5, character Doink the Clown attacked wrestler Crush from behind with phony plaster cast. With paramedics placing a spine board under Crush's back, McMahon gushed about the possibility of Crush injuring his neck and vertebra. Considering the seriousness of recent injury suffered by Dennis Byrd, the script McMahon was working form could have been written only by an insensitive lowlife concerned only with exploiting the misery of others--and all in place to entertain your children." As a wrestling angle, I've seen far worse, but if you actually think about the Byrd injury on 11/30, the prominence of it in the new in New York, and the fact the angle was shot on 12/14, well, it doesn't say anything about what depths will be used that hasn't already been made clear in the past.

(FEBRUARY 8) After the negative press in the New York Daily News, the Crush-Doink angle was toned down on TV. No indication at either TV taping this past week or at Rumble that there even was an angle, and on television this past weekend they said that Crush was fine, the injury wasn't that bad and he'd be back in two weeks. Originally Crush was going to be held out for a long time.

VINCE MCMAHON GETS NEGATIVE PRESS

(FEBRUARY 1) Muscle Beach Newsletter awarded the same Mr. McMahon a partial award as the "Gluteus Maximus of the year. Writer Steve Neece (a former pro wrestler in the early 80s in the Stampede Wrestling circuit) wrote, "This leaves Vince McMahon and the (bodybuilding) supplement industry to battle it out for top honors. There is no doubt that the supplement industry has ripped off the public for hundreds of millions, if not billions of dollars this year by using advertising they knew to be false and dishonest. It is possible that some people may have damaged their health following some of the more crack-brained programs. This is in addition to the ill will it fosters in the public and their distrust that results from it that prevents truly worthwhile nutritional programs from being accepted by the public. Whether Vince McMahon has defrauded anybody through the WWF is debatable. The fans take their chances at the matches. He has ripped off his wrestlers big time and ruined many of their careers. Likewise, he has more than likely ruined the careers of most of the bodybuilders who joined the WBF and damaged the health of several of them with his poorly thought out agenda. It can be said that those that went to his shows and bought his magazine were taking their chances, but those that bought ICOPRO products were conned big-time." Actually there is more that is even nastier, but it's of a personal nature and revolves around unproven rumors and charges.

WCW STARTING FLORIDA TERRITORY

(MARCH 8) Wrestlers in Florida have been told that WCW plans to open a satellite territory with the NWA name, running four to six shows per week, starting in the summer with payoffs in the $100 to $150 per night range. WCW is also trying to increase its Florida syndication which lends credence to this. Don't know if this will be happening, only that wrestlers have been contacted and told about it.

WRESTLING MAGAZINES

(MARCH 8) Expect some shake-ups in the Pro Wrestling Illustrated family. Stanley Weston sold the company some months back to a Pennsylvania firm and the offices are scheduled to be moved from Rockville Centre, NY to a Philadelphia suburb in around April. Already Bob Smith has left for High Society magazine and Roy London has left to work as a WWF staff photographer.

(MARCH 22) The major staff of Wrestling Fury magazine will be based out of Indianapolis. A lot of the newsstand mags see this as an opportunity because of the uncertainty around London Publishing (so-called Apter-mags) over what will happen when the offices move to Pennsylvania in April and who will stay and who will go. An interesting note based on publishers statements for second class mail in the various mags is that Wrestling Main Event this past year apparently has surpassed Pro Wrestling Illustrated as the best selling non-single promotion vehicle magazine. WWF Mag is far and away and largest seller overall. PWI had just over 80,000 listed as its paid circulation, while WME was 89,000, although those figures can be misleading in comparison because the year-end issue if that figure for WME was of that (and the PWI figure definitely wasn't of the year-ender) usually sell far more than the regular monthly issues. WME had a huge increase over the past year to reach that figure while PWI had about a 10-15 percent drop. Most of the other newsstand mags took serious drops in 1992, many by more than 30 percent.

(APRIL 5) A clarification regarding the circulation figures listed here two weeks back for newsstand mags Pro Wrestling Illustrated and Wrestling Main Event. The figures listed for WME were basically worked and also misleading in that they counted issues that had yet to be returned from the newsstand when they listed circulation for the most recent issue at 80,000. The year average lists circulation at 50,000, but that isn't correct either because they only distribute 99,000 and selling 30 percent of distribution is considered extremely good in the newsstand game, so 30,000 to 35,000 is probably closer to accurate. PWI's year average circulation was 91,000 although the figure dropped by the end of the year to 83,000 out of 245,000 printed so circulation of PWI is probably double or slightly more than that of WME. In the more easily calculated subscription list, WME had 602 subscribers while PWI had 6,361 as of the most recent figures.

(APRIL 26) G.C. London Publishing, which puts out the most well-known non-singular promotion wrestling mags on the market, led by Pro Wrestling Illustrated, recently was sold to a Pennsylvania-based company and the move from the long-time headquarters in Rockville Centre, NY to a Philadelphia suburb of Ambler, PA is scheduled to take place this coming week. It was long talked about that the change in ownership and location would result in major changes in magazine content. While that may still occur, the three most well-known names on the editorial staff, Bill Apter, Craig Peters and Stu Sacks are all making the move to Pennsylvania. At least two others, Chris Bernucca and Andy Rodriguez, will continue to write freelance articles for the various magazine titles but will not be making the move or working full-time. Two others, Bob Smith and Roy London, had both left the company in recent months, with Smith now working for Wrestling Main Event, a competing magazine, while London has been working as a staff photographer for the World Wrestling Federation.

WWF IN JAPAN

(MARCH 8) WWF's presence in Japan will take a major turn for the worst over the next two months. Three things, all unrelated to one another, saw its television syndication (which ran Wrestling Challenge in late night spots in only a few small markets and not in Tokyo) announced as being dropped at the end of this month, WOWOW Channel, which broadcasted edited versions of the PPV shows announced Royal Rumble would be the last one it was doing and JVC, which distributed the videos, canceled its deal as well. It is believed another company may pick up the video deal because videos in general are so big. The general reasons for loss of interest was the lack of superstars in Japan that are in the WWF. WOWOW felt Hart vs. Ramon and Hart vs. Michaels meant nothing in Japan. Hogan's return could make the difference in regaining those deals because TV station managers all know Hulk Hogan, but since new schedules have already been announced, if it does happen, it'll take some time.

(JUNE 14) WWF has negotiated a deal with Kyodo-Tokyo, one of the biggest concert promotions companies in Japan, to run shows in Japan on its own. Kyodo-Tokyo has an affiliation with the WWF's local promoter in London, and is now doing market research on the Japanese wrestling market. It is believed Hogan won't work for the WWF in Japan because of his deal with New Japan, which would be a major blow since he'd be the one guy who could sell tickets. Undertaker and Bam Bam Bigelow would then become the biggest names because Bret Hart, Lex Luger and Shawn Michaels mean little in Japan. Also it has long been believed to be difficult to sell tickets without a Japanese babyface on top.

(OCTOBER 5) Tokyo Sports reported the WWF will do two or three shows in Japan in April, 1994 as part of a Far East tour. Vince McMahon was reported as saying that they wouldn't be working with a Japanese office, but would use Japanese wrestlers, and that he would be going to Japan for a press conference to make the announcement of the shows. It is believed they will all be indoor shows in 10-15,000 seat arenas

(NOVEMBER 22) It appears WAR and WWF have put back together their old working relationship. WWF Japanese rep Akio Sato was at the WAR 11/11 show at Korakuen Hall and announced that Tenryu, Great Kabuki and one other WAR wrestler will be appearing in the Royal Rumble. This is likely reciprocation for the WAR top wrestlers being booked on top when the WWF tours Japan in April.

(NOVEMBER 29) Atsushi Onita was invited to be in the Royal Rumble and will accept, so he'll join Tenryu and Kabuki, and in exchange it is expected Onita will appear on WWF cards in Japan next year. Randy Savage was a big hit at the WWF press conference last week in Tokyo, although the press conference announced nothing. Onita is filming a movie in January in Japan which could keep him from doing the Rumble, but is said to be working hard to free that weekend.

(DECEMBER 6) Atsushi Onita has already canceled his appearance in the Royal Rumble and has instead opted to appear on the ECW 12/26 card in Philadelphia.

BRUTUS BEEFCAKE DRAWS RATINGS

(MARCH 15) The return of Hulk Hogan, Ric Flair and Brutus Beefcake, surprisingly in the reverse order, has led some of the best wrestling television ratings since the early part of 1991. The 2/15 edition of Monday Night Raw aka the Doink the Clown show, headlined by the Brutus Beefcake vs. Ted DiBiase match scored a 3.3 rating, making it the seventh highest show on cable television during that week, the first time a regular wrestling show has occupied that slot (a few Clashes have) in recent memory. Ric Flair's return to WCW on 2/27 drew a 3.1 rating, the highest rating of a Saturday show in 13 months. Hogan's television return on the 2/22 Raw did a 3.0, which actually was surprisingly low to me since Raw has been close to that number for the previous several weeks and Hogan's return was heavily hyped and actually drew less viewers than the show the week before, but it's still good compared with the 1.7s and 1.8s that the show as Prime Time Wrestling was doing not all that money months back. There is no question Hogan and Flair returning to the organizations that are almost associated with their respective names has gotten a lot of people who had stopped watching wrestling back tuning in. While this hasn't led to any significant increase in box office revenue, more viewers should eventually lead to that. Hogan's first live appearance, on 3/8 in Charleston, SC, in a tag match with Brutus Beefcake vs. Beverly Brothers, which was announced to the local fans ahead of time because the advance before the announcement wasn't that good, did cause a major surge in attendance as the show drew 7,800 paid.

The challenge for both groups right now is to maintain the television viewing numbers of course, because it's only logical the return of the big names of the 80s would increase viewership for the short-term. More important is that they have to get new acts over big while the fans who have left are in the midst of the short-term regaining of interest. Hogan and Flair are not going to be around forever, nor will them just appearing on television garner the kind of interest in six months that it will today. However, both companies have their best chance to create new stars for the future in front of a larger than usual viewing audience because Hogan and Flair are back on. In the case of Titan, if Hogan becomes the focus of the show for the next six months and he then leaves in October if his TV series is picked up, Titan will be in worse shape next fall than it was this past fall. I can't imagine that mistake being made. I can imagine it being made in WCW, however.

STING AND VADER EXCHANGE WCW TITLE IN UK

(MARCH 22) Sting became WCW champion for the third time on 3/11 in London, England at Wembley Arena when he pinned Big Van Vader catching him with a powerslam as Vader came off the ropes in 16:00 of what was reported to us as a ****1/2 match. It was the first title change outside of the United States in the short history of the title, and it came before the largest crowd to see a WCW event since 1989 and by far the largest gate in company history. This may be a short-term title switch. The WCW British tour, which is continuing at press time, has been a major success along the lines of the recent WWF tours. The Wembley Arena show sold out (11,500 seats) while the next night in Birmingham drew 10,500 and Manchester drew a sellout 8,000. Tickets for the United Kingdom tour, which ended on 3/16 in Dublin, Ireland, ranged from 8 to 22.50 in pounds ($17.50 to $50) so the gates for the shows should have been in the $250,000 to $350,000 range. WCW's involvement with the New Japan Tokyo Dome shows have done gates well in excess of $3 million, however the largest gate of a WCW promoted show was about $190,000 for the Ric Flair vs. Terry Funk match at the 1989 Great American Bash in Baltimore.

(MARCH 29) The WCW heavyweight title switched back on 3/17 in Dublin, Northern Ireland before about 3,000 fans on the final night of the United Kingdom tour. Big Van Vader defeated Sting to begin his third title reign. We've got few details on the match, which from our reports indicate wasn't taped for television. The finish saw a referee bump and Harley Race interfering and hitting Sting with a foreign object leading to Vader scoring the pin with a power bomb. Sting had won the title from Vader just six days earlier at Wembley Arena in London. Don't expect this to be the end of it either. For reasons of which I'm not altogether sure of, there was less interest regarding these two title changes than any other title changes of what would be considered major world titles in recent memory. The title changes were mentioned, but only in passing, on the television show that aired on 3/20, which only will perpetuate this type of situation.

WILD FINISH TO RUSSIAN ROULETTE MATCH

(MARCH 29) The wildest finish of the weekend was for the Russian Roulette match between Kevin Sullivan and Brian Lee. They had a wheel with six choices, similar to the Spin the wheel match, and it ended up being a match where there were four poles put in the respective corners. On each pole was a box. Three boxes were empty, but the fourth box had a spike, and whoever got the spike could use it. Sullivan and Lee found the three empty boxes first, leaving the obvious box left as the one with the gimmick. Both were going for the final box when Night Stalker came down, but Tim Horner cut him off. At this point, with nobody else watching, The Tazmaniac, who hadn't appeared on television for this group yet, ran down and got into the box with the spike, took it and put the spike in a different box. As Lee climbed up to the fourth box, it was also empty, allowing Sullivan to go to the box that now had the spike and get it first. Lee kicked Kevin's hand so the spike was like a loose fumble with everyone going for it. Lee ended up with the spike, but at this point Tazmaniac handed Sullivan a fireball and Sullivan threw fire at Lee and he dropped the spike. Sullivan picked up the spike and used it and scored the pin.

MICHINOKU PRO WRESTLING DEBUT SHOW

(MARCH 29) Michinoku Pro Wrestling, Japan's first attempt at a regional promotion (they promote only on the far Northern Island of Japan based out of Iwate in small towns) ran its first show on 3/16 amidst incredible national publicity. All four television networks ran stories about the local family (it is being run by the family of the Great Sasuke) putting together a wrestling office and going to small towns with the show. Two TV stations are already working on documentaries on Sasuke (23-year-old Masanori Murakawa), one of wrestling's biggest flying daredevils, who the promotion is being built around. Mainstream media outlets really didn't understand the Lucha style with all the wrestlers wearing masks and working a different style then Japanese. They opened to a full house of 1,200 using foreigners El Signo, El Rudo, Rocky Santana, Blackman, Kendo and El Sagrado plus veteran Gran Hamada.

TERRORIST CLAIMS TO BE KILLER KOWALSKI

(APRIL 5) Someone planted a bomb in Australia and when he was arrested, he claimed he was the famous wrestler Killer Kowalski, and the Australian news agencies reported it as if it was the real Kowalski who had planted the bomb.

MARCO MORENO RESIGNS

(APRIL 19) Marco Moreno, the EMLL's booker, handed in his resignation on 4/7 amidst a tremendous amount of local media coverage. Moreno was made booker about nine months ago when Juan Herrera was replaced. Herrera is the new founder of the group PREDESA, and there are some who feel that group working as opposition to EMLL is really a work and that it's just to set up a promotion vs. promotion angle down the road. No reason was given for the change and no replacement was named. Moreno is the father-in-law of Ultimo Dragon. This change took place just three days after the 50th anniversary show at Arena Coliseo which turned into a major fiasco. The show was headlined by a tournament with 16 masked wrestlers in which the losers advance in the tourney and the ultimate loser must remove his mask. They advertised 18 wrestlers in advance, all Mexico City regulars including several big names. They would all be placed in a lottery and two men would be luckily eliminated before-hand while the other 16 would be in the tournament. Because several retired wrestlers were being brought back as part of in-ring festivities and it was such a major show, ringside tickets were raised to $50 and regular ticket prices were tripled. As it turned out, three of the advertised wrestlers weren't on the show which meant one wrestler had to be added, Rey Barbaro, who is a total no-name, and of course, he lost the tournament and his mask, revealing himself to be Manuel Oliveras, age 35. The newspapers ripped this as a fraud the next day and those who attended apparently felt like they were ripped-off big-time. Among the old-timers brought back were Bobby Bonales, El Padron, Rey Mendoza, Enrique Llanes, Juanito Diaz, Blue Demon and 93-year-old Vicky Aguilera, the most famous wrestling fan in Mexico and probably the world. All were given proclamations from EMLL head Chavo Lutteroth.

NWA SHOW DOES BIG BUSINESS

(APRIL 26) What was reported as one of the hottest indie shows of the year took place 4/17 in Minneapolis, drawing 750 fans for a show co-promoted by Pro Wrestling America and Dennis Coraluzzo of New Jersey (promoting under the National Wrestling Alliance banner). The show was highlighted by what I'm told were excellent matches with Road Warrior Hawk going to a double count out with Terry Funk in a match which contained almost nothing inside the ring, and Lightning Kid beating Sabu via DQ in a match filled with unique high-risk moves with Sabu being the most impressive on the show to an audience that had never seen him before. Among the moves he did were a Liger dive over the top with a mid-air flip, an Asai moonsault (technically called a quebrada) and an inventive move where he leaped over the top rope while Kid was on the apron into a sunset flip type of maneuver that ended up turning into a flying power bomb onto the floor. This show was largely raved about by those who saw it live with some even saying Kid vs. Sabu was the best match they had ever seen. Masa Saito from Japan and Chris Candido from New Jersey also worked the undercard which was comprised mainly of Minnesota-based talent. Ed Sharkey was planning on giving Wally Karbo an award at this show for his decades of contribution to the Midwestern wrestling scene, but with Karbo's recent passing away, the award was accepted by his son Steve. Coraluzzo is looking at putting together a return show, although no date was announced. It should also be noted that Hawk gave back $100 of his payoff to a fund to benefit the ill child that the show was planned as a fund-raiser for, which is only being mentioned here because nobody is supposed to know about it.

WWF SUMMER PLANS

(APRIL 26) Judging from interviews that started airing this weekend, it appears the WWF's summer plan is for the 6/13 PPV show from Dayton to be headlined by the first Hogan-Yokozuna title match plus the King of the Ring tournament. Summer Slam in late August, at a site that has yet to be announced (I don't think it will be European if only because 1994 Royal Rumble was scheduled for Europe although those plans may have fallen through) appears to be building toward a Hogan vs. Bret Hart main event. Hart cut an interview on the Raw that aired 4/19 on 4/12 talking about his hit list being Lex Luger, Yokozuna and Hogan, and also listed the same three names on a local syndicated interview that aired in this market over the weekend (which probably ran a week before it should have because in the interview promoting the Hart vs. Luger match in San Francisco, Hart talked about Luger's steel plate in his forearm which wasn't going to be acknowledged in the story line for another week). Unlike in WCW, in the WWF hints aren't dropped unless the plan is to get there. Despite what has been written here the past few weeks, if such a match were to take place at Summer Slam, the only logical ending I can see is a Hart victory. The screw-job where heels attack both and they clean house together burying the hatchet was done at the same show one year ago and would be a letdown if the same basic finish was done a second time. Hogan beating Hart makes no sense because it's doubtful the timing would be right for Hart to be able to elevate himself by losing as he did in last year's SS match with Davey Boy Smith. All the inside speculation I hear is that Hogan is unlikely to do a job for Hart which throws another monkey wrench into the plans, particularly since some behind-the-scenes maneuvering attempts are to elevate Brutus Beefcake ahead of both Bret Hart and Mr. Perfect on the babyface ladder as evidenced by the closing scene at Mania (which didn't air on PPV) with Hogan, Savage, Beefcake and Vince McMahon in the ring together.

(MAY 10) Updated info on King of the Ring and Summer Slam. The King of the Ring show from Dayton, OH on 6/13 will consist of the final eight men in the tournament, five of whom will be Jim Duggan, Bret Hart, Lex Luger, Bam Bam Bigelow and Razor Ramon. Based on house show happenings this past weekend, it appears that Ramon will either turn face at TV before this card, or at this card. Hulk Hogan vs. Yokozuna for the WWF title will headline, with both Brutus Beefcake and Jimmy Hart being in Hogan's corner and them hyping that after Hogan wins, Beefcake will cut Yokozuna's hair off. What will probably be the only two other matches on the show will be Shawn Michaels defending the Intercontinental title against Crush, and an eight-man tag team match with The Nasty Boys & Steiners vs. Money Inc. & Head Shrinkers. Summer Slam will be 8/30 in Detroit and it sure seems likely it'll be a Hogan vs. Hart main event for the title.

(JULY 26) The complete line-up for SummerSlam '93 at the Palace in Auburn Hills, MI on 8/30 will be Yokozuna vs. Lex Luger for the WWF title, Bret Hart vs. Jerry Lawler, Money Inc vs. Razor Ramon & 1-2-3 Kid, Shawn Michaels vs. Mr. Perfect for the Intercontinental title, Rick & Scott Steiner vs. Head Shrinkers for the WWF tag title, Undertaker vs. Giant Gonzalez in a Rest In Peace match (which should be explained in the next week or two on television), Doink I & II vs. Crush & Marty Janetty and Adam Bomb vs. Tito Santana. The other match listed, that has yet to be announced, is Tatanka & Sensational Sherri vs. Bam Bam Bigelow & Luna Vachon in a mixed tag, however Sherri was fired this past week and Luna has a broken wrist, so assume this will be a singles match with Tatanka vs. Bigelow when it's announced on television.

Satoru Sayama Does First Interview in Years

(April 26) Satoru Sayama (The original and legendary Tiger Mask) was on the cover doing an interview in this week's Gong, which is his first wrestling magazine interview in years. Sayama, who quit New Japan in 1983 and quit pro wrestling in 1985, was a forgotten figure in the wrestling world over the past few years but kind of underwent a re-birth in 1992 when a three-volume videotape package with his great matches in New Japan was released and sold millions of dollars worth to young fans who had heard about the legend but were too young to either see or save videotapes of his matches. It was somewhat known that some in New Japan wanted to book Sayama vs. Jushin Liger in Fukuoka Dome, but Sayama, now 35, never said anything about it. In his interview, Sayama said he'd be willing to work with New Japan as a trainer, but he's not a pro wrestler anymore, he's a shooter, and talked of training Koji Kanemoto to become the new Tiger Mask. Sayama said that he likes the current Japanese pro wrestling scene, which is a far cry from his interviews years back in martial arts magazines where he decried the business. He said that Kengo Kimura and Kuniaki Kobayashi had talked with him about returning to New Japan. He also wants the publicity among wrestling fans so he can promote his own shooting style group at Korakuen Hall to a larger audience (his shooting was drawing about 250 per show at Korakuen about two years back and may have disappeared since then since I've heard nothing about them).

Stan Hansen Wins Champion Carnival

(May 3) Stan Hansen captured the Champion Carnival tournament for 1993 by pinning Mitsuharu Misawa in the championship match on 4/21 at the Yokohama Bunka Gym. Hansen won in 20:26 after a power bomb to set up his shot at Misawa's Triple Crown on 5/21 in Sapporo. Since All Japan uses pretty much the same regular wrestlers on every tour, there is little sense of newness even though by and large this group has the stiffest and most realistic and exciting matches in the world. This tourney had some newness with the various upsets along the way, and it was reported to me that the many of the singles matches involving the top workers during this tournament were between four and five stars. Judging from the photos, the guys went past normal bounds to give memorable matches as bloody noses and busted lips were commonplace, and in some matches, in particular the Toshiaki Kawada vs. Kenta Kobashi match, both men came out of the match looking like boxers who had gone 15 rounds with swollen eyes and puffy lips. Hansen and Misawa each finished with 20 points and a 10-2 record in the round-robin to meet in the championship match. Hansen winning was considered a surprise by the majority of fans since they had figured since Hansen beat Misawa in the round-robin, it would be Misawa's turn to even the odds. There was the argument, and the winning one as it turned out to be, that Hansen gaining two consecutive wins would set him up for the logical title match for the next Budokan. The remainder of the standings were: 3. Terry Gordy (9-2-1, 19 points); 4. Steve Williams (9-2-1, 19 points); 5. Kawada (8-2-2, 18 points); 6. Akira Taue (8-3-1, 17 points); 7. Kobashi (5-5-2, 12 points); 8. Johnny Ace (4-8, 8 points); 9. The Patriot (3-8-1, 7 points); 10. Davey Boy Smith (3-9, 6 points); 11. Dan Kroffat (2-10, 4 points); 12. Doug Furnas (2-10, 4 points); 13. Jun Akiyama (0-12 all matches forfeited due to injury).

Kensuke Sasaki in WCW

(May 3) Greg Gagne appeared on World Wide television talking about how during sweeps on World Wide, each week they will have a title match with the computer picking the No. 1 contender for each belt. Then it was announced that the computer picked as the top contender for Dustin Rhodes' U.S. title, Kensuke Sasaki. Even giving not making any sense the broad latitude it needs in wrestling, this really makes no sense. Every fan knows Sasaki doesn't even wrestle for WCW and doesn't wrestle in the U.S. If they know who he is, it's even worse, since the wrestler Kensuke Sasaki doesn't presently even exist. Well, he will exist again since he's coming to WCW in late May under his real name.

(MAY 17) Kensuke Sasaki starts 5/11 and has dates with Rip Rogers, Rude and Maxx Payne leading to the PPV. Sasaki was advertised on all the "A" shows this past week although he wasn't scheduled to arrive until this week. On WCW Saturday night on 5/8 they announced that Sasaki was injured and hinted that Rude did it so Rude would be getting a title shot at Dustin Rhodes' U.S. belt on TV this weekend. Unbelievable lack of attention to details here. Sasaki is said to be injured so he can't appear on a television show that airs 5/15, but is working at all the houses starting 5/11. The only thing that makes it almost acceptable is so few people see the houses so they really don't expose that the angle is b.s. except to only their most loyal fans. Also on that same show in running down the house show, had the pix that ran the previous week so they were running down all the dates and cities that took place last week, although they did also run down events that haven't taken place as well. But TV right now has two major bright spots, the Flair for the Gold segments (second one without Barry Windham was even better than the first) and the tag team antics of the Hollywood Blonds who are the best tag team in the world both when it comes to work and also when it comes to personality. The improvement out of the ring in Steve Austin is tremendous. Although the Dos Hombres angle that aired this past weekend is an age-old deal, it was really entertaining in a campy way.

SAM MUCHNICK UNDERGOES HEART SURGERY

(MAY 10) Sam Muchnick, the last survivor from the original 1948 meeting which formed the National Wrestling Alliance and president of the organization during much of its heyday, underwent open heart surgery on 4/27 and remains hospitalized at press time in stable condition. Muchnick, 87, who promoted wrestling in St. Louis from 1943 through his retirement in 1982, and NWA president for more than two decades, was complaining of chest pains over the weekend and failed a stress test and doctors ordered an operation. He was found with 90 to 95 percent blockage in three arteries and 100 percent blockage in three others. The operation was said to have gone very well and he's expected to be out of the hospital toward the end of this week. Muchnick was for many years considered within the industry as the top promoter in the United States and along with Paul Boesch as the fairest payoff man. A roast had been planned in St. Louis for this coming weekend for Muchnick by Mike Lano and it hasn't been canceled. The roast, and things leading up to it, is a bizarre story in and of itself. Several major names in the industry including Lou Thesz, Nick Bockwinkel and Ted DiBiase are scheduled to appear and from our information will be there as will other major names. The roast, however, has been plagued by so much deception and dishonesty in its advertising, perhaps more in what was said to those asked to come as much as deception to the readers of the wrestling newsletters that plugged the event. So many names were listed as "invited" or even written up as coming unless there was a last-minute emergency before many had even been spoken with, let alone if there was even a remote chance of them coming. Some of the names listed as part of the organizing committee knew nothing of it until hearing from third parties their names were listed.

THE MOUNTIE

(MAY 10) WWF has sent word that they don't want Jacques Rougeau to use The Mountie name on indies, so he's being billed as Canadian Law & Order, formerly known as The Mountie. Apparently this stems from an attempt to look like they're not specifically targeting Kevin "Nailz" Wacholz, who is now being called The Convict instead of Nailz on indie shows for similar reasons.

WWF AND NJPW WORKING TOGETHER

(MAY 24) A minor note from Japan may turn out to be a major note here. It was announced that Masao "Tiger" Hattori will referee the Hogan-Yokozuna match in Dayton. Hattori was the same New Japan referee who did the Flair-Fujinami match in St. Petersburg in 1991. This means one of the following things: 1) It was a deal put together by Hogan to use a heel Japanese ref as a way for him to lose the title via screw-job since he just agreed to do a new movie over the summer which would limit house show appearances and then doesn't have to do a match with Bret Hart at Summer Slam; 2) It will be teased as a heel Japanese ref (in which case some emphasis needs to be put on this beforehand on television) to add a storyline to a match that needs a major storyline to go more than 7:00, but in the end Hogan wins; 3) It may the beginning of a business relationship between the two biggest money promotions in the world, New Japan and WWF, which, if it happens, would cut WCW out of a significant revenue stream and out of Japanese talent, which it never used correctly to begin with, and would enable Titan to use Great Muta, Jushin Liger, etc. on big shows. This scenario is feasible since there has to be some question about continuing the relationship with WCW when the only WCW name New Japan pushes is Sting, and the contract renewed on March 31, 1993 for one year has already technically been violated when Vader (WCW world champion) worked for a rival office in Japan. It should also be noted that Antonio Inoki and Vince McMahon Sr. had a long-time working agreement which dissolved under Junior in the mid-80s when Junior wanted to work with nobody. The WWF's recent business downswing has changed that attitude with working deals with USWA already in evidence.

HOWARD FINKEL

(MAY 24) On the 5/10 Raw, the car windshield that Michaels went through wasn't gimmicked. Actually it was Howard Finkel's car and they did a number on the car, unbeknownst ahead of time to Finkel. It was pretty much done as a practical joke on him.

(JUNE 14) Because they are taping television this coming Monday, Raw, the 6/14 Raw was taped on 6/7. Highlights were Marty Janetty and Doink the Clown doing a double count out, and a birthday celebration for Howard Finkel ending with Jerry Lawler putting Howard's face in the birthday cake. Poor guy, first they total his car, then they make fun of him when he's had an operation, then they put his face in a cake on his birthday. The next thing you know they'll send him down to Memphis and make him run around the ring in his underwear. Sorry, they already did that as well. Guess that's what being a team player is all about.

FLAIR FOR THE GOLD

(MAY 24) Flair for the Gold segment over the weekend with Brian Pillman & Steve Austin was nothing short of incredible. It's funny that these guys have shot past everyone to be the best tag team in the world and they were really just a makeshift team because Chris Benoit's negotiations to come in kept getting tangled.

JEFF JARRETT AND EDDIE MARLIN INJURED IN TRUCK ACCIDENT

(MAY 31) Jeff Jarrett and Eddie Marlin were injured in a truck accident at about 4 a.m. Sunday morning in Dickson, TN while driving from Jonesboro, AR, where they had worked on Saturday night, to Nashville. Apparently Marlin fell asleep at the wheel while driving the ring truck. Both the truck and ring were destroyed in the accident. Marlin and Jarrett were both hurt, although at press time we've heard conflicting reports on their condition. Jarrett is expected to be out of action this week, but other reports indicate it could be longer than that. The accident occurred apparently just a few miles away from the accident site on the same I-40 where manager Sam Bass was killed in the mid-70s.

(JUNE 7) Jeff Jarrett returned to action on 5/28 in Covington, TN after the truck accident a few days earlier. It was probably a little quick since he skipped the next night in Nashville but was scheduled to return for a mixed tag in Memphis on 5/31 where he could probably get by with minimal action. Jarrett was on television on 5/29 telling everyone to wear seat belts and crediting them for saving him, and saying that Eddie Marlin, who was driving the truck, was shaken up but should be back in a few weeks.

(JUNE 14) Eddie Marlin returned to television and they aired a photo of what remains of the truck he and Jeff Jarrett were riding in. From what I was told, from looking at the truck, Marlin and Jarrett are fortunate to be in one piece. Marlin said they had someone watching out for them or they wouldn't have made it.

JUAN HERRERA HIRED AS AAA BOOKER

(MAY 31) Former EMLL booker Juan Herrera was hired this past week as the new AAA booker. Herrera, Antonio Pena and Paco Alonso were the three men in charge when EMLL made its run a few years back and overtook the UWA as the major office in Mexico. There ended up being a three-way split in a sense as Pena left last year to form AAA, and Herrera was fired amidst allegations of improprieties. Just recently Herrera started his own promotion, PREDESA, which after a few weeks was obviously not going anywhere, and in a surprise, was named new booker. The expectations are that Herrera is going to bring with him Atlantis, Sultan Gargola, Canadian Vampire Casanova and possibly Rayo de Jalisco Jr. over the next few weeks and at press time Vampire was scheduled to debut on AAA's 5/28 card at Juan de la Barrera Gym. Emilio Charles Jr. was also on that list however he was at the last minute given the CMLL middleweight title which seems to have put his moving on hold.

WCW SAVING MONEY BY USING LOCAL DJs AS RING ANNOUNCERS

(MAY 31) In addition, they are no longer sending company ring announcers on the road and instead using local DJ's. While this is a savings of money, I've seen enough shows with local DJ's who often don't come across as professional, and often don't even know the names and the characters which gives the entire card an amateurish look. That's the reason they sent company ring announcers on the road in the first place, although it seems more and more obvious there is very little hope for or interest in the house show aspect of the business as it relates to this company. Truthfully, after five straight years of huge money losses on the road, maybe it's for the best.

CACTUS JACK

(JUNE 14) Several complaints were phoned into TBS about the first segment looking for Cactus Jack which aired Saturday. Catherine White was at a mental hospital where they said Cactus has been since the Vader match, but he had escaped without authorization. She interviewed a guy pretending to be Rain Man (the scriptwriter who came up with this trash) and a guy pretending to be Jack Nicholson from "One Flew Over the Cookoo's Nest" (an actor who does Nicholson impressions). The complaints were largely that the segment made fun of mentally ill people. My complaint is that they took an angle that people actually believed, and made sure everyone knew it was just another weekly wrestling angle. Cactus Jack himself underwent major knee surgery about two weeks back and shouldn't be back in the ring for at least six months, although we all know he'll be back a lot quicker than that.

MORALE DOWN IN WWF

(JUNE 14) Morale is way down since the crowds this past week were way down, including several shows that drew less than 1,000 in the Southeast. Since the new Face-to-face segment started, it led to morale being down since these segments are generally taped on Tuesdays, and sometimes run over to Wednesdays, at the offices in Stamford. The guys who live out of town, which most of them do, that do interviews, have what used to be days off having to do the countless localized interviews, which is the downside of doing town-specific promos. In addition, apparently the payoff for Raw is $150 per man, which some are complaining isn't even enough to cover expenses for a day in New York. The guys who work the road regularly and aren't being put over would have the most obvious complaints because they work New York for a relatively small payoff and then are seen doing a job on a widely-viewed television show.

(JUNE 28) Lots of morale problems regarding the "Face-to-face" segments for the same reasons discussed here a few weeks back. This past weekend, with no house shows booked on Sunday, the guys flew from their Saturday night show into New York for a day off Sunday, worked Poughkeepsie Monday for the $150 television payoff, and went to Stamford on Tuesday, so they were spending three days in the most expensive part of the country and earning $150 in total which doesn't come close to even paying expenses. Because the houses have actually fallen since introducing the "Face-to-face" segments that were supposed to increase attendance (I don't believe for a second the segments are causing attendance to drop, just that the forces causing it to drop aren't offset by the new segments) and it means another day away from home and with no expenses paid, one can sense the frustration. At the same time the advertising budgets for promoting the shows locally have been slashed as cost-saving measures which probably have some effect on the crowds being down, which means payoffs are down, which means more frustration since guys don't earn guaranteed money here. There are those who would consider leaving but the realities of the business don't allow it because WCW is no longer offering big money except to a few like Sid Vicious and Ric Flair so WCW isn't an option and there aren't enough spots in Japan, or enough weeks per year offered in most cases, to justify someone with large house payments going there, not to mention that for reasons having to do with talent, Japan is simply not an option to many.

PEGASUS KID WINS BOTSJ

(JUNE 21) Pegasus Kid (Chris Benoit) captured the New Japan Top of the Super Junior tournament which ended on 6/14 in Osaka by pinning El Samurai (Osamu Matsuda) in the finals. However the real story of the tournament is that the planned finish had to be changed because Jushin Liger, the world's showcase lighter weight wrestler, suffered a broken left foot on 6/12 in Chigasaki against Too Cold Scorpio. Liger is expected to be out of action for at least a few months. The "planned" finish no doubt would have had Liger, with six wins going in, beating Scorpio, with five wins. This would have left Liger and Pegasus tied with seven wins in the round-robin going into the finals in Osaka. Pegasus and Eddy Guerrero, both with six wins going in, wrestled the same night in Chigasaki with the winner being guaranteed a spot in the finals, with Kid winning. Since Liger beat Pegasus in their earlier match-up and given that Liger already holds the IWGP junior heavyweight title and the "correct" thing for this tournament to do is to create a new viable contender for him, probably Kid would have pinned Liger had the injury not taken place. That isn't a definite, but it would make the most sense. Generally things are done in New Japan based on what makes the most sense. The injury gave Scorpio a win he wasn't "supposed" to have and left Liger, Scorpio, Dean Malenko, El Samurai and Eddy Guerrero all tied with six points in second place. With Liger out of the picture, they had to add three previously unscheduled matches to the Osaka show, with Malenko making Guerrero submit to the Texas cloverleaf (similar to the scorpion deathlock), Samurai pinning Scorpio, and Samurai pinning Malenko with a huracanrana (similar to Frankensteiner). This put Samurai in the finals with Pegasus, and Pegasus got the pin winning the tournament with a power bomb off the top rope. The final tournament standings were: 1. Pegasus Kid (8-3); 2. Samurai (8-5); 3. Malenko (7-5); 4. Liger (6-4); 5. Guerrero and Scorpio (tied, both 6-5); 7. Norio Honaga and David Finlay (tied, both 5-5); 9. Lightning Kid (4-6); 10. Shinjiro Otani (2-8); 11. Masao Orihara (2-8). Planned standings probably would have been Kid or Liger first at 8-3 with the other in second at 7-4, then Malenko and Guerrero tied for third at 6-4 and Scorpio, Honaga and Finlay tied for fifth at 5-5.

JOHNNY B. BADD SITCOM

(JUNE 21) Atlanta Business Chronicle had an article about plans to create a TV sitcom called "The Main Event" which would star Johnny B. Badd. It's the idea of Sandra Glass, who came up with the idea by observing the characters who train as "Main Event Gym" (owned by Sting and Lex Luger) in Atlanta. The show idea has only reached the stage where a script for the pilot has been completed and they are shopping the script around, so odds against it actually getting on television at this point are astronomical.

ITALIAN STALLION BREAKS WORLD SPAGHETTI EATING RECORD

(JULY 12) Italian Stallion broke his old world spaghetti eating record on 6/26 in Princeton, WV. Stallion ate one pound of spaghetti in 17.2 seconds, breaking his old record of 21 seconds. This mark got a good deal of local publicity and will be in the next edition of the Guiness Book of World Records.

CARLOS COLON RETIRES

(JULY 19) Carlos Colon, 47, announced last week that he was going to retire from wrestling, with his final matches taking place 8/6 through 8/8 against Mr. Hughes, Kimala and Abdullah the Butcher respectively. Colon, long-time co-owner and top babyface for Capitol Sports Promotions (World Wrestling Council) had been for many years the most popular wrestler and biggest drawing card ever in Puerto Rico. Colon, who began wrestling in 1967, worked early in his career as a prelim wrestler in the old WWWF. In the mid-70s, he, along with several other Puerto Rican natives and Bob Marella (Gorilla Monsoon) put together the Capitol Sports office. In later years the company was owned by Colon, Jose Gonzales (Invader #1), Victor Jovica and Victor Quinones. In Colon and the company's heyday during the early 80s, running major stadium shows and drawing 25,000 to 35,000 fans was not unusual, and Colon in his prime probably ranked among the top five drawing cards in the world. Business took a tumble in the wake of the mysterious dressing room stabbing death of Bruiser Brody in 1988, and from that point on never came close to its former levels. Initially Colon was recognized as WWC world heavyweight champion, but in the early 80s the title's name was changed to Universal champion when the group joined the NWA and Ric Flair began defending the NWA title when it was still a touring world title. Colon's biggest rival was always Abdullah the Butcher, but he also traded the Universal title back-and-forth with the likes of Ox Baker, Dory Funk, Hercules Ayala, Ron Garvin, Steve Strong (DiSalvo) and Dick Murdoch among others.

(AUGUST 16) Another area legend, Carlitos Colon, 47, the biggest drawing card ever in Puerto Rico, had what was advertised as his final match ever on 8/8 at Bayamon Stadium, defeating Terry Funk as the main event of the 20th anniversary of the World Wrestling Council promotion. The promotion, and Colon's personal popularity peaked in the early 80s when he often drew crowds in excess of 25,000 for outdoor shows. Colon retired as Universal champion, with a three-night tournament held this weekend in Caguas, Ponce and Baymon to determine the new champion. Greg Valentine use the figure four leglock using the shinguard gimmick he had used years earlier in the WWF to beat Invader #1 in the finals on 8/8 of a tournament that included several international names like Mr. Hughes, Dan Kroffat, Johnny Ace, Warlord and Miguelito Perez. By the way, in a strange case of irony, the booker for the WWC right now is Buck Robley, who was one of Bruiser Brody's best friends.

WCW AMATEUR CHALLENGE

(JULY 26) How many of you gag every time Tony Schiavone brings up this WCW amateur challenge bit? For those who haven't seen it, WCW is telling its viewers that maybe they can be signed to a WCW wrestling contract and to send in a videotape to get the chance. But the tape should only consist of you doing an interview, not wrestling. If anything makes the product seem like schlock to a viewer it is telling them that someone can come off the street and do it and it only depends on how well they talk and that the ability to wrestle isn't even a criterion. The masses aren't going to pay money to see people do things that they either believe anyone could do, or that it doesn't require a special talent to do. Being a good wrestler does require both training and a special talent, although it seems that the people running this organization either want to change that, or simply aren't aware of it to begin with. Can you imagine the equivalent watching a broadcast of any other entertainment event, either sport or otherwise and have the announcers bring up a contest like that?

(AUGUST 16) In the world of wrestling talk shows on radio, several things are going on. Mike Tenay was already contacted by the Sports and Entertainment network due to the number of phone calls from wrestling fans to some of the affiliates. No deal has been worked out, but the Wrestling Insiders show will probably return in some form next month. It would be a good idea for those who listened to contact your local affiliate to ask them to put the show back on because the SEN plan appears to be to send out two feeds, one with a regular sports talk show and one with the wrestling show, and let the affiliate decide which feed to pick up. At this point when the affiliates are making the decision, phone calls and letters would probably be very effective.

WRESTLING INSIDERS RADIO SHOW CANCELED

(AUGUST 9) The Wrestling Insiders nationally syndicated radio show that aired Saturday nights on the Sports and Entertainment Network was abruptly canceled this past week. The show, hosted by Mike Tenay, was dumped Thursday night when Tom Bigby was hired as program consultant for the network. Bigby, who came from WIP in Philadelphia, had a negative image of wrestling and had been quoted about two weeks back in a trade paper when the announcement was made of his hiring that SEN would no longer cover "fringe" sports, which he stated to mean anything other than baseball, football, basketball and hockey. At that point the handwriting was on the wall for the show. People have asked about writing letters, and you can write Bigby c/o KVEG Radio in Las Vegas, but it seems the move to dump all fringe sports programming is part of his long-term plan so it doesn't seem like a letter writing campaign will have much effect, since the popularity of the program wasn't taken into account in the first place was the decision was made. Tenay is working on getting his show back on radio with a new syndication deal.

OLE ANDERSON VS NEWSLETTERS

(AUGUST 9) Ole Anderson completely lost it on the WCW 900 hotline two weeks ago in a tirade against newsletters. He wasn't quite as far gone as Bill Watts was, although he did challenge any newsletter writers to get in the ring with him for $10,000 saying that even though he's 50 he could still take all those skinny guys with skinny arms and skinny butts and thick glasses. I think he's been watching too many Razor Ramon interviews.

(AUGUST 16) There was an awful lot of discussion earlier this week regarding the Ole Anderson hotline segments. On 7/24, Anderson challenged any "rag writers" (who we presume to mean newsletter writers but considering his references to Miami, it seemed to also include Alex Marvez of the Herald) to get in the ring for $10,000, although during the segment he talked about it as reviving the "old challenge" which apparently in his youth in the Carolinas Anderson used to offer $10,000 to any mark who could beat him in 10:00 as a way to show wrestlers were real, although few people alive remember that or would know what the "old challenge" was. On that segment, Anderson appeared to have lost it, although not to the extent Bill Watts did in a similar situation near the end of his run, since it was embarrassing. On 7/31, after Mark Madden (Pro Wrestling Torch/Pittsburgh Post-Gazette) contacted WCW about accepting the challenge, Anderson cut a promo on the 300-pound Madden saying he was fatter than Haystacks Calhoun and that one of the McGuire Twins must still be alive (McGuire Twins were a pair of 750-pounders who I believe have both passed away that did some wrestling in the early 70s). Anderson was actually pretty funny on this one, and tried to work his promo toward drumming up a debate between himself and newsletter writers on the WCW hotline. Madden during the past week faxed WCW a letter asking for his check for $10,000 to get in the ring and Marvez wrote a column in the Herald about Madden accepting the challenge, going on the idea that Anderson, a Vice President with a Turner company, went on the Hotline challenging reporters who criticized him to get in the ring with him and get beaten up. On the 8/7 Hotline, Anderson said basically that he meant it all in fun.

(AUGUST 30) Pro Wrestling Torch columnist Mark Madden's ongoing saga with Ole Anderson hasn't completely died down. WCW attorney Michael Shapiro wrote Madden a letter claiming that Anderson's challenge wasn't given to a specific group and thus wasn't valid, although Madden claims the term Anderson used, "rag writers," is a very specific finite group that he's one of, and Madden wrote a goading column directed at Anderson that will likely be published this week or next.

WWF ROSTER CUTS PLANNED

(AUGUST 9) Major roster cuts will be made over the next few weeks. WWF will be cutting back to one house show per night with the final night of double shots being 8/15. Among the names who will be either cut, leaving, or receiving few dates and staying under contract but working mainly indies, are: Damian Demento (who finished up with Titan this past Sunday), Terry Taylor (who finishes up on 8/6 after the European tour and is likely headed to WCW as a television announcer teaming with Eric Bischoff on the second hour of WCW Saturday Night), Bob Backlund, Tito Santana, Mr. Fuji, Kimala, Giant Gonzalez, Virgil, Blake Beverly, Doink the Clown II (Steve Keirn), Papa Shango, Ted DiBiase (headed to Japan) and Jim Duggan (working part-time).

(SEPTEMBER 6) A lot of the wrestlers who were thought to be being let go are getting a reprieve because Titan is planning on re-starting "B" team shows as early as October. Unlike in the past, they won't be running split evenly balanced crews. All the major stars and angles will appear on loaded shows in major markets. Leftover guys will work WWF shows in 1,800 to 2,500 seat high school gyms with the local school boosters or local charities setting shows up as fund raisers with a 75-25 split.

RACISM IN WCW

(AUGUST 16) On 8/9 at Center Stage, they taped for WCW Saturday night shows airing 8/28 and 9/4. Before the taping they once again confiscated all pro-Tex Slashinger signs, and they also brought in a group of well-dressed female models to sit in the center in front of the camera along with some execs in suits because apparently those in charge don't like the idea of the show airing with so many black children's faces on camera. They are also auditioning for a female wrestling newscaster, and have hired Chris Cruise for Tony Gilliam's old spot doing magazine segments and local house show promos.

WWF TALENT RELOCATING

(AUGUST 16) Titan is wanting the guys to all move to the Northeast to cut down on transportation costs since they'll be basing much of the operation and television out of the Northeast. I was told Randy Savage moved to Connecticut "to set an example" for the rest of the guys, since he was flying in two to four days per week for television and doing a lot of PR work in the Northeast and flying in for that as well so it saves the company a bundle not flying him in so frequently. Was also told Savage has nothing to do with the booking and that Pat Patterson isn't retiring his post. At the same time, Steve Keirn did an interview in Wrestling Flyer saying he was offered a position as Savage's booking assistant when his spot as a wrestler was eliminated. Keirn said he turned it down and wants to revive his Skinner gimmick on independent shows.

VERNE GAGNE DECLARES BANKRUPTCY

(AUGUST 16) Former AWA President and long-time champion Verne Gagne declared bankruptcy on Friday in news that made mainstream media nationwide. Gagne, 67, filed in federal court in Minneapolis largely as protection against a $2 million real estate debt. Gagne got into trouble in a St. Louis Park office building he owned with son Greg and Mark Senn. The chief tenant in the building with Gagne's Minneapolis Boxing & Wrestling Club, which fell eight months behind in rent, and Senn sued Gagne since he personally guaranteed payments on the company's lease which had several years to run. Because he failed to make payments, the office building partnership fell behind in its mortgage payments to Norwest Bank of Minneapolis and the bank filed a $1 million lawsuit a few months ago against the managing partnership. Gagne's attorney stated that his potential liability in the two lawsuits exceeded $2 million, and forced him to file for bankruptcy as protection against the debt, which isn't the same thing as not having any money left to his name. Gagne, in the suit, claimed his only significant asset was his Eden Prairie, MN home worth $300,000, and documents he filed claimed assets of less than $500,000 and debts in excess of $1 million. Gagne came out of the University of Minnesota where he was a football star and a two-time NCAA wrestling champion in a collegiate career that saw him inducted into that sport's Hall-of-Fame. Packaged in his hometown Minneapolis as local All-American hero, Gagne became one of the top babyfaces when wrestling hit it big on the Dumont Network in the early 50s. By 1960, Gagne had a hand in the promotion in Minnesota and the environs and established his own AWA, breaking away from the NWA, in order to make himself world heavyweight champion. The AWA was a thriving promotion during most of the two decades where the title revolved around Gagne, and expanded as far West as Denver, and later San Francisco, North to Winnipeg and into the lucrative Chicago market. Gagne held the title on-and-off until a retirement match in 1981, but made comeback matches as late as 1986. The AWA slowly started going downhill, beginning in late 1983, when its biggest draw, Hulk Hogan, joined the WWF to begin a legendary run which changed the business. The organization finally folded, being unable to keep pace in a changing business, promoting its final show in the summer of 1990. His son Greg, who wrestled for the AWA from 1972 until the company went out of business, now works in the WCW front office.

THE SHOCKMASTER

(AUGUST 23) There isn't much to say about the Clash of Champions on 8/18. The card drew 8,903 fans to the Ocean Center in Daytona Beach, of which about 2,400 were paid. It would be the largest number of people in the building for a WCW show this year, although that's just because fans in the city were more receptive to using the freebies. Because the show was cut to two hours, most of the matches were very short. Nothing dragged because of the time constraints, but nothing had time to build into anything special either. The show did feature the most unintentionally funny and embarrassing moment in recent wrestling history. During the Flair for the Gold segment, Davey Boy Smith and Sting were to introduce their mystery partner for the War Games on 9/19 in Houston. Sting called him The Shack Master, and he came walking through the wall, tripped, and his mask fell off (Fred "Typhoon" Ottman). He had to put the mask on and stood there while Ole Anderson did the Black Scorpion voice for him. It was one of the biggest bloopers on live television in recent memory, and enough to give a marginal show a thumbs down. The surprise was the appearance of both Road Warriors together. Hawk made a last-minute deal to appear as Dustin Rhodes' mystery partner after the deal had seemingly fallen through a week earlier. During the interim, Animal was already contracted. Just a few weeks earlier, largely due to heat between the two of them, Animal no-showed the WWN debut show in Texas so it surprised a lot of people to see them together on the show. Animal won't be back in the ring until February, because that's when his payments stop from his Lloyd's of London disability policy. Apparently the team will reform at that time which is a major shock to a lot of people. WCW officials believe Hawk will start with the company toward the latter part of the year, which is a huge blow to WWN, which had planned to build the promotion around him as a single. Due to the Equalizer, the big pop the Warriors got for their return dissipated into nothing in just seconds. Apparently the wrestlers took the recent steroid test seriously, because the change in physiques in just a few weeks time in around half of the wrestlers who wrestled on the show was noticeable.

(AUGUST 30) If you listen back and turn the volume up high for Fred Ottman's amazing entrance at the Clash, you'll hear Flair, Sting, Sid and Smith all make comments like "Oh, god."

(SEPTEMBER 6) They are changing the Shock Master character to klutz Uncle Fred. They replayed his Clash entrance over and over, then must have aired an interview or something with him unmasking (you couldn't tell from being there live). On the 9/18 show, the main is Flair & Rhodes vs. Rude & Sid, ending when Flair had Rude in n the figure four and Harlem Heat interfered. Sting and Big Fred made the save, but Fred tripped over the guard rail and wiped himself and the rail out before he could actually make the save. During the show, several kids were kicked out of the taping because Big Fred was in the audience and they began chanting "Shock Master" at him. The middle section in front of the cameras was blocked off again for models and suits as part of the "no black kids in front of camera" idea. A lumberjack match was held with Charlie Norris vs. Maxx Payne ending when Shanghai Pierce's interference backfired and caused Payne to lose. Cactus Jack did a run-in attacking both Yoshi Kwan and Harley Race after a Kwan squash and 50-year-old Harley took a great bump out of the ring. Steamboat came out during an Orndorff squash, which wound up with Regal. The two attacked Steamboat with Bill Dundee's umbrella and left him laying, which airs the day before the PPV and probably will be part of the storyline leading to a change. Rhodes was also carried out when he went to save Sting from a double-team attack by Harlem Heat.

(SEPTEMBER 29) They also did a video on WCW Saturday Night this past weekend with Tony Schiavone

interviewing Shock Master in a restaurant, and Shock Master "accidentally" spilled a glass of water all over Schiavone. Overall the Saturday show was weak, with Rhodes-Rude deciding match being only **.
How they can keep airing that clip of Shock Master and expect him to draw buys as a main eventer in the War Games is beyond me.

(OCTOBER 11) An interview aired on television where Shock Master was surrounded by kids who called him Uncle Fred and he blew up a balloon which one of the kids had poured powder in, the balloon popped and he had powder all over his face.

JAKE ROBERTS AND EDDIE GILBERT NO-SHOW

(AUGUST 30) An indie show on 8/19 in Woodstown, NJ saw both participants in the Jake Roberts vs. Eddie Gilbert main event no-show to the dismay of the 500 fans in attendance. A snake was brought to the ring, brought in as a prop for Jake, and ended up going to the bathroom in the ring. That's the danger of using animals that haven't been smartened up to the business.

WWF SHOWS CANCELLED

(AUGUST 4) KPLR-TV, which has aired pro wrestling for a little over 34 years, is canceling the WWF Superstars show effective in a few weeks because of dwindling ratings and viewer complaints about the product. The station aired Sam Muchnick's wrestling show from 1959 until his retirement, and switched to WWF in late 1983--the first station to switch from the existing local promotion to WWF when the national expansion started.

(SEPTEMBER 27) Ch. 17 in Philadelphia was scheduled to dump World Wide, but instead dumped WWF Challenge even though it had higher ratings locally because WCW came back with a better offer than WWF to maintain the show.

PAUL VACHON

(SEPTEMBER 27) Paul "Butcher" Vachon, the younger brother of legendary Mad Dog Vachon and the father of Luna Vachon, is running for Canadian parliament as part of the New Democratic Party, a third party, which has no chance of winning a 10/25 election. You see on television all those election ads where the politician shows his wife and kids. Can you imagine Paul doing an ad showing his brother and his daughter and having them talk? Actually it would become a camp classic.

WWF MOST UNPOPULAR SPORT

(SEPTEMBER 27) After the Dallas-based Sports Management Group's annual survey of the most liked and most disliked sport in the United States found "WWF Wrestling" as the most unpopular sport in the country, Vince McMahon sent a letter to SMG requesting not to be a part of any future surveys. The SMG does bi-annual public opinion polls of sports' popularity and unpopularity for corporate executives who decide what sports to advertise in and what sports celebrities to build campaigns around. The 1991 survey, released just after the WWF did the Persian Gulf War angle also showed WWF No. 1 as most unpopular sport. McMahon wrote in a letter to the group, "We do not wish to be included in your survey because the WWF is not a sport. it is a unique brand of sports entertainment, but I'll reiterate, WWF wrestling is not a sport." For better or for worse, it's comments like this that have taken pro wrestling from getting minimal coverage in the newspapers to getting no coverage whatsoever as sports editors, most of whom don't like pro wrestling because of its obvious worked nature, can justify against the argument that it deserves coverage because of its popularity by saying the leading promoter himself even says that it isn't a sport. Many newspaper sports sections used the WWF's admission years ago in New Jersey that wrestling was pre-arranged entertainment as its reason to completely exclude all wrestling coverage from the sports pages. Of course, given the nature of what a lot of the coverage may have been over the past year, and more so over the next few months, that may not be in McMahon's worst interests.

There was no other pro wrestling promotion or type listed in the survey as sport, so whether those surveyed would have had similar feelings about pro wrestling in general, or it is about WWF in specific, is impossible to know. News wasn't all bad for WWF from the survey. Out of about 110 sports asked about, the WWF finished in the high 40's in terms of popularity. However, to show the weakness of the survey, WWF Wrestling in terms of popularity finished below "Roller Derby," which for all real purposes hasn't even existed since the mid-70s, and even more ridiculous, the survey showed that NBA basketball (No. 9) was less popular then sports like Women's figure skating (2), Women's gymnastics (3), Pairs figure skating (5), Men's figure skating (6), Ice Dancing (7) and Men's gymnastics (8), none of which can show any measurable signs of popularity even in the same stratosphere with WWF wrestling (with the exception of television ratings once every four years for the Olympics), let alone NBA basketball.

(SEPTEMBER 29) The Dallas-based Sports Management Group (SMG) came out with its annual survey of Most and Least Popular Sport in America. Out of about 110 sports surveyed, pro wrestling, which was called "WWF Wrestling" in the questionnaire came out as the Most Hated Sport in the country and 42nd most popular. Similar pre-1984 survey before wrestling so-called mainstream appeal showed it as one of the most disliked sports, but with much greater popularity.

LUDVIG BORGA CONTROVERSY

(SEPTEMBER 29) Some controversy involving Ludvig Borga (Tony Halme). Halme had told Titan months back that he needed October off for the New Japan tag tourney and it was agreed upon, but then he got his schedule which showed him booked the entire month. He was told they'd work things out with New Japan. Within wrestling circles this New Japan tour was much-talked about because Scott Norton would be on the same tour. Last year there was a bar fight between the two in Japan which only lasted three punches, all by Halme, although the story has since evolved that Norton was in no condition to fight, and as the story goes, the big rematch was going to happen sometime this tour. Ever since the fight, wrestlers everywhere have been a little apprehensive about wrestling Halme.

UFC DEBUTS

(OCTOBER 4) Yet another pay-per-view involving a few participants in pro wrestling, although definitely not a pro wrestling PPV will be taking place on 11/12, emanating from Denver. The show, put together by John Milius, the movie director whose credits include "Dirty Harry" and "Conan the Barbarian," will be called "The Ultimate Fighting Championship." The concept is to take a pro boxer, pro wrestler, sumo wrestler, judoka, karate and other martial arts fighters and put them into a one-night tournament, with the idea being to capitalize on the success of martial arts movies depicting the same type of anything goes fight to the finish tournament with men of different fighting styles.

The two names involved that have participated in pro wrestling are Ken Shamrock and Gerard Gordeau. Shamrock is listed in the bios as representing the sport of "shootfighting" rather than pro wrestling. He was a top-notch amateur wrestler and toughman contest winner before being trained by Nelson Royal for pro wrestling several years ago, works as Wayne Shamrock, the top foreigner for the Pancrase promotion in Japan which had its debut show this past Tuesday in Tokyo. Prior to that time Shamrock had worked for All Japan Pro Wrestling, and later switched to the old UWF, and then after the UWF split, worked the past few years for Pro Wrestling Fujiwara-Gumi. The press guide to the tournament lists him as having a 23-2 record, which I believe is actually his record in UWF and PWFG pro wrestling matches. Gordeau, from Amsterdam, is listed as the current world heavyweight champion in savate (foot-fighting). He's also listed as having a 27-4 record, although I have no idea what that entails as when he came to Japan in 1989 they gave him a record that back then included more than 70 fights. He also won a major kick-boxing tournament in Japan about two years back and another famous tournament before his lone UWF match, and was world ranked in judo. His only pro wrestling appearance was a main event match in 1989 on a major UWF card at the Ariake Coliseum in Tokyo, losing to Akira Maeda. The other participants are a 410-pound sumo wrestler from Hawaii who was the first non-Japanese to team with Japanese collegiate sumo championship, the World Kick Boxing Federation (WKBF) super heavyweight champion, the World Ju-Jitsu light heavyweight champion, a former World Kick Boxing Association super heavyweight champion (between WKBA, WKBF, ISKA and WKA, kick boxing seems to have more different organizations with world champions than pro wrestling), the IBF Cruiserweight boxing champ and the Sabaki (I have no idea what Sabaki is although with as many martial arts aficionados among the readership, that question should be answered in a week or two) heavyweight champion. The matches will be five, five-minute rounds fought in a circular pit with no ropes with matches being stopped by knockout, submission, throwing in the towel, unbreakable chokehold or doctor stopping. The only illegal moves are those affecting the eyes and groin, there is no point system and matches go into overtime if they last five rounds without a finish

(NOVEMBER 22) There's an old saying that it isn't the size of the dog in the fight, but the size of the fight in the dog. The 11/12 Ultimate Fighting Championship, a legalized street fight (everything goes but attacking the eyes and groin) involving champion martial artists from different sports emphasized that to the nth degree. The show was an amazing demonstration showing how someone of small stature with incredible technique could subdue much larger champions in combative sports. The event, which was obviously a shoot despite the fact any wrestling fans who didn't see it would question it by the fact that the promoter of the event's brother was the eventual winner. The show, which was a big deal in Denver because a local Tae Kwon Do champion, Patrick Smith, was part of it, drew 7,800 fans (although obviously with significant padding since the gate was $73,000) and thousands more on PPV. It was too early to get an accurate buy rate, although a Los Angeles Times story hyping the event said it needed an 0.5 to break even. The star of the show, and unequivocable convincing winner was a man with 13 inch arms who weighed 176 pounds, Jiu-Jitsu world champion from Brazil named Royce (pronounced Hoyce) Gracie. The fight showed more than anything that boxing and kick boxing because of the many rules that put limitations on defenses they're taught are, at least in this case, no match for a fighter who knows submissions. Ken Wayne Shamrock, the pro wrestler invited from Japan's Pancrase promotion, who lost in the semifinals to Gracie was clearly the only one who had a chance against him. Shamrock beat Pat Smith, the Tae Kwon Do fighter who had some ground fighting techniques but was obviously no match for him. Shamrock quickly took Smith down and started working on the mat in UWF style. In rapid order he got him in an achilles tendon submission hold. After the match Shamrock, who along with Gracie was obviously the most confident man on the show, was asked how fighting Smith compared to his Pancrase matches and said that Smith was much easier to beat then the guys in Japan because of their knowledge of submission maneuvers. The Shamrock-Gracie match was the semifinal, but everyone knew it was really be the championship match because it was obvious from early matches that Dutch savate expert Gerard Gordeau (who himself appeared doing a job for Akira Maeda in a 1989 UWF outdoor spectacular) couldn't match either man once they got on the ground. Shamrock, who trimmed down to 216 but looked like a bodybuilder, had 40 pounds on Gracie which, combined with his own awesome intensity and technique and far superior strength, had commentators (which included football legend Jim Brown and kick boxing legend Bill "Superfoot" Wallace) thinking he had a chance except one familiar with jiu-jitsu who said that once you are on the ground with a jui-jitsu expert, size nor strength is a factor. Shamrock took Gracie down first, but the calm Gracie reversed things and while Shamrock was working to take out the ankle, he left himself open for a choke, something shootfighters don't instinctively think to defend against, and that was it. Shamrock was going crazy in the locker room after (this wasn't on the PPV but from a source who was there) mad about not knowing how to defend against the choke and that being the difference. Gracie had an easier time beating Gordeau in the finals with a chokehold. Depending upon how PPV buys went, the decision will be made on whether to do a second PPV in April. What has been discussed is having another eight-man tournament but without Gracie, and having Gracie fight the winner later in the year, or putting Gracie back in but banning choking. The downside, as Pancrase is evidence of, is that a legit shoot doesn't last long. None of the matches lasted 5:00 and the brutality made UWFI look like a pillow-fight. Despite

Gracie winning with so much ease, and having never been defeated in mixed martial arts matches in Brazil that he's been frequently involved in, one still questions how he's be able to take down a 350-pound powerhouse with wrestling and street fighting skill and experience. Teila Tuli, the sumo wrestler billed at 425 pounds (who looked closer to 350), had his orbital bone broken in his eye and his teeth knocked out by Gordeau's kicks and punches. Gordeau, fighting without gloves, broke his hand on a punch to the eye of Tuli, but still beat a former World kick boxing champ Kevin Rosier, who clearly was blown up in his first match, in his semi.

AKIRA HOKUTO

(OCTOBER 11) Akira Hokuto missed the AJW show as she's still out of action after a broken bone in her back and a recent knee operation. The moral of the story is that All Japan women isn't strong enough to run big arenas for so-called major shows without hot line-ups. The previous three big shows that all either sold out or came close to selling out the big buildings had far stronger line-ups, which seems to be the key, rather than just simply pushing something as a big show. All Japan women have yet another major show on 10/9 at the Tokyo Bay NK Hall, which is the traditional "Wrestlemarinpiad" show, with Hokuto challenging for Aja Kong's World title in the main event. Hokuto at the Nagoya show did announce she was accepting the challenge of Rumi Kazama on 11/9 in Tokyo on an LLPW card in a hair vs. hair match. LLPW has come under much criticism for charging $143 for ringside for this show.

(DECEMBER 20) In a story that really has been somewhat well-known for months behind the scenes, Akira Hokuto of the All Japan Women's promotion, who has to be considered one of the five greatest workers in the history of women's wrestling, announced her retirement after winning the tag team tournament with partner Manami Toyota on 12/10 at Tokyo's Korakuen Hall. Hokuto, whose real name is Hisako Uno, had in her final year become one of the most popular wrestlers in the country because of her gutsy history of working with severe injuries and her ability to make matches dramatic that greatly exceeded almost any women wrestler in history. Hokuto, who turned 26 on July 13th, began wrestling under her real name in the summer of 1985 just before her 18th birthday. Although she started out very skinny, she was given a major push by 1988 where she held the world tag team titles with partner Mika Suzuki (now Suzuka Minami) as the Marine Wolves in the days where All Japan Women gave gimmicky names to all its babyface tag teams. Her career nearly ended at around that point when she took a tombstone piledriver off the middle rope from Yumi Ogura (a move that has since never been tried again in that promotion) and suffered a broken neck. The move was actually the finish of the second fall, however it what turned out to be the thing she was famous for years later, with the broken neck, she continued to work the entire third fall doing all the spots agreed upon beforehand even though it was obvious to everyone in the audience her neck had been severely broken. She was out of action for nearly one year, and came back with a Samurai Ninja type gimmick as a semi-heel as Akira Hokuto. The duo held the WWWA world tag titles from June 18, 1989, beating Bison Kimura & Grizzly Iwamoto, lost them one month later to Yumiko Hotta & Mitsuko Nishiwaki, before regaining them on February 7, 1990 from Iwamoto & Aja Kong. She also held the All-Pacific title on three occasions since 1991, vacating it the final time due to injuries. By 1990 she had pretty well established her reputation for being the best women's worker in the world, although by 1992, Kyoko Inoue and Manami Toyota had improved to the point where all three had a lot of supporters as to who really was the best. In 1993, her spirit became well-known throughout wrestling, even though it was nothing new, for working every night with severe injuries, although even a year or two earlier she was nicknamed the mummy because she was always taped up because of constant elbow and shoulder injuries because she continually did nightly high-risk moves rather than take it easy and let her injuries heal. Even though it was known for most of the year that she would be retiring, the promotion actually gave her the biggest push of her career and she was easily the most popular woman wrestler in the world, particularly after her legendary match at Dream Slam I against Shinobu Kandori. Hokuto will finish highly in both Japanese balloting and Observer balloting for Wrestler of the Year this year, a rarity for a woman. It is expected that a major retirement ceremony, as is the tradition for the top stars of the All Japan women's promotion, will take place for Hokuto on the March 27,

1994 show at the Yokohama Arena.

STEINERS AND DOINK SUSPENSIONS

(OCTOBER 11) The Steiners and Matt Borne worked the tapings even though they have been pulled from house shows. Steiners will be back on the road in the final days of October. The St. Louis Post-Dispatch ran a short on Doink the Clown being suspended and making fun of an apparent WWF policy of allowing wrestlers who are suspended to still wrestle on television, comparing it to the NHL's ludicrous policy of last season when players who were suspended had to serve their suspension time only on days when their team didn't have games. The funny part of the short is that it credited the Wrestling Observer with the item about Borne being suspended, when it was never reported here that such was the case. All I can report is that I've been given denials of Scott Steiner and Borne being suspended, even though it has been reported as such elsewhere (and in the case of Steiner, here initially, although it was retracted last week). The story gets more confusing since "high-ranking WWF officials" have been reported elsewhere as saying the recent suspensions (without any names given) should show everyone that the drug testing enforcement is legitimate. Anyway, if any wrestlers are suspended right now, they were working the television tapings this week, which seems to indicate this is a new policy. It can be justified in that if wrestlers are pulled from house show dates, that is where they make their money and a suspension costs them in the pocket book and is a legitimate punishment. Wrestlers for the most part only earn $150 for television tapings, which in the Northeast barely covers road expenses and in some cases with high-livers doesn't even cover that.

DWAYNE JOHNSON

(NOVEMBER 1) Both the New York Daily News and the Miami Herald (which was syndicated nationally on the Knight-Ridder service) ran stories about University of Miami defensive tackle Dwayne Johnson, talking about him being the son of long-time pro wrestler Rocky Johnson. The New York story didn't mention that he was the grandson of the late Chief Peter Maivia although it was emphasized in the Miami story. He claimed his uncles included Jimmy Snuka, The Head Shrinkers and the Wild Samoans, which I don't believe would actually be blood relatives as much as spiritual. Johnson, who is 6-5, 275, is a redshirt junior who splits time in a rotating foursome at DT and will likely someday end up in pro wrestling.

DAVE MELTZER ILLNESS

(DECEMBER 20) Anyway, here is the situation on me and before starting I want to thank all of you who called or wrote expressing concern. I was scheduled to leave for Japan on 12/1 until 12/11 to attend the six major shows in Tokyo during the week. I'd actually been sick for three weeks beforehand and couldn't shake it, although I didn't feel all that sick except for maybe two days during that period. On the evening of 11/21, I thought I was suffering from appendicitis, although never having had it, I didn't know what it felt like. Anyway, I was in the hospital the next day and they ran tests and I was told the tests didn't show any sign of appendicitis, although I was told that wasn't rare in appendicitis cases, and that if I didn't get better in a few days, to come back in. On Thanksgiving night, looking back, my appendix probably burst but I was at friend's houses and didn't want to say anything and basically was an idiot about the situation since I was in pretty severe pain. But I went home and when I woke up, I didn't feel that bad, which I'm now told isn't rare in those situations either. So five days later I was planning on going to Japan, because I felt only mildly sick and felt if I've got a mild flu, I could have it just as well in Japan as in the United States. The night before, not feeling bad at all, I checked my temperature (which had been hovering at about 99.5 to 100 the previous three weeks, enough to be sick but nothing to get concerned over). The fever was 102, which I actually didn't believe and took twice more because I didn't feel that bad, but it was enough to wake me up to reality and cancel the flight the next morning and reschedule it for two days later and see the doctor. The doctor said he thought I had a stomach flu and couldn't see any reason not to go to Japan in a few days, but then the blood test came back and they ordered me into emergency without telling me much other than my blood didn't look good, which is always thrilling to hear. What had happened was I was suffering from something that may have been peritonitis (I don't know the actual medical term) but I had a major league bad infection that had spread to somewhat of a dangerous degree and they rushed me into a hospital bed, hooked me up to IV's, started draining the infection from my stomach and for two days my temperature was at 104.5, which wasn't pleasant. I wound up spending 14 days in the hospital, totally bed-ridden for most of that time, and filled with tubes, being released two days before this is being mailed and losing about 15 pounds. I don't want anyone to make a big deal over this because after the first few days in the hospital, virtually everyone in there was in a lot worse shape than I was. Anyway, that's the end of this part of the story although I'm still going to need to undergo an appendix operation in about two months, but it'll probably be scheduled later in a week and it shouldn't affect publication because the operation is comparatively minor. I'm not 100 percent physically and probably won't be for a while. I've realized working on this issue just how much stamina it requires, which I never realized until I didn't have any. But I would think by next week when it comes to this newsletter, everything should be back on track for the next issue. Again, I want to thank all of you who called the hospital and left messages and everything because it could have been easy to get real down, and after the first few days I don't think I was ever that down.

MISAWA AND KOBASHI WIN WORLD STRONGEST LEAGUE

(DECEMBER 20) The biggest and most famous tournament of the year in wrestling is All Japan's World Strongest League tournament, which debuted in 1977 and has finished the final series of the year for the promotion ever since. In recent years the tournament has also traditionally been for both the PWF World & International tag team belts since the champions now vacate the belts on the first night of the tourney. Mitsuharu Misawa & Kenta Kobashi captured both sets of tag belts and the tournament by beating Toshiaki Kawada & Akira Taue in the finals before a sellout 16,300 fans on 12/3 at Tokyo Budokan Hall in what some are saying was the best men's tag match of the year. The dramatic finish saw Kobashi finally pin Kawada for the first time after several backdrop drivers in 23:24. The tournament itself came down to three teams going into the final night, the two in the final match and Giant Baba & Stan Hansen. All three teams had cleanly beaten everyone below them, and in the head-to-head matches to that point, Baba & Hansen did 30:00 draws against both Kawada & Taue and Misawa & Kobashi. While traditionally the company has a policy of protecting its legends (Dory Funk, Baba and Abdullah) by keeping them low on the card so as to not having them put in a position more than once or twice a year where they need to put someone over, it is more likely in this case that the tournament was booked this way with Ted DiBiase and Hansen's partner and when DiBiase went down with the neck injury, they didn't want to do anything that would make them have to start what had been carefully (and simplistically) booked and re-do everything. With a 4-0-2 record going into their final match (as opposed to Misawa & Kobashi and Taue & Kawada who were 5-0-1), Baba & Hansen needed and got a win in their match with Steve Williams & Big Bubba Rogers (Bossman) when Hansen pinned Rogers with a lariat. This left Misawa & Kobashi to face Taue & Kawada in a 30:00 time limit. If there was a draw, there would be a three-team playoff after the match, but in the case of a pin, the winner would take the tournament and the loser would fall to third place behind second place Baba & Hansen. Williams & Rogers wound up with a 4-3 record and in fourth place, while Danny Spivey & Johnny Ace, Dan Kroffat & Doug Furnas and The Patriot & The Eagle all were 2-5, losing to the top four and splitting against each other. Tracy Smothers & Richard Slinger, at 0-7, finished in last place.

RIOT IN SMW

(DECEMBER 20) A brawl between several spectators, security guards and wrestlers from Smoky Mountain wrestling on 12/10 in Wise, VA may turn into a major story because of fear that the NAACP may get involved and because in some circles it has been labeled a race riot. According to several live reports, there were actually two separate but connected incidents. During a 3-on-2 tag match with the Bruise Brothers facing Jimmy Del Rey, Killer Kyle (subbing for Tom Prichard who was at home during the week because of a family illness) & Jim Cornette, Cornette was doing the gimmick where he was afraid of the Bruise Brothers and was hiding behind a security guard. A second security guard told Cornette not to do it and Cornette and Del Rey both tried to tell the second security guard that it was part of the act, no doubt without actually saying those words. Anyway, the second security guard, who happened to be black, started arguing with Cornette. At one point one of the three heels was arguing with the security guy who put his finger in the guys face and the wrestler, either Cornette or Del Rey, apparently slapped the guy's finger and may have slapped the guy's nose as well. Moments later Cornette was still arguing and the Bruise Brothers whipped Del Rey into the guard rail, but instead Del Rey delivered a flying forearm to a security guard and the small brawl broke out, Cornette got in the ring to get pinned for the finish and they got out of there. Cornette went to the head of security about getting the guard thrown out, which is what happened. Later in the show, the second security guard came back with new clothes and a half-dozen friends. In addition, in the bleachers several members of the Clinch Valley Community College wrestling team had been heckling the heels all night calling them fake and challenging them to fight. The Battle Royal came down to Tracy Smothers, Del Rey, Kyle and Bobby Blaze. At this point Del Rey was thrown out and as he went by the bleachers, he was getting major league heckled by the wrestling team, some members of which were black and some of whom were white. Del Rey apparently did a Fred Sanford comedy gimmick challenging them to fight and several of the guys jumped down and surrounded him. The Bruise Brothers, who had just been eliminated, came running over and pushing led to shoving which led to punches. Most of the guys on the card wound up in the fray, including Smothers and Kyle who jumped out of the Battle Royal simultaneously. Both Ron Harris and ring announcer Brian Mathews claimed somebody had a knife, although police reports didn't incicate that. As the brawling got going, reportedly a lot of racial epithets were used by a few of the wrestlers, and there were reports of some used earlier in the show by Cornette (who was unable to be reached at press time) but others on the scene claimed Cornette did make racial remarks but it was only backstage. In an article in the Kingport Times-News, it reported fan David Dotson, who witnessed the melee saying Cornette started it by hurling a racial epithet at the second security guard, and after Cornette made the remark, another wrestler (Del Rey) knocked the security guard down. It wound up with the faces and heels brawling side-by-side to get to the heel dressing room. Some fans then went into the face dressing room but by this point units from four different local police departments had arrived to quell the situation. The police escorted all the wrestlers out of town. Wrestlers were asked about pressing charges that night by the police but decided against it. Since that time police have contacted SMW officials and there was fear about filing charges against a few of the wrestlers, since apparently one fan was hurt in the brawl, and of NAACP involvement because it was reported in some circles as a race riot, although those there say that would be a misnomer because wrestlers were fighting both white and black fans, although racial remarks were flowing during the fight which didn't help quell the situation. It is believed the end result of this situation is that SMW won't be running anymore shows in Wise, VA.

CHAPTER FORTY FIVE

INS AND OUTS

MAX MOON

(JANUARY 4) WWF: Max Moon (Tom Boric) was fired. Don't know if he was fired but contractually prohibited from working elsewhere (it's one thing if a guy quits to invoke the con-tract to keep them from going to the opposition but it's another when a guy is fired to use the term suspended to keep him from working) or he can do whatever he pleases, but he's a talented wrestler and WCW should try to use him. Remember that nobody has seen him as Paul Diamond in years since he wore a hood at Kato and Max Moon for so long. He's actually an unseen talented wrestler who hasn't been overexposed nationally, and there aren't too many around who fit that bill.

(JANUARY 20) WWF: Max Moon (Tom Boric) worked the first Monday Night Raw taping on 1/11, which shocked most of the wrestlers when they saw him in the building. Apparently the story behind all this is there was a personal problem between Boric and an-other wrestler and the other wrestler seemed to have been told that it was all settled and Boric was fired, but Boric was never told he was fired, but everyone assumed he was fired. Boric was pulled from all his dates both current and future, had his knee scoped, and missed the past two sets of television tapings with everyone under the assumption he was gone. Anyway, he was brought back to put Shawn Michaels over on television, and supposedly will be back on the road at least on some dates.

(JANUARY 25) WWF: Max Moon (Tom Boric) was brought back to take Lance Cassidy's dates, but they've obviously changed their mind about him since he was doing jobs for Skinner every night.

STEVEN REGAL, ROB VAN DAM & MAX PAIN

(JANUARY 15) WCW: Among the names being looked at to be brought in over the first quarter of 1992 are Steve Regal from England (I've never seen him but have heard he's a good wrestler, Rob Szatkowski (Rob Van Dam) and Max Pain (Darryl Peterson).

(JANUARY 20) WCW: Max Pain (Darryl Peterson) debuted on the TV that aired 1/16. Besides the Steam-boat-Rhodes U.S. title match, they also had Jack over Orndorff via DQ when Vader interfered and Barbarian made the save to set up a tag program. TV for 1/23 includes the debut of Robbie V (Rob Szatkowski) in an underdog challenge and heard he looked pretty good.

(FEBRUARY 1) WCW: Robbie V passed his try-out and I believe has been offered a one-year contract.

(JUNE 7) WCW: Robbie V is reportedly gone although that isn't confirmed, although I doubt many even realized he was here in the first place.

TERRY FUNK

(JANUARY 20) WCW: Terry Funk backed out early last week. He had agreed originally to start in the cage match at the Clash as the original replacement for Van Hammer. Apparently he was offered a short-term deal and decided that if they were to make him look so bad by the way they edited the I Quit match, that if he was only there for a short time, his main role would be to put others over and they'd make him look bad again. Give WCW credit for taping the angle where Cactus Jack turned heel on 1/6 and getting it on the air four days later, in time for everyone to see Jack's turn before the Clash.

(SEPTEMBER 27) WWF: Pat Tanaka will be returning probably this week and Terry Funk was talked with about coming in but that's not a definite. Johnny Gunn has a November try-out scheduled and a Northeastern indie called The Condor (said to be a green muscle-head) will also get a try-out soon.

THE BRITISH BULLDOG

(JANUARY 20) WCW: At one point Davey Boy Smith was scheduled to debut at the Clash, but problems in negotiating a contract release from Titan to work here have postponed his debut but it's a pretty sure bet he'll be in as soon as things are worked out. Apparently he's agreed to work 100 dates during 1992, presumably for $100,000, and they'll cut a separate deal for the European tour(s) where he should mean a lot at the box office.

(JANUARY 25) WCW: Jim Ross reported on the 900 number that the Davey Boy Smith deal could be closed within this week. Our reports are that Smith will debut on 2/16. Apparently WWF has sent Smith a letter saying that he can't use the name British Bulldog or Davey Boy Smith until October.

(JANUARY 25) AJPW: Davey Boy Smith was originally set to debut, but it appears those negotiations have fallen apart. All Japan sources say Smith was offered the same money he was earning when he left Japan for WWF a few years back (between $4,500 and $6,000 per week) and Smith wanted a raise. Supposedly the promotion felt that Smith had become a worse wrestler since he left, not a better wrestler. Anyway, it now looks like Smith will work for UWFI in Japan, which on the surface seems like a bad move. There is more short-term money in UWFI because they'll pay more, although I don't know that Takada vs. Smith is a match "shoot" fans will be interested in. But there isn't the long-term money there because once he finishes his program with Takada, there really isn't much that can be done with him.

EDDIE GILBERT

(JANUARY 20) WCW: Eddie Gilbert's name has been bandied about, perhaps as a manager, although as far as I know no deal has been reached nor is there a starting date, just a lot of rumors and Gilbert has had at least one meeting.

(JANUARY 25) WCW: More talk of Eddie Gilbert coming in but nothing is confirmed other than the name has been talked about in more serious tones than in a long time.

RON SIMMONS

(JANUARY 20) WCW: Ron Simmons worked the house shows this past weekend, but missed the 1/11 television taping that he was originally scheduled to appear on. Presumably the 1/13 angle will "injure" him and he'll be kept out. His contract expires in just a few weeks and who knows what decision will be made. Simmons was reportedly fined $2,000 for missing Charlotte and Philadelphia and has clearly been in the doghouse ever since, which shows how fortunes can turn in this business, because in August he was going to turn the company around.

PAUL ORNDORFF

(JANUARY 20) WCW: Paul Orndorff also signed a one-year contract this past week. He'll finish up with Smoky Mountain on 1/17, and work full-time with WCW, picking up Rick Rude's dates, from that point forward.

MADUSA

(JANUARY 20) WCW: Madusa is definitely gone. Don't know details. I know she wanted to wrestle and the company didn't have ideas in that direction. This is purely speculation, but it would make all the sense in the world, for Madusa to go to WWF and manage Shawn Michaels and feud with Sherri.

(JANUARY 25) WCW: While the differences are said not to be irreconcilable, Madusa is gone now. Basic problem is the difference between the old contracts and new contracts when it comes to medical coverage being removed and the percentage of the money being held back until the review period, Madusa wanted to be more aggressively marketed which I guess the company didn't want to focus on her strongly enough in that way, and also, apparently she wants to wrestle.

SAPPHIRE

(JANUARY 25) USWA: The latest WWF superstar to come into Memphis this week was Sapphire (Juanita Wright). Actually, Honkytonk Man was advertised this week on some spot shows so it looks like he's coming in which is something of a surprise. Anyway, Sapphire was brought in by Bert Prentice who asked her if she used to be married to a man named Bubba Johnson. If you recall, Prentice has been claiming that Bubba Johnson is the real name of Miss Texas, who had a sex change opera-tion. Anyway, Sapphire said she used to be married to Bubba Johnson. Jerry Lawler than came out and brought out who he said Prentice was claiming to be Bubba Johnson, and Miss Texas came out. At that point Sapphire started hitting Prentice saying, "I wasn't married to no women. I'm not gay." At this point both Leslie Belanger and Lauren Davenport jumped Sapphire until Miss Texas made the save. Last week Belanger and Davenport were feuding over Mike Miller, but Miller did an interview and said that both women can be his valets, so that's where that stands.

MARTY JANNETTY

(FEBRUARY 1) WWF: Marty Janetty was fired or suspended which is why Tatanka started his program with Michaels. Max Moon, who had no bookings in the near future, will take Janetty's place on the immediate house shows although Tatanka will over the long range. Sherri never appeared on television so it isn't clear what her role is going to be with Janetty out of the picture. Janetty was on real-life probation for his resisting arrest and possession arrest in Florida last January. I guess this can be called one of those unprofessional conduct deals, and that description is probably pretty accurate.

(FEBRUARY 15) WWF: Marty Janetty was fired because at the San Jose tapings, he was asleep in the dressing room. He claimed he was sleeping, but apparently others felt it was more like passed out. There is some heat among the wrestlers on Ray Stevens, who reported it, because of the belief that Stevens was once a wrestler and all the boys should stick together.

SID VICIOUS

(FEBRUARY 1) WWF: Sid Eudy got his release from Titan Sports this past Friday, which makes me think he'll be in WCW before too much longer. Either way, he's now a free agent and free to take independent dates as well.

(FEBRUARY 22) WCW: I believe WCW send Sid Eudy (Justice/Vicious) a contract this past week. Ole Anderson had been negotiating with Sid regularly for quite a while. Sid just received his WWF release and his Wrestlemania payoff. One of the clauses Eudy wanted in his WCW contract was to not include any provisions regarding Japan. He doesn't want WCW to be able to send him to Japan and wants to make his own separate deal if he wants to work Japan. There were negotiations with All Japan but he asked for $8,000 per week and they offered quite a bit less.

(MARCH 1) WCW: Sid Vicious has a meeting scheduled with Ole Anderson for later this week to try and complete a deal.

(MARCH 8) WCW: Sid (Justice/Vicious) Eudy was in Atlanta on Friday and met with Ole Anderson. Eudy came out of the meeting expecting that he'll be getting an old-style WCW contract with guaranteed money and complete medical benefits including getting paid in full if injured. No deal has been signed, but most feel at this point it is inevitable.

(SEPTEMBER 13) WCW: Biggest news of the past week is that Sid Vicious walked out on 9/1 in Dothan, AL at a television taping, although at press time it appears everything was worked out. Vicious, according to several on site sources, refused to take a drug test (he had missed the mandatory drug test some weeks back because WCW had scheduled him for a public appearance) and said he'd take in a few weeks. Apparently he was told that he'd put it off long enough and if he didn't take it then, he'd be fired, and before being fired, he instead walked out. If it hadn't have been rectified, it would have been a disaster since Vicious was all over the pre-taped television and scheduled for the main event on the next two PPV shows (War Games and a singles main event against Sting at Halloween Havoc) that have already had ad slicks sent to the cable companies.

JOHNNY B. BADD

(FEBRUARY 8) WCW: Johnny B. Badd's WCW contract expires in a few weeks. JBB was on a $156,000 guarantee for his one year deal, and was offered $350 guaranteed plus $150 potential bonus money per event with a 200-event guarantee by Watts. Odds are very good he'll be in the WWF in March with a new name but the same gimmick. He came close to going to WWF last year but it was a little too much money guaranteed on paper at that time to turn down.

(MARCH 1) WCW: Johnny B. Badd had a contract meeting with Bill Shaw, but no deal has been completed and the lines of communication are still open with Titan.

(MARCH 8) WCW: Don't know this as a fact, but presume with his new push and the fact he's working with the bad elbow, that Johnny B. Badd signed a new deal. Badd's television match with Chris Benoit (gone to Australia, then Japan, not certain when/if he'll re-turn) that aired Sunday as JB's best match I've seen to date. It was better than the Steamboat-Windham match which followed.

(MARCH 15) WCW: I believe Johnny B. Badd did sign a new one-year contract although don't have it confirmed. Apparently Badd's main concern was to own rights to use the Johnny B. Badd name in acting endeavors since he's taking acting lessons.

(MARCH 29) WCW: Despite what we reported, Johnny B. Badd hasn't signed.

(APRIL 5) WCW: Johnny B. Badd's contract expires at the end of the month and he's been continuing dialogue with Titan Sports.

(APRIL 12) WCW: Johnny B. Badd did agree to terms for a new contract which reportedly guarantees him $500 per match and a minimum of 200 matches per year, plus a $50,000 sign-ing bonus and a $31,000 wardrobe bonus. Titan had made a major play for him and were still pursuing him as late as this past weekend.

DIAMOND DALLAS PAGE

(FEBRUARY 8) WCW: Dallas Page's contract also expired and he was offered $300 per night with no guarantee as far as the number of dates and Page turned it down because the job offers no way of knowing how much you'll earn without at least a number of dates guaranteed. Page is out with an injury and rumor has it will approach Smoky Mountain when he's healed up.

THE BERZERKER

(MARCH 8) WWF: Add Berzerker (John Nord) to the list of departed. Not sure if he's gone or on temporary leave but he has cut his hair and has gotten a job selling cars in Minnesota.

SEVERAL NEW WWF SIGNINGS

(MARCH 15) WCW: Ron & Don Harris debuted at the 3/8 Center Stage tapings as The Bruise Brothers, Ron & Don, and appear to be groomed to work a program with Keith & Kent Cole. I'm told their matches consisted largely of bearhugs so they didn't look as good as they do with the brawling Memphis style.

(MARCH 22) WWF: Several new faces expected in at or after Wrestlemania. Luna Vachon will start, most likely as a valet for Shawn Michaels, to feud with Sensational Sherri. Luna shaved her head and is being given a new set of extensions for her role as a bizarro type. Bryan Clark, who works SMW as Night Stalker, was the most impressive of the try-outs in the eyes of those who make decisions, and was offered a spot, alt-hough he'll be filling out his SMW commitments until that time. He was scheduled this week to get his new name, costuming, etc. In addition, Kip Sopp and Mike Polchlopec, who worked as the Long Riders for Eddy Mansfield (Kip Winchester & Brett Colt), will start after Mania doing a cowboy tag team gimmick. Mr. Hughes, wearing the sunglasses and suit, got a try-out on 3/9 in Augusta, GA, as did a boxing Turtles tag team and Mike Shaw.

(MARCH 29) WWF: Night Stalker was supposed to fly up this week and get his new gimmick. There was talk, but not finalized, of him doing a Vampire gimmick. I wonder where that idea came from?

(APRIL 5) WWF: Add Mike Shaw and Ron & Don Harris to the list of those who have been offered contracts of late. Assume Shaw will sign, as there is nowhere better for him to go, and Harris Brothers have already signed after jumping from WCW after just a week or so.

(APRIL 12) WWF: Debuting at TV 4/5 in Phoenix were The Mad Monk (Mike Shaw), who immediately was put into a program with Typhoon as he attacked him with a wooden staph, The Smoking Guns (Long Riders from IWF doing a cowboy tag team gimmick), Ron & Don Harris and Mr. Hughes (who worked several televised matches so he got the job). Working dark matches were Butch Beardon (who may have been Night Stalker), Lightning Kid (who did a job for Louie Spicolli in a non-televised match) and a guy named Tex Deaton (who did a job for Brooklyn Brawler, but who is definitely not Joel Deaton).

(APRIL 19) WWF: Mike Shaw debuted on television as a babyface called Friar Ferguson. He had ear-lier in the week worked the television tapings on Monday as a heel called The Mad Monk, but at the Tuesday taping was turned face because there was fear of heat from religious groups. The gimmick came off really lame.

(MAY 3) WWF: Ron & Don Harris failed their audition here and seemingly burned their bridge with WCW, so it looks like they're back in the indies.

(MAY 5) WWF: Several newcomers were at the television tapings on 5/4 in Worcester, MA and 5/5 in Portland, ME. Among them were Johnny Polo (Scotty Flamingo) as a heel man-ager from a rich California family who is managing Atom Bomb (Bryan "Night Stalker" Clark) from Three Mile Island, who wears goggles and black rubber gloves to the ring. They show footage when Bomb comes to the ring. Also getting try-outs included Big City Mike, who works New England indies as Man Mountain Mike (Rick Martello), a 465-pounder reminiscent of Rochester Roadlock, Tazmaniac, Colin Scott, a former NFL lineman from Australia and the Harlem Knights as a babyface rapper tag team. Knights were pushed as if they were in. They debuted a segment on Challenge called "The King's Court" with Jerry Lawler and Scott was his first guest and they ended up in the ring with Scott cleaning house on Lawler, and looking terrible in doing so. Scott is said to be about 6-7 but he's never been in a ring before, similar to Kevin Nash when WCW tried to debut him on a live Clash. Do I see Jim Ross' fingerprints? Friar Ferguson was nowhere to be seen and word is that gimmick has been scrapped but they may use Mike Shaw with a new gimmick. It was one of the worst gimmicks in memory.

(JUNE 28) WWF: Bastion Booger debuted on television losing to Virgil. He'll win this week's re-match. I don't know who Mike Shaw lost a bet to or who he screwed over in an-other lifetime to have to wear that costume and get his hair cut like that.

(JULY 19) WWF: Several newcomers debuted at the tapings on 7/6 in Wilkes-Barre, PA and 7/7 in Salisbury, MD. The biggest push was to a 320-pound heel named Ludwig Borge (New Japan's Tony Halme), doing an aryan (but from Finland rather than Germany) anti-American gimmick. They handed out little American flags before the tapings and seemingly are going to push the American patriot vs. Foreign menace angle as the backbone of the promotion once again. Nikolai Volkoff was back as the Soviet-American babyface. A new tag team called The Quebecians was brought in as heels, billed as Jacques & Pierre, wearing Mountie-like outfits. Jacques is former Mountie Jacques Rougeau, while Pierre is Pierre Ouellet, a 280-pounder from St. Catherines, Quebec, who has had few if any matches and was really green. Rex King & Steve Doll got a push as a heel tag team called "Well Done." King's new ring name is Tim Dunn, while Doll's is Steve Well. The two already have done a television job for the Smoking Gunns so they look to be in the Beverly Brothers old slot.

THE BIG BOSSMAN

(MARCH 29) AJPW: Biggest news from the promotion, unconfirmed, is that Ray Traylor (Big Bossman) has signed as a regular. Traylor definitely has negotiated of late with both All Japan and New Japan, so it looks as though his WWF stint is winding to a close. If Traylor does come in, he won't be using the Bossman gimmick and will instead revert back to his former ring name of Big Bubba Rogers.

(MAY 24) AJPW: Big Bossman's working this tour was canceled. He was going to work as Big Bub-ba Rogers, his pre-WWF ring name that he used with this group and NWA several years back. No reason was given, but the assumption is that All Japan only wants to bring in foreigners that they can use as regulars, and Bossman decided not to sever ties with Titan so All Japan probably had no interest in using him.

REPO MAN

(APRIL 5) WWF: Repo Man (Barry Darsow) finished up this past weekend and will be doing indies and apparently is getting into selling car alarms which is kind of humorous given his character.

DUTCH MANTELL

(APRIL 5) WWF: With the Bruise Brothers already bolting for WWF, Dutch Mantell's shot at coming in (they had talked about making him their manager) went out the window. There had been talk of him doing color, but the "he's too country" forces won out over the "he's a good commentator" forces.

(JULY 19) USWA: Dutch Mantell was scheduled to start with USWA on 7/5, but that morning he received a phone call from both Lawler and Jerry Jarrett telling him that he wasn't needed and all future dates were canceled. At the arena they announced Mantell lost his match via forfeit. Lawler was furious at Mantell for appearing on 7/3 on the Wrestling Insiders radio show, which airs in Memphis, and talking about Christopher as Lawler's son. Jarrett was also mad about Mantell appearing on the Real Wrestling Hotline with people like myself and claimed Dutch was "exposing the business" by doing Mike Tenay's radio show and doing his "Ring of Dreams" camp. This qualifies Lawler and Jarrett as two of the biggest hypocrites in wrestling. Lawler has done Wade Keller's radio show and been interviewed in several newsletters, while Jarrett himself was recently interviewed in Keller's Pro Wrestling Torch newsletter and were as much if not more open in those interviews than Man-tell was on the radio show, not to mention Jarrett's business relationship with a company (Titan) that has testified before state legislatures around the country that pro wrestling was pre-determined entertainment. The term protecting the business has been obsolete for a while, but those who throw that term around shouldn't be living in glass caves. Besides, does anything publicly "expose the business" more than Jerry Lawler's heel character on one television show and face character on an-other simultaneously, praising people on one show that he feuds with on another.

(JULY 26) USWA: A clarification from last week's story regarding Dutch Mantell being fired. Jerry Lawler never phoned up Mantell to fire him. Jerry Jarrett called Mantell up to fire him and Mantell called Jarrett back and asked for a reason and Jarrett apparently said it was because Lawler was upset about him doing Mike Tenay's radio show the previous Saturday and in the course of the conversation it came out that Brian Christopher was Jerry's son. Lawler later claimed that he wasn't even listening to the show and that had nothing to do with Mantell being let go, and that he had nothing to do with the booking since Jarrett is handling the booking. Lawler claimed it was because Mantell hadn't bought the burro which was the gimmick Jarrett wanted him to bring to the ring as the Lost Dutchman or something of the sort. As far as the hypocrite label, that's still pretty well deserved based on Lawler blaming others for exposing the business when his own company's business prac-tices and his own heel/face on different television shows do that more than any radio show possibly could.

TULLY BLANCHARD

(APRIL 5) WCW: Among the plans for Slamboree is a reunion of the Original Four Horseman (Ole Anderson, Flair, Arn Anderson and Tully Blanchard). Blanchard, 39, who has been working as a preacher since retiring from wrestling three years ago, has made noises about wanting to come back although to say that anything more than prelim-inary feelers have been sent would be premature.

(APRIL 19) WCW: Tully Blanchard reached an agreement to come in, with his first appearance being at Slamboree which will lead to working house shows in June. I believe Blanchard will re-form his tag team with Arn Anderson as babyfaces. Blanchard, who had been working as a preacher since retiring from wrestling in 1990, had said numerous times that he wouldn't return to wrestling and had been critical of the profession in some newspaper interviews.

(APRIL 26) WCW: I don't believe a deal is completed with Tully Blanchard but negotiations are underway. Supposedly he's being offered a $500 per night deal and he's looking for an old-fashioned yearly contract.

(MAY 10) WCW: Latest on Tully Blanchard this week is that he's not coming in because he's mad that he was offered less money than Johnny B. Badd and Jim Neidhart were given and less than Tom Zenk is earning. Of course that could all change by the time you read this.

(JUNE 21) WCW: There are reports that Tully Blanchard sent WCW a letter two weeks before the last PPV saying that he wasn't going to be there and not to advertise him.

TAMMY FYTCH

(APRIL 26) SMW: Debuting at the television taping was Tammy Fytch (real name Tammy Sytch), who according to the storyline has filed a sexual discrimination suit against Smoky Mountain Wrestling for having no female employees. She said she was a college student from Hilary Clinton's alma mater and talks about Hilary as her personal hero. On one interview, she was asking Dixie Dynomite if she could become his manager and said that she wants to be just like Hilary Clinton, taking a nobody all the way to the top. Dynomite turned her down.

SEAN MOONEY

(APRIL 26) WWF: Sean Mooney will be gone once his contract expires. I believe that's only about a week or two away. Gene Okerlund is already doing Events Centers but word we get is that is only temporary.

123 KID

(MAY 3) WWF: Lightning Kid was hired and started at the 4/26 Raw losing in a squash submission fashion twice to Doink the Clown (not sure if it was different Doinks in the two matches) without getting any offense in. The Manhattan fans reacted surprisingly big when he came out with his name on his trunks since it's a hardcore audience, but that fact will have to be ignored when it airs on television 5/3 since he got squashed and got no offense in and was supposed to be just another faceless unknown jobber. It looks like Kid will be a babyface and be both the youngest (20) and lightest wrestler (est. 200) to get a push in WWF probably in more than a decade. He'll start as a regular after his June New Japan tour.

(MAY 10) WWF: Lightning Kid will be using the name Kamikaze Kid, which is the name they billed him as in his debut getting squashed by Doink the Clown. That is definitely a unique method of pushing someone.

(MAY 17) WWF: Lightning Kid was on Raw again 5/10, this time using the name Cannonball Kid and got squashed with no offense against Hughes, who is now managed by Harvey Whippleman. Show highlight was the open where Perfect and Michaels had a great brawl in the parking lot before the show which included Michaels foot going through a gimmicked windshield. Michaels then had a lumberjack match with Duggan for the title which saw him come to the ring on crutches, but Perfect at-tacked him and his leg was suddenly fine. Michaels took about 20 minutes worth of great bumps for Duggan making the thing watchable and even pretty good at times. Finish saw Yokozuna legdrop Duggan and throw him in the ring, but before Michaels could get the pin, Perfect jumped in and started brawling with him so Duggan lost via DQ. All the lumberjacks got in and it ended up with Duggan cleaning house with his 2x4. From start to finish this was reminiscent of UWF from Tulsa.

(MAY 24) WWF: Also on the show, Sean Waltman, this time simply wrestling as "The Kid," scored the first jobber upset in WWF history (I've been waiting seven years to see some-one introduce a new star in this manner) by pinning Razor Ramon. It was set up as the typical squash with Kid selling every move big, and after Ramon missed a move, Kid did a moonsault bodyblock off the top rope for the pin. Waltman, who had worked as Kamikaze Kid and Cannonball Kid on the previous two shows in doing total squash jobs for Doink the Clown and Mr. Hughes, got no offense in again before his pinning move. This will be the fourth shot Janetty has received with the WWF, being fired once after the second day he was in, a second time after his arrest on cocaine possession and resisting arrest charges in Tampa in January of 1992, and a third firing after the Royal Rumble when he was either sleeping or passed out in the locker room. Janetty had been negotiating not only with WWF and WCW, but also with Japan and the as-yet-unnamed promotion that Paul E. Dangerously is booking all in the past two weeks. The final decision was probably made within the last week since it changes storylines that were already in progress and were to be further advanced on upcoming television tapings.

(MAY 31) WWF: Sean Waltman, whose ring name seems to change every week, is booked on house shows after his Japan tour starting late June under the name Cannonball Kid, against Terry Taylor.

(JUNE 7) WWF: Razor Ramon continually ups the money on each TV show in his challenge to "The Kid" whose name changes on a weekly basis, this past week being "The 1-2-3 Kid." Of course since Sean Waltman is in Japan until 6/14, the money will continue to rise until that point.

BONI BLACKSTONE

(MAY 17) WWF: Boni Blackstone debuted at the tapings doing stand-up interviews, and she'll also do the former Events Center segments which are now called "Face to Face." The segments have the two foes that wrestle each other at the local arena do simultaneous split-screen promos insulting each other. They are also doing them market specific as the promos that aired here this week for example talking about the Bret Hart vs. Lex Luger match had both men insulting each other but talking specifically about the Cow Palace. The lines they use are pretty much the same for all arenas as in other markets they cut virtually the same promo just talked about the specific arena. Doing all those individually rather than the old method of doing generic interviews and having the announcer do wrap-arounds mentioning the town has to be incredibly time consuming as the top guys probably have to cut 30 new sets per week instead of just a few the old way. Most of the big names will be in studio every non-syndicated taping Tuesday after Raw doing the promos which cuts one day off of time spent at home. Still, the new method seems a lot more effective for building heat and hopefully should reflect on attendance, which is still lagging.

(MAY 24) WWF: Boni Blackstone aired on television this weekend for the first time doing stand-up live interviews. In her first week she was already better than Raymond Rougeau.

(NOVEMBER 8) WWF: Both ring announcer Mike McGuirk and television interviewer Boni Blackstone have been let go. McGuirk was told the company wanted to cut back on transportation expenses.

THE NASTY BOYS

(MAY 17) WWF: Nasty Boys are on a suspension but were still talked about on Raw so they'll be brought back.

(MAY 31) WWF: Nasty Boys will be on their suspension or hiatus or whatever the technical term is for about another eight weeks so, as was announced on television, Smoking Gunns will be taking their place on the PPV in an eight man tag teaming with Steiners against Money Inc. & Head Shrinkers.

(JUNE 28) WWF: Nasty Boy Brian Nobbs was on the Wrestling Insiders radio show Saturday night and said he was no longer with the WWF and is looking for indie bookings.

(JULY 17) WCW: Nasty Boys as heels managed by Missy Hyatt debut at the WCW tapings. Expect them to be pushed as the No. 1 heel tag team ahead of the Hollywood Blonds. Go try and figure.

TOM ZENK & SHANE DOUGLAS

(MAY 31) WWF: Nasty Boys are on a suspension but were still talked about on Tom Zenk and Shane Douglas also received their notice. It's not necessarily a firing although it does mean if they stay it won't be under their existing money deal. In the case of Zenk that's hardly a surprise, since he had all but disappeared from television and the "A" team shows, and management one year ago wanted to get rid of him but sent him his notice after his contract had already rolled over for another year. In the case of Douglas, I guess it just shows how much value is placed on having the best match on the card every night, standing out at the major shows and making significant improvements in-ring performance.

SABU

(JUNE 14) WCW: Sabu received a try-out on 6/3 in Port Huron, MI. They actually did a match with Sabu vs. local wrestler Mad Max Anthony before any fans were in the building. Sabu broke Anthony's nose doing a moonsault. Sabu was told they would fly him to Atlanta for another try-out, this time in front of fans.

(SEPTEMBER 6) WCW: Sabu received word from WCW that they weren't going to bring him in. Let me get this right. Charlie Norris, Thunder & Lightning, Harlem Heat all passed their try-outs and Sabu failed his.

(OCTOBER 5) WWF: Sabu got a try-out at the taping but didn't look good beating Scott Taylor, who is one of the best of the face jobbers. Sabu was the only newcomer at TV the first night.

(NOVEMBER 1) WWF: Sabu looked much better at the second (where he was pinned by Owen Hart in an excellent match) and third night of television tapings and was offered a job, but turned it down because it would have meant he'd have to give up his FMW job and he's staying loyal to Onita for giving him his first career break.

GANGREL

(JUNE 21) WWF: David Heath, who was originally selected by WCW to be offered a developmental contract, instead did a try-out match in Columbus, OH for WWF and looked okay, but they had him put over jobber Kevin Kruger. If he gets the job, expect him to be given the Vampire gimmick.

SENSATIONAL SHERRI & TED DIBIASE

(JUNE 28) WCW: Reportedly before making his deal with Japan, Ted DiBiase tried to get a $250,000 deal to come to WCW but was turned down.

(JULY 5) WWF: Sensational Sherri gave notice and will be leaving first week of September. She's going to enroll in beauty college in the fall and will be available for weekend indie dates. That's why Luna Vachon's role has been changed to being Bam Bam Bigelow's manager, and also why the Sherri-Luna feud, which started out hot, was so quickly cooled off.

(JULY 26) WWF: Sensational Sherri was fired this past week. Funny thing about it was it was report-ed in the Torch that was mailed out Wednesday, but Sherri didn't even find out un-til two days later when she was called just before she was about to get on the plane to Philadelphia for her booking that night. With Luna Vachon out with the broken wrist and unable to wrestle until after Sherri's quitting date of 9/8, Titan really had no use for her left.

(SEPTEMBER 13) WWF: The new WWF Magazine didn't have a story, as promised last month, on David Shults, blaming deadline pressure but promised it would run a story similar to last month's Billy Graham story in an upcoming issue. The magazine also acknowledged both Ted DiBiase and Sensational Sherri leaving the federation, saying Ted left "to pursue other endeavors" and Sherri left for beauty school. It wished both luck in the future and also pretty much closed the book on the Million Dollar Man gimmick saying DiBiase has lost much of his wealth due to bad investments, I guess paving the way for an eventual face turn if he decides to come back. In the past, WWF never acknowledged wrestlers when they were gone.

RANDY SAVAGE

(JULY 26) WWF: Randy Savage is moving to Connecticut from Florida to work full-time in the office on the booking side. Rumors were flying all week that Savage was the top candidate to become new WWF booker, although at press time all we've been able to confirm is that Savage will have a hand in the booking.

THE QUEBECERS

(JULY 26) WWF: While I'm not certain of this, I believe Jacques Rougeau's partner Pierre Oulette formerly worked in Puerto Rico under the name Killer Karl Wallace. The Quebec heel team starts on the road 10/6. Jacques has claimed to the local Montreal media that he signed a two-year $1 million contract, although those in wrestling who read those printed reports are howling with laughter and that figure. This past week they cut a song with the line "We're not the Mounties."

TNT & VAN HAMMER

(AUGUST 2) WWF: TNT from Puerto Rico and Van Hammer both got try-outs at the WWF tapings in Utica. TNT put over Glen Ruth while Hammer, using the same ring name as in WCW but working as a heel, put over Virgil. With ratings sweeps over by the time these tapings air, the number of competitive matches taped for syndication was whittled down to almost zero.

SGT. SLAUGHTER

(SEPTEMBER 27) WWF: With cutbacks necessary because of cutting back to running only 3-4 house shows per week (they in the past often ran more shows than that on specific days), Sgt. Slaughter was let go as a road agent.

GLENN JACOBS

(NOVEMBER 1) WWF: Also getting a try-out both nights is Sid Vicious-clone Glenn Jacobs, who will be the Black Knight at the Survivor Series. I believe all three nights with the unknown muscle types. Jacobs had worked Florida indies as Sid Powers and Jim Powers and Memphis as Doomsday (currently) and Christmas Creature. Black Knight debuted during a Bret Hart vs. Lawler cage match on 10/19 in Glens Falls. After a ref bump, Knight went into the cage and pulled Lawler out the door, but before the ref could see Lawler having escaped, Owen Hart ran in and threw Lawler back in. As Knight was destroying Owen on the floor, Bret managed to escape and win.

MR. PERFECT

(DECEMBER 6) WCW: There is no indication Mr. Perfect is coming back at any time in the near future. Apparently he was upset at being bypassed for the IC title that he thought was promised him, although in reality Ramon was a lot more popular. He received an offer from WCW to do Clashes and PPVs but not house shows.

LARRY MATYSIK

(DECEMBER 6) WWF: Larry Matysik, who had been the WWF's promoter in St. Louis dating back to 1983, was fired this past week in what was said to have been another budget cutback, although it came just days after a spot show drew 700 fans near St. Louis. Matysik was a long-time television announcer and assistant to Sam Muchnick in the old St. Louis NWA office during the 70s and early 80s.

CHAPTER FORTY SIX

1993 YEAR IN REVIEW

House Show/TV Business In 1993 Compared With 1992

WWF	'92H	'92TV	'93H	'93TV
January	6,580	2.50	3,660	1.80
February	6,240	2.50	3,410	2.30
March	6,690	2.60	4,040	2.00
April	3,570	2.40	3,200	2.00
May	4,150	2.10	3,650	2.00
June	3,900	2.00	2,610	2.10
July	3,990	2.20	3,100	2.00
August	3,250	2.10	4,620	2.10
September	3,280	1.90	4,130	1.70
October	3,310	1.70	3,290	2.00
November	2,840	1.90	3,300	2.10
December	3,210	1.90	3,430	2.40
EST YEAR AVG	4,250	2.15	3,540	2.05

In comparing WWF business from 1992 to 1993, besides the obvious 16.7% decline in average house show attendance for the year, and almost surely a greater decline in overall house show revenue during the same period because of running far less house shows over the year period (down from an estimated 550 to probably just under 400), is that the decline in interest in the WWF product has to this point been quelled. For the most part, interest was way down during the early part of the year as compared with the year before. In April of 1992, that was the beginning of the fallout of the scandals, loss of Hulk Hogan, more serious steroid testing that resulted in many of the top guys either shrinking noticeably or leaving over the summer which all resulted in the huge decline in WWF business. This trend largely continued through the early part of 1993 and into the summer. August and September average attendances are misleading because during that period WWF was often cut down to just one loaded house show per night and running many fewer shows, concentrating on the bigger buildings which are going to draw bigger crowds. By the end of the year, it was clear the house show business decline was over, and things were steadying and even beginning to show some improvement, particularly when it comes to television ratings. Early signs don't point to a significant change in arena attendance during 1994, but it appears television ratings in 1994 will probably be above the levels of both 1992 and 1993. This slowing down the rate of decline and showing signs of reversing the trend is more limited to the company rather than an industry-wide barometer of improvement, as looking at WCW house shows.

WCW	'92H	'92TV	'93H	'93TV
January	2,120	2.70	1,590	2.20
February	2,090	2.40	1,690	2.60
March	2,660	2.50	1,770	2.40
April	2,340	2.20	1,520	2.00
May	1,790	2.10	490	1.90
June	1,780	2.00	825	2.00
July	1,960	2.10	655	2.00
August	2,380	2.00	700	2.50
September	1,720	1.80	640	2.10
October	1,180	1.80	600	2.00
November	1,210	2.20	370	2.40
December	930	2.20	640	2.00
EST YR AVG	1,850	2.17	960	2.18

A few years back, one of the bookers for a then-major and now out-of-business wrestling promotion got a hold of all the TV ratings numbers for the various wrestling companies in all the different markets. The time period here was the late 1980s when there were a half-dozen or so promotions that had significant national syndication. In looking at the ratings and comparing them with house show business done in the different markets, the conclusion he came up with was there was absolutely no correlation. The conclusion made no sense, but he found instances of cities with tremendous local TV numbers that didn't draw, cities where one promotion would draw twice the TV numbers as a competing one yet the competing one would triple the house show attendance of the one with twice the TV audience, etc. Overall, WCW's house show business was cut in half from last year, and the percentage decline has been the greatest over the past few months. Overall, TV ratings for the year are almost exactly the same as the previous year, with much of the period where ratings were better than last year coinciding with the period house show business took its greatest fall.

AJPW	'92H	'92TV	'93H	'93TV
January	3,000	6.70	2,720	4.50
February	2,090	4.70	2,080	3.90
March	3,200	4.40	3,210	3.80
April	3,460	4.20	3,280	3.30
May	3,715	4.00	3,270	3.50
June	3,110	4.20	3,400	2.90
July	2,690	4.40	2,920	2.40
August	2,400	4.50	2,300	2.80
September	2,530	3.50	3,130	3.10
October	3,020	3.50	2,710	2.80
November	4,100	4.20	3,320	3.20
December	4,030	4.80	4,680	3.50
EST YR AVG	3,110	4.43	3,090	3.31

Yet another example of ratings and house show business having little correlation. All Japan ratings nosedived this past year. Part of this was due to the abnormally high ratings the show had in late 1991 and continuing through the first few months of 1992. The weekly show aired from 12:30 a.m. to 1:25 a.m. on Sunday nights, which is a terrible time to draw a large audience, and the January 1992 rating, as an example was close to a 70 share of the homes watching television for all four shows that month. So even with this decline in ratings, you are still taking about All Japan's weekly TV show drawing an astronomical share of the audience that is awake watching television during the time slow. As a comparison, Monday Night Raw over the past three months has averaged a 2.9 rating which is a 4.3 share because it's on during a time slot when so many are watching. That type of rating share isn't going to be able to be maintained over the long haul. However, any television sport in which the rating drops 25% over a full season would be in a panic. All Japan won't panic, and can cite the lack of decline in arena business as a reason not to, plus the idea that over the course of 1993, it packed 77% of its arena shows. But as a comparison, if next season, NFL football has its TV ratings drop 25% on NBC (throwing the Fox vs. CBS factor out the window), the fact its stadium attendance stays almost the same would not quell the panic that would go through the industry.

NJPW	'92H	'92TV	'93H	'93TV
January	3,280	N/A	2,000	8.20
February	4,090	6.70	5,170	6.10
March	3,160	8.10	4,170	6.10
April	2,890	5.50	9,800	6.00
May	2,710	7.10	3,240	8.40
June	3,350	7.10	4,650	6.00
July	3,490	6.50	3,480	6.60
August	9,110	6.50	8,300	6.10
September	3,160	N/A	4,610	N/A
October	3,340	6.30	2,850	5.80
November	2,710	7.00	2,430	5.00
December	3,950	7.40	3,450	6.80
EST YR AVG	3,770	6.82	4,510	6.46

Once again, no correlation between a significant (16.4%) attendance increase and a slight decline (5.2%) in television viewership. New Japan boomed this year with the interpromotional feud with WAR creating all the new "dream" match-ups. As the "dream" matches ran their course, combined with the weakest foreign crew in the company's history, the boom subsided largely after the September series, particularly in the weak tag team tournament. Most feel the quality of the New Japan house shows, particularly the headline matches, was the lowest in years because the WAR and Skinheads vs. New Japan feuds. New Japan sold out an estimated 70% of its house shows this past year, slightly up from last year, which is a lower percentage than All Japan, but they booked a substantial number of larger arena shows during the year. Of the major promotions, New Japan drew the greatest average attendance, the largest gates and had the best television ratings during the past year. Signs going into the year because of the feuds no longer being fresh and weak foreign talent are that its 1993 success will be difficult to duplicate.

1994 is going to be an interesting year because it's becoming more and more apparent that the world is becoming a smaller place. Instead of ignoring what goes on in its industry in other parts of the world as virtually all promoters of the past had done, events of the past few weeks have indicated more cooperation with the various groups. The next round of technology changes in the television industry, which is a few years away in this country, is certain to have a profound effect of making the world a smaller place as well.

Both WCW and AAA have had reps visit Japan in recent months. Eric Bischoff of WCW went to Japan in November to attempt to put together a deal that had fallen apart between WCW and New Japan. While no deal has been signed that we know of and reports we get are that New Japan isn't willing to pay the type of price it has in the past for WCW talent, the groups are willing to do a degree of talent exchanges which would hopefully augment each side's major shows. As mentioned last week, Rick Rude (why Rick Rude is one of life's great mysteries; although no more mysterious that Mocho Cota being a drawing card in Mexico) goes to New Japan for a week in March, and in exchange, Great Muta will come to WCW in April including headlining the 4/17 Spring Stampede PPV show from the Rosemont Horizon against Ric Flair.

AAA's Antonio Pena, Octagon, El Hijo del Santo and Fuerza Guerrera visited Japan as well during the first week of the year. Konnan wasn't on the trip, despite what was reported here. One of the magazines had a photo of Konnan with Atsushi Onita but apparently the photo was an old photo. On 1/3, Pena (AAA booker) met with Onita (FMW President). The next day he met with Seiji Sakaguchi and Antonio Inoki at the New Japan post-Tokyo Dome party, and set up a business meeting with Sakaguchi for the next afternoon. Sakaguchi, Masa Saito along with prelim wrestler Black Cat and Pena's international liaison Jimmy Suzuki (serving as a translators) met the next day and made a verbal agreement to work together. New Japan apparently wanted to send its young wrestlers to work in Mexico to gain experience at the different style before bringing them back and giving them a push. Unlike every other promotion in the world, New Japan has its unique way of developing talent, one which some would say is responsible for developing more top-quality talent than any other method in the world. With a few rare exceptions, what New Japan does is debut rookies underneath and they generally do jobs, or trade wins with other rookies of the same experience. After a year, or two, or three, or whenever they begin to show signs that they are ready to move up to the next level, they are sent away. The feeling is that fans see them as prelim wrestlers and won't take them seriously in a pushed role after seeing them do so many jobs. So they leave for a year or two, gain experience at another style (years back, New Japan would send young wrestlers mainly to Calgary and UWA in Mexico, but also on occasion to U.S. regionals or to Otto Wanz in Europe), grow their hair long or get a new ring costume or a new ring name, and comeback, this time with a push and the fans accept them as having paid their dues and as being ready to take their place among the top stars. With UWA struggling financially, New Japan would literally be sending people to starve if they sent wrestlers there, and Calgary and the regionals don't exist anymore, so there is only Otto Wanz. An agreement was made to send Tiger Mask (Koji Kanemoto) to AAA and future young wrestlers would be sent there to gain seasoning.

This is a system that I believe would benefit WCW greatly as well. WCW has stifled the careers of many new wrestlers in the past few years because of pushing them before they are ready, which ends up in fans rejecting them, and having no place to learn. If WCW were to work with New Japan and when they find someone they believe to be a prospect, to use them as a jobber without a gimmick on small shows early, then send them to Japan for a year or two, and bring him back with a push, that way the first time the public sees them with a push, they'll have a few years under their belt and hopefully won't be rejected by the public for not knowing their craft. The other advantage is if the wrestler can survive two years in Japan, the odds are he'll come back as a skilled talent and have more respect for wrestling. If he can't survive Japan and comes home, the promotion will find out quickly just how dedicated the wrestler is to becoming the best they can be, looks be damned, before giving him the four-year guaranteed contract, promising him the world title, and sending him to Europe to go berserk.

That evening, Pena went to the FMW show to shoot an international interpromotional angle that will probably lead to a joint FMW/AAA stadium show later this year. Pena, Octagon, Santo and Guerrera were introduced to the crowd early in the Korakuen Hall show and sat at ringside. During a tag match, Michinoku Pro's Great Sasuke did a quebrada (Asai-moonsault to the floor) on Ginsei Shinzaki, and in following through, crashed into Guerrera at ringside. The two started brawling and had to be separated. The next day before the Korakuen Hall show, a press conference was scheduled to further the angle. Pena, Guerrera, Sasuke and Onita were there. Pena apologized for what happened claiming they weren't there to interfere with the matches. Onita said there was no need to apologize as it was just something that happened and it was nobody's fault. Sasuke then apologized saying he should have been more careful before crashing into Guerrera. Guerrera then made he had no reason to apologize, that he was sitting there minding his own business when Sasuke crashed into him, then threw a coke in his face and the two brawled again. Three days later Sasuke came to Guadalajara to work the AAA show, however due to visa problems, he wasn't able to work the main event and instead they just did another angle in the ring where he and Guerrera got into it again to set up a feud for both countries for later in the year.

Pena also met with the All Japan women's office and they made a verbal agreement to send wrestlers to AAA, with the first name mentioned as going to tour being Bull Nakano. No contracts were signed in any of these cases, only verbal agreements made. Whether these meetings will result in substantial talent trading has been agreed to but isn't definite. Because of major cultural differences between Mexico and Japan as far as how businessmen in each country operate, these deals aren't definite until they happen. One of many roadblocks to Pena being the Vince McMahon of the 1990s, as many believe he wants to be, is that many wonder if he'll be able to adapt to so-called international business speed and rules rather than the ways of doing business in Mexico, which are slower, laid-back, and virtually nothing gets done until the last minute. As has been mentioned here, in Mexico, most card line-ups aren't even announced until the Monday before the show, and virtually all tickets are walk-up. In Japan they often have cards put together, especially for big shows, months in advance. The U.S. is somewhat in between. For these agreements to work, the AAA will have to be able to conclude all business negotiations far enough in advance that the Japanese can get things done at their pace.

Whatever rumors there were about WCW eliminating or even cutting back on house shows have to be thrown out the window since the company signed Zane Bresloff, the WWF's leading independent house show promoter for the past nine years. Many believe the signing of Bresloff will result in the fiercest war between WWF and WCW in a few years because this deal pretty well guarantees a far more aggressive approach WCW will take to booking major arenas that it had been locked out of in the top markets. In addition, knowing egos involved, with Gene Okerlund, Bobby Heenan and Bresloff all jumping in rapid fashion, one would think that WWF would be looking for a big coup in return of its own. It appears WCW getting into the Rosemont Horizon in suburban Chicago for the 4/17 PPV show (moved from Asheville, NC), a building they had been unable to book shows in for seven or eight years, is a result of Bresloff's relationship with the building as the long-time WWF local promoter. Bresloff, a former rock & roll promoter, handled most of major and medium-sized markets in the Western part of the United States with the exception of Detroit, Milwaukee, St. Louis, Texas and Northern California for Titan. He is also said to be responsible for many of the promotional contacts the WWF has made overseas and was the local promoter for the Wrestlemania III live show at the Pontiac Silverdome, which drew the largest pro wrestling crowd ever. While unconfirmed, it is believed that WCW will attempt to once again run house shows on more of a national basis, particularly in major markets like New York, Chicago and Los Angeles. The truth of the matter is that no local promoter is any better in the long-run than the product he is promoting. A bad promoter can screw up promotion of a good product, and a good promoter may be able to get people out once or twice for a bad product but in the long run, if people aren't interested in the product, where the ads are placed and publicity ideas aren't going to help much. With all the money WCW is spending on announcers, promoters, tour expansion, booking more expensive arenas, and expensive television production tricks that are more distracting than effective, they had better put some money into getting more performers who can perform and figuring out how to get those who can over to where people care about them. In an unrelated move, in that the planning stages for this had taken place before any of the aforementioned changes had happened, WWF is going to send several name wrestlers to SMW for SMW's house show on 3/10 in Marietta, GA, a suburb of WCW's home base of Atlanta.

Despite all the emphasis on house shows these moves indicate, it is still PPV revenue that is going to be the main revenue source in this country of presenting live events. In 1993, WCW drew about $7.56 million on seven PPV events as opposed to around $3 million on more than 300 house show dates. While estimated profit is haphazard, the PPV shows probably did $2.5 million in profit while the house shows certainly lost a lot more than $2.5 million. WWF was a little more balanced, drawing about $16.1 million on five PPV dates and another $19 million on about 400 or so house show dates. Of course the cost of gambling in the PPV arena are higher. UWFI, which ran a 1:50 PPV show (as opposed to more than two hours for WWF and WCW) on tape rather than live, had built in costs in excess of $850,000. Even if the figure is slightly lower for WCW, and based on higher production costs, at least as much advertising, going live and a longer show, if anything it should be a higher break-even. That means if buy rates fall to consistent 0.3 to 0.4 level, the profit margin in that medium would be gone. If what they tell us about technology changes is accurate, in not too many years, many cable systems will be carrying 500 stations. Despite the belief of many that pro wrestling is already overexposed on television, with 500 stations in a market, that is going to mean a lot more pro wrestling, in terms of variety, on television in years to come, not less, despite inevitable ratings declines that will occur. The apparent success of the different and unknown UWFI on PPV and ethnic regional success AAA has already had in the U.S. has opened the eyes of several international promotions on running in the United States on PPV where an 0.5 buy rate is worked right can be profitable. The idea of an international promotion trying to put together a U.S. tour, with the exception of AAA or EMLL on a regional basis, would be a waste of effort when PPV is the only way it can bring a return on the investment. The potential drawing power of AAA on PPV is a question mark to be sure, particularly on a national basis, however dismissing it outright would be ignoring a very important fact. Traditionally, in the United States, it has been the heavyweights in boxing that were the biggest draw. Occasionally, with the most recent example being when Ray Leonard was in his prime, a middleweight fighter captures the nation's fancy and becomes boxing's top draw. Right now boxing is the No. 1 sport on PPV in the United States as far as biggest grosses, however wrestling is No. 2, and still a more consistent product. The biggest draw on PPV in the United States today among boxers, wrestlers, or even Howard Stern fans, is Julio Caesar Chavez, a lighter weight boxer whose appeal is largely ethnic. His success says that dismissing AAA's chances on PPV because "Mexicans don't have the money to buy PPV" or because it is too ethnic in appeal is ignoring the obvious. Chavez vs. Pernell Whitaker outdrew Holyfield-Bowe by a wide margin.

Inevitably with 500 stations, Japanese wrestling is going to air in the United States. It would be surprising it hasn't thus far except the "wrestling is wrestling" mentality among those who would make the decision to put it in. Which companies and their potential for doing business here varies. None are a sure thing. All Japan, with the most Americans in key positions and best workrate on top might seen like it has the best chance, but the company is also the most conservative around and seems to be the one that would be the last one to try something new. New Japan would be more likely to try, but if a deal is reached with WCW, it may not want to compete with its business partner and instead may, as in the past, offer Dome shows to WCW to air as small-time PPV events. FMW, with its bizarre gimmickry, would have the best chance of drawing PPV buys based on airing something nobody has seen, if it first were to be able to draw a regular following for its product. But it doesn't run television in its own country and despite the fact it has been very successful there because of the outrageous gimmicks, it would have no chance here without television. There is already a link between Pancrase and the Ultimate Fight people. UWFI, if the figures were accurate, had significant success (although probably no financial success) on the first show, but whatever momentum was picked up has already been blown by lack of follow-up and there is no talk whatsoever about a second show, which originally was supposed to air in March, which also makes me skeptical of the released figures. All Japan Women already have discussed plans to try and do a PPV in the U.S. of the 11/10 Tokyo Dome show, although that is dependent upon getting national exposure on television (they have put together a series of one hour shows with no announcing track and English graphics for U.S. syndication and will attempt to sell the show in this country) and garnering a following at that point. It is a unique product and one completely unlike anything that has ever been done before in this country. All Japan women had a brief run in the mid-80s on the small Tempo Cable network, but the station had little national penetration so it never was clear whether that brief run was successful or not. Unlike the mid-80s, when the appeal of All Japan women was based on something culturally different from the U.S. and Japan (Japanese teenager girls worshipping women jocks as role models rather than Americans teenager girls that worship TV actors and rock stars rather than female jocks), the group draws the same wrestling fans as the other groups, which except for how they are educated and income strata, are not all that different in their make-up than American wrestling fans. Of course that is something that has been around for 25 years on television drawing at times incredible ratings, but it has really once been since 1990 that the women's wrestling in Japan has been successful drawing the wrestling fan audience. The group, if it gets on TV in the U.S. or not, is already planning on bringing back several American women to work full-time in 1994.

The television situation of pro wrestling not only in Mexico, but in the United States on the Galavision cable, has changed once again. To understand the situation, a little background needs to be in order. EMLL a few years back signed a multi-year contract with Televisa, the leading network in Mexico (equivalent to ABC, NBC and CBS combined) to broadcast its weekly program. Pena, who was then the EMLL booker, quit and formed AAA, with Televisa as his backer. In short order, Televisa pulled EMLL off U.S. television (with the exception of Local Ch. 22 in Los Angeles) and put AAA on in its place. However, because of the contract, Televisa aired both EMLL and AAA throughout Mexico. About two months back, Televisa moved EMLL from a prime slot to a late Thursday night slot, and then last month canceled it altogether, which was potentially a crippling blow to the office. That cancellation was short-lived, apparently because of the long-term binding contract, and EMLL is back on television on Saturday nights in Mexico. In addition, on the Saturday night Galavision two hour wrestling show that aired on 1/15, one hour was EMLL taped from 1/4 and 1/7 at Arena Colieso and the other hour was AAA taped 1/7 from Morelia. The Sunday show was the fifth year-in-review show airing major main event matches from both EMLL and AAA. With television back in the United States, it seems a good bet that EMLL will attempt to run, perhaps as early as April, in the Los Angeles market.

On the same night as he lost the WWF tag title, 1-2-3 Kid suffered what appeared to be a serious leg injury, perhaps a break, when taking a bump over the top rope being eliminated in the 1/17 Royal Rumble in Madison Square Garden. In the prior match on the card, Kid & Marty Janetty's one-week reign as WWF tag champs ended against The Quebecers. WWF attempted a risky live voice-over from the studios (if that was the case, if not they attempted an even riskier talking about something that hadn't happened yet in the middle of a snowstorm that kept several wrestlers from appearing) of the first part of the Monday Night Raw show, with two on-site phone calls from Stan Lane who reported live during the show about the title change. Unfortunately, it didn't go smoothly as the sound mixing was a mess, causing almost inaudible commentary for the first half of the show. The tag title match, described as equally as good as the match the previous week, went 21:24 ending with Kid on the top rope when Johnny Polo shook the ring rope and Kid crotched himself, fell into the ring, and was pinned after a double-team move. In the Rumble, Kid was eliminated and laid on the ground for several minutes, with most believing he was just selling the bump. Finally paramedics came out (this wasn't a work because they had already done one stretcher job earlier in the card with Tatanka and WWF isn't about to do two worked stretcher jobs on the same show) and Kid signalled that he thought his leg was broken. At press time we haven't been able to get any updates on his situation other than he was in the hospital Monday night.

Sam Menacker, who was a wrestler, promoter and later a television wrestling announcer for many different promotions around the world, passed away on 1/7 at a hospital in his home town of Springfield, IL. The cause of death is unknown. Menacker, 79, was probably best known for his stints as Jim Barnett's television announcer in Australia in the late 1960s when Australia was a wrestling hotbed, and later in the 1970s for Dick the Bruiser out of Indianapolis. Menacker, who at one time was married by women's wrestling champion June Byers, was originally a baseball player, a catcher in the New York Yankees system before World War II. After serving five years in the Army, he drifted into pro wrestling, and then became an announcer for Stu Hart in Calgary and out of Boston for a show called Bedlam in Boston, and later for Barnett out of Detroit. He later became a promoter in El Paso, TX, before stints in Australia and Indianapolis (which during the early 70s was also broadcast in Detroit during the famous NWA/WWA promotional war), and had a short run as television announcer for Sam Muchnick in St. Louis. While in Indianapolis, Menacker would still wrestle occasional gimmick matches against the likes of heel managers Bobby Heenan and Eddie Creachmann. After Bruiser had pretty well run Indianapolis into the ground, Menacker resurfaced in the mid-80s as the announcer for Stampede Wrestling, and after that stint retired to Illinois around 1985. Although he developed in his youth a reputation as something of a television wrestling genius, by the 70s his announcing style would have been comparable to Gorilla Monsoon. Menacker, because of his gangster looks, played the heavy in several fight movies including "Mighty Joe Young, "Sounder" and "Foreign Legend" and was the lead mob heel in Verne Gagne's attempt at a motion picture in 1973 called "The Wrestler."

Aside from numerous major out of the ring stories, most of a negative nature, 1993 can be concluded as a year not of change as most figured it would be going in, but of status quo and largely spinning of wheels. The dramatic downturn in wrestling of 1992 levelled off in the United States with the exception of WCW house show attendance, which actually continued dropping a staggering to this point. WWF attendance is well down from pre-Spring 1992 levels, but has actually made slight gains from the depths it fell to at this time last year. Both companies are celebrating and trumpeting television ratings increases about now, but in looking at history of ratings, the cold weather traditionally brings increases. While both groups are up just under 10 percent as compared with last year at this point, which it should be noted was the worst year in the history of wrestling television ratings, both groups are considerably below November 1991 levels. Of more concern (see business comparisons) is that while the Weekly Raw ratings are way up from the Prime Time show of one year ago and the All-American ratings are up as well, and the ratings for the pre-Survivor Series special increased nearly 20 percent, the money machine this is all supposed to lead to, the Survivor Series itself, fell an estimated 41 percent, a staggering figure, in buy rate from the previous year.

Just a few years ago, PPV was looked at as the golden goose of pro wrestling. There was concern about the long-term profitability of house shows, and it's questionable if any major American promotion actually made money doing house shows this past year. But the PPVs were windfalls and all signs pointed that they would become more so as the number of homes wired for PPV continued to increase. Over the past few years, the number of homes have continued to increase, but number of buys have dropped about 25 percent per year. Both groups tried to make up for this decrease by adding more shows. This appeared to be working until November, when both groups hit all-time lows with two shows scheduled just four days apart. Despite those who say otherwise, a definite lesson was told with Battle Bowl and Survivor Series. Enough of the PPV audience for both groups is cross-over, that scheduling shows that close together badly hurts both shows. Second, because of the proliferation of these shows, they are less and less special and people are picking and choosing now more than ever. While each group had one spectacular PPV this year, WWF with the King of the Ring and WCW with SuperBrawl, and overall quality, particularly toward the end of the year was declining both in crowd interest, quality of matches and overall creativity. The WWF shows are all profitable, while WCW's Battle Bowl may have been its only show of the year to fall below that level. But if there is another year of dropping buy rates, WCW is going to right on the edge, and as buy rate history has shown, WWF is about 18-24 months behind being in the league of what the current WCW buy rates are. Neither group is cutting back on PPV shows next year, which somewhat assures the panacea we all thought PPV would be for the major wrestling companies is not going to be achieved.

In Japan, things were somewhat different. Live attendance for about a half-dozen different promotions all hit high water marks this past year. I can recall just six years ago being in Japan and the attitude among the promotions is that the most people any wrestling match could possibly draw would be a little over 20,000. Nobody even thought about booking baseball stadiums for shows. Now even small promotions without television can book baseball stadiums and draw crowds of double that. The most traditional of all major promotions, All Japan, continued to book its major shows at Budokan Hall, and sold out every show to the tune of 16,300, usually about a month in advance. However, to take advantage of the demand for tickets, Budokan shows, which used to be quarterly, were increased to seven per year. Unlike American PPVs, this increase in the big shows didn't result in a decrease in interest level. However, the traditional All Japan approach was a killer when it came to television ratings. Despite having the best matches on television for any company in the world on a consistent basis, the repetitive nature of these matches combined with a bad time slot (12:30 a.m. Sunday nights, often moved back 30 to 60 minutes due to other programming) dropped TV ratings 40 percent over the past two years. This decrease doesn't seem to have meant a whole lot at the box office, and there is no sign at all that anyone is panicking or even considering changing the successful formula. However, this year's tag team tournament was the least interesting in history, and didn't draw at the level of previous years and the group needs to add some new faces to the mix to abate staleness, no matter how great Kenta Kobashi, Mitsuharu Misawa and Toshiaki Kawada put out every night.

New Japan from a business standpoint was easily the promotion of the year. From selling out the Tokyo Dome in January, to drawing 55,000 at the Fukuoka Dome in May, to drawing night-after-night of megagates in

August and September, this group did more major shows than ever before, and did them as successfully as any promotion has in years. However, New Japan got stale as the year went on. The tag team tournament series in October through early November was largely a flop, and the late November/early December tour only had an average amount of interest in what is traditionally the hottest period for wrestling in Japan. Television ratings also started to decline, particularly after the disappointing in-ring Fukuoka Dome show. The promotion was largely built around the influx of Genichiro Tenryu, a long-time superstar for All Japan who had been with SWS and WAR for the past several years. Tenryu, who at one-time was the most popular wrestler in Japan, saw his popularity fade badly being involved with two promotions with little appeal. However, when put in the New Japan rings, it created a series of prospective dream matches with Riki Choshu, Tatsumi Fujinami, Keiji Muto, Masa Chono, Shinya Hashimoto and Antonio Inoki. Tenryu was used carefully throughout the year and not exploited. He split two singles matches with Riki Choshu, winning the first as he needed to for long-term credibility as a serious challenger in 1993 to all the top stars rather than being a 1980s wrestler. He then won two major singles matches with Hashimoto and another with Chono, and another against Hiroshi Hase, to make up for a first time loss to Fujinami (which set up his beating Fujinami). The first match with Inoki was held off until the Tokyo Dome, and singles matches with Muto are still to come. Tenryu, like Choshu and Fujinami, are nowhere near the wrestlers they were six or seven years ago, but they are big names well-known to the general public, and when carefully booked in well promoted singles matches with logical booking, it spelled New Japan's most successful year to date.

What is the most impressive about today's Japan wrestling isn't the success of All Japan and New Japan, but the number of groups in a geographically small country, many presenting a totally different product from the others, all enjoying success. FMW, with little in the way of quality wrestling, presents the Atsushi Onita show, filled with barbed wire and heavy juice on a nightly basis, and was largely successful, peaking for the May 5 show against Terry Funk that drew 41,000 fans. Onita drew in excess of 25,000 fans for another stadium show against Mr. Pogo, and at the end of the year sold out a 12,500 seat indoor building for his final major show of the year for a match with Mitsuharu Matsunaga. While Onita's personal popularity is nowhere close to what it was two years back, he still has drawing power when it comes to putting together a major show. The only period FMW faltered badly this year was when Onita was in the hospital after jumping into a polluted river in the winter with several open wounds from a just completed match. Pogo and Matsunaga had been the top two stars with the rival W*ING group, a promotion that finished the year, but largely struggled. W*ING featured even more bizarre gimmick matches, like the ring surrounded by a bed of nails, ring surrounded by fire, and barbed wire baseball bats which led to legitimate serious injuries. At the other end of the spectrum where the so-called "shoot" groups, UWFI, PWFG, Rings and Pancrase. PWFG, which still ran shows during the year, was largely dormant and not a major factor on the scene, with its leader, Yoshiaki Fujiwara, more remembered for his occasional big show appearances on New Japan shows. UWFI almost surely, on an average drew more fans to its events than any wrestling promotion in the world. If someone was to do a study of all the main event wrestlers in the world, and rate them by how well the shows they headlined drew, to determine who really is the biggest drawing card of them all, I'd be willing to bet No. 1 in 1993 would be Nobuhiko Takada. UWFI, which signed a "pro wrestler" type in Big Van Vader, later called Super Vader for copyright reasons, and slowly, methodically built to the dream match with Takada. The heavily-advertised show drew 46,168 fans, the largest pro wrestling crowd for a wrestling company in the world without television since the heydey of the legendary UWF in 1989 at the Tokyo Dome. However, on the surface, there seems nothing on the horizon for UWFI that can do anywhere near that business. UWFI also did a PPV show in the United States in October, which had shocking success in at least some parts. However, whatever momentum and interest that was gained by the PPV show which was well received, was lost because of a lack of anything done as follow-up promotion. Rings, which is largely the Akira Maeda show, didn't have a strong year largely because Maeda missed most of the year with reconstructive knee surgery. Rings was the favorite promotion of the true Japanese hardcore wrestling fan because it was the most believable of all, but may turn out to be the one hurt the most in the end because of Pancrase Wrestling. Debuting late in the year, Pancrase was the latest of many groups which touted their wrestling to be on the level, without predetermined finishes. But if it wasn't, it fooled more people than ever before. Although UWFI liked to push itself as the real deal, and it is stiff as hell, a lot of fans took him as a more realistic looking New Japan rather than like Rings, which Maeda incessantly tried to push as having nothing to do with and not being pro wrestling, to the point that virtually nobody but himself who had previous ties to pro wrestling was used. However, Pancrase, which its one minute matches, exposed Rings. What that will mean to Rings, particularly with Maeda back, is unknown. But Pancrase managed to parlay its image into a crowd of nearly 10,000 in Kobe for Minoru Suzuki vs. Maurice Smith, and has looked into booking bigger buildings including perhaps the Tokyo Dome in 1994. Several other groups started up this year or continued from last year, although they are all way back in the pack.

The best wrestling held anywhere is undoubtedly on the major cards of the All Japan women's promotion. It appeared the group peaked in interest back in 1985, when The Crush Gals reigned supreme as the heroines for Japanese teenage women. The audience changed and the product changed greatly, and built up to another peak year in 1993. It's been said numerous times, and probably will be for years to come--Dream Slam I was the greatest pro wrestling live event ever held, and Dream Slam II nine days later wasn't far behind. Japanese women wrestling in 1993 will be forever remembered for those two shows. But All Japan women also ran successful major shows at Budokan Hall, Osaka Castle Hall and Sumo Hall. Not everything came up roses, as the Wrestlemarinpiad and Nagoya shows were disappointments, and with the woman who turned into the heart and soul and focal point of the promotion retiring, the line-ups for 1994 on paper just don't have that zing to it. Ideas are going to have to be good because attempting a Tokyo Dome show next November is going to be umpteen times harder than selling out a 25th anniversary show in Yokohama Arena. Because of cross-promotional help, JWP had its most successful shows to date, twice selling out the Yokohama Bunka Gym (5,500 seats) for matches against All Japan women, and LLPW similarly packed 4,500 into a Tokyo building in November when Rumi Kazama put her hair up against Akira Hokuto.

Tokyo Sports announced this past week its highly political and nationalistic but most publicized awards for pro wrestling in Japan. Tenryu was named MVP. Tenryu vs. Riki Choshu from 1/4 Tokyo Dome was named Match of the Year. Misawa & Kobashi were named Tag Team of the year. Kobashi was named Best Performer. Masakatsu Funaki was named Best Technical Wrestler. Shinya Hashimoto was given the Fighting Spirit prize. Giant Baba was given an award for wrestling his 5,000th match in Japan. Shinjiro Otani & Ginsei Shinzaki were named co-rookies of the year. The late Motoshi Okuma was given a Meritorious Service Award. All Japan Women Corp. were named promotion of the year, and Great Sasuke was named Most Popular Newcomer.

Mexico had an up-and-down year finishing with perhaps the biggest news story of them all. EMLL, which just recently had been moved to a late Thursday night time slot from a prime weekend slot, was canceled by Televisa effective immediately. This leaves the country's and world's oldest and still in many ways largest (in terms of number of wrestlers and number of cards promoted during the year and probably in terms of total attendance) group without any television exposure. AAA is as topsy-turvy as wrestling promotion's can get. Still unable to run in many locales and arenas because EMLL has buildings locked up, it wasn't until early this year that AAA could run in Mexico's media capital and largest city, Mexico City. At that point, the promotion caught fire, selling out the 10,500 seat Juan de la Barrera Gym every Friday night, with the rock stars and movies stars in the front row, and with some of the greatest matches ever held in Mexico. The momentum peaked by selling out the 48,000-seat Plaza de Toros on 4/30 for TripleMania. At that point, with the company's top draw, Konnan El Barbaro, out of action because of a retirement stipulation in losing the main event to Cien Caras, attendance fell off in Mexico City. Even attempts on putting on weekly major stip (hair, mask or title) matches failed to increase attendance, and crowd heat got worse and it reflected in the television product with the weak reactions and noticeable empty seats. An August tour of California was an incredible success. Finally in November, with Konnan back in action, AAA started touring the Northern part of the country that it abandoned when it hit big in Mexico City, and was packing them in again. AAA always seems to have huge plans, such as the plan of running 40 house shows next year in the United States in 13 different cities, and running Europe and Puerto Rico and tying in with Japan. The success in California has been in many ways staggering, as the two shows in

November in Los Angeles and San Jose drew three times as much money in this as WCW did the same entire month. But in many ways it seems the long term planning is at best hazy. EMLL seemed on the ropes for much of the year, but rebounded with a 18,000 sellout house for the Anniversary show in October and another big house for the year-end blow-out. The loss of television will hurt, particularly when it comes to touring, but most feel the promotion will be around forever.

CHAPTER FORTY SEVEN

SUPERCARD SUMMARY

WCW/NJPW SUPERSHOW III

The third annual Japan Super Show, taped 1/4 at the Tokyo Egg Dome, which began airing on 3/7 as a WCW PPV show and will continue to air for about two weeks, was scheduled to be headlined by a match between the Steiners and the Hell Raisers (Hawk & Power Warrior) for the IWGP tag team title. Just a few days before the show was to air, and several weeks after the voice-overs and editing had been completed, Titan Sports sent a letter threatening legal action against WCW if the match aired. While I don't know the exact wording of the letter, I believe the basic claim is that the Steiners contract with WCW expired on November 30, 1992, the Steiners signed a WWF contract which gives Titan exclusivity on booking, televising, merchandising, etc. in mid-December, or before January 4, 1993 when the match was taped, so therefore they were of the belief that WCW didn't have the right to air the match. The first reports I'd heard were that WCW felt it had the right to air the match and were going to ignore the threat because it had a signed deal with New Japan Pro Wrestling to broadcast the show, the match was part of the show, and the Steiners did have a deal with New Japan Pro Wrestling which included both participating and being televised in the match (which has already appeared on television in Japan). Apparently on Friday, in an 11th hour meeting, Turner legal and WCW reversed their field and pulled the match, which had been the feature match in all the advertising of the show, from the PPV. Advertising of the show with the Steiners-Hell Raisers continued to air up until show time on Request TV and also the match was plugged as the show's feature match on Saturday's TBS show. In fact, the advertising may still be continuing on Request since the show is scheduled for several more air plays.

The PPV aired as scheduled, but with no mention even made of the match that had the most appeal and was the only match that had been pushed. To make matters even worse, to fill the hole in the broadcast left by the elimination of the match, WCW added the opener from the Dome show (Koki Kitahara & Masao Orihara & Nobukazu Hirai vs. El Samurai & Akira Nogami & Takayuki Iizuka) into the semi-main event slot on the PPV show, which in and of itself wasn't that bad because it was a pretty hot match. What was bad was that with Jim Ross having quit the company, and with Tony Schiavone doing other WCW television work that day in West Palm Beach, it left the announcing chores to Eric Bischoff. Suffice to say it was among the most embarrassing moments in wrestling announcing history and by itself was almost enough to give the show a major thumbs down. Bischoff came in with no introduction saying that Ross and Schiavone "were at the sushi bar" and only called two names during the match. He had all six names obviously in front of him on a piece of paper because he mentioned the six mens' names in conglomeration twice, with significant mispronunciation of most, but never pointed out who was who individually. The two names he did call when they were in the ring were El Samurai (the easy one, since he was wearing a mask) and Orihara (who he called Hirai the entire match). When the others were in the ring, he bullshitted his way through it without mentioning any names, and mentioning very few moves except the obvious dropkicks and power bombs and "back heel round kick" (which he used for every kick used during the match, even though almost none of them were back heel round kicks). He told fans that the next match coming up was Sting vs. Tatsumi Fujinami even though Sting's opponent was Hiroshi Hase. Even more pathetic about this is that both Nogami and Iizuka had appeared on major WCW shows in 1992, and Iizuka's performance in his lone appearance (Wrestle War '92 in Jacksonville) was quite memorable.

Bischoff also called the crowd 67,000 when Ross and Schiavone had given the realistic 63,500 throughout the show, the same figure he had used in the magazine segments in syndication when discussing the Muta-Chono title change. It's the old wrestling axiom, even when the truth is impressive enough, lie anyway. Before even addressing the question of advertising a certain match as the PPV headliner without checking the legality status of such, then after pulling it, never even making an acknowledgement of it during the telecast, the question has to be raised as to the professional pride of the newly-named Executive Producer of WCW. The argument can (and I'm sure will) be made that the majority of those viewing the show didn't know the difference between the six Japanese either and many probably didn't care, although that was certainly not the opinion of those who called here. However, if I'm watching the NAIA women's basketball championship game on ESPN next week between Midwestern State University of Wichita Falls, Texas and Simon Fraser University of Vancouver, British Columbia (these are just two NAIA schools that popped into my head. I have no idea how good their women's basketball programs are), I won't know the names of any of the participants on either team, nor will nearly everyone who would be watching the game on television. Would the announcers dare be so unprofessional as to go on the air and never call who had the ball, who was taking the shot, and instead of faking their way through the game? They could, you know, if they had no professional pride in what they did. They'd probably never work again on ESPN afterwards, but much of the audience probably wouldn't care anyway. Since this is wrestling and WCW, the rules are different. Some free advice next time someone is in this situation if there ever is a next Japan Super Show on PPV, it takes one phone call to Chris Zavisa or Steve Sims or any of the many dozen of well-known fans who know all the names, know their favorite moves, and know the storyline of what's going on in Japan, and maybe 90 seconds to two minutes of conversation max and you'd have more than enough info to do the thing as a professional would. But only someone with professional pride in their on-air work would think that way before going on with the show. Hopefully it won't happen again. This is going to come off as being very hard on someone for something minor, but the problem really isn't just that Bischoff went on the air without knowing or more importantly, caring enough to know anything about what he was about to talk about, but what doing that is indicative of.

As for the show itself, comparing the taped version to the live version, I'd call it better than adequate. Four of the six matches that aired were good (Sting vs. Hiroshi Hase, Jushin Liger vs. Ultimo Dragon, Masa Chono vs. Great Muta, six-man tag). Ron Simmons vs. Tony Halme and Dustin Rhodes & Scott Norton vs. Masa Saito & Shinya Hashimoto were the exceptions. The latter was a lot more clumsy up close than it was seeing it live from the distance (a great distance, I should add). Special effects were barely evident on the tape although they were spectacular at the live show, but most were edited out. Unlike the first show in 1991, there were many crowd shots amplifying the size of the crowd which gave the impression this was the big deal that it was. Jim Ross, in his final WCW appearance, and Tony Schiavone ranged from pretty good to barely okay. They actually made Liger-Ultimo Dragon into a better match by explaining the submissions and making the boring early matwork into a storyline as part of each man's strategy. Ditto Sting vs. Hase. There were the minor factual errors (calling Tony Halme an ex-kick boxer when he was an ex-boxer) offset by the surprising understanding of storylines (getting across that Liger vs. Dragon was a dream match between wrestlers from different promotions that fans had been waiting years to see). They even explained the personality difference in Japan between the Great Muta and Keiji Muto, although they called his real name Kenji Muta. They got across the status Masa Saito has in his country as a senior star and even gave Hiroshi Hase a personality. On the downside, one of Ross' final television remarks before what may be an extended hiatus was, in pretending they were there live doing the show, saying he couldn't wait to get home so he could get a burger for less than $20, which, while the same Japanese stereotype directly out of the movie Mr. Baseball, is ridiculous in reality since you can get the same burgers and fries at MosBurgers and McDonald's in Japan for $2 to $3 that you get in the States for only a little less.

WCW CLASH OF THE CHAMPIONS XXII

The latest Clash of Champions on 1/13 from Milwaukee seems to be a show I'm in the minority when rating. I really enjoyed the show. There were only a few negatives, and most of them were over in the first ten minutes. The show drew an estimated 3,500 at the Mecca Arena, which was set up for 6,000, although I'm relatively sure way over half of that was paper. The crowd looked good enough on television because they placed them heavy into the section facing the cameras. The show sent a lot of subtle messages out, but after watching it, I almost think because they do so much and make things so confusing, that unless you read the Observer, it's impossible not only to follow all the angles they do, but even to understand what they say during some of the interviews.

Well, at least in the first few minutes. The show opened with Bill Watts, who was obviously booed. Watts talked about teaming with Crusher in Milwaukee (who was the biggest draw in the city for years) against Larry Hennig and Harley Race in his last appearance in the city, and that was when Ric Flair was breaking in. The chronology is way off, since Hennig & Race teamed regularly until around 1968, and I'd be pretty sure Watts stayed in the AWA as a regular for a few years after Race had left for the Central States and occasionally came for big shows for a few years after that. Flair didn't even break in until December of 1972. It sure dated Watts, because most people think of Flair breaking in as being really ancient history, since any 30-year-old would remember Flair on top when they were a teenager and someone 25 would remember Flair on top probably the first time they ever saw a wrestling show. Then they started talking about an incident, and never actually told anyone what it was (that's why you need an Observer to follow this promotion so you would at least know the angle because most viewers must have been really confused) and that Erik Watts was suspended. Then Erik Watts did an interview and didn't make it clear what was going on, either. Talking about Erik Watts in the spotlight is becoming an old topic and everything that can and should be said has already been said. But all those points were emphasized as he looked really out of place once again.

WWF ROYAL RUMBLE '93

The annual WWF Royal Rumble took place on 1/24 in Sacramento's Arco Arena. The show drew an estimated 1.2 to 1.3 buy rate based on very preliminary estimates (Titan's share would be approximately $2.85 million if those estimates are accurate). With the exception of the Tuesday in Texas PPV in 1991, it would be the lowest buy rate of any Titan PPV show in history, a drop of 10 to 15 percent from the previous low, the 1992 Survivor Series, which, it should be noted, also had a higher price tag so it's a double whammy. I thought the build-up to the show was done about as well as it could be, so even with the upturn in television ratings and slight increases at the houses, the PPV side of the industry continues to decline almost on a show-by-show basis. The live event sold out legitimately about five days before show time, drawing 16,000 fans (about 15,000 fans paying $187,000), which would be I believe the second largest gate ever in Northern California (I believe Hogan vs. Kimala once drew $189,000 in Oakland around 1986) and would be the largest actual crowd in Northern California for wrestling since the early 60s during the Ray Stevens heyday. Since I attended the show live, I haven't seen the PPV broadcast yet. Based on talking the several people who have seen both, the show came off better on PPV then it did live. Most of the responses to the poll from those who attended live were thumbs in the middles and thumbs downs, while from those who was it on PPV the thumbs ups were well above 50 percent. My feeling is it was better than a typical house show from WCW or WWF and in no way was it a bad card, but in comparison with other PPV shows that I've seen live, it wasn't as good as most. I'd give it a thumbs in the middle. The only thing I have seen thus far on tape is the El Gigante (now called The Giant Gonzales) angle with Undertaker (since they played it on the big screen in San Jose at the Superstars taping), and it was much better on tape than it was live and they seemed to have done a great job in miking the crowd, which has often been a negative on PPV shows. This was not a hot crowd after the first two matches, with the exception of four or five spots. But in talking with people, you wouldn't have known it from watching the PPV. Usually the reverse is true. Anyway, if you're surprised at the number of thumbs downs, it is because so many readers that called in attended live, and what they saw was really nothing special of a show. The undercard was pretty good, but the Rumble itself was much worse than the previous two years.

The problems were twofold. Usually the Rumble is carried by one or two of the super workers who kind of take control so the bad workers are left in the shadows, so to speak. In the past, Curt Hennig, Bret Hart, Shawn Michaels, Randy Savage, Roddy Piper and of course Ric Flair last year would carry the focus of the fans while the rest is just background music. This year, there was nobody who put on the killer performance. Flair was good and kept things interesting, and his elimination was actually the loudest pop of the entire show. But once he was eliminated, with the exception of the Undertaker angle which was intriguing, it was really dead until the final minutes. The final minutes were well booked and very exciting, particularly considering Savage vs. Yokozuna doesn't sound like a promising match-up. But in between a hot seven minutes at the end and a fairly good first 15:00 were about 40 minutes of a Battle Royal going nowhere with a lot of non-charismatic people. The lack of talent depth really showed. And don't even get me started on Bob Backlund. If you look up the term not over in the dictionary, you'll see his picture.

AJW DREAM SLAM I

All Japan Women pulled off the biggest promotion in the group's history, setting several records with its 25th anniversary "All-Star Dream Slam" show 4/2 at the Yokohama Arena. As expected, the show drew the largest crowd in the history of both the promotion and women's wrestling in Japan with a sellout 16,500 fans (some seats were blocked off for the ramp and other special effects in an arena that normally holds 17,010 for wrestling), of which 15,000 were paid. While this wasn't the largest crowd ever to see an all-women's wrestling show (I believe the record was set by a card headlined by Mildred Burke in another generation of 19,000), it may have been the largest anywhere in the world over the past 40 years. While a Japanese record crowd was expected, a sellout wasn't. About 5,000 of those tickets were walk-ups, with huge lines forming early in the afternoon. While we don't have a gate figure for the card, I was told that with the high scale ticket prices ($255 ringside) that it was in the neighborhood of what New Japan has done when it packs the arena (New Japan with the same ticket prices has done $1.5 million in the building although I doubt the gate was quite at that level). The only money figure that I do know is that sales of the program alone were $68,000 and they were sold out before the first match began. Certainly they shattered and probably more than doubled the previous gate record for a women's wrestling show anywhere in the world set by the same promotion in same building four years earlier for the Chigusa Nagayo retirement card. In addition, it was believed to have been the longest wrestling show in the history of Japan, starting at 6:30 p.m., with the final match ending at 12:21 a.m. Traditionally major shows in Japan end around 9 p.m., and I believe this was the first regular starting house show to last past midnight (W*ING did a New Years Eve show starting at 11 p.m. that lasted past Midnight this past year and JWP did a live television shoot from 1:30 to 5 a.m. last August). Between 12,000 and 13,000 fans were still there for the finish of the main event, with a large clump leaving just as the final match was getting started because the final train to Tokyo left at midnight. Since the bouts consisted of All Japan women facing wrestlers from other promotions in each match, with the promotional rivalries and egos involved, some matches had cooperation problems. All the women debuted new ring outfits so make it seem like this was different from the every-day show. From an audience standpoint I'm told it was considered one of the most spectacular shows ever in Japan. A videotape of the show is expected to be released in three or four weeks, which will be a three-video series lasting six hours.

This show got more publicity than any women's show in the past decade, as the next morning's Tokyo Sports devoted the first two-and-a-half pages of the sports section to photos and stories on the card. Several mainstream media sources, due to the crowd for this show, have tried to proclaim that there is a new popularity boom for All Japan women (some of the wrestling writers are trying to get it mainstream so it becomes self-fulfilling prophesy because when you tell people enough that something is the hot new thing, often it becomes the next hot thing). The same night as this card saw the first clean pin by Toshiaki Kawada over Stan Hansen during the Champion Carnival plus the Tatsumi Fujinami vs. Great Kabuki first singles match ever with the Great Muta's gimmick on the line relegated to small stories on page three and four respectively, both of which would have normally been given significant coverage. All-Star Dream Slam II on 4/11 in Osaka is being planned for a four-hour long, ten match card, with the promotion trying to peak again for 8/25 at Budokan Hall.

WWF WrestleMania IX

The biggest and most publicized wrestling show of the year in the United States ended with a unique twist--two WWF title changes in about two minutes. Hulk Hogan ended a surrealistic Wrestlemania with the WWF title by legdropping Yokozuna (Rodney Anoia) in 21 seconds, just moments after Yokozuna had pinned Bret Hart, ending a Wrestlemania that promised little on paper and delivered even less.

The WWF's third Wrestlemania held in conjunction with a gambling center fell victim in terms of crowd reaction to a similar, but not quite as extreme fate as the two worst Wrestlemania's of the past, numbers Four and Five held at Trump Plaza in Atlantic City. By and large the crowd came to see Hulk Hogan, and not wrestling, so there wasn't much interest or even knowledge of the underneath angles, hence little heat for any of the actual wrestling. The only big crowd reactions were reserved for the ring entrances (and musical exits) of Hogan, Undertaker and Bret Hart. It was also the day that the WWF formally abandoned its direction of the past six months, and decided its future was its past, in surprisingly building things around Hogan as WWF champion.

There of course has been the expected negative reaction to Hart losing the title. Things have to be looked at from a business perspective. Inside the ring for the quality of his matches on a consistent basis, Hart had done as good a champion as he probably could have under the circumstances. His interviews were also a lot better than one would have expected of him before he won the title. If one is to be judged deserving of something by the quality of their work, Hart did not deserve to have the title taken from him. However, this is the entertainment business, not the construction business. Plenty of people in the entertainment business who are great in their craft live permanently in the shadow of more charismatic people who don't have anywhere near their talent in the same profession. In pro wrestling, that's the case as much if not more than any other form of entertainment. Hart gained a lot in stature and in popularity and one can argue that there was a small increase in recent months at the box office, but realistically that is largely the seasonal gains that take place the first quarter of every year rather than an increase in his drawing power. This formula wasn't working at the box office. It really never did. It has a lot more to do with the state of the business than Bret Hart. But Hulk Hogan is a proven draw. The WWF needed his box office juice to maintain its position in its entertainment world. He had a lot of bargaining chips on his side because of it when he chose to return.

The reaction to the double title switch, if it even holds up that way, on one hand has cheapened the title more than ever before because of the constant hot-shotting on nearly every PPV and switching over the past 18 months, was largely negative. If the title is taken away, it'll be almost a repeat of the Tuesday in Texas angle that was just run in the fall of 1991. If it isn't, the manner cheapened the title and eliminated one obvious PPV gate with Hogan vowing to regain the title. But the most important thing for the credibility of a major title is for it to be the focus of the promotion and what everyone is gunning for. As long as Hogan is around, he'll be the focal point. If Hogan is around, and not involved as either the champion or top contender makes the belt secondary to whatever Hogan is involved in. That still doesn't satisfy the argument that if they don't change things they will have killed the obvious PPV gate with Hogan as a challenger simply to pick up whatever few extra buys they can on 4/12 for a replay showing by advertising two title changes. Even though the majority of reaction here has been strongly negative regarding the direction change, it has to be acknowledged that this was the right move for business this summer. One can argue that it was only the right move short-term and the company has to build for long-term. Hogan's presence overwhelms anyone else getting over as the next superstar, which was largely the argument WWF sources had been espousing to me while the company was at its box office depths in the winter as to why it would be counter-productive for Hogan to return, almost until the day Hogan re-signed.

Hogan coming back after the weak buy rate of Royal Rumble was the acknowledgement that building for life without Hogan wasn't working yet with the biggest show of the year on the horizon. Hogan's return, which it appears what happened at Mania was a large part of the deal, pretty much ended the direction tried with Bret Hart. At the same time, there are so many unpredictable variables surrounding this business that are completely out of the control of those running the business that short-term planning and getting the quick money may be the smartest direction of all because long-term planning may be fruitless. If that's the case, going with Hogan on top is the right choice because on an immediate basis, he and the title belt together (whether he is wearing the belt or simply the top contender for it and eventually wins it) should draw more than either without the other. From most accounts, the finishes for the key matches were so secretive that the wrestlers' themselves didn't know until the afternoon of the card (although I'm sure Hogan wasn't among the list of those who didn't know) which has its pluses and minuses. The minuses are when nobody knows, word can't leak out. The pluses are that when the wrestlers themselves don't know, they can't plan their match out ahead of time and results in a match that could be a lot better than it turns out to be (Perfect vs. Luger in particular may have been victimized by this).

On television Monday night, they announced that Yokozuna was filing a protest and that a ruling would be made on television as to the future of the title. The ads for the replay of Mania on 4/12 PPV talk about seeing the title change hands twice in the same night at the greatest Wrestlemania ever (is there even one person alive who believes that?). They could hold the belt up and give it to the winner of the 6/13 PPV tournament, go back to Yokozuna, or keep things the way they are. As of press time, it's still a state secret, but if a change is going to be made, it won't happen until after the replay show. Hogan didn't work the tapings Monday night in Phoenix (nor was he scheduled for Tuesday in Tucson) and nothing at the show gave any indication one way or another about the status of the title.

As for the show itself, it's hard to make an argument this was worth the $29.95. With the poor lighting, the show lacked the visual impressiveness a mega-show should have. It certainly lacked the wrestling action. The majority of the matches were bad and none were the excellent memorable type matches one expects to see at least one of on the so-called biggest show of the year. The booking, while unique with the double title change, the manner of doing so did little for credibility of the title. Whatever creativity there was with the double Doink finish was lacking when it came to several other finishes, most notably the other two title matches. It seemed the endings consisted of one "how can we get out of this" after another. Being overly creative is okay for one or two matches as the exception to the rule. But an entire show of those endings kills the uniqueness and impact that screw-jobs should have individually and turns these type of match endings into having the impact they've had the past few years in WCW. Zilch, as I presume will be the impact most of the finishes will have. Although there was talk about magic during the Doink finish, the best magician was Jim Ross, who showed up and nearly made 350 pound Gorilla Monsoon disappear. Ross did a great job as an announcer, since he appeared totally familiar with every angle and what he needed to get across which is no easy feat considering he's only been with the company for one week. Ross interacted well with Bobby Heenan. Heenan's and Shawn Michaels' performances (just coming back from a shoulder separation) were the only "biggest show of the year" calibre acts on the entire show. As has been the case the past few years on major WWF shows, there were timing problems with the early matches running long (after all these years, how do they constantly have this problem show-after-show?). The Kimala-Bigelow match was canceled (like anyone really missed it) and several of the matches later in the card were cut short on time so planned out sequences were on the cutting room floor so to speak.

On the positive side, the local promotion of the event was nothing short of spectacular. Many were surprised that such a preponderance of the crowd was families from Las Vegas, largely to see Hulk Hogan, which had to do with the immense amount of local publicity. The day before the show, an autograph session was held with several wrestlers, the biggest name of which was Undertaker, which drew an estimated 6,000 people to Caesar's. A brunch was held the day of the show, complete with an angle where Lex Luger attacked and KO'd Bret Hart (an angle which was acknowledged several times on the telecast yet played no part whatsoever in the storyline of the main event). Most of the crew was in town several days early to do local publicity and almost all came across in a positive manner.

We've got little in regard to PPV buy rate reports which are the most important figures as to whether the show was a success or failure other than talk that it was the lowest Mania ever, but that was a given going in, with several surprising reports around the country of cable systems not even carrying the event claiming a lack of interest (including systems in Chicago and Beverly Hills which says something about its perceived current upscale appeal, but is unexplainable since even at a worst-case scenario this show was going to do better on PPV than anything aside from a major boxing title fight). Live, the show drew an announced crowd of 15,045 fans, very few of which were freebies, which was pretty much a full house but I don't believe it was a sellout. At match time they were still selling $50, $100 and $150 tickets although the way the seating was set up, there didn't look to be room for many more. The live gate was reported to me by two sources between $1 million and $1.2. So the live gate was actually only about $50,000 to $200,000 less than last year's Mania in the much larger Hoosier Dome with more than four times as many humans in attendance because of the higher scaled ticket prices. It will no doubt be the only million dollar gate of the year in the U.S., but it may not have been the highest live gate of the weekend. For those who want to make plans early, tentative word is next year's Mania will take place in Madison Square Garden. Anything in wrestling one year from now has to be labeled as tentative.

AAA TripleMania I

Triple Mania, headlined by the loser must retire match between Konnan El Barbaro (Carlos Espada) vs. Cien Caras (Carmelo Reyes), the top babyface and heel in the country, drew a sellout 48,000 fans of which between 42,000 and 45,000 were paid, or about the 12th largest verified paid attendance in pro wrestling history. It was either the largest or second largest paid attendance for pro wrestling in North America in the past three years and broke all existing crowd and gate records for Mexico. It was also the largest crowd to see any event at the Plaza de Toros, traditionally a bullfighting arena but it also houses big name concerts and boxing matches, since a boxing match in the 50s. Tickets were priced from $39 (120,000 pesos) ringside down to $1.70, so the gate was nowhere near the level of some of the biggest WWF or Japanese gates, but was probably in the $400,000 range. The average working person in Mexico earns about one-eighth of what someone in the U.S. would earn so in relation to average income, the tickets aren't as cheap as they sound.

The media nationwide reported the crowd at 62,000 which will be the number the show will be associated with for evermore. The media coverage was similar to a world title boxing fight or an NFL football game in the U.S., to the point that Cien Caras and Konnan were on all the network newscasts the day of the show and the top-rated newsmagazine show in the country (equivalent to "60 Minutes") ran a feature on the card the last week. The promotion was based around heavy television advertising on Televisa, the largest network in Mexico and the network which airs this group's television show. The advance was about 47,000 tickets, but it didn't actually sellout until the day of the event. At least 5,000 fans were turned away at the door. There were no major problems stemming from that as was feared going in based on the biggest show in 1991. One of the previous biggest crowds in recent memory in Mexico, a Cien Caras vs. Rayo de Jalisco Jr. mask vs. mask match at Arena Mexico in 1991 where Caras lost his hood, there was so much demand for tickets after the building had sold out that those wanting in overpowered security and barged into the building without tickets midway through the card and congregated in the upper deck. The combination of 6,000 more fans than capacity and people jumping up and down caused serious structural damage to the building and caused it to close down for a few months. What was interesting also was the huge amount of fans cheering the heels, which has been an AAA trademark of late even with "rudo" sections of the crowd heavily cheering the heels at the regular Friday night cards.

After the third match on the card, Jake Roberts was brought to ringside. Even though he had done a few heel promos on television, he was largely cheered at first as being an American superstar. Some people recognized him and others didn't. He then did an interview talking about how he was the best wrestler around and put down the country of Mexico and Mexican wrestling and wrestlers in general. He then said he wanted to challenge the winner of the main event, who he hoped would be Cien Caras, and grabbed his crotch and gave the crowd the "up yours" which resulted in chants of "culero" (asshole) at him. Roberts watched the rest of the card from a fifth row seat and the TV cameras constantly showed him sneering at the quality of the wrestling and I heard raves about his facial expressions all night in getting himself over instantaneously.

Surprisingly, the crowd was split when the main event started. An estimated 40 to 50 percent of the crowd was cheering Caras vehemently. The kids, particularly the teenagers, and the women were cheering for Konnan. The older fans, particularly the men, were heavily pro-Caras. The older fans are more traditional in that they like the older wrestlers that they are familiar with rather than the new flashes in the pan, and are also more nationalistic. Caras is Mexican and Konnan isn't, and Caras even though a heel has been around for about 19 years and is a fixture on top. They were heavily pro-Caras and there were a lot of Mexican flags waving for him. As you can figure with that kind of a crowd mix, it was Perro Aguayo, who is popular with every audience, that received the most thunderous cheers on the show. Konnan came out surprisingly with midget wrestler Mascarita Sagrada as his second, which made sense based on what the storyline was. In the third fall of the main event, after several near falls, Roberts came to ringside. He acted like he was trying to give Caras advice but Caras kept ignoring him. As Caras finally jumped out of the ring to confront Roberts, Konnan attacked Caras. Sagrada, who was in the vicinity, was then jumped by Roberts and punted around the ring. At this point heel Caras goes to save Sagrada (who wound up doing a stretcher job) and he and Roberts exchange blows until Roberts hits him with a black glove (remnants of the late referee Gran Davis) and gives him a DDT. Konnan and Roberts started brawling outside the ring with Konnan getting the advantage and while this was going on, Caras' brother threw him into the ring and Konnan was counted out, losing the match. Roberts never actually entered the ring because promoter Antonio Pena didn't want to test prospective problems because he didn't have a work permit and had he interfered in the ring, the EMLL could have possibly caused him governmental headaches.

At this point a lot of the kids and women started crying, and promoter Antonio Pena cued a song called "Las Galodrinas" to be played over the speakers. The song is famous in the country as the saddest song there is and reminds people of funerals and other sad occasions and many people cry whenever they hear the song, so before you knew it, about 30,000 people were crying, making it one of the most emotional finales to a wrestling show ever. As Konnan left the ring for the "final" time (as if), he was hugging the kids who were crying. This all took place between 12:30 and 12:45 a.m. since the show lasted so long. After the show there was so much heat that there were an estimated 5,000 fans waiting outside the heel dressing room at 3 a.m. for Roberts, before they finally got the crowd to disperse and could get Roberts safely out of the building. Obviously, based on the finish, Konnan will be returning at some point, but it looks as though that won't be for about two months. After the show at about 2 a.m., with several thousand fans near the face dressing room, they already began hinting of a letter writing campaign to bring back Konnan, so I guess that's the direction they are going. The very tentative plan seems to be for Konnan vs. Cien Caras in a hair vs. hair match in the same building around September or October, and holding off the inevitable Konnan vs. Jake Roberts Mexico City match until Triple Mania II.

Under normal scheduling, this card would have aired on television in Mexico City on 5/2 and in the United States on 5/9. However, it had been announced earlier in the week, as a means to guarantee filling the building, that the show wouldn't be televised this weekend and in the slot that will air on 5/9 they instead aired a card taped 4/25 from Villahermosa from a bullring with Konnan vs. Caras on top going to a double count out in a non-stipulation match. Triple Mania will air on television in Mexico City as a special wrestling show on 5/21 on Televisa, for those who have dishes, although I don't know the time slot at press time. I've been unable to confirm if the show will air in the United States although it was speculated it would air during the normal Galavision wrestling time slot on 5/23. There is also a lot of talk about AAA running shows as soon as June or July in the United States, as well as talk of a major card in Tijuana (across the border from San Diego) during the same time frame.

Based on what I'm told, the wrestling on this card would be considered good under normal Lucha Libre standards and a spectacular overall show with the rock bands playing and laser light shows. But according to two regulars that were there live that the wrestling itself was below the standard of the typical Friday night card at Juan de la Barrera Gym. It was confirmed that a lot of the wrestlers were really nervous, with the noted exception of Aguayo, who has seen and done everything that can be done in a ring already, and thus had the best match on the show. Most didn't try new moves or the ultra-spectacular moves that have become commonplace on the regular shows because they didn't want to screw up moves in front of so many. It was far and away the largest crowd that just about all of them had ever performed in front of and was the most publicized show in the country's history. The pressure took the work level down just a peg. I'm told almost all the matches were good, just that none were of the spectacular level that some of the Friday night mid-card matches have reached over the past few months.

Results from the undercard saw: 1. Martha Villalobos & Pantera Surena & Wendy beat Lola Gonzales & Vicki Caranza & La Rosa in an all-action match. La Rosa was the highlight; 2. Winners & Super Calo & El Salsero beat May Flowers & Rudy Reyna & Baby Sharon; 3. Volador & Misterioso & Rey Misterio Jr. beat Tony Arce & Vulcano & Rocco Valente in what was the second or third best match on the show; 4. Octagon & El Hijo del Santo & Villano III beat Fuerza Guerrera & Heavy Metal & Rambo; 5. Lizmark retained the Mexican Light heavyweight title in a strange finish over La Parca. La Parca, a heel, was the best worker on the show based on what I was told and was cheered like crazy and this was said to have been a great match. The match went about 20:00 when La Parca got the pin but just before the three count, Lizmark got his shoulder up. That was "supposed" to be the finish, a controversial one to give Lizmark something to complain about. Anyway, apparently they forgot to inform the commission what they were going to do, because the Box y Lucha commissioner saw Lizmark complain and made a fuss and ordered the match re-started because Lizmark had his shoulder up. Pena came out and what was agreed to was they would go another 15:00 and if Lizmark could win during that time period, he'd retain the title, but if he couldn't, then Parca could keep the title. They went 15:00 so apparently Parca would get to keep the title but somehow via a referees decision, Lizmark was ruled the winner. The ending was every bit as confusing as it reads; 6. Mascara Sagrada & Love Machine (Art Barr) & Mascarita Sagrada beat Jerry Estrada & Blue Panther & Jerrito Estrada in a mixed match. The main focus of this was the Blue Panther vs. Love Machine long-time feud. Machine kept going for the piledriver, which is illegal in Mexico, and the ref kept stopping him. Finally Panther gave Machine a piledriver and was disqualified and Machine did a stretcher job and will be kept out of action for two or three weeks; 7. The semifinal before Konnan-Caras was a hair vs. mask match with Aguayo vs. Mascara Ano 2000. Aguayo bled buckets as he always does in the big matches and this was the wildest match and had the most heat. Not only was Aguayo drenched in blood, so was the mat, and there were puddles everywhere. Mascara's brother Universo 2000 interfered in the early falls. Aguayo won in 28:00 and Mascara first ran away, but was forced back into the ring and announced that he was Jesus Reyes (younger brother of Cien Caras/Carmelo Reyes which was well-known) and 34 years old.

WCW SLAMBOREE '93

After years of American promotions ignoring all history of their business, suddenly, in the wake of declining viewer interest, both major promotions are in a race to see who can bring up the most nostalgia. WCW scored first last September with its 20th anniversary Clash of Champions drawing a 3.7 rating, which was much higher than most of the recent Clashes have done. The WWF seemingly beat WCW to the punch on one idea by announcing a Hall of Fame and Andre the Giant as the first inductee, since it was known within the industry it was going to announce its own Hall of Fame this past weekend. WCW attempted the biggest score based on nostalgia with a PPV show primarily advertised on that theme with some great (and a few not-so-great) segments on television building up that premise.

The reaction to Slamboree '93, the night of the legends was mixed overall. It's not a show that is going to have any effect on the current business trends, either positively or negatively. Personally, I'd give the show a very mild thumbs up because the three main matches delivered great action, the bad matches were kept short, and it was fun seeing wrestling history all of a sudden not become a forbidden subject to talk about. But there were serious negatives. The show lacked any momentum from start to finish. The finishes were almost all mindless, which made the matches with the current wrestlers seem more like a good house show effort rather than a major card designed to change and further storylines. Little was done effectively to build up anything for the future, although Davey Boy Smith came out stronger than before.

There were far too many substitutions on a major card, some of which could and should have been announced ahead of time. Trying to pretend one of the substitutions didn't happen by pretending someone who wasn't on the card was in a title match by putting a hood over his replacement is a little too fraudulent. When that happened in California in 1977, the promoter nearly lost his license and the wrestlers involved had to pay legitimate heavy fines to the state athletic commission because it was taken as a serious matter of fraud, although false advertising is so frequent in wrestling now as compared with 16 years ago that it'll be considered simply every-day business by most. And how about Scott Norton's replacement? Granted, they were in a lurch when a guy walks out before a PPV, and they did at least get it announced on television the day before about the change in the match, but that Sting-Nailz deal was a 5:00 fiasco which was a waste of the company's most popular wrestler on a major show. And most of all, whose idea was it to introduce all the legends before the PPV show started? With all the money spent to bring all the guys in, which was probably close to the entire live gate, the least they could have done was give them nice introductions so older viewers in the television audience could see a close-up of people who entertained them years ago. Seven weeks ago, All Japan women did this exact same thing and handled it perfectly, which seemingly means that WCW would find a way to screw up the easy one.

The basic story on Norton allegedly is that they had offered him $2,000 for the match with Sting and they wanted him to put Sting over. Norton saw that he wasn't booked on the television shows that would air after Slamboree when they taped Monday through Wednesday and must have thought it was a quickie blow-off since he had just arrived and it was is first major show. Since his business is Japan where he's a top star, he may have thought it wasn't good for his primary job to put Sting over on a major U.S. card. Whatever the reasons, lawyers got involved, and on Friday, negotiations had broken off and Norton went home.

Even though the advance was poor, the house for television was well-dressed to where it at least looked respectable. There were 7,008 in the building, with 3,722 paid, which is pretty bad for a PPV but considering how the advance looked, it wasn't unexpected. The paid attendance was actually lower than the previous regular Omni house show, although that show had a $1 ticket price so the comparison isn't really fair and the gate was lower than this. The live gate was $37,000 which is a little better than most Omni shows over the past year. Starrcade at the Omni, in comparison, did $70,000. No PPV numbers at press time, but from all indications, this would be among the lowest ever.

The show opened with all the legends in the ring but no announcements made as to who was who. In a lot of cases it was obvious who they were, but if he hadn't have done the interview, who would have guessed that reject from Crosby, Stills and Nash was Bugsy McGraw? Maxx Payne played the guitar during the open. Then they announced that "The Prisoner" had done something to Scott Norton and that he'd be facing Sting. On television on Saturday they had announced that Nailz (Kevin Wacholz) had injured Norton (who legitimately walked out over a money dispute earlier in the week) and would be facing Sting. Sounds like a last minute threatening legal letter came from Connecticut which caused them not to use the Nailz name, which is the subject of some legal volleyball right now. However, it was almost science fiction as the ultra-prepared Tony Schiavone, who did his best job ever on a major show, suddenly developed a major memory loss during that match as he acted as if nobody knew who the Prisoner was or his background, despite the fact he had to know that almost everyone watching knew both, especially since he wore the same ring outfit down to the nightstick as with Titan. I guess the WCW jokesters got their little revenge by announcing Prisoner from Green Bay, WI, which is where Mr. Wacholz allegedly did that number on Vince McMahon which has resulted in a lawsuit and a counter-suit. Jesse Ventura was announced as being hospitalized, which was legitimate. He was replaced by Larry Zbyszko, who did a pretty good job as well. Ventura was complaining Saturday morning at his Minnesota home of leg pains and went to a local hospital where it was diagnosed as blood clots in the leg. He was attributing it to wearing ultra-tight knee pads in his movie costume filming "Demolition Man." Ventura was expected to be released from the hospital on Monday or Tuesday.

WWF KING OF THE RING '93

The first King of the Ring pay-per-view show, as opposed to the first King of the Ring tournament, featuring

Yokozuna winning the WWF title from Hulk Hogan and Bret Hart going over in the tournament was largely praised as the best WWF pay-per-view show since the 1992 Summer Slam show from London. Ironically, the star of that show, Bret Hart, who apparently went in with an injured ankle and came out hurt enough that he missed the next night's television taping, was almost a one-man show this time, making the difference between a largely uneventful show and a very good one.

However, the big news was Hogan putting Yokozuna (Rodney Anoia of San Francisco doing a sumo wrestler gimmick) over to make Yokozuna into a two-time WWF champion. As many have noted, the WWF is turning into a Memphis style promotion with more frequent angles, title changes and new scenarios created, which make it more intriguing for a hardcore audience and harder to follow for a casual audience. Since the overall casual interest has decreased so much over the past year, this may not be the worst idea. An example of this was a second title change in as many nights as Rick & Scott Steiner won the tag team titles from Money Inc. on 6/14 at the Wrestling Challenge tapings in Columbus, OH.

The Hogan-Yokozuna title switch apparently sets up a rematch between the two at the Summer Slam show on 8/30 at the Palace in Auburn Hills, MI. An angle after Hart won the King of the Ring tournament seems to set up a match with Jerry Lawler. One would expect the logical scenario coming out of this would be for Hogan to either regain the title outright, or come up with a strong showing since he put Yokozuna over in a big way and obviously didn't do that if he wasn't trying to make someone strong so it means more when they lose to him. By teasing the bodyslam, Hogan can get a "moral" win by doing the slam and winning via count out without regaining the title, if the decision is made that his outside wrestling commitments won't allow him to work enough dates to make it feasible for him to be champion. This also explains Hogan's comments in Japan about the WWF title, since he knew when he did those interviews that he was going to lose (which from all accounts was his choice since he made the contact with Masao Hattori to be referee and do a heel ref screw-job finish) and apparently wanted to make it seem that it wasn't high on his list of priorities so it wasn't really a big loss, at least to the Japanese who know Yokozuna as Kokina, not a major headliner. Hogan had asked Hattori to referee the match, which had been announced in Japan but never in the U.S. Apparently Hattori's role as explained by Hogan was to be the Japanese heel ref to screw Hogan out of the title.

For unexplained reasons (the only one given was the fact that the original finish was in the Wrestling Observer, but that holds no water since WWF policy as opposed to WCW policy has always been to not change storylines and scenarios because of this newsletter and this newsletter never printed the finish beforehand, only hinted at different scenarios), but given that it was apparently former WWF wrestler Akio Sato of the original Orient Express tag team who got to participate in the angle as the photographer, the real reason seems more to be Japanese internal politics vis a vis Sato vs. New Japan. One week before the show, Hattori received word that they weren't bringing him in. The original screw-job scenario of changing the title was replaced by having a photographer, Sato, shoot a flash of fire out of his camera into Hogan's eyes, blinding him, and making him a victim of a legdrop at 13:11. The storyline that Hogan had proposed, and whether this is how it will go or not I don't know, was that he would lose to set up becoming a six-time champion at Summer Slam. By how strongly he put Yokozuna over, I have to believe that was in his mind for the Summer Slam finish when he was in the ring at King of the Ring. If he wasn't going to regain the title, he'd have dominated the body of the match before losing rather than given Yokozuna virtually the entire match.

Hart, who had the three best matches on the show and was put over the strongest of anyone as a babyface, is being groomed to eventually win the title, either from Hogan or Yokozuna. It appears this is more of a long-term story that may be put off until Wrestlemania, rather than pushed immediately.

The show itself drew a legitimate sellout of about 6,500 paid and just under $80,000 at the Nutter Arena in Dayton, OH. Although in typical WWF fashion it was announced one week out that all tickets at the live event were sold out, the card actually didn't sellout until the night of the show. No word at press time on PPV, but most expect it to fall between the 1.0 and 1.5 percent level. Going head-to-head with the NBA finals did nobody any favors, not to mention the game they went head-to-head with is now being called in some circles the greatest basketball game in history. In 1993, that is probably very close to if not equally as stiff competition as running a PPV head-to-head with the World Series, as WCW often has during Halloween Havoc, although in looking back, surprisingly, even going head-to-head with the World Series doesn't seem to have nearly the effect on the buy rate as one might ascertain. A replay of the show is scheduled on PPV on 6/22.

The show had a strong overall storyline, in that looking at the show in hindsight, it seemed to be a better and more significant show than it actually felt like while it was going on. My own feeling after watching the show and getting the poll results is I was surprised that the thumbs up percentage wasn't between 80 and 90 percent. There was an opinion expressed on many callers that they could only give a one man show a thumbs in the middle. It also seemed more like watching a serious event as opposed to a fantasy show, with the emphasis on the wrestling and in many ways seemed to have the flow of some of the WCW PPV shows when Jim Ross was formatting them. The crowd, which largely stayed until the final match even though Hogan was put on in the middle of the card (in the past when Hogan was put on early, it meant an early departing crowd for the final main matches), didn't seem on television to react strongly to much aside from Hogan's ring entrance and a few big climactic spots and finishes. The show was a more hardcore wrestling show than most of the Titan shows, with mainly clean finishes and only one bizarre screw-job in the Hogan match and a preposterous screw-job in the Crush match.

My feeling is the announcing wasn't bad, but it was below the standard of most recent PPV shows. Jim Ross was okay but below his usual standard. I can't find any fault with his performance although the interplay between the three wasn't as smooth as at Wrestlemania. Bobby Heenan was below par as well. He told a few jokes, most of which were predictable, and wasn't anywhere near as funny as he usually is. The chemistry with Randy Savage just didn't work on this show. It always seemed ill at ease every time he tried to get in something to say. Savage also suffers from his patter being to simple and predictable and without enough varying points to not get stale in a two-and-a-half hour broadcast. Then when he did, it always seemed like he really didn't know what he wanted to say, just that he wanted to talk but had no cogent point to make.

WCW BEACH BLAST '93

Beach Blast on 7/18 came and went. That's about all the impression the show seems to have left. The card, which based on reaction here seems to have garnered the least amount of interest in any major promotion PPV to date. From all accounts the show was well promoted in the area with a cross-promotion with a local casino, which paid WCW $10,000 for a site fee. The 10,000 seat Gulf Coast Coliseum in Biloxi, MS was nearly filled, with about 8,600 fans, of which nearly 4,000 were paid, many with a $5 GA ticket, so the gate was $33,000. Even with freebies, that is the most people put in a building for WCW in quite a while.

I'm in the minority here giving the show a thumbs up, because I enjoyed the work rate in most of the matches and none of the matches were poor. There were no excellent matches either, and with the exception of Big Van Vader doing a moonsault with a herniated disc, there was little that will be remembered about the show in the months to come. Whatever historical implications Ric Flair regaining the NWA title should have had going on seemed to be an enormous letdown when actually viewing it, which again emphasizes one more time how there are too many titles in wrestling and almost all of them have zero meaning. The crowd looked good on television and reacted well early in the show, during matches with wrestlers that haven't to this point been given a major push. In hindsight, it appeared the big mistake on the show was going with two straight long matches. While both were well-worked, there was a point about 18:00 in during the Blonds vs. Arn Anderson & Paul Roma match where the crowd seemed to lose a lot of interest, even though the hottest spots of the match actually came after that point. Dustin Rhodes vs. Rick Rude was solidly worked, but I also believe this match hurt the show more than any other. Rude does not have the repertoire to do a 30 minute match on a PPV show (where inherently you need to deliver more moves and action than you do on a house show), and it was a big mistake to do two falls. The resulting draw, while no surprise, left the show flat. It stayed flat for the Flair-Windham match. The tag match ended the show on both a hot and logical note. However, the single most important thing in the finish and one of the two key points that should have been remembered about the show (the other being the NWA title change), was that Smith had scored a clean pin on the world champion and thus was the logical contender for the title. Since the Vader-Smith match headlines the next Clash, the Smith pinning Vader finish was totally logical booking, which is such a rarity it was almost a surprise. However, that point wasn't even referred to after the pin, let alone was the point driven home by the announcers as it should have been to start building the momentum for the Clash. The pyrotechnics that opened the show were hot, but they should have used the pyro to emphasize the major spots on the card (Flair and Smith's wins) rather than use it all to build an artificial pop to open the show. As for the company's new steroid policy, this show pretty well confirmed everything. The steroid policy is in place and it's working. The only thing is that this show emphasized what the real policy, as opposed to the written policy, really is. That is, if you aren't on steroids, you aren't allowed anywhere near the top on PPV cards.

WWF SUMMERSLAM '93

Summer Slam '93 was a show of several surprises, although not all of them were good. The best performer on the show was a guy who only was in the ring for 6:32 and didn't do all that much once he was in (Jerry Lawler). The second best performer on the show was a retired wrestler who has never even worked for the promotion (Bruce Hart). And the best performer in the ring was a guy from another promotion who was only there as a negotiating favor and there don't appear to be any plans to bring back (Jimmy Del Rey). If anything was shown at Summer Slam, it was that the show quality of WWF pay-per-views can be greatly helped by using performers from other territories, because I'd hate to think of what the show would have been if you took Jerry Lawler and the Heavenly Bodies off it. I wouldn't call the show a bad one, but did give it a minor thumbs down. It came nowhere close to what it was built up as going to be. The WWF's strengths, as far as production and smoothness of the telecast were evident, but the biggest strength was the attempt to camouflage yet another in what is turning into a consistent stream of screw-job finishes in PPV main events. For all the heat WCW took for same, there was never a period when Dusty Rhodes booked WCW when seven of the previous eight PPV shows had the advertised main event end with a screw-job finish. The only difference is the WWF does a better job of dressing things up through audience manipulation (this is meant as a compliment). By dropping the balloons and having the faces run in to congratulate Luger as if he'd won the title, and by never making an announcement inside the building about the title not changing hands, the initial confusion and later disappointment about such a poor finish to the main event would never come across to the viewer at home. In fact, from our reports, it didn't really hit the live audience until they started leaving the building.

There is a very logical business reason to not change the title. The biggest money match the company thinks it has for Wrestlemania is Yokozuna vs. Luger. But it can't draw a Wrestlemania buy rate with Yokozuna as the challenger. The scenario that seems to make sense is for Luger to be denied a title shot (since McMahon made a point of saying he'd be getting one and everything said in that manner is a set up for misdirection) because of the no return clause, and then being forced to win the Royal Rumble to get the shot at Mania, which he would. Whether it was a good or bad decision (and it was a decision made many weeks ago to not change the title) will be determined by the fall business. As for as major positives, the entire angle with Lawler and the Hart Family was the highlight of the show, and the Steiners-Heavenly Bodies delivered about as much as they could given the time constraints. Vince McMahon did a phenomenal job of announcing during the Luger-Yokozuna match which made it seem a lot better than it really was, but Bobby Heenan wasn't at top form and new interviewer Joe Thaller (replacing the departed Gene Okerlund) only showed that you can't parody a parody (Okerlund). And the six-man tag match (Smoking Gunns & Tatanka vs. Head Shrinkers & Bam Bam Bigelow) was good.

The list of negatives is longer: 1) It is a huge mistake for announcers to promise any specific match is going to be one of the great matches of all-time because that leads to disappointment because of inflated expectations. They can promise a title switch or revenge because that is in control of the scriptwriter, but promising a classic makes the classic match seem expected rather than a bonus, not to mention that no matter who is in the ring, you can't just snap your fingers and expect they'll both be at their best. Anyway, Michaels vs. Perfect was promised as a classic over-and-over, and then didn't deliver at all. It was a good match if judged by the standards of two ordinary wrestlers in that spot, but because of pre-match build-up, a huge disappointment. I think it's also becoming more and more obvious that those who believe Curt Hennig is one of the top wrestlers in the world pay more attention to what someone has done years in the past rather than what goes on in the ring today; 2) Ted DiBiase didn't carry Razor Ramon to a good match; 3) IRS vs. 1-2-3 made no sense on several different levels; 4) Ludvig Borga is terrible; 5) Giant Gonzalez makes Ludvig Borga seem like Kenta Kobashi; 6) While Luger and Yokozuna did about as well as they could do, it was ridiculous to have them go that long because it exposed that Luger is no Bret Hart; 7) While it would be foolish to call any crowd of 19,000 in the year 1993 a disappointment, the fact they failed to sellout after spending so much time and money on pushing Luger and dropping tickets down to a $5 bottom for kids shows that while the "Call to Action Campaign" was a success, it was not an overwhelming success.

AAA/IWC La Revancha

Using any words except overwhelming success to describe "La Revancha" would be misleading. It was an eye-opening experience that everyone involved in the wrestling business at the top level should have seen. But the success only asks more questions about where does it go from here. There clearly is an audience, and one much larger than anyone suspected, for Lucha Libre shows in areas where 1) There is a large spanish speaking population and 2) Where the AAA television show is available to that population. While in no way comparable to the Los Angeles show, the 8/27 show in San Jose, drew a near sellout to the SUREC Arena of 4,500 paying $93,000. It nearly doubled the previous best ever gate in the city set by the WWF for a television taping in February. It was also a major success overall and a hot house show. WCW, for example, hasn't drawn a gate as large as the San Jose show in this continent since 1990. The key in both markets was not only the large spanish population base, but the AAA's television show availability to that audience. In contrast, the 8/29 show in San Diego, which drew 2,500 paying $46,000, wasn't a big success (although the gate was larger than any WWF show in the market since March 1992) because although the area has the spanish population, it appeared that the Galavision cable wasn't on the systems that reached that audience. In Los Angeles and San Jose, the fans were familiar with every wrestler, every angle and every personality involved. In San Diego, it was a crowd that came to see wrestling and they got hooked into the storylines of the matches so a lot of the guys got over, but nobody was over strong to begin with. Things that got reactions such as things related to recent angles or heel ref El Tirantes and some of the big names didn't get the reaction.

Most people watching AAA for the first time don't know what to make of it. Some of the moves look great, but the transitions look "wrong" because you'd be used to watching American style. Admittedly some of the spots are really hokey, but then again, if you look at things logically, the only groups whose work style isn't filled with hokey unrealistic spots would be UWFI and Rings. If you just concentrate on the storylines and presentation, AAA is very similar to WWF. Heavy on the glitz, although delivering more on the substance. Strong on symbolization and one-dimensional gimmick characters who are nothing like what they portray, rather than presenting its stars as multi-dimensional human beings. The only difference is in AAA, it's the Americans who are the foreign menaces and it's the Mexican flag that keeps getting waved. Just like the WWF's top foreign menace is really an American (Yokozuna), AAA's top Mexican star (Konnan) is really also really an American of Cuban birth who represents Mexico. Konnan is AAA's answer Lex Luger although he seems to have more charisma and fire and has an ability to connect with the crowd better. He's gained 30 pounds in the last few weeks while Luger has lost it, and probably for at least partially similar reasons. Perro Aguayo is Randy Savage, right down to the frizzies, but with a forehead like Atsushi Onita. Cien Caras, well I just don't get it. He's probably drawn more fans this year than any heel in the world, which should make him by that criteria the winner for heel of the year. But as the top heel, it looks like everyone cheers him in Mexico, although as a heel in San Jose, nobody cheered him. I have no idea why anyone would even care one way or another. Rey Misterio Jr. is 1-2-3 Kid, except everyone sells for him and he gets more of a push. Jake Roberts is Jake Roberts. Love Machine & Eddy Guerrero are the Hollywood Blonds. Machine being Pillman and Guerrero being Austin. Psicosis isn't Jushin Liger, but he wears the same outfit and does work like Liger's evil twin. La Parka is anything but a comic book character and looks like nothing but one. Arturo Rivera is Bobby Heenan and Alfonso

Morales is Jim Ross, except he doesn't talk as much about football. Blue Panther is Dory Funk Jr. in his prime, but now he's Ted DiBiase after a face turn. Heavy Metal is Negro Casas' younger brother but looks like Janet Jackson's younger brother. And Mascarita Sagrada is anything but the Macho Midget.

The rules of Lucha are also different. Most matches are called trios matches, known in the U.S. as six-man tags. They are usually two of three falls. One member of each team is designated as the captain. When someone is knocked out of the ring, a member of his team can replace him without having to tag. To win a fall, one must either pin or make submit either the captain, or two members of the team, so fall sequences often end with two, and sometimes three pins or submissions. It creates the scenario at the end of most falls where they fight 10:00 to gain a fall, but the second pin usually takes a matter of seconds. If you think about it, it seems to make no sense, but that's how they've been doing it for decades so you just have to accept it as part of the game. The best matches are highlighted by topes (to-pays), which are dives out of the ring. The storylines are kept to pretty basic traditional feuds. The moves themselves are the most creative in wrestling, although also the most unrealistic. The actual psychology of the matches live isn't that different (faces start strong to get the crowd behind them, heels pick on one member of the face team to draw heat, hot tags, building toward a finish), but the means to that end are totally different. In AAA, the heavy, and I mean heavy emphasis, is that the heels leave with heat and send the fans home frustrated which in theory would mean leaving them with baited breath wanting to come back to see the heel taste his own medicine. This is different than the major Japanese offices, where it is presented as athletic competition with clean winners and losers rather than morality play, or the U.S. where it is morality play but in recent years the idea is to send people home happy and the heels taste their own medicine every night.

Where to go next? Last summer's run of major Lucha Libre shows in Los Angeles show this crowd isn't necessarily a one-time fluke. Anyone in the building Saturday would probably agree with the assessment that with correct booking into a major climactic match that a major blow-off show at the Los Angeles Coliseum with Konnan vs. Roberts with the right stipulation has the potential to break the Blassie-Tolos record. Still, by presenting a show that was so strong in line-up, execution and presentation, let alone crowd reaction, a standard has been set that logically can't be lived up to. Logically you can't sellout every show, but with strong line-ups and coming on a regular enough basis, and booking from show-to-show doing consistent $75,000 to $100,000 houses should be a piece of cake. If the promoters start expecting consistent business at the $200,000 level and budget things that way, this, like all recent prior major Lucha promotions in Los Angeles, will burn out. The idea for Antonio Pena, the AAA President, and his American partners, Ron Skoler and John Arezzi, seems to be to run U.S. tours of three or four cities every few months. The next tour is scheduled for the weekend of 11/12 to 11/14 with the probable main event for next time in Los Angeles being Roberts & Terry Funk teaming with either Machine or Page against Konnan & Cien Caras & Aguayo. Pena seemed to be leaning toward the idea of running Los Angeles four times per year and running other Southwestern markets a little less often.

WCW FALL BRAWL '93

The biggest story that came out of WCW's Fall Brawl PPV, came four days before the show even took place in a Charlotte courthouse. In a series of scenes more reminiscent of a television drama than what would expect real life to be like, the National Wrestling Alliance, Inc., a group of several promoters worldwide, but only one of whom at present even has so much as a television show and none that run a full-time promotion, were attempting to gain a temporary restraining order against WCW to keep them from advertising the Ric Flair vs. Rick Rude match as a world heavyweight title match of any kind. The NWA believed it would, should the match and result take place as scheduled, create the idea among wrestling fans that Rick Rude was the NWA champion since Rude was scheduled to win the belt synonymous with the title and which had up until one week before the event been billed as a match for the NWA championship. On September 1, WCW withdrew as a member of the NWA. The NWA board of directors, which by the NWA by-laws, controls and has the decision-making power over the NWA world heavyweight title, refused to sanction the title change and at their annual convention on 9/3 decided to take control of the championship and create a new champion.

Several of the NWA members were led to believe an out-of-court settlement was reached in principle on 9/14, when WCW led NWA lawyer Ed Lyons to believe they were accepting NWA's proposal that would allow WCW to go through with the Flair-Rude title change provided WCW agrees to have Rude drop the title clean to a wrestler of the NWA's choosing on an NWA house show before January 31, 1994. There were several other provisions as well, which included WCW being forbidden to do anything that would discredit the NWA name or title and would give the NWA the possession of the championship belt. If Rude wouldn't do the clean job to the wrestler of the NWA's choosing, WCW would agree to pay the NWA $100,000 per day in damages. Early the next morning, the NWA lawyers were told that there might be a problem because WCW was concerned that Rude wouldn't agree to do the job and obviously if that was the case, the price for that in daily penalties was way too steep. The counter-offer was made that the Flair-Rude match would be billed as being for the "World heavyweight title" and the result of the match would go as planned, but that on the broadcast the announcers would read a disclaimer that this match wasn't an NWA world heavyweight title match and that the National Wrestling Alliance did not sanction this event as a title match, which apparently the NWA was still willing to accept.

Later that morning, WCW pulled out from negotiating a settlement and announced it had hired Faison Hicks to represent them in the court case for the temporary restraining order scheduled for that afternoon. Hicks had represented both the NWA and WCW in a 1991 case it won against Vince McMahon and the WWF belt over the NWA belt which resulted in the judge ruling that Ric Flair could no longer wear either the NWA belt or the facsimile NWA belt (when McMahon ordered a duplicate replica belt created for Flair when it was believed Flair would have to return the belt to the NWA/WCW). In the aftermath of that case, Flair was paid $28,000 by WCW for his NWA title belt, which Kip Frey and Seiji Sakaguchi agreed to use to revive the NWA title as a recognized championship with a tournament in August, 1992 in Tokyo, won by Masa Chono. In September of 1992, the NWA, which at the time really consisted of two promotions, WCW and New Japan Pro Wrestling although several other former promoters had kept their memberships active, held its convention. At the convention Sakaguchi was named as NWA President. On or around October of 1992, Bill Watts, who replaced Frey as WCW Vice President in charge of Wrestling Operations, drafted a letter, which was believed by NWA counsel to have been a bill of sale for the physical championship belt from the NWA to WCW for the $28,000 already paid by WCW, representing the NWA, to Flair, which was signed by Sakaguchi as NWA President. Apparently nobody from the NWA actually saw that letter or knew of its contents other than it was known about a bill of sale letter for what had become known in the industry as the "Ric Flair championship belt" to WCW. What wasn't known was that letter, written by Watts and signed by Sakaguchi also gave WCW all "intellectual rights" to use the name NWA. The NWA's counsel was first informed of the contents of the letter during its arguments Wednesday afternoon before U.S. District Judge Richard Voorhees for the restraining order against the match billed as a world title match. The letter was the key in the judge turning down the NWA's claim and allowing the match, advertising of it as a world title match, and the scheduled result, to all go on as planned. The only thing Voorhees ruled is that WCW would be prohibited from calling the match on the PPV show as an NWA title match, which WCW wasn't going to do at this point anyway. The NWA members were scheduled to be discussing the situation later this week as to whether they will challenge the validity of the letter in court, since NWA attorneys claim that NWA bylaws specifically state any such transaction and the belt itself is controlled by the Board of Directors, which were never informed about nor approved the letter. However, with the exception of gaining possession of the "Ric Flair belt," it is not known what can be gained. The title switch to Rude for what all wrestling fans will believe is the NWA championship did take place on 9/19 in Houston, although the initials NWA were never used on the broadcast, but to virtually all wrestling fans watching the show, they believed they were watching an NWA title match and that they had seen the NWA title change. On the air, it was simply referred to as "The World heavyweight championship" and presented as if it were the premier title in the promotion since Vader's title was called just "WCW title" and downplayed heavily. The result can't be erased in the minds of wrestling fans who saw the match or eventually will hear or read of the result by virtue of wrestling publications and wrestling television shows even if an expensive court fight would wind up with the letter being overturned. The NWA can and will likely at some point name a new world champion, but that title in its initial stages would lack the credibility to fans it would have if the champion won it from Rude or whomever, and that in-ring title switch isn't going to take place.

The Charlotte Business Journal in an issue that came out prior to the PPV show had an article about the legal fight between NWA and WCW over the Flair-Rude title match. The story revealed the result of the Flair-Rude match with Rude winning and talked about the television that had been done months back with Rude holding the belt and talking about his win over Flair.

At least some NWA members were also upset at information from its convention in regard to Road Warrior Hawk, Terry Funk and Ted DiBiase being the three discussed as being recognized as next NWA champion that was reported both here and in Pro Wrestling Torch. As was expected by many when those names went public, WCW re-opened negotiations with both Hawk and DiBiase during the week, which some within the NWA believe is largely based on knowledge they were being considered to be NWA champion. Hawk agreed to work several dates in November, the television tapings in Orlando, the 11/17 Clash from Tampa and the 11/20 Battle Bowl PPV show from Pensacola. Reportedly WCW will allow Hawk & Animal (whose business partnership break-up has been smoothed over by Minneapolis attorney Mark Levine, who is merchandising Road Warrior gimmicks) to maintain their merchandising rights and allow them advertising time in exchange for both men appearing on several shows. Animal still won't be wrestling, but will be appearing alongside Hawk on those shows as he did at the recent Clash. DiBiase and WCW negotiated during the week but the negotiations broke off mid-week. DiBiase didn't get the money offer nor the number of dates he was after. The numbers we were given was that DiBiase wanted $100,000 to $125,000 for a 100-date deal and WCW didn't want to make that commitment which should tell you something about future contract negotiations with a lot of wrestlers because there aren't a lot of DiBiase-calibre performers in this country. He was also told his first match back would be a 30:00 draw with Dustin Rhodes in a U.S. title match at the Halloween Havoc PPV show (which would have replaced the scheduled Steve Austin in the spot), which he apparently didn't feel like was the appropriate way to begin with a new promotion.

Fall Brawl was the worst major show thus far in 1993. The matches were sluggish. The booking was unimaginative. The matchmaking itself was downright pathetic. It looked pathetic on paper going in, and the result was even worse than what would have been expected from the line-up. Some of the best talent in the company (Brian Pillman, Steve Austin, Chris Benoit) was left home while the parade of new, uncharismatic, mechanical and largely untalented "big guys" were brought out to no fan reaction. The only performers on the card who showed even a semblance of a good performance were Ric Flair and Rick Steamboat, and they weren't anywhere close to at their best either. The crowd, while larger than WCW has ever drawn in Houston, was the deadest major show crowd in a long time. The show drew about 4,500 fans in the 6,000 seat Astro Arena. No word right now on the gate and how much of it was papered, although the advance indicated it wasn't a heavily papered house.

UWF-I SHOOTFIGHTING: IT'S REAL!

No television exposure, no mainstream media publicity, no interviews, no known personalities, a style completely unfamiliar and no hard-sell Events Center-like segments to hype the show sounds like a recipe for a disastrous failure in the pay-per-view arena. Complete disasters aren't unheard of, either. Both the LPWA and the Herb Abrams UWF tried PPV shows in recent years that drew less than 3,000 buys nationally. In the case of the latter, that was with main eventers who were at least known commodities to most wrestling fans, but with a product with little television exposure except on third-world Sports Channel cable stations. Even Vince McMahon's attempt to promote a bodybuilding pay-per-view event last June, using his own huge syndicated and cable wrestling network as the springboard, hyping it to the level of one of his wrestling PPVs and creating a one-hour weekly cable bodybuilding show specifically to hype the PPV and personalities involved in it, ended in disaster with approximately 4,500 buys nationally. So, logically, what chance did a Japanese promotion doing "shoot-style" wrestling with none of the above have in garnering PPV buys?

Plenty, at least according to Joe Hand, whose Front Row Entertainment promoted the PPV portion of the event to the United States and Canada. Hand claimed the Union of Professional Wrestling Force International (UWFI) PPV show garnered roughly 100,000 buys (which would be an 0.48 percent buy rate). If this number is accurate, and keep in mind tradition when it comes to PPV numbers announced by the companies producing the show, it not only would have to be considered a huge success, but by wrestling industry standards, be considered a success of mind-boggling proportions. It would be slightly more buys than WCW's Fall Brawl on 9/19 in Houston, which drew an estimated 0.46 percent buy rate and 95,000 buys which had all the aforementioned promotional advantages. The most recent WWF PPV event, SummerSlam, which was one of the best hyped PPV shows ever, did an estimated 265,000 buys (1.2 percent buy rate). Hand reported that the buy rate numbers he received were not consistent system-by-system, with the variation by systems ranging from 1.1s down to 0.2s, and said he was most impressed with the showing in Quebec (better than one percent) since his show went head-to-head with the American League Championship Series game involving the Toronto Blue Jays. Highlights of the PPV were scheduled to air nationally on the syndicated George Michael Sports Machine show and a segment is scheduled on UWFI for the TV-show "Hard Copy."

Hand said the show garnered a small profit. If the 100,000 buys is accurate, at a $14.95 price tag, the promotion's gross on the event would be $673,000. In an earlier interview, Hand said his company was budgeting $895,000 for expenses, of which $285,000 would go to advertising. In late October the show will be replayed, rather than a new PPV show broadcast since UWFI doesn't have another show between now and late October. The UWFI's next major show will take place 12/5 at the 48,000-seat outdoor baseball stadium in Tokyo, but won't air on PPV in this country because Request and Viewer Choice didn't have an available date for airing a lot more than the fact that the main event would be unable to be broadcast on that specific show. A second PPV show will air in February 1994, and Hand, who claims the next show will do an even more illogical 1.5 buy rate (if it does, Hand's company will make a $1.7 million profit on the event and it would beat out every wrestling PPV event next year except Wrestlemania), is planning on running quarterly PPV shows next year.

Others in the wrestling industry with PPV contacts strongly dispute these numbers, citing areas where the UWFI show did only one-fourth the number of buys as recent WCW shows and less than one-twentieth of WWF shows. On the other hand, several callers from various parts of the country left messages saying the phone lines were jammed attempting to order the show and they were unable to get through, reports that we haven't received of late from either WWF or WCW PPV shows. In Pittsburgh, one group that phoned in poll results noted they had to wait until the replay show to view it because of the inability to get through all the busy signals representing last-minute buys. I was stunned that the number of our poll responses ran ahead of the pace of most recent WCW and WWF PPV shows, when I was expecting responses at about 25 percent of the level of the major PPVs, even though the audience reading this publication would be far more likely to purchase an international wrestling PPV event than any other audience. As of press time, we were awaiting independent information from a variety of sources and insider PPV industry newsletters as to their read on the show's buys. There is no doubt that the advertising of the event as "real wrestling," largely on sports broadcasts the week before the event, created more mainstream curiosity in this event than any wrestling PPV show in recent years with perhaps the exception of Wrestlemanias. The question going into the event was whether that curiosity would translate into buys. The real big question now is whether the people who bought the show are interested in seeing the product again, and whether that audience can sustain itself through quarterly shows. If the 100,000 figure is accurate, it was largely based on the curiosity of seeing pro wrestling that was purporting to be "real," since only a microcosm of that audience would have ever seen UWFI on tape beforehand or have any knowledge of its wrestlers, none of whose names were used in marketing the event. Whether that curiosity can be turned into interest in the style and the competitors and whether the audience that purchased the event found it interesting enough to want to see it again will determine whatever long-term fate UWFI wrestling has in the United States. Based on our totally unscientific poll, the prospects of return business among those who saw the show look bright.

To understand what is UWFI, one first has to look at how it became what it is. This story dates back to 1982, when New Japan Pro Wrestling was the most successful pro wrestling company in the world. New Japan was coming off a banner year, selling out 90 percent of its house shows and drawing 20 ratings weekly on Saturday night from 8 to 9 p.m. on the countries' No. 2 network. The company's biggest star and countries' most famous and most popular wrestler at the time was Antonio Inoki, although with names like Andre the Giant, Hulk Hogan, Riki Choshu, Tatsumi Fujinami, the original Tiger Mask (Satoru Sayama), Dynamite Kid, Abdullah the Butcher and Dick Murdoch as regular main eventers and the best crop imaginable of potential superstars underneath, this was hardly a one-man band. Nevertheless, the underneath wrestlers weren't getting paid what they felt was fair, with the claim later coming out that the New Japan profits were going to finance Inoki's outside of wrestling money-losing business, in particular a cattle farm in Brazil. Inoki's popularity was viewed by the consensus as the major cog in the successful wheel. But when he was injured and had to take several months off wrestling, the group continued to sellout virtually every show. Many of the wrestlers saw this, combined with their pay level, and revolted, going public with their claims that Inoki was using his power of controlling the company to take money the wrestlers should be getting and funneling it into his outside losing businesses. When this went public, Inoki was forced to resign as company President (although he eventually reclaimed his power), but was allowed to stay in the company as its top star. Hisashi Shinma, the Chairman of the Board of New Japan and Inoki's long-time personal business manager (and at the time figurehead president of the WWF as well), took the major hit in the fallout of the scandal and was forced out of the company. Sayama, whose popularity set the stage for the role lighter weight wrestlers would eventually play in Japan, had retired from wrestling, perhaps fearing reprisals, after he had set the wheels in motion for the scandal to eventually go public. He then wrote a book, called "kay-fabe," which exposed pro wrestling as pre-planned entertainment.

At the time, Akira Maeda was a high-card wrestler who would lose to Fujinami, Choshu, Inoki, Hogan, etc., have non-finishes with the Murdoch, Kengo Kimura and Masked Superstar level wrestlers and beat most everyone else. Shinma had originally recruited Maeda to New Japan when he saw him as a teenager in a karate tournament. With his height, looks and athletic ability, Shinma had groomed Maeda to be the heir to Inoki's throne. With Shinma thrown out, he decided to form his own wrestling company in April of 1984 called the Universal Wrestling Federation, with Maeda as his top star. Maeda brought along with him his best friend, Nobuhiko Takada, a young wrestler who had shown flashes of brilliance as a prelim wrestler and it was well-known would be an eventual world junior heavyweight champion, and Kazuo Yamazaki, even smaller, but groomed to be a factor eventually as a junior heavyweight. Shinma also signed up veterans Rusher Kimura, who had a big-money feud with Inoki a few years earlier, and Ryuma Go. Later Osamu Kido and Yoshiaki Fujiwara joined. In the gym, Fujiwara, who for most of his New Japan career had been a jobber but had suddenly received a push by the company exploiting his reputation as a "shooter" within the business, was known as the master of submission moves and the No. 1 pupil of Karl Gotch, "The God of Professional Wrestling," as he was known in Japan. The group ran shows using the New Japan style of wrestling, but with only moderate box office success, for about three months. Several of the wrestlers at this time already, likely under the influence of Fujiwara, who was the group's elder statesman so to speak, wanted to switch to a more reality-based moves group, but Shinma and some of the older wrestlers like Rusher Kimura and Ryuma Go were against the move. At the time, the manager of Sayama's business affairs contacted the group and offered Sayama, who would by far be the biggest box office draw they could ever hope to get besides Inoki himself. As part of the provisions, Sayama took the stance that he'd only join the promotion if Shinma, the founder, was expelled, stemming from the heat regarding the scandal. The group, feeling it needed Sayama's drawing power more than Shinma's brain, agreed to those terms. This left the group run by head-strong younger wrestlers, all trained by Gotch, who wanted to change pro wrestling to largely a vision of Gotch's wrestling, based on incorporating unspectacular looking but legitimately painful if actually applied "real" submission holds into the product. Kimura and Go immediately quit, thinking the style would be death at the box office. Since several of the remaining wrestlers also had either karate or kick boxing backgrounds, they incorporated kicks, body punches and open-hand face blows with the palm and slaps into the new style. To say the new product took Japan by storm would be inaccurate. The "different" product, which was not as realistic looking and was far more dramatic than today's "shoot style," gained a cult following in Tokyo where it overflowed Korakuen Hall for every event with the hardcore UWF-maniacs selling the 2,000-seat arena out faster than the two major promotions could at the time. They would sell standing room tickets the day of the event, and often they would draw 900 to 1,200 SRO fans which in a building that small made the fans stuffed in as tight as a Tokyo subway during rush hour. Maeda in particular decried all other wrestling promotions as being "fake" but that UWF was real. Largely for that reason, it became the favorite group of Tokyo hardcores who believed UWF wrestling to be the real thing. Matches ended out of nowhere with submission maneuvers that fans, once they became educated to it, would put on each other and realize were unbreakable. In addition, the blistering stiff kicks to the head and body were like nothing ever seen before in pro wrestling rings and gave it even more of an aura of authenticity. Under any scrutiny it was obvious it was a much more realistic-based and some of the kicks were as brutal as anything in a boxing or kick-boxing match and far stiffer work than had ever been seen in Japanese wrestling before. But it was still a work. The group had a minimal following outside of Tokyo, largely due to the inability of the public to understand the style and no television to get it over. Eventually there were all kinds of behind-the-scenes troubles, scandals and money problems, and even a gangland-style murder that aired live on television involving Sayama's apparent mobster business associates. Sayama retired again, this time for good, and in September of 1985, the UWF ran its final card and closed shop. Sayama eventually opened a gym and trained young men in his new sport, which he called "shooting." It achieved little in the way of visibility or popularity since he himself never competed. Ironically, of all the groups that claimed to be "shooting," Sayama's unknown group of students was the only one that ever really was.

Maeda, Fujiwara, Takada, Kido and Yamazaki returned to New Japan in January 1986 for one of the most eventful 12 months of Japanese wrestling history. Remember that Maeda in particular had decried pro wrestling as being fake in the press and at the UWF matches. He had bad-mouthed Inoki in particular as not being a real wrestler as before the UWF shows he'd challenge Fujinami (New Japan's best worker and No. 2 native behind Inoki in the pecking order) to come to the UWF rings and wrestle with no ropes (for no rope escapes of submission moves) "for real" and then mockingly say something to the crowd to the effect of, "You know why I say Fujinami and not Inoki" and everyone in the crowd laughed together. Now, because he had no other job and because his previous statements and cult popularity could be used to draw incredible money for New Japan, he was back working for Inoki's company. Inoki and Maeda never did have their long-awaited singles match which would have easily set what would have been an all-time gate and attendance record in Japan, because Maeda would never agree to put Inoki over. But Maeda had several singles matches during that year that were memorable. Once at Korakuen Hall, which quickly became known as Maeda and the UWF's home court so to speak when in New Japan rings, he was booked against Kerry Von Erich. The UWF audience came specifically to see Maeda destroy an American superstar "worker." When they worked an even match ending in a double count out, fans stormed out of the building furious even though there were two matches left in the card. Another match with Andre the Giant became infamous in wrestling lore. Maeda also knocked-out Keiji Muto in a bar fight that was well publicized. He also participated in the most successful mixed match in history beating kick boxer Don Nakaya Neilsen on the undercard of an Inoki-Leon Spinks mixed match which drew the largest television audience for pro wrestling in Japan in many years (a 28.9 rating in Prime Time). The UWF wrestlers started appearing regularly on New Japan television, thus the chicken wings, Fujiwara armbars or wakigatamaes, cross-knee locks, achilles tendon holds, etc. started getting over to the general public as finishing maneuvers. The entire New Japan style of fast-paced high flying and big moves was changed with the submission moves incorporated into the style. Because of the strong UWF personalities, New Japan had a banner year at the box office and more heat than ever at the arenas. However, during that same period, its TV ratings nosedived to the point where TV-Asahi moved wrestling from prime time to Saturday afternoon, where it remains today. Many attributed the declining ratings to the casual audience not understanding or wanting to see all the unspectacular but realistic submission moves after years of the spectacular fast-paced style New Japan had become famous for.

In November, 1987, there was an event known forever as "the shoot kick." Heat had been building up behind the scenes between Riki Choshu, a former Olympic games wrestler who had become a legend in New

Japan, and Maeda as the annual tag team tournament was starting out. While the general public knew nothing was up, word had spread that trouble might develop between the two amongst the Tokyo hardcores, and the place would be during a six-man tag team match on Maeda's home court, Korakuen Hall, on November 19. Troubles built up when it became apparent neither was going to sell to make the other look good. Finally when Choshu held Kido in a scorpion deathlock, Maeda came in the ring and with Choshu defenseless because his arms were holding Kido down, blasted him in the eye with a kick that broke two bones underneath his eye. The match largely fell apart at that point although Takada did jump in and do the prescribed finish for Choshu's lariat. Maeda was immediately suspended from New Japan and with Choshu injured, the tag team tournament, traditionally the highlight tour of the year, became anti-climactic. About one month later, New Japan gave Maeda the terms to allow him to return. He'd be suspended for several more months from Japan, although they would set up a tour of low-paying unrealistic-style Mexico as "punishment" that he'd have to fulfill. In addition, upon returning he'd have to put both Choshu and Inoki over in singles matches. Maeda wouldn't accept the terms, and got financing to re-start the UWF.

Few gave the UWF much hope of surviving. Interest in pro wrestling in Japan in 1987-88 was in a decline, largely due to the predictability and frequent non-finishes of main event matches and the public belief that the wrestlers were more mercenaries going to the highest bidder because of several wrestlers jumping promotions which in old-style Japan where people kept jobs for life, was against the cultural mores of the time. The first UWF didn't make it and never gained much of an audience outside Tokyo. The group debuted at Korakuen Hall on May 12, 1988 and sold all tickets out in 15 minutes. Over the next two years, the UWF was the hottest promotion in the world, selling out virtually every show, most of the time the first day tickets were put on sale. Its most successful show was on November 29, 1989 at the Tokyo Egg Dome. They sold 40,000 tickets for $2 million the first day tickets went on sale, blistering all previous records for one-day sales (the SummerSlam '92 at Wembley Stadium sold more tickets the first day they went on sale although with much lower ticket prices). The show drew 60,000 fans live, at the time the third largest crowd in pro wrestling history and a record at the time in Japan, and $2.9 million, which was an all-time world record at the time. It also was put on closed-circuit television in nine locations, drawing another 15,000 fans. Between live tickets, merchandise sales and closed-circuit revenue, the show grossed $5.6 million, which is a record never topped to this day in Japan. The promotion cooled off a little in 1990, but still sold out most of its shows. However, a promotional dispute between Shinji Jin, the company President, and Maeda, at the end of 1990, wound up with the group suddenly folding.

As important it is in examining this facet of wrestling to cite the success of the UWF's shows, it is probably more important to note the affect UWF had on the major pro wrestling groups in Japan, because if it gains a foothold or success here, a question is begging to be answered. Will the major and minor promotions, as the major promotions in Japan did successfully, change their style to incorporate successful facets of UWF to create stronger wrestling companies, or will they simply ignore it? Of course, UWFI is a long way from gaining a foothold here. In 1986, when Maeda and company came back to New Japan and appeared weekly on network television, it exposed and got over many new submission holds. This caused the style of wrestling to change. Many moves previously thought of as "dead-time" or "rest-holds" became "near-submissions" so it changed, because matches didn't need to contain as many spectacular moves and flying moves to escape "dead-time," the entire style and psychology of matches changed. In addition, stiff, fast kicking became incorporated into pro wrestling. At the beginning, it resulted in a slight-decline in television viewership because matches were slower, but it seems to have been a successful formula over the long run. In 1988, when the UWF blew by everyone in the wrestling business, it caused All Japan and New Japan, left in their dust, to re-evaluate their business. Both groups, All Japan in particular, eliminated the screw-job ending from the repertoire. All Japan, which used to end its main event competitive matches largely with double count outs to protect stars and egos, ended every, as in 100 percent every, match with a clean finish. After several months of doing so, this largely turned their arena business around and is responsible for the current atmosphere at its shows. New Japan never quite got to 100 percent, but easily 95 to 98 percent of its matches end with clean finishes as well, and the crowd reaction to the few that don't is decidedly negative. New Japan's current status in the wrestling world speaks for itself. There are many that feel the single most important factor, and admittedly there are dozens of them, for WCW's abysmal house show attendance is that so many fans were turned off and eventually turned away from the company because of unsatisfying finishes at both the house show and on major cards.

Although the UWF crew had always stuck together from the beginnings in 1983, differing offers to differing personalities saw Maeda and his "younger-brother" Takada break up "the family." Maeda formed a promotion called "Fighting Network Rings," which he proclaimed wasn't pro wrestling and was 100 percent real. To get over that point, he used nobody ever associated with traditional pro wrestling in his company, relying largely on foreign ex-sambo (amateur submission style, also known in some circles as Soviet judo) wrestlers, kick boxers and karate champions with himself as the main draw. While most insiders in Japan accept that occasional "shooting matches" occur in Rings prelim matches (as have happened in the past in All Japan women matches when they put the gloves on), the key matches aren't. Fujiwara formed Pro Wrestling Fujiwara-Gumi with the backing of Hachiro Tanaka, who also owned SWS. PWFG eventually folded with Fujiwara returning to New Japan, although they now promote in Korakuen Hall one show every few months using mainly Florida independent wrestlers. The main PWFG wrestlers, Masakatsu Funaki, Wayne Shamrock and Minoru Suzuki started their own promotion called Pancrase that debuted last month, claiming to be real shooting with winners and loser not predetermined. Takada got backing and formed UWFI, taking most of the old UWF wrestlers with him.

UWFI soon signed American scientific wrestling legends Lou Thesz, Billy Robinson and Danny Hodge and flew them in for their big shows as this sort of thing adds credibility in Japan. When the shows started selling out Budokan Hall in Japan, interest in expanding to the United States started, which eventually led to this PPV show.

Positives and Negatives of the show:

- Match quality was a positive. Most of the matches were good when judged against the limitations the style would allow. Based on reactions we've heard, to the untrained eye, they appeared to be real, or at least real enough to not insult someone trying to suspend their disbelief, which is necessary for this style to make it. Obviously a trained eye would see things differently, but its audience isn't going to consist of many people with a trained eye. This is also a potential negative. If this group gains any sort of real popularity next year, too much popularity will be its albatross because if it gets too popular, eventually mainstream media will discover it isn't what it claims to be which would be a lot more damaging to something worked this style than an American style where largely everyone knows what it is going in and realism is no longer an issue.

- Production wasn't good. The show had no creativity. It simply aired eight matches, with no announcers building up what was coming next or even mentioning any of the matches that were coming up until after the sixth match when they previewed the final two matches. It's ludicrous that neither Takada or Albright's name were never even mentioned until six matches had been completed. Since this was largely an audience unfamiliar with any aspect of what this was or who the people were that were doing it, it desperately cried out for an instructional video demonstrating several submission holds so the action on the mat as they struggled to break clasped arms and pull the arm into a short-arm scissors wasn't viewed as "dead time" rather than a "near finish." They also needed to highlight four or five of the wrestlers (Koslowski, Tamura, Albright, Takada and Scott) to whet the public's appetite and give them an idea who the stars are when the show began so people had things to look forward to and needed more clips showing them in action, their big moves, etc. They needed interviews with Americans talking about the style and their upcoming matches, particularly Koslowski, Albright and Scott or even Badnews if he wanted to make a comparison of it with traditional pro wrestling. Films of some of the Japanese in training, perhaps showing all-out kicks to the heavy bag or to protected sparring partners, would get over the power in their feet. If that story Gene Pelc said during the show about Takada kicking the machine and it registering more force than someone hitting it with a baseball bat is true, then that clip should have been shown. I guarantee it would make everyone respect Takada as a bad-ass and a real world champion, both of which are necessary for the company to gain any significant following. They needed to show clips of Takada's previous wins, in particular Trevor

Berbick since everyone knows him, and Koji Kitao (which actually did air although nobody would have known because it was just one guy kicking a big guy who went down) since there is some general public knowledge of sumo wrestling in the United States because of Chad "Akebono" Rowan. They needed to show Tamura beating Matthew Saad Muhammad since the match only went 25 seconds and Muhammad had a pretty decent boxing name to sports fans. They needed to show Koslowski clips from the Olympics, Albright destroying people on previous shows, and films of Billy Scott taking on James Warring to give him credibility as a challenger. If this is to be successful, the eventual success depends on marketing personalities, getting them over, and then airing matches with them against each other. The public won't pay to see boxing matches on PPV with personalities that they don't know, but boxing matches on PPV with "over" personalities (Chavez-Whitaker), even among lighter weight guys, draw three times as much money on PPV as Wrestlemania nowadays, let alone any other wrestling events. Things like doing tale-of-the-tapes for both guys on the screen together before every match would have added to the interest of each match

- The announcers failed to get over the Japanese as anything other than nice guys who are nameless, faceless kicking and submission machines. Does anyone who viewed the show remember the difference between Tamura, Kanehara, Anjyo or Kakihara? The only name that came out of the show with any remembrance would be Takada.

- Play-by-play man Jim Dougherty was pretty bad, and was crucified among callers after the show. Besides his constant knocking of pro wrestling in America, which got old, and his mentioning about how "you've never seen slow-motion on pro wrestling before" when it's actually prevalent every week, he only seemed slightly familiar with the subject. Gene Pelc, who handled color and is part of the promotion was very good overall. His talking about strategies, particularly in Koslowski-Kakihara, made the matches more interesting. Still, even he failed to do anything that would enable to audience to differentiate between the Japanese. In addition, some of the athletes on this show have some incredible real athletic credentials. While in some cases they were superimposed on the screen, they were never emphasized. Even though his performance was awful and he's too old and came in out of shape, Badnews Allen was a legend in the world of judo before he was a pro wrestler which is largely the reason he works for this group. All four men in the tag match have tremendous credentials in amateur wrestling and Koslowski and Severn's record books are lengthy. Lou Thesz was good in doing color the final two matches in that he was enthusiastic, but unless you were a hardcore pro wrestling fan, you wouldn't have known who he was and his credentials as well needed to be given since you have to assume this audience was largely sports fans who were curious about something and with no knowledge of any aspect of it.

- The majority of the thumbs downs were more because they didn't like the style because of what it wasn't, and for the most part, what it couldn't be (no babyfaces and heels, no overt angles, a "boring" style) and maintain the legit aura which is its only drawing point. Several thumbs downs came from workers and promoters of the independent nature who ranged from mildly unhappy to downright outraged at the constant knocking of American style as being staged and rehearsed during the broadcast. Even many who voted thumbs up and enjoyed the show themselves questioned whether the style would be marketable in the United States.

WWF Survivor Series '93

S.S. drew a sellout 15,509 fans in the Boston Garden, all but a few hundred paid, for a gate that would be estimated around $180,000. The show sold out in about an hour when tickets were first put on sale, although the building had actually been more than half sold out before the box office had even opened by pre-sale mail orders. The anticipation of the first PPV show ever in Boston somehow didn't live up to its execution, as the crowd was strong in the opener, largely lost interest over the next two matches, reacted in a mixed way to a comedy match and was largely flat for the main event except for a short sequence with Undertaker and Yokozuna. Part of this was blamed on the poor sound system within the building, as fans couldn't hear Ray Combs' extended monologue and that was the point the live crowd turned off of the show. Part was blamed on

Shawn Michaels replacing Jerry Lawler in the second match, which no matter how hard they tried, virtually killed all interest in the match. Part was blamed on the idea of presenting something called the Smoky Mountain tag team title match to Northeasterners who no doubt view that terminology as something out of the latest Beverly Hillbillies movie, and part was blamed on the fact that no matter how much it is pushed, Lex Luger and Ludvig Borga just don't cut it in their respective positions. Overall I thought the show was only a slight thumbs down, better than both the previous Clash and the Battle Bowl. Actually most of the wrestling was fine and with the exception of the match played for laughs, nothing was that bad, but when it was over, there was nothing on the show that days later was memorable. The best description is it reminded me of a bad Mexican show which had long matches, few good workers, and somehow the good workers didn't do much either.

WCW STARRCADE '93

Ric Flair's 11th (or 10th, or 12th, depending on what you consider a world title and what you're willing to accept and ignore when it comes to wrestling history) world title victory was easily the most memorable of all his title wins, and created a unique emotional moment almost foreign to American wrestling.

In what was easily the best job of build-up for a single match in the five-year history of WCW, Starrcade '93, by virtue of a horrible situation that took place two months earlier in England, was switched from the planned Vader losing the WCW title to Sid Vicious, to Vader losing the title to Flair in a match where Flair put his career on the line. The result was what was announced as a sellout at the Charlotte Independence Arena (actually about 300 shy of capacity, probably with less papering than at any recent WCW major shows). The report we got was the house was $65,000, which is more than any WCW house in a long time, but still indicates they needed significant paper to fill the building even with all the hype nationally and in the local media because Flair is a major celebrity in town and friends with key writers and sportscasters. Most likely it also resulted in as good a PPV buy rate as WCW could be capable of getting at this stage or any stage in the foreseeable future, although based on our response as far as numbers of calls, it doesn't indicate the 0.8 that some people were hoping for. But in fairness to the company, once they were forced into changing the main event, they did everything possible to not only make it work, but did a unique promotional job using the media and pushing Flair like never before. Ironically, just days before the event, something happened in the build-up that just a few years earlier would have been regarded as an absolute disaster, but in today's wrestling world was almost not even worthy of a notice.

In a snafu the likes that seems to happen with alarming regularly with the company, a PPV ad that ran one week before the show in the trade magazine Multi Channel News, featured an ad not for Starrcade, but for SuperBrawl (2/20/94) listing the main event as Flair defending the title against Vader in a Thundercage match. Ad slicks for that match had been sent to cable companies around the country well before hand, so anyone within the cable industry with any interest in wrestling knew the result, but then again, any fan with a brain should have been able to easily figure it out as well. But the topper was three days later when the New York Daily News, which is I believe the largest circulated daily newspaper in the country, showed the ad for Super Brawl mentioning the snafu with the headline, "You Can Bet on it," saying the ad gave away that Flair was going to win the title four days later and said if you need some extra holiday cash, bet the ranch on Flair, if you can find someone to take the bet. Ironically, or perhaps not, the same newspaper ran a lengthy story on Flair the day before, treating Flair and pro wrestling as if it were a shoot. In addition, the ads in local newspaper TV Guides around the country for the show were still listing Vader defending against Vicious as the main event. If this was just one year ago and Bill Watts was still in charge of WCW, he'd have pulled out what little hair he had left, torn apart several sections of the office, and probably have to be heavily sedated in order to keep from changing the finish. But it's one year later and nobody cared, and quite frankly, I doubt if affected the number of buys for this show one iota.

In the weeks leading up to the show Flair delivered some of the best interviews of the decade, and WCW backed it up by getting footage of other sports stars, most notably Charles Barkley, plugging the match and building up Flair. The television, while giving some build-up to other matches, focused on the main event in a manner telling everyone that this match was not the typical PPV main event, thus making it not a typical PPV show, and effectively got the match and thus the show over as an extra special event. The show itself, sold as a one-match show, delivered because of that. There were no expectations for the undercard, which was fortunate, because nothing underneath delivered. Because of that, it was a $24.95 PPV show with only one good match out of eight, but was still a solid, in fact a major, thumbs up.

The undercard was made a backdrop for hyping the main event, similar to a boxing PPV. While the unique setting and uniqueness of the hype is something that neither WWF nor WCW could possibly duplicate more than once every few years (if even that, because how many enduring figures will this business produce that reach the level of Flair, let alone how many are capable of putting on the performance that created this emotion?), other aspects of building drama (showing the guys entering the arena, interviews with the main eventers interspersed throughout the card rather than just immediately before the match) for the main event to make it seem special could be done for the world title match on most PPV shows effectively. Once a year, for the big match, they could even build interest by having interviews with the other leading wrestling personalities in the group analyzing and predicting a winner. In this case, having the other faces and heels both talk about Flair and his legacy would have been a nice added touch. At this PPV, the maudlin approach to "what could have been" Flair's final match ever at one point bordered on being overdone.

The show opened with a series of photos of Flair from early childhood through what appeared to be college football, a newspaper clipping of the 1975 small airplane crash that he was in with Johnny Valentine and Bob Bruggers (both of whom never wrestled again) and some others where he broke his back, and then showed clips of him in the ring from previous Starrcade main events. They aired a clip of Vader arriving in the building and working out in the ring hours before the show started. They then went to Flair's house showing Flair, wife Beth and three of his four children in an emotional setting trying to get over the idea that this really could be his last ride to his final match. Flair was then shown getting into a limo with Gene Okerlund and they talked in a manner leading you to believe it was going to be his last match. After the opener, they showed another clip of them riding to the building with more last match talk (at this point it bordered on being overdone) and finally showed them arriving at the building.

The match itself was excellent when it came to drama and heat largely because of the Charlotte crowd/hometown Flair tie-in and the build-up. It would have been a great match in any case, but not one that would be remembered for years. The match never had the heart-stopping close calls that made nearly every nightly Flair match during the mid-80s, nor did it have the brutality that Vader's PPV matches with Sting or Cactus Jack had or the level of heat and action of every big show Kenta Kobashi match this year. But as a total performance, and by that I don't mean bell-to-bell performance but pre-match build-up to post-match interview performance, it probably was both the best and most memorable of Flair's entire career. This was also a night where Gene Okerlund to a lesser extent got over this as something special because he tried to act largely out of character, and a main event where Tony Schiavone did the best announcing job of his career. Whether this was the last real hurrah or a career rebirth, either for WCW and/or Ric Flair, will be answered by crowd reactions over the next few weeks. But no matter which it is and what the future of WCW is, Flair's role in wrestling history as its greatest all-around performer of all-time, which was solidified many years ago, was defined on this night. It was the night where his versatility, interview ability and obvious love for his sport took center stage above any wrestling match. If it seemed real at times, it probably was because with the exception of what actually went on in the ring (which was really brutal in its own right), an awful lot of it was.

CHAPTER FORTY EIGHT

THE BIG SHOWS DIRECTORY

NEW JAPAN TOKYO DOME

(JANUARY 4, TOKYO, JAPAN)

ATTENDANCE: 63,500 sellout

LIVE GATE: $3.5 million

HIGHLIGHTS: 1. Takayuki Iizuka & Akira Nogami & El Samurai (Osamu Matsuda) b Nobukazu Hirai & Masao Orihara & Koki Kitahara (Tatsumi Kitahara) 15:11 ***1/4; 2. Shiro Koshinaka & Masashi Aoyagi & Great Kabuki (Akihisa Mera) & Akitoshi Saito b Super Strong Machine (Junji Hirata) & Hiro Saito & Norio Honaga (Nobuo Honaga) & Tatsutoshi Goto 14:20 ***1/2; 3. IWGP jr. heavyweight title: Jushin Liger (Keiichi Yamada) b Ultimo Dragon (Yoshihiro Asai) to win title 20:09 ***3/4; 4. Ron Simmons b Tony Halme 6:10 *1/2; 5. Sting (Steve Borden) b Hiroshi Hase 15:31 ***1/2; 6. Masa Saito & Shinya Hashimoto b Dustin Rhodes (Dustin Runnels) & Scott Norton 13:57 **3/4; 7. IWGP & NWA heavyweight titles: Great Muta (Keiji Muto) b Masa Chono to retain IWGP title and win NWA title 19:48 ****1/4; 8. IWGP tag title: Hawk (Michael Hegstrand) & Power (Kensuke Sasaki) Warrior DCOR Rick & Scott Steiner (Robert & Scott Rechsteiner) 14:38 ****; 9. Tatsumi Fujinami b Takashi Ishikawa 11:41 ***1/2; 10. Genichiro Tenryu (Genichiro Shimade) b Riki Choshu (Mitsuo Yoshida) 18:14 ****

WCW CLASH OF THE CHAMPIONS

(JANUARY 13, MILWAUKEE, WI)

ATTENDANCE: 4,000 (1,500 paid)

LIVE GATE: $14,000

TELEVISION RATING: 2.90

THUMBS UP/DOWN/MIDDLE:
77.29% / 17.2% / 9.9%

BEST MATCH: 161 - Ricky Steamboat & Shane Douglas vs. Brian Pillman & Steve Austin, 26 - Chris Benoit vs. Brad Armstrong

WORST MATCH: 57 - Cactus Jack vs. Johnny B. Badd, 51 - Wrecking Crew vs. Tom Zenk & Johnny Gunn

HIGHLIGHTS: 1. Jack (Michael Foley) b Badd (Mark Merro) *; 2. Too Cold Scorpio (Charlie Skaggs) b Scotty Flamingo (Scott Levy) **1/4; 3. Benoit b Armstrong (Robert James Jr.) ***; 4. Wrecking Crew (Al Greene & Marc Laurinaitis) b Zenk & Gunn (Tom Brandi) **1/4; 5. NWA & WCW tag titles: Steamboat (Richard Blood) & Douglas (Troy Martin) b Pillman & Steve Austin-DQ 13:00 ***3/4; 6. Cage match: Sting & Dustin Rhodes b Barry Windham & Vader (Leon White) & Paul Orndorff 11:00 ***1/4

WWF ROYAL RUMBLE '93

(JANUARY 24, SACRAMENTO, CA)

ATTENDANCE: 16,000 sell out

LIVE GATE: $187,000

EST. BUY RATE/REVENUE:
1.2 / $2.80 million

THUMBS UP/DOWN/MIDDLE:

49.2% / 35.5% / 15.2%

Best match: 208 - Shawn Michaels vs. Marty Jannetty, 65 - Royal Rumble

Worst match: 223 - Bam Bam Bigelow vs. Big Bossman, 52 - Royal Rumble

Highlights: 1. Rick & Scott Steiner b Beau (Wayne Bloom) & Blake (Mike Enos) Beverly 10:34 ***; 2. IC title: Michaels (Michael Hickenbottom) b Janetty 14:20 ****; 3. Bigelow (Scott Bigelow) b Bossman (Ray Traylor) 10:10 *; 4. WWF title: Bret Hart b Razor Ramon (Scott Hall) 17:52 ***1/4; 5. Yokozuna (Rodney Anoia) won Royal Rumble 61:18

WCW SUPERBRAWL III

(*February 21, Asheville, NC*)

Attendance: 6,500 sellout

Live gate: $55,000

Est. buy rate/revenue: 0.5 / $0.98 million

Thumbs up/down/middle: 95.2% / 0.2% / 4.6%

Best match: 146 - Sting vs. Big Van Vader , 121 - Chris Benoit vs. Too Cold Scorpio

Worst match: 171 - Dustin Rhodes vs. Maxx Payne, 129 - Davey Boy Smith vs. Bill Irwin 129

Highlights: 1. Brian Pillman & Steve Austin b Marcus Bagwell & Erik Watts 16:34 ***; 2. Scorpio b Benoit 16:57 ***3/4; 3. Smith (David Smith) b Irwin 5:49 1/4*; 4. Falls Count Anywhere: Cactus Jack b Paul Orndorff 12:17 ****; 5. Ricky Morton & Robert Gibson (Ruben Kane) b Stan Lane & Tom Prichard 12:52 ****; 6. U.S. title: Rhodes b Payne (Darryl Peterson)-DQ 11:18 -1/2*; 7. NWA title: Barry Windham b Great Muta to win title 24:10 *1/4; 8. Strap match: Vader b Sting 20:54 ****1/4

AJPW BUDOKAN HALL

(*February 28, Tokyo, Japan*)

Attendance: 16,300 sellout

Live gate: $850,000

Highlights: 1. Mighty Inoue (Sueo Inoue) & Masao Inoue b Takao Omori & Mitsuo Momota; 2. Dan Kroffat (Phil LaFond) & Doug Furnas b Black Hearts (Tom Nash & David Johnson); 3. Dory Funk b Kurt Beyer; 4. Giant Baba (Shohei Baba) & Rusher Kimura (Masao Kimura) & Yoshinari Ogawa b Haruka Eigen & Satoru Asako & Ryuma Izumida, 5. The Patriot (Del Wilkes) & The Eagle (George Hines) b Steve Williams & Rob Van Dam (Rob Szatkowski); 6. Terry Gordy b Jun Akiyama ***; 7. PWF jr. hwt title: Masa Fuchi b Tsuyoshi Kikuchi ****; 8. Kenta Kobashi b Danny Spivey ***1/2; 9. Stan Hansen b Toshiaki Kawada ****3/4; 10. Triple Crown: Mitsuharu Misawa b Akira Taue ****

AJW DREAM SLAM I

(*April 2, Yokohama, Japan*)

Attendance: 16,500 sellout

Live gate: $1.2 million

Highlights: 1. Plum Mariko & Hikari Fukuoka b Sakie Hasegawa & Kaoru Ito 16:31 ****1/4; 2. Yoshika Maedomari & Eriko Tsuchiya b Terri Power (Terri Polk) & Saemi Numata 7:42 *; 3. Kaoru (Kaoru Maeda) & Ultima Tigrita (Esther Moreno) b Tomoko Watanabe & Mima Shimoda 14:41 ***3/4; 4. Rumi Kazama & Miki Handa b Suzuka Minami (Mika Suzuki) & Etsuko Mita 22:27 ***1/2; 5. WWWA martial arts title: Bat Yoshinaga (Eriko Yoshinaga) b Susan Howard; 6. Devil Masami (Tenjin Masami) b Chigusa Nagayo 17:28 ***3/4; 7. Kyoko Inoue & Takako Inoue b Cutie Suzuki (Yumi Suzuki) & Mayumi Ozaki 16:44 *****; 8. Bull Nakano (Keiko Nakano) & Aja Kong (Erica Shishedo) b Eagle Sawai (Tomoko Sawai) & Harley Saito (Sayori Saito) 14:08 ****; 9. Dynamite Kansai (?) b Yumiko Hotta 16:42 ***3/4; 10. Akira Hokuto (Hisako Uno) b Shinobu Kandori 30:27 *****; 11. WWWA tag title: Manami Toyota & Toshiyo Yamada (Toshinori Yamada) b Megumi Kudo & Combat Toyota 28:14 ****

SMW BLUEGRASS BRAWL

(*April 2, Pikeville, KY*)

Attendance: 2,000 sellout

Live gate: $14,000

Highlights: 1. Robbie Eagle (Rob Kellum) b Rip Rogers; 2. Mongolian Stomper (Archie Gouldie) b Rob Morgan; 3. Tim Horner b Night Stalker (Bryan Clark)-DQ; 4. Singapore Spike match: Brian Lee b Kevin Sullivan; 5. Chain match for SMW title: Tracy Smothers b Dirty White Boy (Tony Anthony to win title); 6. Three team street fight: Bobby Eaton & Tom Prichard & Stan Lane won over Robert Fuller (Robert Welch) & Dutch Mantel (Wayne Cowan) & Jimmy Golden and Arn Anderson (Marty Lunde) & Ricky Morton & Robert Gibson

WWF WRESTLEMANIA IX

(*April 4, Las Vegas, NV*)

Attendance: 15,045 (paid est. 14,000)

Live gate: $1.1 million

Est. buy rate/revenue: 2.0 / $5.50 million

Thumbs up/down/middle: 12.8% / 78% / 9.2%

Best match: 180 - Shawn Michaels vs. Tatanka, 118 - Rick & Scott Steiner vs. Headshrinkers

Worst match: 132 - Razor Ramon vs. Bob Backlund, 89 - Undertaker vs. Giant Gonzalez

Highlights: 1. IC title: Tatanka (Chris Chavis) b Michaels-COR (Michaels retained title) 18:13 ***1/2; 2. Steiners b Head Shrinkers (Sam Anoia & Solofa Fatu) 14:22 **1/3; 3.

Doink the Clown (Matt Osborne) b Crush (Bryan Adams) 8:28 *1/2; 4. Ramon b Backlund 3:45 -*; 5. WWF tag title: Ted DiBiase & IRS (Larry Rotunda) b Hulk Hogan (Terry Bollea) & Brutus Beefcake (Ed Leslie)-DQ 18:27 **; 6. Lex Luger (Larry Pfohl) b Mr. Perfect (Curt Hennig) 10:56 *1/4; 7. Undertaker (Mark Callaway) b Gonzalez (Jorge Gonzalez)-DQ 7:33 *1/4; 8. WWF title: Yokozuna b Bret Hart to win title 8:55 ***; 9. WWF title: Hogan b Yokozuna to win title :21 DUD

AJW DREAM SLAM II

(*April 11, Osaka, Japan*)
Live attendance: 6,500
Highlights: 1. Sakie Hasegawa b Hikari Fukuoka ****; 2. Leo Kitamura (Mami Kitamura) & Mikiko Futagami & Utako Hozumi b Kaoru Ito & Saemi Numata & Tomoko Watanabe ***; 3. Bat Yoshinaga & Terri Power b Rumi Kazama & Miki Handa **1/2; 4. Combat Toyota & Megumi Kudo b Etsuko Mita & Mima Shimoda ****; 5. Yumiko Hotta & Kyoko Inoue & Takako Inoue b Cutie Suzuki & Plum Mariko & Boirshoi Kid ****1/2; 6. Suzuka Minami b Harley Saito ***1/2; 7. Bull Nakano b Chigusa Nagayo ****1/4; 8. Shinobu Kandori & Eagle Sawai b Aja Kong & Akira Hokuto ****; 9. WWWA tag title 2/3 falls: Dynamite Kansai & Mayumi Ozaki b Manami Toyota & Toshiyo Yamada to win titles *****

AAA TRIPLEMANIA

(*April 30, Mexico City, Mexico*)
Attendance: 48,000 sellout (45,000 paid)
Live gate: $400,000
Highlights: 1. Martha Villalobos & Pantera Surena & Wendy b Lola Gonzales & Vicki Caranza & La Rosa; 2. Winners & Super Calo & El Salsero b May Flowers & Rudy Reyna & Baby Sharon; 3. Volador & Misterioso & Rey Misterio Jr. b Tony Arce & Vulcano & Rocco Valente; 4. Octagon & El Hijo del Santo & Villano III b Fuerza Guerrera & Heavy Metal & Rambo; 5. Mexican Light hwt title: Lizmark b La Parka via referees decision; 6. Mascara Sagrada & Love Machine & Mascarita Sagrada b Jerry Estrada & Blue Panther & Jerrito Estrada; 7. Hair vs. mask: Perro Aguayo b Mascara Ano 2000 (revealed as Jesus Reyes); 8. Career vs. career: Cien Caras b Konnan El Barbaro-COR

NJPW WRESTLING DONTAKU

(*May 3, Fukuoka, Japan*)
Attendance: 55,000
Live gate: $2.5 million
Highlights: 1. El Samurai & Takayuki Iizuka & Akira Nogami b Hiroyoshi Yamamoto & Satoshi Kojima & Osamu Nishimura 15:01; 2. Michiyoshi Ohara b Akitoshi Saito 9:26; 3. Brutus Beefcake b Masa Saito 8:35; 4. Great Kabuki & Masashi Aoyagi & Kuniaki Kobayashi & Shiro Koshinaka & Kengo Kimura b Ashura Hara & Takashi Ishikawa & Super Strong Machine & Tatsutoshi Goto & Hiro Saito 11:26; 5. Tiger Mask (Koji Kanemoto) b Jushin Liger 14:25 ***1/4; 6. Sting NC Scott Norton 9:16; 7. Yoshiaki Fujiwara b Hiroshi Hase 12 11 *1/2; 8. IWGP tag title: Hawk & Power Warrior b Shinya Hashimoto & Masa Chono 12:22 **; 9. Hulk Hogan b Great Muta 15:55 **; 10. Antonio Inoki & Tatsumi Fujinami b Riki Choshu & Genichiro Tenryu 26:25 ***1/4

FMW KAWASAKI STADIUM

(*May 5, Kawasaki, Japan*)
Attendance: 41,000 (32,000 paid)
Live gate: $1.8 million
Highlights: 1. Eiji Ezaki b Koji Nakagawa 10:03; 2. Rie Nakamura b Keiko Iwame 10:45; 3. Elimination tag match: Eagle Sawai & Utako Ozumi & Yasha Kurenai & Midori Saito & Mikiko Futagami b Miwa Sato & Eriko Tsuchiya & Yoshika Maedomari & Kumiko Matsuda & Yukie Nabeno 25:52; 4. The Sheik (Ed Farhat) & Sabu (Terry Eskar) b Dr. Looser (Len St. Clair & Dr. Hannibal (Steve Gillespie) 6:53; 5. Great Sasuke (Masanori Murakawa) & Kendo & Battle Ranger b Espantos IV & V & Super Delfin (Hiro Wakida) 20:22; 6. Shinobu Kandori b Victoria Kazuniya 5:18; 7. Combat Toyota & Megumi Kudo b Manami Toyota & Toshiyo Yamada 22:17; 8. No rope barbed wire tornado street fight loser leaves town death match: Ricky Fuji & Big Titan (Rick Bogner) & The Gladiator (Mike Alfonso) b Katsuji Ueda & Great Punk (Katsutoshi Niiyama) & Tarzan Goto (Munenori Goto) 9:31; 9. Gregori Veritchev b Leon Spinks 8:09; 10. Explosive barbed wire match with exploding ring: Atsushi Onita b Terry Funk 12:14

WCW SLAMBOREE '93

(*May 23, Atlanta, GA*)
Attendance: 7,008 (3,722 paid)
Live gate: $37,000
Est. buy rate/revenue:
0.5 / $1.15 million
Thumbs up/down/middle:
36.6% / 33.2% / 30.2%
Best match: 112 - Big Van Vader vs. Davey Boy Smith, 112 - Hollywood Blonds vs. Dos Hombres
Worst match: 174 - Sting vs. The Prisoner, 50 - Brad Armstrong & Thunderbolt Patterson vs. Baron Von Raschke & Ivan Koloff
Highlights: 1. Too Cold Scorpio & Marcus Bagwell b Bobby Eaton & Chris Benoit 9:23 **3/4; 2. Sid Vicious (Sid Eudy) b Van Hammer :35 DUD; 3. Wahoo McDaniel (Ed McDaniel) & Blackjack Mulligan (Bob Windham) & Jim Brunzell DDQ Jimmy Snuka (James Reiher) & Don Muraco & Dick Murdoch 9:25 *3/4; 4. Patterson (Claude Patterson) & Armstrong b Von Raschke (James Raschke)

& Koloff (Jim Parris) 4:40 1/2*; 5. Dory Funk drew Nick Bockwinkel 15:00 **1/4; 6. Rick Rude (Richard Rood) & Paul Orndorff b Dustin Rhodes & Kensuke Sasaki 9:41 **; 7. Sting b The Prisoner (Kevin Wacholz) 5:16 -*; 8. Cage match for NWA & WCW tag titles: Brian Pillman & Steve Austin b Dos Hombres Rick Steamboat (Richard Blood) & Shane Douglas (Tom Zenk under a mask) 16:05 ***1/2; 9. NWA title: Barry Windham b Arn Anderson 10:56 ***1/2; 10. WCW title: Smith b Vader-DQ ***3/4

AJPW BUDOKAN

(JUNE 1, TOKYO, JAPAN)
Attendance: 16,300 sellout
Live gate: $850,000
Highlights: 1. Mitsuo Momota b Takao Omori; 2. Giant Kimala II (Benjamin Peacock) b Ryuma Izumida; 3. Dan Kroffat & Doug Furnas b Al Perez & Kurt Beyer; 4. Giant Baba & Rusher Kimura & Mighty Inoue b Abdullah the Butcher (Larry Shreeve) & Masa Fuchi & Haruka Eigen *1/4; 5. Tsuyoshi Kikuchi & Satoru Asako b Yoshinari Ogawa & Masao Inoue ***1/4; 6. The Patriot & The Eagle & Joel Deaton (Joseph Jones) b Steve Williams & Richard Slinger (Richard Aceslinger) & Barry Horowitz, 7. Stan Hansen b Terry Gordy **; 8. PWF & Intl tag title: Akira Taue & Toshiaki Kawada b Mitsuharu Misawa & Kenta Kobashi 29:12 ****3/4

WWF KING OF THE RING '93

(JUNE 11, DAYTON, OH)
Attendance: 8,000 sellout (7,000 paid)
Live gate: $78,000
Est. buy rate/Revenue:
1.1 / $2.6 million
Thumbs up/down/middle:
71.0% / 15.7% / 13.3%
Best match: 305 - Bret Hart vs. Mr. Perfect, 39 - Bret Hart vs. Bam Bam Bigelow
Worst match: 98 - Jim Duggan vs. Bam Bam Bigelow, 77 - Hulk Hogan vs. Yokozuna
Highlights: 1. Hart b Razor Ramon 10:27 ***; 2. Perfect b Mr. Hughes (Curtis Hughes) -DQ 6:02 *1/4; 3. Bigelow b Duggan 4:59 1/4*; 4. Tatanka d Lex Luger 15:00 **1/4; 5. Hart b Perfect 18:55 ****1/4; 6. WWF title: Yokozuna b Hogan to win title 13:11 *1/2; 7. Rick & Scott Steiner & Smoking Gunns b Head Shrinkers & Ted DiBiase & IRS 6:49 *; 8. IC title: Shawn Michaels b Crush 11:14 *1/2; 9. King of Ring final: Hart b Bigelow 18:11 ***3/4

WCW CLASH OF THE CHAMPIONS

(JUNE 16, NORFOLK, VA)
Attendance: 6,000 (2,000 paid)
Live gate: $20,000
TV rating: 2.6

Thumbs up/down/middle:
71.4% / 18.6% / 9.6%
Best match: 165 - Ric Flair & Arn Anderson vs. Brian Pillman & Steve Austin, 44 - Barry Windham vs. Too Cold Scorpio
Worst match: 99 - Ron Simmons vs. Dick Slater, 71 - Steve Regal vs. Marcus Bagwell
Highlights: 1. Simmons b Slater 3:56 1/2*; 2. Regal b Bagwell 6:18 *1/2; 3. NWA title: Windham b Scorpio 12:53 ***3/4; 4. Big Van Vader & Rick Rude & Sid Vicious b Sting & Davey Boy Smith & Dustin Rhodes 10:59 ***; 5. 2 of 3 falls for NWA & WCW tag titles: Flair (Richard Fliehr) & Arn Anderson b Pillman & Austin-DQ (Pillman & Austin retain belts) 21:15 ****

WCW BEACH BLAST '93

(JULY 18, BILOXI, MS)
Live attendance: 8,600 (4,000 paid)
Live gate: $33,000
Est. buy rate/revenue:
0.5 / $1.18 million
Thumbs up/down/middle:
36.7% / 45.8% / 17.5%
Best match: 137 - Sting & Davey Boy Smith vs. Big Van Vader & Sid Vicious, 53 - Brian Pillman & Steve Austin vs. Arn Anderson & Paul Roma
Worst match: 80 - Maxx Payne vs. Johnny B. Badd, 55 - Ron Simmons vs. Paul Orndorff
Highlights: 1. WCW TV title: Orndorff b Simmons-DQ 11:15 *3/4; 2. Too Cold Scorpio & Marcus Bagwell b Tex Slashinger & Shanghai Pierce (Mark Canterberry) 12:46 **3/4; 3. Lord Steven Regal b Erik Watts **; 4. Badd b Payne 4:52 *; 5. NWA & WCW tag title: Pillman & Austin b Anderson & Roma (Paul Centopani) 26:14 ***3/4; 6. U.S. title Iron Man Rules: Dustin Rhodes d Rick Rude (title held up) **; 7. NWA title: Ric Flair b Barry Windham to win title 11:21 **1/2; 8. Sting & Smith b Vader & Vicious 16:41 ***3/4

AJPW BUDOKAN

(JULY 29, TOKYO, JAPAN)
Attendance: 16,300 sellout
Live gate: $850,000
Highlights: 1. Satoru Asako b Takao Omori; 2. Rusher Kimura & Mighty Inoue & Mitsuo Momota b Joel Deaton & Yoshinari Ogawa & Ryuma Izumida; 3. Pete Roberts & Richard Slinger b Mark & Chris Youngblood (Mark & Chris Romero); 4. Giant Baba & The Destroyer (Dick Beyer) & Kurt Beyer b Masao Inoue & Haruka Eigen & Masa Fuchi; 5. Tsuyoshi Kikuchi & Jun Akiyama b Dynamite Kid (Tom Billington) & Johnny Smith (John Hindley); 6. Steve Williams & Terry Gordy b Kendall Windham & Johnny Ace (John Laurinaitis) *; 7. Akira Taue b Big Bubba (Ray Traylor)

*1/2; 8. Stan Hansen b Kenta Kobashi 22:35 *****; 9. Triple Crown: Mitsuharu Misawa b Toshiaki Kawada 25:53 ****

WCW CLASH OF THE CHAMPIONS
(AUGUST 18, DAYTONA, FL)
Attendance: 8,903 (2,400 paid)
Live gate: $20,000
TV rating: 3.8
Thumbs up/down/middle:
36.1% / 46.6% / 17.3%
Best match: 108 - Davey Boy Smith vs. Big Van Vader, 49 - Rick Steamboat vs. Paul Orndorff
Worst match: 71 - Johnny B. Badd vs. Maxx Payne, 54 - Dustin Rhodes & Road Warrior Hawk vs. Rick Rude & The Equalizer
Highlights: 1. WCW tag title: Arn Anderson & Paul Roma b Steve Austin & Steve Regal (subbing for injured Brian Pillman) to win belts 9:52 ***; 2. Too Cold Scorpio b Bobby Eaton 5:26 **1/2; 3. Mask vs. guitar: Badd b Payne 2:41 1/2*; 4. WCW TV title: Steamboat b Orndorff to win title 8:31 ***; 5. Ric Flair & Sting b Awesome Kong (Dwayne McCullough) & King Kong 2:14 *; 6. Rhodes & Hawk b Rude & Equalizer (Bill Dannenhauser) 7:41 1/2*; 7. WCW title: Vader b Smith 11:11 ***1/2

SMW K-TOWN SHOWDOWN
(AUGUST 20, KNOXVILLE, TN)
Attendance: 2,780
Live gate: $18,000
Highlights: 1. Bobby Blaze b Dirty White Boy (White Boy failed to pin Blaze in 10:00) **1/4; 2. Loser has to wear a diaper: Tim Horner b Chris Candido-DQ ***; 3. SMW title: Brian Lee b Mongolian Stomper **1/2; 4. Singapore spike match: Big Bossman b Kevin Sullivan ***1/2; 5. Four tag team elimination match: Bruise Brothers (Ron & Don Harris) won over Ricky Morton & Robert Gibson, Steve & Scott Armstrong (Steve & Scott James), and Tom Prichard & Jimmy Del Rey (Jim Richland) ****; 6. Bob Armstrong (Robert James Sr.) b Jim Cornette ****

FMW NISHINOMIYA STADIUM
(AUGUST 22, OSAKA, JAPAN)
Attendance: 25,000
Live gate: $1.6 million
Highlights: 1. Masato Tanaka b Mr. Chin 5:29; 2. Koji Nakagawa b Chiaki Matsuyama 2:58; 3. Combat Toyota & Shark Tsuchiya (Eriko Tsuchiya) & Crusher Maedomari (Yoshika Maedomari) b Kumiko Matsuda & Keiko Iwame & Nurse Nakamura (Rie Nakamura); 4. WWWA midget title: Little Frankie b Tomezo Tsunonkake to win title 5:23; 5. Ricky Fuji b Mercurio 6:10; 6. Yasha Kurenai b Yukie Nabeno 8:50; 7. Onita Jr. (Akihito Ichihara) & Terry Boy b Cockroaches I & II (Amigo Ultra & Genghis Khan) 12:40;

8. Megumi Kudo & Miwa Sato b Aja Kong & Kaoru Ito 18:25; 9. Great Sasuke & Taka Michinoku & Battle Ranger b Super Delfin & Ginsei Shinzaki & Gran Naniwa 22:56; 10. Street fight: Big Titan & The Gladiator b Katsuji Ueda & Sambo Asako 9:51; 11. Katsuji Ueda b Leon Spinks 6:43; 12. Stretcher match: Terry Funk & Tarzan Goto b The Sheik & Sabu 6:21; 13. No rope barbed wire exploding ring explosive match for World Brass Knux title: Atsushi Onita b Mr. Pogo 12:45

AJW BUDOKAN
(AUGUST 25, TOKYO, JAPAN)
Attendance: 14,500 (12,500 paid)
Live gate: Unknown
Highlights: 1. Midori Endo & Yasha Kurenai & Otaku Hozumi b Chikako Shiratori (Chikako Hasegawa) & Numacchi (Saemi Numata) & Tomoko Watanabe 15:42; 2. Candy Okutsu & Boirshoi Kid b Asari (Masami Watanabe) & Infernal Kaoru (Kaoru Maeda) 13:02; 3. Bull Nakano & Suzuka Minami & Mima Shimoda & Bat Yoshinaga & Etsuko Mita b Leo Kitamura & Eagle Sawai & Harley Saito & Miki Handa & Yukari Osawa 14:54; 4. Takako Inoue b Cutie Suzuki 18:17; 5. Toshiyo Yamada & Kaoru Ito b Megumi Kudo & Yukie Nabeno 14:23; 6. Shinobu Kandori b Kyoko Inoue 17:44; 7. Plum Mariko & Mayumi Ozaki & Hikari Fukuoka b Manami Toyota & Yumiko Hotta & Sakie Hasegawa 25:09; 8. All-Pacific title: Akira Hokuto b Rumi Kazama 15:51; 9. WWWA title: Aja Kong b Dynamite Kansai 22:54

AAA LA REVANCHA
(AUGUST 28, LOS ANGELES, CA)
Attendance: 16,742
Live gate: $243,000
Highlights: 1. Super Boy (Sergio Torres) b Thunder Machine (Augie Loya) 4:12 DUD; 2. Lover Boy & El Mercenario (Louie Spicolli) & Pat Tanaka b Piloto Suicida & Mando Guerrero & Mercurio 9:56 **1/2; 3. Mascarita Sagrada & Octagoncito b Espectrito & Jerrito Estrada 23:18 ****; 4. Psicosis & Heavy Metal & Jerry Estrada b Misterioso & Volador & Rey Misterio Jr. 24:36 ***3/4; 5. Octagon & El Hijo del Santo & Blue Panther b Love Machine & Eddy Guerrero & Fuerza Guerrera 23:56 ****; 6. Konnan El Barbaro won triangular match over Cien Caras & Jake Roberts ****1/2

WWF SUMMERSLAM '93
(AUGUST 30, AUBURN HILLS, MI)
Attendance: 20,000
Live gate: $215,000
Est. buy rate/revenue:
1.3 / $3.1 million
Thumbs up/down/middle:

48.0% / 29.9% / 22.1%

Best match: 161 - Steiners vs. Tom Prichard & Jimmy Del Rey, 133 - Bret Hart vs. Jerry Lawler

Worst match: 177 - Undertaker vs. Giant Gonzalez, 96 - Lex Luger vs. Yokozuna

Highlights: 1. Razor Ramon b Ted DiBiase 7:32 *1/2; 2. WWF tag title: Rick & Scott Steiner b Prichard & Del Rey 9:28 ***1/2; 3. IC title: Shawn Michaels b Mr. Perfect-COR 11:20 ***; 4. IRS b 1-2-3 Kid (Sean Waltman) 5:44 **1/4; 5. Hart b Doink the Clown-DQ 9:05 *1/2; 6. Lawler b Hart-DQ 6:32 ****; 7. Ludvig Borga (Tony Halme) b Marty Janetty 5:15 1/2*; 8. Undertaker b Gonzalez 8:04 -*; 9. Smoking Gunns & Tatanka b Head Shrinkers & Bam Bam Bigelow 11:15 **3/4; 10. WWF title: Luger b Yokozuna-COR (Yokozuna retains title) 17:58 **3/4

AJPW BUDOKAN

(*September 3, Tokyo, Japan*)

Attendance: 16,300 sellout

Live gate: Est. $850,000

Highlights: 1. Takao Omori b Mighty Inoue; 2. Abdullah the Butcher & Giant Kimala II b Thunder & Lightning; 3. Dan Kroffat & Doug Furnas b Tracy Smothers & The Eagle; 4. Giant Baba & Rusher Kimura & Mitsuo Momota b Ryuma Izumida & Haruka Eigen & Joel Deaton; 5. Jun Akiyama & Tsuyoshi Kikuchi & Satoru Asako b Masa Fuchi & Yoshinari Ogawa & Masao Inoue **3/4; 6. Kenta Kobashi b The Patriot ***1/4; 7. PWF World & Intl tag titles: Stan Hansen & Ted DiBiase b Toshiaki Kawada & Akira Taue to win belts **3/4; 8. Triple Crown: Mitsuharu Misawa b Steve Williams ****

WCW FALL BRAWL '93

(*September 18, Houston, TX*)

Attendance: 6,000 (3,500 paid)

Live gate: $35,000

Est. buy rate/revenue:

0.46 / $1.07 million

Thumbs up/down/middle:

1.1% / 91.4% / 7.5%

Best match: 166 - Ric Flair vs. Rick Rude, 54 - Rick Steamboat vs. Lord Steven Regal

Worst match: 86 - Ice Train vs. Shanghai Pierce, 68 - War Games

Highlights: 1. WCW TV title: Regal b Steamboat to win title 17:05 *3/4; 2. Charlie Norris b Big Sky (Darryl Karolet) 4:34 DUD; 3. Too Cold Scorpio & Marcus Bagwell b Paul Orndorff & The Equalizer 10:46 *1/2; 4. Ice Train (Harold Raines) b Pierce 3:27 -*; 5. WCW tag titles: Nasty Boys (Brian Yandrisovitz & Jerry Seganowich) b Arn Anderson & Paul Roma to win titles 23:58 *1/4; 6. Cactus Jack b Yoshi Kwan (David Ashford-Smith) 3:38 *3/4; 7. NWA title: Rude b Flair to win title 30:47 **3/4; 8. War Games:

Sting & Dustin Rhodes & Shock Master (Fred Ottman) & Davey Boy Smith b Harlem Heat & Sid Vicious & Vader 16:39 *1/2

NJPW YOKOHAMA ARENA

(*September 23, Yokohama, Japan*)

Attendance: 17,000 sellout

Live gate: $1.5 million

Highlights: 1. Shinjiro Otani & Satoshi Kojima & Dean Malenko (Dean Simon) b Tatsuhito Takaiwa & Yuji Nagata & El Samurai; 2. Brutus Beefcake b Black Cat; 3. Black Tiger (Eddy Guerrero) b Tiger Mask; 4. Scott Norton & Hercules (Raymond Fernandez) b Akira Nogami & Takayuki Iizuka; 5. Hiromichi Fuyuki & Koki Kitahara b Manabu Nakanishi & Masa Chono; 6. Shinya Hashimoto b Jake Roberts (Aurelian Smith Jr.); 7. IWGP jr hwt title: Jushin Liger b Masao Orihara; 8. Tatsumi Fujinami & Tokimitsu Ishizawa b Yoshiaki Fujiwara & Yuki Ishikawa; 9. Hulk Hogan & Great Muta b Hawk & Power Warrior *1/2; 10. Genichiro Tenryu b Hiroshi Hase ***3/4

NJPW OSAKA CASTLE HALL

(*September 26, Osaka, Japan*)

Attendance: 16,000 sellout

Live gate: Unknown

Highlights: 1. Manabu Nakanishi & Yuji Nagata b Satoshi Kojima & Tokimitsu Ishizawa; 2. Shinjiro Otani & El Samurai b Black Cat & Dean Malenko; 3. Scott Norton & Hercules b Brutus Beefcake & Jake Roberts; 4. Hawk & Power Warrior b Takayuki Iizuka & Akira Nogami; 5. Masao Orihara b Tiger Mask; 6. Non-title: Black Tiger b Jushin Liger; 7. Masa Chono b Yoshiaki Fujiwara; 8. Shinya Hashimoto b Hiroshi Hase; 9. Hulk Hogan b Keiji Muto; 10. Tatsumi Fujinami b Genichiro Tenryu

EMLL 60TH ANNIVERSARY SHOW

(*October 1, Mexico City, Mexico*)

Attendance: 18,000 sellout

Live gate: $125,000

Highlights: 1. Jaque Mate & Kahos I & Javier Cruz b El Brazo & Brazo de Oro & Brazo de Plata-DQ, 2. Canadian Vampire Casanova (Ian Hotchkinson) & Pegasus Kid (Chris Benoit) & King Haku (Uliuli Fifita) b Mocho Cota & Pierroth Jr. & Black Magic (Norman Smiley)-DQ ***1/4, 3. Hair vs. hair: Negro Casas (Jose Casas) b La Fiera ***3/4, 4. Mask vs. mask: Atlantis b Mano Negra (revealed as Jesus Rosales) **3/4

UWFI SHOOTFIGHTING

(*October 4, Osaka, Japan*)

Attendance: 5,900

Live gate: Unknown

Est. buy rate/revenue:

0.48 / $730,000
Thumbs up/down/middle:
76.4% / 15.8% / 7.9%
Best match poll: 105 - Nobuhiko Takada vs. Billy Scott, 93 - Salman Hashimikov & Vladimir Berkovich vs. Gary Albright & Dan Severn
Worst match poll: 215 - Kazuo Yamazaki vs. Bad News Allen, 29 - Hashimikov & Berkovich vs. Albright & Severn
Highlights: 1. (dark) Mark Silver b Kazushi Sakuraba 7:14; 2. Tsunemitsu Kanehara b Tommy Cairo 3:49; 3. (dark) Yoshihiro Takayama b Tom Burton 11:12; 4. Jean Lydick b Greg Bobchick 7:37; 5. Yoji Anjyo b Tatsuo Nakano 9:22; 6. Dennis Koslowski b Masahito Kakihara 8:55; 7. Kiyoshi Tamura b Yuko Miyato 8:19; 8. Yamazaki b Allen (Allan Coage) 13:34; 9. Hashimikov & Berkovich b Severn & Albright 13:09; 10. UWFI title: Takada b Scott 13:00; 11. (dark) Super Vader b Naoki Sano 6:20

AJW WRESTLEMARINPIAD '93

(OCTOBER 9, TOKYO, JAPAN)
Attendance: 6,000
Live gate: Unknown
Highlights: 1. Etsuko Mita & Tomoko Watanabe & Nummachi b Mikiko Futagami & Mitsuki Endo & Carol Midori; 2. Captain falls match: Cutie Suzuki & Plum Mariko & Hikari Fukuoka & Boirshoi Kid b Mima Shimoda & Kaoru Ito & Chikako Shiratori & Chapparita Asari 27:49; 3. Shinobu Kandori & Yasha Kurenai b Takako Inoue & Sakie Hasegawa ***1/2; 4. Bull Nakano & Reggie Bennett b Yumiko Hotta & Suzuka Minami; 5. Kyoko Inoue b Devil Masami; 6. Manami Toyota b Mayumi Ozaki ****; 7. Dynamite Kansai b Toshiyo Yamada; 8. Aja Kong b Akira Hokuto **1/2

AJPW BUDOKAN HALL

(OCTOBER 23, TOKYO, JAPAN)
Attendance: 16,300 sellout
Live gate: Est. $850,000
Highlights: 1. Mitsuo Momota & Mighty Inoue b Masao Inoue & Yoshinari Ogawa; 2. Dan Kroffat & Doug Furnas b Tsuyoshi Kikuchi & Satoru Asako; 3. Dory Funk & Tamon Honda b Joel Deaton & Kendall Windham; 4. Giant Baba & Jumbo Tsuruta & Rusher Kimura b Haruka Eigen & Ryuma Izumida & Masa Fuchi; 5. Steve Williams & Big Bubba b Danny Spivey & Johnny Ace; 6. The Eagle & The Patriot b Akira Taue & Takao Omori; 7. Ted DiBiase b Jun Akiyama **3/4; 8. Toshiaki Kawada b Kenta Kobashi 29:37 ****3/4; 9. Triple Crown: Mitsuharu Misawa b Stan Hansen 22:10 *1/2

WCW HALLOWEEN HAVOC '93

(OCTOBER 24, NEW ORLEANS, LA)
Attendance: 6,000 (3,000 paid)

Live gate: $30,000
Est. buy rate/revenue:
0.5 / $1.17 million
Thumbs up/down/middle:
62.4% / 21.4% / 16.2%
Best match: 245 - Vader vs. Cactus Jack, 31 - Nasty Boys vs. Marcus Bagwell & Too Cold Scorpio
Worst match: 282 - Harlem Heat & Equalizer vs. Ice Train & Charlie Norris & Shock Master, 9 - Davey Boy Smith vs. Steve Regal
Highlights: 1. Ice Train & Shock Master & Norris b Harlem Heat & Equalizer 9:45 *; 2. Paul Orndorff b Rick Steamboat-COR ***1/2, 3. WCW TV title: Regal d Smith 15:00 **3/4; 4. U.S. title: Dustin Rhodes b Steve Austin 14:23 **3/4; 5. WCW tag title: Nasty Boys b Scorpio & Bagwell to win titles 14:36 ***1/2; 6. Sting b Sid Vicious 10:41 **3/4; 7. Int world title: Rick Rude b Ric Flair-DQ 19:22 ***1/4; 8. Death match: Vader b Cactus Jack 15:59 ****3/4

WCW CLASH OF THE CHAMPIONS

(NOVEMBER 10, ST. PETERSBURG, FL)
Attendance: 6,000 (1,700 paid)
Live gate: $17,000
TV rating: 3.3
Thumbs up/down/middle:
22.2% / 62.1% / 15.6%
Best match: 246 - Brian Pillman vs. Steve Austin, 77 - Ric Flair vs. Vader
Worst match: 156 - Shockmaster vs. Equalizer, 140 - Rick Rude vs. Road Warrior Hawk
Highlights: 1. Intl world title: Rude DCOR Hawk 5:41 -**; 2. Shock Master b Equalizer 2:28 -*; 3. WCW TV title: Lord Steven Regal b Johnny B. Badd 6:23 *; 4. Austin b Pillman 9:11 ***3/4; 5. U.S. title: Dustin Rhodes b Paul Orndorff **1/4; 6. WCW tag title: Nasty Boys b Sting & Davey Boy Smith 8:30 **; 7. WCW title: Flair b Vader-DQ (Vader retains title) 9:32 ***1/4

AAA/IWC LA LUCHA DEL HONOR

(NOVEMBER 12, LOS ANGELES, CA)
Attendance: 12,500 (11,600 paid)
Live gate: $195,000
Highlights: 1. Psicopata (Mando Guerrero) & Crazy Boy b Piloto Suicida & Mercurio 8:22 *1/2; 2. Louie Spicolli & Vandal Drummond (Kurt Brown) b Super Boy & Capitan Oro 9:33 *1/2; 3. El Mexicano & Torero & Winners b Baby Sharon & May Flowers & Rudy Reyna 24:48 1/2*; 4. Misterioso & Volador & Rey Misterio Jr. b La Parka & Espectro Jr. & La Mommia 26:30 ***1/4; 5. El Hijo del Santo & Octagon & Mascara Sagrada b Heavy Metal & Jerry Estrada & Fuerza Guerrera ****; 6. Jake Roberts & Love Machine & Eddy Guerrero b Konnan El Barbaro & Perro Aguayo & Blue Panther 24:40 ****

WCW BATTLE BOWL

(NOVEMBER 20, PENSACOLA, FL)
Attendance: 7,000 (3,000 paid)
Live gate: $30,000
Est. buy rate / revenue:
0.27 / $674,000
Thumbs up / down / middle:
13.1% / 82.4% / 4.5%
Best match: 68 - Battle Royal, 46 - Ric Flair & Steve Austin vs. Too Cold Scorpio & Maxx Payne
Worst match: 80 - Dustin Rhodes & King Kong vs. Awesome Kong & Equalizer, 13 - Hawk & Rip Rogers vs. Davey Boy Smith & Harlem Heat Koal
Highlights: 1. Cactus Jack & Vader b Harlem Heat Kane & Charlie Norris 7:34 *1/2; 2. Johnny B. Badd & Brian Knobs b Erik Watts & Paul Roma 12:56 3/4*; 3. Shock Master & Paul Orndorff b Rick Steamboat & Steve Regal 12:26 **; 4. King Kong & Rhodes b Awesome Kong & Equalizer 5:55 -***; 5. Sting & Jerry Sags b Ron Simmons & Keith Cole 13:14 *1/2; 6. Flair & Austin b Scorpio & Payne 14:31 **3/4; 7. Rick Rude & Shanghai Pierce b Marcus Bagwell & Tex Slashinger 14:50 -*; 8. Hawk & Rogers b Smith & Harlem Heat Koal 7:55 DUD; 9. Vader won Battle Royal 25:33 ***1/2

WWF SURVIVOR SERIES

(NOVEMBER 24, BOSTON, MA)
Attendance: 15,509 sellout
Live gate: $180,000
Est. buy rate / revenue:
0.82 / $2.08 millon
Thumbs up / down / middle:
21.4% / 68.7% / 9.9%
Best match: 158 - Ricky Morton & Robert Gibson vs. Tom Prichard & Jimmy Del Rey, 57 - Razor Ramon & Randy Savage & Marty Janetty & 1-2-3 Kid vs. Rick Martel & Adam Bomb & Diesel & IRS
Worst match: 206 - Four Doinks vs. Bam Bam Bigelow & Bastion Booger & Head Shrinkers, 66 - Hart Brothers vs. Shawn Michaels & Knights
Highlights: 1. Janetty & 1-2-3 Kid & Ramon & Savage (Randy Poffo) b IRS & Diesel (Kevin Nash) & Martel (Richard Vigneault) & Bomb (Bryan Clark) 26:58 **3/4; 2. Bruce & Keith & Bret & Owen Hart b Michaels & Knights (Barry Horowitz & Greg Valentine & Jeff Gaylord) 30:57 *1/2; 3. SMW tag title: Prichard & Del Rey b Morton & Gibson to win titles 13:43 ***1/4; 4. Four Doinks (Men on Mission--Bobby Horne & Nelson Frazier & Bushwhackers--Robert Miller & Brian Wickens) b Bigelow & Head Shrinkers & Booger (Mike Shaw) 10:58 DUD; 5. Lex Luger & Steiners & The Undertaker b Quebecer Jacques (Jacques Rougeau Jr.) & Crush & Yokozuna & Ludvig Borga 27:59 **1/2

AJW CASTLE HALL

(NOVEMBER 28, OSAKA, JAPAN)
Attendance: 9,600
Live gate: unknown
Highlights: 1. Tomoko Watanabe b Candy Okutsu ***; 2. Harley Saito & Leo Kitamura b Numacchi & Chikako Shiratori DUD; 3. Japanese jr. title: Chapparita Asari b Mitsuki Endo to win title ****; 4. Kyoko Inoue b Yukie Nabeno *; 5. Japanese tag title: Sakie Hasegawa & Kaoru Ito b Yasha Kurenai & Mikiko Futagami ***1/2; 6. Bull Nakano b Hikari Fukuoka ***; 7. Aja Kong b Eagle Sawai **1/2; 8. Captains fall elimination match: Dynamite Kansai & Mayumi Ozaki & Devil Masami & Plum Mariko b Akira Hokuto & Suzuka Minami & Mima Shimoda & Etsuko Mita ****1/2; 9. All Pacific title: Toshiyo Yamada b Manami Toyota 30:47 ****; 10. UWA tag title: Yumiko Hotta & Takako Inoue b Shinobu Kandori & Miki Handa 21:49 ***1/2

AJPW BUDOKAN

(DECEMBER 3, TOKYO, JAPAN)
Attendance: 16,300 sellout
Live gate: $850,000
Highlights: 1. Masao Inoue b Takao Omori; 2. Tamon Honda & Yoshinari Ogawa b Satoru Asako & Jun Akiyama; 3. Mitsuo Momota & Mighty Inoue & Rusher Kimura b Haruka Eigen & Ryuma Izumida & Masa Fuchi; 4. Abdullah the Butcher & Giant Kimala II & Tracy Smothers b Dory Funk & The Patriot & The Eagle; 5. Danny Spivey & Johnny Ace b Dan Kroffat & Doug Furnas; 6. Stan Hansen & Giant Baba b Big Bubba & Steve Williams; 7. Tag tourney championship for PWF and Intl tag titles: Mitsuharu Misawa & Kenta Kobashi b Toshiaki Kawada & Akira Taue 23:24 ****3/4

UWFI JINGU STADIUM

(DECEMBER 5, TOKYO, JAPAN)
Attendance: 46,168 sellout
Live gate: Unknown
Highlights: 1. Badnews Allen b Kazushi Sakuraba; 2. Tom Burton b Jean Lydick; 3. Hiromitsu Kanehara b Greg Bobchick; 4. Yoshihiro Takayama b Tommy Cairo; 5. Masahito Kakihara b Tatsuo Nakano; 6. Mark Silver & Kazuo Yamazaki b Naoki Sano & Yuko Miyato; 7. Billy Scott b Yoji Anjyo; 8. Kiyoshi Tamura b Dennis Koslowski; 9. Salman Hashimikov & Vladimir Berkovich b Dan Severn & Gary Albright; 10. UWFI title: Nobuhiko Takada b Super Vader

AJW ST. BATTLE FINAL

(DECEMBER 6, TOKYO, JAPAN)
Attendance: 11,500 sellout

Live gate: Unknown

Highlights: 1. Leo Kitamura & Otaku Hozumi b Tomoko Watanabe & Chikako Shiratori; 2. Little Frankie b Buddha Man; 3. Japanese jr. title: Candy Okutsu b Chapparita Asari to win title, 4. Japanese tag title: Miki Handa & Yasha Kurenai b Sakie Hasegawa & Kaoru Ito ***1/2; 5. Combat Toyota b Suzuka Minami; 6. Bull Nakano & Etsuko Mita & Mima Shimoda b Hikari Fukuoka & Cutie Suzuki & Plum Mariko 20:36 ***1/2; 7. Takako Inoue & Kyoko Inoue & Yumiko Hotta b Harley Saito & Rumi Kazama & Eagle Sawai ***1/4; 8. WWWA title: Aja Kong b Megumi Kudo 22:34 ***3/4; 9. WWWA tag title: Manami Toyota & Toshiyo Yamada b Dynamite Kansai & Mayumi Ozaki to win titles 25:33 *****; 10. Shinobu Kandori b Akira Hokuto 21:15 ****

WCW STARRCADE '93

(DECEMBER 27, CHARLOTTE, NC)
Attendance: 8,000 (7,000 paid)
Live gate: $62,000
Est. buy rate / revenue:
0.55 / $1.35 million
Thumbs up / down / middle:
66.7% / 22.0% / 11.3%
Best match: 327 - Ric Flair vs. Vader
Worst match: 164 - Shockmaster vs. King Kong, 62 - Sting & Hawk vs. Nasty Boys
Highlights: 1. Paul Orndorff & Paul Roma b Too Cold Scorpio & Marcus Bagwell 11:45 *3/4; 2. Shock Master b King Kong 1:34 -*; 3. WCW TV title: Steve Regal d Rick Steamboat 13:10 *3/4; 4. Cactus Jack & Maxx Payne b Tex Slashinger & Shanghai Pierce 7:48 *1/4; 5. U.S. title 2/3 falls: Steve Austin b Dustin Rhodes to win title 15:30 **3/4; 6. Intl world title: Rick Rude b The Boss (Ray Traylor) **; 7. WCW tag title: Sting & Hawk b Nasty Boys-DQ (Nasty Boys retain titles) 29:11 **; 8. WCW title: Flair b Vader to win title 21:11 ****1/2

CHAPTER FORTY NINE

WRESTLING OBSERVER NEWSLETTER AWARDS

CATEGORY A AWARDS

The following are the results of the 1993 Wrestling Observer Newsletter readership awards, along with a listing of all previous winners in the various categories. Winners determined by points voted on a 5-3-2 basis. First place votes in parenthesis.

WRESTLER OF THE YEAR

1.	Vader (169)	1,163
2.	Kenta Kobashi (84)	672
3.	Bret Hart (61)	495
4.	Toshiaki Kawada (52)	466
5.	Ric Flair (46)	436

HONORABLE MENTION

Mitsuharu Misawa 325, Akira Hokuto 241, Stan Hansen 165, Nobuhiko Takada 163, Manami Toyota 131, Shawn Michaels 96, Genichiro Tenryu 91

PREVIOUS WINNERS

1980 - Harley Race, 1981 - Ric Flair, 1982 - Ric Flair, 1983 - Ric Flair, 1984 - Ric Flair, 1985 - Ric Flair, 1986 - Ric Flair, 1987 - Riki Choshu, 1988 - Akira Maeda, 1989 - Ric Flair, 1990 - Ric Flair, 1991 - Jumbo Tsuruta, 1992 - Ric Flair

MOST OUTSTANDING WRESTLER

1.	Kenta Kobashi (224)	1,530
2.	Manami Toyota (66)	568
3.	Toshiaki Kawada (13)	492
4.	Jushin Liger (39)	440
5.	Vader (42)	411

HONORABLE MENTION

Bret Hart 316, Akira Hokuto 287, Shawn Michaels 245, Mitsuharu Misawa 131, Sabu 110, Ric Flair 74

PREVIOUS WINNERS

1986 - Ric Flair, 1987 - Ric Flair, 1988 - Tatsumi Fujinami, 1989 - Ric Flair, 1990 - Jushin Liger, 1991 - Jushin Liger, 1992 - Jushin Liger

BEST BABYFACE

1.	Atsushi Onita (116)	875
2.	Sting (85)	774
3.	Bret Hart (81)	672
4.	Konnan El Barbaro (59)	579
5.	Mitsuharu Misawa (37)	442

HONORABLE MENTION

The Undertaker 359, Ric Flair 208, Perro Aguayo 193, Tracy Smothers 96, Razor Ramon 92, Nobuhiko Takada 91, Cactus Jack 85

BEST BABYFACE PREVIOUS WINNERS

1980 - Dusty Rhodes, 1981 - Tommy Rich, 1982 - Hulk Hogan, 1983 - Hulk Hogan, 1984 - Hulk Hogan, 1985 - Hulk Hogan, 1986 - Hulk Hogan, 1987 - Hulk Hogan, 1988 - Hulk Hogan, 1989 - Hulk Hogan, 1990 - Hulk Hogan, 1991 - Hulk Hogan, 1992 - Sting

BEST HEEL

1.	Vader (201)	1,275
2.	Jerry Lawler (95)	823
3.	Yokozuna (23)	338
4.	Cien Caras (12)	256
5.	Jake Roberts (18)	228

HONORABLE MENTION

Rick Rude 216, Shawn Michaels 216, Love Machine 118, Brian Christopher 80, Dirty White Boy 79, Brian Lee 68

BEST HEEL PREVIOUS WINNERS

1980 - Larry Zbyszko, 1981 - Don Muraco, 1982 - Buzz Sawyer, 1983 - Michael Hayes, 1984 - Roddy Piper, 1985 - Roddy Piper, 1986 - Michael Hayes, 1987 - Ted DiBiase, 1988 - Ted DiBiase, 1989 - Terry Funk, 1990 - Ric Flair, 1991 - The Undertaker, 1992 - Rick Rude

FEUD OF THE YEAR

1.	Jerry Lawler vs. Bret Hart (136)	966
2.	Misawa & co. vs. Kawada & co. (76)	663
3.	Vader vs. Cactus Jack (66)	637
4.	WAR vs. New Japan (19)	289
5.	Bob Armstrong vs. Jim Cornette (31)	238

HONORABLE MENTION

Rock & Roll Express vs. Heavenly Bodies 233, Sting vs. Vader 177, Konnan El Barbaro vs. Cien Caras 157, All Japan Women vs. JWP 119, Konnan El Barbaro vs. Jake Roberts 117, Tracy Smothers vs. Dirty White Boy 106, El Hijo del Santo vs. Heavy Metal 102

PREVIOUS WINNERS

1980 - Bruno Sammartino vs. Larry Zbyszko, 1981 - Andre the Giant vs. Killer Khan, 1982 - Ted DiBiase vs. Junkyard Dog, 1983 - Freebirds vs. Von Erichs, 1984 - Freebirds vs. Von Erichs, 1985 - Ted DiBiase vs. Jim Duggan, 1986 - Hulk Hogan vs. Paul Orndorff, 1987 - Jerry Lawler vs. Austin Idol & Tommy Rich, 1988 - Midnight Express vs. Fantastics, 1989 - Ric Flair vs. Terry Funk, 1990 - Jumbo Tsuruta vs. Mitsuharu Misawa, 1991 - Tsuruta & company vs. Misawa & company, 1992 - Moondogs vs. Jerry Lawler & Jeff Jarrett

TAG TEAM OF THE YEAR

1.	Brian Pillman & Steve Austin (133)	1,124

2.	Tom Prichard & Jimmy Del Rey (111)	972
3.	Manami Toyota & Toshiyo Yamada (122)	751
4.	Mitsuharu Misawa & Kenta Kobashi (8)	318
5.	Rick & Scott Steiner (12)	249

HONORABLE MENTION

Dan Kroffat & Doug Furnas 185, Toshiaki Kawada & Akira Taue 148, Hawk & Power Warrior 107, Too Cold Scorpio & Marcus Bagwell 103, Head Hunters 102, Ted DiBiase & Stan Hansen 87, Dynamite Kansai & Mayumi Ozaki 72, Terry Gordy & Steve Williams 63

PREVIOUS WINNERS

1980 - Terry Gordy & Buddy Roberts, 1981 - Terry Gordy & Jimmy Snuka, 1982 - Stan Hansen & Ole Anderson, 1983 - Ricky Steamboat & Jay Youngblood, 1984 - Road Warriors, 1985 - Dynamite Kid & Davey Boy Smith, 1986 - Bobby Eaton & Dennis Condrey, 1987 - Bobby Eaton & Stan Lane, 1988 - Bobby Eaton & Stan Lane, 1989 - Shawn Michaels & Marty Jannetty, 1990 - Rick & Scott Steiner, 1991 - Mitsuharu Misawa & Toshiaki Kawada, 1992 - Terry Gordy & Steve Williams

MOST IMPROVED

1.	Tracy Smothers (74)	518
2.	Marcus Bagwell (47)	379
3.	Sabu (35)	254
4.	Steve Williams (19)	162
5.	Jun Akiyama (10)	126

HONORABLE MENTION

1-2-3 Kid 122, La Parka 121, Too Cold Scorpio 103, Brian Lee 90, Jimmy Del Rey 86, Heavy Metal 77, Chris Candido 75, Mayumi Ozaki 73, Eddy Guerrero 71, Brian Christopher 62, Satoru Asako 60, Sakie Hasegawa 60

PREVIOUS WINNERS

1980 - Larry Zbyszko, 1981 - Adrian Adonis, 1982 - Jim Duggan, 1983 - Curt Hennig, 1984 - The Cobra (George Takano), 1985 - Steve Williams, 1986 - Rick Steiner, 1987 - Big Bubba Rogers, 1988 - Sting, 1989 - Lex Luger, 1990 - Kenta Kobashi, 1991 - Dustin Rhodes, 1992 - El Samurai

MOST UNIMPROVED

1.	Rick Rude (76)	553
2.	Sid Vicious (55)	374
3.	Lex Luger (30)	307
4.	Mr. Perfect (36)	297
5.	Ric Flair (27)	187

HONORABLE MENTION

Hulk Hogan 150, Keiji Muto 145, Barry Windham 111, Randy Savage 103, Ron Simmons 74, Konnan El Barbaro 73, The Undertaker 70

PREVIOUS WINNERS

1984 - Jimmy Snuka, 1985 - 1985 - Sgt. Slaughter, 1986 - Bob Orton, 1987 - Butch Reed, 1988 - Bam Bam Bigelow, 1989 - Jim Duggan, 1990 - Sting, 1991 - Davey Boy Smith, 1992 - Randy Savage

MOST OBNOXIOUS

1.	Vince McMahon (83)	734
2.	Eric Bischoff (68)	473
3.	Dusty Rhodes (44)	403
4.	Sid Vicious (41)	385
5.	Gorilla Monsoon (11)	197

HONORABLE MENTION

Hulk Hogan 158, Gene Okerlund 65, Mark Madden 60

PREVIOUS WINNERS

1981 - Gene LeBelle, 1982 - David Crockett, 1983 - Vince McMahon, 1984 - Vince McMahon, 1985 - Vince McMahon, 1986 - Vince McMahon, 1987 - David Crockett, 1988 - Dusty Rhodes, 1989 - Dusty Rhodes, 1990 - Vince McMahon, 1991 - Herb Abrams, 1992 - Bill Watts

BEST ON INTERVIEWS

1.	Jim Cornette (239)	1,521
2.	Ric Flair (101)	895
3.	Jerry Lawler (47)	640
4.	Arn Anderson (5)	172
5.	Brian Christopher (7)	164

HONORABLE MENTION

Cactus Jack 103, Bob Armstrong 85, Bret Hart 69

PREVIOUS WINNERS

1981 - Lou Albano and Roddy Piper (tied), 1982 - Roddy Piper, 1983 - Roddy Piper, 1984 - Jimmy Hart, 1985 - Jim Cornette, 1986 - Jim Cornette, 1987 - Jim Cornette, 1988 - Jim Cornette, 1989 - Terry Funk, 1990 - Arn Anderson, 1991 - Ric Flair, 1992 - Ric Flair

MOST CHARISMATIC

1.	Ric Flair (75)	724
2.	Atsushi Onita (76)	719
3.	Sting (83)	711
4.	The Undertaker (57)	497
5.	Sid Vicious (27)	222

HONORABLE MENTION

Konnan El Barbaro 217, Canadian Vampire Casanova 145, Perro Aguayo 121, Mitsuharu Misawa 120, Bret Hart 107, Hulk Hogan 95, Nobuhiko Takada 64

PREVIOUS WINNERS

1980 - Ric Flair, 1981 - Michael Hayes, 1982 - Dusty Rhodes and Ric Flair (tied), 1983 - Ric Flair, 1984 - Ric Flair, 1985 - Hulk Hogan, 1986 - Hulk Hogan, 1987 - Hulk Hogan, 1988 - Sting, 1989 - Hulk Hogan, 1990 - Hulk Hogan, 1991 - Hulk Hogan, 1992 - Sting

BEST TECHNICAL WRESTLER

1.	Hiroshi Hase (107)	821
2.	Jushin Liger (94)	787
3.	Kenta Kobashi (66)	663
4.	Manami Toyota (70)	658
5.	Bret Hart (47)	366

HONORABLE MENTION

Nobuhiko Takada 221, Shawn Michaels 174, Steve Regal 156, Eddy Guerrero 122, Akira Hokuto 120, Blue Panther 73, Wild Pegasus 69, Ric Flair 62, Negro Casas 61

PREVIOUS WINNERS

1980 - Bob Backlund, 1981 - Ted DiBiase, 1982 - Tiger Mask (Satoru Sayama), 1983 - Tiger Mask (Satoru Sayama), 1984 - Dynamite Kid and Masa Saito (tied), 1985 - Tatsumi Fujinami, 1986 - Tatsumi Fujinami, 1987 - Nobuhiko Takada, 1988 - Tatsumi Fujinami, 1989 - Jushin Liger, 1990 - Jushin Liger, 1991 - Jushin Liger, 1992 - Jushin Liger

BRUISER BRODY MEMORIAL AWARD (BEST BRAWLER)

1.	Cactus Jack (159)	1,141

2.	Vader (87)	873
3.	Stan Hansen (62)	840
4.	Atsushi Onita (40)	385
5.	Sabu (33)	367

HONORABLE MENTION

Terry Funk 253, Toshiaki Kawada 61

PREVIOUS WINNERS

1980 - Bruiser Brody, 1981 - Bruiser Brody, 1982 - Bruiser Brody, 1983 - Bruiser Brody, 1984 - Bruiser Brody, 1985 - Stan Hansen, 1986 - Terry Gordy, 1987 - Bruiser Brody, 1988 - Bruiser Brody, 1989 - Terry Funk, 1990 - Stan Hansen, 1991 - Cactus Jack, 1992 - Cactus Jack

BEST FLYING WRESTLER

1.	Jushin Liger (209)	1,358
2.	Rey Misterio Jr. (97)	837
3.	Manami Toyota (78)	652
4.	Sabu (49)	651
5.	Too Cold Scorpio (36)	544

HONORABLE MENTION

1-2-3 Kid 278, Great Sasuke 275, Ultimo Dragon 153, Eddy Guerrero 138, Brian Pillman 93, Heavy Metal 74, Oro 60

PREVIOUS WINNERS

1981 - Jimmy Snuka, 1982 - Tiger Mask (Satoru Sayama), 1983 - Tiger Mask (Satoru Sayama), 1984 - Dynamite Kid, 1985 - Tiger Mask (Mitsuharu Misawa), 1986 - Tiger Mask (Mitsuharu Misawa), 1987 - Owen Hart, 1988 - Owen Hart, 1989 - Jushin Liger, 1990 - Jushin Liger, 1991 - Jushin Liger, 1992 - Jushin Liger

MOST OVERRATED

1.	Sid Vicious (189)	1,172
2.	Lex Luger (49)	458
3.	Hulk Hogan (47)	318
4.	Ludvig Borga (10)	207
5.	Yokozuna (12)	162

HONORABLE MENTION

The Undertaker 136, Cien Caras 133, Tatanka 114, Hercules Fernandez 81, Shock Master 72, Dustin Rhodes 65

PREVIOUS WINNERS

1980 - Mr. Wrestling II, 1981 - Pedro Morales, 1982 - Pedro Morales, 1983 - Bob Backlund, 1984 - John Studd, 1985 - Hulk Hogan, 1986 - Hulk Hogan, 1987 - Dusty Rhodes, 1988 - Dusty Rhodes, 1989 - Ultimate Warrior, 1990 - Ultimate Warrior, 1991 - Ultimate Warrior, 1992 - Erik Watts

MOST UNDERRATED

1.	Bobby Eaton (52)	528
2.	Wild Pegasus (46)	453
3.	Terry Taylor (35)	399
4.	Sabu (26)	274
5.	Too Cold Scorpio (33)	188

HONORABLE MENTION

1-2-3 Kid 180, Owen Hart 163, Psicosis 157, Brad Armstrong 145, Tracy Smothers 108, Chris Candido 74, Rick Steamboat 60

1980 - Iron Sheik, 1981 - Buzz Sawyer, 1982 - Adrian Adonis, 1983 - Dynamite Kid, 1984 - Brian Blair, 1985 - Bobby Eaton, 1986 - Bobby Eaton, 1987 - Brad Armstrong, 1988 - Tiger Mask (Mitsuharu Misawa), 1989 - Dan Kroffat, 1990 - Bobby Eaton, 1991 - Terry Taylor, 1992 - Terry Taylor

BEST PROMOTION

1.	All Japan Pro Wrestling (159)	1,472
2.	All Japan Women (172)	1,284
3.	New Japan Pro Wrestling (87)	912
4.	Smoky Mountain Wrestling (74)	638
5.	AAA (32)	461

HONORABLE MENTION

World Wrestling Federation 320, Union of Wrestling Force International 109, Frontier Martial Arts Wrestling 97, Eastern Championship Wrestling 95, World Championship Wrestling 94

PREVIOUS WINNERS

1983 - Jim Crockett Promotions, 1984 - New Japan Pro Wrestling, 1985 - All Japan Pro Wrestling, 1986 - Mid South Sports, 1987 - New Japan Pro Wrestling, 1988 - New Japan Pro Wrestling, 1989 - Universal Wrestling Federation Japan, 1990 - All Japan Pro Wrestling, 1991 - All Japan Pro Wrestling, 1992 - New Japan Pro Wrestling

BEST WEEKLY TELEVISION SHOW

1.	All Japan Pro Wrestling (241)	1,570
2.	Smoky Mountain Wrestling (73)	903
3.	WWF Monday Night Raw (96)	849
4.	New Japan Pro Wrestling (33)	405
5.	AAA (32)	393

HONORABLE MENTION

WCW Saturday Night 202, Eastern Championship Wrestling 160, USWA 90 minute show 116, WWF Superstars 96

PREVIOUS WINNERS

1983 - New Japan World Pro Wrestling, 1984 - New Japan World Pro Wrestling, 1985 - Mid South Wrestling, 1986 - Universal Wrestling Federation (Mid South), 1987 - CWA 90 Minute Memphis Wrestling, 1988 - New Japan World Pro Wrestling, 1989 - All Japan Pro Wrestling, 1990 - All Japan Pro Wrestling, 1991 - All Japan Pro Wrestling, 1992 - All Japan Pro Wrestling

MATCH OF THE YEAR

1.	Toyota & Yamada vs. Kansai & Ozaki (4/11) (121)	790
2.	Steve Williams vs. Kenta Kobashi (8/31) (115)	771
3.	Akira Hokuto vs. Shinobu Kandori (4/2) (55)	451
4.	Cactus Jack vs. Vader (10/24) (33)	434
5.	Stan Hansen vs. Kenta Kobashi (7/29) (40)	397

HONORABLE MENTION

Hikari Fukuoka & Cutie Suzuki & Dynamite Kansai & Mayumi Ozaki vs. Aja Kong & Kyoko Inoue & Takako Inoue & Sakie Hasegawa (7/31) 192, Sting vs. Vader (2/21) 168, Lightning Kid vs. Sabu (4/17) 165, Shawn Michaels vs. Marty Janetty (7/19) 147, Stan Hansen vs. Toshiaki Kawada (2/28) 130, Toshiaki Kawada vs. Kenta Kobashi (4/14) 115, El Hijo del Santo vs. Heavy Metal (10/29) 96, Winners & Rey Misterio Jr. & Super Calo vs. Jerry Estrada & Heavy Metal & Psicosis (1/29) 95, Bret Hart vs. Mr. Perfect (6/11) 82, Mitsuharu Misawa vs. Toshiaki Kawada (3/27) 81, Atsushi Onita vs. Terry Funk (5/5) 66, Devil Masami vs. Bull Nakano (4/18) 61, Rick & Scott Steiner vs. Tom Prichard & Jimmy Del Rey (8/30) 60, Heavy Metal & Psicosis & Picudo vs. Winners & Super Calo & Rey Misterio Jr. (2/14) 60

PREVIOUS WINNERS

1980 - Bob Backlund vs. Ken Patera, 1981 - Pat Patterson vs. Sgt. Slaughter (4/21), 1982 - Tiger Mask (Satoru Sayama) vs. Dynamite

Kid (8/5), 1983 - Ric Flair vs. Harley Race (11/24), 1984 - Freebirds vs. Von Erichs (7/4), 1985 - Tiger Mask (Mitsuharu Misawa) vs. Kunaki Kobayashi (6/12), 1986 - Ric Flair vs. Barry Windham (2/14), 1987 - Ricky Steamboat vs. Randy Savage (3/29), 1988 - Ric Flair vs. Sting (3/27), 1989 - Ric Flair vs. Ricky Steamboat (4/2), 1990 - Jushin Liger vs. Naoki Sano (1/31), 1991 - Rick & Scott Steiner vs. Hiroshi Hase & Kensuke Sasaki (3/21), 1992 - Dan Kroffat & Doug Furnas vs. Kenta Kobashi & Tsuyoshi Kikuchi (5/25)

ROOKIE OF THE YEAR

1.	Jun Akiyama (274)	1,515
2.	Bobby Blaze (39)	368
3.	Smoking Gunns (20)	349
4.	Juventud Guerrera (20)	333
5.	Duane Koslowski (21)	261

HONORABLE MENTION

Men on a Mission 143, Dan Severn 108, Ice Train 65, Manabu Nakanishi 60

PREVIOUS WINNERS

1930 - Barry Windham, 1981 - Brad Armstrong and Brad Rheingans (tied), 1982 - Steve Williams, 1983 - Road Warriors, 1984 - Tom Zenk and Keiichi Yamada (tied), 1985 - Jack Victory, 1986 - Bam Bam Bigelow, 1987 - Brian Pillman, 1988 - Gary Albright, 1989 - Dustin Rhodes, 1990 - Steve Austin, 1991 - Johnny B. Badd, 1992 - Rey Misterio Jr.

MOST MANAGER

1.	Jim Cornette (362)	1,860
2.	Tammy Fytch (17)	512
3	Ron Wright (5)	325
4.	Paul E. Dangerously (7)	261
5.	Harley Race (4)	233

HONORABLE MENTION

Johnny Polo 134, Mr. Toyota 109

PREVIOUS WINNERS

1983 - Jimmy Hart, 1984 - Jimmy Hart, 1985 - Jim Cornette, 1986 - Jim Cornette, 1987 - Jim Cornette, 1988 - Jim Cornette, 1989 - Jim Cornette, 1990 - Jim Cornette, 1991 - Sensational Sherri, 1992 - Jim Cornette

BEST TELEVISION ANNOUNCER

1.	Jim Ross (123)	1,025
2.	Tony Schiavone (52)	708
3.	Bob Caudle (57)	538
4.	Vince McMahon (41)	427
5.	Akira Fukuzawa (70)	391

HONORABLE MENTION

Arturo Rivera 120, Dr. Alfonso Morales 87

PREVIOUS WINNERS

1981 - Gordon Solie, 1982 - Gordon Solie, 1983 - Gordon Solie, 1984 - Lance Russell, 1985 - Lance Russell, 1986 - Lance Russell, 1987 - Lance Russell, 1988 - Jim Ross, 1989 - Jim Ross, 1990 - Jim Ross, 1991 - Jim Ross, 1992 - Jim Ross

WORST TELEVISION ANNOUNCER

1.	Gorilla Monsoon (137)	927
2.	Eric Bischoff (89)	734
3.	Cory Macklin (64)	375
4.	Vince McMahon (19)	345
5.	Jay Sulli (32)	212

HONORABLE MENTION:
Todd Pettengill 127, David Webb 125, Randy Savage 120, Jim Dougherty 101, Tony Schiavone 100, Jim Ross 71, Gene Okerlund 67

PREVIOUS WINNERS
1984 - Angelo Mosca, 1985 - Gorilla Monsoon, 1986 - David Crockett, 1987 - David Crockett, 1988 - David Crockett, 1989 - Ed Whalen, 1990 - Herb Abrams, 1991 - Gorilla Monsoon, 1992 - Gorilla Monsoon

CATEGORY B AWARDS
Winners determined by first placed votes.

BEST MAJOR WRESTLING CARD
1.	AJW Dream Slam I (4/2)	229
2.	WCW SuperBrawl '93 (2/21)	92
3.	AJW Dream Slam II (4/11)	61
4.	AAA TripleMania (4/30)	37
5.	New Japan Tokyo Dome (1/4)	34

HONORABLE MENTION:
WWF King of the Ring (7/13) 14, WWF Summer Slam (8/30) 12, All Japan (2/28) 9, WCW Halloween Havoc (10/24) 6

PREVIOUS WINNERS
1989 - WCW Baltimore Great American Bash (7/23), 1990 - WWF/New Japan/All Japan U.S. and Japan Wrestling Summit (4/13), 1991 - WCW Wrestle War (2/24), 1992 - All Japan Women Wrestlemarinpiad (4/25)

WORST MAJOR WRESTLING CARD
1.	WCW Fall Brawl (9/19)	116
2.	WCW Battle Bowl (11/20)	108
3.	WWF Wrestlemania IX (4/4)	70
4.	WWF Survivor Series (11/24)	33
5.	WCW Clash of the Champions (11/10)	6

PREVIOUS WINNERS
1989 - WWF WrestleMania (4/2), 1990 - WCW Clash XIII (11/20), 1991 - WCW Great American Bash (7/14), 1992 - WCW Halloween Havoc (10/25)

BEST WRESTLING MANEUVER
1.	Vader - Moonsault	92
2.	Too Cold Scorpio - Splash	49
3.	Manami Toyota - Quebrada outside ring	37
4.	Ultimo Dragon - Asai moonsault	27
5.	Manami Toyota - Ocean Cyclone suplex	25

HONORABLE MENTION
Marcus Bagwell - Buff Blockbuster 16, Great Sasuke - Sasuke Special 16, Juventud Guerrera - Air Juvi 13, Ultimo Dragon - Running Liger Bomb 12, Bret Hart - Figure Four around post 11, Chaparita Asari - Sky Twister Press 11, Rey Misterio Jr. - Springboard Plancha into Huracanrana on Floor 9, Shinjiro Otani - Springboard DDT 8, Ultimo Dragon - Asai Moonsault 6

Bret Como - Comotizer 21, Sabu - Sunset flip out of ring into power bomb 15, Akira Hokuto - Northern Lights bomb 14, Rey Misterio Jr. - Frankensteiner off top rope 13, Chapparita Asari - moonsault 13, Rey Misterio Jr. - flip tope 10, Tiger Mask - Frankensteiner off rope 10, Scott Steiner - Frankensteiner 8, Steve Williams - backdrop driver 7, Scott Steiner - suplex piledriver 6

PREVIOUS WINNERS
1981 - Jimmy Snuka - Superfly Splash, 1982 - Super Destroyer (Scott Irwin) - Superplex, 1983 - Jimmy Snuka - Superfly Splash, 1984

- Davey Boy Smith - Power Clean in combination with Dynamite Kid Dropkick off the top rope, 1985 - Tiger Mask (Mitsuharu Misawa) - Tope with mid-air flip, 1986 - Chavo Guerrero - Moonsault Bodyblock, 1987 - Keiichi Yamada (Jushin Liger) - Shooting Star Press, 1988 - Keiichi Yamada (Jushin Liger) - Shooting Star Press, 1989 - Scott Steiner - Frankensteiner, 1990 - Scott Steiner - Frankensteiner, 1991 - Masao Orihara - Moonsault off top rope to floor, 1992 - Too Cold Scorpio - Scorpio Splash

MOST DISGUSTING PROMOTIONAL TACTIC

1.	Cactus Jack Amnesia Angle	81
2.	WWF 900 number scams	64
3.	WWF xenophobic angles	37
4.	WCW handling of Vicious/Anderson	36
5.	WCW exploding boat video	26

HONORABLE MENTION

WCW continual false advertising of talent 13, Hogan getting WWF title 10, Lex Luger American hero drug-free push 10, WCW giving away storylines/title switches in Orlando 10, WCW pushing steroid guys 9, Flair plugging Sid Vicious on Clash 9, WCW amateur challenge 6

PREVIOUS WINNERS

1981 - LeBelle Promotions usage of The Monster saying he was built in a laboratory, 1982 - Bob Backlund as WWF champion, 1983 - WWF pretending Eddie Gilbert had re-broken his neck after original neck injury in a car accident, 1984 - Blackjack Mulligan faking heart attack by Championship Wrestling from Florida, 1985 - Usage of Mike Von Erich's near fatal illness to sell Cotton Bowl tickets, 1986 - Equating an angle of Chris Adams' blindness with the death of Gino Hernandez by World Class, 1987 - World Class' handling of Mike Von Erich's death, 1988 - Fritz Von Erich fake brush with death by World Class, 1989 - Jose Gonzalez babyface push by WWC, 1990 - Atsushi Onita stabbing angle with Jose Gonzalez, 1991 - WWF exploiting Persian Gulf War for WrestleMania angle, 1992 - Erik Watts push

BEST COLOUR COMMENTATOR

1.	Bobby Heenan	212
2.	Jesse Ventura	86
3.	Dutch Mantel	47
4.	Larry Zbyszko	14
5.	Jerry Lawler	13

PREVIOUS WINNERS

1986 - Michael Hayes, 1987 - Jesse Ventura, 1988 - Jesse Ventura, 1989 - Jesse Ventura, 1990 - Jesse Ventura, 1991 - Paul E. Dangerously, 1992 - Bobby Heenan

READERS PERSONAL FAVORITE WRESTLER

1.	Ric Flair	84
2.	Manami Toyota	27
3.	Vader	24
=3.	Shawn Michaels	24
5.	Jushin Liger	22
=5.	Sabu	22

HONORABLE MENTION

Heavy Metal 15, Bret Hart 13, Cactus Jack 13, Toshiaki Kawada 12, El Hijo del Santo 12, Negro Casas 11, Hiroshi Hase 11, Jerry Lawler 11, Arn Anderson 10, Mitsuharu Misawa 9, Nobuhiko Takada 8, Toshiyo Yamada 6

PREVIOUS WINNERS

1984 - Ric Flair, 1985 - Ric Flair, 1986 - Ric Flair, 1987 - Ric Flair, 1988 - Ric Flair, 1989 - Ric Flair, 1990 - Ric Flair, 1991 - Ric Flair, 1992 - Ric Flair

READERS LEAST FAVORITE WRESTLER

1.	Sid Vicious	112

2.	Hulk Hogan	39
3.	Shockmaster	26
4.	The Equalizer	17
=4.	Jose Gonzales	17

HONORABLE MENTION

Tatanka 8, Ludvig Borga 8, Ice Train 6, Bushwhackers 6

PREVIOUS WINNERS

1984 - Ivan Putski, 1985 - Hulk Hogan, 1986 - Hulk Hogan, 1987 - Dusty Rhodes, 1988 - Dusty Rhodes, 1989 - Ultimate Warrior, 1990 - Ultimate Warrior, 1991 - Hulk Hogan, 1992 - Erik Watts

WORST WRESTLER

1.	The Equalizer	103
2.	Giant Gonzalez	98
3.	Sid Vicious	38
4.	Shockmaster	26
5.	Bastion Booger	15

HONORABLE MENTION

Jim Duggan 11, Diesel 8

PREVIOUS WINNERS

1984 - Ivan Putski, 1985 - Uncle Elmer (Stan Frazier), 1986 - Mike Von Erich, 1987 - Junkyard Dog, 1988 - Ultimate Warrior, 1989 - Andre the Giant, 1990 - Junkyard Dog, 1991 - Andre the Giant, 1992 - Andre the Giant

WORST TAG TEAM

1.	Colossal Kongs	97
2.	Bushwhackers	52
3.	Harlem Heat	51
4.	Keith & Kent Cole	22
5.	Scott Norton & Hercules	18

HONORABLE MENTION

Quebecers 8

PREVIOUS WINNERS

1984 - The Crusher & Baron Von Raschke, 1985 - Uncle Elmer (Stan Frazier) & Cousin Junior (Lanny Kean), 1986 - Junkyard Dog & George Steele, 1987 - Jimmy Valiant & Bugsy McGraw, 1988 - Nikolai Volkoff & Boris Zhukov, 1989 - Warlord & Barbarian, 1990 - Giant Baba & Andre the Giant, 1991 - Giant Baba & Andre the Giant, 1992 - Bushwhackers

WORST TELEVISION SHOW

1.	GWF on ESPN	77
2.	WWF Mania	58
3.	WCW Main Event	53
4.	WCW Saturday Night	38
5.	IWCCW	35

HONORABLE MENTION

WCW Power Hour 32, WCW Pro 25, WCW World Wide 19, WWF Superstars 15, Eastern Championship Wrestling 9, WWF All-American 8

PREVIOUS WINNERS

1984 - WWF All-Star Wrestling, 1985 - Championship Wrestling from Florida, 1986 - California Championship Wrestling, 1987 -

World Class Championship Wrestling, 1988 - AWA on ESPN, 1989 - ICW Wrestling, 1990 - AWA on ESPN, 1991 - Herb Abrams UWF, 1992 - GWF on ESPN

WORST MANAGER

1.	Mr. Fuji	171
2.	Harvey Wippleman	57
3.	Paul Bearer	17
4.	Missy Hyatt	16
5.	Col. Rob Parker	15

HONORABLE MENTION
Harley Race 10, Teddy Long 10

PREVIOUS WINNERS
1984 - Mr. Fuji, 1985 - Mr. Fuji, 1986 - Paul Jones, 1987 - Mr. Fuji, 1988 - Mr. Fuji, 1989 - Mr. Fuji, 1990 - Mr. Fuji, 1991 - Mr. Fuji, 1992 - Mr. Fuji

WORST MATCH OF THE YEAR

1.	Four Doinks vs. Bigelow, Booger, Headshrinkers (11/24)	63
2.	Undertaker vs. Giant Gonzalez (8/30)	41
3.	Rick Rude vs. Hawk (11/10)	40
4.	War Games (9/17)	34
5.	King Kong & Rhodes vs. Awesome Kong & Equalizer (11/20)	27
=5.	Sting vs. The Prisoner (5/23)	27

HONORABLE MENTION
Shock Master vs. Equalizer (11/10) 20, Undertaker vs. Giant Gonzalez (4/4) 8

PREVIOUS WINNERS
1984 - Fabulous Moolah vs. Wendi Richter (7/23), 1985 - Fred Blassie vs. Lou Albano, 1986 - Roddy Piper vs. Mr. T (4/2), 1987 - Hulk Hogan vs. Andre the Giant (3/29), 1988 - Hiroshi Wajima vs. Tom Magee (4/21), 1989 - Andre the Giant vs. Ultimate Warrior (10/31), 1990 - Sid Vicious vs. Night Stalker (11/20), 1991 - P.N. News & Bobby Eaton vs. Terry Taylor & Steve Austin (7/14), 1992 - Rick Rude vs. Masahiro Chono (10/25)

WORST FEUD OF THE YEAR

1.	Undertaker vs. Giant Gonzalez	61
2.	Johnny B. Badd vs. Maxx Payne	54
3.	Lex Luger vs. Ludvig Borga	51
4.	Dusty Rhodes vs. The Assassin	45
5.	Lex Luger vs. Yokozuna	18

HONORABLE MENTION
Erik Watts vs. Arn Anderson 11, Hulk Hogan & Brutus Beefcake vs. Money Inc. 10, Konnan El Barbaro vs. Cien Caras 9, Yokozuna vs. Jim Duggan 9, Crush vs. Doink the Clown 8

PREVIOUS WINNERS
1984 - Andre the Giant vs. John Studd, 1985 - Sgt. Slaughter vs. Boris Zhukov, 1986 - Machines (Andre the Giant & Bill Eadie) vs. King Kong Bundy & John Studd, 1987 - George Steele vs. Danny Davis, 1988 - Midnight Rider (Dusty Rhodes) vs. Tully Blanchard, 1989 - Andre the Giant vs. Ultimate Warrior, 1990 - Ric Flair vs. Junkyard Dog, 1991 - Hulk Hogan vs. Sgt. Slaughter, 1992 - Ultimate Warrior vs. Papa Shango

WORST ON INTERVIEWS

1.	Mr. Fuji	33
2.	Scott Steiner	30

3.	Lex Luger	15
4.	Yokozuna	14
5.	Harley Race	10

HONORABLE MENTION

Paul Roma 8, Dustin Rhodes 8

PREVIOUS WINNERS

1984 - Jimmy Snuka, 1985 - Thunderbolt Patterson, 1986 - Mike Von Erich, 1987 - Bugsy McGraw, 1988 - Steve Williams, 1989 - Ultimate Warrior, 1990 - Ultimate Warrior, 1991 - Ultimate Warrior, 1992 - Ultimate Warrior

WORST PROMOTION

1.	World Championship Wrestling	251
2.	Global Wrestling Federation	70
3.	World Wrestling Federation	16
4.	Eastern Championship Wrestling	13
5.	W*ING	11

HONORABLE MENTION

IWCCW 9

PREVIOUS WINNERS

1986 - AWA, 1987 - World Class, 1988 - AWA, 1989 - AWA, 1990 - AWA, 1991 - Herb Abrams UWF, 1992 - GWF

BEST BOOKER

1.	Jim Cornette	135
2.	Riki Choshu	98
3.	Shohei Baba	92
4.	Vince McMahon	41
5.	Eddie Gilbert	27

HONORABLE MENTION

Paul E. Dangerously 25, Jerry Jarrett 14

PREVIOUS WINNERS

1986 - Dusty Rhodes, 1987 - Vince McMahon, 1988 - Eddie Gilbert, 1989 - Shohei Baba, 1990 - Shohei Baba, 1991 - Shohei Baba, 1992 - Riki Choshu

PROMOTER OF THE YEAR

1.	Shohei Baba	127
2.	Vince McMahon	102
3.	Antonio Pena	66
4.	Jim Cornette	63
5.	All Japan Women	41

HONORABLE MENTION

UWFI 20, Atsushi Onita 19, Tod Gordon 17, Jerry Jarrett 9

PREVIOUS WINNERS

1988 - Vince McMahon, 1989 - Akira Maeda, 1990 - Shohei Baba, 1991 - Shohei Baba, 1992 - Shohei Baba

BEST GIMMICK

| 1. | The Undertaker | 80 |

2.	Doink the Clown	58
3.	1-2-3 Kid	24
4.	Hollywood Blonds	22
5.	Tammy Fytch	19

HONORABLE MENTION:

Yokozuna 18, Razor Ramon 18, Skinheads 11, Crybaby Chris Candido 11, Dr. Looser 9, FMW exploding ring 8

PREVIOUS WINNERS

1986 - Adrian Street, 1987 - Ted DiBiase Million Dollar Man, 1988 - Rick Steiner Varsity Club, 1989 - Jushin Liger, 1990 - Undertaker, 1991 - Undertaker, 1992 - Undertaker

WORST GIMMICK

1.	Shockmaster	86
2.	Bastion Booger	32
3.	Friar Ferguson	28
4.	Doink the Clown	27
5.	Prince Kharis	25

HONORABLE MENTION:

Rio Rogers 17, Los Payasos 14, Ice Train 11, Dink 9, American Original Lex Luger 8, The Narcissist Lex Luger 6, Lord Steven Regal 6

PREVIOUS WINNERS

1986 - Adorable Adrian Adonis, 1987 - Adorable Adrian Adonis, 1988 - Midnight Rider (Dusty Rhodes), 1989 - Ding Dongs, 1990 - Gobbledy Gooker, 1991 - Oz, 1992 - Papa Shango

MOST EMBARRASSING WRESTLER

1.	Bastion Booger	82
2.	Shockmaster	38
3.	Doink the Clown	34
4.	Bushwhackers	26
5.	The Equalizer	23

HONORABLE MENTION:

Giant Gonzalez 18, Hulk Hogan 18, Prince Kharis 17, Los Payasos 13, Men on a Mission 11

PREVIOUS WINNERS

1986 - Adrian Adonis, 1987 - George Steele, 1988 - George Steele, 1989 - Andre the Giant, 1990 - Dusty Rhodes, 1991 - Van Hammer, 1992 - Papa Shango

Printed by Amazon Italia Logistica S.r.l.
Torrazza Piemonte (TO), Italy